WITHDRAWN
FROM
UNIVERSITY OF PLYMOUTH
LIBRARY SERVICE

D1765208

World
culture
report
1998

World culture report 1998

Culture, creativity and markets

UNESCO Publishing

UNIVERSITY OF PLYMOUTH
Item No. 900 3922374
Date 1 2 JUL 1999 Z
Class No. 306 UNE
Contl. No. 9231034901
LIBRARY SERVICES

Director of Research: Lourdes Arizpe
Special Editors: Louis Emmerij, Paul Streeten
Executive Co-ordinator: Ann-Belinda S. Preis
Research Assistant: Paola Leoncini Bartoli
Publication Editors: Monique Couratier, Malachy Quinn
Graphs and cover: Marina Taurus, Terry McKinley
Design and layout: Jean-Francis Chériez

The authors are responsible for the choice and presentation
of the facts contained in this report and for the opinions
expressed therein, which are not necessarily those of
UNESCO and do not commit the Organization.

The designations employed and the presentation of material
throughout this publication do not imply the expression of
any opinion whatsoever on the part of UNESCO concerning
the legal status of any country, territory, city or area or of
its authorities, or concerning the delimitation of its frontiers
or boundaries.

Published in 1998 by the United Nations Educational,
Scientific and Cultural Organization,
7 place de Fontenoy, 75352 Paris 07 SP, France
Text composed by Éditions du Mouflon,
94270 Le Kremlin-Bicêtre, France
Printed by Darantiére, 21800 Quétigny, France

ISBN 92-3-103490-1

© UNESCO 1998

Preface

Culture shapes the way we see the world. It therefore has the capacity to bring about the change of attitudes needed to ensure peace and sustainable development which, we know, form the only possible way forward for life on planet Earth. Today, that goal is still a long way off. A global crisis faces humanity at the dawn of the twenty-first century, marked by increasing poverty in our asymmetrical world, environmental degradation and short-sightedness in policy-making. Culture is a crucial key to solving this crisis. That is why UNESCO decided to develop a new tool, the *World Culture Report*, to provide a worldwide analysis on which new policies can be based.

When we speak about culture, we are looking at ways of living as individuals and ways of living together. A 'living culture' is one which – almost by definition – interacts with others, in that it involves people creating, blending, borrowing and reinventing meanings with which they can identify. UNESCO is committed to preserving and protecting what its Constitution calls 'the fruitful diversity of cultures'.

What are the prospects for the world's diverse cultures in an increasingly interconnected world undergoing extraordinarily rapid change? Uniformity is often seen as the inevitable result of the processes of globalization that are so strongly marking the end of this century. But we are also witnessing a trend towards fragmentation which drives people apart. What is certain is that we cannot afford to lose any of the world's multitude of cultures and that their survival depends on their peaceful and creative coexistence.

Complex systems draw their strength from diversity: genetic diversity in a species, biological diversity within an ecosystem, cultural diversity in human communities. Each culture constitutes a unique mode of interpreting or relating to a world so complex that the only hope of knowing it or dealing with it is to approach it from as many perspectives as possible. Our task is to ensure that people enjoy freedom for their own culture and have knowledge and understanding of other cultures. In both cases, this can only be accomplished through an active and positive respect for the differences between all cultures whose values are tolerant of others. It is a task we all share, from the individual level to the governmental and international level. On the success of this undertaking depends the shape our common future will take.

There has never been a better way to protect each person's and each group's cultural identity than by fostering mutual respect. In the minds of those who drafted and signed UNESCO's Constitution in 1945, the reason for developing the means of communication was to advance 'the mutual knowledge and understanding of peoples'. By promoting 'the free flow of ideas by word and image', it was hoped to banish the 'suspicion and mistrust between the peoples of the world through which their differences have all too often broken into war'. Mutual knowledge, free flow, differences . . . UNESCO, in its mission to build a culture of peace, is unequivocally concerned with diversity and reciprocity. It is my sincere hope that the *World Culture Report* will prove to be another stepping stone on the path to peace.

Federico Mayor
Director-General of UNESCO

Acknowledgements

Irma Adelman
Benjamin Barber
William J. Baumol
Jos Becker
Annette Bernardi
Irmgard Bontinck
Lord Meghnad Desai
Bruno S. Frey
Mwangi wa Githinji
Héctor Hiram Hernández Bringas
Mark Jamieson
Louis Yasushi Kikuchi
Paul McPhie
Hans-Peter Müller
Patrick O'Keefe
Alfred Smudits
Johan Verweij
Gilberto Villlamarín

Special thanks to

The Government of the Netherlands
The Netherlands National Commission for UNESCO
The Danish Development Agency (DANIDA),
    Copenhagen
The Social and Cultural Planning Office (SCP),
    Rijswijk (Netherlands)
The United Nations Research Institute for Social
    Development (UNRISD), Geneva

UNESCO Secretariat

Guiomar Alonso Cano
Mirta Caifano-Romero
Pilar Chiang-Joo
Elvira Cross-Frías
Rosa Guerreiro
Maria-Cristina Iglesias
Jean-Yves Le Saux
Hafida Ouhajjou
Michèle Rabadeux
Marielle Richon
Win Tennakoonge

Contents

11 Foreword *Lourdes Arizpe*

13 List of tables and graphs

15 General introduction

Part One. Culture and economic development

22 Introduction

25 Chapter 1. Culture and economic development *J. Mohan Rao*

    ☐ The Asian financial turmoil in perspective *Louis Emmerij* 27

    ☐ The incidence of child labour *J. Mohan Rao* 30

    ☐ The decline of birth rates in Europe and elsewhere *J. Mohan Rao* 38

    ☐ Asian values and economic growth *Amartya Sen* 40

Part Two. Global sociocultural processes

50 Introduction

54 Chapter 2. Equal yet different *Alain Touraine*

    ☐ 'I don't sell bread, only yeast . . .' (Miguel de Unamuno) *Gisèle Halimi* 60

64 Chapter 3. Cultural possibilities *Robert Borofsky*

    ☐ The global in the local *Ann-Belinda S. Preis* 66

    ☐ 'Convivencia': the goal of conviviability *Lourdes Arizpe* 71

76 Chapter 4. Cultural rights and indigenous peoples: the Sami experience *Ole Henrik Magga*

85 Chapter 5. Culture and indigenous rights *Henriette Rasmussen, Inger Sjoerslev*

93 Chapter 6. Culture and sustainability *Melissa A. Leach*

    ☐ Forests in West Africa *Melissa A. Leach* 96

    ☐ Environmental degradation in the Himalayas *Melissa A. Leach* 98

    ☐ Population growth, sustainable development and the environment *Sergey Kapitza* 100

105 Chapter 7. Cities, culture and globalization *Elizabeth Jelin*

    ☐ Urbanization and globalization *Fu-chen Lo, Yue-Man Yeung* 108

    ☐ The destruction of the Old Bridge of Mostar *Azzeddine Beschaouch* 116

    ☐ A case of local democracy: the 'participatory budget' of Pôrto Alegre (Brazil) *Elizabeth Jelin* 122

125 Chapter 8. Culture and democracy *Adam Przeworski*

    ☐ Democratization and women's rights in the South African Constitution: the challenge of African customary law *Ronald Thandabantu Nhlapo* 132

147 Chapter 9. Culture, ethics and globalization *Yoro K. Fall*

Part Three. Creativity, markets and cultural policies

154 Introduction

157 Chapter 10. Cultural policy options in the context of globalization *Néstor Garcia Canclini*

    ☐ Cultural policies in post-Soviet Russia *Nickolay Anastasyev* 160

    ☐ Cultural policies in Japan *Michihiro Watanabe* 174

    ☐ 'Culture is about having a future' *European Task Force on Culture and Development (Council of Europe)* 177

183 Chapter 11. Global creativity and the arts *Catharine R. Stimpson, Homi Bhabha*

193 Chapter 12. The role of music in international trade and economic development *David Throsby*

    ☐ World Music: the relocation of culture *Martin D. Roberts* 204

210 Chapter 13. Cultural and economic development through copyright in the information society *Milágros del Corral, Salah Abada*

222 Chapter 14. International standards for cultural heritage *Lyndel V. Prott*

    ☐ International standards: an African perspective *Folarin Shyllon* 232

237 Chapter 15. Heritage and cyberculture: what cultural content for what cyberculture? *Isabelle Vinson*

    ☐ Minority heritage: a priority for the networks *Isabelle Vinson* 242

    ☐ Cyberculture and infoethics *Philippe Quéau* 244

Part Four. Public opinion and global ethics

250 Introduction

252 Chapter 16. Public opinion and global ethics: a descriptive study of existing survey data *Adriaan van der Staay*

    ☐ A search for common values *Yersu Kim* 254

Part Five. Methodology: building cultural indicators

314 Introduction

317 Chapter 17. Culture, freedom and independence *Amartya Sen*

322 Chapter 18. Measuring the contribution of culture to human well-being: cultural indicators of development *Terry McKinley*

333 Chapter 19. Cultural indicators of well-being: some conceptual issues *Prasanta Pattanaik*

    ☐ Cultural statistics within a developed statistical system (Australia and Canada) *Barry Haydon* 336

Part Six. Implications for policy

343 Recasting cultural policy

Part Seven. Statistical Tables and Culture Indicators

349 Measuring culture: prospects and limits *Leo Goldstone*

352 List of Statistical Tables and Culture Indicators

357 Statistical Tables

485 Index and sources of the Culture Indicators

Lourdes Arizpe
Assistant Director-General for Culture,
UNESCO

Foreword

The publication by UNESCO of a *World Culture Report* was the first recommendation of the Report of the World Commission on Culture and Development, *Our Creative Diversity*. Its task is to survey recent trends in culture and development, monitor events affecting the state of cultures worldwide, construct quantitative cultural indicators, highlight good cultural practices and policies and analyse specific themes of general importance accompanied by policy suggestions. Mr Federico Mayor, Director-General of UNESCO, agreed that it should be published on a biennial basis by UNESCO, being written by an independent team of scholars.

This report is significant in that it is interdisciplinary in nature: governments and the general public consistently point to the need to address issues from the viewpoint of various specialized fields. Because it is a new hybrid field, first delineated in *Our Creative Diversity*, no state-of-the-art review is possible as yet. The present report is, in effect, a first step towards the construction of such an art.

Following as it does the general framework and guidelines of *Our Creative Diversity* and the UNESCO principle of promoting intercultural dialogue, the report accordingly must practise what it preaches. It sets out to be as intercultural as possible in that authors from many different cultures have been invited to contribute to it. There can be no question of the report providing certainties by taking sides on culturally defined assumptions: it strives, rather, to go beyond that to examine the nature of phenomena related to culture and development in the contemporary scene by providing hard and comparative data in this field. Some of these data and the accompanying interpretations will, it is hoped, provide an effective counter to chauvinistic views, confused arguments and political manipulation of ethnicity regarding issues in these fields.

In view of the fact that the report is breaking new ground, many of its findings and proposals should be regarded as preliminary in nature. It is vital none the less that governments, intellectuals, artists and cultural activists should review and utilize these findings for activities and policies that have practical outcomes.

Specifically, quantitative indicators and indices of culture and development should be tried and tested in order to come up with more precise statistical categories and methodologies to enable governments to collect the necessary data in this field. As will be seen in the tables, data have yet to be collected in many areas and, importantly, new phenomena have yet to be named.

Both the constitutive and the instrumental aspects of culture, as set out in *Our Creative Diversity*, are discussed in the different chapters here. For instance, the report explores the manner in which culture is used to define development and identities, in other words 'who we are', 'where we come from' and, equally importantly, 'where we are going'. It also investigates ways in which culture can be usefully integrated into economic activities to bring about improvements in people's income or well-being through cultural industries, the arts and crafts markets and employment.

UNESCO particularly welcomes this report which extends the discussion of actions that are planned in pursuance of the programme of the Culture Sector as a follow-up to *Our Creative Diversity*. It is set in the new context of economic interdependence, global creativity, the changing role of the state and the rise of new communication and information technologies. Its analysis also reaches into emerging areas that are of concern to governments in regard to culture and its relations to global economic policies, ethnic and linguistic pluralism, urban interculturalism, sustainability, democracy and global ethics.

Any issue as close to our hearts as culture must inevitably fuel impassioned controversy. We have chosen to break new ground, using the most reliable data available, from a decentred standpoint. We would much rather see people flaring up and galvanized into debate and action upon reading this report than sing them to sleep with bland, repetitive statements.

Moving with the times, this report should be regarded as an ongoing project, a lifelong, interactive, distance dialogue, in much the same way as education must henceforth be. The narrator now builds the situations as she or he goes along. And while a number of voices are creating new realities here, it is to be hoped that very many others will in due course join in this new creative process. Policy-makers will be the winners if they can help to foster this.

The canvas of this report has been painted by many hands including some members of the World Commission on Culture and Development who support its scientific work: Yoro Fall, Kurt Furgler, Keith Griffin, Elizabeth Jelin, Chie Nakane, with Adriaan van der Staay of the Social and Cultural Planning Office in the Hague. The report team also included Louis Emmerij, Paul Streeten, Dharam Ghai, Leo Goldstone, David Throsby and Terry McKinley.

Mr Federico Mayor, Director-General of UNESCO, has made this report possible by steadfastly upholding its independence, and Mr Javier Pérez de Cuéllar, former President of the World Commission on Culture and Development, gave encouragement and words of advice. A strong intellectual commitment to the *World Culture Report* came from Mahbub ul Haq and other members of the Steering Committee for the Follow-up of *Our Creative Diversity*. The financing of the report was generously provided by the Government of the Netherlands.

The report also benefited from the expertise of many UNESCO specialists whose commitment to and unfailing belief in the ideals of the Organization are a shining example of intercultural co-operation.

List of tables and graphs

Tables

1   Mega-cities of the world: population (millions) in 1994 and 2015 (estimated)   106

2   Observed rates of transitions (by lagged per capita income and lagged rate of economic growth)   136

3   Cases when democracy was overthrown (by per capita income and the perpetuators)   136

4   Religions and regime transitions: dynamic probit model   141

5   Ethnolinguistic fractionalization and regime transitions: dynamic probit model   142

6   Breakdown (hours) of television programmes broadcast in Latin America and the Caribbean (by country of origin)   166

7   Flow of television programmes towards Latin America and the Caribbean   166

8   World revenues from music publishing ($ million) (1994)   196

9   World sales of music recordings (1995)   197

10   Trends in music recording sales (1986–96 and forecast 2001)   198

11   Percentage share of music recording sales, (by region, 1991, 1996 and forecast 2001)   198

12   Major music piracy markets (1995)   200

13   Exports and imports of musical goods and services: Australia (1991/92) and the United Kingdom (1993)   201

14   Means and standard deviations (logits) for various measures of satisfaction (1995)   259

15   Means and standard deviations (logits) for various values to be taught to children (1993)   264

16   Opinions on marriage and divorce (1994)   270

17   Opinions on sexual freedom in standard deviations (logits) and in mean percentages (1994)   271

18   Various satisfactions (1995, 18 countries)   278

19(a)   Trust in people and various satisfactions (1990–93, 42 countries)   279

19(b)   Trust in people and various satisfactions (1990–93, 6 regions)   280

20   Comparison between the present world and that of the past and the future (1995, 17 countries)   281

21(a)   Important qualities to be taught to children (1990–93, 40 countries)   282

21(b)   Important qualities to be taught to children (1990–93, 6 regions)   283

21(c)   Important qualities to be taught to children (by gender, 1990–93, 6 regions)   284

22(a)   Approval of the human rights movement, interest in politics and geographical identification (1990–93, 42 countries)   285

22(b)   Approval of the human rights movement, interest in politics and geographical identification (1990–93, 6 regions)   286

22(c)   Approval of the human rights movement by education (1990–93, 6 regions)   287

23(a)   Rank order of countries on intolerance scale and tolerance towards some specific groups (1990–93, 42 countries)   288

23(b)   Rank order of countries on intolerance scale and tolerance towards some specific groups (1990–93, 6 regions)   289

23(c)   Rank order of countries on intolerance scale and tolerance towards some specific groups (by age, 1990–93, 6 regions)   290

24   Opinions on the way society treats men and women and opinions on the change of women's social position (1995, 22 countries)   291

25(a) Attitudes towards paid work for married women (1990–93, 41 countries)   292

25(b) Attitudes towards paid work for married women (1990–93, 6 regions)   293

25(c) Attitudes towards paid work for married women (by gender, 1990–93, 6 regions)   294

26(a) Opinions on marriage and divorce (1994, 24 countries)   295

26(b) Opinions on marriage and divorce (1994, 6 regions)   296

26(c) Opinions on marriage and divorce (by age, 1994, 6 regions)   297

27(a) Opinions on sexual freedom (1994, 24 countries)   298

27(b) Opinions on sexual freedom (1994, 6 regions)   299

28(a) Environmental attitudes (1992, 24 countries)   300

28(b) Environmental attitudes (1992, 6 regions)   301

29   Opinions on the state of the environment (1988–89, 16 countries)   302

30   Publication of books   326

31   Consumption of cultural goods and services (music albums, films, cultural paper)   327

32   Production of long films   327

33   Educational attainment   330

34   Means of communication (newspapers, telephone lines, TVs and computers)   331

Graphs

1   Percentage believing that most people can be trusted (1990–93)   36

2(a) Comparing countries in terms of communication: letters sent abroad per person (1995)   43

2(b) International telephone calls: minutes per person (1995)   44

2(c) Fax machines per 10,000 persons (1992–95)   46

3   Cultural attitudes to women's employment: female labour force participation rate as a percentage of male labour force participation rate (1995)   56

4   Multilingual peoples: countries where over fifty languages are spoken (1996)   68

5   Televisions per 1,000 persons (1995)   107

6   International migrants: percentage of total population (1990)   112

7   Teaching and practising tolerance (1990–93)   130

8   Number of books published per 100,000 persons (1991–94)   163

9   Percentage of imports in total films distributed (1990–93)   168

10   Cultural television programmes: percentage of total programmes (1989–94)   171

11   Most-translated authors (1994)   187

12   Disseminating the world's culture through its languages (1994)   188

13   National popular music as a percentage of all popular music (1996)   199

14   Internet hosts per 10,000 persons (1996–97)   216

15   Parties to UNESCO World Heritage Conventions (1997)   227

16   Financial satisfaction (1994)   261

Map

Map of the distribution of indigenous peoples throughout the world   78

General introduction

At the turn of the last century, most people in the world lived in villages and would not have met a foreigner from a remote culture in their life. Today, at the turn of this century, most people come into contact with persons from other cultures every day. Images of other cultures fill the television and film screens, and in work places, streets and markets, people meet traders, migrants, travellers and refugees constantly, particularly in cities. In the space of one hundred years, cultural interaction around the world has increased dramatically.

Culture has evolved as a continuum in which particular cultures or aspects of particular cultures have blended or differentiated at various times. In the course of their long evolution most cultures have developed distinct terms for 'foreigners' and codes of conduct on how to behave towards them. But today, with neighbours in a typical twenty-floor building using different languages and practising different religions, their children none the less attend the same schools; or when trade is continuous among multicultural partners, the traditional codes for dealing with 'others' break down and new ones have to be developed.

There are various responses to such situations, which are being reproduced everywhere in the world. People may seek security in 'traditional' cultures, feeling that cultural contact is a threat to existing patterns and ways of life. Yet there is no way in which cultural patterns can be 'preserved' when there are dynamic processes of change under way. Some people may express fear and sorrow for the 'loss' or transformation of traditional culture, and indeed this concern is constantly being heard in international meetings and in local and national gatherings.

Other people may be stimulated by this new challenge and go forward, changing and adapting as well as persuading others to adopt some of their new ways. There are those, however, who want to impose their culture or religion on others.

What is new about these patterns of cultural contact and exchange? The globalization of world markets is advancing at a very fast pace in this last decade of the twentieth century. Financial markets, economic systems and information exchanges are leaping across borders and frontiers. Some authors even see globalization as a process that is leading to the gradual disappearance of borders and institutions, including the territorial state. This may be considered somewhat far-fetched in so far as there are clear indications that the notion of globalization does not involve a linear process.

In fact, there are a number of multiple and complex processes under way. If in financial markets there are trends towards opening national boundaries and the emergence of powerful actors that do not reflect national or state allegiances, much of what is happening is linked to the process of 'internationalization', i.e. the opening of frontiers between nation-states that continue to lead an autonomous existence although they are increasingly interactive.

The recognition of the multiple dimensions of globalization and internationalization – whether frontiers are dissolved, become more permeable yet continue to exist, or become encompassed in larger units (e.g. regional blocks) or decentralized in smaller ones with increasing autonomy – is crucial today to an understanding of cultural processes and to the discussion of cultural diversity.

In this report we challenge the common implicit assumption of culture as a homogeneous, integral and coherent unit. Such units have existed only intermittently, if at all, in the historical context of the evolution of cultures. Cultures can no longer be examined as if they were islands in an archipelago. The contemporary globalization of economic, political and social life has resulted in even more cultural penetration and overlapping, the co-existence in a given social space of several cultural traditions, and in a more vivid interpenetration of cultural experience and practice. Modern media and transportation technologies, travel and tourism have accentuated and accelerated processes that have been in motion throughout history.

In order to capture the fluid character of relationships between cultures and the realization that cultural flows are not territorially bound, notions such as 'creolization', 'hybridity', and 'cultural complexity' have emerged in the vocabulary of contemporary social science.

Although the classic vision of unique cultural patterns arguably has some merit, its limitations are serious. The most important weakness is that it emphasizes shared patterns at the expense of processes of change and internal inconsistencies, conflicts and contradictions. In contrast to the classic view which posits culture as a self-contained whole made up of coherent patterns, culture is now conceived as a mass of interplaying stimuli.

Cultural contact and exchanges have not always been harmonious and equitable. There are of course differences in power, globally and locally, and we live in a world of multiple polarities. There is cultural interchange as opposed to a one-way flow, although the process of interpenetration may at times be unequal. The global is visible in the local, but each locality absorbs global influences in distinctive ways. One could look at specific local spaces and conditions, and search for the ways in which these spaces can creatively adapt, react, resist or transform the threats and opportunities that come from the outside. In that vein, there is clearly a growing diversity of local patterns in handling globalization, i.e. what may be termed the diversity of the local in the global.

In more general terms, therefore, the question to ask is 'How do multiple cultures coexist in an interactive world?' Many different groups are trying to answer this question, including governments, political leaders and researchers. In a communication- and information-driven era, all individuals and communities should be able to make their own choices. Already, such choices are becoming wider in scope and content, especially in urban settings. Yet the ability to make cultural choices involves certain prerequisites – to be free from hunger and physical violence, and to be able to make one's own choices – and we cannot say that these are being met in all parts of the world.

Furthermore, individuals and communities may have a choice as to their local cultural identity, although the boundaries of their choice are inserted within those of larger groups commanding allegiance: the nation-state, micro- or macro-regional cultures, linguistic groups or spiritual communities. In this way, cultural identities today overlap many linguistic, religious, geographical and political entities. People's lives are made up of multiple allegiances in the workplace and the market place, just as the images and texts of television, films and the Internet multiply the networks in which they are enmeshed.

In spite of this increasing exposure to diversity, the fear of foreigners, ancestral or contemporary, is a very real feeling that has led to conflict, war and genocide in recent years. Beyond fear, however, is the fact that conflict has frequently resulted from attempts by one group to dominate or subordinate another. It is not enough, then, to call on governments and communities to be tolerant and to respect 'the other'. New social and governing arrangements must be found to allow expression of cultural diversity, while keeping a common purpose and resolve to enable people to live together and co-operate.

Conflict is often viewed as destructive of the social order. But conflict, or at least some forms of it, can also be regarded as a pillar of democratic societies, as the glue that holds them together. Conflicts can provide society with the 'social capital' it needs to be kept together. Some authors have made a beginning in distinguishing between conditions when conflict is destructive and when constructive. One may distinguish between conflicts about more/less, such as the distribution of income, and conflicts about either/or, such as abortion. Conflict arises inevitably with change. Globalization and technical progress benefit some countries, some regions, some sectors and some groups, and harm others. In free societies, those who suffer will tend to organize themselves and attempt to regain their position. They will be supported by those who agree with them from a sense of social justice or sympathy. One group is motivated by self-interest, the other by solidarity or a sense of fairness or fellow-feeling. The strength of democratic societies may derive from this combination and from the conflicts to which it gives rise.

If poverty comprises many more dimensions than lack of income and includes deprivation of education and health services, social exclusion, lack of employment, discrimination against women, environmental degradation (of the soil, water, forests and climate), insecurity, violation of human rights, lack of voice in the counsels of society, and lack of cultural expression, the chances of conflict over its reduction and eradication are greatly increased. Income can be divided in different proportions and is therefore easier to negotiate and to compromise on than decisions that are subject to an either/or. Ethnic, linguistic, religious and gender divisions and disagreements on voting rights give rise to non-divisible conflicts. Unfortunately, it seems that these types of conflict which are not readily amenable to negotiation and compromise are now on the increase.

Globalization reduces the confrontations between capital, management and high skills on the one hand, and capital and labour on the other by enabling the former to opt out by going abroad. 'The community spirit that is normally needed in a democratic market society tends to be spontaneously generated through the experience of tending the conflicts that are typical of that society', writes Albert Hirschman.[1] And Dani Rodrik goes on to ask: 'But what if globalization reduces the incentives to "tend" to these conflicts? What if, by reducing the civic engagement of internationally mobile groups, globalization loosens the civic glue that holds societies together and exacerbates social fragmentation? Hence globalization delivers a double blow to social cohesion – first by exacerbating conflict over fundamental beliefs regarding social organization and second by weakening the forces that would normally militate for the resolution of these conflicts through national debate and deliberation'.[2]

The present report attempts to convey the various levels and approaches that can be adopted in looking at cultural diversity in the world today.

Some people argue in favour of the elimination of cultural diversity. Since individuals interact and co-ordinate their actions through culture, cultural diversity can interfere irritatingly with time and effort-saving. But apart from this practical argument against diversity, there are several strong arguments in its favour.

Above all, cultural diversity is here to stay. But in addition to its inevitability, diversity is desirable for several reasons. First, diversity is valuable in its own right as a manifestation of the creativity of the human spirit. Second, it is required by principles of equity, human rights and self-determination. Third, in analogy to biological diversity, it can help humanity to adapt to the limited environmental resources of the world. In this context diversity is linked to sustainability. Fourth, it is needed to oppose political and economic dependence and oppression. Fifth, it is aesthetically pleasing to have an array of different cultures. Sixth, it stimulates the mind. And seventh, it can provide a reserve of knowledge and experience about good and useful ways of doing things.

But we are not confined to merely celebrating diversity. We can see it at work, as a majority of people become involved in the challenge of interculturality, that is, the ways in which diverse groups can and should live together, in a shared world. We can see an increase in cultural exchanges and hybrids; in the protection of one's own culture, as the current attention and appreciation that

cultural heritage has received in the last decade; in new creative forms – the chicano muralist art in the United States and the Indian theatre experience are examples of the creative use of elements of traditional cultures to fashion new meaning, a pattern that is becoming common, specially in certain urban districts of large cities. New languages are springing up as old ones are becoming muted. This is certainly true of music, and it is equally true of painting, sculpture, theatre and, most of all, films, video and the new multimedia.

However, besides these creative forces of interculturality, the current world scene is also witness to numerous struggles for control over resources that too often are presented as cultural or ethnic conflict. The challenge here is to find ways in which interculturality can handle conflict and create spaces and institutions of cultural 'conviviality'.

A major issue examined in this report is what has been described as a tendency to produce a single homogeneous global culture, most often ascribed to increasing economic globalization. But there is of course a counter-current, i.e. increasing cultural diversity and creativity. When uniformity entails a blunting of the creative edges of cultures, it is clearly negative and implies loss and cultural impoverishment. However, when uniformity results, say, in the establishment of international standards for cultural activities – ranging from the recognition of basic rights of minorities and indigenous groups to copyright agreements or UNESCO's world heritage sites – and involves many groups and voices democratically in the decision-making process, it undoubtedly becomes positive.

A word of caution is needed before considering the contents of this report. Ambivalence and multiple interpretations and meanings are part and parcel of culture and cultural analysis. The same principle applies to the present work. Our intention is to put forward issues and questions and to come up with some answers, even though they may not all be final or absolute answers, based on authority or on forced consensus. The debatable nature of the subject-matter of this report implies the need to convey some of the same cultural pluralism that the report itself praises. Hence the plurality of authors, and the plurality of views, albeit at times at odds with one another.

The report starts with a discussion of the interrelationship between economic and financial policies on the one hand, and cultural diversity and uniformity within countries and regions on the other. Is there still room for differences in the paths taken for economic and social development in the face of the tremendous forces of globalization? Have cultural and institutional factors been taken into account when economic development strategies have been adopted or imposed? These are some of the questions considered in Part One.

Part Two outlines several major world trends and processes, including the logic of equality and difference at an abstract level and at that of concrete intercultural encounters. These concern mainly the conditions of indigenous cultures and populations, the diverse understanding of environmental issues, cultural heterogeneity and encounters in the face of the urban explosion, and the link between cultures and democracy. The evidence presented seems to point to a creative tension between homogenization trends at the macro-level and local wisdom and diversity at the micro-level.

Part Three considers the impact of global markets on culture, and assesses the role of cultural policy in managing the direction of economic and cultural change. Can global markets provide new opportunities for creativity, not only in the arts but also in economic management, innovation and technology ? The chapters here look especially at the role of cultural policy in fostering cultural industries in conditions of increased internationalization, managing cultural heritage and providing new forms of copyright protection in an era of cyberculture.

Part Four presents an interesting attempt to translate the abstract concept of global ethics into measurable attitudes through the use of public opinion data from many countries assembled and analysed by the Dutch Social and Cultural Planning Office. Some reference is made to the themes of the various chapters in the report. This part also touches on the complex relationship between culture and ethics.

Part Five contains a discussion of methodological issues that arise in devising cultural indicators. The construction of cultural indicators of well-being is, indeed, a major conceptual and empirical challenge. There is also a discussion of the arguments for and against the construction of a composite index of cultural achievement. Heterogeneity and richness of cultural manifestations do not lend themselves easily to the design of a single composite index. Yet the challenge is left open for future work in successive issues of the report. Data for a wide range of cultural indicators in many countries are included.

Implications for policy are the subject of Part Six of the report. Culture is being increasingly invoked to account for both the successes and failures of development. Such assertions call for an in-depth analysis of the relationship between culture and development and of the role of diversity in economic success, social opportunity, political stability and conflict-resolution. The evidence points to the need for democratic institutions to favour a more participatory culture and more democratic political structures open to diverse voices and interests within nation-states. Policy projections should include experimental forms of creative conviviality to foster recognition of national and local cultural values in economic management with full participation of all social actors through new partnerships at all levels.

Part Seven analyses the question of the collection and comparison of statistical data on culture and development. Stressing the complexity of cultural indicators, it goes on to emphasize the need to broaden the scope of measurable and reported

aspects of world culture beyond the mere production
and consumption of cultural goods in terms of the
market economy. This part discusses the limitations
of designing a monolithic cultural development
index that would reinforce the current bias between
developing and developed countries to the detriment
of cultural diversity. Finally, a series of statistical
tables accentuates the dearth of basic cultural
indicators in many countries, which hampers the
comparability of data.

The overall implications of the various forms
of evidence examined in the report is that there is far
more global and local creativity of every kind than
many people believe. Globalization and
homogenization are not synonymous, nor is the
latter inevitable or even likely. Many local cultures
and art forms are stimulated by intercultural contact
and by global markets, rather than crushed by them.

Notes

1.   A. O. Hirschman, 'Social Conflicts as Pillars of
Democratic Societies', *A Propensity to Self-Subversion*,
Cambridge, Massachusetts, and London, Harvard
University Press, 1995.
2.   D. Rodrik, *Has Globalization Gone Too Far?*,
Washington, Institute for International Economics, March
1997, p. 70.

Part One
Culture and economic development

Introduction to Part One

In Part One of the first *World Culture Report* we have chosen to look at the cultural assumptions of development models, or rather at economic and social policies worldwide. Can we say that the range of development models has progressively narrowed over time and that with the increased level of internationalization and globalization the room for manœuvre has diminished even more? Is there room today for different approaches to development and, if so, what is the role of culture?

Part One of the report thus defines culture in a broad manner, as a way of life and a way of living together. This includes the values that people hold, tolerance for others (race and gender), outward as opposed to inward orientations and inclinations, and so on. Of course culture can also be defined in a narrower sense (as in subsequent Parts of the report) as an expression of art, music, literature and so forth.

Western ethnocentrism has customarily been employed as the implicit basis of thinking about development. The paradigm equating development to modernization and modernization to Westernization has long been, and still is, the conventional wisdom, although it has been recognized that there are several alternative strategies of development. One of the many paradoxes that has accompanied internationalization and globalization is that local peculiarities are now being stressed more than before. Globalization stimulates localization, it would appear. Or rather, globalization leads to cultural interpenetrations which, in turn, lead to a multiplication of permutations and the growth of new 'local' cultures. Cultural pluralism is increasingly becoming an all-pervasive feature of societies, and ethnic identification is often a normal and healthy response to pressures of globalization. The impression of growing global uniformity may, therefore, be misleading as people turn more and more to culture as a means of self-definition and mobilization.

Could it be, therefore, that globalization marks the true beginning of a search for a range of

development models based on local differences? We say 'local' rather than 'national', because almost all societies are multicultural in composition and it would therefore be wrong to equate cultural identity with national identity. Cultural freedom – as pointed out in *Our Creative Diversity* – 'leaves us free to meet one of the most basic needs, the need to define our *own* basic needs'. But while defining one's own basic needs is one thing, the way to attain them – through economic and social policies – is quite another. It is easy to imagine a situation in which the bundle of basic needs is defined very differently from one culture to another, but in which the model, i.e. the policies through which to reach these different bundles, is not essentially different from one culture to another.

Our contention can be summarized in the following points:
- Western culture has held an iron grip on development thinking and practice;
- this influence has tended to increase during the last twenty or so years through the force of global markets, in particular financial ones; but
- there do exist alternative development models based on a different cultural, institutional and historical background; and
- such alternatives are likely to multiply in the era of globalization, in spite of appearances, which may paradoxically witness greater diversity than uniformity.

Japan has consistently held its own view on the question of globalization, development models and culture. It runs along the following lines: globalization does not imply that a universal model or uniform set of rules as set forth in the current economic and financial orthodoxy (which has spread from the United States and Europe to Latin America, Eastern Europe and parts of Africa) will eventually spread to all parts of the world. The world will, therefore, not become homogeneous, either economically or culturally. The Japanese view holds that localization, or an identification with local

cultural values, is proceeding hand in hand with globalization.

The current orthodoxy – the so-called uniform model – consists of pluralistic congressional or parliamentary democracy on the political front, and of the neoclassical market economy on the economic one. Most mainstream economists tend to apply this universal model unilaterally to all countries, neglecting the historical, institutional and cultural backgrounds of the countries in question. But there have always been doubters who recognize the plurality of economic systems, institutions and cultures, and emphasize the interaction among them. For them the key concept is not uniformity, but rather diversity and interaction. In this connection Japan, and other East Asian countries, are distinctive in that they modernized and industrialized their systems while at the same time retaining their own traditions and culture.

It has been argued by many economists that deregulation must be implemented as intensively, simultaneously and speedily as possible on many fronts. But such an approach implicitly assumes that Anglo-American institutions and social environments complementary to these institutions are already in place or can be very quickly established by enlightened reformers with the help of consultants and international organizations.

Overlooking the validity of different cultures and the evolutionary processes of history has frequently led to confusion and the collapse of the existing order rather than to reform. The alternative would be strategic deregulation of some selected sectors while retaining controls in other sectors, at least at the outset. How can proper macroeconomic policies be conducted if the necessary infrastructure, such as a central banking system and an effectively governed enterprise system, do not exist? Forcing a uniform model on diverse country and cultural situations may endanger the economic future of these countries as well as that of the world at large. We seem to be at a crossroads now, where alternative approaches have to be pursued and diversity rather than uniformity must be chosen.

The point to be made is that each region would be well-advised to establish its own model of capitalism and democracy. Indeed, each region will have to do so if one accepts the general idea of path dependency, i.e. the notion that the future is strongly influenced by the past. We do not live in a timeless, a-historical world. The world should gain from systematic diversity rather than suffer from the confusion and possible catastrophe caused by forceful applications of a universal model. Uniformity ultimately is impoverishing.

Caution, however, is of the essence and we should not indulge in too extreme a form of cultural relativism. Extreme relativism can very easily degenerate into barren nihilism or dangerous anarchism. What is important here is to capture the totality of the system with diverse elements, in other words, globalization with local differences.

We should aspire in future to an interconnecting global system linking all regions or countries of the world while respecting their diverse cultures and their own special socio-economic systems. This does not necessarily mean that we observe widely divergent models, but that above all we should not impose the uniform model that is now being pressed on developing countries and on countries in transition.

The least we can say is that the specific historical experiences of Africa or Latin America are likely to imply that the systems will differ in some important respects from the Anglo-American model, just as the French, Italian and Spanish configurations differ from the German model. More and more developing countries argue that societies differ in their particular path of development; that each society has its own political and social structures and cultural values; that the role of the state and the substance of national policies vary according to the needs and requirements of each society's political and social structure and cultural values; and therefore

that what is appropriate to one society may not be appropriate to another.

The need for a differentiated approach has long been obvious, in view of the remarkable success of the East Asian development experience – notwithstanding the 1997 financial panic. Moreover, we must confront the disquieting fact that many countries that have adopted the current orthodoxy over the past fifteen to twenty years are experiencing worsening income inequality and sometimes greater poverty and reduced employment. Similar phenomena have of course also been observed in countries that have not accepted the current orthodoxy but have participated in the process of globalization, such as China. So that while the causal linkages are not well understood, the association between globalization and economic orthodoxy and the accentuation of problems of inequality and poverty is a cause for serious concern.

If one of the priorities is, according to *In from the Margins* (Council of Europe, Strasbourg, 1996, p. 9), 'to bring the millions of dispossessed and disadvantaged in from the margins of society and cultural policy in from the margins of governance', then bringing these two together by adapting the development models according to the needs, institutions, history and culture of different societies is an absolute necessity.

The scope for manœuvre is not large, but wider than one might at first sight suspect. This scope involves institutions, consumption habits, land rights, access to markets, distribution systems, economic democracy and so forth. The growing internationalism and globalization will provide diversity at least as much as they impose uniformity.

Chapter 1
Culture and economic development

J. Mohan Rao
Professor, Specialist in Development Economics,
University of Massachusetts, Amherst
(United States)

'As the global age dawns . . . questions linking culture, development and globalization are no less pressing than other vital questions about our common future . . .'

Culture and development in a global age

Despite the vast expansion in the world's capacity to produce material goods and services over the past two centuries, economic growth remains a powerful imperative today. The power of this imperative seems self-evident in the poorer nations of the world which hold a large majority of the world's population. According to World Bank projections, the number of people classified as 'absolutely poor', most of whom reside in the less-developed countries, will have grown at virtually the same rate as world population itself during the final decade of the millennium (Jolly, Rosenthal and Tokman, 1994). But even in some of the richest countries on the planet, levels of unemployment and underemployment, of economic insecurity and vulnerability, remain stubbornly high. There are also troubling signs of growing income and wealth inequalities in many countries, both poor and rich, a trend that worsens feelings of economic deprivation and social inadequacy even if average incomes continue to grow.

Economic expansion since the Second World War has ushered in a truly global age, an age of rapidly increasing international economic interdependence in the form of cross-border flows of trade, investment, finance and technology. In addition, this process of globalization has received a strong boost over the past decade or two as numerous governments have chosen (or been compelled) to liberalize their economies internally and externally.

The impact of globalization and liberalization is hardly limited to the economic and political levels only. Economic globalization has greatly increased the international interchange of information, ideas, beliefs and values. Although political-economic effects – on states, firms, workers and consumers – are understandably immediate and palpable, globalization may also have a wide and profound impact at the level of cultures (in the sense of people's shared beliefs and attitudes, lifestyles and values). But the relationship between economy and culture is by no means a one-way street. Given that the world is characterized by great cultural diversity, cultures can also be expected to influence each other through global interchange and react upon the process of local and global economic change. Such interchange and interaction may facilitate or hinder economic growth; it may also be a prime source of cultural assimilation or conflict. And if economic growth in a globalized setting has the capacity not only to transform individual and collective ways of living but also to transform the very basis of our evaluations of these alternative modes, we must ask how economic change can be promoted without denying valuable elements in a country's tradition.

To be sure, conventional economics has championed globalization and liberalization virtually unconditionally. In particular, liberal economics advocates a rigidly uniform model of economic institutions and public policies whether for rich or poor nations. This is based on the claim that the mutual economic gains for all nations participating in international markets are maximized when such markets are free from interventions and policy-imposed impediments. Analogous arguments support non-interventionism in domestic markets as well. Indeed, without protectionist and other barriers to their smooth functioning, global and domestic markets are expected, in this view, to equalize productivities, prices and incomes both within and across nations. Although employed ubiquitously, these arguments and the economic models on which they are based are not universally accepted. A major objection is that globally integrated markets cannot be expected to produce symmetric gains for both weak and strong economies. There are powerful economic forces that make for and sustain unequalizing rather than equalizing development both within and among nations. These forces are deeply implicated in the huge economic differences across nations that exist today and which, on average, have visibly increased over the past four decades. Similarly, nations inherit diverse problems

and diverse resources (both economic and social) from their histories. It should hardly be surprising if they should wish or need to deal with their situations in diverse ways. Especially for poor countries, harnessing the opportunities presented by markets and technologies requires: (a) strategic state interventions in markets and long-term management of the economy on both the internal and external fronts, and (b) the constitution of participative communities at various levels rather than a policy of state minimalism as defined by liberal orthodoxy. Yet, for both rich and poor nations alike, globalization appears to be reducing the space available for the pursuit of autonomous policies. Some see in this development the possibility, indeed the likelihood, of political and economic crises that will require a turn away from the now-dominant neo-liberal prescriptions of unregulated globalization and liberalization (Greider, 1997). How can nations create for themselves the political and economic capabilities to pursue whatever they see fit to value?

The austere one-dimensionality of liberal economics is not, however, the only source of growing worldwide unease about globalization. As national policies and institutions come increasingly under the scrutiny of global financial markets, as fiscal and labour regimes are bent to the growing imperative of 'international competitiveness', as cherished traditions and lifestyles appear increasingly to be threatened, the sense of national autonomy is gradually losing potency. Some observers are worried that the juggernaut of economic globalization will produce a culturally uniform world, a world of one-dimensional men and women that, like monocropping agriculture, will have lost its creative potential and adaptive resilience. Once again, globalization has its champions who draw hope from the very same trend that the distinctions and differences, both egregious and insidious, that have for long divided the human family will at last have been overcome and the basis for much-needed global co-operation laid. But this hope seems to rest on the

The Asian financial turmoil in perspective[1]

For years, if not decades, politicians and experts alike have praised the 'East Asian development model' even if they have not agreed on the components of the model. Indeed East Asia witnessed *annual* per capita GDP growth during the thirty-year period 1965–95 of 6.6% for the four 'Tigers' (i.e. the Republic of Korea, Taiwan, Singapore and Hong Kong), 5.6% for China and 3.9% for South-East Asia, as compared to 1.9% for South Asia, 2.1% for the OECD, 0.9% for Latin America and 0.2% for sub-Saharan Africa.

Suddenly last summer, many Asian currencies depreciated sharply, stock exchange valuations collapsed, and politicians and experts denounced corrupt local customs, weak banking systems, lifetime employment, etc., as the causes of the débâcle.

WHAT ACTUALLY HAPPENED?

The Asian currency crises of 1997 are not a sign of the end of rapid economic growth in Asia but rather a recurring – if difficult to predict – pattern of financial instability that often accompanies rapid economic growth. Just as Indonesia, Malaysia and the Republic of Korea rapidly recovered from financial crises in the 1970s and 1980s, so the Asian economies are likely to resume rapid growth within two or three years. Indeed the currency crises originated from misaligned exchange rates, which were severely punished by market forces in a liberalized and globalized economy. Long-term fundamentals remain sound.

The West is currently enjoying a disproportionate share of world income, but its share will diminish as global market forces penetrate even more deeply into Asia. By 2025, Asia will probably regain its long-enjoyed place at the centre of the world economy. Asia may account for up to 60% of world income by that time, with the West's share falling from around 45% today to between 20 and 30%.

These long-term projections might seem heedlessly optimistic in the face of the economic shocks now buffeting Asia, but the currency upheavals probably reflect short-run financial considerations aggravated by destabilizing speculation rather than a long-term crisis of regional economic growth. The major part of the explanation is that many East and South-East Asian countries came to peg their currencies to the US dollar during the 1990s, even though the region's trade depends not just on exports to the United States, but on the European and Asian markets too. After mid-1995, the US dollar began to appreciate sharply vis-à-vis the yen and the major continental European currencies. As a result, the Asian currencies also appreciated sharply against the yen, European and other currencies, such as the Chinese yuan. In effect, Asian exporters became increasingly uncompetitive and priced themselves out of the European and Japanese markets. They were also facing stiff competition from China which had devalued the yuan in early 1994. As a result of all this, its growth of exports began to fall and countries ran increasingly large balance-of-payment deficits. Naturally, exchange rates came under pressure.

There is a second, related aspect of the financial crises. In the mid-1990s a rising share of foreign capital inflows appears to have been attracted to speculative investment in real estate. Following financial market deregulation in many countries, Asian commercial banks borrowed dollars from abroad and lent the funds domestically to real estate developers. So, when property markets weakened in 1996 and the currencies declined in value in 1997, the banks were hit by non-performing loans, and many faced insolvency.

The currency crises probably will have continuing negative effects on the health of the banking system and on investment by the construction sector for two or three years, so that growth during 1997 and 1998 will be slower than in previous years. The crises also underscore the need for better regulation and supervision of the financial markets as a condition for more stable growth in the future.

Looking forward, the currency crises (appropriately dealt with) do not call into question the underlying strategy of the region or the medium-term growth prospects.

Louis Emmerij
Economist, Special Adviser to the President,
Inter-American Development Bank (IDB),
Washington, D.C. (United States)

as yet unfulfilled expectation that global inequalities will progressively disappear. For its part, liberal economics tends either to treat culture as a negligible epiphenomenon of the economy or as an expression of the scope for individual choice (which free markets are presumed to promote and cater to).

But the pursuit of individual ends with individual means which the market encourages and thrives on does not ensure that social arrangements required for furthering individual and collective ends will be met. Cultural freedom in the sense of our collective capacity 'to meet one of the most basic needs, the need to define our own basic needs' (World Commission on Culture and Development, 1995) does not even enter the liberal lexicon. Yet this most basic of our needs is now threatened by both global pressures and global neglect. This threat to cultural freedom cannot but mean a threat to democracy and community. Will globalization produce cultural harmony or cultural contradictions within and among nations? Conversely, can global cultural diversity and freedom be preserved without harming creative advance for the world as a whole?

As the global age dawns, these questions linking culture, development and globalization are no less pressing than other vital questions about our common future such as the growing fragility of the global environment. It can scarcely be doubted that viable answers can only be found through the creative exercise of our collective freedom. Our collective freedom can be preserved and promoted only through the conscious application of that very freedom.

The creative role of culture

Social life plays not only an instrumental role in the development of individuals' capabilities but also has an important constitutive role and independent value. Social relations impinge on individuals' capabilities and on the criteria by which individuals make their choices. In particular, the experience of well-being may be inter-subjective rather than individualistic: thus action may be driven by social envy and empathy, not just egoistic motives of the individual. In such a case, human development would have to be defined and measured in social/relational terms by taking account of such interdependence. If interdependence varies over time and space, then, the concept of human development cannot be uniform over all such situations. Even if we took human development to refer only to individual functionings and not to feelings, there is no reason to suppose that individual capabilities and functionings are not socially influenced also. The functionings of individuals may be governed by inter-personal relations among them in families, firms, various other forms of collective organization and communities at large. This would be the case, for example, in situations where power and influence are exercised. Even apart from the interdependence of valuations and of functionings, social life may also strongly condition the specific beliefs and values by which individuals make their choices. Indeed, social individuals typically develop beliefs and preferences about how society itself should be constituted. If any of the above channels of social conditioning holds, then there exists no unified measure of human development that, in general, is invariant over time or across societies.

While demographic and material features of the environment have been invoked to explain various cultural practices in economistic terms, the basic question is not resolved thereby. For example, it can be argued that although the rise in dowry rates in India in recent decades seems to conflict with the fact that the female/male population ratio has been adverse and deteriorating over the same period, it can be none the less accounted for by the acceleration of population growth: because men tend to marry women considerably younger than themselves, accelerating population growth has served to reduce further a low ratio of men to women in the relevant population cohorts (Bagchi, 1996). Such economic determinism, however, can in

no way explain the observation that marriages require dowry in some parts of the world but not in others (or that marriages may require bride-price instead). Marshall Sahlins (1976) provides an even more mundane example to establish this point. It may be contended, in functionalist fashion, that forks and knives are more blunt than they might 'usefully' be so as to guard against accidental injuries. But this does not tell us why forks and knives came into vogue in the first place.

These considerations show that individualistic constructions in economics and politics achieve coherence in explaining social outcomes precisely by ignoring the contingent or endogenous elements in individual values and beliefs. Does all this then point to a notion of development that must be regarded as just a dimension of culture whose forms are 'ultimately determined by cultural values' (UNRISD–UNESCO, 1997, p. 5)? This seems to be implied if culture constitutes the individual and therefore determines the sorts of choices the individual is likely to make.[2] It is not merely that human development focuses on individual achievements whilst culture has a collective aspect: if this were all, then, one could 'add up' the two aspects to get a comprehensive notion of social development. Rather, what is being implied is that the very content of development, whether at the individual or group levels, ceases to be extraneous to culture.[3]

But it is equally pertinent to examine critically this notion of culture as a unitary and shared totality, sufficient unto itself and having no external referent, determining but itself undetermined. If the economy and economic development are part of a people's culture, what then is the social basis of culture itself? If cultures, in the sense of collective beliefs and attitudes, norms and values, did not vary significantly across social contexts or over time, then, they could not possibly be important to either understanding economy–culture interactions or in defining a general concept of development. It is

precisely because they do vary that cultures acquire significance for social understanding and evaluation. Cultures – as shared complexes of values, beliefs or behaviours – are certainly not immortal. They seem eminently subject to social construction, contestation and evolution.

Moreover, cultures are rarely, if ever, totalizing and monolithic even within social groups that may appear tightly knit and stable. In any real society with even a modicum of complexity – in terms of specialization, differentiation and hierarchy of status, power and wealth – values, beliefs and behaviours may be differentiated and actively contested, not simply shared. Just as important, beliefs-values are learnt but the opportunities and incentives for learning will be socially differentiated. This differentiated learning also creates cultural memory, a repertoire of beliefs and values that each society accumulates during the course of its own particular history. Cultural evolution is thus a socially differentiated process of learning in which a society draws upon its historical past and engages its political present. The construction and contestation of cultures takes place everywhere in society not excluding the so-called economic and political domains: beliefs and values are not independent of the structures of economic and political institutions. But neither is the construction of social institutions independent of beliefs and values held, i.e. there is no reason to suppose that social institutions do not express culture.

If neither institutions nor cultures are trans-historical but, instead, evolving and mutually determining, then, what might the determining parameters be? Outside the individualistic approach, two polar models of social evolution may be distinguished. At one end, we may suppose that cultural and institutional factors specific to each society are the main explanation for differences in social and economic evolution: each society's past governs its path of evolution. This is a model of path dependence in which historical contingency plays a

The incidence of child labour

The heavy incidence of child labour in South Asia provides an excellent example where attempts to describe social stasis and change using economic categories or cultural categories in isolation fail to convince. Governments in many Third World nations contend that child labour cannot be cured overnight and must therefore be endured. Two main arguments underpin their case (and that of other articulate segments of their populations) against a ban on child labour. For one, child labour is not as great a burden as it had been in the heyday of the Industrial Revolution in the West, for most child workers work alongside and in their families, and thereby acquire the skills of traditional occupations. For another, poverty compels the poor to rely on the labour and income of their children for bare survival; hence compulsory education would amount to unconscionable coercion. Economic growth provides the way out of these constraints of poverty. As the economy develops, large-scale enterprises using hired labour and modern technologies will grow and this growth will be at the expense of low-technology family operations. As growth and technological competition intensify, increasing fractions of the labour force will be absorbed by the modern sector, thus generating a growing demand for education and skills. In short, the disappearance of child labour, in this perspective, is simply an economic phenomenon, just another universal pattern of development.

Others argue that this economic-determinist position simply ignores the role of culture if it is not actually wrong. Historically, compulsory education has been introduced in many countries and regions that had low levels of income and widespread poverty (Japan, China, the two Koreas; in South-East Asia too as also Sri Lanka; Germany, New England and Sweden; and the communist countries). According to Weiner (1996), 'theologies and ideologies' were critical determinants in the development of compulsory education in all of these countries. In India, by contrast, 'policy-makers continue to be mired in a set of views that preclude their taking the necessary steps to get children into school and out of the labour force'. Nor have 'the actors that have mattered elsewhere' been sufficiently engaged politically (p. 3014). In other words, beliefs that would be conducive to universal education have not been championed by those in a position to do so. While this explanation relies strongly on cultural specificities, culture's moorings in the broader society need also to be taken account of. Our analysis remains incomplete if we fail to ask who will gain and who will lose from the abolition of child labour in India.

Not surprisingly, economic interests in the perpetuation of child labour are divided along class lines. The middle and upper classes gain both from policies that ignore the education of poor children (as available educational resources are allocated to higher education) and from the labour of these children who are available to work in their households.[4] Some believe that, in addition, the introduction of compulsory education must also mean the abridgement of parental choice. Contrary to the dominant view that child labour is a matter of economic necessities, a survey found a systematic difference between the children and their parents: the girls interviewed 'did not regard their parents' decisions about their schooling as choiceless' (p. 3008). In other words, parents gain at the expense of their own children.

But how do parents gain at all from putting their children to work? A common view is that parents gain directly from the added income due to their children's labour and, by extension, that poor parents have

additional children for this reason. This ignores the obvious fact that such contribution comes many years later in the child's life; in the initial phase, children are consumers of parental resources without contributing to production and this is followed by another phase over which they remain net consumers (that is, consume more than they contribute). Only beyond this gestation period can children make a positive income contribution to their parents. But at the high rates of interest at which capital is usually available to their parents, a net loss on the investment in children seems all but certain. Hence, the real economic 'function', if any, that children may perform for their parents is not so much in raising their incomes but in reducing their economic insecurity, particularly in old age. During the years when a couple are young and healthy, the probability of economic misfortune is generally low; they can therefore, by having more children, choose to suffer a reduction in their 'standard of living' during these years for a reduced probability of misfortune in later years when they are less, and their children more, able to support the family. Indeed, sustenance in old age when there is no other alternative and when the poor wholly discount any savings they might manage to accumulate for themselves may be sufficient reason to invest in children. It is in this light that the 'choices' that poor people make must be seen: it is not because children can be used as workers that they are produced; it is because they are produced that children are used as workers. But children must share their parents' poverty, a burden that may be partly relieved by child labour.

But there is a further wrinkle to the analysis of interests that deserves mention. Individual interests and collective interests may not coincide. Though individual couples may view their children's earnings as beneficial to their families, a high incidence of child labour may well detract from the employment opportunities and earnings rates of adults creating a sort of low-level equilibrium trap in which child labour and poverty reinforce each other. Similarly, there may be a conflict between the short-run and long-run interests of employers. Thus, in a number of industries, 'the availability of low skilled low-wage children has reduced the incentives of businessmen to acquire the sophisticated technologies that would enable them to make export-quality products' (p. 3009). In this case, keeping the market for child labour open actually constricts long-term business and economic growth.

To sum up, it is evident that both cultural and economic factors are germane to an understanding of the prevalence of child labour. The successful abolition of child labour and achievement of universal primary education is not an inexorable law of economic development that operates like a physical law. Beliefs, perhaps even values, that stand in their way have to be transformed. However, such cultural transformations depend on the particular histories and inheritances of different societies. Patterns of existing inequality create vested interests which inhibit emancipatory ideologies and prevent political action for human development. In the Indian case, deep inequalities of income and class are heavily compounded by the inherited inequalities of caste and other forms of social stratification. Yet, we should not identify class interest with the interest of individual members of that class. When the two deviate, individual behaviour and even beliefs may run counter to class interests. In these circumstances, again, the transforming power of cultural politics and culture change become evident.

J. Mohan Rao
Professor, Specialist in Development Economics,
University of Massachusetts, Amherst (United States)

major role. At the other end, it may be supposed that all societies can be fitted within a common model yielding a common, path-independent solution.

In recent years, historicist or path-dependent explanatory models have gained some favour. A valuable example is Barrington Moore's (1987) attempt to explain patterns of authority and inequality in the United States, the former USSR and China. He argues that there exists 'an historical relationship between these three societies and their [respective] predecessors. This relationship goes a long way toward providing an explanation of the character of authority and inequality in each of the three societies. Each society was reacting against its historical predecessor, trying to improve on it by avoiding or reducing earlier forms of unjust authority and inequality' (p. 104). Such reactions required changes in institutions as also in beliefs and values. In each of these societies (and Moore avers the argument can be generalized at least to other democratic-capitalist and authoritarian-socialist societies), there has been an endemic tension between a general reluctance to accept social hierarchy, conflict of interest between groups and the social inequalities that both hierarchy and conflict generate and, on the other, historically specific pressures for the acceptance of the same.

While each conception, the general model as well as the historicist one, is deterministic in its own way, neither seems to allow any genuinely autonomous role for human agency. Even cultural evolution as 'learning' implies learning from determinate objects or experiences. Deterministic accounts of culture and economy leave no room for free human agency whether in constructing economic and political institutions or in choosing beliefs and values. At the same time, however, no society seems wholly exempt from the influence – in the form of constraints and possibilities – of its own history. But the important point is that the contingencies of beliefs and values are resolved contextually, i.e. in a narrative rather than an

explanatory way, or posited in ad hoc fashion.[5] In short, the determining parameters are amorphously specified if specified at all.

Social science abounds in attempts to explain social phenomena on the basis of general principles akin to the 'laws of nature' of classical physics. With much ingenuity, social scientists have sought to persuade themselves and others that there exist real patterns in the raw data of social history that conform with their preferred 'laws of society'. It is probably fair to say that the results have been tantalizing rather than wholly convincing: enough pattern for the persuaded and enough noise for the unpersuaded to perpetuate a dialogue among the deaf.

Experience shows that our beliefs affect our choices and that our choices have profound consequences. Experience does not prove, of course, that we can choose our beliefs 'freely' though they seem to imply such freedom. It may be that our beliefs themselves are determinate consequences of our actual experience of the world, an experience that may not be captured with sufficient precision by the authors in the above examples. But the elementary human notion of controllability (and with it the notion of responsibility, individual or collective) over future development would be meaningless in the absence of an intent to control. Beliefs without intentionality are not meaningful in terms of our own experience. On the other hand, intentionality without beliefs cannot lead to purposive action. Accepting a role for intentionality or creativity does not imply a denial of inherited constraints or necessities. Such a dualistic picture of freedom and determinism does not seem any less reconcilable with the facts of social life than deterministic models.

Such a picture also allows room for meaningful politics and social evolution. By contrast, liberal economic theory has no place for politics. As the economist Abba Lerner remarked : 'An economic transaction is a solved political problem. Economics

has gained the title of queen of the social sciences by choosing solved political problems as its domain' (1972, p. 259). That is to say, only solved political problems permit determinate economic predictions to be made. Does this necessarily imply that 'unsolved political problems' do not have determinate solutions? It might be argued that political solutions derive from a particular history and so are heavily influenced by the minutiae of history (path determinism) rather than being indeterminate. But the alternative hypothesis, emphasizing the narrative rather than the determinative element in politics, would suggest an evolutionary dynamic in which agency, both individual and collective, has an autonomous and 'creative' role.[6] Both economic evolution and cultural change fit into this dynamic with politics – in the sense of thought and action that may change the very parameters of thought and action – assuming a central role in both. Politics here becomes just a shorthand expression for the creative role of agency in social evolution.

A global route to harmony and equality?

Viewed as a process increasing international resource and goods flows, globalization has been a major feature of world economic growth over the past half century. This process has accelerated, especially in respect of finance capital, during the past decade or two. Major impetus for globalization has come from both technological and policy changes. The costs of transactions across national frontiers – the movement of money, knowledge and materials – have been greatly reduced by the information and communication revolutions. Several rounds of international trade negotiations have reduced traditional trade barriers while liberalized regimes for capital flows have been put in place in a number of countries. Many among the economies of the South and in Eastern Europe have shifted policies, in some cases radically, towards opening up their economies to global markets.

It has been argued that by many measures, the world economy was more integrated in the late nineteenth century than it is today (Rodrik, 1997). But such comparisons cannot be sustained without further investigation. It is true that labour movements, in the form of mass migrations from the Old World to the New, were substantially higher during the nineteenth century than they are today. Similarly, net capital outflow relative to GNP was much higher in the United Kingdom prior to the First World War than at any time since. But a large share of these labour and capital flows was restricted to the same group of countries which today account for the lion's share of goods flows. The significance of capital and labour movements in such a comparison cannot be considered apart from trade flows. Economies may be 'integrated' by goods flows even in the absence of any factor movements. Turning to trade volumes relative to national incomes, measured openness in the United States and in Europe peaked before the First World War, fell sharply between the wars and trended upward after the Second World War. By this measure, the advanced economies of the world are not any more open in 1997 than they were in 1897. But per capita incomes in these advanced economies are many times higher today and, as a result, the share of services, which tend to be far more non-tradable than goods, is considerably higher. Hence, even constant trade ratios represent a significant increase in openness.

The policy changes furthering globalization have themselves been conditioned by the pattern of economic growth and accompanying institutional changes. Though the unravelling of the monetary arrangements of the post-war era in 1971, the productivity growth deceleration of the advanced capitalist countries starting in the late 1960s and the oil price increase of 1973 had a definite impact on the shape of international economic relations during the past two decades, these are themselves best seen to have been effects of prior causes. The latter are located in the crumbling of the particular political-economic regime (termed Fordism) in the advanced capitalist countries that maintained stable national and international regimes of rapid growth (the Golden Age).[7] As Fordism successfully diffused from the United States to Western Europe and Japan, high growth was led and sustained by rising wages which enlarged home markets in the advanced capitalist countries. The coincident growth of home demands, together with United States hegemony and the Bretton Woods institutions, also ensured the rapid growth of international trade without threatening conflicts between external and internal balance. The convergence of productivity and income levels in Europe and Japan to those prevalent in the United States accelerated the growth of intra-industry trade and investments. Protectionist barriers to trade also came down in successive rounds. In other words, converging incomes produced market integration, not only the other way around.

As a group and individually, countries in the South enjoyed respectable rates of economic growth during the Golden Age. Growth in the ex-colonies surpassed their dismal performance during the colonial era. This difference was not simply due to the global economic environment of the Golden Age alone; rather, a large if variable share of the difference must be accounted for by the transition from colonialism to sovereignty and the developmental role of the state. The growth momentum was maintained even through the 1970s in part because of better export prices for many raw material exports. Whereas the first oil price increase had produced a severe crisis of macro management in the advanced capitalist countries, the recycling of petro-dollars to the South also supported continuing growth there. But the eventual crash turned out to be far more costly in the South, particularly in sub-Saharan Africa and Latin America, than the earlier one had been in the North. It was brought on by the crushing rise in interest rates and the sharp adverse movement in the South's terms of trade which followed the Reagan-Volcker policies of the early 1980s.

The growing flow of global transactions has not

been conducted in a rudderless market vacuum. On the contrary, it is strongly associated with deliberate national and international economic restructuring. In the North, 'flexibility' has been actively promoted by conservative policies: the political assault on the Fordist compromise and the welfare state, through macro and micro policies, has permitted capital to pursue the new rationality of flexible restructuring. This political-economic environment has enabled footloose capital to wrest further concessions from both labour and the state. In the South, straitened fiscs (reflecting the internal transfer problem arising from the debt crisis) have undermined state capacities to pursue indigenous models of modernization or to sustain and expand anti-poverty programmes. Conditionalities imposed by international creditors, in the form of orthodox stabilization and structural adjustment programmes, have been the major instrument for opening up these economies to the winds of global competition.

The cultural correlates of economic growth

The rapid and sustained growth of incomes is undoubtedly a hallmark of the modern era. It is also characteristic of our epoch that each generation expects and generally wishes to do better materially than its predecessor. And not infrequently, moderns tend not to differentiate between 'being better off' and 'being better'. Not surprisingly, we place high value on innovation and creativity. By contrast, economic growth prior to 1800 was excruciatingly slow, episodic and subject to rapid reversals. Arguably also, the desire for steady material progress was quite alien to pre-modern societies; on the contrary, ancients typically tended to recall a golden if mythical past and to admire if not worship their ancestors. Hence, premodern societies lived by the weighty influence of 'custom' and 'tradition'.

At least broadly, therefore, economic performance is correlated with our beliefs and our values, in short our cultures. Are our desires, like our prophesies, sometimes self-fulfilling (which would

account for the correlation)? If so, cultures may be seen to have an instrumental role in economic growth. Or, do we get inured to the performance of our economies (which too could explain the correlation)? If so, economic change would appear to produce us, i.e. our cultures.

Based on his studies of the economic development of the now advanced countries, Simon Kuznets (1966) concluded that uniformities in the patterns of economic growth were considerable and encompassed a wide range of economic phenomena and indicators. A sustained rate of growth together with these patterned regularities came to be called modern economic growth. In Kuznets' view, modern economic growth was to be accounted for by the waves of scientific discovery and technological invention in the modern period which lead to the transformation of economic organization and productivity. Like most conventional economists, Kuznets saw capitalism as the necessary institutionalization of technological forces. But he also observed that this transformation was accompanied by the breakdown of traditional ideas, beliefs and values.

Apart from a quantum increase in the growth rate, the uniformities that Kuznets (and his followers) described include the following:
• investment acceleration (a doubling or even tripling in the rate of saving and investment);
• the demographic transition (a steep decline in both mortality and fertility rates but with a considerable lag in the former causing a demographic explosion);
• the industrial transition (a large rise in the income share of industry at the expense of agriculture followed later by a rise in the share of services at the expense of industry);
• urbanization (a massive shift in the relative weight of rural and urban dwellers in favour of the latter); and
• rise of large-scale, bureaucratically organized enterprises at the expense of small, family-run firms.

In this light, capitalist development in non-European regions would be seen as a process of diffusion of technologies and associated economic institutions out of Europe. The clear implication is that culture is only an epiphenomenon which can neither impede nor hasten such a transition.

This view is of course at odds with Weber's influential thesis that the rise of the Protestant ethos – a change in religious beliefs and attitudes that also altered the ethics of work, family, material pursuits and community – promoted the advance of capitalism in the West. The implication that only appropriate changes in culture, of the sort the West experienced, could generate a capitalist economy became the dominant view among sociologists. How then was capitalist development elsewhere to be explained? In most cases, it could be attributed to culture change (Westernization) following contact with the West (through missionary work, settlement, trade and aid with or without political dominion and colonialism); in a few, autochthonous substitutes to Protestantism were perceived to support indigenous capitalist development. Conversely, cultural inertia or resistance was supposed to account for failures of economic growth.

Capitalism and markets, and the behaviours they give rise to, are hardly instituted in identical ways even among the advanced economies of the world. Even a casual glimpse at the advanced market economies shows that there are great and persistent differences in their economic and social institutions. The employment relationship; retailing; inter-firm co-operation versus competition; business-government relations; and consumer loyalty to national products and companies – these crucial elements in economic performance cannot be derived as the logical implications of market forces alone. Ideology and culture are also implicated. Policies towards social security reveal sharp and significant differences. The rate of personal saving in Japan is far above that prevalent in Western countries despite similarities in income levels. Japan, the United States,

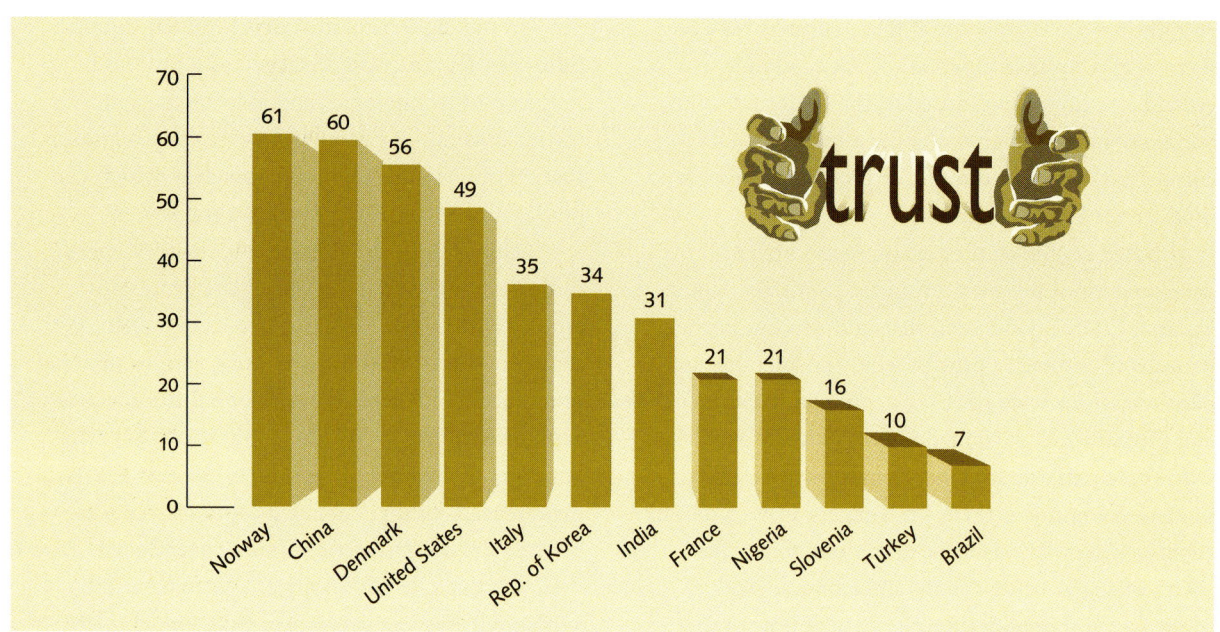

GRAPH 1
PERCENTAGE BELIEVING THAT MOST PEOPLE CAN BE TRUSTED (1990–93)
Source: A. van der Staay (see Chapter 16, Table 19(a), of the present report).

the United Kingdom and Scandinavia, to take four archetypal examples, enjoy or suffer from radically different histories of conflict between employers and employees and institutions for conflict-resolution. Rules of job tenure and regulations of employers' rights to lay off or retrench workers define deep differences in the functioning of labour markets.

Such differences only grow in importance when poor countries are added to the universe of comparisons. Regularities in the statistical patterns of economic development may be interpreted not as exclusive, determinate and 'normal' patterns of development but as the result also of asymmetric culture contact in politically and economically unequal settings. Similarly, both economic and cultural globalization or homogenization may be actively, i.e. politically, contested. In this sense, market forces are no more automatic than people are automatons.

Consistent with the Weberian world view, pre-industrial societies have been portrayed as 'zero-sum systems'.[8] Lack of growth must mean, so the argument goes, that somebody's gain is necessarily somebody else's loss. Cultural beliefs in stagnant agrarian societies became adapted to maintaining a stable social balance. Thus, social status is hereditary whilst social stability is sought to be secured through a denial of earthly aspirations. Norms of social sharing rather than of private thrift and accumulation come to prevail. The Protestant Reformation helped break the hold of such traditional culture in the case of Western Europe and helped it, over the next few centuries, to advance well ahead of Southern Europe. Norms in favour of thrift, determination and hard work are taken to reflect the values of autonomy and economic achievement whilst norms of obedience, religious faith and tolerance and respect of other people

suggest values of conformity to tradition. Inglehart and his colleagues constructed an Index of Achievement Motivation for a sample of countries using survey data on the aforementioned norms. They found a strong correlation between this Index of Achievement Motivation and the rate of economic growth during 1960–89. Hence their conclusion that economic growth is determined not only by political and economic institutions (e.g. policies and investments in education) but also by cultural factors such as attitudes to thrift.[9]

Apart from the value of thrift to economic growth, mutual trust among a citizenry is also considered by many to be a powerful factor promoting economic growth and international competitiveness (Alain Peyrefitte, cited in NYFER, 1996). Some even take it to be an essential if variable and rarely acknowledged foundation of a market economy. Conversely, the instrumental value of trust for economic growth appears to be threatened by the growing depersonalization of transactions in the electronic age. As with thrift, the statistical correlation between the level of trust in fellow citizens and the average economic growth rate is found to be positive and robust (NYFER, 1996, p. 25).[10]

But several caveats are in order as regards these statistical regularities that may be taken to support a cultural rather than an economic understanding of economic growth. First, cross-cultural quantification of such delicate variables as the level of thrift, trust or personal integrity have been based on self-assessments by people in each society and may reflect varied standards as much as varied performance across these societies. Second, correlations do not establish causality and alternative interpretations of these correlations are usually possible. Finally, there is a danger that such correlations may prove 'too much': if culture determines economic performance, then, how do countries with values unfavourable to growth ever get out of the rut?[11]

Globalization and culture: assimilation or diversity?

It might have been possible once upon a time to imagine cultures as being separated from one another, with room to breathe and to develop independently, but technological change in transport and communications has for centuries been dissolving time and space, breaking down the barriers which surround even the most isolated cultures. This process has accelerated dramatically in the last fifty years and is part of a wider tendency toward globalization. One consequence is that cultures are coming into increasingly close contact with one another.

This interaction between cultures has been going on for a long time, and before considering the implications for the contemporary world, it is worth glancing back at history. It would be fatuous to claim that technological change and cultural interchange that follows it have been universally beneficial. Development has been uneven and, more important, the impact of cultural interchange has often been asymmetrical, some groups and cultures losing absolutely, not just relatively. Central Asia, for instance, long occupied a strategic position on caravan trade routes connecting China with the eastern Mediterranean and Europe. Its cities of Samarkand, Bukhara and Khiva (now in Uzbekistan) were centres of economic, political and cultural activity where the arts and architecture, the natural sciences and mathematics and theology flourished. Beginning in the fifteenth century, the development of transoceanic transport, however, made overland transport through Central Asia unprofitable and the region fell into a steep decline. The maritime regions of Asia were brought into closer contact with Europe while parts of the interior of Asia became increasingly isolated.

Closer contact, however, has been a mixed blessing. Whether one considers the explosive conquests of Islam beginning in the seventh century,

The decline of birth rates in Europe and elsewhere

A key pattern of modern economic growth is the inverse relationship between income levels and birth rates. It may be taken to imply support for an economic theory of fertility behaviour. But such a view is disputed not only in the context of development in non-European nations but even with reference to European history. Fertility decline in historical Europe cannot be firmly correlated with precise levels of variables such as child mortality, urbanization, education or income levels. The transition occurred at widely different values for these 'economic' indicators of the 'demand' for children. Variations in fertility decline were greater across 'cultural' groups than within (Coale and Watkins, 1986). The most important lesson deriving from these studies is not that economic forces do not matter but that the transformative power of economic forces may be limited much or little by factors specific to each context, i.e. cultural-historical factors that define beliefs, norms and other behavioural constraints.

Compared to historical Europe, developing countries today are experiencing a significantly more rapid rate of change in reproductive behaviour (Watkins, 1989). The explanation for this fertility decline has been founded on two major factors: improvements in contraception technologies and their availability to users; and a decline in the desired number of children in response to economic and social change (respectively the supply-led and demand-led hypotheses). In the demand-led view, changes in people's material conditions of living produce changes in the desired number of children; this change in demand also calls forth the requisite supply of children (which implies that contraceptive practice is demand-led). But as with historical Europe, accelerated fertility decline in developing countries cannot be explained by demand factors or economic variables alone.

The supply-led hypothesis has lately been broadened to include not merely new technology availability but also the power of new ideas or norms of behaviour to propagate themselves in a population through a process of cultural diffusion. In this view, therefore, 'supply' creates its own demand. An analysis of fertility behaviour in Bangladesh seeks to show that it is mainly the acceptance of birth control (and the concomitant access to control technologies), not economic changes (such as improved levels of living or changing occupational and rural/urban distribution of the population), that supports the decline (Cleland et al., 1994). In this connection, it should be noted that urbanization itself is not a purely economic process; it may also entail changes in consumption norms and lifestyle norms. More broadly, fertility behaviour appears to be driven by forces that are unique to our times. The speed and spread of information transmission has intensified producing large-scale demonstration effects on beliefs and behaviour. Similarly, notable improvements in reproductive technology have also contributed. Such observations may be taken to be supportive of the view that the very linkage between fertility and economic variables (the so-called demand for children) may have been transferred through culture contact with the West during the modern era.

J. Mohan Rao
Professor, Specialist in Development Economics,
University of Massachusetts, Amherst (United States)

which from the epicentre of Arabia covered the whole of the Middle East, all of North Africa and the Iberian peninsula in Europe; or the westward migration of the Mongol 'hordes' of the thirteenth century, which ended at the Danube River and the outskirts of Budapest; or the unrelenting expansion of Western Europe from the fifteenth century onwards to virtually every corner of the globe, cultural exchange seems more like a one-way street than a dual-carriage highway. Cultural contact often has been a by-product of military encounters and has been associated with violence, pillage, war, enslavement, conquest, colonialism and imperialism (Elsenhans, 1991). It has led to the introduction of alien diseases to those who had no natural resistance to them and, in some cases, to the decimation of indigenous populations. It has contributed to the spread of racism;[12] occasionally it has resulted in genocide; more often it has led to the destruction of pre-existing social structures and the system of beliefs that sustained them.[13] Historically, globalization often had a fatal impact.[14]

Yet there is another side to the story: cultural contact was indeed a mixed blessing. The initial effects of cultures rubbing against one another may well be accurately described by the phrase 'a fatal impact',[15] but the longer-term effects were more positive. Contacts between cultures led to a myriad of exchanges and adaptations that were of benefit to all parties. Consider foodstuffs and primary commodities. Latin America gave us maize, potatoes, the tomato and natural rubber; Ethiopia and Yemen gave us coffee; China gave us tea and noodles (which the Italians transformed into pasta), and so on. The world's pharmacopoeia similarly draws on botanical products from many different regions. The same is true of our domesticated animals.

In our own time, the making of the 'global village' points to reductions not merely in the effective physical distances across peoples but also, at least in a certain sense, in the effective 'cultural' distances. Satellite communications and television transmit news, views and images at electronic speeds and directly, without the local intermediation and the cultural filters of yesteryear. A great deal of this information exchange is underwritten by advertising and marketing and, in turn, conveys the images that make such underwriting commercially profitable. Just as numerous local languages are disappearing, traditional ways of life too are being abandoned: Western-style fast foods replace indigenous alternatives; mega brand names (again, mostly Western if Japan is included as an honorary Western nation) such as Coca-Cola or Levi's push out local substitutes; North American pop music and forms of entertainment render the practitioners of local performing arts jobless and their skills extinct. Apart from converging preferences in dress, music and entertainment, certain subcultures relating to drugs, crime and corruption have also spread.

Cultural assimilation of this sort is one of the defining aspects of contemporary globalization. Its economic correlates, if not causes, seem fairly clear. It is especially pronounced among urban youth, a fact which portends even greater global acculturation in the future. Compared to the late nineteenth century, demographic and urban transitions have proceeded much further to produce major shifts in family structures, a larger proportion of youth who now spend an increasing proportion of their time in schools and away from family work, and wider diffusion of urban living patterns. Just as important, many traditional skills and occupations have disappeared to be replaced by modern occupational structures and by makeshift work on the fringes of modernized urban society. In many parts of the world, growing discretionary incomes at least in the hands of burgeoning 'middle classes' have fuelled consumerism and consumer aspirations.

Another feature of such convergent modernization is that it has taken the form of Americanization. According to Pieterse (1996), American culture's appeal grows out of the ongoing intermingling of its multiple cultures, many of which

Asian values and economic growth

The last few decades have seen remarkable economic progress in East Asia. Despite the current financial crisis, the achievements remain extremely impressive. What began as a unique achievement in the case of Japan has gradually become a general accomplishment of Asia in general and of East Asia in particular. This success has been accompanied by the emergence of new theories on the role of Asian culture in achieving economic success as well as political distinction. The former draws directly on the experience of fast economic development in a number of Asian economies, i.e. Japan, the Republic of Korea, Taiwan, Hong Kong, Singapore and now China. An emerging theory attributes these successes partly – even largely – to the role of Asian cultural values, and in particular to Confucianism.

This question is of some importance. If there really is something remarkable about the contribution of Confucian or other Asian values in promoting economic development, should such a causal linkage not give rise to a cultural evaluation in terms of the economic potential of such values? Why should the *World Culture Report* not benefit from the 'science' of value-based explanations of economic growth?

These claims are not, however, particularly easy to vindicate. Indeed, value-based accounts of economic performance are often quite arbitrary, and the Asian story is no exception. The industrial revolution occurred first in Europe, not Asia: even before that, the changes known as the European Renaissance had been transforming the face of Europe – beginning with Italy – before similar mutations occurred in Asia. For a very long time, people wondered what made the European values so productive of social results. Such questioning followed closely on readings about economic, political and military power such as Samuel Johnson's novel *Rasselas* (1759), which speaks of the northern and western nations of Europe as being 'in possession of all power and all knowledge, whose armies are irresistible, and whose fleets command the remotest parts of the globe'. Many people at the time wondered what values and which knowledge had permitted Europe to get so far ahead of Asia and the rest of the world.

However, Japan then emerged as a major economic and military power and was subsequently included in the world of privileged values. In the first half of the twentieth century, the question was asked as to why Japan was the only non-Western country to have become a major industrial nation. Why did modern industrial capitalism arise in one East Asian society and not in another? Why Japan, and not China? The particular norms, traditions and values of Japan – from the martial Samurai heritage to its family-centred business traditions – began to receive attention.

Then things moved further. Some other Asian countries and regions – Hong Kong, Singapore, the Republic of Korea and Taiwan – began to prosper and won admiration as Asian successes. Inevitably, then, the Samurai gave way to shared traditions on the eastern edge of Asia. This economic development has been followed more recently by the rapid transformation of

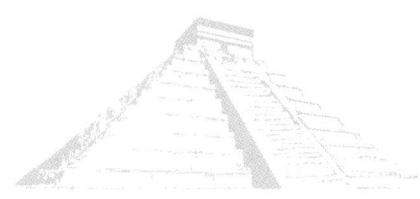

the Chinese economy and society. Attention has now shifted to the special virtues of Confucianism, i.e. the cultural tie binding China, Japan and much of East Asia.

However, Thailand too then forged ahead at remarkable speed. Its cultural background is Buddhist rather than Confucian. Japan too has had much Buddhism in its past (and present), as has Korea and China, and Buddhism is a radically different tradition from Confucianism. The Indonesian economy too was expanding, until very recently, quite rapidly. That country has, of course, an Islamic present and much Buddhist and Hindu as well as Muslim cultural achievements in the past. And even more recently the giant economy of India has started to move forward fast: India now has a substantially faster GNP growth rate than Europe and America and is second only to East and South-East Asia. Past accounts of sluggishness due to the special values of these regions are giving way to explanations of economic dynamism, with the identification of *other* values and *other* connections (the fact that India has perhaps the longest accounting tradition in the world has now been dusted up and presented as a causal explanation).

In raising doubts about explanations of Asia's economic success in terms of Asian values, it is not my purpose to argue that we have learned nothing about the role of values from the spread of economic growth and development in Asia and its superior economic performance. I think some important lessons have emerged, but these do not include anything as grand as the special fitness of Asian values to modern economic growth. The most important lesson here may be a negative one, i.e. that European culture is not the only road to modern success. To appreciate the importance of this lesson, we have to return to the time when European civilization appeared to be the sole route to industrial success, and the focus was on 'The Protestant Ethic and the Spirit of Capitalism' – to quote the title of Weber's classic study. We now know that other values work too – and often work better – and this is the lesson that has been emerging over the last century, beginning with Japan's remarkable economic progress.

However, the disestablishment of an earlier pro-European prejudice must not be confused with the establishment of a new asymmetry of values – this time in favour of Asia, against Europe. As the Japanese economy has reached and in some respects surpassed levels of economic prosperity earlier experienced only in the West, its growth rate has started to moderate, and no doubt similar slowing will occur also in other Asian economies which have levels of per capita real income that are still low by European standards. There have, of course, been special features in East Asian development, including a bigger role of education and skill formation, and the use of a more friendly – and collaborative – relation between the market and the state. But these are not special features of 'Asian values' as such – nor things that other countries cannot follow with equal ease.

Amartya Sen
Economist and Philosopher;
Master, Trinity College, Cambridge (United Kingdom)

are themselves imports. 'This is a culture where the grammars of multiple cultures mix and this intercultural density may constitute part of the subliminal attraction of American popular media, music, film, television' (p. 1393). While such subtle features of American culture may account for its marketability, a purely market-based explanation for the appeal of American consumerism and its artefacts can be advanced that seems more persuasive. American business has enjoyed two overwhelming advantages from its home market: first, the American mass market matured decades before consumer markets elsewhere did; second, it is much larger than national markets elsewhere. As a result, products, brand names and their images originating there have enjoyed the advantages of an early start and a highly competitive testing ground. These advantages have been furthered by the growth of direct foreign investment where, too, American companies, assisted by the might of American foreign policy, remain dominant. Though both advantages have been diminishing over time, the Americanization of tastes reflects their cumulative effect in the post-war era.

But what are we to make of these tendencies towards consumption and lifestyle convergence? Are they merely a superficial form of cultural assimilation which leave undisturbed the 'deeper' sources of diverse cultures, i.e. their varied beliefs and values? Do they threaten to destroy the diversity that has been the gift of cultural creativity? One difficulty in assessing whether cultural convergence is 'deep' or 'shallow' is that there are no reliable markers of culture comparable, say, to statistics on economic performance; even if these could be identified, there would be no natural basis for weighting and aggregating them into any overall index.[16] What is clear is that scholarly assessments as well as 'real world' reactions vary a great deal.

In many parts of the world, growing cultural interchange has increased peoples' awareness of cultural diversity and identities. And, as in the past, reactions have depended on the perceived degree of

openness and the terms on which a culture interacts with other cultures. That is, whether the relationship is one of subordination, domination and exploitation or one of equality, mutual respect and beneficial exchange. In some cases, cultural assertiveness against perceived external threat underlies ethnic and nationality movements that have erupted in our times. Indeed, Huntington (1993) has elevated the idea of cultural inertia and civilizational conflict arising from it to the level of the fundamental defining feature of an emerging epoch. He views a globalized economy as giving rise to fierce economic competition among 'civilizations' that retain differentiated cultures; in other words, globalized economic competition without global cultural convergence. The whole view is based on the premise that the particularist cultures of the non-Western world seek to modernize without Westernizing and runs counter to both an economic theory of cultural convergence ('patterns of development') as well as to a cultural theory of economic convergence (culture diffusion). Instead, cultural differences remain frozen in time whilst economies seek to converge. But this reification of culture completely misses the evolutionary/historical element in politics, culture and the economy we emphasized above. Similarly, it ignores the fact that some of the most important 'culture' conflicts today are internal to the 'civilizations' that Huntington takes to be immutable.

While there is some truth in the view that issues of cultural domination remain important today, cultural interchange in the modern world is also a two-way exchange. Whilst homogeneity has certainly increased in some areas of life, the scope for making diverse choices has also undoubtedly risen. Capital, technology and even labour circulate globally. Science is universal and accessible to all to a greater degree then ever before. Ideas, information and knowledge are transmitted much more rapidly and more widely than in the past. The result is that people can make creative recombinations of available options. This evidently is true at any given location,

14.2	*Saudi Arabia*
11.3	*Lesotho*
9.9	*Sweden*
7.7	*Jamaica*
4.2	*Spain*
3.6	*Costa Rica*
2.5	*Denmark*
1.8	*Honduras*
1.5	*Egypt*
1.4	*Botswana*

World	1.3
Developing countries	0.7
Industrial countries	4.2

GRAPH 2(a)
COMPARING COUNTRIES IN TERMS OF COMMUNICATION: LETTERS SENT ABROAD PER PERSON (1995)

Source: Statistical Table 10 in Part Seven of this report.

Graphs 2(a) and 2(b) compare ten countries with respect to letters sent abroad and international telephone calls. Graph 2(c) does the same for ten other countries with respect to fax machines. All three media – letters, telephones and faxes – have the potential to enhance communication tremendously among people of different cultures.

The media gap between industrial and developing countries is smallest for letters sent abroad, i.e. industrial countries send only six times more than developing countries. Some developing countries, such as Saudi Arabia and Lesotho, far outstrip the average even for industrial countries.

With respect to international telephone calls, industrial countries average fourteen times more minutes per person than developing countries. Sweden averages 108 minutes per person, for example, in sharp contrast to Egypt, which averages only 2. Averaging considerably more are developing countries such as Jamaica (22 minutes per person) and Botswana (20 minutes per person).

Developing countries still lag significantly behind industrial countries with respect to the use of fax machines, i.e. they have only about one-fiftieth the number of machines on average. The United States and Japan have the highest numbers (539 and 480). By contrast, Kazakhstan and Kenya have the lowest (2 and 1).

as more and more ways of life learn to coexist, and it is also true globally, as cultural interpenetration multiplies the number of permutations and in the process creates new ways of life, new cultures.

Whether growing cultural interchange is viewed as a threat or opportunity (and whether as a homogenizing force or a source of increasing diversity), it cannot be separated from the forces of economic globalization. At least at the present juncture, it is fair to say that there is growing unease about globalization in rich and poor countries. As

national policies and institutions come increasingly under the scrutiny of global financial markets, as fiscal and labour regimes are bent to the growing imperative of 'international competitiveness', the sense of national autonomy is gradually losing potency. This is exacerbated, in many cases, by the cultural dislocations of growing globalization. But this cannot be easily separated from the alienation and powerlessness that come from rapid economic changes, whether they originate at home or across borders, which lead to loss of traditional

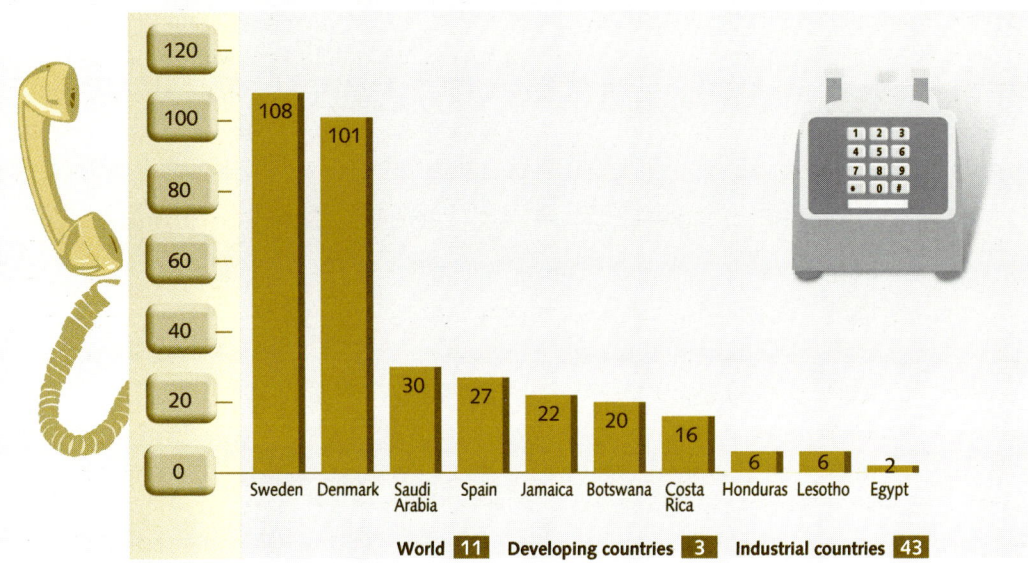

GRAPH 2(b)
COMPARING COUNTRIES IN TERMS OF COMMUNICATION: INTERNATIONAL TELEPHONE CALLS,
MINUTES PER PERSON (1995)
Source: Statistical Table 10 in Part Seven of this report.

occupations, livelihoods, habitations and communities. A good deal of cultural globalization has differential impacts on rural versus urban populations, young versus old, men versus women, rich versus poor, and so forth. As different groups make their choices, traditional identities and social relationships are upset, producing further effects on politics and society. Under the circumstances, group identities and loyalties tend to be exploited by different groups and leaders for their own political purposes. Inter-group divisions may also be exploited in ways which promote neither cultural well-being nor economic development. The recent spate of challenges to established governments and nation-states, of old and new identity and ethnic conflicts, and of regional and class conflicts in various parts of the world have, of course, diverse sources: economic collapse, political democratization, upheavals of war, ecological displacements and the like. Ethnicity

sometimes has led to violent conflict and it is not always clear that such conflict does not express considerable disaffection from the economic and political institutions of a given society. But the opportunities as well as challenges emanating from a globalizing world economy play direct and indirect roles in these emerging contradictions.

As nations, rich and poor, experience the cumulative and growing influence of international trade and resource movements on their national economic and political arrangements, many of them are likely to come under pressure to seek ways of preserving their own social norms and institutions, within their own borders, the better to socially 'embed' economic relations. Alternatively or in addition, they will seek to constrain international economic relations through internationally enforced standards.[17] Global standards presuppose a minimal set of globally shared ethical premises (and hence a

modicum of cultural convergence). But it is far from clear how such convergence is to be assured, much less how it might be enforced. Meanwhile, there is no assurance that the economic process of globalization can be sustained in political-social terms.

It is true that there is a remarkable degree of convergence in the actual economic policy regimes that have been put in place in countries North and South, East and West. In a sense, this represents the most important form of 'cultural' convergence that we have been witness to. But this aspect of cultural convergence is not so much a consequence of globalization as the hoped-for cause of economic convergence that is yet to be. Nor is there any assurance that people will concur in the economic and cultural consequences that may follow in its wake. Domestic market systems are embedded within domestic political and social arrangements. By contrast, the global market system is not embedded in comparably cohesive political and social arrangements. Meanwhile, by elevating the goal of competitiveness, globalization tends to undermine the ability of states to maintain national arrangements and commitments and hence could be socially destabilizing. Optimists who foresee global market integration as the engine of global economic and cultural convergence therefore advocate neo-liberal policies in both rich and poor nations. But they blithely ignore the very real possibility that unfettered markets may upset the internal social equilibrium in ways that will then endanger globalization itself.

Some believe that the global expansion of markets is already undermining social cohesion and is therefore headed towards a major political and/or economic crisis (Greider, 1997). In the advanced countries, the source of the tensions may be the growing inequality of incomes (including, or perhaps especially, earned incomes) and the fraying of social safety nets while in the developing world there are multiple threats from fiscal retrenchment, jobless growth, worsening environmental problems,

increased wage inequalities, increased economic uncertainty without social safety nets, and so on. We have recently witnessed widespread protests and resistance to a new law in the Republic of Korea which does away with regulations on employers who will lay off or dismiss their workers. The law, which was initially passed surreptitiously by a conniving government and parliament, has been justified in the name of the need to assure Korean competitiveness in world markets. There is continuing uncertainty over the domestic socio-political implications of currency integration in Europe; the uncertainty is breeding active political conflict and resistance, in France for example. There is a growing movement in India to limit the international property rights regime from incorporating new life forms and for extending it to include community rights in traditional medicines and inherited biodiversity. There are also powerful potential conflicts across the rich/poor divide over such issues as labour standards, environmental standards and human rights, to name but these.

Human vulnerability and suffering form a central and recurrent theme of nearly all cultural traditions. It is the source of the virtually universal ethic to alleviate suffering as also of the injunction, though expressed variously, that one should treat others as one would want to be treated oneself. The authors of *Our Creative Diversity* note that this principle can provide the sheet anchor for a global ethics. This is cause for hope. On the other hand, the fast-paced growth of international interdependence is increasingly structured by weakly regulated markets and large corporate organizations. In consequence, a wide range of problems has come to the fore – the slow erosion of the welfare state, threats to local and global environments, national systems of food security in jeopardy, systematic violation of labour standards, abuses of human rights, double standards in medical and scientific ethics, and many others. This should be cause for concern. Can the hope for a global ethics be effectively tapped to meet our

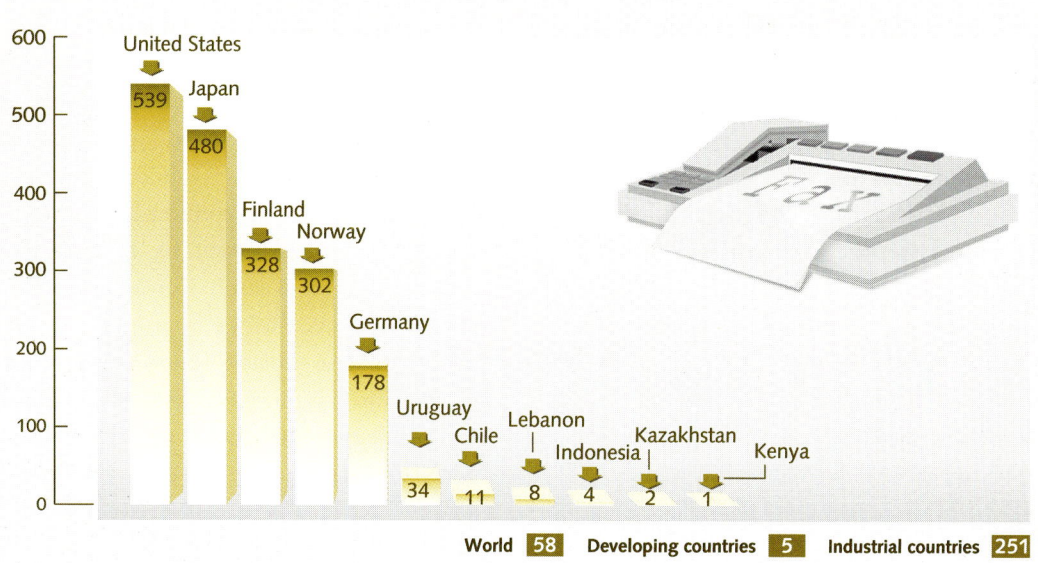

GRAPH 2(C)
COMPARING COUNTRIES IN TERMS OF COMMUNICATION: FAX MACHINES PER 10,000 PERSONS (1992–95)
Source: Statistical Table 10 in Part Seven of this report.

growing global concerns? Translating the promise into reality will require the construction of concrete global standards that elicit the commitment of people everywhere. Finding the strategic and operational means by which global markets will be moored to a global ethics will become the central political and economic challenge of the world community in the coming decade.

Notes

1.   Partly based on S. Radelet and J. Sachs, 'Asia's Bright Future', *Foreign Affairs*, November/December 1997.

2.   This implication holds even if the term 'culture', as in the present discussion, is used narrowly and in an analytically useful way to denote: (a) beliefs and values shared by a group, and (b) the group identity that such beliefs-values may define, rather than in the broad sense as the entire gamut of individual and collective ways of living, including beliefs, values and social institutions.

3.   As the authors of *Our Creative Diversity* (World Commission on Culture and Development, 1995) noted:

'Culture's role is not exhausted as a servant of ends . . . but is the social basis of the ends themselves. Development and the economy are part of a people's culture'.

4.   Although education is a key prong of the Human Development Index, it seems clear that the realization of this capability among a population may constrict the rights of some while enhancing the rights of others, i.e. that human development as the enhancement of people's choice sets loses meaning unless an ethical/cultural basis for aggregating different individuals' well-being or capabilities is introduced.

5.   Emile Durkheim, for example, deployed the notion of 'collective unconscious' in this way.

6.   The term is used in its value-neutral sense, i.e. creation need not be benign, beautiful or true.

7.   Recent accounts of the constituents of the Fordist Golden Age and of the paths out of that regime of accumulation are given in Boyer (1995) and Lipietz (1995).

8.   See Inglehart, Granato and Leblang (1995).

9.   But Ingelhart and others are advisedly cautious about interpreting the correlations as causal relations. For example, rather than high economic growth being the

effect of a culture valuing thrift, hard work and economic success, it well may be the cause of the latter. Indeed, it is noteworthy that despite persistent differences in the professed norms of Southern and Northern Europe (or Catholic and Protestant nations), there has been a remarkable convergence of living standards between these regions in the post-war period.

10.   Similarly, Putnam (1993) has tried to show that differences dating back to the Middle Ages in regard to citizenship and co-operation versus familial orientation and egoism explain differences in the quality of life and economic achievements in the various provinces of Italy.

11.   Consider attempts to understand the phenomenal success of the Japanese economy. Some scholars have attributed the Japanese success to its Confucianism and its Shintoism which made for citizenship based on a powerful sense of loyalty and a working class prepared to co-operate with rather than contest the authority of their bosses. The same sort of co-operativeness informs the Japanese indigenous system for advancing technological capabilities. Yet, these arguments must be tempered by the obvious fact that China, the original home of Confucianism, lagged well behind Japan in the race to catch up with the West.

12.   For an analysis of how scientific and technological achievement became a measure of the value of a civilization in the eighteenth century, justifying the right to 'civilize' inferior 'races' and to dominate the world, see Adas (1989).

13.   For a study of how this continues today in the Amazon, see Lewis (1988).

14.   The phrase is borrowed from Moorehead (1996).

15.   The effects of European expansion and the 'development of underdevelopment' are discussed in Griffin (1969) and Frank (1966).

16.   This is not to say that cultural indicators and some sort of aggregate of them cannot contribute useful information. On the contrary, our argument underlines the need for such indicators if our understanding of culture under globalization is to be advanced on an empirical basis.

17.   This is already happening on an accelerating scale in many important areas of concern – regulation of the conditions of labour, of the use and abuse of natural resources and the environment, of the behaviour of transnational corporations, etc. Such action, whether internationally co-ordinated or not, involves diverse interests, rights, powers and ethics. For an analysis of conflict and interests in evolving global standards, see Rao (1996*b*).

Bibliography

ADAS, M. 1989. *Machines as the Measure of Men.* Ithaca, Cornell University Press.

BAGCHI, A. K. 1996. Contextual Social Science: or Crossing Boundaries. *Economic and Political Weekly,* Vol. 31, No. 43, pp. 2875–82.

BOYER, R. 1995. Capital–Labour Relations in OECD Countries: From the Fordist Golden Age to Contrasted National Trajectories. In: J. Schor and J. You (eds.), *Capital, the State and Labour: A Global Perspective.* Aldershot, Edward Elgar and UNU Press.

CLELAND, J. G.; PHILLIPS, J. F.; AMIN, S.; KAMAL, G. M. 1994. *The Determinants of Reproductive Change in Bangladesh.* Washington, D.C., The World Bank.

COALE, A. J.; WATKINS, S. C. 1986. *The Decline of Fertility in Europe.* Princeton, Princeton University Press.

ELSENHANS, H. 1991. *Development and Underdevelopment: The History, Economics and Politics of North–South Relations.* New Delhi, Sage Publications.

FRANK, A. G. 1966. The Development of Underdevelopment. *Monthly Review,* No. 18.

GREIDER, W. 1997. *One World, Ready or Not — The Manic Logic of Global Capitalism.* New York: Simon & Schuster.

GRIFFIN, K. 1969. *Underdevelopment in Spanish America.* London, Allen & Unwin.

——. 1996. Culture, Human Development and Economic Growth. (Riverside, University of California). Unpublished.

GRIFFIN, K. (ed.). 1996. *Social Policy and Economic Transformation in Uzbekistan.* Geneva, International Labour Organisation.

GRIFFIN, K.; KHAN, A. R. 1992. *Globalization and the Developing World: An Essay on the International Dimensions of Development in the Post-Cold War Era.* New York, United Nations. (United Nations Development Programme: Human Development Report Occasional Papers, No 2.)

HUNTINGTON, S. P. 1993. The Clash of Civilizations. *Foreign Affairs,* Vol. 72, No. 3, pp. 22–49.

INGLEHART, R.; GRANATO, J.; LEBLANG, D. 1995. The Effect of Culture on Economic Development: Theory, Hypotheses and Some Empirical Tests (Ann Arbor, University of Michigan.) Unpublished.

JOLLY, R.; ROSENTHAL, G.; TOKMAN, V. 1994. Foreword: A Challenge of Poverty. In: R. van der Hoeven and R. Anker (eds.), *Poverty Monitoring: An International Concern.* New York, St Martin's Press.

KUZNETS, S. 1966. *Modern Economic Growth*. New Haven, Yale University Press.

LERNER, A. 1972. The Economics and Politics of Consumer Sovereignty. *American Economic Review*, No. 62.

LEWIS, N. 1988. *The Missionaries*. London, Secker & Warburg.

LIPIETZ, A. 1995. Capital–Labour Relations at the Dawn of the Twenty-First Century. In: J. Schor and J. You (eds.), *Capital, the State and Labour: A Global Perspective*. Aldershot, Edward Elgar and UNU Press.

MOORE JR., B. 1987. *Authority and Inequality under Capitalism and Socialism: USA, USSR and China*. Oxford, Clarendon Press.

MOOREHEAD, A. 1966. *The Fatal Impact: An Account of the Invasion of the South Pacific, 1767–1840*. London, Hamish Hamilton.

NEEDHAM, J. *Science and Civilization in China*. Cambridge, Cambridge University Press. (Various years.)

NOLAN, P. 1997. China's Rise, Russia's Fall. *Journal of Peasant Studies*, Vol. 24, Nos. 1–2, pp. 226–50.

NYFER. 1996. *Institutions, Values, Norms and Growth*. Breukelen, NYFER Forum for Economic Research.

PIETERSE, J. N. 1996. Globalization and Culture: Three Paradigms. *Economic and Political Weekly*, Vol. 31, No. 23, pp. 1389–93.

——. 1994. Globalization as Hybridization. *International Sociology*, No. 9.

PUTNAM, R. (with Robert Leonardi and Raffaella Nanetti). 1993. *Making Democracy Work: Civic Traditions in Modern Italy*. Princeton, Princeton University Press.

RAO, J. M. 1995*a*. *Labor and Liberalization in Less Developed Countries*. Geneva, ILO. (Employment Paper No. 1.)

——. 1995*b*. *The Market for the State: Rules, Discretion, Rent-Seeking and Corruption*. Amherst, University of Massachusetts. (Department of Economics Working Paper No. 1995–3.)

——. 1996*a*. *Globalization: A View from the South*. Geneva, ILO. (Paper prepared for the Employment Department.) Unpublished.

——. 1996*b*. *Local Development in a Globalizing World*. Bangalore, HIVOS (Humanistisch Instituut voor Ontwikkelingssamenwerking, Netherlands).

RAWLS, J. 1971. *A Theory of Justice*. Cambridge, Harvard University Press.

RODRIK, D. 1997. *Has International Economic Integration Gone Too Far?* Washington, D.C., Institute for International Economics.

SACHS, J.; WARNER, A. 1995. Economic Reform and the Process of Global Integration. *Brookings Papers in Economic Activity*, No. 1, p. 118.

SAHLINS, M. 1976. *Culture and Practical Reason*. Chicago, Chicago University Press.

SCHWARTZ, H. M. 1994. *States Versus Markets: History, Geography and the Development of the International Political Economy*. New York, St Martin's Press.

SEN, A. 1990. Development as Capability Expansion. In: K. Griffin and J. Knight (eds.), *Human Development and the International Development Strategy for the 1990s*. London, Macmillan.

UNDP. *Human Development Report*. New York, Oxford University Press for UNDP. (Various years.)

UNRISD–UNESCO. 1997. *Towards a World Report on Culture and Development: Constructing Cultural Statistics and Indicators*. Paris and Geneva, UNRISD–UNESCO. (Occasional Paper Series on Culture and Development.)

WALLIS, J. 1997. Ironically the Volunteerism Summit Excluded a Key Voice. *Boston Globe*, 20 May.

WATKINS, S. 1989. The Fertility Transition: Europe and the Third World Compared. In: J. M. Stycos (ed.), *Demography as an Interdiscipline*. New Brunswick and Oxford, Transaction Publishers.

WEINER, M. 1996. Child Labour in India: Putting Compulsory Primary Education on the Political Agenda. *Economic and Political Weekly*, Vol. 31, Nos. 45–6, pp. 3007–14.

WORLD COMMISSION ON CULTURE AND DEVELOPMENT. 1995. *Our Creative Diversity*. Paris, UNESCO.

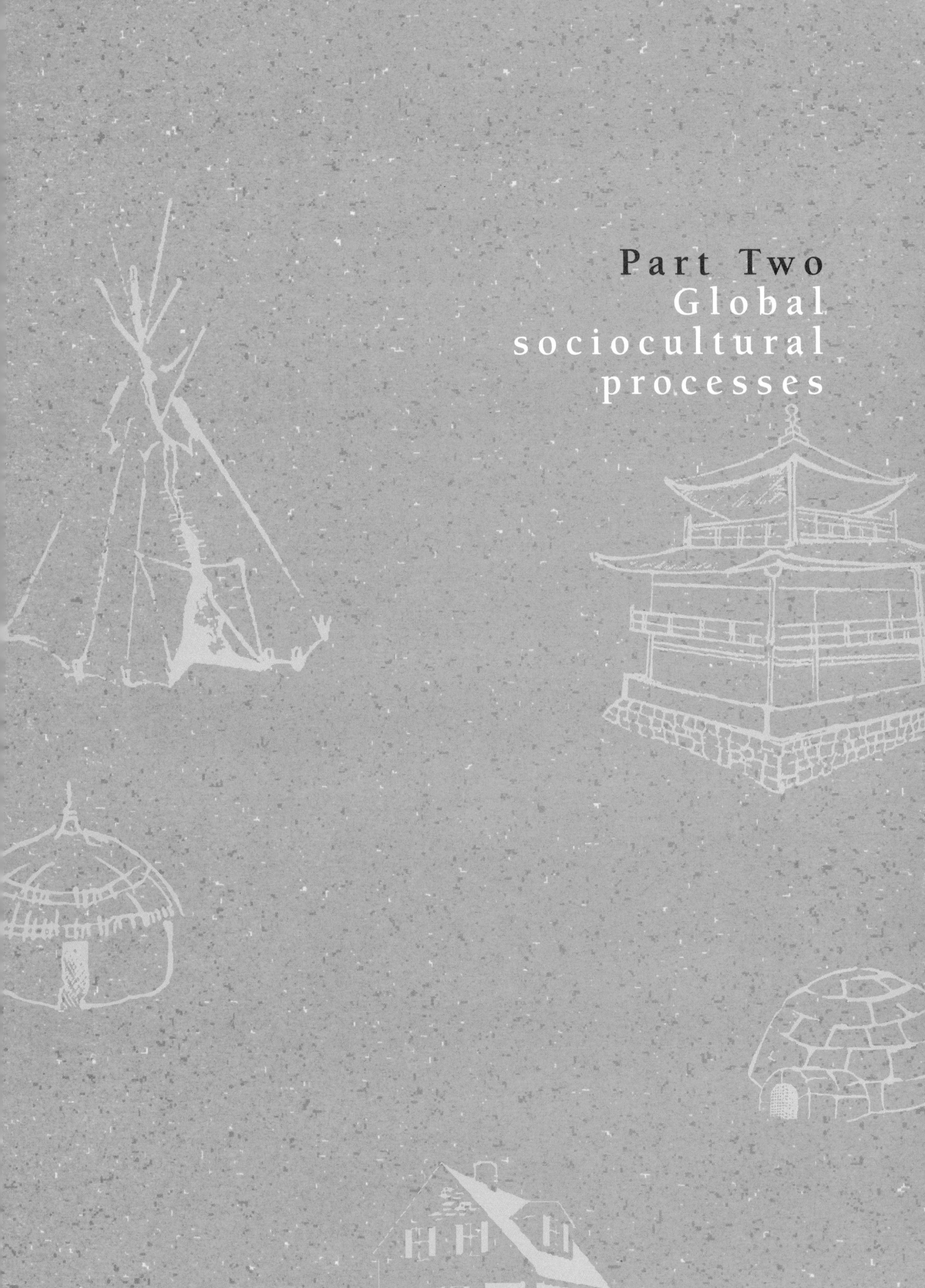

Part Two
Global
sociocultural
processes

Introduction to Part Two

The world today is experiencing some major changes in terms of societal, cultural and political processes. Some of the trends and dynamics of these processes are discussed in this part of the report: issues of equality and difference among peoples, the definition and recognition of indigenous peoples and their rights, the recognition of differences in cultural traditions and the mechanisms for intercultural conviviality, issues of sustainability, urban growth and the role of cities as places for interculturalism and for creativity, and the spread of democratic practices around the world.

These are issues that deal first of all with relations between people, individually and collectively. They stem from recognition of the 'hard fact' of diversity, that is, that women and men, people with different cultural backgrounds and practices, with different ideas and different ways of life and economic resources, share their living space, and have to find ways to deal and cope with each other.

Three levels of analysis may be proposed for consideration of these matters. The first involves the ways in which 'ourselves' and 'others' are defined in the process of interaction (identifications and identities). The second involves looking at the ways in which people share the world and their more localized environments with 'others', i.e. how patterns of exchange, 'conviviality', conflict and negotiation, togetherness and mutual enrichment occur – and what can be learned in terms of the overall horizon of a sort of 'conviviability'. The third concerns the ways in which peoples and societies organize themselves to handle diversity, and the lessons that can be learned regarding the need to build institutions to enhance and promote cultural creativity in the world of the future.

These chapters analyse trends and processes that are actually present in the real world. Trends that exist and which can be considered as 'data' upon which policy choices and alternatives have to be based. These are the common threads in the chapters

in Part Two. All of them start by assuming diversity and interaction among various cultural groups and individuals, and look from there at ways in which life and 'conviviality' are or could be organized.

This is the subject of Touraine's chapter at a more global and theoretical level. Touraine sifts through the main paradigms and ideas that inform the ways in which societies have dealt with the combination of equality and difference. The basic question is to know how one should combine the universality of rights with the acknowledgement of particular social interests and cultural values, a question that has ever accompanied humankind. The challenge that humanity faces nowadays is one of transcending extreme solutions, i.e. 'the disappearance of all differences in a mass society, or the direct clash of these differences and communities'. His call is 'to affirm the right of all human beings to choose their path, to combine equality and difference in their journey through life, in the construction and defence of their personal life'.

Seen at the most general level, Touraine's way is to create space for the construction of personalities capable of innovation, with room for identities and a sense of belonging.

At the practical level of intergroup relations, Borofsky analyses the current dilemmas faced by interculturality: the fear of losing cultural 'traditions' in the process of globalization, the relationship between cultures, modernity and development, the need for identities and belonging – as well as the discursive use of ethnicity in political conflict and violence on the world stage. They propose a new concept, that of 'conviviability' or the ability of groups and peoples to share creatively the increasingly open spaces that cultural contacts create, and thus pose the challenge of constructing institutional spaces that could foster and promote that needed and desired conviviality.

Practical and institutional aspects of the recognition of difference and the need for rules of conviviality is what Magga's paper brings out in the

context of the cultural rights of indigenous peoples. Equality and difference are not abstract principles but rather practical matters related to the specific rights of the Sami people: land rights and other resources, political institutions (the Sami Council and Parliament), cultural self-determination, language, education, mass media and management of cultural heritage. In fact, in analysing the case of the Sami people, Magga brings out the need to recognize multiple layers of belonging: the Sami people are asking for the right to take advantage of 'local, pan-Sami, and Nordic opportunities'. For instance, in relation to education, 'the goal is to ensure that children reach a level of functional bilingualism that will empower them to function smoothly in Sami cultural and social settings as well as in those of the majority, as exercised anywhere in the country in question'.

Indigenous peoples' rights, related to the protection of territories, self-organization and the acquisition of self-determination, are also analysed in the chapter by Rasmussen and Sjoerslev. What all these cases show is the claim and the search for legitimate institutions to guarantee identification with communities and the collective cultural rights of existing groups, as well as rights relating to wider senses of belonging and cultural contact. In this sense, the logic of 'multiple layers of belonging' and the search for legitimate institutions to protect rights apply to many situations where collective cultural diversity prevails – ethnicities and religious groups, immigrants and their diasporas, and so on.

Cultural diversity is the framework that Leach uses in exploring environmental issues, but with a very special twist. The author contrasts local ecological knowledge, meanings and social organizations with the idealized views in which these are often framed in 'globally defined environmental agendas or the goals of externally defined campaigns'. Her chapter shows that the images that dominate international policy debates are, however, also based on particular cultural perspectives. Their effectiveness for international action comes from 'crisis narratives' and the ecological discourse in which these are framed. Inhabitants of local environments and external expert agencies very often have different understandings of what the environmental issues are. Yet they are not equal partners in defining the terms of the debate, and there is a real danger in that 'the imposition of global orthodoxies and analysis over different environmental values and notions of sustainability can infringe not only on local livelihoods, but also on cultural freedom, in a deeply decivilizing process'. Hence the author's final call for democratization of the policy process, thus recasting 'citizen participation and the sustenance of cultural diversity in far more political terms, with self-determination in knowledge, ideas and organization at their core'. Here again is a call for participatory institutionalized spaces where diverse voices and interpretations have the right to make themselves visible, and the need for mechanisms to articulate the multiple interests and voices that are present.

The chapter on urban culture designates cities and urban environments as the historically constructed sites of interculturality, diversity and creativity. In so far as current demographic trends are leading to a continuous process of urbanization and metropolitanization of the world in which growing proportions of the world population are living in large cities, and given that these populations are increasingly made up of diverse cultural groups, with roots both in the local environment and in migratory diasporas, it is logical that cultural diversity and creativity will continue to increase. The challenge that the world is facing, therefore, is to create and consolidate spaces, spheres and institutions that will foster and promote the multiplicity of ways of belonging in urban areas, coupled with the spaces and expressions of interactions between 'different' people: conviviality and cultural creativity in all sorts of hybrid forms (new languages, music, art and other forms of expression), based however on sharing

spaces rather than on conflict, violence and discrimination against the 'other'.

The chapter on culture and democracy poses a question that is at the heart of much international debate at present, i.e. 'whether democratic institutions can function in all cultural environments or we must accept that some cultures are compatible only with various forms of authoritarianism'. In spite of strong culturalist traditions and views in the history of political thought and in current political debates, empirical evidence strongly supports a non-culturalist view of democracy. Democratic stability shows a strong association with development or wealth (per capita income) and none at all with cultural traditions (taken as religions). At the same time, research shows that there is no clear relationship between transitions from dictatorship and any other factors. As the authors state, 'dictatorships just seem to run many risks and to die for a broad variety of reasons'.

The strong evidence that the effective existence of democratic institutions is not correlated with culturally defined differences sends a clear signal, i.e. that no society can refuse democracy on the grounds that it is incompatible with its culture, or, in the words of the authors, 'there is little, if anything, that should lead us to believe that cultural obstacles to democracy are immovable'. Thus, any essentialistic view of culture – this particular discussion relates to the current debates on world religions – is quite misplaced. Not only are cultural traditions multi-faceted: they are not a one-off phenomenon and are constantly being invented and reinvented. 'Cultures are made of cloth but the fabric of culture drapes differently in the hands of different tailors.' In fact, rather than see cultural priorities and differences in the threatening light of 'clashes of cultures', democratic institutions can provide the very means to channel and give them expression.

Finally, the chapter on ethics, culture and globalization argues that contemporary ethical requirements are intricately linked to the current

process of globalization in culture, communication and the economy. The complexity of the concept of ethics calls for the identification of a number of standards, some more urgent than others, that need to be observed by societies and states. A major stumbling block here is the confusion between rights and values, and between morals and ethics. The chapter discusses the effectiveness of human rights as an issue raised by ethics in the context of globalization and shows how the logic of rights must necessarily lead to a logic of responsibility.

In sum, the message to be drawn from the analysis and perspectives presented in the chapters in Part Two is relatively clear and consistent, i.e. cultural diversity is here to stay, and the creativity derived from diversity can flourish, avoiding violence and authoritarianism. Yet considerable imagination is needed to build the participatory institutional spaces where diverse voices can express themselves, whether in the management of local environmental issues, the organization of local urban life, or the operation of political institutions of functioning democracies.

Chapter 2
Equal yet different

Alain Touraine
Sociologist, École des Hautes Études
en Sciences Sociales (EHESS);
Founder of the Centre d'Analyse
et d'Intervention Sociologiques (CADIS),
Paris (France)

'If the technical
world and the
world of cultural
identities have
grown further and
further apart,
only the individual
has the means
to bring them
together
again . . .'

Social interests
and cultural values

Our collective experience is strongly marked by two
recent changes: one is the new industries which act
on culture and the personality by creating languages,
images, representations of the world and of
ourselves. The other is the entry into the world
economy of populations which have undergone
modernization not by a gradual process but suddenly,
while continuing to live in their former social and
cultural conditions. On the one hand, therefore, we
can no longer consider that men create their
technical or economic environment since it is
henceforth the cultural industries – education, health
care and information in particular – which create
new representations of the human being, and on the
other hand, we discover that it is possible to
innovate not only with things new, as the West
believed, but also with things old, by mobilizing the
cultural and social resources of each country to
enable it to enter the global economic system.

This dual change means that today the most
visible problems and those which give rise to the
greatest conflicts, dramas and hopes are cultural
problems, while what we used to call social problems
seem to be better controlled in the industrialized
countries and less central in the developing
countries, where the conditions of modernization are

more important than the internal problems of an
industrial society still in the making.

If it is true, however, that cultural problems
have got the upper hand over social problems proper,
and that claims to cultural rights carry more weight
than claims to social rights, in both cases we are
faced with comparable choices. Modernity always
appears as a break between rational action vis-à-vis
the world on the one hand, and therefore
disenchantment with it, and awareness of the self on
the other, be it in the form of the moral
individualism of Kant or in that of a community
identity. And in any event it is the call to politics, to
the willful action of society on itself, which alone can

save the unity of our personal and collective experience.

In the two great historical situations considered, that in which social problems prevail and that in which cultural problems are more to the fore, the same question arises: how does one combine the universality of rights with the acknowledgement of particular social interests and cultural values? Without the universality of rights a culture shuts itself off in its difference, and often in the idea of its superiority, while technical and economic activity is reduced to the management of means placed at the service of a political will. This brings us to what Weber called the war of the gods, and what is in fact the war of nations, states and peoples.

The question as to how one can give real content to the affirmation of universal rights has been answered in three main ways.

The first is to maintain the call for universal rights, i.e. for citizenship, in the name of God, of Reason or of History, at the risk of accepting social inequalities or cultural repression. The second, on the contrary, is to affirm the universal value of a particular culture, and consequently to reject all pluralism and to do away with minorities. The third is to extend the idea of civic rights to that of social or cultural rights.

At the time of the first industrial era, which affected only a few countries in the Western world, these three responses produced in the one case a highly legal 'republicanism' which was indifferent or hostile to the demands of the working classes; in the second case, on the contrary, the will to create a society of workers and even a dictatorship of the proletariat; and in the third instance, the creation of an 'industrial democracy', as the English call it, a change which took the form elsewhere, or later, of social democracy and the Welfare State. The important thing for us today is to reformulate these three responses to adapt them to the problems raised by the affirmation of cultural rights.

Three responses

The first response, attractive especially to the countries which have the oldest political and democratic traditions, and particularly France, is the defence of the universalism of culture and therefore the rejection of minorities, which at best means a very open society which identifies with universal values. To a certain extent this is what happened in the United Kingdom or in France, at least when these countries were in a superior position, and not threatened as they are today by the redistribution of wealth and production in the world. In an even more central manner, this vision was destroyed by the principal action of the women's movements, i.e. the affirmation that the terms 'man' and 'human rights' have no expression other than the man/woman duality, so that equality and difference, the universal and the particular, are henceforth inseparable.

The second response, similar to the idea of a society of workers or a dictatorship of the proletariat in industrial society, is search for purity and homogeneity, often through authoritarian means or by isolating communities one after the other in the name of a boundless cultural relativism. In certain countries, like the United States, this is reflected in the importance of identity politics. In other, less privileged countries, it has led to the rise of the kind of fundamentalism that serves as a springboard for authoritarian regimes.

Is it possible to find a third path, similar to the one which led to industrial democracy in the first industrial societies? This simple question sums up the most important problem of our societies. Just as in the Europe of the nineteenth century the key problem – the social issue – was that of the domination of the working class, today the central problem is that of combining cultural pluralism with the participation of everybody in a technico-economic world in which all countries participate. Several solutions have been proposed.

The first solution, the aesthetic response, is the

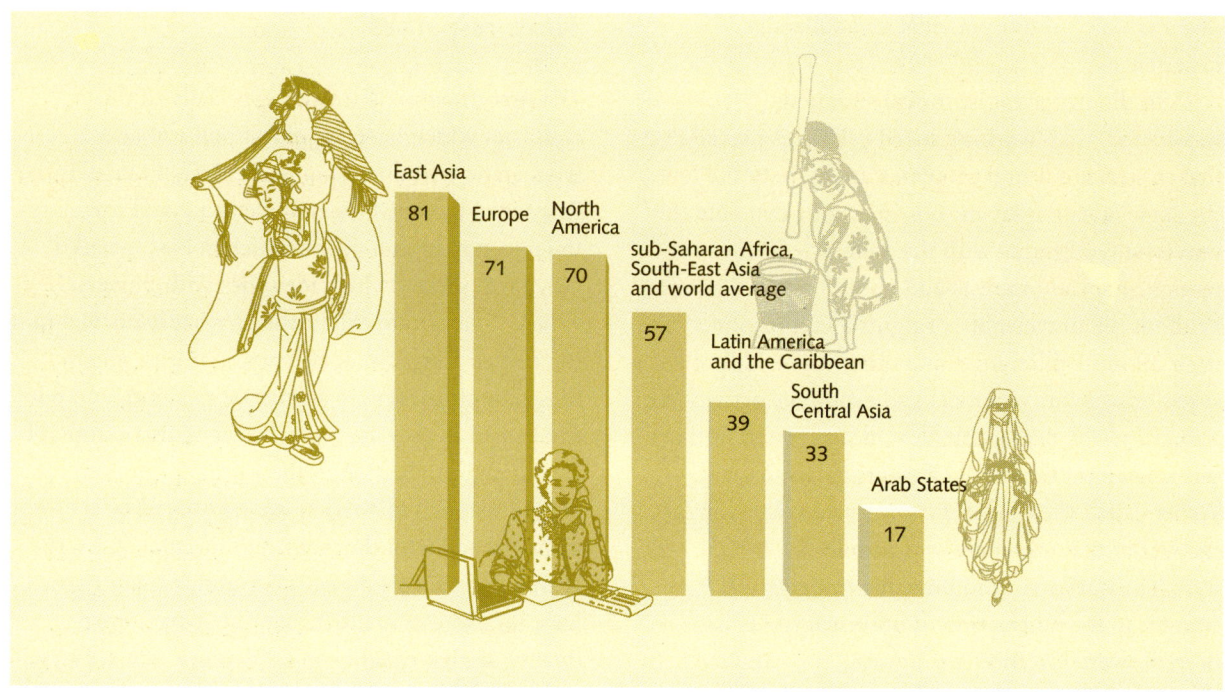

GRAPH 3
CULTURAL ATTITUDES TO WOMEN'S EMPLOYMENT: FEMALE LABOUR FORCE PARTICIPATION RATE AS A PERCENTAGE OF MALE LABOUR FORCE PARTICIPATION RATE (1995)

Source: International Labour Organisation.

The extent of female employment is a reflection not only of economic development, but of culture too. Industrial countries on the whole have higher female employment than developing ones, although the region with the highest figure is East Asia, because of China. Similarly Latin America and the Arab States show a considerably lower figure than sub-Saharan Africa: this is due to the influence of cultural attitudes on the economy.

recognition of cultural diversity and curiosity for other cultures, which can also help to cast a critical eye on oneself, like Montesquieu in his *Persian Letters*. It was during the Industrial Revolution that the interest in Antiquity developed, and it was the economic boom of the post-war period which saw the rapid development in many countries of museum and exhibition attendance. And whereas initially these attracted above all an audience interested in retracing their origins, particularly in the case of Europe, in Rome, Greece and above all Egypt, we are witnessing the development of museums presenting objects from cultures which are said to be different,

or representative of the 'primitive arts', to use Jacques Chirac's expression. But the limits of this aesthetic response are evident, for this recognition of different cultures is all the easier when they are far away and have no effect on our everyday lives and social relations.

The second solution consists in looking beyond the differences and seeking the same universally applicable principles in all cultures. This is the spirit which prevails in all ecumenical encounters, like the one organized by Pope John Paul II in Assisi, and several activities organized by UNESCO to encourage mutual recognition of different cultures. Are we not

all concerned by the same fundamental questions? Where do we come from? Where are we going? Do all the major religions not agree on the need to respect life and to treat all human beings equally? True, this response often appears absurd, and religions have been at the origin of as many wars as they have ecumenical conferences, as Samuel Huntington points out. Nevertheless, the Enlightenment continues to appeal to all those who place communication, i.e. relations, above production. This position is best illustrated today in German philosophy, with Habermas and Apel, and their search for the universal conditions of communication between the different protagonists. It is difficult to see, however, how communication and mutual recognition can be achieved between individuals or social groups in situations of inequality, domination or dependence. Is this not a reversion to the illusions of republicanism and consequently the rejection of the cultural rights of certain categories in the name of the universality of political rights?

We must therefore seek another solution, along the lines of the slow, difficult and ever partial creation of an industrial democracy in the first countries to undergo capitalist modernization. A difficult quest which may even seem impossible to many people in a fast-moving world without a principle and without a centre, and where it seems more rational to accept a diversity regulated by market forces alone. This is the post-modern position, both radical in its deconstruction of all the universalist principles accused of being the ideologies of the dominant countries or classes, and ultra-liberal since only the market can assure communication without integration.

It appears to me, however, that an answer can be found. If the technical world and the world of cultural identities have grown further and further apart, only the individual has the means to bring them together again, or even feels the need to do so, since his oneness, the coherence of his personality,

are threatened by this separation. And this combination is possible because it is a matter of linking the world of the means, to which everybody is party, and that of the ends, the values, which are increasingly different. Universalism is therefore no longer to be sought in a higher principle, in the manner of those who, with Hannah Arendt, seek to rebuild politics and its principle of equality over and above social inequalities, but on the contrary in the need of each individual and each community to be defined at the same time by identities and by participation in the technico-economic world.

This idea takes us beyond the solutions envisaged. It means recognizing cultural diversity, affirming the cultural rights of all, and of minorities in particular, and therefore combining equality and difference. Renowned anthropologists like Clifford Geertz or Louis Dumont have claimed that these two terms are incompatible. And indeed they are, within a strongly anchored social system with its ever-present hierarchies, where differences lead to inequalities. In an open society, however, where the regulating principles disappear, the only sources of inequality are either economic or military, so different cultures can combine with an economic world which is not egalitarian by referring to what I call the subject, i.e. the will of each individual to be an actor, combining instrumental action and cultural identity.

This claim triggers an immediate objection: if this construction of the subject is personal, does it not remain confined to private life, while public life is abandoned to economic inequalities and the war of the gods? But this objection is so evident that it is easy to dismiss, for no social actor can assert the right to be a subject without acknowledging that everyone has the same right. And more immediately, an actor can be a subject only in relation to another actor whom he or she recognizes and who recognizes him or her as a subject. As a matter of fact we cannot define democracy today other than as the political system which protects and encourages mutual recognition by actors in their effort to combine their participation in the technico-economic world with the protection of their cultural identity. One example is enough to illustrate this. When a minority finds itself in a society, for example when immigrants arrive to work and live in a society different from their own, their integration cannot be achieved by merging them with the host society or by isolating them in their community; it can be achieved only by equal access to work and income and by recognizing their identity. To quote Simmel, they must be integrated as foreigners, i.e. as both equal and different. In practice the opposite often happens: we encourage inequality by confining immigrants to unskilled jobs, precariousness and unemployment, and at the same time expect them to resemble us and to forego the distinctive marks of their cultural identity.

Cultural identity and democratic management

Similar reasoning can be applied to categories other than ethnic origin, such as religious or sexual categories. In the case of religion, it means going beyond mere tolerance, which encloses religious beliefs in the private sphere, and beyond secularity, which sees religious behaviours as inferior and irrational. Religious minorities must be allowed to participate in economic life while at the same time asserting their religious identity, which in turn must increasingly define itself in its own terms and not because historically it belongs to a community most of whose standards are their own and cannot be justified or explained by religious beliefs.

In the realm of sexual behaviour, in many countries we have witnessed great progress in recent years in the recognition of homosexuals, not only in the recognition of a difference but above all as a special facet of the relationship each of us seeks to establish between sexuality and culture, as we rid ourselves of the puritanical, repressive ideas on which Western culture was long based.

If we discard warlike stances that proclaim the need to create pure, homogeneous communities, which can lead only to totalitarian societies defined by their battle against the enemy within, there are two main answers to the question at hand: the affirmation of a higher political order, based on equality of all citizens, as opposed to inequality of the social actors, or in a completely different direction, a call to manage differences by recognizing that everybody has the right to combine technical activity and cultural identity in a world where we no longer believe that economic modernization and rationalization in particular necessarily lead to the triumph of a type of moral, belief or social organization. The thinking of Max Weber did not explain the cultural foundations of the modern age but the cultural reasons for a certain type of modernization – capitalism, i.e. the breaking of all the bonds that linked the economy to cultures and forms of social organization. Today we have arrived at societies which are technical, i.e. operational and instrumental, imposing no culture, no form of social organization. And at the same time we are witnessing a host of different forms of modernization, whereas formerly many people thought that there was only 'one best way', as Taylor put it, and that the newly industrialized countries should follow in the footsteps of the countries which preceded them on the road to modernization.

This combination of a cultural identity, particularly an ethnic or religious one, and a democratic management guaranteeing and strengthening the right of each individual to become a subject, almost always occurs in practice in a national context, and the national conscience is never reduced to the functioning of democratic institutions at the service of universal rights. The opposition traditionally established between the nation-institution *à la française* and the nation-community German-style has an analytical value but does not really describe reality. On the German side, from Herder to Fichte, the creators of the German

national conscience were strongly influenced by the philosophy of the Enlightenment and wanted Germany, as well as France and the United Kingdom, to be able to identify with reason and progress. On the French side, the idea of the nation was constantly, from Michelet to Renan and Charles de Gaulle, a carnal, emotional reality, a feat of memory even more than of principles and institutions. A nation-community can be expected to reject minorities more easily. And so it does: Germany makes it much more difficult than France to acquire citizenship, for example; but in all the countries of Europe, including France and the United Kingdom, the national conscience is strongly linked to a 'local' conscience, a sense of belonging to a restricted community, a region or a smaller unit. This is not very different from the American situation, where the strong national conscience combines with awareness of belonging to a nationality of origin. Ethnicity is therefore by no means in opposition with nationality: on the contrary, it is when the national conscience is more democratic that the ethnic (be it national or religious) conscience can combine with it. The clearest case in the Western countries is that of the Jews, who have associated a strong sense of community with a very strong sense of national belonging. If one defines the nation only by its representative institutions, there is a risk of leaving the sense of national belonging in the hands of populists or demagogues.

This remark needs elucidation. It is only right that increasing doubt should be shed on the claim to universality of the model which Europe invented and implemented at the beginning of its modernization. This model was not based only on rationalization but also on what it implied, namely the greatest possible separation of the rational and the non-rational, concentrating at the summit of society everything that could be considered rational and placing everything considered irrational in a position of inferiority or dependence. Whence the dichotomous representations which have dominated life and thinking in the West. The adult male individual, safe from need or even owner of his home, was considered as the bearer of modernity, while children, women, dependent workers and colonies were considered to be dominated by their passions. Reason versus belief, interest versus passion – these highly hierarchized oppositions have dominated the Western world. They explain both the extraordinary success of the countries which applied this vision, not least the United Kingdom, and the violence of the internal conflicts of these societies based on repression and at the same time calculation.

The history of the last 100 years has been marked by the revolt of the dominated: workers, colonies, women and perhaps now children too, since we have begun to take children's rights seriously. A great movement is afoot, which I have called 'the reshaping of the world'. It affects each and every one of us: cultural traditions like the imagination or sexuality, and the body in general, are invading the preserve of rational calculation and weakening the capitalist vision which protected rational enterprise from any pressure from the lower orders. What was previously separated and hierarchized is tending to draw closer together and to communicate. How, in a world where the domination of one class over another, where the colonial order and the dependent role of women have been rightfully and violently called into question, can we possibly support the idea of a society governed by reason, by abstract equality, over and above all social and cultural differences and singularities? The destruction of the old inequalities cannot lead to the confused idea of a global melting pot, or to the feeble and hopeless image of a world united in mass consumption. It must lead only to the recognition by everyone of the great movement towards the reshaping of the world, and therefore towards dialogue between cultural identities and instrumental reason, divested henceforth of the role of legitimizing the power of a class or a nation. The action of the ecologists in this sense has been most important, as

'I don't sell bread, only yeast . . .'
(Miguel de Unamuno)

Is woman part of nature, or of culture? But why the question, since she is fully half of humankind, the one known as the *other* half (since there has to be another half) as opposed to *the* half, the one that *matters*, the male half? The story of her debarment from responsibility and the democratic process gives us our first answer to these questions.

The roots of the problem have yet to be explored. The problem is such that even now, at the dawn of the third millennium, with a technological revolution enabling women and men to patrol the galaxies, perhaps even to combat AIDS and to conceive through *in vitro* fertilization, sexual inequality is still with us in one form or other around the world.

The World Conference on Women (Beijing, 1995) showed up the appalling situation of all those who are deprived of progress and well-being: 70% of the 1,300 million human beings living in absolute poverty are women. The work done by women – they do fully two-thirds of the world's work without any payment (as against a quarter for men) – is 'invisible', as though, in the words of Isabel Larguia, the Cuban sociologist, it was 'a secondary sexual feature of women'.

In very many countries, women are still alienated from their bodies – they cannot decide when to have children, or not to be 'sold' to a husband in childhood, or not to be raped – and so suffer the maltreatment of their class and sex.

Women are the victims rather than the subjects of political authority, unlike men. Politics, like religion, is still the preserve of men. Women fill only 6% of ministerial posts in the world. Only 11% of parliamentarians are women. And in 55 countries women are barred, or virtually so, from public office.

This outright dismissal, this age-old discrimination that is so deeply entrenched in institutions and people's minds, that is so sweeping (after all, it affects fully half of the human race) and so absurd (are men alone capable of governing?), emanates from the monotheistic religions, Genesis and the curse placed on the woman who sinned.

Certain eighteenth-century philosophers, those who reduced women to natural objects and thence to sexual objects, following the example of the Church Fathers (Tertullian called the female genitals the 'devil's door'), held that they were not entitled to education. Silvain Maréchal, the egalitarian communist and disciple of Baboeuf, published a lampoon soon after the French Revolution entitled *Women Shouldn't be Taught How to Read*. The philosophers of the Enlightenment decreed, in the name of Reason, the segregation of social roles. Diderot, Rousseau and Voltaire reduced the role of woman to that of a housewife. Men enacted and applied the law. Women, confined to the home, were in charge of morals.

Yet segregation is a kind of apartheid, unjust and intolerable. The culture of one of humankind's most brilliant centuries – that of humanist philosophy and of the French Revolution – sanctioned this separation unequivocally. A misleading brand of universalism sheltered it for centuries. Because for centuries the rights of man, which were purportedly universal, in other words the rights of all humankind, in fact were those of men alone. And, indeed, of only a small number of those.

The weaknesses of universalism were accompanied by syllogisms whose apparent rationality invited scorn and repression. Accordingly, if every man is identical and interchangeable with all the others in the world, then multiculturalism has no meaning and all difference is proscribed. Was it not in the name of *homo universalis* that nineteenth-century colonial expeditions were organized to convey the humanistic ideals of the Revolution to populations that were different? Was it not in fact with the object of bringing the benefits of the

Enlightenment and of civilization (universal and, naturally, white and Western) to those remote 'others' – those good or evil savages, those good-for-nothings, those children – that the subjugated peoples' demands for equal rights were swamped in blood and scorn? Not to mention the fact – yet another grave imperfection of the system – that in France it did not prevent the Members of the Constituent Assembly in 1789 from upholding slavery (it had to await the Constitution of 1848 to be finally abolished). It was universalism – of the sort that Étienne Balibar, the philosopher, called 'extensive' – that very largely built empires and justified colonial dominion.

Thus the Declaration of the Rights of Man and of the Citizen created a strangely limited, 'restricted' citizen. Sartre was right when he wrote that behind the abstract man of the Declaration stands the bourgeois of 1789. The individual is therefore a man (not a woman), white (and not coloured), and a bourgeois (not a peasant or a colonized person). This shaky universalization did not take long to rebound. It muzzled women who protested against inequality, who refused the identification of humankind as an all-male preserve and who pointed out that it was they, after all, who bred and perpetuated humankind. Yet they were still being told they were equal. The difference due to sex was denied and blotted out.

The result is that the world and its future are now in the hands of men. Up to 90%. And what is the upshot of it all?

Is the earth blue like an orange, as Eluard wrote? Or red with the blood of genocides from the Sho'ah to Rwanda, not forgetting Bosnia? Or is it the atmosphere with the ozone layer perforated and dwindling, its cardinal constituents all spoiled? Following the international Rio Summit Conference on the future of our planet, and the Denver Conference of June 1997, the heads of state – all men? – adjourned. Without having accomplished their mission. They had done nothing about the greenhouse effect (the international corporations had successfully protested with one voice), nothing about the ozone-layer damage, nothing about pollution. Total failure.

An environment left to the tender care and destructive power of unrestrained industrialization, the power of the lobbies and their profits. A starved world in which 75% of the inhabitants live in a state of absolute poverty (women, of course, being hardest hit), while 358 billionaires (in US dollars) own more than the earnings of half of the world's populations. While at the same time, on the same planet, human rights go on shrinking. Could things possibly be worse? If universalism is to be humanistic, then reasoning should be the other way round.

Let us begin with the (undeniable) observation that humankind is sexed and that this unique distinction, upon which its survival depends, implies, for purposes of genuine universalism, that the two halves accede – equally – to power. This is the price of democracy. Anything else is a mere travesty. Equality here denotes parity. In other words as many women as men involved in decision-making: war, the environment, hunger, unemployment, nuclear energy . . . it is as much women's responsibility too.

This will lead to a genuine cultural blend. An alternative culture produces an alternative democracy and vice versa.

It seems to me that UNESCO's cardinal role today is to achieve a dual utopia (in the sense of a universal project), i.e. history produced by men and women in equal and integral parts, and politics dialectically linked to culture.

Aimé Césaire was right when he said that politics would not be worth an ounce of effort if they were not warranted by a cultural project.

Gisèle Halimi
Lawyer; President of the Feminist Movement
'Choisir – La Cause des Femmes';
Author; Former Ambassador of France to UNESCO

they defend both the survival of the world and the diversity of its species and cultures. Only in this way is it possible to achieve sustainable development, of which cultural diversity and respect for personal and collective projects are central features.

Numerous obstacles prevent us from progressing faster along this path, but the main obstacles are those which render us powerless in the face of the dissociation of the global economy and individual cultures, leading to the disappearance or the dissolution of all the social and cultural projects, all the active visions of development.

Choices and obstacles

We must find a way round the impossible choice between the mass culture which unites the world in the consumption of the same products and the differentialism which confines us all in closed communities unable to communicate with one another other than through the market or through war. An impossible choice indeed, but one many of us are faced with in a world where the centre is defined by the intensity of trade, data flows and especially financial exchanges, and the periphery by the frontiers erected by communities increasingly obsessed by the threats bearing down on them.

It is easy to understand the dangers of this situation, because we have already experienced them. At the beginning of the century we witnessed an expansion of world trade even greater than what we call globalization today. At that time too, just as today, new industrialized countries emerged (Japan and Germany). This triumph of financial capitalism led to some dramatic confrontations: not only a fight to the death between the nations of Europe, but also revolutions in peripheral countries or those which were beginning to take part in the capitalist exchanges, such as China, Mexico or Russia, which sometimes led to forms of nationalism conducive to a degree of modernization, and sometimes to totalitarian regimes.

Today we live under the illusion that the American model can be generalized, that a complementarity can and must exist between the major modern technical, economic and financial networks and a cultural fragmentation that has enabled numerous minorities to affirm their identities but has made communication between minorities increasingly difficult. In the United States this cohabitation was made possible both by the resounding economic success and by the strength of the institutions and legal mechanisms which have long sought and achieved integration in a society made up of people from a wide variety of origins. However, not only does the American situation remind us of the violence of the conflicts it has engendered, even recently, but the other parts of the world are perfectly aware of their powerlessness to deal with such an explosive situation, which can easily lead to the collapse of all the institutions and of any possibility for organized community life.

However, the conclusion towards which these remarks about the present and the past lead us is that above all we must avoid choosing between two extreme solutions: the disappearance of all differences in a mass society, or the direct clash of these differences and communities. On the contrary, we must learn to combine the two. UNESCO has been seen to do this quite well in the major debates on democracy, development, education and, above all, human rights, combining universalist principles with cultural differences and with the participation of everybody in economic activity and exchanges. The idea which must never be sacrificed is that peace within each society and between societies cannot exist without the recognition, first and foremost, of a universalist principle which prevails over both the instrumental reason which rules the economy, and cultural diversity. We must respect the attachment of many people to the solutions developed by Greek democracy, to the key place given to citizenship, but how can we satisfy such a principle of order when we live in a time of movement, change and multiplicity of cultural and economic exchanges? Is

it not time, instead of seeking a higher principle of order, to affirm the right of all human beings to choose their path, to combine equality and difference in their journey through life, in the construction and defence of their personal lives? Just as we must resist the superficial arguments of those who predict the imminent disappearance of states and all forms of control over an economy which knows no frontiers and obeys no laws, it is also true that the image of the Greek city or of our modern states, especially in Europe and the two Americas, regions which have believed in the overwhelming power of the law and education, has been weakened. This means that in the wake of the great capitalist revolution that has unfurled across the world in the last twenty years we must build new political and social mediations to limit the now patent and dangerous dissociation of an economy which operates on a global scale and cultural identities increasingly enclosed in the defence of a threatened essence.

And how could one fail, in addressing UNESCO, to stress the implications of such a thought for education? The West has long upheld a vision based on the *Bildung*, i.e. on access for young people to higher values, such as truth, beauty and good, with which each country tended to identify and which led us to transmit knowledge and values rather than to prepare children for life. Is it not high time that we focused education on young people to help them not to lose their distinctive features in the name of universalism, but on the contrary to live and to innovate, combining technical activities and cultural and psychological motivations? Education must not be merely a means of strengthening society: it must also serve to build personalities capable of innovating, resisting and communicating, affirming their universal right, and acknowledging that of others, to participate in the modern technical age with their own personalities, memories, languages and desires. If we do not push such solutions forward the world will experience greater turmoil than was ever caused by the class struggle.

Chapter 3
Cultural possibilities

Robert Borofsky
Anthropologist; Professor of Anthropology,
Hawaii Pacific University (United States)

'. . . culture may
be viewed
as a creative
force for
embracing
and coping
with change.'

Abounding culture

Culture has become one of the most popular words in our global vocabulary. It is repeatedly referred to in local, national and global media. But it is not always clear what the central concept being discussed is. One hears references to Indonesian national culture, for example, but also to Javanese, Batak and Balinese culture within Indonesia as well as to northern Balinese and southern Balinese culture. How can culture refer to all of these groups at the same time? In addition, one hears references to a culture of violence, of poverty, of drugs, of anorexia and of the jet set. How does one make sense of such phrases? 'It has gotten to the point that when you hear the word "culture",' the Ghanaian scholar Appiah notes, 'you reach for your dictionary.' Perhaps we need to reframe the discussion.

The present chapter's basic themes may be summarized as follows:

First, culture is a concept, not a reality. It is an idea that has developed over the past two centuries and is substantially linked to notions of political solidarity, particularly that of the nation-state. Culture has neither substance nor taste, although people can touch and taste a whole range of things that they label as culture.

Second, culture, as a concept, frequently embodies a contradiction. On the one hand, historically, it incorporates a political agenda of homogenization. It implies that people living in a particular locale, a specific state, act in the same general way. It affirms a group's identity by encircling it with a boundary. On the other hand, if one looks carefully at the behaviour patterns being delineated, one realizes that they are not really circumscribable and, moreover, are constantly changing. Attempts to trace such boundaries are akin to trying to encage the wind.

Third, the previous two points set the stage for discussing two alternative ways of reflecting on the concept of culture: (a) regarding culture as something to be preserved from the past – as something once bounded and, if possible, to be kept so – is the more established view of the matter; and (b) alternatively, culture may be viewed as a creative force for embracing and coping with change. Such a view helps to reinforce social solidarity within groups. This approach, however, draws unity from common visions for the future, building on the past and present to reach sought-after goals. Critically, this perspective tends to dampen conflict: people are more open to differences and changes around them.

These points deserve to be examined in greater detail: they involve a number of significant subtleties that need to be addressed.

Culture is a concept

Despite the fact that people talk of culture as being something 'real', as something that exists 'out there', it is, in fact, an intellectual construct[1] used for describing (and explaining) a complex cluster of human behaviours, ideas, emotions and artefacts. Scholars have been making this point for decades. The anthropologist Lowie, for example, wrote in 1937 that 'culture is invariably an artificial unit segregated for purposes of expediency' (1937, p. 235). Kroeber made a similar assertion in 1945 (Kroeber, 1945, p. 90). And recently, the widely respected anthropologist Geertz observed: 'To describe a culture . . . is not to set out some odd sort of object . . . It is to try to induce somebody somewhere to look at some things as I have been induced, by journeys, books, witnessings, and conversations, to look at them' (1995, pp. 61–2).

The point that culture is a concept – not an actual reality – can also be exemplified by noting the wide variations in the manner in which people use the term. Goodenough states: 'The term culture has a long history of meaning different things to different people' (1989, p. 93). Or to quote the sociologist Parsons: 'In anthropological theory there is not what could be called close agreement on the definition of culture' (1951, p. 15). Williams suggests that 'Culture is one of the two or three most complicated words in the English language. This is so partly because of its intricate historical development, in several languages, but mainly because it has now come to be used for important concepts in several distinct intellectual disciplines and in several distinct and incompatible systems of thought (1976, pp. 76–7).

An easy way to see this is to read through a book entitled *Culture: A Critical Review of Concepts and Definitions* by Kroeber and Kluckhohn (1952) which contains over 150 definitions of culture.[2]

Rather than getting drawn into arguments about what *is* and *is not* culture and instead of seeking one essential meaning (or meanings) for the concept, it would be wiser, perhaps, to take a pragmatic perspective and ask: What concrete problems do people tend to address when they refer to culture? Building on the report on culture and development, published by UNESCO in 1995, *Our Creative Diversity*, one might well highlight three of these.

First, people repeatedly voice concern about the loss of cultural values and cultural identity. From the First World to the Third (as well as the Fourth), the complaint is often the same: modern life tends to disrupt traditional foundations of meaning and identity. The Kenyan economist Mwale, for example, calls for a decolonization of the African mind, for a cultural identity independent of the West (Useem, 1997, p. A48). Intriguingly, despite the fact that each case refers to a culturally specific situation, the complaint is understood around the world. Complain about the problem in Thailand, and Japanese and Indonesian visitors will understand; complain about it in Guatemala, and Brazilians and Canadians will sympathize.

Second, culture also comes into play in discussions regarding economic development. Culture is seen as emphasizing an alternative set of priorities from the market – as stressing the humane and inspiring in life and/or the caring for others. Today is not the first time market economies have dramatically reshaped social life. The same occurred in England and the United States in the 1800s. 'The Great Transformation', Polyani (1944) called it. That market calculus has now returned, in revised form, in relation to economic development and 'neo-liberal' reforms. Questions are repeatedly raised as to what cultural values are lost in the march toward full market economies and globalization.

Third, culture also comes into play in discussions of ethnic conflict. The conflicts between, for example, Hutu and Tutsi (in Rwanda), Bosnians and Serbs (in the Balkans), Moslem and Hindu (in

The global in the local [3]

The much publicized Unity Dow court case in Botswana is a good illustration of the interface and tension between international standards and local customs. What the case shows is that, rather than see international standards (in this case, involving discrimination against women) as impositions from outside, they only become effective when local actors mobilize them as resources in conflicts that unfold and have to be solved within the local (national) institutional and cultural scene.

The case drew its immediate significance from the fact that it was the first time in the history of the country that a woman challenged the government in court. The case, known as *Dow* v. *State of Botswana*, had its origins in amendments to the Citizenship Act that were enacted in 1984 when the government decided to restrict the categories of persons who could become citizens through birth or descent.

Unity Dow, a prominent Gaborone lawyer and a leading member of the feminist organization Emang Basadi ('Stand Up Women'), had married an American citizen, Peter Nathan Dow, before 1984. They had three children, two of whom were born after 1984 and were therefore affected by the amendments to the Citizenship Act. Under the amended Act, the two children were not citizens of Botswana, even though they were born there

and had lived there all their lives, and even though their mother was a citizen of that country.

In November 1990, Unity Dow decided to challenge the Citizenship Act in court. She argued that her children were denied Botswana citizenship because her husband was a non-citizen. She also contended that if a Botswana male had married a woman from outside Botswana, his children would have been granted citizenship without difficulty.

From the beginning the case was viewed as a test, intended to set a precedent for future legal action on behalf of women. In June 1991 Judge Horowitz delivered a 24-page verdict. Writing that in matters of human rights he was compelled to take a generous interpretation of the law, the Judge found for Unity Dow and declared the relevant sections of the Citizenship Act 'null and void'. He accepted that Unity Dow had been discriminated against on the basis of her sex and had thereby been denied fundamental rights to liberty, protection from being subjected to degrading treatment, and protection from restrictions on her freedom of movement – all arguments put forward by Dow's lawyer.

Reactions to the verdict were swift and divided largely along gender lines. Supporters of Unity Dow hailed it as a breakthrough for women, hoping that the

India), and Tamil and Sinhalese (in Sri Lanka) are all portrayed as being rooted in age-old cultural differences. Culture becomes a way for explaining – almost justifying – ethnic violence and conflict today.

Trapped in a contradiction

It is important to realize that the concept developed in a particular historical context – nationalism – which framed culture as a homogenizing, unifying force that, ultimately, supported the state. As developed in Germany during the nineteenth century, the cultural concept involved the search for a unifying identity among the politically fragmented and disempowered German middle class. 'With the slow rise of the German bourgeoisie from a second-rank class to the bearer of German national consciousness . . . from a class which was first

obliged to perceive or legitimize itself primarily by contrasting itself to the courtly-aristocratic upper class, and then by defining itself against competing nations', culture evolved, Elias (1994, p. 25) suggests, into an identity-marker of German political unity.

We see this process at work in modern states too. Many Third World nation-states are formed of disparate groups. Claiming an underlying cultural unity for the nation helps legitimize and strengthen the state. By holding up nationally shared ideals, nationally shared visions of life, internal divisions are muted. Culture, in this sense, acts as the 'tie that binds' people together within a political unit.

But this framing of the cultural concept faces two central problems or, to put it more aptly, two realities. First, no culture is an island unto itself. 'No culture is a hermetically sealed entity', as *Our*

government would now move swiftly to change all discriminatory laws. Government ministers, however, who seemed to speak for the vast majority of men on this issue, vehemently attacked the decision as an unacceptable affront to Tswana culture.

Two weeks after the judgement, the government announced its decision to contest it; it indicated that it would launch an appeal before a five-member panel of the High Court, and that meantime the relevant sections of the Citizenship Act would continue in force. The government further signified that, should the appeal fail, it would consider moving to amend the Constitution to allow gender discrimination. As a statement from the Attorney-General said, it might become necessary to 'ensure that the Constitution reflects the popular norms of Botswana'. In December 1991, however, the appeal was heard by the full bench of the High Court, which in July 1992 upheld Justice Horowitz's judgement.

The Unity Dow court case thus touches directly upon the 'cultural values' and 'rights' anatagonism in international human rights debates. It has structural equivalents in many parts of sub-Saharan Africa where numerous women's movements, organizations and networks presently place women's rights high on the agenda, as forcefully evidenced during the 1993 World Human Rights Conference in Vienna.

The case exemplifies the fact that there is no 'Botswana culture' in the sense of a unitary whole, a bounded entity, to which human rights may be said to apply, or not to apply. This culture is itself being vehemently contested, negotiated and debated.

Furthermore, in the process of negotiating what (women's) human rights in Botswana are, or ought to be, the question of power is very much present. Various forms of knowledge are manipulated by different actors in specific contexts in pursuit of certain ends.

Finally, human rights as culture in action in and around the Unity Dow court case is constituted by many voices from within and outside Botswana itself. This clashes conspicuously with old perceptions of the autonomy and integrity of territorially based cultures. It suggests at the same time that the traditional relativist view of human rights as being particularly 'Western' can no longer be sustained.

Human rights have now clearly become part of a far wider, globalized cultural network of perspectives with a much more creative interplay, and women like Unity Dow and her feminist supporters certainly consider them to be theirs.

Ann-Belinda S. Preis
Anthropologist; Executive Co-ordinator,
World Culture Report, UNESCO

Creative Diversity puts it. 'All cultures are influenced by and in turn influence other cultures' (World Commission on Culture and Development, 1995, p. 54). There is always a sense of relation[4] in the cultural concept – it is not simply 'the X', but rather 'the X' in relation to 'the Y', the French to the British, the British to the Germans, the Thais to the Burmese, or the Vietnamese to the Chinese. 'To think of ethnicity in relation to one group and its culture', Barth intimates, 'is like trying to clap with one hand. The contrast between "us" and "others" is what is embedded in the organization of ethnicity: an otherness of the others' (1995, p. 13).

While contemporary rhetoric may imply that each culture is pristine unto itself, there is considerable evidence to evince the fact that cultures are subtle mixtures of indigenous and foreign

influences. 'The amount of cultural material . . . of foreign origin which gradually accumulates within any one culture', Kroeber (1948, p. 257) observed in an extensive study of the subject, 'may . . . be said to be normally greater than what is originated within it.'

Careful study indicates that there is always a host of foreign 'imports' within a culture although – and this is important – these may, over time, gradually become perceived as part of the culture itself. Only careful historical study uncovers their origin. The range of examples is full of surprises: the Hawaiian ukulele is Portuguese, the glass on Western windows was invented by the Egyptians, porcelain comes from China, and our modern toilets derive from Rome. The indigenous and the foreign, it is clear, are repeatedly entwined within a cultural group.

People embrace the world in a multitude of

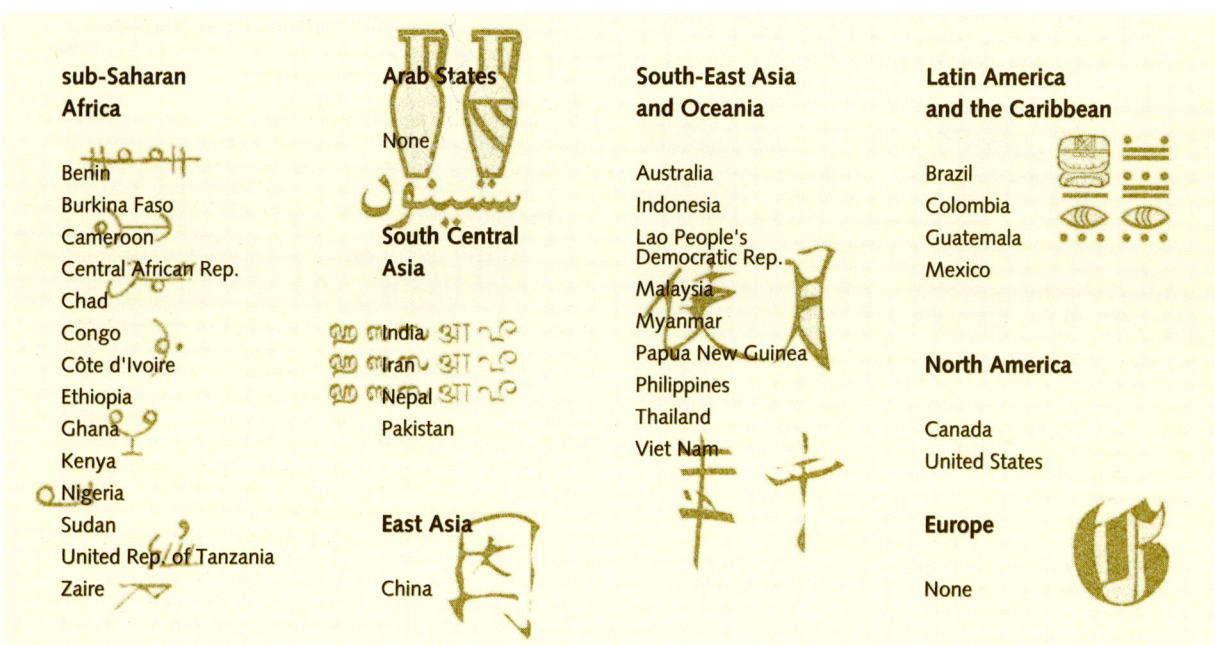

sub-Saharan Africa	Arab States	South-East Asia and Oceania	Latin America and the Caribbean

None (Arab States)

sub-Saharan Africa	South Central Asia	South-East Asia and Oceania	Latin America and the Caribbean
Benin		Australia	Brazil
Burkina Faso		Indonesia	Colombia
Cameroon		Lao People's Democratic Rep.	Guatemala
Central African Rep.	India	Malaysia	Mexico
Chad	Iran	Myanmar	
Congo	Nepal	Papua New Guinea	
Côte d'Ivoire	Pakistan	Philippines	**North America**
Ethiopia		Thailand	
Ghana		Viet Nam	Canada
Kenya			United States
Nigeria	**East Asia**		
Sudan			**Europe**
United Rep. of Tanzania	China		
Zaire			None

GRAPH 4
MULTILINGUAL PEOPLES: COUNTRIES WHERE OVER FIFTY LANGUAGES ARE SPOKEN (1996)
Source: SIL (Summer Institute of Linguistics), *Ethnologue*, 13th ed., edited by B. F. Grimes, Dallas, Texas, 1996, and *CEL* (the *Cambridge Encyclopedia of Language*), edited by D. Crystal, 1996.

Of the thirty-four countries with a rich multilingual tradition (i.e. more than fifty languages in daily use), two-thirds are to be found among the developing countries of sub-Saharan Africa, South-East Asia and Oceania. Sub-Saharan Africa alone provides fourteen of these countries. By contrast, not one of the fifty-three countries of Europe and the Arab States is found in this table although three non-European industrial countries are represented.

ways. They draw on the cultural resources of their own communities. Not only that, they also draw on other sources, weaving a variety of threads from diverse experiences into coherent frameworks of meaning. What makes these threads truly 'indigenous' – part of a group's culture – is not the fact that they are indigenous or foreign in origin, but the manner in which they are woven together. 'They gave us the language', says a character in Kureishi's novel *The Black Album,* referring to the British occupation of India, 'but it is only we who know how to use it' (in Iyer, 1997, p. 27). 'Indian English is not just a savory stepmother tongue to hundreds of millions of Indians and not just an invaluable memento of a centuries-long mishmash,' Iyer

suggests. It is 'a grand and distinct product' of Indian culture (ibid.).

A second 'reality' of culture is its fluid nature.[5] 'A country's culture,' *Our Creative Diversity* asserts, 'is not static or changeless . . . it is in a constant state of flux' (World Commission on Culture and Development, 1995, p. 24). Some people talk of culture as an age-old tradition, passed on unchanged from generation to generation. But cultures need to change constantly if they are to remain meaningful to the living.

Take Pukapuka, a small Polynesian atoll in the Cook Islands, as an example. The island has a reputation among Polynesians and anthropologists alike for being rather traditional, preserving its

traditions better than most places in the Pacific. Yet a careful study of its traditions shows that these are constantly changing, constantly being updated (Borofsky, 1987). The process is often a very subtle one. People puzzle over certain traditions, trying to make sense of them. Whatever traditions seem unclear are 'cleaned up', interpreted (and reinterpreted) in order to make them understandable. That such reinterpretations constitute 'changes' only becomes clear when one compares the historical records with those of today. Rather than ask why traditions change, we might well turn the question round: Why should cultural traditions not change? Times change and so does people's understanding. If one is going to preserve cultural traditions to make them live in the present, then one has to alter them. There is an irony here: in order to preserve traditions, the living often transform them but, in transforming them to make them meaningful to themselves, they are able to pass them on to others – to preserve them for posterity.

Hobsbawm and Ranger (1983) call this process the 'invention of tradition'. Change or, more precisely, responding to change is part of the human condition – which is perhaps why our rhetoric often tries to ground the present in the past. It adds continuity to that which, in fact, is only partly continuous.

One might well concur with the nation-state's mission – to overcome local diversities and provide a national identity; but the way such unity is phrased – as homogeneous, as unchanging and as bounded – brings it face to face with contradictions it cannot overcome. People's ideas, traditions and productions tend to be mixtures of internal and external elements. And despite rhetoric to the contrary, they are frequently fluid because the past – if it is to stay meaningful – has to make sense in an ever-changing present.

Thinking about culture: two options

Trying to preserve cultural homogeneity and cultural boundaries against change

The above insight perhaps helps to explain why culture has become such an explosive issue around the world today. For political groups seeking to affirm cultural homogeneity – as a way of legitimizing an identity that brings different people together – it is a never-ending task to silence parts of their past, emphasizing this and excluding that: a Sisyphean task, perhaps, at the best of times, but now, with globalization, an overwhelmingly difficult one.

As the power of nation-states to conduct their Sisyphean labours (i.e. building national communities) weakens under the onslaught of economic globalization, it is becoming increasingly difficult to affirm culturally homogeneous nations. Nation-states often need more than just positive affirmations to create their cultural communities. They need enemies – people to be continually mobilized against – to conceal ambiguities, diversities, divergences and conflicts among their constituents. To put it succinctly, they must have someone or something to fight against. Mobilizing people against 'others' is a convenient way of legitimizing political power and developing a cadre of followers.

Let us take the case of Rwanda. Desforges, reviewing three books on the subject, writes:

Prunier, Keane and McCullum all rightly reject the simplistic analysis of the genocide as a manifestation of age-old tribal hatreds. As Prunier writes, 'Tutsi and Hutu have not been created by God as cats and dogs, predestined from all eternity to disembowel each other . . .'. The three authors recognize that Hutu and Tutsi are not tribes, but social strata, speaking a common language, bound by shared customs, living interspersed in a nation that they created together. All conclude that the killing campaign was systematic and planned, the result of an organized and ruthless exploitation of fear and ethnic loyalty by leaders who were in danger of losing power. (1997, p. 27)

This option often draws culture into acting as a tool for political mobilization that, in reinforcing ethnic identity, easily trips over into vilification of and, thence, violence towards others.

Affirming culture as a creative ongoing process

If one affirms the two 'realities' of culture noted above, i.e. its multiple engaging and fluid character, one can reframe the cultural concept, focusing on how cultural values and identity manage to survive difficult and changing times. Where boundaries form the core of the concept of Option 1, creativity forms the core of that of Option 2.

However, this does not mean that all cultures directly encourage creativity. A distinction should be made between relatively open and relatively closed communities[6] in this regard. Communities situated towards the open end of the continuum embrace the interrelational, fluid cultural dynamics discussed above, whereas communities placed towards the closed end tend to obscure, not to say deny them. Following the pattern of Option 1, ambiguous delineations in relatively closed communities tend to become reframed as boundaries, boundaries as borders, and borders as barriers. Obviously, there are limits to the extent to which such 'closed' groups can be excluding and exclusive. (Ultimately they can only regulate, not completely prohibit, outside influences. Nor can they prevent change.) Still, people's understandings and identities gradually grow 'out of joint' with the rest of the world. Pamuk describes one such case, as follows:

[The] cultural climate can be described as a kind of mental silence. Since people have lost their memories and their relationships with their cultural neighbours, the entire country has acquired the crudeness, inflexibility and the slovenliness which often occur in those who live alone . . . In my childhood, foreigners, and those different from ourselves, were spoken of with scorn and ridicule. Artists were similarly scorned and pitied unless they were either rich, famous, or important enough to be imprisoned.

In order even to deserve pity, they were expected to think like the majority. Nobody was curious about other cultures or about knowledge for knowledge's sake. (1997, p. 34)

With this open–closed continuum in mind and focusing on open communities, it may be of some use to return to the problems discussed above regarding culture, dealing first with the issue of cultural identity loss. It is intriguing to realize that cultural identity rarely gets 'lost' in relatively open societies. There is repeated talk of loss, certainly. But there is often a vibrant remaking/reaffirming of values and identity going on. In fact, one can conceive of the talk of loss as being one of the engines pushing the creative remaking/reaffirming process forward. It represents a mobilizing call to action. Americans driving Swedish Volvos do not become Swedes any more than Swedes wearing Michael Jordan T-shirts become Americans. But what does happen is that each group's interaction with the other reflects back on itself, encouraging each one to refine, remake and reaffirm its cultural identity in creative ways. This is the point that Goldstein and Rayner emphasize: cultural identity is 'strengthened through a process of continuous interaction with other collectivities – a process that requires each community to see itself from the perspective of others, and incorporate those perspectives through the prism of its own consciousness in a continuous reflexive process' (1994, p. 381).[7]

This brings the discussion round to the second problem, i.e. alternatives to a market mentality. Capitalism, despite the way it is spreading around the globe, is not free from cultural contexts. It is embedded in them[8] – not only relating to a particular mode of conducting business but, more critically, relating to a basic need for stability. It flourishes in a secure social environment where rules for organizing labour and property do not continually change, and where million-dollar investments are not washed away in a single night.

The rhetoric of development frequently encourages inflated promises of the possible in Third

'Convivencia': the goal of conviviability

Sustainability cannot be achieved without conviviability. People cannot manage the natural environment rationally if the 'way they live together' forces them to be hungry, greedy or destructive. We need a new model of human relationships for sustainable development.

New concepts are necessary now that governance, social and gender structures are changing as a result of globalization and the rise of social and cultural movements that cut across borders. Nation-states are reorganizing the decision-making and participation of their diverse constituencies. This is transforming the way in which individuals handle multiple allegiances related to languages, cultures and national identities. The decentering of knowledge and information is also leading people to redraw the maps of understanding that bind them to different realms of everyday life.

Governability is clearly useful as a general principle to shape this reorganization, but it implies a top-down approach to societies. What happens when the political borders of units being governed do not coincide with cultural boundaries? The latter may delineate larger groups, as in the case of the Kurds in the Middle East, or smaller ones, since most countries in the world are multicultural. Religious boundaries are also being redrawn the world over. Will all of these be incorporated into new political philosophies? It would appear that social and cultural dynamics must be understood and shaped with other tools, new ones that do not exist as yet.

The World Commission on Culture and Development defined culture as 'ways of living together'. This is the reason why *Our Creative Diversity* stated that culture is at the core of sustainable development. More than 80% of phenomena that are creating risks for our survival as a species are anthropogenic, that is, originate in human actions. Yet thinking on sustainability has focused almost exclusively on the direct relationships of humans to the natural environment, while the indirect ones – human-to-human relationships – are dealt with as a totally separate issue of governability to be analysed and decided on according to separate models of reality.

Yet we know that co-operation in human relations is a prerequisite for sustainable development. Fulfilling today's human needs while preserving and protecting the natural environment for future generations requires equitable and harmonious interactions between individuals and communities. Frequently, the debates on these issues revolve around the degree of primacy that should be given to either the environmental or the human issue. What is needed is a new model that integrates both issues in the same way that they are imbricated in reality.

People in many places, even when they are aware and willing to protect the natural environment, find it impossible to do so because of economic, political or cultural dislocations. Eliminating these pressures calls for good governance, organizing people through democratic processes. But it also requires proper conviviability or 'convivencia', that is, reorganizing cultural allegiances to enable human beings with different ideals of a good life to live together compatibly in a living biosphere. The term 'convivencia' reflects this in the sense in which it was used in Spain in the fifteenth century to betoken the peaceful coexistence of Christians, Jews and Muslims. It comes from the Latin word *convivere*, first used by Seneca and other Roman authors, to denote bringing people together at a banquet. 'Vivencia' in Spanish also means gaining experience of the world, so 'convivencia' means not only living side by side, but experiencing life together.

'Convivencia' could serve as the guiding principle for the cultural transition that we must live through in the Global Age. Such a concept could also serve as a performance marker both for governments and for civil society.

Lourdes Arizpe
Anthropologist;
Assistant Director-General for Culture, UNESCO

World countries. In a volatile world of unmet promises and possibilities, the creative affirmation of cultural identity offers a way, none the less, for developing meaning and solidarity, and for re-orienting life away from an economic calculus towards alternative, more personally empowering frames of reference. Following *Our Creative Diversity*, one might well agree that culture 'is not a means to material progress: it is the end and aim of "development" seen as the flourishing of human existence in all its forms and as a whole' (World Commission on Culture and Development, 1995, p. 24).

The third problem noted above regarding culture – inter-ethnic conflict[9] – often puzzles. There is no doubting the horrors that such conflicts generate. Yet they often do not make sense, in view of the inter-relational, fluid 'realities' of culture. Many of the combating groups have frequently been living together for decades, even centuries, in relative peace. Why, then, does such brutality suddenly erupt? Attributing a cultural basis to the conflict is to ignore more history – the periods of peaceful interaction – than it takes into account.

One needs to realize that 'culture' in such contexts is often used as a political tool by individuals for their own aggrandizement – for whipping up popular passions to achieve political ends. As noted, that was the case in Rwanda. Careful analysis suggests the same holds for the recent ethnic conflicts in the former Yugoslavia as well as in Russia (see Tishkov, 1994, 1995, 1997).

Policy implications

Following the above discussion, the following four recommendations may be made directly to policy-makers.

First, greater emphasis should be placed on the recognition of each culture's resources for dealing with change. Museums and historical publications should not only focus on a culture's past, but on how people overcome changing challenges. The process of coping with change should be regarded as central to 'culture'.

Second, cultural creativity should be encouraged through the sponsoring of artists and exhibitions. Creativity should not be disconnected from a culture's traditions but seen as an intimate part of them. Innovative cultural works that build on traditions – in the remaking/reaffirming sense noted above – need to be encouraged. Drawing on others, beyond one's cultural 'borders', should be seen as a critical part of this process, and as fostering a culture's own dynamic qualities. There should be more openness to exploration, greater stress on creativity, and more ways to make cultural traditions come alive in the present.

Third, governments need to refocus the issue of development/cultural relations away from statistical measures of economic success – such as per capita increases in income – towards a broader array of concerns. Over-promising as to the results of development merely leads to frustration and instability. Rather than assuming that economic development brings about culturally meaningful lives, it might be wiser to focus on culturally agreed goals – such as fostering community stability and meaningful lives; some thought should be given to ways in which economic development – as a means to an end rather than an end in itself – can foster these.

Finally, it should be emphasized that cultural coexistence is the general global norm. There are thousands of cultural groups around the world. And when one thinks of the ethnic 'hot spots' – Bosnia, India, Rwanda, Sri Lanka, for example – it is clear that only a relatively limited number of groups are caught up in intense, violent conflict at any one time.

One has to speak the truth in order to face the political ploys of aggrandizing politicians. Policy-makers and scholars should not allow mere rhetoric about seeming 'age-old' cultural conflicts to act as a disguise, excuse or justification for violence. The huge cost of such conflicts should also be emphasized. Both Bosnia and Rwanda, for example,

have been economically devastated. Ethnic conflicts tend to benefit a very few. For the others, there is only misery. For far too long people have let themselves be carried away by the rhetoric of small groups of aggrandizing politicians in respect of culture and cultural purity. It is time to move on.

Notes

1. Regarding culture's constructed nature, refer for example to: Abu-Lughod (1991), Anderson (1991), Barth (1995), Bhabha (1994), Brightman (1995), Burke (1978), Clifford (1986, 1988, 1997), Clifford and Marcus (1986), Elias (1994), Foster (1988), Gates (1997), Geertz (1973, 1983, 1995), Gellner (1983), Gilroy (1993), Hackney (1994), Herbert (1991), Jenks (1993), Kahn (1989), Lévi-Strauss (1964), Lowie (1937), Rabinow (1988), Rosaldo (1989), Said (1989, 1993), Turner (1993) and Williams (1976, 1983).

2. Regarding various definitions of culture, refer for example to: Arnold (1960 [1869]), Bhabha (1994), Bloch (1994), Borofsky (1994), Brightman (1995), Goodenough (1989, 1994), Goody (1994), Hannerz (1996), Herbert (1991), Herskovits (1948), Jenks (1993), F. Keesing (1958), R. Keesing (1981, 1994), Kincaid (1997), Kluckhohn (1951), Kroeber (1945), Kroeber and Kluckhohn (1952), Lowie (1937), Parsons (1951), Radcliffe-Brown (1922), Tylor (1958 [1871]) and Williams (1976).

3. Partly based on A.-B. Preis, 'Human Rights as Cultural Practice . . .', *Human Rights Quarterly*, Vol. 18, No. 2, May 1996, pp. 286–315.

4. Regarding the inter-relational nature of culture, refer for example to: Alvarez (1995), Anzaldua (1987), Appadurai (1996), Barth (1995), Clifford (1997), Gilroy (1993), Goldstein and Rayner (1994), Gutiérrez-Jones (1995), Hannerz (1996), Haraway (1988), Lévi-Strauss (1963), Robins (1996), Rorty (1989), Rosaldo (1989), Wolf (1982) and the World Commission on Culture and Development (1995).

5. For the fluid nature of culture, refer for example to: Borofsky (1984), Burke (1978), Cohn (1980), Foster (1988), Gilroy (1993), Hobsbawm (1983), Hobsbawm and Ranger (1983), Lévi-Strauss (1966), Rosaldo (1989), Wolf (1982) and the World Commission on Culture and Development (1995).

6. Regarding culturally open and closed communities, refer for example to: Horton (1993), Goldstein and Rayner (1994), Popper (1962) and Soros (1997).

7. Regarding the effect of inter-cultural relations in 'open' cultural communities and the notion of one group culturally overwhelming another, refer for example to: Gates (1997), Iyver (1997), Pells (1997) and Sahlins (1992, 1994). In respect to issues of cultural hegemony, in relation to the distinct case of colonization, refer for example to: Gramsci (1971), Cohn (1996) and Comaroff and Comaroff (1991).

8. Regarding the issue of embedding the economy in culture, refer for example to: Dalton (1968), Kaplan (1968), Polyani (1944), Sahlins (1972) and Soros (1997).

9. Regarding ethnic and cultural conflict, for detailed, in-depth studies refer for example to: Connor (1994), Tishkov (1994, 1995, 1997) and Tambiah (1994, 1996).

Bibliography

ABU-LUGHOD, L. 1991. Writing against Culture. In: R. Fox (ed.), *Recapturing Anthropology*, pp. 137–62. Santa Fe, School of American Research Press.

ALVAREZ, R. 1995. The Mexican–U.S. Border: The Making of an Anthropology of Borderlands. *Annual Review of Anthropology*, No. 24, pp. 447–70.

ANDERSON, B. 1991. *Imagined Communities*. New York, Verso.

ANZALDUA, G. 1987. *Borderlands/La Frontera*. San Francisco, Spinsters/Aunt Lute.

APPADURAI, A. 1996. *Modernity at Large*. Minneapolis, University of Minnesota Press.

ARIZPE, L.; PAZ, F.; VELAZQUES, M. 1997. *Culture and Global Change: Social Perceptions of Deforestation in the Lacandona Rain Forest*. Ann Arbor, University of Michigan Press.

ARNOLD, M. 1960. *Culture and Anarchy*. Cambridge, Cambridge University Press. (First published in 1869.)

BARTH, F. 1995. Ethnicity and the Concept of Culture. Nonviolent Sanctions and Cultural Survival. *C.I. Affairs* (Harvard), Spring, pp. 13–22.

BHABHA, H. 1994. *The Location of Culture*. New York, Routledge.

BLOCH, M. 1994. Language, Anthropology, and Cognitive Science. In: R. Borofsky (ed.), *Assessing Cultural Anthropology*, pp. 276–82. New York, McGraw-Hill.

BOHANNAN, P. 1992. *We, the Alien: An Introduction to Cultural Anthropology*. Prospect Heights, Waveland.

BOROFSKY, R. 1987. *Making History*. New York, Cambridge University Press.

——. 1994. *Assessing Cultural Anthropology*. New York, McGraw-Hill.

BRIGHTMAN, R. 1995. Forget Culture, Replacement, Transcendence, Relexification. *Cultural Anthropology*, Vol. 10, No. 4, pp. 509–46.

BURKE, P. 1978. *Popular Culture in Early Modern Europe*. London, Temple Smith.

CLIFFORD, J. 1986. Introduction, Partial Truths. In: J. Clifford and G. Marcus (eds.), *Writing Culture*, pp. 1–26. Berkeley, University of California Press.

——. 1988. *The Predicament of Culture*. Cambridge, Harvard University Press.

——. 1997. *Routes*. Cambridge, Harvard University Press.

CLIFFORD, J.; MARCUS, G. (eds.). 1986. *Writing Culture: The Poetics and Politics of Ethnography*. Berkeley, University of California Press.

COHN, B. 1980. History and Anthropology: The State of Play. *Comparative Studies in Society and History*, Vol. 22, No. 2, pp. 198–221.

——. 1996. *Colonialism and Its Forms of Knowledge*. Princeton, Princeton University Press.

COMAROFF, J.; COMAROFF, J. 1991. *Of Revelation and Revolution*. Chicago, Chicago University Press.

CONNOR, W. 1994. *Ethnonationalism*. Princeton, Princeton University Press.

DALTON, G. (ed.). 1968. *Primitive, Archaic and Modern Economies*. New York, Anchor.

DESFORGES, A. 1997. No More Corpses on the Road. *Times Literary Supplement*, 15 August, pp. 26–7.

ELIAS, N. 1994. *The Civilizing Process*. Cambridge, Massachusetts, Blackwell.

FOSTER, S. W. 1988. *The Past is Another Country*. Berkeley, University of California Press.

GATES, H. L. 1997. Applying the Corrective. *The Boston Book Review*, Vol. 4, No. 4, pp. 4–6.

GEERTZ, C. 1973. *The Interpretation of Cultures*. New York, Basic Books.

——. 1983. *Local Knowledge*. New York, Basic Books.

——. 1995. *After the Fact*. Cambridge, Harvard Univ. Press.

GELLNER, E. 1983. *Nations and Nationalism*. Oxford, Blackwell.

GILROY, P. 1993. *The Black Atlantic*. Cambridge, Harvard University Press.

GOLDSTEIN, J.; RAYNER, J. 1994. The Politics of Identity in Late Modern Society. *Theory and Society*, Vol. 23, No. 3, pp. 367–84.

GOODENOUGH, W. 1989. Culture, Concept and Phenomenon. In: M. Feilich (ed.), *The Relevance of Culture*, pp. 93–7. New York, Bergin & Garvey.

——. 1994. Toward a Working Theory of Culture. In: R. Borofsky (ed.), *Assessing Cultural Anthropology*, pp. 262–73, New York, McGraw-Hill.

GOODY, J. 1994. Culture and Its Boundaries: A European View. In: R. Borofsky (ed.), *Assessing Cultural Anthropology*, pp. 250–60. New York, McGraw-Hill.

GUTIÉRREZ-JONES, C. 1995. *Rethinking the Borderlands*. Berkeley, University of California Press.

HACKNEY, S. 1994. Organizing a National Conversation. *The Chronicle of Higher Education*, 20 April, p. A56.

HANNERZ, U. 1996. *Transnational Connections, Culture, People, Places*. New York, Routledge.

HARAWAY, D. 1988. Situated Knowledges. *Feminist Studies*, Vol. 14, No. 3, pp. 575–99.

HERBERT, C. 1991. *Culture and Anomie: Ethnographic Imagination in the Nineteenth Century*. Chicago, University of Chicago Press.

HERSKOVITS, M. 1948. *Man and His Works*. New York, Knopf.

HERZFELD, M. 1997. *Cultural Intimacy*. New York, Routledge.

HOBSBAWM, E. 1983. Introduction: Inventing Tradition. In: E. Hobsbawm and T. Ranger (eds.), *The Invention of Tradition*, pp. 1–14. Cambridge, Cambridge University Press.

HOBSBAWM, E.; RANGER, T. (eds.). 1983. *The Invention of Tradition*. New York, Cambridge University Press.

HORTON, R. 1993. *Patterns of Thought in Africa and the West*. New York, Cambridge University Press.

IYER, P. 1997. English in India: Still All the Raj. *New York Times Book Review*, 10 August, p. 27.

JENKS, C. 1993. *Culture*. New York, Routledge.

KAHN, J. 1989. Culture, Demise or Resurrection? *Critique of Anthropology*, Vol. 9, No. 2, pp. 5–25.

KAPLAN, D. 1968. The Formal–Substantive Controversy in Economic Anthropology: Reflections on Its Wider Implications. *Southwestern Journal of Anthropology*, No. 24, pp. 228–51.

KEESING, F. 1958. *Cultural Anthropology, The Science of Custom*. New York, Rinehart.

KEESING, R. 1981. *Cultural Anthropology: A Contemporary Perspective*. New York, Holt, Rinehart & Winston.

——. 1994. Theories of Culture Revisited. In: R. Borofsky (ed.), *Assessing Cultural Anthropology*, pp. 301–10. New York, McGraw-Hill.

KINCAID, J. 1997. Culture and Irony. *New York Times Book Review*, 16 March, p. 14.

KLUCKHOHN, C. 1951. The Concept of Culture. In: D. Lerner and H. D. Lasswell (eds.), *The Policy Sciences*, pp. 86–101. Stanford, Stanford University Press,

KROEBER, A. L. 1945. The Ancient Oikoumene as an Historic Culture Aggregate. *Journal of the Royal Anthropological Institute*, Vol. 75, pp. 9–20.

KROEBER, A. L.; KLUCKHOHN, C. 1952. Culture, A Critical Review of Concepts and Definitions. *Papers of the Peabody Museum* (Harvard University), Vol. 47, No. 1.

LASS, A. 1988. Romantic Documents and Political Monuments: The Meaning-Fulfillment of History in 19th-Century Czech Nationalism. *American Ethnologist,* Vol. 15, No. 3, pp. 456–71.

LÉVI-STRAUSS, C. 1963. *Structural Anthropology.* New York, Basic Books.

——. 1964. *Tristes Tropiques.* London, Atheneum.

——. 1966. *The Savage Mind.* Chicago, University of Chicago Press.

LINDSTROM, L. 1982. Leftamap Kastom: The Political History of Tradition on Tanna (Vanuatu). *Mankind,* Vol. 13, No. 4, pp. 316–29.

LOWIE, R. 1937. *The History of Ethnological Theory.* New York, Holt.

PAMUK, O. 1997. On the Periphery. *Times Literary Supplement,* 8 August, p. 34.

PARSONS, T. 1951. *The Social System.* London, Routledge & Kegan Paul.

PELLS, R. 1997. The Local and Global Loyalties of Europeans and Americans. *The Chronicle of Higher Education,* 2 May, p. B4.

POLYANI, K. 1944. *The Great Transformation.* Boston, Beacon Press.

POPPER, K. 1962. *The Open Society and Its Enemies.* Princeton, Princeton University Press. 2 vols.

RABINOW, P. 1988. Beyond Ethnography: Anthropology as Nominalism. *Cultural Anthropology,* Vol. 3, No. 4, pp. 355–64.

RADCLIFFE-BROWN, A. R. 1922. *The Andaman Islanders.* Cambridge, Cambridge University Press.

RENAN, E. 1939. What is a Nation? In: A. Zimmern (ed.), *Modern Political Doctrines,* pp. 186–205. London, Oxford University Press.

ROBINS, K. 1996. Interrupting Identities: Turkey/Europe. In: S. Hall and P. Du Gay (eds.), *Questions of Cultural Identity,* pp. 61–86. Thousand Oaks, California, Sage.

RORTY, R. 1989. *Contingency, Irony and Solidarity.* Cambridge, Cambridge University Press.

ROSALDO, R. 1989. *Culture and Truth: The Remaking of Social Analysis.* Boston, Beacon Press.

SAHLINS, M. 1972. *Stone Age Economics.* Chicago, Aldine.

——. 1981. *Historical Metaphors and Mythical Realities.* Ann Arbor, University of Michigan Press.

——. 1985. *Islands of History.* Chicago, University of Chicago Press.

——. 1992. Historical Ethnography. Vol. 1 of *Anahulu: The Anthropology of History in the Kingdom of Hawaii.* Edited by Patrick Kirch and Marshall Sahlins. Chicago, University of Chicago Press.

——. 1994. Goodbye to Triste Tropes: Ethnography in the Context of Modern World History. In: R. Borofsky (ed.), *Assessing Cultural Anthropology,* pp. 377–94. New York, McGraw-Hill.

SAID, E. 1989. Representing the Colonized: Anthropology's Interlocutors. *Critical Inquiry,* No. 15, pp. 205–25.

——. 1993. *Culture and Imperialism.* New York, Vintage.

SOROS, G. 1997. The Capitalist Threat. *The Atlantic Monthly.* Vol. 279, No. 2, February, pp. 45–58.

TAMBIAH, S. 1994. The Politics of Ethnicity. In: R. Borofsky (ed.), *Assessing Cultural Anthropology,* pp. 430–41. New York, McGraw-Hill.

——. 1996. *Leveling Crowds.* Berkeley, University of California Press.

TISHKOV, V. 1994. Inventions and Manifestations of Ethno-Nationalism in Soviet Academic and Public Discourse. In: R. Borofsky (ed.), *Assessing Cultural Anthropology.* pp. 443–52. New York, McGraw-Hill.

——. 1995. 'Don't Kill Me, I'm a Kyrgyz!', An Anthropological Analysis of Violence in the Osh Ethnic Conflict. *Journal of Peace Research,* Vol. 32, No. 2, pp. 133–49.

——. 1997. *Ethnicity, Nationalism and Conflict in and after the Soviet Union: The Mind Aflame.* London, Sage.

TREVOR-ROPER, H. 1983. The Invention of Tradition: The Highland Tradition in Scotland. In: E. Hobsbawm and T. Ranger (eds.), *The Invention of Tradition,* pp. 15–41. New York, Cambridge University Press.

TURNER, T. 1993. Anthropology and Multiculturalism: What is Anthropology that Multiculturalists Should be Mindful of It? *Cultural Anthropology,* Vol. 8, No. 4, pp. 411–29.

TYLOR, E. B. 1958. *Primitive Culture.* New York, Harper. (First published in 1871.)

USEEM, A. 1997. An Era of Painful Self-Examination for Many Intellectuals in Africa. *Chronicle of Higher Education,* No. 10, October, pp. A47–8.

WILLIAMS, R. 1976. *Keywords.* New York, Oxford Univ. Press.

——. 1983. *Culture and Society, 1780–1950.* New York, Columbia University Press.

WOLF, E. 1982. *Europe and the People Without History.* Berkeley, University of California Press.

WORLD COMMISSION ON CULTURE AND DEVELOPMENT. 1995. *Our Creative Diversity.* Paris, UNESCO.

ZIMMERMANN, W. 1995. The Choice in the Balkans. *The New York Review,* 21 September, pp. 4–7.

Chapter 4
Cultural rights and indigenous peoples: the Sami experience

Ole Henrik Magga
Linguist; Head of the Sami Parliament of Norway;
Expert on Sami culture

'. . . The right to self-determination . . . is not synonymous with the right to a separate state.'

Nordic policies

The World Commission on Culture and Development has pointed out the urgent need for securing the cultural rights of indigenous peoples. Such peoples are directly and heavily dependent on their lands, meaning that policies and legislation cannot be limited to the protection of a people's right to cultural expression alone, but must also guarantee the fundamental material basis for the existence of their communities.

The Commission expressed strong support for the process initiated by the Human Rights Commission regarding the drafting of a United Nations Draft Declaration on the Rights of Indigenous Peoples, which aims at developing greater international protection for indigenous peoples (World Commission on Culture and Development, 1995, p. 71).

The Sami (also spelled Saami, and previously known as Lapps) are an indigenous people numbering between 60,000 and 100,000 who are dispersed across a wide area in four countries: Finland, Norway, Sweden and Russia. Invasions by other peoples and the establishment of nation-states led to the division of the Sami territory. Colonization was a slow process, which is why the Sami's situation differs greatly in the four countries. The Sami have been the victims of harsh assimilation policies. For example, Norway, where the majority of the Sami live, launched a systematic Norwegianization programme at the end of the nineteenth century, using every means available – economic, legislative, educational and religious – as weapons in a 'cultural war'.

After the Second World War, Finland, Norway and Sweden revised their previous minority policies with regard to the Sami, recognizing in principle, and backing by constitutional guarantees, the right of the Sami to preserve and develop their culture. However, translating the new ideas into practice has been a long, slow process and Sami culture is still highly vulnerable. Moreover, there are fundamental differences in the minority policies of the three countries (see World Commission on Culture and Development, 1994). The Sami situation is still uncertain in Russia, where few changes seem to have been incorporated into the legislation or implemented in policy form since the fall of the Soviet regime.

The Sami Council is an umbrella organization for individual Sami NGOs. Ever since it was founded in 1956, the Sami Council has invested considerable efforts in developing transborder co-operation on

Sami cultural expression and on legal protection for the Sami culture and people. The eighth Nordic Sami Conference (1971) summarized the basis of a Sami cultural policy programme in the following opening statement, often quoted in the Sami political arena:

We are Sami and we will remain Sami. For this reason, we are neither greater nor lesser than other peoples in the world. We are a people with a territory of our own, a language of our own, and a culture and social structure of our own. (Sillanpää, 1994, p. 60)

Since 1986, the Sami Council has been working on the wording of an updated agreement on Sami rights – a Sami Convention or a Nordic Sami Treaty – with the four states in which they live.

Based on a recommendation from the Nordic Co-operation Agency for Sami and Reindeer-Herding Affairs, the Ministers from Norway, Sweden and Finland responsible for Sami affairs in their respective countries decided in principle to open negotiations on a Sami Convention in 1995. The Sami Parliaments of the three countries were invited to take part in the preparations, Norway being asked to initiate the project. The Sami have still not lost sight of their initial ambition to have all four Sami homeland states become party to a convention. However, for the time being, the most realistic approach is to begin with the three Nordic countries, and leave the door open for Russia to join in at a later stage.

Background and justification for a Sami Convention

When borders were drawn up between Denmark and Norway and between Sweden and Finland in 1751, legislators agreed on an addition to the border treaty entitled the 'Lapp Codicil' aimed at the 'preservation of the Lapp nation' (Smith, 1987, p. 21). The main purpose of the codicil was to protect the rights to land use of nomadic Sami, primarily the Sami reindeer-breeders, who were dependent on transborder migration. The Reindeer Grazing Convention of 1919 between Norway and Sweden

(last amended in 1972) contains more detailed provisions on grazing and migration rights. However, both these agreements are of limited value for the broader protection of Sami cultural rights. Despite the fact that other international instruments such as the Human Rights Convention of 1966 are binding for the Nordic countries, and Russia, and the fact that Norway ratified ILO Convention 169 concerning Indigenous and Tribal Peoples in Independent Countries in 1989, there is still a need to define more precisely and explicitly each country's joint and several obligations in respect of the Sami people.

There can be little doubt that Norway's Sami have made the most progress in terms of securing legal protection for the Sami culture and political clout for Sami demands. One direct result of this progress is a 1988 amendment (110A) to the Norwegian Constitution: 'It is incumbent upon the government authorities to take the necessary steps to enable the Sami population to safeguard and develop their language, culture and social life.'

In 1996, Finland added a special clause to its Constitution (51A) regarding the status of the Sami: 'Given their status as an indigenous people, and pursuant to the law, the Sami shall be accorded cultural autonomy in their homelands on matters relating to their language and culture.' This is a clear reinforcement of the Sami's position in Finland. It is also noteworthy that the expression 'an indigenous people' is embodied directly in the Constitution.

Although there are no special provisions about the Sami in Sweden's Constitution, a general provision about minorities states that the opportunities of ethnic, linguistic and religious minorities should be promoted in order to maintain and develop their cultures and societies.

In practice, Sweden has a long history of respect for Sami rights, even though these are limited to the reindeer-herding Sami being entitled to manage their own grazing areas, and entitlement to fishing and hunting rights on Sami grazing lands. In recent years, it would appear that Sweden's national

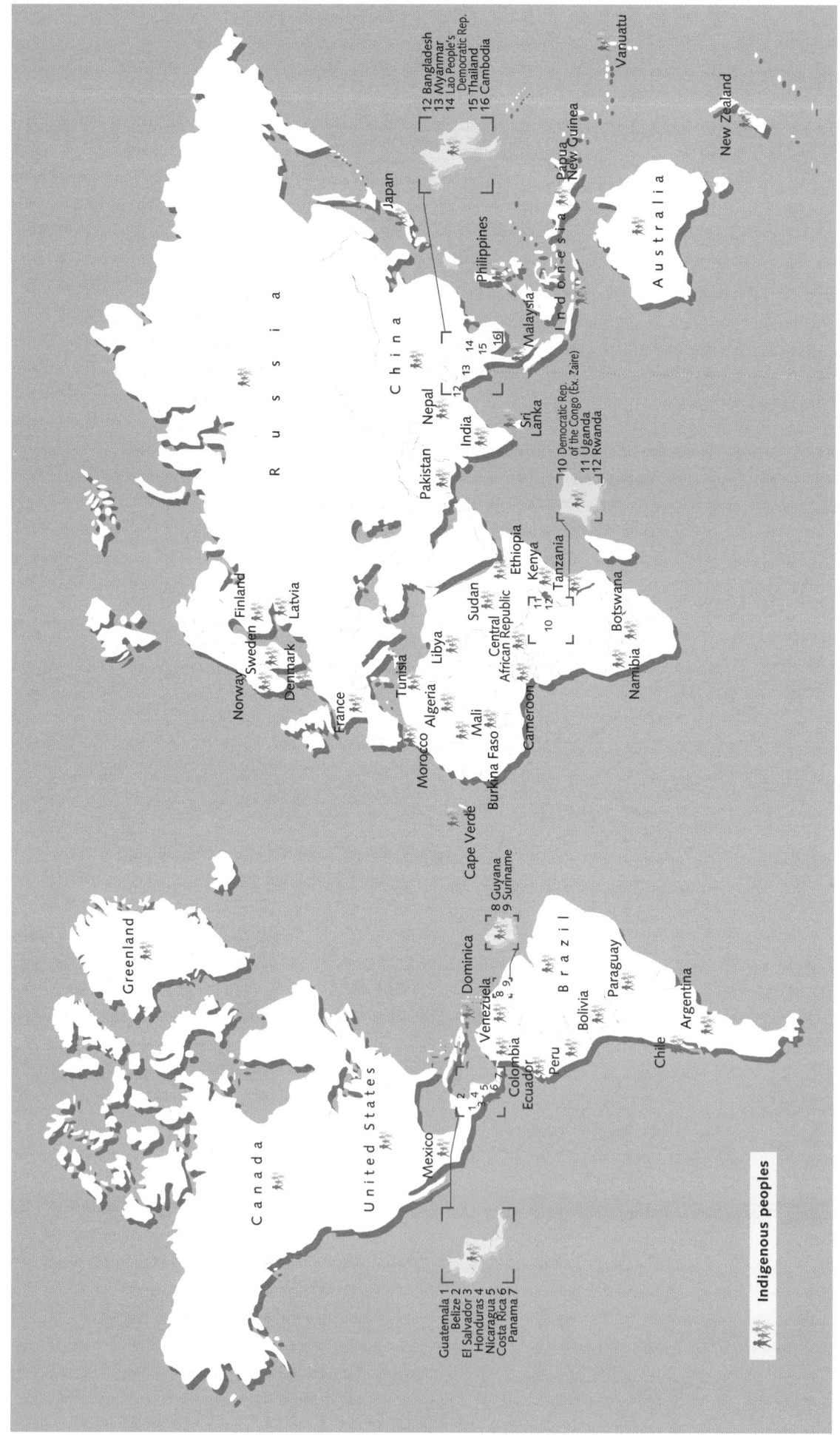

MAP OF THE DISTRIBUTION OF INDIGENOUS PEOPLES THROUGHOUT THE WORLD

Source: The geographical location of indigenous peoples as indicated here is part of an ongoing research process based on the data on, and the working definition of, indigenous peoples commonly agreed within the United Nations system. The information has been collected from the documents of the United Nations Economic and Social Council and the United Nations General Assembly.

Indigenous peoples

Guatemala 1
Belize 2
El Salvador 3
Honduras 4
Nicaragua 5
Costa Rica 6
Panama 7

8 Guyana
9 Suriname

10 Democratic Rep.
   of the Congo (Ex. Zaire)
11 Uganda
12 Rwanda

12 Bangladesh
13 Myanmar
14 Lao People's
   Democratic Rep.
15 Thailand
16 Cambodia

authorities have decided to undermine the material basis for the Sami culture by taking away their right to administer the hunting of small game on Sami grazing lands.

A supplementary document issued by the ministerial meeting in Reykjavik that laid the foundation for the convention-drafting efforts of Norway, Sweden and Finland reads:

The fact that the Sami people are spread across Norway, Sweden and Finland places upon these countries a shared responsibility for preserving and developing the Sami's basis for economic, linguistic and cultural development. If, as a people, the Sami are to preserve their common Sami identity and act as one nation, irrespective of national borders, it is important to underscore the three countries' joint responsibility for and shared obligations to the Sami.

To achieve the most viable development of Sami culture, language and society, it is absolutely essential that these three countries make concerted efforts to ensure that, within certain limits, the Sami can govern their development themselves. (Dikkanen, 1997, p. 4)

The Sami Council was very active in the work on ILO Convention 169 concerning Indigenous and Tribal Peoples in Independent Countries, which was adopted in 1989, and ratified by Norway in 1990. Clearly, the ILO convention has been a model for the Sami Council's ideas about a Sami convention, as has the Draft Declaration on the Rights of Indigenous Peoples prepared by the United Nations Working Group on Indigenous Populations under the auspices of the Human Rights Commission.

Cultural rights

The general notion of cultural rights is a very broad and complex one under international law. Article 27 of the Universal Declaration of Human Rights and Article 15 of the International Covenant on Economic, Social and Cultural Rights cover:

. . . the right to take part in cultural life, the right to enjoy the benefits of scientific progress and its applications, the

right to benefit from the protection of the moral and material interests resulting from any scientific, literary or artistic production of which the beneficiary is the author, and the freedom indispensable for scientific research and creative activity. (Eide, 1995, p. 32)

The important aspect of cultural rights – and of crucial interest in connection with cultural rights of indigenous peoples – is the right to preserve the cultural identity of minority groups guaranteed under Article 27 of the International Covenant on Civil and Political Rights (CCPR):

In those states in which ethnic, religious or linguistic minorities exist, persons belonging to such minorities shall not be denied the right, in community with other members of their group, to enjoy their own culture, to profess and practise their own religion, or to use their own language.

There are comparable provisions in Article 30 of the Convention on the Rights of the Child and Article 1 of the United Nations Declaration on the Rights of Persons Belonging to National Ethnic, Religious and Linguistic Minorities. However, cultural rights are not a separate category in the Sami Council's Draft Convention. It would be extremely difficult to make such distinctions, given the closely interwoven nature of the connections between the various types of rights, as pointed out by numerous experts in the theory of international law (e.g. Eide, 1995).

The principle of cultural self-determination and autonomy

The Draft Convention proposes that the Sami's right to cultural self-determination and autonomy be incorporated into the constitutions of the countries involved. This has not yet been done in Russia or Sweden. The respective nation-states would be jointly and severally responsible for ensuring that the Sami could fully express their culture, economic interests and language. It should be noted that the right to self-determination, as advocated by the Sami Council and other indigenous peoples' organizations, is not synonymous with the right to a separate state.

It is important to point this out clearly because the term 'self-determination' often generates suspicion and uncertainty. Working to obtain a convention between independent states is, in itself, an expression of precisely this view. ILO Convention 169, which the Sami Council supports fully, contains an explanation that clarifies this issue: 'The use of the term "peoples" in this Convention shall not be construed as having any implications as regards the rights which may attach to the term under international law' (Art. 1).

Otherwise, the Sami Council's Draft Convention indicates that the term 'self-determination' should carry the same meaning in the draft as it does in the United Nations Draft Declaration on the Rights of Indigenous Peoples which, on this particular point, follows ILO Convention 169. The doctrine of self-determination has an 'internal' ramification for the state, namely that a state should guarantee that all peoples living within its borders should be entitled to take part in governing their own economic, social and cultural development.

To facilitate the practice of self-determination in various areas, including the right to consult the national authorities of the different countries, the Sami should have the right to establish elected legislative bodies. Such bodies have been set up in the Nordic countries, but not in Russia. The criteria as to who should have the right to vote in the elections for such a legislative body should be set by the Sami themselves and should be identical in the different countries. The countries should be obligated to support co-operation between the Sami legislative bodies and also to support the establishment of a joint Sami legislative body.

No obstacles should be placed in the way of transborder co-operation.

The material basis for a culture

The cultures of indigenous peoples are closely linked to the natural resources in their homelands. Accordingly, protecting a people's moral right to cultural expression is not sufficient in itself. This is the most singularly important argument in the efforts of indigenous peoples to protect and preserve their cultural heritage.

In accordance with Article 27 of the CCPR, the Norwegian Government has, in principle, acknowledged its obligation to ensure the material basis for Sami culture. The grounds underlying the proposal for the Act relating to the Sameting (Sami Parliament) are described as follows:

. . . the State must be regarded as obliged to give active support to minority groups and, moreover, that the term 'culture' in Article 27 must be interpreted to also include the material prerequisites for the culture . . . The interpretation indicates that the State takes on an obligation to constructively help ensure that the Sami people have the conditions necessary to be able to cultivate their culture and language. (Proposition to the Odelsting, No. 33, 1986–87. English translation from Sillanpää, 1994, p. 143)

ILO Convention 169, which is binding on Norway, contains the least ambiguous provisions in all international law regarding the rights of indigenous peoples to land and natural resources:

The rights of ownership and possession of the peoples concerned over the lands which they traditionally occupy shall be recognized. In addition, measures shall be taken in appropriate cases to safeguard the rights of the peoples concerned to use lands not exclusively occupied by them, but to which they have traditionally had access for their subsistence and traditional activities. Particular attention shall be paid to the situation of nomadic peoples and shifting cultivators in this respect. (Art. 14, para. 1)

The rights of the peoples concerned to the natural resources pertaining to their lands shall be specially safeguarded. These rights include the right of these peoples to participate in the use, management and conservation of these resources. (Art. 15, para. 1)

The Sami are of the opinion that large parts of Sami territory were acquired by others illegally. Throughout the post-war era, the Sami have striven to secure their territories through the judicial and

executive branches of the government. Ideally, all areas that have ever been used by the Sami should be either returned to them or compensated for. The Sami would, however, regard it as more realistic if they were permitted to keep what is left of their lands at the very least. In the 1960s, some progress was made on the land question in individual cases, but since then, numerous cases have been lost in the courts: for example, the famous case of the 'Taxed Mountain' in Sweden in 1981, and the Aursund case in Norway in autumn 1997. The reason is obvious: the laws were promulgated in accordance with the interests of the majority, many of them at a time when the authorities had an uncooperative attitude towards Sami culture, favouring their own culture. A new understanding and a new basis in law has to come about if justice is to prevail.

Even though the principles are quite clear, it has proved difficult to translate them into practice, even in Norway which has ratified the ILO Convention. This is why the question of the Sami's right to maintain the material basis for their culture remains unresolved in all the Sami homeland countries. From the legal point of view, any injustice, provided it is practised over a sufficiently long period of time, stands a good chance of becoming sanctioned by law. The Sami Council's Draft Convention places considerable emphasis on the question of land rights, discussing it in a separate chapter along the lines of the principles embodied in ILO Convention 169. Collateral to the land issue is the question of economic development rights: reindeer-herding, for instance, plays a special role in large parts of the Sami homelands, especially in the south, making it an industry for which the Sami maintain exclusive rights in Norway and Sweden. Many other activities, including aspects of freshwater and ocean fishing, handicrafts, farming and hunting, are strong carriers of the Sami cultural heritage and should be protected by law as part of the rights of indigenous peoples.

Language

Language is such a key element of Sami culture that the Sami's long-term existence as a nation is contingent on its maintenance and development.

Language rights are explicitly mentioned in the Draft Convention, and the Sami Council has been working for a long time on evolving ways of protecting and preserving the language as well as ensuring legal protection for it. From the Sami point of view, the status of the Swedish language in Finland is a good model for what it should be possible to achieve with the Sami language in each of the countries in which it is spoken. Legal provisions regarding the Sami's right to their own language were adopted in Finland and Norway in 1992 (Greller, 1996, pp. 90–4). Russia and Sweden have not so far made such legal provisions. The Sami Council's Draft Convention refers specifically to the legislation in Finland and Norway on the Sami language as well as to relevant international provisions.

The right to use the Sami language for official purposes is first and foremost motivated by the practical need for equal services for Sami speakers in different areas of community life (see the Norwegian Act No. 78 of 21 December 1990 related to the Sami). Language rights should provide:

• that persons be entitled to address queries to the authorities in the Sami language and to receive a response in Sami;

• that notices and announcements from public bodies that affect all or parts of the population be made public in the Sami language and that laws and regulations that affect the Sami be translated into Sami;

• that persons be allowed to use Sami in the courts and when dealing with the police;

• that persons be allowed to use Sami to protect their own interests when in contact with local and regional public health and social services institutions;

• that persons be entitled to hold or attend church services in Sami;

•   that Sami have the same status as the majority language in the whole or parts of the municipal administration in municipalities where Sami account for a certain proportion of the population;

•   that students who speak Sami receive instruction in Sami throughout the nine years of their mandatory education and that children whose native tongue is Norwegian be instructed in Sami as a subject in Sami areas;

•   that prison inmates be allowed to speak Sami with their own family.

It should not be necessary to have to describe oneself as 'helpless' in order to avail of such services. These rights should apply to all Sami speakers, thereby obviating the need for public agencies to check individuals' needs for services in Sami.

A language is best preserved and developed when it is used throughout the community. Languages reserved exclusively for use in the private sphere will ultimately wilt and die. This consideration is vital to the formulation of language policy.

Language rights are specially important as a prerequisite for other rights (Skutnabb-Kangas and Phillipson, 1994, p. 2). Some progress has been made in obtaining Sami language rights, although the languages of many other minorities in Europe enjoy far better protection than Sami receives under law in Finland and Norway. Nor is it any mean feat to ensure that language laws operate properly. However, the point now is to obtain the same rules for language rights in all the Sami homeland countries, and to back up those rights with resources sufficient to make the laws effective.

Education

In many areas, the educational system has been and continues to be the authorities' most powerful instrument of deculturalization. The school system, particularly at primary level, is still geared mainly to ensuring that children become members of the majority culture. The Sami language was first introduced into the school system as recently as the 1970s.

The Sami Council developed a Sami educational programme which was adopted in 1989 and has the following main objectives (Sami Council, 1991, pp. 8–9):

•   The upbringing and education of Sami children and young people shall be based on the principle that the Sami, as a people, are equal to other peoples. Children and young people should be brought up to have a Sami identity. The upbringing and education of children and young people instil in them both the will and the knowledge to fulfil the common aims adopted by the Sami.

•   Through upbringing and education, children and young people shall adopt the Sami people's cultural heritage and general human values. The education of Sami children and young people should attach priority to the legacy of Sami values, the protection of nature and efforts to promote international peace.

•   The education of children and young people shall be a natural function of Sami society, fulfilling the basic needs of the Sami community through its very existence in terms of Sami culture.

•   Students should be given an education about the world around them, gaining an understanding of the status of Sami in society and the status of the Sami people among other peoples. Students should be trained to work together and with others. Sami educational programmes should pay special attention to co-operation across national borders. Students need to be made aware of existing co-operation programmes between the Sami and other indigenous peoples.

•   Young Sami should be brought up to want to live and work in Samiland. Students should receive the education and training they need to enable them to earn a living as Sami, and to take advantage of local, pan-Sami and Nordic opportunities.

These objectives underscore the Sami Council's demands for the right to learn Sami in school and take adult education courses with common Sami curricula, common Sami teachers' training programmes and obligatory information on Sami life for all students in the majority societies. As regards schools for Sami students and schools for those belonging to the majority cultures in the respective

countries, there shall be equality in principle, although the systems need not necessarily be identical. The elementary school system is a particularly appropriate tool for preserving and developing the Sami language, culture and society, and shall, accordingly, protect and pass on the legacy of Sami culture and knowledge. The elementary school for Sami children and young people shall equip the coming generation to function well both in Sami society and in the majority society. The goal is thus to ensure that children reach a level of functional bilingualism that will empower them to function smoothly in both Sami cultural and social settings and those of the majority.

The Nordic countries have gradually been moving in the direction mapped out by the Sami Council. A new elementary school curriculum was approved in Norway in 1997. In a variety of ways, the new curriculum satisfies many of the principles laid down in the Sami Council's educational policy. Accordingly, the general curriculum for elementary schools in Norway now incorporates some material on Sami culture. The next step will be to have the same principles introduced into all schools in all Sami homeland countries.

Mass media

There are currently two Sami-language newspapers published twice weekly in Norway, and a monthly Sami-language magazine published in Finland. A monthly Sami newspaper is published in Sweden, though it is mainly in Swedish. Sporadic attempts have been made to publish Sami magazines for children and young people. A monthly religious magazine in Sami has been published in Norway for nearly a hundred years. A Norwegian-language newspaper in Norway is subsidized as though it were a 'Sami' newspaper, but this is more for historical and political than for cultural reasons. As for books, some twenty-five to thirty titles are published in Sami each year. The national radio/TV broadcasters have Sami desks that co-operate efficiently. There are

about six and a half hours of Sami radio broadcasts each day in Norway, but the figures are significantly lower in Finland and Sweden. Sami TV broadcasts are few and far between. However, some regularity has been achieved in the broadcasting of children's programmes in Norway (Solbakk, 1997).

It is generally agreed that the media have a tremendous impact on the Sami language, the development of Sami democracy and the preservation and development of the Sami identity. The right to exercise media in the Sami language is one of the most important cultural rights for Sami society. The Sami Council has not specified any particular objectives or goals regarding the exact scope of media development. However, the Sami organizations and the Sami parliaments have continually stressed the importance of the following: a daily newspaper in Sami, preferably as a pan-Sami measure; newspapers in Sami languages other than Northern Sami; more newspapers and books for children, and daily television broadcasts.

With the benefit of Nordic co-operation, it should not be unrealistic to foresee the establishment of a Sami radio station and eventually even a Sami TV station. The Norwegian State Broadcasting Corporation (NRK) has invested considerable efforts in Sami radio in Norway, and is currently working with these further objectives in mind.

Cultural heritage

For many groups of indigenous peoples, the past and its symbols are amongst the most important unifying issues in the struggle for self-determination. The way in which any nation defines and articulates itself is vital to its growth. A nation's historical and cultural heritage is a repository for definitions of its character and identity. The point is not just to recapture its own history, but to create its own character and identity.

Discussions as to whether particular heritage sites in Sami areas are Norwegian *stricto sensu* or Sami reveal that such relics are closely linked to the sense of identity. The Sami initiative in heritage work is one aspect of a cultural struggle in which precisely this question about rights to one's own past figures significantly. The right to the land goes hand in hand with the right to the past.

Against this background, the development of a system for Sami cultural heritage protection in Norway is at least a very interesting – not to say unique – example of how the ambitions of the World Commission on Culture and Development have been put into practice in this area. As a significant contribution to the Sami people's influence and control over their future, the Sami Parliament was given responsibility for the administration of Sami heritage sites from 1994 onwards. The right to a past, the right to a present and the right to a future are basically the same thing. It is all a matter of the right to a life – both as an individual and as a people.

Although cultural relics are not given specific mention by the Sami Council in the framework of a Sami Convention, it is extremely important to establish the principles that should apply to the administration of Sami heritage sites in each individual country.

Framing the challenges

Cultural rights span a wide range, and the above description has by no means been exhaustive. The Sami Council has also mentioned respect for Sami values, Sami beliefs and the Sami community, as well as for the Sami environment and a certain degree of circumspection in the recruitment of Sami to the armed forces, as being elements of importance for the protection of the Sami cultural heritage. The Sami should be entitled to establish and develop their own institutions in order to preserve and exercise their cultural rights.

The object of a Sami Convention is similar to that of ILO Convention 169, namely: 'promoting the full realization of the social, economic and cultural rights of these peoples with respect for their social and cultural identity, their customs and traditions, and their institutions' (Art. 2.2.b).

A special agreement in the form of a convention would have a stabilizing effect by rendering it impossible to alter the Sami's situation in the short term or on the basis of passing political fluctuations. A convention would have a unifying effect on the Sami and, naturally, a notable symbolic value for a nation that has few such unifying symbols from the past. Such a convention would also introduce a completely new element into the international arena. To the best of my knowledge, no comparable agreements exist between other countries anywhere in the world. This poses a great challenge, initially to Norway, Sweden and Finland, but also to Russia in the longer term.

Bibliography

DIKKANEN, G. 1997. *Arbeidet med en nordisk samekonvensjon.* (Unpublished MS.)

EIDE, A. 1995. Economic, Social and Cultural Rights. In: A. Eide, C. Krause and A. Rosas (eds.), *Economic, Social and Cultural Rights.* Dordrecht.

GRELLER, W. 1996. *Provision and Regulation of the Sami Languages.* Chippenham.

Lov om Sametinget og andre samiske rettsforhold. Proposition to the Odelsting, No. 33, 1986–87.

SAMI COUNCIL. 1991. *The Sami Education and School Policy Programme.* Ohcejohka.

——. 1995. *Forslag till samekonvention.* Ohcejohka. (Unpublished MS.)

SILLANPÄÄ, L. 1994. *Political and Administrative Responses to Sami Self-Determination.* Helsinki.

SMITH, C. 1987. The Sami Rights Committee: An Exposition. Self-Determination and Indigenous Peoples. Copenhagen. (IWGIA doc. No. 58.)

——. 1996. *Loven og livet.*

SKUTNABB-KANGAS; PHILLIPSON (eds.). 1994. *Linguistic Human Rights.* Berlin/New York.

SOLBAKK, J. T. 1997. Sami Mass Media. In: H. Gaski (ed.), *Sami Culture in a New Era.* Karasjok.

WORLD COMMISSION ON CULTURE AND DEVELOPMENT. 1994. Majority–Minority Relations. *Diedut* (Kautokeino), No. 1. (Seminar report.)

——. 1995. *Our Creative Diversity.* Paris, UNESCO.

Chapter 5
Culture and indigenous rights

Henriette Rasmussen
Educator and journalist; Chief Technical Advisor, Project
for the Rights of Indigenous and Tribal Peoples,
International Labour Office (ILO), Geneva (Switzerland);
Former Minister for Social Affairs and Labour in the Home
Rule Government (Greenland)

Inger Sjoerslev
Anthropologist; Senior Lecturer, Institute of Anthropology,
University of Copenhagen; Former Director,
International Work Group for Indigenous Affairs (IWGIA),
Copenhagen (Denmark)

'. . . indigenous
peoples also want
the freedom
to maintain and
recreate culture,
and to adapt cultural
and social forms to
the new conditions
of intensified
interaction with
the surrounding
world.'

Globalization, identity and rights

Cultural diversity, pluralism and a creative and
dynamic multicultural world are unthinkable
without encompassing indigenous peoples in the
global cultural landscape. Indigenous peoples
number more than 300 million individuals and are
stakeholders of more than 5,000 cultures and
languages.[1] They regard themselves as custodians of
their territories and maintain that biodiversity and
cultural diversity are closely linked. Although the
contention that 'we belong to the Earth, the Earth is
our Mother' has become a standard phrase in much
indigenous rhetoric, it contains a deep truth about
conceptions of belonging, special attachment to land,
and non-proprietory thinking about natural
resources.

We shall argue below that cultural rights and
the preservation and strengthening of cultural
diversity cannot be separated from the strengthening
of political, economic and general human rights, and
the combating of marginalization. Self-determination
is a key concept in the discourse on the role of
indigenous peoples in the global development
process and the flourishing of cultural diversity.
Equality and dignity can be maintained, and the
decolonization process can be completed, only
through the acquisition of self-determination by
indigenous peoples.

From the outset, however, it must be recognized
that indigenous peoples face a myriad of problems in
the contemporary world. In their day-to-day
conditions for survival and defence of their
territories, the majority are confronted with the
consequences of economic globalization. Policies to
increase productivity, to build infrastructure, and to
create conditions for foreign and domestic investment
in industrial production have led to natural resource
exploitation in indigenous peoples' areas. This has
meant greater encroachment on indigenous
territories, and the ensuing dissolution of indigenous
communities, urbanization, the displacement of
hundreds of thousands of indigenous people, leading
to what may be termed an indigenous diaspora.

Furthermore, indigenous peoples suffer from being stereotyped by the non-indigenous world. In much the same way as refugees, they are pictured as 'raw humanity' (Malkki, 1996) or as embodiments of 'culture' representing human and cultural diversity, rather than as active agents in a social-cultural world. Like refugees, who are not asked questions about history and politics but are seen as speechless victims in need of help, indigenous peoples – Andamans, Igorots, Inuits, Pygmies – are regarded as cultural specimens. They are seen as 'closer to nature', yet in other contexts they are regarded as a threat to the environment. This has led to the creation of national parks in areas that have for generations been inhabited by indigenous peoples who have lived in unproblematic interaction with the same wildlife.

The present situation of indigenous organizations – as reflected in the pan-indigenous movement, the increasing involvement in national-level politics, a stronger involvement with foreign donors, governments and non-governmental organizations (NGOs) – affects not only the organizational structure and political strategies, but also processes of self-identification, perceptions of 'indigenousness' and the ways and means through which indigenous cultures are articulated and reflected. The increased necessity of manoeuvring in many different 'worlds' at once calls for implicit creations of new cultural and social forms, and explicit, sometimes even strategic, articulations of culture and tradition.

In examining such transformations it is important to bear in mind that indigenous peoples would not have been 'indigenous' if it had not been for certain historical and political processes. 'Indigenousness' is not an inherent characteristic; it implies a discourse on rights. The notion of culture in relation to indigenous peoples thus raises important questions of identity construction and the strategic use of concepts such as tradition and authenticity. Here, the danger of 'essentializing'

culture needs to be noted. By emphasizing identity as a construction, tradition as an invention, and warning against the danger of essentialism leading to ethnic conflicts, modern anthropologists and other experts critically question the legitimacy of indigenous leaders' increasing use of the concept of culture, authenticity and tradition (Becket, 1996; Rogers, 1996).

However, the contemporary renaissance of indigenous identities also has to be understood within a global/local context, in which the articulation of culture and 'indigenousness' is a reaction to global forces and influences, from hard-core economic and political pressures and demands, over the change and dissolution of social forms, to cultural influences and inspirations from the outside through media, tourism and so forth (Friedman, 1996). International alliances and pan-indigenous movements are necessary survival strategies.

Last but not least, the question of cultural rights and individual versus collective rights is an underlying question in all dealings with the indigenous issue. In their struggle for rights, indigenous peoples claim respect for both individual and collective rights. Thus, in recent years the 's' in peoples has been increasingly emphasized in order to indicate the right to be accepted as a collective identity, i.e. a people with rights to self-determination according to internationally established conventions.

The whole issue of collective rights is, however, not very well understood. Nor is the formulation of cultural rights by indigenous peoples themselves (and in general) well explained. Public opinion tends to see indigenous rights as cultural rights and the protection of indigenous rights as mainly the preservation of cultural diversity. Like threatened animal species – who often seem to receive more sympathy and attention than threatened human beings – peoples and cultures must be preserved for the sake of cultural diversity.

This is not the position of most indigenous

leaders involved in international political and human rights work, however. The majority want individual rights and the protection of cultural and collective rights in the form of self-determination, which they see as the right to determine their own development, whether this means modernization or preservation of traditional lifestyles or both. Their primary concerns are thus related to the protection of territories, self-organization and the acqusition of self-determination.

The following three cases from Greenland, Australia and Brazil illustrate different aspects of the problems and potentialities surrounding indigenous peoples in the world of today. They have been chosen for their substantive significance and not on the basis of either their current political importance or their numerical importance. In Greenland, the focus is on the role of language in culture, and on those possibilities for cultural maintenance and reflection that were offered through the colonization process. The Australian example illustrates the close relationship between the preservation of culture and basic human rights; and the Brazilian case points to the role of outsiders – whether exploiters or supporters – in indigenous peoples' self-identification and articulation of culture.

Culture and language

Among indigenous and tribal peoples there is today a growing awareness of the need to preserve their languages, and there is a strong urge for the use of indigenous languages in education. Whether in French Guyana, where the work for creating a writing system has been initiated among the Kalina,[2] or in Alaska where the Alaskan Language Commission has introduced bilingual education, this has, among many other positive achievements, resulted in the restitution and revival of indigenous languages.[3]

The Greenland Inuit have a long history of European colonization. When the Norwegian missionary Hans Egede arrived in 1721 for the purpose of christening the remaining Vikings, he met the Inuit, and thus christened them instead, as the Vikings had been gone for several hundred years. Egede had a hard time converting the Inuit to Christianity, however, and disagreements between him and the Inuit resulted in a rebellion led by the Shamans who claimed superiority in their knowledge of the spirit world. Unfortunately, Egede eventually humiliated and prohibited the Shamans from practising, thereby creating a wide gap in the spiritual and intellectual culture of the West Greenlandic Inuit, who were the first to be christened.

In spite of this, however, the Inuit were very impressed by the Bible and by the fact that information could be stored in print, and books subsequently aroused an enormous interest among the hunters. Egede, and his sons after him, learned Greenlandic and spread Christianity in Greenland where it exists up to the present. Thanks to some far-sighted and respectful colonizers, the Greenlandic Inuit language very early achieved a writing system, thus ensuring the early documentation of myths, legends and magic songs. The Inuits' love of storytelling, legends, drum songs, religiously related poetry, music, dance and games was thus preserved and passed down to the present generation.

The newspaper *Atuagalliutit* ('Served for reading') was founded in 1861 and distributed once a year to different villages. The paper contained old stories, hunters' stories, translations of old Danish stories and books, religious writings, messages from the authorities, tabloids about royalties, and finally what might be called illustrated 'world news'. In Greenland we thus find not only one of the oldest newspapers in the world, but also one printed in an indigenous language. *Atuagalliutit* is still the main national newspaper in Greenland. It has had a tremendous impact on the spiritual development of Greenlandic society and contributed to the survival of the cultural and intellectual heritage of the Inuit in this region.

Atuagalliutit also created an early tradition for political debate among the Inuit. Due to the efforts of the Greenlandic political movement during the turmoil of the Danish development era in the 1950s and 1960s, there is now a legislation in the Greenlandic Parliament ensuring the use of Greenlandic. Greenlandic is, according to the Home Rule Act, the main language. Danish, which is the first foreign language, is fully taught too, and both languages are used in administrative practice. The legislation on education recommends that Greenlandic be used as the language of instruction, and the court system tends to use it as well. In order to secure the status of the Greenlandic language, however, there is still a need to develop updated educational materials and to update existing dictionaries, while computerization would certainly improve the chances of survival of the language into the twenty-first century (Petersen and Olsen, 1985).

The pan-Inuit organization, Inuit Circumpolar Conference (ICC), is attempting to create a common writing system among all the Inuit of the Arctic, i.e. the Greenlandic, Canadian, Alaskan and Siberian Inuit. The intention is not to suppress other languages; in Greenland, for instance, there is widespread recognition that a thorough knowledge of these is necessary in order to communicate with the outside world. The case of the Inuit thus reflects the potentials, as well as the dangers, of all that goes on in the space of colonial encounters, the contact zone (Pratt, 1992; Clifford, 1997). Colonizers and missionaries brought death and loss of Shamanistic culture, but at the same time they provided the tools, in the form of the alphabet, printing technology and written archives, for coming generations to preserve and reflect on their culture.

Culture and human rights

The importance of cultural continuity, and the close interlinkage between culture and rights in indigenous communities, is clearly and tragically revealed in the report of the Australian Human Rights and Equal Opportunity Commission (1997): *Bringing them Home*. The report is an account of the Commission's inquiry – which collected evidence from 535 indigenous people throughout Australia – into the so-called 'stolen generation': between 1910 and 1970 about one in ten indigenous children were forcibly removed from their families and communities across the nation.

The history of the Australian Aboriginals is a history of battles over rights to land, food and water sources, and a history of often violent race relations, discrimination, derogation and forced labour. The motives for removal of indigenous children from their families (by government and missionaries) were to 'inculcate European values and work habits in children who would then be employed in service to the colonial settlers' (Ramsland, quoted in *Bringing them Home*, p. 27). The perception was that the children sent away to work for non-indigenous people would be of 'mixed descent' and over time 'merge' into the non-indigenous population.

The report documents the emotional and psychological effects of the forced removal, and reveals, through oral and written evidence, how this affected the individual, the family, the culture from which the children were removed, and the whole of society. The children forcibly removed from their Aboriginal families, lineage, culture, language and land were brought to foster homes, orphanages, missionary schools, or were adopted by white families who were often ignorant of, or consciously neglected, Aboriginal heritage, values, customs and history. The children suffered the traumatic consequences of identity loss, and in very many cases were not – although this was the alleged intention – absorbed into and accepted by the white society. They were often discriminated against and marginalized.

A decline in the rates of removal of indigenous children only set in after the policy platform of Aboriginal self-determination was initiated in 1972. However, in order to make land claims, the current

Australian land rights legislation requires proof of some linkage to Aboriginal culture and language. Native title can be claimed only by members of an identifiable community who are entitled to the land under the traditional laws and customs, as currently acknowledged and observed, of that community. And the only persons entitled to claim native title are those who can show biological descent from the indigenous people entitled to the land. In addition to the psychological consequences of the sense of non-belonging, the 'stolen generation' thus suffers the loss of the basis necessary for claiming their rights.

In much modern and post-modern academic thinking about culture and belonging, the metaphor of 'routes' is preferred to that of 'roots'. The reason is that the latter implies a static and bounded notion of culture that could become dangerous and develop into racism and ethnic absolutism and lead to conflict (Clifford, 1997). It is true that in the modern world, travel, cross-cutting of boundaries and the search for new routes are the concern of an increasing number of the world's inhabitants. At the same time, however, there is no doubt that both indigenous and non-indigenous people need the possibility of, and space for, creating forms of cultural continuity. It is this very possibility that was taken away from the Australian Aboriginals, with effects that have been likened to genocide. As the Commission's report says: 'Official policy and legislation for Indigenous families and children were contrary to accepted legal principles imported into Australia as British common law and, from late 1946, constituted a crime against humanity' (p. 275).[4]

Indigenous culture and external intervention

While some cultures and languages may disappear due to contemporary global processes, the global tendency towards cultural homogenization should not be deemed irreversible. The processes that accompany cultural and economic globalization are complex, and an understanding of the indigenous perspective in the context of global cultural diversity must be based on thorough investigation and research. It may seem anachronistic, and even futile, to speak about pre-contact cultures today, more than 500 years after Columbus, and after several years' of recognition that no culture is an island. However, the recent discovery of a tiny population in the Brazilian state of Rondônia may be regarded in a sense as an epitome of the present situation of indigenous peoples.

In September 1995, two Indians, a man and a woman, finally met the workers of FUNAI, the Brazilian state organ for the service of the Indians. The occasion was videotaped and subsequently shown on television. Ten years previously, loggers in the area had already reported Indians shooting arrows at the tractors entering their hunting grounds. A small population of twenty-five Indians was thought to live in this area, quite close, in fact, to a number of large, modern farms. Nevertheless, their presence was not confirmed until 1995, when satellite photos revealed a small village, and FUNAI managed to contact them. The language of the newly encountered persons was identified with some difficulty as related to the practically extinct Kanoé, still spoken by a 70-year old man and six or seven other individuals. With their help, some communication became possible, and another village inhabited by six persons, calling themselves Akuntsu, was located nearby. The male members of this tiny isolated group wore shorts made of salt sacks. They knew that they were not alone. Their neighbours had been their neighbours for years, knowing little more than the existence of the other. The same year, two areas of three square kilometres, surrounding the newly discovered villages, were demarcated and legally protected (Instituto Socioambiental, 1996, p. 539).

The 210 groups of indigenous peoples living in Brazil have increased in number in recent years and now total some 280,000 individuals, distributed in over 4,000 villages and settlements. They represent a tiny but significant 0.2% of the total population. The Brazilian Indians are not disappearing, and are protected by a national legislation constitutionally guaranteeing land inhabited by Indians. However, in spite of the fact that a substantial amount of indigenous land has been demarcated since 1990, 85% of indigenous lands still suffer some kind of invasion. Invaders are typically big landowners, gold diggers, loggers, woodcutters and landless rural workers (Ricardo, 1996–97).

On the one hand the Brazilian Indians live under constant threat of invasion owing to the richness of their resources and the lack of legal protection and implementation of the laws, and on the other they lack the power to sanction trespassers. At the same time, they suffer the consequences of living in geographically inaccessible areas, making health assistance, educational support and the marketing of their products costly and difficult. This affects their culture in profound ways and jeopardizes their prospects of maintaining cultural forms and traditions and establishing harmonious cultural interactions in the contact zones.

Underlying any effort to sustain cultural modes and traditional social patterns is the recognition and securing of territorial rights. The efforts to guarantee these, however, quite often do not lie in the hands of the Indians themselves. A host of non-indigenous organizations, individuals, church organs, development and environment NGOs, researchers, universities and 'indigenistas' are ready to help. Goodwill and outsiders' help is necessary, yet misdirected 'goodwill' can also be detrimental to the cause, and the claim to represent the interests of Indians should ideally only be made by Indians themselves.

The question of indigenous representation therefore cannot be understood without improving our knowledge of the whole field of intermediaries. In different ways, outsiders seek to influence internal indigenous policies, and indigenous leaders are forced to find new allies, to organize along new lines,

make new alliances with NGOs, universities and public agencies, and bypass old relationships of dependence on the state (Ricardo, 1997). This means that today's contact zones are radically different from those of colonial times. They are spaces where the NGOs are active, where the indigenous peoples are beginning to organize, where missionaries, government representatives, environmentalists, educationists and so forth interact, and where new forms of practice emerge with crucial implications for cultural continuity and creativity.

Towards self-determination

Indigenous organizations have increased substantially in numbers over the past ten to twenty years.[5] They have sprung up in response to the need to deal with the political and economic forces that threaten indigenous resources and territories, and to organize in order to obtain access to the goods and development possibilities offered by the national and international society. This has implications both for indigenous culture itself and for the culture created in the contemporary contact zone, i.e. the interface between the indigenous communities and the majority society, represented by 'indigenistas', experts, supporters, church people, environmentalists and researchers, among others.

Modern communication technology has played an essential part in creating such new organizational forms. The fact that an increasing number of contemporary indigenous organizations have access to communication technology in the form of fax and e-mail, and communicate with each other – as well as with supporters and policy-makers in other parts of the world – has provided a solid basis for the appearance of a growing international indigenous movement. Hence, the new indigenous organizations should be regarded not merely as a political, but also as a cultural phenomenon, i.e. as part of an ongoing and creative cultural practice.

In such new contexts, reflexiveness – or the ability to move smoothly between 'cultures' – seems

to be the only hope for the survival of indigenous cultures. Aside from a very few isolated groups, such as the Akuntsu in Brazil, for example, a lack of perception of the outside world is a thing of the past for indigenous societies and cultures. A conscious attitude to one's own culture, and a knowledge of and familiarity with, the culture of local, national and global neighbours, is a precondition for cultural survival in the world of today.

When indigenous peoples recreate their traditions reflexively, this is accompanied by new forms of self-organization. Within the global space, new borders are consciously created, sometimes with the strategic use of 'tradition' and 'indigenousness', including stereotypes from feathers to spiritual prayers. This is not only understandable from a political or even survival point of view; it is also an expression of the very dynamics of culture and therefore ought to be viewed as being just as 'authentic' as any classical ritual, prayer or headgear.

In the cultural process, specific social forms – a ritual, for example – may be recreated or 'reinvented', and former implicit cultural rules and notions may become articulated. This can be called forth by political pressure or by involvement with newly acquired knowledge of a global international discourse on rights. This articulation of culture is not, however, a complete breakaway from more implicit traditional forms, and it does not necessarily lead to 'essentialism' and ethnic absolutism, although the dangers of this must be constantly kept in mind.

Some forms of reflexiveness may be more ingrained in social processes than others. The important question to ask is what kinds of changes in cultural articulation can be identified in situations where indigenous peoples are socially marginalized or displaced, and their subsistence threatened. For example, when do erstwhile social forms deteriorate, thereby preventing physical attachment to land from being maintained? Under what circumstances is culture forced to become an issue in a strategic political struggle? What happens in the encounter

with a global discourse, a Western discourse, or a development discourse? And, not least, how can knowledge about such processes be used to improve development strategies for indigenous peoples?

These questions cannot be answered easily, but it is important to acknowledge that when indigenous peoples claim self-determination, this implies the right and freedom to develop new forms of self-organization and cultural practices. Faced with the challenges of interactions in the modern contact zones, indigenous peoples do not wish to be regarded as a 'living museum'. They ask for the recognition of their rights to determine their own pace of development, wishing to stay on their land without being threatened by dislocation, pollution or enslavement. Yet, indigenous peoples also want the freedom to maintain and recreate culture, and to adapt cultural and social forms to the new conditions of intensified interaction with the surrounding world.

With a few exceptions, indigenous peoples have no wish to secede from the state. They regard self-determination as a platform for interaction, as a mechanism to achieve some form of self-organization in the indigenous communities, and as the right to practice their own language and culture, but within the context of the nation-state.

Cultural diversity will exist where there are cultural and political spaces for creativity and negotiation. A positive development in the indigenous world will require the creation of spaces for the negotiation of new social and organizational forms, and this is what self-determination means. For indigenous peoples, a safe context primarily means defended and secured territorial rights and the possession of the necessary skills to interact and negotiate with the surrounding societies of neighbours, nations and beyond.

In creating such spaces, culture should not be the basic argument. Cultural creativity and pluralism may perhaps be regarded as humanity's reward for dealing successfully with the ideas of rights, equality and common as well as culture-specific values. Yet human beings and their rights must be the main argument. When people – and peoples – are left in peace to develop and cultivate their individual and social creativity, culture will take care of itself.

Notes

1.   Figures are cited from various United Nations documents (Seufert-Barr, 1993), material published by ILO in connection with the International Decade of the World's Indigenous People (Tomei, 1994), and the IWGIA Yearbooks.

2.   Personal communication from Felix Tiouka, Awala Yalimapo, French Guyana, who in 1997 engaged a linguist to introduce education in the Kalina languages.

3.   The Alaska Native Language Centre, based in the University of Fairbanks, initiated in the 1970s bilingual education in native languages and introduced orthographies or reforms of these. This led to the establishment of language commissions in several regions of Alaska.

4.   At the fifteenth session of the United Nations Working Group on Indigenous Populations, 28 July to 1 August 1997, the Federal Minister for Aboriginal and Torres Strait Islander Affairs expressed his regret for the wrongs of the past. At the time of writing, however, the Australian Government had not made any official response to the report. So far, it has rejected calls for financial compensation to Aboriginal children taken away from their families. At the Australian Reconciliation Convention in May 1997, the Australian Prime Minister, Mr Howard, voiced his sorrow (*The Australian*, No. 10, 27 May 1997). However, Aboriginal leaders, and the Chairman of the Stolen Children Inquiry, Sir Ronald Wilson, have criticized the Prime Minister and the government for not making any commitments to follow up their expressed moral attitude. A Council for Aboriginal Reconciliation was set up in 1991 and the process of reconciliation will continue for some years to come.

5.   The increase in the number of indigenous organizations and individuals who attend in the international negotiation of indigenous rights is, among other things, revealed by the number of attendants in the United Nations Working Group on Indigenous Populations, which in 1997 had around 1,000 attendants (United Nations doc. E/CN.4/Sub.2/ Ac.4/1997/INF1: List of Attendants).

Bibliography

Australian (The). No. 10, 27 May 1997.

BECKET, J. 1996. Contested Images: Perspectives on the Indigenous and Ecological Movements. *Identities: Global Studies in Culture and Power*, Vol. 3, Nos. 1–2.

BERTHELSEN, C. 1976. *Oqaluttualiaativut taalliaativullu.* Atuagkat, Det Grønlandske Forlag.

CLIFFORD, J. 1997. *Routes: Travel and Translation in the Late Twentieth Century.* London, Harvard University Press.

COBO, J. M. *A Study of the Problem of Discrimination Against Indigenous Populations.* New York, United Nations. (United Nations doc. E/CN.4/Sub.2/1986/7/Add.4. para. 379.)

FRIEDMAN, J. 1996. The Politics of De-authenticification: Escaping From Identity. A Commentary on *Beyond Authenticity* by Mark Rogers. *Identities: Global Studies in Culture and Power*, Vol. 3, Nos. 1–2.

HUMAN RIGHTS AND EQUAL OPPORTUNITY COMMISSION. 1997. *Bringing Them Home: National Inquiry into the Separation of Aboriginal and Torres Strait Islander Children from Their Families.* Sydney.

INSTITUTO SOCIOAMBIENTAL. 1996. *Povos Indigenas no Brasil, 1991–95.* São Paulo.

IWGIA. *The Indigenous World 1996–97* (IWGIA Yearbook). Copenhagen, IWGIA.

MALKKI, L. 1996. Speechless Emissaries: Refugees, Humanitarianism, and Dehistorization. In: Olwig and Hastrup (eds.), *Siting Culture: The Shifting Anthropological Object.* New York.

OLDENOW, K. 1959. *Printing in Greenland.* Copenhagen.

PETERSEN, R.; OLSEN, C. C. 1985. *Contemporary Problems of Preservation and Development of Arctic Culture in Greenland.* (Unpublished.)

PRATT, M. L. 1992. Imperial Eyes: Travel Writing and Transculturation. London.

RICARDO, B. 1997. Brasil. *The Indigenous World 1996–97.* (IWGIA Yearbook). Copenhagen, IWGIA.

ROGERS, M. 1996. Beyond Authenticity: Conservation, Tourism and the Politics of Representation in the Ecuadorian Amazon. *Identities: Global Studies in Culture and Power*, Vol. 3, Nos. 1–2.

SEUFERT-BARR, N. 1993. Seeking a New Partnership. *UN Chronicle* (New York, United Nations), June.

TOMEI, M. 1994. *Indigenous and Tribal Peoples and the ILO.* Geneva, International Labour Office.

Chapter 6
Culture and sustainability

Melissa A. Leach
Social anthropologist; Fellow, Institute of Development Studies,
University of Sussex, Brighton (United Kingdom)

'Achieving environmental sustainability . . . will require a democratization of expertise in the very definition of environmental issues and problems . . .'

Environment: development debates

Environmental concerns are now highly prominent in debates about global development and futures, whether in international policy circles or among populations influenced by increasingly global media. Following the United Nations Conference on Environment and Development (UNCED) in Rio de Janeiro in 1992, international agendas are being set to address problems such as desertification, deforestation, biodiversity loss and climate change. The extent to which similar environmental problems appear to recur across the world, the transnational nature of many environmental problems, and the ultimate sanction that there is 'only one earth' on which we all face a tragedy of the commons, suggest the truly global nature of the environmental crisis, and the need for universal scientific values and a global environmental ethics to respond to it. More than any other important contemporary discourse, the debate on the environment has adopted the concept of the global as both 'motive and motif'.[1]

Yet global environmental problems have local origins and impacts. Recognizing this, an international consensus – represented in UNCED's Agenda 21, for instance – advocates decentralized, local solutions. Cultural diversity attracts international attention in this context, and global

environmental debates now generally embrace the notion that 'traditional' forms of knowledge and organization have contributed to environmental sustainability in many localities. They can be learnt from and built upon.

This recognition that culture is significant in mediating people/environment relations is certainly an advance on approaches, still present, which view environmental issues in purely technical terms, or conceive of environmental problems simply in terms of imbalances between sheer numbers of people and overall resource availability. Equally, community-based and locally grounded approaches to sustainable development can, in many circumstances, offer significant advantages over approaches relying on state control or market-based solutions to environment and development problems.

While endorsing the growing attention to 'culture' in environment/development debates, the present chapter also questions the ways in which it has been incorporated. To set the scene for this argument, the chapter begins by illustrating how people interact with local environments – with their 'surroundings', as the environment can be broadly defined – in culturally grounded ways. Frequently, diverse cultural perspectives have been harnessed selectively, and with distortion, to suit globally defined environmental agendas which, rather than being shared or universal, actually reflect the priorities of those in positions of power. Yet local realities and alternative cultural perspectives can offer very different views from the orthodoxies on which global environmental agendas rest. The latter, and the science and notions of environmentalism with which they are associated, are equally partial, cultural perspectives. This poses a challenge not only for the ways that 'culture' is used, understood and defined, but also for approaches to the governance of environment and development processes.

Local cultural knowledge

Much research now illustrates the culturally diverse and creative ways in which people interact with their environments. In many rural and urban localities, people are directly dependent on environmental resources and services for their lives and livelihoods. Many local environmental concerns and representations are technical; they are about manipulating the environment for livelihood ends. Yet as work on ethno-ecology has shown, technical concepts are not merely utilitarian, but are embedded in broader sets of ideas and beliefs: ways of thinking about and understanding the world. Environmental processes and phenomena have a material existence in and of themselves, but the meanings which people impose on them are always socially and culturally constructed.[2]

When African farmers describe and manipulate the soils and vegetation which are basic to agricultural livelihoods, for instance, they use culturally embedded concepts. Kinship terms such as 'companionship' or 'brotherhood' may be used to describe situations in which particular trees, crops or weeds coexist; equally, terms such as 'killing' or 'struggle' can be used to describe competitive suppression, whether in fallows or crops. Soil fertility may be described in terms of heat and cold, damp and dry, hard and soft, with farmers managing these attributes to balance their qualities. Such vocabularies find echoes and gain their meaning in the broader frames in which people understand their world and their place in it, and which might include phenomena – such as kinship and social relations – which Western science would not treat as 'environmental'. For example, Kuranko-speaking farmers in West Africa use the term *tombondu* to refer to a soil which has acquired softness, 'oiliness' and 'maturity' through prolonged, intensive cultivation. Literally meaning 'abandoned settlement', the term makes metaphorical reference to the way old village and hamlet sites acquire such characteristics through habitation, gardening and rubbish disposal. The concepts of oiliness and maturity are also applied to girls who have completed their initiation rites, establishing them as fertile women; within this broader frame of reference, then, *tombondu* soils are 'initiated' through work into a newly fertile, productive status.

Because of their cultural embeddedness, local idioms used to categorize and explain ecological phenomena frequently do not translate easily into those of Western environmental science. For example, scientists have often assumed that farmers do not manage for crop diseases, because when presented with diseased specimens, they may fail to either distinguish diseases or to consider crop ill-health in terms of disease – presumably because they cannot see the disease vector. However, farmers may have other frameworks for understanding and

influencing crop health. Farmers in the Bwisha area of Kivu, in the former Zaire, for instance, consider rain, dew and humidity to have particular cooling and putrefactory qualities, and manage for these – the conditions in which disease develops – in their cropping, by altering sowing time, weeding, variety selection and so on. Understandably, they refer to fungicides within this cultural framework as 'medicines against the rain'.[3]

In many cultural settings, the concepts used to describe ecological processes are also used to describe aspects of people's health and fertility. Thus where Western science conventionally draws its boundary between body and field, local beliefs may draw causal links which cross-cut such boundaries. For example, several West African peoples believe that if a woman who is menstruating or in the early stages of pregnancy enters a stream or pond as part of a fishing group, both the fishing and her future fertility will be ruined. Equally, a hunter's fortunes can be influenced by his wife's sexual activities; if she engages in adultery while he is hunting, a hunter in Sierra Leone's forests will say that 'the bush will close' and he will kill nothing.[4]

Such examples give some indication of how within particular cultural understandings, people's behaviour and relationships can have direct consequences for the 'natural' environment and vice versa. In this sense, a network of conceptually linked processes and causal relationships cuts across the division between 'nature' and 'society' or 'culture', so basic to European thought. Unsurprisingly, claims to authority over such linked ecological and social processes can be central to local political dynamics. The power of the leaders of territorial cults in Central and Southern Africa earlier this century rested strongly on their claims to manage environmental and human fertility concerns. Power relations in women's and men's initiation societies along Africa's Upper Guinea coast rest on claims to gender-specific knowledge and claims to power over respective ecological domains.

Knowledge, ideas and beliefs concerning ecological relations are neither static, nor necessarily shared by the members of a particular society. Knowledge may develop through a creative interplay between theory and practice, and through interaction with ecological processes that are themselves dynamic. And it may develop through local processes of debate between people whose opinions reflect their positions in social and political relations. Whereas in the forest–savannah transition zone of Guinea, West Africa, elders of landowning lineages tend to associate the existence of large trees in peri-village forests with the foundation of settlements by their ancestors, reflecting a domain in which they have relative authority; young women tend to explain them as the overgrown fence poles of kitchen gardens, reflecting their relative powerlessness in lineage affairs and their more everyday concerns with kitchen gardening.

At one level, therefore, particular environmental understandings might be associated with a particular 'culture': with a particular society, or with a broad regional tradition encompassing subtle local variations on common themes.[5] But it is equally important to recognize diverse cultural perspectives within any given local setting. These may be associated with axes of local social difference: by gender, age, caste, kinship position, socio-economic status or occupation, for instance, and can be the stuff of local debate. The notion of cultural perspective also allows for the recognition of commonalities, coalitions and alliances across localized cultures, in a globalizing world in which the idea of 'cultural boundaries' has become even more problematic. Such alliances may be grounded in aspects of common experience: for example, those engaged in commercial logging from urban and rural backgrounds in South-East Asia and in Latin America might share similar perspectives on forests as a source of valuable timber. Alliances can also be forged around environmental phenomena as shared political symbols, as when forest-dwellers in

Forests in West Africa[6]

The forest–savannah transition zone of West Africa has, since early colonial times, been portrayed as undergoing rapid deforestation. 'Islands' of forest in a sea of grassland are assumed to be relics of once-extensive natural forest cover, the climax vegetation for the zone's humid climate, progressively destroyed by local farming and fire-setting for hunting and pastoralism. This supposed human disturbance to natural vegetation has led government policies and international aid programmes to restrict land-use practices supposed to be environmentally damaging through regulations and fines, while state agencies have taken control over threatened 'natural' trees. Some forest patches have been singled out for more community-based forms of conservation, on the grounds that they are 'sacred' forests culturally preserved amid secular destruction around them.

But at least in the Guinea forest, local cultural perspectives strongly contradict this view of progressive 'savannah-ization', presenting an opposed, even reversed, reading of the landscape. Villagers describe how forest patches, far from being relics of destruction, have been created by themselves or their ancestors in savannahs, whether the emphasis is on tree planting, settlement foundation and forests as early war fortresses

(as elderly men frequently suggest) or on the gradual vegetation-enhancing effects of gardening, household waste and the grazing of domestic animals (as others, including many women, imply). Many forest-building and expanding practices are essentially of an everyday kind, grounded in villagers' practical ecological knowledge and the fundamental idea that land is improved through use and work. Forests are not 'sacred' in local thought, even though they can be sites for initiation activities and ancestral veneration. Many local farming and early-burning practices have enhanced the progressive expansion of forest into savannah over the last century; a change confirmed by historical sources such as comparative air photographs and archival descriptions. Yet scientists and administrators have repeatedly overlooked such evidence in favour of data supporting their conviction of deforestation. The latter both conforms with dominant scientific theories and supports particular economic and political interests, not least the revenues to be derived from government-controlled trees.

Melissa A. Leach
Social anthropologist;
Fellow, Institute of Development Studies,
University of Sussex, Brighton (United Kingdom)

Malaysia's Penan unite with northern environmental activist groups to valorize medicinal plants, deploying this value symbolically in campaigns for rainforest preservation.[7] Because they are produced through, and are supportive of, particular relations of power, these cultural perspectives can usefully be seen as 'discourses' on environment; an argument which will become clearer later in this chapter when discussion focuses on the relationship between environmental knowledge and material practices.

Much international attention has focused on cultural diversity in ecological knowledge. It is sometimes argued that non-industrial societies possess a 'primitive ecological wisdom' which could offer pointers towards sustainable future ways of life; or that detailed indigenous knowledge of soils, plants, animals and so on offer vital resources for global struggles to develop sustainable food

production systems, conserve biodiversity and so on. Alternatively, localized, culturally specific knowledge is seen as important to fine-tune or adapt generalized technologies to local settings. Such arguments underlie the creation of international networks and centres to record and preserve indigenous knowledge. However, such efforts frequently portray knowledge as static and 'traditional', associated with particular cultures; ignoring the intra- and transcultural diversity and dynamism discussed above. Equally, they often take an evaluative perspective: culturally specific knowledge is selected and valued in so far as it is recognizable in the terms of Western science, or in so far as it is seen as useful to address globally defined environmental agendas or the goals of externally defined campaigns. At the extreme, local knowledges may be re-packaged in scientized terms, or within romanticized notions of

'sacred wisdom', such as to become unrecognizable to those who spawned them, suppressing local creativity.[8] Taking cultural diversity seriously requires a far more comparative approach.

Culture, institutions and sustainability

While work on environmental knowledges treats culture largely in terms of ideas and beliefs, its arguments are often used in support of those made from a slightly different strand of work, emphasizing the way local organizations and institutions can promote environmentally sustainable practices.

This strand of work has been highly influential in bringing cultural concerns into international environment and development debates. In some formulations, including the ecosystems approaches to cultural ecology which became popular from the 1960s, culture is seen as having adaptive value in the maintenance of the environment. Thus, it is argued, culturally defined norms about co-operation, religious institutions and so on serve to regulate human impact on surroundings so that people/environment relations remain harmonious. These arguments are not dissimilar to those made in discussions of common property. The latter developed as a counter to earlier views that people were inclined always to maximize their use of resources for individual gain, leading inevitably to a 'tragedy of the commons', and necessitating privatization or state control if resources were to be sustainably maintained. The counter-arguments build on evidence that local institutions, frequently underlain by shared values and a sense of 'community', can enable people to co-operate to conserve and manage resources sustainably, whether these be fisheries, water resources, or grazing lands.

Linked with arguments about environmentally benign knowledge systems, these arguments about organization have contributed to or rejuvenated a view of 'ecocultures': that certain peoples, principally non-industrial, possess forms of knowledge and organization which mean their ways of life are more harmoniously integrated with their environment, and thus sustainable. Such claims, particularly, are often made for remote 'forest peoples', 'hunter-gatherers' and 'tribals'. Other societies may 'traditionally' have maintained such harmony, but have seen it ruptured by external economic or political forces: the imposition of inappropriate state regimes and the undermining of traditional authority; commercialization; modernity; or new urban aspirations. It can be argued, then, that (a) certain local culture/environment systems are adaptive or sustainable; (b) the world has much to learn from these; (c) those which are adaptive should be conserved; and (d) on the precautionary principle, and similar to arguments used about biodiversity, it is important to retain cultural diversity to avoid the loss of systems which, in the future, might be valued. Some of these ideas are already embodied in national and donor policies and programmes: for instance in 'cultural reserve' in biodiverse rainforest areas, or in community-based sustainable development which seeks to support or rebuild traditional, environmentally sustainable institutions.

However, some of the same problems which suffuse the treatment of ecological knowledge also apply here. First, there are problems with the view of 'cultures' as shared, bounded wholes, relating to single, static environments. Rather than a community of homogeneous interests, there may be an assortment of people who, with different livelihoods and different socially defined responsibilities, might give priority to very different environmental goods and services within ecologies that are also diverse and variable. In a watershed in Rajasthan, for example, the same hillsides are valued by women of scheduled castes for gathering saleable wild foods; by Rajput women as a convenient source of fuelwood; by men to plant trees for cash sale of poles, and by livestock-raising groups as common grazing grounds. Evidently, such diverse values can come into conflict.

Second, then, how people use and manage environments depends on the ways they can come to

Environmental degradation in the Himalayas[9]

The Himalayas have been portrayed as a region of environmental crisis par excellence. Dominant views hold that local farming and fuelwood collection practices lead to the depletion of tree cover. Encouraged by rapid population growth, the deforestation frontier is pushed further and further out from settlements onto more mountainous and marginal land, where it leads to soil erosion. This progressive degradation is felt not only locally, but also downstream, with soil erosion and landslides blamed for flooding on the Nepalese and Indian plains below. This crisis has provided the justification for a variety of government interventions aimed at restricting shifting cultivation and halting deforestation, and for large inputs of international aid into mountain Nepal.

However, detailed research among mountain farmers reveals some very different perspectives. Farmers generally do not interpret the region's ongoing environmental change as degradation or crisis caused by their practices. Rather than degrade land in response to population growth, they have, through active agricultural innovation and tree planting, been able to intensify production on parts of their land in sustainable ways. While donors and scientists have treated landslides as an indicator of ecological collapse, some farmers consider them advantageous – and even trigger them deliberately – to fertilize valley bottom lands. Furthermore, many of the erosion processes attributed to careless farming can be reinterpreted as due to long-term tectonic changes. Indeed, a critical review of empirical evidence for and against environmental degradation reveals a vast diversity of possible measurements and interpretations. Depending on the data selected, the Himalayas can appear to be about to become totally denuded, or about to succumb to a vast increase in tree cover, or anything in between. Farmer-induced ecological collapse is only one possible interpretation among many; nevertheless it has commonly been selected by many aid organizations and governments because it matched their own policy objectives.

Melissa A. Leach
Social anthropologist;
Fellow, Institute of Development Studies, University of Sussex, Brighton (United Kingdom)

access and control particular resources and services, and perhaps struggle with others to do so. Many social and political relationships and institutions, both local and not so local, are involved in these processes and shape their ecological outcomes. To focus on 'culture' as knowledge and ideas is to ignore these, and thus assume falsely that environmentally benign beliefs translate into environmentally benign practice. To adopt a definition of 'culture' so broad and holistic as to conflate all within 'ways of life' is to lose analytical insight. For instance, it may be important to recognize that people fell trees or allow soils to degrade because of their insecure tenurial status as tenants, despite their knowledge of the soil degradation which might ensue. Broader scale processes – state policies, changes in market prices and so on – interact with these local institutional dynamics in affecting patterns of environmental change. Such processes have a profound impact which tends to be underplayed by analysis framed in

terms of culture and external rupture to local, culturally determined sustainability.

Finally – but crucially – an evaluative perspective has dominated international debates about the cultural determinants of environmental change, and the value of 'conservationist' cultures. Thus 'ecocultures' have tended to be valued selectively to the extent that they support environmental values and trajectories of change which are compatible with those in global debates. Do they, for instance, contribute to combating serious known problems such as tropical deforestation, biodiversity loss or desertification? Many studies of the social and cultural dynamics of environmental change – of deforestation or soil degradation, for instance – frame their analyses uncritically without questioning the 'reality' of these processes. In this, they support a view of such broad environmental problematics as shared, global preoccupations, and of the science that underlies

them as universal, objective and neutral. Serious attention to diverse cultural perspectives can question these global orthodoxies in quite fundamental ways, showing them, and their underlying science, to be partial cultural perspectives grounded in particular relations of power.

Global science and environmentalism as cultural perspectives

In fact, the orthodox views of environmental change which currently dominate international policy debates are, themselves, particular cultural perspectives. Notions such as desertification or deforestation, and the views that they are occurring in particular places, rest on evidence which fails to describe the whole of a problem.

The perspectives which inform the dominant positions in international science and policy are just as cultural as the local perspectives which sometimes prove to counter them. Like land users' perspectives, they are partly rooted in experience – albeit different experience – of ecological processes. They embody particular ideas, beliefs and values concerning the environment and people/environment relations; they employ particular concepts, vocabularies and theories of causation; and they emanate from particular institutional contexts. Indeed, that a relatively small number of orthodoxies have come to dominate in international circles, including donors, governments and the Northern public, seems to reflect significant convergences in economic and funding interests, influencing education and training.

The scientific ideas which underlie these perspectives are clearly not universal or neutral. Formal science is itself culturally produced, as shown by research which takes the approaches once used to study the cultural perspectives of remote rural peoples into the world of laboratory scientists, climate or land-use modellers, or into the meetings in which they debate their findings.[10] Indeed, work on critical science now emphasizes that all attempts to understand ecological processes reflect cultural

ideas or social or political agendas.[11] Different and partial scientific knowledge not only theorizes environmental change in different ways, but also carries very different implications for how human agency in environmental change is understood, and hence for resource claims and policy. Particular scientific theories have underpinned dominant positions in international policy debates; for instance the notion of 'carrying capacity' – and thus of overstocking by pastoralists – as a justification for conventional rangeland policy, and for controlling the movement of pastoralists.

While an empirical contrast between the perspectives of formal science and those of lay publics may be evident, formal science, too, is far from consensual. Many global environmental problems, involving long and distant causal chains and complex processes, are the subject of debate within the international scientific community. Major shifts in the theoretical underpinnings of ecological science have also given rise to new debates, and opposed positions, in understandings of ecological systems, in particular around the divergence between conventional, linear perspectives on change and dynamic, non-equilibrial perspectives which emphasize uncertainty, conjuncture and contingency. This latter set of shifts (what some have heralded as the 'new ecology') theoretically opens the way for a greater pluralism in environmental science; a pluralism in which diverse cultural perspectives and local knowledge may find a voice. In practice, however, it is striking how far older ecological theories continue to dominate in administrative and policy circles.

The cultural perspectives which drive current environment-development agendas can be seen to be produced through particular political and economic relations. Frequently, they reflect the institutional histories of colonial and donor regimes. And they clearly have material effects; to put it simply, as Roe has done, 'crisis narratives are the primary means whereby development experts and the institutions for which they work claim rights to stewardship over

Population growth, sustainable development and the environment[12]

Population growth has now practically reached the peak point of the transition to a stabilized world population for the foreseeable future, the full transition period being from 1965 to 2050. The transition is remarkably brief, if we compare it with the million years of our development; yet one-tenth of all those who have ever lived will experience this period of rapid change. The pace and width of the transition are due to interactions in the global population and are the outcome of the complex behaviour of a highly non-linear dynamic system. During this eventful period of eighty-five years the population of the world will multiply by three and grow much older. It is incontestably the most critical and singular period ever experienced by humankind, which all through the ages has followed a stable and persistent pattern of growth. This pattern is now very rapidly evolving towards that of a stabilized world population. In fact, it simply cannot switch over faster from expansion to saturation (barring an all-out nuclear war or extraterrestrial intervention) and it is this rapid change that should to be kept in mind in any attempt to understand the global problems now facing the world.

Since the 1992 Rio de Janeiro Conference on Development and the Environment the concept of sustainable development has emerged as a significant landmark in the international debate on world affairs. Five years later a review conference was held in New York: it revealed difficulties, not to speak of a split in attitudes towards development and the environment between developed and developing nations. The consensus reached in Rio is now being challenged: the reasons for differences in attitudes have to be looked into, taking into account the population transition.

All the world's land, food, energy and wealth distribution shows that the world population system is very far from any equilibrium. This is a most important point, indicating as it does the relationship of such distribution to rapid growth, enhanced as a country approaches the demographic transition. On the other hand, the evolution of this distribution shows that in the process of growth the world population system was dynamically sustainable – otherwise it could not have evolved consistently for a million years in the way that it has.

It may be assumed that the global population system is an open one and has enough resources to support its development in the foreseeable future. The first indication of a global shortage will be a more uniform pattern of the use of resources. At this tempo, the next century promises to be crucial for humankind in negotiating the final stage in its adaptation to the

land and resources they do not own. By generating and appealing to crisis narratives, technical experts and managers assert rights as 'stakeholders' in the land and resources they say are under crisis'.[13]

Such external claims over resource management and control can have deleterious consequences for local livelihoods. They can marginalize or alienate people from natural resources over which they previously enjoyed access and control, perhaps directly undermining their ability to secure food or income. This has sometimes been the case, for instance, with policies to exclude people from externally managed forest or wildlife reserves, or to confine pastoralists to fenced paddocks. Where inhabitants must, out of necessity, continue to use resources claimed by external agencies, they often find themselves subject to taxes or fines which render them more resource-poor. In some cases, the assertion of professionalized claims over land and resources has also had adverse ecological consequences. For example, external prohibitions on the setting of bush fire in Guinea undermined

stabilized state of the future and then, hopefully, moving on to a sustainable pattern of development. By then all progress will have to be reckoned by means other than that of numerical growth, the stereotype of development that dominated humankind for a million years, i.e. tens of thousands of generations. *History and our present experience show that the software, our ideas and values, evolve much slower than the hardware which for ages was geared for maximum growth and productivity.* Under the pressure of rapid development these long entrenched attitudes will have to change. Of all factors, this is probably the one most central to resolving the issue of sustainability.

These ideas and concepts provide the historic context for considering sustainability of biodiversity of the biosphere. As recent environmental research shows, it may be expected that biodiversity will be largely lost during the period of rapid growth, as happened in the developed world two or three generations ago during the first stage of the population transition, i.e. the stage of rapid growth. Today it is the very rapid growth of the developing world that is seen by many as the principal menace to the global environment, and biodiversity in the first place as a short-term factor when compared with the long-term environmental issues. The sheer rate of growth and the rapid transition to a stabilized new world are competing factors that will determine the

outcome and state of the world in the foreseeable future. What can and will to a certain extent resolve these issues is the change of values, determining people's patterns of social behaviour. At the peak rate of the present stage of development, material growth far outbalances the development of humankind's software.

The difference in our values and ideas and of our material development are influenced to a great extent by the processes of globalization. If the spread of technology, money and industrial know-how are accelerating development, the corresponding diffusion of appropriate ideas and values is lagging. The sheer complexity of the global society is complicating matters still further, for it takes considerable time for our social habits and customs to become established and even longer for international institutions to evolve. The time-scales involved may be traced from the fact that it takes nine months to produce a human's hardware, but at least twenty years to programme or educate a human being. These are the fundamental biological and human constants that finally determine both our personal development and the fate of humankind. Ultimately, it is the interplay and balance of mind and matter that will resolve our predicament.

Sergey Kapitza
Physicist; Professor, P. L. Kapitza Institute
for Physical Problems, Moscow (Russian Federation)

inhabitants' early-burning strategies, risking greater fire damage by late dry season fires.

Cultural perspectives on environment, in this light, are perhaps best understood as shaped by discourses.[14] The notion of discourse draws attention to the ways that particular ideas come to embody relations of power, and reproduce them. It emphasizes that power-knowledge has real practical consequences.

The growth in global environmentalism as a form of discourse involving large sections of the

world's population is significant both as a phenomenon, and in its effects. Broadly defined as a concern to protect the environment through human responsibility and effort, environmentalism can itself be seen as a particular cultural perspective (or set of perspectives, as it encompasses many strands) in the sense that it reflects particular ways of understanding the world and one's place within it. It can be seen as a transcultural discourse par excellence, emerging through and in turn playing a role in globalization, by reducing social distance, compressing the world.[15]

Yet in the globalization of environmentalist discourse, we might ask whose perspectives are represented and whose are excluded?

The globalization of environmental discourse has been greatly assisted by growth in global information flows, including the mass media. The mass media do not simply transmit messages to their audiences about the 'real world'. Rather, they participate in constructing environmental issues in particular ways, by transmitting culturally specific 'messages' which are subsequently decoded and given meaning by their audiences according to their pre-existing cultural frames of reference.[16] Through these communicative processes there appears to be an in-built tendency for the media to generate 'crisis' narratives with respect to environmental issues. As Burgess argues:

The power to define the meanings of landscapes and places, plants and animals, renewable and non-renewable resources is being contested in new and fascinating forms of cultural politics conducted primarily through the mass media: take, for example, the alliance between actors, musicians, Brazilian Indians, pop-music promoters, conservation organizations, the media industry and the mainly young consumers who buy records to support the campaign against the destruction of the Amazonian rainforest.[17]

A dominant strand in global environmental discourse emphasizes more global integration as the best way to protect the environment. This discourse has a number of particular effects. It legitimizes the need for international, global mechanisms to address environmental problems; it justifies the assertion of global rights and claims over resources such as biodiversity, rainforests and so forth on the grounds that they are global patrimony, over and above local claims; and it supports a reliance on development and Western science as a solution to environmental problems. While arguments for public participation (as in Agenda 21) and for support of cultural diversity may be made from within this discourse,

they are seen as part of – and as means to achieve – agendas already set by global agencies.

Although inhabitants of local environments may participate in the production of ideas about environmental change, they do so with less power to define the terms of debate. As token participants in global and national fora, they may have little chance to express alternatives to the dominant viewpoint. Equally, it is not uncommon for rural inhabitants in their interactions with development fieldworkers to confirm outsiders' preconceived ideas, given the power relations which operate at such 'interfaces'. Such confirmation may arise out of fear, suspicion, or a desire to remain on good terms by accepting what is being offered. Relations of authority and the memory of past experience structure these interactions. More significantly, land users may also selectively adopt outsiders' environmental idioms and turn them to their own advantage in struggles over identity and resource control. For example, in Guinea, externally derived images of forest loss are invoked by villagers in discourse about ethnicity, to identify themselves respectively as 'forest people' or 'savannah people' in ways which – in colonial and now modern Guinea – have political significance, despite the very different practical ecological knowledge which they invoke in other contexts.

The bases for localized discourses of resistance to globalized environmental perspectives exist. Many of the diverse cultural perspectives found among land users, contain the seeds of such discourses. A strand of global environmental discourse would seem to support such localized perspectives, in the form of broad arguments that advocate eco-friendly localism.[18] In contrast with the dominant views outlined above, these hold that development is a Northern conspiracy which has damaged the environment, and that the replacement of local cultural perspectives by Western science is ecologically destructive. They advocate opting out of globally defined agendas for sustainable development in favour of local self-determination, in forms of

development grounded on communal values, subsistence perspectives and indigenous knowledge, with women's knowledge and perspectives – ecofeminism – frequently seen as key. But these broad anti-globalist positions can in themselves be seen as defined by dominant global discourse, having developed in opposition to it. And many of the positions that they uphold – such as the myth of 'primitive ecological wisdom' – equally risk imposing globally defined values on local cultural diversity, overriding people's own experiences and realities.

Democratizing environmental knowledge

To sum up, cultural perspectives on ecological processes and people/environment relations are as diverse as are the world's ecologies and the historical experiences of their inhabitants. Diversity encompasses the concepts and vocabularies through which ecological processes are understood; the institutions and forms of sociocultural organization through which environmental goods and services are accessed, controlled and struggled over; the way in which particular aspects of the environment are valued, and even the ways that 'nature' and 'culture', or people and environment, are categorized and bounded. Cultural perspectives are discourses in the sense that they are produced through and supportive of power relations, and can have material effects, supporting particular positions in struggles for control over environmental goods and services.

In the context of globalization, and through convergences in information flows, scientific ideas and economic and political concerns, international debates about environment and development have come to be dominated by a powerful set of global orthodoxies. In keeping with the ideas of Western science and contemporary environmentalism, these frame environmental problems and set agendas for sustainable development in such a way as to admit cultural diversity only on their own terms. In this process – and paradoxically, sometimes through the very conservation and development programmes which claim to build on and encourage local environmental knowledge and organization – localities are reproduced within global discursive images. Land users' own perspectives and creativity are thus silenced, or pushed into reformulation as discourses of resistance.

Much current discussion of the cultural dimensions of globalization values the apparent spread of consciousness of a shared earthly ecosystem as an important manifestation of an emerging global culture. Science and the scientific ethos of grounding policies and decisions on empirical evidence and proof are also gaining global ground, and are frequently seen to provide a neutral, universal basis on which political decisions can proceed. Yet these trends risk contradicting principles of democratic participation and support of a global civic culture, if this supposed 'global environmental consciousness' and universal, neutral science are not themselves subjected to cultural critique. For if the arguments and evidence presented in this chapter are valid, global environmentalism and its supportive science come to be seen as at least partly the product of particular, Western-dominated cultural traditions and relations of power. The imposition of global orthodoxies and analysis over different environmental values and notions of sustainability can infringe not only on local livelihoods, but also on cultural freedom, in a deeply decivilizing process.

No single culture or set of cultural perspectives holds the key to understanding and addressing the complex environmental challenges which the world faces now, or will face in the future. Achieving environmental sustainability – and certainly environmental sustainability which is compatible with livelihoods and citizenship for the world's populations – will require a democratization of expertise in the very definition of environmental issues and problems. It will require the bringing together of diverse pieces of knowledge into 'hybrid' forms that shed light on different issues from diverse angles; and it will require a science-policy process that while grounded in a realist conception of environmental change, embraces the plurality of partial, cultural perspectives held on any issue, with explicit recognition of the political or economic agendas which may inform them. This highlights the challenge to develop greater understanding of the culture and politics of global science and policy institutions, with a view to defining where room for manoeuvre or space to recast debates might lie. And it recasts citizen participation and the sustenance of cultural diversity in far more political terms, with self-determination in knowledge, ideas and organization at their core.

Notes

1.   K. S. Milton, *Environmentalism: The View from Anthropology*, London, Routledge, 1996, p. 13.

2.   This position differs from the pure cultural determinism which is sometimes associated with ethno-ecology, and which holds that there is no 'environment' independent of cultural constructions of it.

3.   See J. Fairhead, *Indigenous Technical Knowledge and Natural Resource Management in Africa: A Critical Review.* (Paper prepared for SSRC Conference on African Agriculture, Dakar, January 1992.)

4.   See M. Leach, *Rainforest Relations: Gender and Resource Use Among the Mende of Gola, Sierra Leone,* Edinburgh, Edinburgh University Press, and Washington, Smithsonian Institution, 1994.

5.   See J. Vansina, *Paths in the Rainforest: Toward a History of Political Tradition in Equatorial Africa,* London, James Currey, 1993.

6.   See J. Fairhead and M. Leach, *Misreading the African Landscape: Society and Ecology in a Forest Savanna Mosaic,* Cambridge and New York, Cambridge University Press, 1996.

7.   J. P. Brosius, 'Endangered Forest, Endangered People: Environmentalist Representations of Indigenous Knowledge', *Human Ecology*, Vol. 25, No. 1, 1997, pp. 47–69.

8.   A. Agarwal, 'Dismantling the Divide Between Indigenous and Scientific Knowledge', *Development and Change,* Vol. 26, 1995, pp. 413–39; see also Brosius, op. cit.

9.   See M. Thompson, M. Warburton and T. Hatley, *Uncertainty on a Himalayan Scale: An Institutional Theory of Environment Perception and a Strategic Framework for the Development of the Himalaya,* London, Ethnographica, Milton Ash Publications, 1986; J. Ives and B. Messerli, *Himalayan Dilemmas: Reconciling Conservation and Development,* London, Routledge, and New York, United Nations University, 1989.

10.   See, for example, B. Latour, S. Woolgar and J. Salk, *Laboratory Life: The Construction of Scientific Facts,* Princeton, New Jersey, Princeton University Press, 1986.

11.   See, for example, R. Bhaskar, *Scientific Realism and Human Emancipation,* London, Macmillan, 1986; D. Haraway, 'Situated Knowledge: The Science Question in Feminism and the Privilege of Partial Perspective', *Feminist Studies,* Vol. 14, No. 3, 1988, pp. 575–99.

12.   Partly based on S. P. Kapitza, 'The Phenomenological Theory of World Population Growth', *Uspekhi-Physics,* Vol. 39, No. 1, 1996, pp. 57–72.

13.   E. Roe, 'Except-Africa: Postscript to a Special Section on Development Narratives', *World Development,* Vol. 23, No. 6, 1995, pp. 1065–70.

14.   'Discourse' has a variety of connotations in academic debate and everyday usage; the sense meant here is closest to that in the work of Foucault (e.g. M. Foucault, 'Power/Knowledge: Selected Interviews and Other Writings, 1972–1977', Brighton, The Harvester Press.

15.   See Milton, op. cit.

16.   J. Burgess, 'The Production and Consumption of Environmental Meanings in the Mass Media: A Research Agenda for the 1990s', *Transactions of the Institute of British Geographers*, N.S. 15, 1990, pp. 139–61.

17.   Ibid., p. 141.

18.   For example, W. Sachs, *Global Ecology, Conflicts and Contradictions,* London, Zed Books; M. Miss and V. Shiva, *Ecofeminism,* London, Zed Books, 1993.

Chapter 7
Cities, culture and globalization

Elizabeth Jelin
Sociologist and researcher, Consejo Nacional de Investigaciones Científicas y Técnicas (CONICET)
and Faculty of Social Sciences, University of Buenos Aires (Argentina), with the assistance of Alejandro Grimson

'There is nowadays a global system of cities, and this requires us to look at the world as "one world".'

Urbanization in a global era

Since Babel, the city has been the symbol of the tension between cultural and linguistic integration on the one hand, and diversity, confusion and chaos on the other. The city has also been the symbol of change and innovation. Current processes of globalization undoubtedly impact on cities and their cultural life. What happens to cities with the changes in communications, information and transport technologies? How do demographic patterns of urbanization, new forms of urban poverty and environmental threats combine their influence with the technological revolution?

This chapter will look at cities through a cultural lens. Everyday city life involves a constant interplay between the global and the local. Furthermore, cities are the meeting places of diverse peoples: 'natives', migrants and tourists, groups with various levels and depths of belonging. The chapter will show cities as the loci of cultural diversity and interculturality, and therefore of cultural creativity.

The twentieth century is the century of urbanization and city life. Never before in the history of humanity has urban life been so prevalent, and the turn of the century will find us in an urban world, with pockets of rural life. The passage from one situation to the other is a complex phenomenon,

involving major technological, economic, social, political and cultural dimensions.

In 1950, 29.3% of the world population lived in urban areas; in 1994 it reached 44.8%, and the estimates for the year 2025 are that 61.1% of the world population will be living in urban areas.[1] That change is coming about through three mechanisms: the massive movement of people from the countryside to towns and cities; 'natural' population growth of city dwellers; and the spatial expansion of cities and towns, incorporating adjoining rural areas to urban growth.

There are wide variations among countries and regions: the most developed areas of the world became urbanized earlier, and by now three-quarters of their population live in urban areas, a proportion that is expected to grow to 84% in the next thirty years. The least-developed countries have 21.9% of their population in urban areas, and this proportion will grow to 43.5% in 2025. Thus, the process of world urbanization is still in the making.

Obviously, mega-cities (here taken to mean cities with more than 8 million people) differ from those of less than 500,000 inhabitants. The mega-cities of the world are growing rapidly, particularly in Asia. In 1950, only New York and London fitted the category. In 1994, there were 22 cities of that size, and 16 of them were in the less-developed regions of the world.

Actually, a double process is under way: urbanization, implying growth of towns and cities, and 'metropolization', i.e. the growth of the largest urban concentrations. In some parts of the more developed world, a counter-trend is also taking place, namely the de-concentration of population from some mega-cities into suburban areas or smaller cities, first experienced in the United States and later in some European countries and Japan. Thus, some important cities in Europe and the United States have reduced their populations in the last twenty years: Milan reduced its population by 23%; Naples by 17%; London by 10%; Pittsburgh by 7.4%, and Cleveland by 8.4%. In the future, this counter-urbanization may occur in less-developed areas of the world. In fact, the rate of growth of mega-cities in Latin America already slowed down during the 1980s.

What difference does it make whether one lives in a rural area, in a small city, or in a mega-city? Because of better communications and global access to new technologies, differences tend to blur in some respects, provided rural residents have the opportunity to access this global communicative network. Gaps are still extremely large. UNESCO's statistics show that in the early 1990s, there were about ten TV sets per 1,000 inhabitants in the least developed countries in the world. Rural illiterate women have practically no access to TV, radio or movies. More than continuums and gaps, what we have is clefts and ruptures.

There is nowadays a global system of cities, and this requires us to look at the world as 'one world'. At the top, a transnational business class is

TABLE 1
MEGA-CITIES OF THE WORLD: POPULATION (MILLIONS) IN 1994 AND 2015 (ESTIMATED)

Rank	1994	2015
1.	Tokyo (26.5)	Tokyo (28.7)
2.	New York (16.3)	Bombay (27.4)
3.	São Paulo (16.1)	Lagos (24.4)
4.	Mexico City (15.5)	Shanghai (23.4)
5.	Shanghai (14.7)	Jakarta (21.2)
6.	Bombay (14.5)	São Paulo (20.8)
7.	Los Angeles (12.2)	Karachi (20.6)
8.	Beijing (12.0)	Beijing (19.4)
9.	Calcutta (11.5)	Dacca (19.0)
10.	Seoul (11.5)	Mexico City (18.8)
11.	Jakarta (11.0)	New York (17.6)
12.	Buenos Aires (10.9)	Calcutta (17.6)
13.	Osaka (10.6)	Delhi (17.6)
14.	Tianjin (10.4)	Tianjin (17.0)
15.	Rio de Janeiro (9.8)	Metro Manila (14.7)
16.	Lagos (9.7)	Cairo (14.5)
17.	Delhi (9.5)	Los Angeles (14.3)
18.	Karachi (9.5)	Seoul (13.1)
19.	Paris (9.4)	Buenos Aires (12.4)
20.	Cairo (9.4)	Istanbul (12.3)
21.	Moscow (9.2)	Rio de Janeiro (11.6)
22.	Metro Manila (9.0)	Lahore (10.8)
23.		Hyderabad (10.7)
24.		Osaka (10.6)
25.		Bangkok (10.6)
26.		Lima (10.5)
27.		Teheran (10.2)
28.		Kinshasa (9.9)
29.		Paris (9.6)
30.		Madras (9.5)
31.		Moscow (9.3)
32.		Shinnying (8.6)
33.		Bangalore (8.3)

Source: United Nations, 1995.

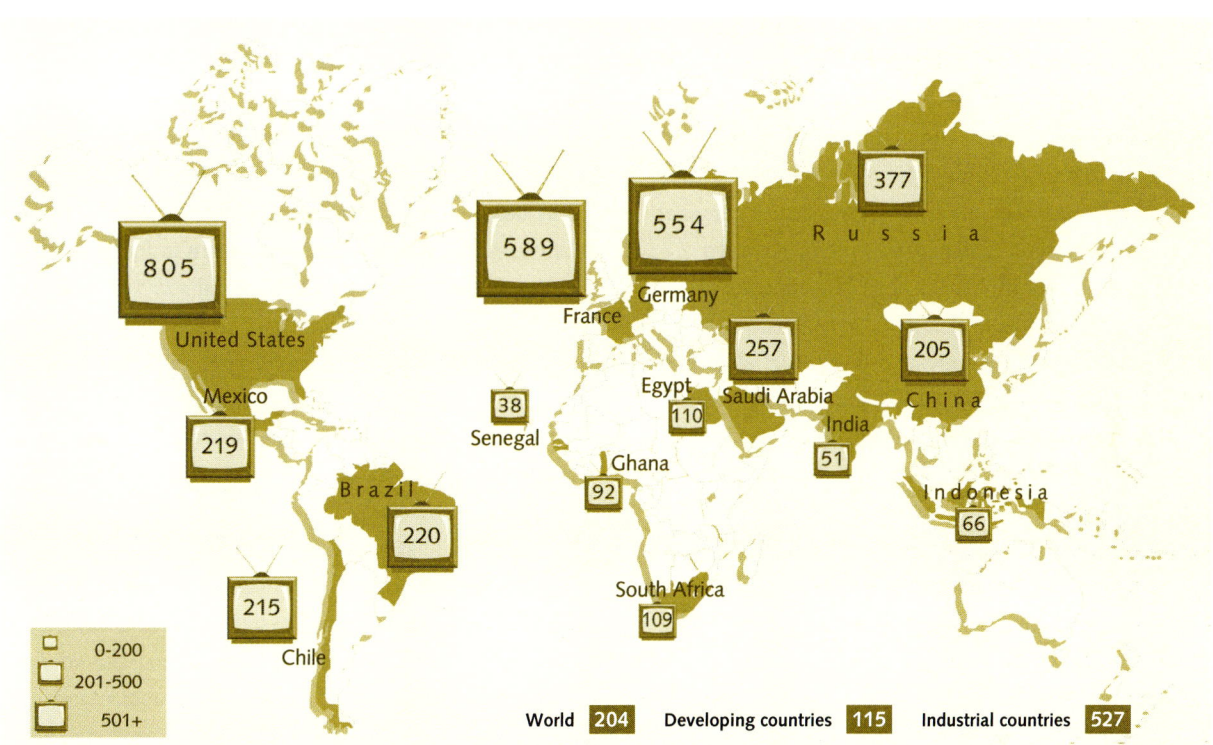

GRAPH 5
TELEVISIONS PER 1,000 PERSONS (1995)
Source: Statistical Table 2 in Part Seven of this report.

Television is increasingly displacing radio as the primary means of receiving information and entertainment, even in developing countries. In 1995 there were 115 televisions and 185 radios for every 1,000 persons in developing countries. In 1980, there were over 16 times more TVs in industrial countries than in developing countries; in 1995, the ratio had fallen to little more than 5.5 times more.

The highest density of TVs is in the United States, i.e. 805 sets per 1,000 persons. Other industrial countries, such as France and Germany, have significantly fewer, and Russia has 377. The increase in TVs has been slow in industrial countries – only 1.7% per annum between 1980 and 1995. Some relatively poor countries, such as China, now have at least 1 TV for every 5 people. In many such countries, TVs are increasing dramatically. Between 1980 and 1995, televisions per person in China increased annually by 145%; in India, by 71%; some countries in sub-Saharan Africa saw comparably high percentage increases: 126% in Ghana and over 200% in Senegal.

developing, with new cultural patterns associated with these globalizing trends. The work culture of this class is cosmopolitan, embedded in the internationalization of cities. One of their multiple identities is 'global', which is in fact a very local and restricted category. They may show a concern with tradition, with identity and with indigenization. As King puts it in reference to architects and urban planners (but it could be generalized to apply to

others), there is a 'thematization and diffusion of "universal" ideas concerning the appropriateness of being unique in a context' (King, 1995, pp. 226–7).

Global norms and forms of institutional, spatial and symbolic signs of the international business class conform in most ways to the norms and forms manifest in the same institutions of the hegemonic states in the world order (United States, Japan, Germany). These spatial signs are the 'landscapes of

Urbanization and globalization

At the beginning of the twentieth century, 150 million people lived in urban settlements, representing less than 10% of the world's population. As the century draws to a close, the world's urban population has increased twentyfold to nearly 3,000 million, i.e. almost half the world's population. Asia accounted for the lion's share (47.5%) of the world's population in 'million' cities and had 143 of such 'million' cities. Asia also has thirteen of the world's twenty-three mega-cities of at least 8 million inhabitants.

Three major urban trends have been observed at the close of the present century. First, contrary to most predictions, population growth rates have slowed down for many cities in developing countries. The largest cities in these countries grew far more slowly in the 1980s than during the previous two decades.

Second, the world is less dominated by very large cities than had been forecast. Less than 5% of the world's population lived in mega-cities in 1990. The prediction that cities such as Calcutta and Mexico City would grow to gigantic conurbations of 30 to 40 million inhabitants has not come true.

Third, the links between urban change and economic, social, political and cultural change are not clear. Some large and rapidly growing cities have been well-managed and serviced, while some of the worst physical conditions have beset small towns.

Several tendencies in shaping the urban future of the third millennium can be discerned. First, the progressive urbanization of the globe is certain. It has been estimated that in the first decade of the twenty-first century more than half the world's population will be living in urban settlements. Second, there will be growing interaction between urbanization and globalization. Globalization is a multifaceted process of drawing countries, cities and people ever closer together through increasing flows of goods, services, capital, technology and ideas. The world cities have come to the fore because they perform special functions in the new global economy. The third characteristic of the urban future is the likely continuing devolution of powers and responsibilities to local authorities and civil society. This process began in the 1990s when traditional modes of urban governance were found wanting and existing institutions could not adequately deal with the old and new urban problems.

In a globalizing world, countries and cities are increasingly linked in interdependent and interlocking relationships. While world cities are important in their own right in a world order in which national boundaries fail to stop cross-border flows of capital, people and ideas, subregional economic entities have emerged. Called 'growth triangles', some neighbouring territories involving several countries have sought creative economic co-operative development. Examples of successful growth triangles in Asia are those known as Southern China, with the participation of Hong Kong, Guandong, Fujian and Taiwan, and SIJORI, including Singapore, Johor (Malaysia) and Riau Island (Indonesia). These two growth triangles are centred, respectively, on the world cities of Hong Kong and Singapore. A variant of this theme of subregional development is what some scholars call region-states. They produce sound economic development in some regions that may be parts of a country or may involve several countries.

Another spatial expression of rapid economic development in the global economy are the urban corridors which have been observed in East Asia, Europe and elsewhere.

Globalization has not been a boon to all cities. While it has brought new opportunities and wealth to some cities, it has marginalized others. The marginalized city can be found anywhere in the world, but especially in Africa. It is outside the cyberways, lacks the requisite information infrastructure and is generally not able to plug into the global economy.

Four common features characterize cities in all parts of the world.

First, urban unemployment remains high. This explains the phenomena of 'area boys': unemployed, able-bodied men, sometimes drug-dependent, in Lagos, and 'parking boys', in Nairobi.

Second, urban infrastructure is often inadequately maintained even in developed countries. Water and sewer systems fail in Chicago and Washington, and electricity on the Eastern seaboard. In developing countries the problems are often much worse. Poor infrastructure has led to problems in water supply, urban sanitation and transport. The urban poor suffer most.

Third, environmental problems, especially air, water and noise pollution have grown in many cities of the developing world.

Fourth, growing social conflicts, such as homelessness and crime, plague many cities. These are the result partly of growing competition for jobs and partly of the freer movement of people.

In the next century, the relevant unit of economic production, social organization and knowledge generation will be the city. World cities will be especially influential in shaping the development of the global economy. Technological advances and easy access to information will enable cities to evolve more efficient ways of production, capitalizing on the cheapest sources of materials.

In the information age that has just begun, cities act as generators, processors and depositories of knowledge. Knowledge is generated by research, discovery and innovation. As knowledge is a highly valued resource, cities will be in competition to generate knowledge. The knowledge industry, science parks, technological development zones, technopolies and others will be further developed in the cities of the future.

Cities of the future will have more freedom. Greater freedom will be enjoyed by individuals and institutions because they will be networked electronically. Wired interactions will supplement face-to-face contacts. This will affect urban lifestyles as people can work at home, shop by computers and travel with credit cards. The clamour for greater participation and democracy will see more attention and resources devoted to non-governmental, community-based organizations. Cities of the future will have the opportunity of reorganizing themselves socially and institutionally. With the knowledge and wisdom that humankind has inherited from our ancestors and with new technologies and resources, there is no reason to believe that we are not prepared to face our urban future which is both a daunting challenge and a window of opportunity.

Fu-chen Lo
Economist; Deputy Director, Institute of Advanced Studies,
United Nations University, Tokyo (Japan)

Yue-Man Yeung
Geographer and Asian Cities Specialist;
Professor of Geography, Chinese University of Hong Kong,
and Director, Hong Kong Institute of Asia-Pacific Studies
(China)

power' (Zukin, 1991), reproducing transnational symbolic forms and styles, often designed by the same international architects, furniture and appliance designers, and fashion trends (King, 1995, pp. 225–6). In terms of lifestyle, the new social aesthetic in everyday life linked to higher income implies a 'new vision of good life. Hence the importance, not just of food but of cuisine, not just of clothes but of designer labels, not just of decoration but of authentic objets d'art' (Sassen, 1991, p. 335). Cosmopolitanism implies the idea of de-territorialization, not only of international capital but of ethnic groups and political forms transcending territorial boundaries and identities (Appadurai, 1990).

What happens with the rest of the social structure? Are middle and working classes also globalized in the same sense? The changes in the global economy, including increasing flexibility in patterns of capital accumulation imply changes in the structure of the labour market and in the organization of production (Harvey, 1993). There are new forms of industrial organization, as well as the return of older forms of subcontracting and informal work. Yet, these patterns of organization have very different meanings in different places, and may intensify the segmentation of the labour market. They constitute subordinate forms of integration of populations into the process of globalization – through employment in global industries and through migrant labour. Seen from the top, these labour conditions imply 'flexibilization' of labour markets. From the bottom, they are experienced as uncertainty in lifestyle and life chances. Integration into the global economy for these workers is not accomplished through the use and consumption of global technology, but rather through putting together the chips that will allow the informational globalization of the others. At times, they involve strategies of survival of the unemployed or peoples discriminated against (e.g. Haitians in New York), while at other times they are mostly new immigrant

groups, trying to enter the capitalist system or to evade taxes. As will be discussed below, these patterns usually involve the reinforcing or even the recreation of ethnic lines.

This 'double bind' of globalization is what Castells (1995) discusses as the 'informational city': an interconnected world, where societies and spaces relate to each other through new networks of communication. The space of flux of capital and of the transnational business class coexists with the space of the experience of daily life for the majority of the people. This second space is each time more local, more territorial, more tied to an identity, a neighbourhood, an ethnicity or a nation. While the space for identity is each time more local, the space for function is each time more global. These processes imply the existence of a 'dual city', with contrasting social and economic structures. Structural dualism pervades a series of areas or dimensions: growth in information, industrial decline, degradation and requalification of the labour force, differentiation between formal and informal labour – all these produce different lifestyles, different patterns of family life, different uses of the urban space. However, it does not produce two different social worlds; rather a variety of social universes, fragmented and with no clear definition of boundaries, but with little communication between them.

At the higher end of the social scale, there is a connection with global communication . . . At the other extreme, local segmented networks, often ethnically defined, use their ethnicity as their most valued resource to defend their interests and their very being . . . This leads to socially discriminated, territorially segregated and culturally segmented communities . . . (Castells, 1995, p. 321)

This perspective of the world economy and of the process of globalization leads towards spatial differentiation, towards dualisms and fragmentation, diversity within and among cities in the world, but with some principles of order: a global capitalistic

system, a global hierarchy of power and control. Diversity is not chaos: there are power relations that transcend nation-states and territorial units; there is a 'geography of cultures', grounded in historical traditions and local identities. The current historical challenge is not to allow this diversity to degenerate into tribalization, fragmentation and xenophobia.

Cities in history

Aksum (in northern Ethiopia) was established in the first century A.D., and was linked to commerce in the Roman world, with a port on the Red Sea (Adulis). Conversion of its kings to Christianity (fourth century) brought the city and its cultural elites into the European world (with translations of the Bible and of literary works from Greek, Arabic and Syriac into Ge'ez). (Gugler, 1996, p. 214)

Spain imagined its colonial empire as a network of cities. . . . From its very inception, the city already had this role assigned to it. Establishing a city, more than just erecting a physical city, meant creating a society. And that compact, homogeneous and militant society had to produce its surrounding reality, matching its elements – natural and social, indigenous and exogenous – to those of the pre-established design, forcing and limiting them wherever necessary. . . . The network of cities had to create a Hispanic, European and Catholic America; but above all, it had to create a colonial empire in the strict sense of the term, that is, a dependent and expressionless world, a periphery of the metropolitan world, which it had to reflect and follow in all its actions and reactions. (Romero, 1976, pp. 9–14)

In a historical perspective, internationalization and globalization are not new phenomena in the world. Neither is their link to cities and urban settlements. Cities were established at crossroads of long-distance trade, especially where trade arrived after having crossed a major obstacle – the sea, deserts or mountain ranges. They derived their power and resources from control over long-distance trade and from control over production processes for that trade. The arrival of European traders in other parts of the world led to the development of ports, and

allowed coastal states to control production for trade. Both the control of trade routes (the silk route in Asia, for instance) and colonial rule were urban-based, setting the patterns for the development of different urban systems, linked from their inception to international phenomena.

In the first place, urban life emerged in the world with commerce and exchange, from local market places linking cities with their immediate hinterlands to world trade centres managing the world distribution of some goods. Second, cities were always the sites of government and power. The imperial cities, East and West, with their palaces, courts and sponsorship of artistic developments, could only exist on the shoulders of bureaucratic structures and administrative sites geared to collect the taxes needed to support city life and imperial splendour. Third, cities were also the places of freedom, where people could escape personal bondage and feudal attachments and (according to historical circumstances) slavery and serfdom. Cities are, after all, the cradle of citizenship, of autonomous individuals bearing rights and duties to each other and to the legitimate state authorities. Armies and conquest were always part of the story: fortified citadels to defend the locality from invaders; armies accompanying the tax collectors in the hinterlands and in the subjugated cities. Often, demands of religious hegemony and conversion were the fellow travellers of invading armies.

Economics, politics, culture (including religion) and force have been the ingredients of the emergence and transformation of cities and systems of cities, and some patterns show the strength of historical continuity.

Amidst rapid economic, social, political and demographic change, there are some elements of continuity in settlements. The average size of the world's largest cities may have changed enormously but their location has changed much less. For instance, in most of the world's regions, there is a perhaps surprising continuity in the list of the largest cities and metropolitan areas; more than

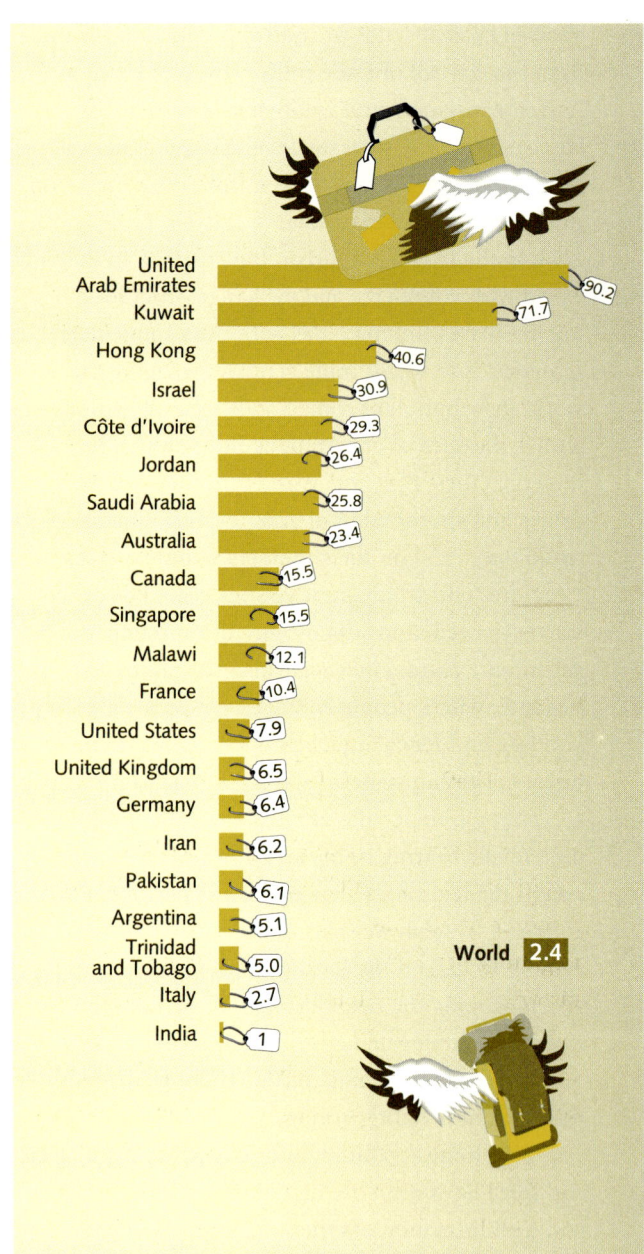

United Arab Emirates — 90.2
Kuwait — 71.7
Hong Kong — 40.6
Israel — 30.9
Côte d'Ivoire — 29.3
Jordan — 26.4
Saudi Arabia — 25.8
Australia — 23.4
Canada — 15.5
Singapore — 15.5
Malawi — 12.1
France — 10.4
United States — 7.9
United Kingdom — 6.5
Germany — 6.4
Iran — 6.2
Pakistan — 6.1
Argentina — 5.1
Trinidad and Tobago — 5.0
Italy — 2.7
India — 1

World 2.4

GRAPH 6
INTERNATIONAL MIGRANTS: PERCENTAGE OF TOTAL POPULATION (1990)

Source: Statistical Table 26 in Part Seven of this report.

Between the middle of the nineteenth century and the start of the Second World War, about 60 million people moved overseas from Europe – 40 million to the United States alone. Until 1914, governments imposed almost no controls on migration. Between 1914 and 1945, however, migration was discouraged, principally for security reasons. After the war, migration rose again because of labour shortages in Europe and elsewhere. But with recession in the 1970s, restrictions were again tightened and continue to be applied. Migration has slowed appreciably in the 1990s.

Nevertheless, international migrants are a large share of the total population in many countries. In Australia, for instance, this share is over 23%, and in Canada over 15%. In other industrial countries, the shares are lower: about 6% in Germany and the United Kingdom, for example. In the United States, the largest recipient of migrants, the percentage is about 8%.

A number of developing countries are host to a large number of migrants. This is especially true of the Arab States because of their labour shortages: in Kuwait international migrants make up almost three-quarters of the population, and in Jordan and Saudi Arabia about 26%. There are also large proportions of migrants in a number of countries in sub-Saharan Africa. In Côte d'Ivoire, the largest recipient in the continent, the share is about 29%, and in Malawi about 12%.

Many of the migrants are motivated to move for economic reasons. The falling cost of travel facilitates their movement. Migration should be viewed positively, not only economically but also as a basis for cultural interaction and interchange. However, the reality that migrants often face is resentment from native-born populations – supposedly for taking their jobs – and discrimination.

two-thirds of the world's 'million-cities' in 1990 were already important cities 200 years ago while around a quarter have been important cities for at least 500 years. (UNCHS, 1996, pp. 13–14)

The effects of economic, political and demographic forces have always been dependent on the development of communications and transport technologies. Whatever side one takes in the debate as to whether we are living through a unique period of globalization or whether there were times when global integration (both economically and politically) was more intense than now, there is no doubt that the technological revolution in communications and transport changes the nature of the phenomenon. In fact, as the pace of communications and transport hastened, space and distance became less central, and cities could grow. Nowadays, when face-to-face communications can be replaced by electronics, will spatial location lose its significance altogether?

People and flows: migration, ethnicity, identities

Movements of people to cities, be it from other places of the same country (internal migration) or from other countries (international migration), has been a constant feature of urban history.

People move in the search for better employment opportunities, for more and better services, for the 'push' factors implied in a worsening of rural conditions in large parts of the world (Africa south of the Sahara, especially). Studies show that there is a growing flow of female rural-to-urban migration, especially young women who migrate to enter the labour force as domestic servants (a trend that was common in Latin America a few decades ago and that is becoming more dominant in Africa and parts of Asia). In areas where Islam is the dominant religion, women tend to migrate as part of their family role, i.e. following their husbands. In general, decisions to migrate are the result of a more complex set of circumstances among women than

men, including economic reasons (a growing trend), family duties, and the search for personal autonomy and greater opportunities, including education (FNUAP, 1996).

International migration also influences the process of urbanization and city growth. To the factors affecting internal migration should be added migration for political reasons, and the difficulties that migratory regulations may imply for exit and entry into specific countries. It is quite clear that international migration is part of the process of the globalization of labour markets. It is also quite clear that the movement is much more open and much more free for capital and for goods than for labour, where protectionist policies are widespread, and barriers to immigration are on the rise (Bhabha, 1997).

Migration and the transformation of territorial bonds

Migratory flows have been highly significant in history.

The slave trade and European settlers in the Americas, Indian and Chinese merchants and bonded labourers in various parts of the world, and migratory flows of all sorts, have produced the historical accumulation of layers of immigrants, creating a tradition of migrant communities in cities, with varying degrees and diverse styles of integration and segregation in the host communities. There is a wide variation in the composition of migrant communities, in their relationships to the communities of residence and to the countries of origin. All these change according to the meanings that migration has for different cultural groups and to the changes in the cost-benefit balances which come into effect (transportation is now easier and faster, while rules and regulations may be making immigration more difficult). In fact, international migration has never been synonymous with a 'melting pot'. There have been histories of assimilation – in ideology and in practice (Todd,

1996) and histories of segregation, discrimination and genocide.

Seen 'from below', that is, from the perspective of the migrants, networks and circuits in which transnational migrants and refugees are implicated constitute transnational or globalized social spaces. In these spaces, transnational forms of political organization, mobilization and practice are coming into being (Smith, 1995, p. 249). It is a form of 'transnational grassroots politics', a counterpart of the new 'global entrepreneurial class', transcending both the urban level of analysis and the reference to the nation-state.

This type of politics has strong historical and traditional roots. Internationalist ideologies – socialism and communism, international workers' organizations and various forms of grassroots Christianity and other religious movements – have travelled across continents and transcended national boundaries since time immemorial. Independence fighters in colonial times and political exiles all through history were often trained and retrained among the progressive elites in the centre, to return then to their home countries with new messages and new political strategies. In so far as movement is easier and communications are instantaneous, the spatial extension of households and ethnic communities across national borders is producing new patterns of cultural and political action and resistance by transnational migrants and refugees, who in some ways partake of two nation-states, while in other ways they may be moving beyond both. These are communities that have a 'bifocal imagination', not tied to one single territory, but rather in a constant state of drawing and redrawing images and identities for themselves (Appadurai, 1996).

With new means of communications, film, television and video bring powerful images of possible future lives into villages, besides the traditional tales of homecoming migrants (Appadurai, 1996). The imagined and talked-about possible world may lead to further migration – one significant way to deal with increasing poverty and worldwide inequality ('Fantasy is now a social practice'). Whether dreams and expectations will be fulfilled, however, is always an open question, full of uncertainties. Human mobility offers the possibility to act out these fantasies peacefully and as an assertion of the positive side of the human condition. They may also have their dark side:

In 'Who Are the "Good Guys"?' (Smith and Tarallo, 1995), the role of global fantasies in the form of images of power, wealth and violence appropriated from Kung Fu movies was played out in the 'representations of self' and in the demands made by four young Vietnamese hostage-takers in a Good Guys electronics store in Sacramento, California, before several hostages were shot and three of the refugee youths were killed by a county sheriff's department SWAT team while acting out their global fantasies. One of the demands of these youths, who were small children when Saigon fell in 1975, was for a helicopter to allow them to fly to Vietnam to fight communists. (Smith, 1995, p. 254)

Processes of maintaining, restoring and reinventing cultural and ethnic identities are open. Diversity and heterogeneity are the rule. There are cases where the 'there' (from where one comes) exists as a possibility for returning, or even for visiting, and cases where these possibilities are non-existent. At times, migrants spread and disperse themselves in the cities in which they live; in others, processes of re-territorialization take place, in the form of ethnic neighbourhoods and streets (the 'Little . . .' and the 'Chinatowns' of the major cities of the world). There may be struggles – at times violent – to recapture spatial territories, and symbolic struggles to assert cultural identities. Circular migrants who move back and forth (between Mexico and the United States, for instance) create new social spaces for identity formation and the production of meaningful social action in their multiple territorial anchorages. There are also cases of movements that use global resources for their local politics, including international issue

networks (Sikkink, 1996) and the confluence of various movements and identities in one single place (Smith, 1995, pp. 258–63).

Multiculturality and ethnicity

The degree of multiculturality in world cities varies, with long-term historical processes of cultural contact and struggles as a background to current reality. Demographically, in most cities there is a numerically dominant population from the host society, which at times is multicultural itself, and a usually highly heterogeneous 'foreign born' (and of foreign descent) population, coming from a variety of ethnicities, religions and cultures and arriving in different historical circumstances. To understand degrees of heterogeneity and variation among cities, one has to draw on the political economic frame of world-systems and on the culturally oriented frame of globalization. Longer-term historical processes and political frames of post-colonialism and post-imperialism are also crucial for understanding social and cultural phenomena in cities.

The political dynamics and changes in labour-market conditions may intensify cultural pressures to maintain and recreate ethnicity – or even to create one if needed. Thus, in Pakistan, where provincial 'nationalisms' offer to local populations an array of intermediate institutions, the numerically small but politically and economically visible group of people who had migrated into Sindh province after partition, excluded from claiming such provincial identity, started to construct a new sense of 'nationality' on the sole basis that their parents had been immigrants. With no shared language or ethnic affiliation, these youngsters speak of the *mohajir* nation (*mohajir* is the Urdu word for migrant). The political party representing their interests ends up filling the gap between the state and a dislocated immigrant community that does not have a coherent tradition to refer to (Shaheed, 1995; World Commission on Culture and Development, 1995, p. 56). In Mexico City, a new cultural development

involves the *concheros*, groups of young urban residents who devote themselves to music and dance based on pre-Columbian practices and names.

Ethnicities and diversity leave their marks on urban space. Yet, 'the public display of individual or collective cultural identities through the use of distinctive building types, shapes, forms, construction materials, methods, colors, finishes, and qualities has . . . differential impact on cities' (King, 1995, p. 224). When there is a dominant spatial culture, such as the grid in New York City, the impact of cultural diversity is less than in other cities, like Bombay or Delhi, that have a much wider variety of historically and culturally constructed physical and spatial environments (King, 1995, p. 224). Even the same spatial layout, like the grid with the main plaza in Latin America, may reflect different combinations of indigenous and European cultural models and meanings (Low, 1993).

New waves of foreign immigrants in large cities may appropriate working-class vernacular housing, transforming it into the 'vernacular' of the newcomers, adapting housing and community public spaces to their cultural preferences, their kinship structures, their religious institutions and their aesthetical styles. In this way, a statement about symbolic cultural identity is being made. This is the case, for instance, with the Portuguese in Toronto, Puerto Ricans in New York, and Bangladeshis in London (King, 1995, p. 226). In this context, the current wave of 'the politics of identity' gives new meaning to cultural diversity, which tends to become the currency for exchange. There is re-territorialization in ethnic neighbourhoods with their symbolic places and institutions. The notion of frontier reappears inside the city, in so far as the multiplication of ethnic identifications becomes enmeshed in the multiplicity of territories, in social inequality and in differential access to urban services. 'Here' and 'there' become highly significant, both inside the city, in reference to the 'original' territories, and in the wish to be somewhere else.

The destruction of the Old Bridge of Mostar

In 1993 the Old Bridge of Mostar was deliberately destroyed. Extremists chose not to recognize the beauty and achievement of the bridge as a treasure of the human spirit but rather as a link between the Muslim and Croat communities and a symbol of Bosniac Muslim heritage. The ancient city of Mostar, built entirely of local materials, is outstanding for its housing and monuments assembled harmoniously over the centuries according to geographical and economic circumstances. In the seventeenth century the city contained about 1,000 houses for a population of some 12,000. Mostar is still a hive of arts and crafts and a major trading centre.

The old Mostar bridge (Stari most), one of the last monumental works to be erected under Süleyman the Magnificent, was built in 1566 by Mimar Hajruddin, a pupil of the renowned Ottoman architect Sinan. Prior to its destruction by artillery in November 1993, it consisted of a graceful hump-backed arch with an opening of 28 metres, being 30 metres long and 4 metres wide. At low water the structure stood fully 20 metres above the Neretva. This crossing-point between east and west in the old city was flanked by two fortified towers, i.e. the Halebija on the right bank and the Tara on the left, both erected in the seventeenth century under Ottoman rule. From the time of its construction and in view of its original single vaulting, it was regarded as a masterpiece of art and architecture.

This unique work of art inspired poets and never failed to impress travellers. In the second half of the sixteenth century a Mostar poet compared the arch across the river to a rainbow. A French visitor in 1658 regarded the construction as a miracle, and as more daring and impressive than the Rialto in Venice. An Austrian author wrote at the beginning of this century that if he had to choose the most beautiful bridge in the world, he would name the ancient Mostar bridge without hesitation.

Prior to the Austro-Hungarian occupation of Bosnia and Herzegovina (1878), a whole wealth of tradition attaching to Bosniac Muslim culture was associated with the bridge. The memorable call to prayer was made by the muezzin from the top of the tower at the left-bank end of the bridge. The other tower contained a spacious room which provided a salon for the more cultured of the Mostar citizens: this is still so fresh in people's memories that, following the civil war, it has now been reopened as a café in an attempt to recapture some of the gaiety of the past. When the weather was good and

There is a re-territorialization brought about by de-territorialization. Displacement gives rise to new meanings attached to urban territories, and also to other cultural creations such as movies, theatre and literature. These cultural dynamics may lead to the emergence of new cultural conflicts, at times violent. At the same time, by providing new contents to artistic forms, they may become commodified in the form of ethnic neighbourhoods, ethnic restaurants, ethnic music, attracting investments from the international business community and international tourism of the new cosmopolitan elite.

In sum, there is a simultaneous growth of a mass culture through the media and the flourishing of ethnic cultures. These two aspects of cultural transformations of cities are part of wider processes of construction of identities based on differential access to, and consumption of, symbolic goods – both local and global. How do the two relate to one another? Some claim that cultural differences 'persist' because different groups receive and process mass media and cultural industry products from the perspective of their own identities. Also, because there is a diversification of supply of symbolic goods, generating new cultural differences, although within the homogenized communicational framework

particularly during Muslim feasts, young people and children used to love diving from the top of the bridge into the waters of the Neretva. This daring tradition was restored in 1995.

However, the fact that the former communist regime regarded Bosniac Muslims as an ethnic group in the same way as the Serbs and Croats only made the eternal 'Balkan problem' even worse. Although they were very largely Slav in origin and language and were converted to Islam in the fifteenth century – a mass conversion that historians attribute in particular to the persecution endured by the Bogomils, a Christian dualist sect held in contempt by both the Orthodox Serb and Croat Catholic Churches – the Bosniac Muslims were regarded none the less by extremists of every hue as having been assimilated.

Such extremists wished to retain nothing of the economic and urban expansion of Mostar which was the fruit of efforts made during the Ottoman period (fifteenth to nineteenth century). In fact they regarded both religious monuments (mosques, madrasas and mausoleums) and civil ones (hammams, souks and bridges) as evidence of foreign occupation and culture.

The Old Bridge was the most famous of all such monuments and among the main features of the Ottoman city. It was tragically marked down for destruction as the locality's chief symbol – the symbol of a culture and of a blend of cultures – although it was no longer of any economic or strategic importance. It is conceivable too that this symbol was amplified by the image – raised to the status of a myth at the gates of Western Europe – of a city with oriental overtones and which was much vaunted to tourists and universally admired by them at a time when tourism in former Yugoslavia prospered under Marshal Tito.

The Old Bridge was destroyed, not for military reasons, but to obliterate people's cultural roots. The highly symbolic sense of the destruction of the Old Bridge lies not only in the fact that it constituted a physical linkage beween two communities and, through these, between two cultural and historical references, the East and the West: the bridge actually represented, in the fullest sense, the connection that today's communities still maintained with a period when, despite their diversity, they had a common past.

Azzeddine Beschaouch
Archaeologist and historian of Classical Antiquity;
Chargé de Mission, Culture Sector, UNESCO,
Member of the Institut (Académie des Inscriptions
et Belles-Lettres, Paris (France))

determined by technology – TV and satellite communications – that, in the end, organize social relations around the world in a homogeneous way.[2] Diversity can also be seen as a consequence of the practices of resistance on the part of subordinate classes (Scott, 1992). There are forces towards heterogeneity within the very logic of capitalist transformation. The key issue is to look at the inherent tensions of the processes of differentiation and homogenization, rather than trying to find indicators that would show that the balance is tipped in one or other direction.

The celebration of diversity and policies of multiculturalism cannot answer the question about the practical meaning of these ethnic identifications. The vast majority of unskilled workers share an excluded social space, highly fragmented in terms of ethnicity, building defensive communities that struggle against each other to gain a larger share of services and to preserve the functional basis of their social networks – a significant resource in low-income communities (Castells, 1995, p. 320). Economic restructuring leads to the configuration of a series of socially discriminated communities, territorially segregated and culturally segmented, that cannot constitute a class because of the extremely high diversity in the evolving relations of production. It seems to be easier to develop fundamentalist (tribal-like) affirmations of identity, culturally and territorially defensive, protective and limited, than to engage in open conflict with the powerful, whose power is expressed in domination through flows rather than through the control of specific spaces (Castells, 1995). The geography of cultures may then degenerate into tribalization, fragmentation and xenophobia.

Cities are the places of diversity, of encounters with strangers, of recognition of an 'I' distinct from the 'them'. The trend towards globalization, towards an interconnected and interdependent 'one world', implies simultaneously and as part of the same process a reaffirmation of cultural differentiation and of localized and national identities. This is always the case, in so far as the human condition involves a sense of belonging to a political community. In fact, human beings are part of communities, not of the human species in the abstract. What this means is that

there is no other road towards universality besides the one that passes through particularism. Only those who master a specific culture have the opportunity to be understood by the whole of humanity . . . Command of one culture is indispensable for individuals to thrive and flourish: acculturation is possible and at times beneficial; de-culturation is always a threat. (Todorov, 1991, p. 434–5)

Spaces and places

Building a city depends on how people combine the traditional economic factors of land, labour and capital. But it also depends on how they manipulate symbolic languages of exclusion and entitlement. The look and feel of cities reflect decisions about what – and who – should be visible and what should not, on concepts of order and disorder, and on uses of aesthetic power. (Zukin, 1995, p. 7)

Building a city means building spaces of dialogue and interaction, of interdependence, of co-ordination and of power relations. Urban culture is a collective creation. Interaction and encounters are its base, encounters that occur among different people,

among strangers, encounters that take place in 'public'.[3] In so far as globalization processes entail the spread of market relations, the question is who will ensure the vitality of public debate and public dialogue, as conditions for collective creativity and cultural vitality.

The vitality of the public sphere, expressed in the creativity of public spaces, is a converging point of consideration for people from different disciplines and commitments: democratic theory and practice based on public deliberation about the goals and means of society and about the role of the state and the contents of citizenship; the concerns expressed by many (from communications to social policies, from feminism to human rights) about the shifting boundaries between private and public; the constant redefinition of the realm of public goods, the responsibilities for the global commons and for collective services, so much influenced by the push towards 'privatization'. More specifically, urban planners and local authorities, concerned with their ability to shape (literally and metaphorically) public spaces and public activities.

There are many examples of local activities and policies geared to foster this vitality. Fiestas and ethnic festivals in cities are not a new phenomenon. Since flows of migration began, ethnic groups have maintained their ties to their origin through two types of rituals: going back to their communities for the ritual festivals and occasions; introducing urban-based festivals that recreate their ethnic identification. Urban festivals of minority groups, however, are not a simple reproduction of what went on before in their communities. They have new contents and new meanings. They express diversity in the large cities; they also are a message directed to the 'others', mainly to the dominant culture from which the group feels estranged.

For more than twenty years, each October, Bolivians in Buenos Aires have been celebrating the Fiesta de Nuestra Señora de Copacabana. The day of the Fiesta, about ten thousand people, coming from different parts of the city,

concentrate in a neighborhood where Bolivians have been a majority for over thirty years. In the morning, there is Mass in the Nuestra Señora de Copacabana church, and then small rockets go up in the sky, carrying Bolivian, Argentine and Vatican flags. There is a procession, and then dances (around thirty-five different groups) representing different historical moments and diverse ethnic, class and regional origins. The Fiesta is an occasion for cultural identification in the urban scene, expanding each year, and attracting increasingly Argentine visitors. It is not the conservation of an ancestral past but the staging of the lived relationship between that history and the migratory present. It is a way to relate to the dominant society, an act of affirmation of a visible presence in the city, counteracting the daily experience of discrimination, stigma and invisibility. What makes this Fiesta especially interesting is that the Virgin of Copacabana has been designated as the 'patron of Bolivian immigrants to Argentina'. Yet there is no 'national' patron Virgin in Bolivia. Actually, multiculturalism and ethnic pluralism are defining traits of Bolivian society, and this diversity is also present among the migrants. As with the dances, the surrounding Fair offers food and crafts typical of a variety of regions of Bolivia. What is not conceived and perceived as a unity in the country of origin (it is not easy to imagine 'Bolivianness'), is culturally constructed 2,000 kilometers away, in Buenos Aires. (Grimson, 1997)

What begins as an in-group activity – the fiesta as an affirmation of cultural identity, restaurants, groceries and neighbourhoods as tools to maintain and carry on daily patterns of living – can easily turn into something different: attracting outsiders as 'customers of ethnic difference', 'invading' other parts of the city to assert more firmly the presence and visibility of the group. Based on celebrating difference, be it ethnic or other (including newer cultural identifications such as gender, sexual orientation and others), there are a great number of events that combine private profit enterprises, community organizations and city government sponsorship. Fifth Avenue in Manhattan is now the scene of a growing number of parades, with growing numbers of people participating in them. And the

gay parade in Sydney has become a major tourist attraction in the Pacific region.

Urban violence: a cultural phenomenon?

It is not the city that generates violence: poverty, political and social exclusion, and economic deprivation are all working against the solidarity that would enable city inhabitants to live together peacefully despite their conflicts. (Pinheiro, 1993)

Data indicate that at least once every five years, more than half of the world's population living in cities are victims of a crime of some kind. The most common one is crime against property (UNCHS, 1996, p. 123). Yet, urban violence (including murder, assault, rape and domestic violence) is on the increase throughout the world, with large variations according to regions. It is lowest in Asia and highest in Africa and in some parts of the Americas.

Urban violence is the result of many factors: inadequate incomes, overcrowded housing, insecure tenure and lack of social support that generates conditions of exclusion and tension. The attraction of goods continuously on display and the ostentatious display of luxury generate frustration. There is also the anger generated by oppression in all its forms, including the destruction and debasement of cultural identities, racism and discrimination. On the other hand, guns are increasingly easy to obtain, there is violence on television, and there is drug trafficking: they too generate violence. Beyond these factors that are usually mentioned and analysed in the literature, there is a highly significant effect of the nature and quality of street life, including the physical design of housing areas, informal supervision of public areas, and a clear visual definition as to who has the right to use it and is responsible for its maintenance (UNCHS, 1996, p. 125).

The levels of urban crime, both against property and people, are bringing about changes in the spatial arrangements of cities, increasing social and spatial segregation. There is a new economics of privatized security and a new 'aesthetic of fear'. For example, during the early period of growth of São Paulo (1890–1940), there was considerable urban concentration. Social heterogeneity, discrimination and segregation were based on housing type, with moral concerns about hygiene and illness (one new middle-class neighbourhood was called Higienópolis). Cleaning up the centre of the city implied pushing working classes to the periphery. The next stage (1940–80) brought about a clear centre–periphery differentiation: spatial segregation of rich (in the well-serviced centre) and poor (in the outskirts) coupled with some movements to improve living conditions in the periphery. The 1980s witnessed economic recession, an increase in violent crime and fear, bringing about a new model of segregation based on the notion of security.

From 1980 to 1987, 217 buildings were constructed in Morumbi [a rich area of São Paulo], corresponding to 49,972 units, mostly luxury. However, the novelty there is not only the volume of construction, but more importantly the type of buildings. Most of them are residential complexes of either houses or high-rises called 'closed condominiums'. They offer the amenities of a club, are always walled, have as one of their basic features the use of the most sophisticated security technology, with the continual presence of private guards. Moreover, because they were competing in a restricted market, the developers used their imagination to endow each apartment complex with 'distinguishable' characteristics: in addition to imposing architecture and foreign names with an aristocratic touch, they have exotic features such as one swimming pool per individual apartment, three maid's bedrooms, waiting rooms for drivers in the basement, special rooms for storing crystals, and so on. All this luxury contrasts with the view from the apartments' windows: the thousands of shacks of the *favelas* on the other side of the high walls which supply the domestic servants for the condominiums nearby. (Caldeira, 1996, p. 63)

Fear of crime is helping to create distance and separation among social groups. At one level, the fear of violence and crime is associated with the 'talk of crime' (commentaries, narratives, jokes) which contributes both to counteract and to magnify violence. It establishes polarities (good versus evil) emphasizing prejudices, creating a distance and excluding whatever is different. At another level, people's reaction to the increase of fear, in a context in which the institutions of order become violent themselves and are perceived to be unreliable, is to adopt private means of security, such as hiring private security guards, adopting new surveillance technology and supporting vigilante operations. Streets are empty, not for walking. Encounters in public areas become increasingly tense and even violent because they are framed by people's fears and stereotypes. Tension, discrimination and suspicion are the new marks of public intercourse.

As the spaces for the rich face inwards (not only their homes but also office and shopping complexes), the outside space is left for those who cannot afford to go in. The modern public space of the streets is increasingly the area abandoned to the homeless and the street children. Contrary to the modern public space constituted in accordance with ideals of equality, commonality and the reference to a notion of universality, the new public space which is being formed in São Paulo is structured on the basis of principles of separateness, and an emphasis on irreconcilable differences (Caldeira, 1996, p. 65).

São Paulo is not alone in this pattern. In the United States, there is a real threat to public culture coming from the 'politics of everyday fear'. The modern egalitarian principle of open access is destroyed. Common popular answers include a call to 'get tough with crime', and a growing privatization and militarization of public space. Currently, private security firms exceed in employment the public law-enforcement agencies. In California, there are 3.9 private security employees for every public security employee. Also, as a feature of the shift towards privatization, partnerships between private and

public security are growing significantly, including 'private' patrolling of public parks (Zukin, 1995).

There are informal etiquettes for survival in public spaces, including 'street-wise' scrutiny of passers-by. Ethnicity – a cultural strategy for producing difference – survives on the politics of fear, by requiring people to keep their distance from certain aesthetic markers. These markers vary over time. Like fear itself, ethnicity and race become an aesthetic category, in a move that identifies body and moral soul, skin colour and the forms adopted by cultural life (Todorov, 1989).

Public policy:
towards new partnerships

Cities have been blamed for many evils and hardships in human life. There are also blessings, advantages and assets in city life. The challenge is to act so as to eliminate evils and enjoy the assets. Who is to act? How?

Three urban and political processes come together in Barcelona: the democratization of municipal government, the physical transformation of the city and the formulation of a city project that meets with the broad approval of civil society. . . . Geographical decentralization through the creation of districts was undoubtedly the most important political act of the early years of municipal democracy, together with the urban policy of creating public spaces and amenities in all barrios. . . . The democratic city government quickly made a special effort to restore or create an attractive urban environment by many different means: improving the city's appearance and security, creating small parks wherever possible, encouraging neighbourhood and city-wide festivals, reviving traditions (such as processions and carnivals). . . . Cultural projects (such as museums, exhibitions and concerts) and sporting events – later to culminate in the 1992 Olympic Games – constituted a particularly important feature of this policy of integration and promotion. . . . The aesthetic aspect of urban projects . . . fulfil three functions, the first being to give the city, as a whole and at neighbourhood level, a sense of unity. . . . The second function is to demonstrate the quality of public administration. . . . The third

function of urban aesthetics is to bring out the most distinctive and attractive features of the city – an invaluable element in city marketing. . . . The embellishment of a city is not just a good thing: it is a sound investment . . . (Borja, 1996)

The current debate about policy and action is based on a tripartite model: the state, market forces and 'society' (often with the added 'civil', often referred to as 'the third sector'). There is no single formula that will assure success in combining the three actors; the actors themselves are quite different in nature, according to historical, political and economic conditions. And the issues they have to confront and act upon are also diverse. Can anything be said under these conditions?

Current world political and economic conditions have led to a heated debate about the role of governments. The demise of centrally planned economies does not involve the disappearance of governments. The state is the final guarantee of citizenship rights and responsibilities for everybody. For the urban inhabitant, so dependent on public goods, on collective services and collective consumption for everyday life, the quality of city administration and governance are paramount.

Most human activities take place outside the direct realm of government action, although regulated by state norms and institutions. It is the role of the state to provide an 'enabling environment' that supports and encourages the development of multiple forms of human activities, of individuals, households, communities, businesses and voluntary organizations (UNCHS, 1996, p. 424).

The emphasis of 'enabling policies' has received considerable support from the growing recognition that democratic and participatory government structures are not only important goals of development but also important means for achieving such development. Participation and enablement are inseparable since popular priorities and demands will be a major influence on the development of effective and flexible enabling policies. (UNCHS, 1996, p. 424)

A case of local democracy: the 'participatory budget' of Pôrto Alegre (Brazil)

Pôrto Alegre is a large city in southern Brazil (population 3.5 million in the mid-1990s). Like many urban areas of Brazil, during the last decades it has experienced an exponential growth of its population, a significant increase in economic performance and a major change in the organization of everyday life. Since 1989, the city government has developed a very interesting institution, the *orçamento participativo* (participatory budget). It involves a process by which a good part of the municipal budget of each year is decided by bodies that deliberate and discuss, with representation according to city district and to five thematic areas (city planning and urban development; economic development and taxation; education, culture and leisure; health; and transportation). The process is evolving and is gradually altered each year, so that it cannot be said to have a definite and final structure.

The process started in 1989, when the PT and its allies won the municipal elections. The newly elected city government and neighbourhood organizations jointly decided to carry out a survey of urban demands. In the first surveys, the accumulation of societal demands was much greater than the budgetary and administrative capacity of the government. Faced with this hard fact, the city developed a participatory system to set priorities and decide expenditures of a significant proportion of the city budget. The structure involves a Budgetary Council, composed of delegates of each of the sixteen city districts, specialists in five thematic areas, and delegates of some specialized agencies, which bring to the Council the demands of their constituencies, who participate in assemblies to discuss the issues involved. On the basis of a process of negotiation, the Council establishes (and constantly reviews) the criteria for decision-making (evaluating proposals according to priorities given to areas or themes, to the degree of poverty of the city district, to the number of people to be affected, etc.). After several years, the experience is described by actors and observers as a success, a model to be developed in other urban contexts.

Active participation of the citizenry implies recognizing the multiplicity of actors and the web of social and political forces at work, improving the transparency of decisions and the accountability of public officials. Yet no city government by itself, whatever its political commitments, could have achieved what the Pôrto Alegre experience did without counting on societal actors – in this case based on pre-existing but changing neighbourhood organizations. One of the unforeseen features of the process is that, given the discrepancy between pre-existing districts and the spatial scope of neighbourhood organizations, city districts were re-drawn. As a consequence, traditional community leaderships were reshuffled, a feature that turned out to be crucial in the democratization process. Community organizations now gained their legitimacy on the basis of their ability to mobilize and persuade, and not solely on their links to official recognition and political patronage. In the new institutionalized open spaces for debate and decision, a leader has to be able to discuss proposals in open assemblies, and not in the back alleys of traditional power or hidden in the offices of bureaucrats.

What can the presentation of this case show us in more general terms? In the first place, there was a pre-existing experience of neighbourhood organizations that started to press their demands. This was already a step in the direction of empowerment. Second, accountability and transparency of governmental action (in this case, at the city level) are achieved through active participation 'all the way', rather than through centralized decision-making that is then 'monitored' or 'audited' by independent expert bodies. Rather than confront the different actors – political leaders, city officials, experts in urban services, popular movements – the strategy is one of sharing responsibility in decision-making and in the implementation of such decisions. And third, as some authors have claimed (Baierle, 1996), the experience entails the seeds of new ways in which power is instituted and politics is enacted.

Elizabeth Jelin
Sociologist and researcher, Consejo Nacional de Investigaciones Científicas y Técnicas (CONICET) and Faculty of Social Sciences, University of Buenos Aires (Argentina)

Good governance means setting the rules and establishing the spaces where the various demands and interests (often with conflicting goals) can be expressed, and where negotiation and implementation can be accomplished. It does not directly refer to investment capacity, but rather to the capacity to manage change and to set the framework for democratic processes of community-based decision-making.

Cities are growing, and the world population is going to be increasingly concentrated in urban areas. Cities are, therefore, becoming the most important spaces for cultural diversity, cultural contact and cultural creativity. This diversity presents the challenge to find the institutional means to ensure peaceful and democratic interculturality.

Notes

1.   These and the following quantitative data are taken from *World Urbanization Prospects: 1994 Revision*, New York, United Nations, 1995.

2.   In several parts of the world, ethnic minorities and migratory groups are using the new communications technologies — from radio, music CDs and video-clips to Internet — as vehicles for their effort to revitalize or recreate 'traditional' identities.

3.   From a theoretical perspective, a key concept is that of the *public sphere*, the symbolic open arena where people engage in a dialogue and debate about the meaning of their shared life conditions (Calhoun, 1991). Although the concept has strong roots in liberal democracies of the West, it has much wider implications, in so far as it brings into question issues concerning *who* is entitled to discuss and decide *what* is to be discussed and decided in societal collective realms. Issues of citizenship and the contents of rights and duties are at the heart of the matter (Jelin and Hershberg, 1996; Jelin, 1997).

Bibliography

APPADURAI, A. 1990. Disjuncture and Difference in the Global Cultural Economy. In: M. Featherstone (ed.), *Global Culture: Nationalism, Globalization and Modernity.* Newbury Park, Sage.

——. 1996. *Modernity at Large: Cultural Dimensions of Globalization.* Minneapolis, University of Minnesota Press.

BAIERLE, S. G. 1996. *A explosão da experiencia: Emergencia de um novo principio ético-político nos movimentos populares urbanos em Pôrto Alegre.* (Mimeo.)

BHABHA, J. 1997. Enforcing the Human Rights of Citizens and Non-citizens in the Era of Maastricht: Some Reflections of the Importance of States. In: B. Meyer and P. Geschiere (eds.), *Globalization and the Construction of Communal Identities.*

BORJA, J. 1996. The City, Democracy and Governability: The Case of Barcelona. *International Social Science Journal* (Paris, UNESCO), No. 147, March.

CALDEIRA, T. 1996. Building up Walls: The New Pattern of Spatial Segregation in São Paulo. *International Social Science Journal* (Paris, UNESCO), No. 147, March.

CALHOUN, C. 1993. Nationalism and Civil Society: Democracy, Diversity and Self-determination. *International Sociology*, Vol. 8, No. 4, December.

CASTELLS, M. 1995. *La ciudad informacional.* Madrid, Alianza.

GRIMSON, A. 1997. *Relatos de la diferencia y la igualdad: Los bolivianos en Buenos Aires.* Buenos Aires. (Unpublished MS.)

GUGLER, J. 1996. Urbanization in Africa South of the Sahara: New Identities in Conflict. In: J. Gugler (ed.), *The Urban Transformation of the Developing World.* New York, Oxford University Press.

HARVEY, D. 1993. *Condição Pós-moderna.* São Paulo, Edições Loyola,

JELIN, E.; HERSHBERG, E. (eds.). 1996. *Constructing Democracy: Human Rights, Citizenship and Society in Latin America.* Boulder, Westview Press.

KING, A. 1995. Re-presenting World Cities: Cultural Theory/Social Practice. In: P. Knox and P. Taylor (eds.), *World Cities in a World-system.* Cambridge, Cambridge University Press.

LOW, S. M. 1993. Cultural Meaning of the Plaza: The History of Spanish-American Gridplan-Plaza Urban Design. In: R. Rotenberg and G. McDonogh (eds.), *The Cultural Meaning of Urban Space,* Westport, Bergin & Garvey.

PINHEIRO, P. S. 1993. Reflections on Urban Violence. *Urban Age*, Vol. 1, No. 4, Summer.

ROMERO, J. L. 1976. *Latinomérica: Las ciudades y las ideas.* Mexico City, Siglo XXI.

SASSEN, S. 1991. *The Global City: New York, London, Tokyo.* New Jersey, Princeton University Press.

SCOTT, J. C. 1992. *Domination and the Arts of Resistance: Hidden Transcripts.* New Haven, Yale University Press.

SHAHEED, F. 1995. *Parallel and Intermediary Institutions within Nation-States.* (Paper prepared for the World Commission on Culture and Development.)

SIKKINK, K. 1996. The Emergence, Evolution and Effectiveness of the Latin American Human Rights Network. In: E. Jelin and E. Hershberg (eds.), *Constructing Democracy: Human Rights, Citizenship and Society in Latin America.* Boulder, Westview Press.

SMITH, M. 1995. The Disappearance of World Cities and the Globalization of Local Politics. In: P. Knox and P. Taylor (eds.), *World Cities in a World-system.* Cambridge, Cambridge University Press.

SMITH, M.; TARALLO, B. 1995. Who Are the 'Good Guys'? The Social Construction of the Vietnamese 'Other'. In: M. Smith and J. Feagin (eds.), *Bubbling Cauldron: Race, Ethnicity, and the Urban Crisis.* Minneapolis, University of Minesota Press.

TODD, E. 1996. *El destino de los inmigrantes: Asimilación y segregación en las democracias occidentales.* Buenos Aires, Tusquets.

TODOROV, T. 1989. *Cruces de culturas y mestizaje cultural.* Júcar Universidad.

——. 1991. *Nosotros y los otros.* Mexico City, Siglo XXI.

UNCHS (United Nations Centre for Human Settlements). 1995. *An Urbanizing World: Global Report on Human Settlements.*

UNFPA (United Nations Fund for Population Activities). 1996. *The State of World Population.* New York, United Nations.

UNITED NATIONS. 1995. *World Urbanization Prospects: The 1994 Revision.* New York, United Nations.

WORLD COMMISSION ON CULTURE AND DEVELOPMENT. 1995. *Our Creative Diversity: Report of the World Commission on Culture and Development.* Paris, UNESCO.

ZUKIN, S. 1991. *Landscapes of Power: From Detroit to Disney World.* Berkeley and Los Angeles, University of California Press.

——. 1995. *The Cultures of Cities.* Cambridge, Blackwell.

Chapter 8
Culture
and democracy

Adam Przeworski
Political scientist and sociologist; Professor,
Department of Politics, New York University
(United States)
in collaboration with José Antonio Cheibub,
University of Pennsylvania,
and Fernando Limongi,
University of São Paulo (Brazil)

'. . . there is little, if anything, that should lead us to believe that cultural obstacles to democracy are immovable.'

Democracy and a 'democratic culture'

Does democracy have to rely on a 'democratic culture' in order to exist and endure? And, if so, are particular cultural patterns either more or less compatible with such a 'democratic culture' and accordingly conducive or counter to democracy?

In one view, i.e. 'non-culturalist', culture exerts no causal power with regard to democracy. No democratic culture is needed for a country to establish democratic institutions and none to sustain them. In the 'weakly culturalist' view, a democratic culture is required for democracy to emerge or to endure, but the question of the compatibility of this democratic culture with the traditions of particular societies is moot, since these traditions are malleable, subject to being invented and reinvented. Thus, the democratic culture can flourish even in those cultural settings that appear hostile to it. Finally, in the 'strongly culturalist' view, some cultures are simply incompatible with democracy. Different countries, therefore, must seek different political arrangements.

What is thus at stake is whether democratic institutions can function in all cultural environments or whether we must accept that some cultures are compatible only with various forms of authoritarianism.

This is a hard question to answer. It is subject to strongly held conflicting beliefs and the evidence required to adjudicate between them is difficult to come by. All we can do is to reconstruct these rival views and to cite some facts. Our general conclusion is sceptical. We think that economic and institutional factors are sufficient to generate a convincing explanation of the dynamic of democracies without any recourse to culture. And we find empirically that at least the most obvious cultural traits, such as the dominant religion, have little relevance for the emergence and durability of democracies. Hence, while there may be good reasons one should expect cultures to matter, the available empirical evidence provides little support for the view that democracy requires a democratic culture.

We begin with a brief history of culturalist views and then analyse them more systematically. The question here is whether democracy can emerge and endure only if it is supported by some definite cultural patterns. Are some specific aspects of culture necessary for democracy and, if so, which and how? We also develop an explanation that does not rely on culture and show that this explanation is supported by some facts. Later, we ask whether particular cultures can be assessed to be more or less compatible with democracy and then examine empirically whether these cultures, crudely identified in terms of dominant national religions, affect the emergence and the survival of democratic regimes. A discussion of some normative issues closes the chapter.

Is a specific kind of culture, i.e. 'democratic', necessary for democracy to emerge and endure? We first present a historical sketch of positive answers to this question and introduce some distinctions among them. Then we juxtapose these answers to a view that does not rely on culture.

A history of culturalist views

Montesquieu, in *Lettres persanes* (1721) and then in *De l'esprit des lois* (1995 [1748]), was the first to argue that each form of government requires definite cultural patterns to be present if it is to endure and function effectively.[1] Each form has a ruling principle: despotism rests on fear, monarchy on honour, and republic on virtue. These principles are what makes each form of government function ('ce qui le fait agir', *EL*, III, 1).[2] They have to be in turn consistent with other elements of culture. According to Versini (1995, p. 24–5), Montesquieu's list evolved gradually as he was learning about the experience of different countries: in *Pensées* No. 645 of 1737–38, the cultural elements included 'la religion', 'les mœurs et les manières'; in *De l'esprit des lois*, these first (*EL*, XIX, 4) became 'la religion', 'les exemples des choses passées', 'les mœurs', 'les manières', and later on 'la religion des habitants', 'leurs inclinations', 'leurs mœurs', 'leurs manières' and 'des rapports entre elles'. This is an open-ended list: ultimately everything seems to matter, from marital institutions, to celibacy of priests, to religious toleration.

Moreover, the cultural causes are not the only ones: climate is crucial as is the quality of land, size of the territory, and 'commerce' (the economy).

What, then, causes what? Versini (1995, p. 38) claims that 'les causes morales sont finalement "dominantes" dans *De l'esprit des lois*'. But he infers this conclusion only from the final order of topics discussed by Montesquieu, not from any explicit statements to this effect. Montesquieu sometimes uses only the language of compatibility, not of causality, as in 'Quel est le législateur qui pourrait proposer le gouvernement populaire a des peuples pareils?' (*EL*, XIX, 2). Yet, he is looking for 'l'ordre des choses' (*EL*, XIX, 1). Then, a little below, he observes that 'Plusieurs choses gouvernent les hommes . . .' and 'A mesure que, dans chaque nation, une de ces causes agit avec plus de force, les autres lui cédent d'autant' (*EL*, XIX, 4). Throughout he emphasizes that laws educate; they are not just an effect. Hence, neither the causal relations between principles, on the one hand, and cultures, on the other, nor between laws and principles, are obvious.

Montesquieu's comparative study of forms of government – for this is what it was – presage the difficulties culturalist views have had to face ever since. The first one is to identify those features of culture that matter for the form of government. The second is to determine the causal links between the economy, political institutions and culture.

Montesquieu's general hypothesis acquired a developmentalist perspective in the writings of Scottish moral philosophers, who 'transformed Montesquieu's states of society into an elaborate sequence of stages in the historical development of civil society in order to account for the process for which a new word had to be coined, namely, civilization' (Collini, Winch and Burrow, 1983, p. 18). The twist they gave was to think of cultures as progressing from primitive to civilized and to claim that some forms of political life can be sustained only among the latter. Political institutions, in their view, could not be simply invented *ab ovo*, introduced by design, but had to correspond to feelings of sympathy, habits of sociability and deference and a learned sense of public utility.

This issue – 'To What Extent Forms of Government are a Matter of Choice' – gave the title to the first chapter of J. S. Mill's *Considerations on Representative Government* (1991 [1861]). Mill did believe that some cultural patterns are incompatible with democracy: 'A rude people, though in some degree alive to the benefits of civilized society, may be unable to practice the forbearances which it demands; their passions may be too violent, or their personal pride too exacting, to forego private conflict, and leave to the laws the avenging of their real or supposed wrongs' (p. 15). People may find the representative form of government repugnant, they may desire it but be unwilling or unable to fulfil its conditions, or may be technologically unprepared to exercise it. Yet Mill (pp. 18–19) insisted that these conditions are malleable: 'These alleged requisites of political institutions are merely facilities for realizing the three conditions . . . it is an exaggeration to elevate these mere aids and facilities into necessary conditions. People are more easily induced to do, and do more easily, what they are already used to; but people also learn to do things new to them.' People may be unprepared for democracy but they can be taught to behave as democrats.

The complicated issue is the direction and the chain of causality. To the extent to which they distinguished technology, wealth and culture understood as beliefs and habits, and culture understood as appreciation of ideas and symbols, most developmentalist views, from Adam Smith (Winch, 1978, Chap. 3), through most stage theories (Comte, Maine, the Cambridge 'comparative politics' school, Toennies and Durkheim to cite just some), to the contemporary modernization theory, were ambivalent about the chain of causality that moved civilizations from one stage to the next. Was it material progress that drove culture and political institutions, or cultural transformations that advanced material progress and forms of government?

The modern attempt to resolve these issues was the book by Almond and Verba (1965 [1963]), which also ushered in a new methodology. Almond and Verba began by observing that while technological aspects of Western culture were easy to diffuse to the new nations, Western political culture was less apparently transmittable. And there is a causal relation between culture and democracy: 'If the democratic model of the participatory state is to develop in these new nations, it will require more than the formal institutions of democracy. . . . A democratic form of participatory political system requires as well a political culture consistent with it' (p. 3). While Almond and Verba accepted that, in the general vein of modernization theory, economic development is necessary for democracy, they claimed it was not sufficient, as evidenced by the fact that the correlations found by Lipset (1959) were far from perfect. Thus they criticized Lipset for ignoring the psychological basis of democratization (p. 9).

For Almond and Verba culture furnishes the 'psychological basis' of democracy. Moreover, as distinct from Laswell (1946) and other studies in the psychoanalytic vein, theirs was a mentalistic psychology. Culture is the 'psychological orientation toward social objects' (p. 13). 'When we speak of the political culture', Almond and Verba explain, 'we refer to the political system as internalized in the cognition, feelings, and evaluations of its population.' And, finally, 'The political culture of a nation is the particular distribution of patterns of orientation toward political objects among the members of the nation.'

Given this conceptualization, culture can be studied by asking questions of individuals and the culture of a nation is nothing but a distribution of the answers. The methodological innovation was to characterize what used to be studied as 'the national character' by examining national history or as 'the modal personality' by inquiring into patterns of child-rearing by asking people what they knew, liked and valued. Thus, even if Almond's and Verba's study was criticized extensively on conceptual and methodological ground (Barry, 1978; Wiatr, 1979), it gave rise to a new industry.

Asking people questions about their knowledge of political institutions, their preferences for systems of government, and their evaluations of political processes, actors and outcomes, is now a routine activity all around the world. Answers to these questions are interpreted as harbingers of democratic stability and are often read nervously: Brazil, for example, seemed to verge on the brink in 1991 since only 39% of the respondents thought that democracy is always the best system of government, as contrasted with, say, Chile where, in 1990, 76% did. The open question is whether such answers to questions do in fact predict whether democracy survives or falls.

The culture Almond and Verba identified as democratic, the 'civil culture', bore an uncanny resemblance to what one would expect to find in the United States, so it was not surprising that the United States best fits the ideal of democratic culture, followed by the United Kingdom. And since democracy in these countries was older – more stable – than in Germany, Italy or Mexico, the central hypothesis of the study withstood the test of evidence: a particular kind of political culture is required for a stable democracy.

Inglehart (1990) and Granato, Inglehart and Leblang (1996) attempted to validate this approach. Inglehart's (1990) 'civil culture' consists of three indicators: (1) interpersonal trust, (2) life satisfaction, and (3) support for revolutionary change (which is expected to be detrimental to democracy). He and his collaborators found that these variables, when taken together, are statistically related to the number of continuous years of democracy between 1900 and 1980 and between 1920 and 1995 in a sample of twenty-four countries. Yet doubts remain (Jackman and Miller, 1996): Is this an appropriate measure of democratic stability? Can one draw such

inferences on the basis of a sample heavily biased in favour of long-lasting democracies? What is the direction of causality?

Muller and Seligson (1994) reanalysed Inglehart's data, adding some Latin American countries, to identify the direction of causality. They concluded that, if anything, it is democratic stability that breeds the democratic culture, rather than vice versa. They also observed, as did Jackman and Miller, that Inglehart's indicators of 'civil culture' do not go together: trust is independent of the preference for gradual change, while life satisfaction has little to do with 'democratic culture.' They found that interpersonal trust is an effect of democratic stability and does not affect democracy in turn, while the inclination to gradual change is unrelated to long-term experience of democracy and does have a positive effect on democracy. Even this finding, however, appears sensitive to the composition of the sample of countries.

Indeed, one limitation of the survey approach is that it lends itself better to the question of democratic stability than to the issue of whether democracy is more likely to be established in societies that have some particular cultural features. Dictatorships rarely, typically only in their dying agony, allow survey researchers to ask questions about democracy. Hence, survey evidence concerning political attitudes under dictatorships is scant, making it difficult to determine whether democrats beget democracies or democracies spawn democrats. Maravall (1995) found that support for democracy did increase in Spain between 1966 and 1976 and in Chile during the last years of Pinochet, while support for the military declined in Brazil between 1972 and 1990, concluding that: 'In all these cases, democracies were preceded by an increase of the number of democrats' (p. 17). Yet Schmitter and Karl (1991) argued that it is democracy that breeds democrats, not vice versa.

What is it about culture that matters, and how?

As this brief historical sketch indicates, the view that democracy requires a definite cultural basis has many lives. Something about culture seems necessary for democracy to emerge or endure. But what? Montesquieu thought it was an irrational motive force ('les passions humaines qui le font mouvoir', *EL*, III, 1) – fear, honour, virtue – which, in turn, reflect religions, mores and manners. Stage theorists looked for feelings, habits, as well as for a rational sense of public utility. Mill was more systematic, distinguishing between a preference for democracy, the temperamental characteristics necessary to sustain it and a sense of community. Almond and Verba looked at beliefs, affects and evaluations of the political process and political outcomes. Inglehart wanted to know whether people are satisfied with their lives, whether they trust each other, and whether they like revolutionary changes. Other survey researchers inquired whether people value democracy per se, regardless of the conditions with which it has to cope and the outcomes it generates.

This ambiguity, and the confusions it engenders, are most apparent in Weingast's (1997) attempt to reconcile apparently rival explanations of democratic stability. Weingast set himself to demonstrate that for democracy to be stable, citizens must adopt a shared view of what constitutes illegitimate actions by the state and must be prepared to act against the transgressions of these limits were they to occur. The first task requires a co-ordination of beliefs, and the second a co-ordination of actions. The first problem is settled when citizens focus on the limits prescribed by the constitution or specified by explicit political pacts. The second is solved when, fearing that they would suffer in the future from state encroachments, citizens put up a united front against illegitimate actions of the state, even if they currently benefit from them. Thus, in the end, democracy is stable when individuals are prepared to rebel in unison whenever the state transgresses some definite limits.

What, then, is the role of culture in supporting this democratic equilibrium? Weingast (p. 253) is careful to emphasize that his is not a causal story, in which values would make democracy stable, nor the reverse. A particular culture and democratic stability are just different aspects of situations in which a society resolves its co-ordination dilemmas. But what exactly are the aspects of culture that support these situations? At the first level, two are prominent: a consensus about the limits of legitimate state actions and a common sense of 'duty' to defend it.[3] But to pacify everyone, Weingast also characterizes them as 'consensus on values and stable democracy' (p. 246), 'consensus over the rules' (p. 257), 'esteem' for limits to state actions (p. 251), 'trust' (p. 257), and 'mutual tolerance' (p. 257). This is a purely linguistic operation and merely muddles the issue.

Yet if culturalist views are to furnish a compelling explanation of the origins and life of democracy, they must specify what it is about culture that matters and how. Let us first distinguish different aspects of culture that may matter.[4]

First, people value democracy per se, regardless of the outcomes it generates. They want to bring it about and they defend it against threats because democracy is based on political equality (Toqueville), because it is an expression of liberty (Dunn, 1992), or for whatever non-instrumental reason. They believe that democracy is unconditionally the best (or the least bad) system of government, they say so when asked, or act as if they so believed.

Second, people see it as their duty to obey outcomes resulting from rules to which they 'agreed'.[5] We put 'agree' in quotation marks, since the agreement in question can be putative: people would have chosen these rules had they been consulted. Democracy is then legitimate in the sense that people are ready to accept decisions of as yet undetermined content, as long as these decisions result from applying the rules. Even if they do not like them,

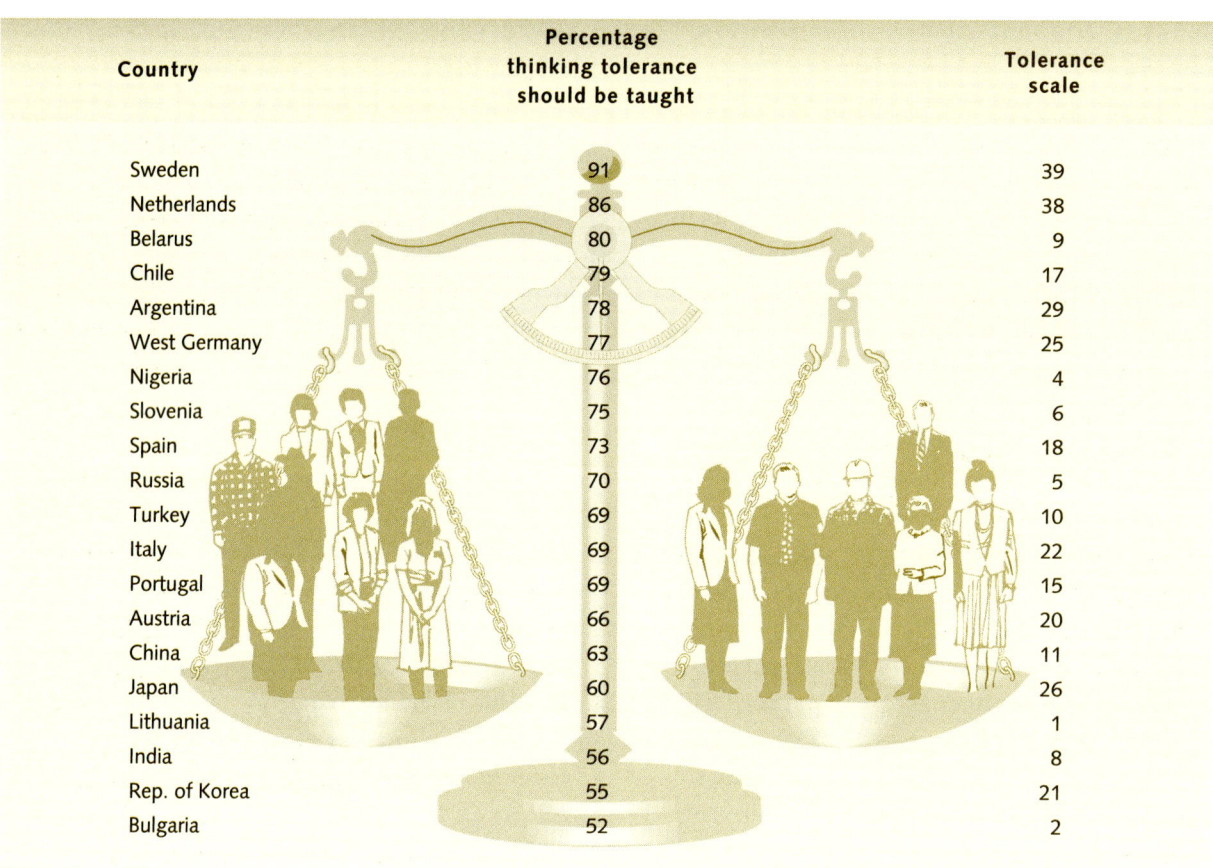

Country	Percentage thinking tolerance should be taught	Tolerance scale
Sweden	91	39
Netherlands	86	38
Belarus	80	9
Chile	79	17
Argentina	78	29
West Germany	77	25
Nigeria	76	4
Slovenia	75	6
Spain	73	18
Russia	70	5
Turkey	69	10
Italy	69	22
Portugal	69	15
Austria	66	20
China	63	11
Japan	60	26
Lithuania	57	1
India	56	8
Rep. of Korea	55	21
Bulgaria	52	2

GRAPH 7
TEACHING AND PRACTISING TOLERANCE (1990–93)
Source: A. van der Staay (see Chapter 16, Tables 21(a) and 23(a), of the present report).

people comply with the outcomes of the democratic interplay because they result from applying rules they accept. Neubauer (1967, p. 225) claimed that 'socialization into the "rules of the game"' is a precondition for democracy. The theory of political obligation has a second variant, one that emphasizes participation, rather than rules. In this version, people see it as their duty to obey outcomes in the making of which they had a chance to participate. Equally with all others, they had an opportunity to make public their reasons (Cohen, 1997) or at least to vote, and having had this opportunity makes the outcomes normatively binding. 'Participatory culture' is then the key to democratic stability.

Third, people have values and perhaps temperamental characteristics ('democratic personality', in the language of the 1950s) that support it. Lipset (1959, p. 153) maintained that 'if a political system is not characterized by a value system allowing the peaceful "play" of power . . . there can be no stable democracy'. These characteristics may include 'republican virtue', trust,[6] empathy, tolerance, moderation, or patience. People may love the collectivity above themselves; they may trust that the government will not take an unfair advantage of them even if it is in the hands of their adversaries; they may be ready to respect the validity of views and interests different from theirs; they may

be willing to accept that others should also have rights; or they may be willing to wait for their turn.

Fourth, what may matter for democracy to be possible is not so much what people share but that they do: 'consensus'.[7] J. S. Mill (1991, p. 230) was perhaps the first to contribute to the long line of arguments to the effect that: 'Free institutions are next to impossible in a country made up of different nationalities. Among a people without fellow-feeling, especially if they read and speak different languages, the united public opinion necessary to the working of representative government cannot exist.' Unless people share basic characteristics, such as language, religion, or ethnicity, they do not have enough in common to sustain democracy. But homogeneity with regard to such basic characteristics is not sufficient: 'agreement' about some basic values, rules of the game, or what not is required for democracy to function (Dahl, 1956; Lipset, 1959; Eckstein, 1961).[8] Thus, Weingast (1997, p. 254) thinks that democracy is unstable in Latin America because 'Latin American states are not characterized by a common set of citizen values about the appropriate role of government'.

The consensualist argument sometimes points to national traditions of decision-making. Thus, the medieval Scandinavian village council (*thing*) is cited as indicating that Scandinavians were prepared to embrace democratic parliaments (Esposito and Voll, 1996, p. 22). Yet this argument cuts both ways: evocations of the same tradition of consensual decision-making in Indonesia or in Africa are used to claim that the culture is hostile to democracy, which entails conflicts rather than consensus.

Clearly, these cultural underpinnings of democracy need not be mutually exclusive. Even if some may be more important in bringing democracy about and others in making it last, any or all of them may be necessary for people to struggle for democracy when they live under dictatorship and to support it actively once it is established. But if culturalist views are to have an explanatory power,

they must distinguish and specify. Otherwise, it will never be possible to conclude that culture does not matter.

The second issue concerns causality. For even if all the enduring democracies were found to share a definite 'democratic culture', this observation would not be sufficient to determine which, if either, comes first: democratic culture or democratic institutions. At the risk of being pedantic, we need to distinguish causal chains that may connect economic development, cultural transformations, and political institutions.

First, culture causes both development and democracy, whatever the causal connection between the latter two elements. This is what we mean by a 'strongly culturalist' view. Protestantism is one candidate for a culture that promotes both development and democracy (see below); at least this was the view of Lipset in 1994. In turn, Catholicism, in the view of Wiarda (1981), impedes both development and democracy in Latin America.[9] Confucianism was seen not so long ago as an obstacle to both, but now it appears to be good for development while still being considered by some, notably President Lee Kuan Yew of Singapore, as antithetical to democracy.

Second, both development and culture are needed independently for democracy to be possible. And even if development generates some cultural transformations, these transformations are not sufficient to generate the democratic culture, which is, in turn, necessary for democracy to emerge and survive. This was the view of Almond and Verba, discussed above, still a strongly culturalist view.

Third, a particular culture is necessary for democracy to be possible, but this culture is automatically generated by economic development. Lipset (1959, 1960) described several ways in which development generates cultural preconditions for democracy: by promoting moderation and tolerance, and allowing the lower strata to 'adopt longer time perspectives and more complex and gradualist views

Democratization and women's rights in the South African Constitution: the challenge of African customary law

A fundamental question is to know how notions of culture and cultural diversity should be accommodated in constitutional structures that actively seek to promote the values of democracy and fundamental rights such as equality, non-discrimination and human dignity. Tracing a link between culture and African customary law, especially African family law, and the provisions in the South African Constitution relating to African customary law and fundamental rights reveals some inevitable tensions between the different sets of provisions, centred primarily around the question of women's rights and gender equality.

It is now fairly well-documented that the major point of friction between customary laws and practices on the one hand, and individual rights on the other, is the matter of patriarchy. One could easily compile a list of cultural practices, all related to marriage and supported by customary law, which may be the source of tension. Such a list would probably include: courtship rituals (where, among some peoples, the practice of 'mock abduction' of the woman may sometimes mask real coercion); age and consent (which brings in concerns not only about 'child betrothal' but also about customs and rituals of submissiveness which cloud the question of the genuineness of consent even for women of age); marriage consequences (including built-in gender inequality); divorce grounds and procedures (sometimes characterized by power inequalities between the spouses, as when the wife cannot sue to end her own marriage and has to persuade her guardian to intervene), and the status of widowhood (under which, in addition to customs such as the levirate, some mourning rituals are an affront to human dignity). As mentioned earlier, to the majority of people who live under these systems such practices are no more than 'our way of life', something that represents familiar pathways through the business of

day-to-day living. To the lawyer these practices constitute 'possible unconstitutionality'.

The question that arises directly is whether these practices are necessarily doomed to extinction simply because they may be incompatible with certain provisions of the constitution. I wish to suggest that the answer should be 'Not necessarily', a response whose somewhat inconclusive tenor calls for an explanation and a legal strategy.

To say that incompatibility with the provisions of the constitution should not 'necessarily' disqualify a cultural practice from protection is to say several other things besides. Firstly, establishing incompatibility with the constitution is itself an involved task that cannot be undertaken lightly. Secondly, it suggests that other factors, legal and non-legal, may be relevant in making the decision. And thirdly, it broadly hints at the fact that the limitation clause (s. 36) is likely to play an important part in the decision.

The strategy proposed is a two-pronged approach to the problem of accommodating culture in an 'open and democratic society based on human dignity, equality and freedom'. The first prong refers to cultures themselves and their need to adapt to changing imperatives: the second suggests judicial and legislative methods of realizing the goals of a constitution that attempts to entrench cultural rights against the background of strong individual entitlements.

To take just one field, the value of the extended family is too entrenched in African thinking to brook serious challenge. It simply is not possible to abolish the role of the wider family and the community in marriage. However, creative ways of ridding value of the discriminatory content of its expression may have to be found. The conflicting interests of fathers and their lineages on the one hand, and mothers and their children on the other, will have to be resolved. The values implicit in the institution of the extended family are worth retaining; alternative formulae may, however, have to be found to express these values in ways that are non-discriminatory. In matters of child custody and other rights over children, for example, the compelling justification for preferring fathers (and even grandfathers) to the exclusion of the mothers has been considerably weakened by changed economic and social conditions. The pointed depersonalization of mothers is not logically necessary to achieve the social ends of the extended family.

Creativity is going to be required on the part of both the courts and the lawmakers. The interests to be balanced in this process are the claims of the majority to a higher profile for their culture (especially after decades of its denigration and suppression by the colonial and apartheid states) on the one hand, and the need, on the other, to prevent the protection of 'pockets of oppression' where some African women under the yoke of culture will suffer more disabilities than their counterparts of other races. The commitment to human rights should be as genuine as the commitment to cultural diversity. To achieve this the two competing world-views, Western and African, should start off as notionally equal.

With a constitution which now requires balance in everything, a practice-by-practice assessment of cultural behaviours is implied. At the end of the day, a particular practice must be ousted only if after careful consideration it is found to be in fact a violation of the constitution, not on the assertion of someone who finds it unfamiliar or unusual, but on merit.

There are encouraging signs that the courts are willing to grapple with the issues of customary practices that may not sit comfortably within a Western value system but nevertheless have to be accommodated according to the constitution. Thus, while it is more usual to use the constitutional notion of human dignity in defence of individual rights, it does not seem far-fetched to conceive of the notion of human dignity being central in a court's assessment of a practice like *lobolo*, for instance (*lobolo* is the transfer – or any negotiation regarding the transfer – of cattle, other forms of livestock or other valuable consideration from the family of the groom to the family of the bride as part of the marriage process).

The legislative option can achieve even more. Sensitive law reform can coax customary law into the constitutional era without alienating its adherents or

forcing a confrontation between so-called Western values and African values. A significant start has been made by the South African Law Commission when, in proposing the long-overdue legal recognition of customary marriages, it also recommends compliance with many of the provisions of the Convention on the Elimination of All Forms of Discrimination Against Women. The proposal includes minimum ages for customary marriages; it makes consent of the parties a central requirement; it repeals laws enshrining inequality of the spouses; it ushers in full property rights for wives and equalizes the position of the spouses in respect of contractual capacity, standing in court, grounds for divorce and custody and guardianship of children. It does all this while steadfastly refusing to 'Westernize' customary marriage out of all recognition. Sensitive and sensible law reform of this kind may yet succeed in giving effect to the somewhat contradictory provisions of the constitution.

It is possible to accommodate culture and cultural arrangements in the context of a modern constitution without sacrificing fundamental rights, even in sensitive areas such as that of women's human rights. The password is balance, balance based on equal commitment to genuine cultural diversity and to human rights. Balance is easier to strike where no single value system is attempting to dominate others. Adherence to this principle makes it easier to focus on the positive aspects of the indigenous system, in other words the creativeness of African family forms and the social solidarity that they engender.

Constitutions need to earn the respect of indigenous peoples by fostering a sense of belonging. Where this is achieved, national energies are released to tackle development issues in ways that are not possible when a significant part of the population is alienated.

Ronald Thandabantu Nhlapo
Professor in Law, University of Cape Town (South Africa);
Member, South African Law Commission and Chairperson,
Project Committee on the Harmonization
of the Indigenous Law and the Common Law, Pretoria
(South Africa)

of politics' (1959, p. 83). Clearly, in this view cultures, in plural, are sufficiently malleable to become 'modernized' along with other aspects of societies as an effect of economic development. Thus, the causal chain goes from development, through culture, to democracy. This is a 'weakly culturalist' view.

Fourth, a particular culture is necessary for democracy to endure but this culture emerges as an effect of democratic institutions once they are in place. This was the view of J. S. Mill who, as we stated above, thought that while people prefer doing what they know how to do, they can be taught to do new things. The educational impact of laws was the persistent theme of Montesquieu as well as of Tocqueville. In this view, we should expect all enduring democracies to have the same political culture, and for such culture to emerge as a consequence of democratic institutions and support them in turn.

Fifth, in the non-culturalist view, democracy emerges and endures independently of culture. Democracy may or may not generate cultural homogeneity but culture has no causal impact on the durability of democratic institutions.

Given the paucity of data about culture, the first three explanations cannot be tested systematically for a large number of countries. However, the non-culturalist explanations can indeed be.

A non-culturalist explanation

The non-culturalist view is strongly supported by evidence. In this view, democracy persists because the relevant political forces are better off, in terms of pure self-interest, complying with its verdicts rather than doing anything else. Even if the losers in the democratic competition would be better off in the short run rebelling rather than accepting the outcome of the current round, they face sufficiently large benefits in the future rounds and a sufficient chance to win and are therefore better off continuing to comply with the democratic verdicts. Similarly for

the winners. Democracy is then an equilibrium because the conflicting political forces find it in their best interest to comply with its verdicts (Przeworski, 1991, Chap. 1).[10]

To tell one stylized story (Przeworski, 1996), take a political actor, collective by definition of 'political', who considers whether to participate in the democratic game – with some chance of winning elections and some share of discretionary spoils in case of winning – or to fight for dictatorship at some cost to the productive endowments and with some chance of becoming a dictator. The choice then is between getting some share of income if staying under democracy or taking the chance of fighting for dictatorship with the hope of getting all of the discretionary income but at the cost of a temporary destruction of some wealth. This is thus a choice between a 'part of more' and 'the whole of less' (both of which are lotteries).

Now make one or both standard economic assumptions. Suppose that political actors value increases in consumption progressively less, the wealthier they already are. Thus the gain from winning the struggle for dictatorship is smaller in a wealthy society. In turn, if the production function has diminishing returns to productive endowments, the 'catch-up' from destroying a part of them during the war for dictatorship is faster at lower levels of wealth. Hence, in poor countries the value of becoming a dictator is greater and the accumulated cost of destroying capital stock is lower. In wealthy countries, the gain from getting all rather than a part of total income is smaller and the recuperation from destruction is slower. As a result, struggle for dictatorship, 'rebellion', is more attractive in poorer countries. It is perhaps more obvious that rebellion is also more attractive for those political forces which expect to get a smaller share of income under democracy.[11]

This simple model leads to several empirical predictions: (a) the probability that a democracy endures should increase in current and future wealth;

(b) the probability that a democracy endures should be higher when no political force completely dominates the political system; and (c) in very poor countries, democracy should be subverted by the incumbents of governmental offices as well as those out of office; in countries with medium level of wealth, democracy should be subverted more often by outsiders ('losers') than by incumbents; and in wealthy countries democracy should be supported by winners as well as by losers.

Examine now some empirical patterns concerning almost all democracies that existed at any time between 1950 and 1990.[12]

The most striking fact is that no democracy ever fell, during the period under our scrutiny, regardless of everything else, in a country with a per capita income higher than that of Argentina in 1976.

The probability that democracy survives increases monotonically with per capita income. In countries with per capita income under $1,000, the probability that a democracy would die during a particular year was 0.1216, which implies that its expected life was slightly above 8 years. Between $1,001 and $2,000, this probability was 0.0556, for an expected duration of about 18 years. Above $6,000, democracies could expect to last for ever.[13]

Moreover, democracies, in particular poor democracies, are highly vulnerable to economic crises. The expected life of a very poor democracy that experiences one year of economic decay is only 5.4 years. Yet very poor democracies – those under $1,000 in per capita income – are about equally likely to survive when income grows as are richer democracies – those between $1,000 and $3,000 – when their income declines.

Several other factors affect the survival of democracies but they all pale in comparison with per capita income. Two are particularly relevant for the rational choice perspective. First, it turns out that democracies are more likely to endure when no party controls a large share of legislative seats, i.e. more than two-thirds. Secondly, democracies are most

stable when the heads of governments change every so often, more frequently than once in five but less frequently than once in two years. These two observations – and both are statistically justified in multivariate analyses – add up to the second fact: democracy is more likely to survive when no political force dominates completely and permanently. When one party has unchecked control over the legislature or when chief executives stay in office for a long time, democracies are less stable.

Finally, the instances in which democracies were subverted follow the pattern predicted by the model: poor democracies (those under $1,000 per capita income) are overthrown by incumbents as well as by those out of power, democracies in countries with incomes between $1,000 and $6,000 are much more likely to be subverted by outsiders, and wealthy democracies are not overthrown by anyone.[14]

Obviously, there are always alternative interpretations. One would be that income is just a proxy for education and more educated people are more likely to embrace democratic values. But, while the accumulated years of education of an average member of the labour force, the measure of educational stock one possesses, does affect the probability of survival of democracy independently of income, the effect of income survives when education is controlled for and is twice as significant statistically.

Finally, we find no evidence of habituation to democracy. The fact that a democracy has been around does not increase its chances of remaining around. Democracies become 'consolidated' if the conditional probability that a democratic regime will die during a particular year given that it survived thus far (the 'hazard rate') declines with its age, so that democracies are more likely to survive the longer they have lasted. Without any exogenous variables this is true, but once per capita income is controlled for, the hazard rates become independent of age, meaning that for a given level of

TABLE 2
OBSERVED RATES OF TRANSITIONS (BY LAGGED PER CAPITA INCOME AND LAGGED RATE OF ECONOMIC GROWTH)

Level growth	All			Dictatorships			Democracies		
	PJK	TJK	N	PAD	TAD	N	PDA	TDA	N
–1 000	0.0147	15	1 019	0.0063	6	945	0.1216	9	74
G<=0	0.0193	9	467	0.0091	4	440	0.1852	5	27
G>0	0.0109	6	552	0.0040	2	505	0.0851	4	47
1 001–2 000	0.0321	32	997	0.0242	18	745	0.0556	14	252
G<=0	0.0447	14	313	0.0313	7	224	0.0787	7	89
G>0	0.0263	18	684	0.0211	11	521	0.0429	7	163
2 001–3 000	0.0325	16	493	0.0261	8	306	0.0428	8	187
G<=0	0.0522	7	134	0.0341	3	88	0.0870	4	46
G>0	0.0251	9	359	0.0229	5	218	0.0284	4	141
3 001–4 000	0.0201	7	349	0.0146	3	205	0.0278	4	144
G<=0	0.0303	3	99	0.0172	1	58	0.0488	2	41
G>0	0.0160	4	250	0.0136	2	147	0.0194	2	103
4 001–5 000	0.0339	8	236	0.0469	6	128	0.0185	2	108
G<=0	0.0500	3	60	0.0588	2	34	0.0385	1	26
G>0	0.0284	5	176	0.0426	4	94	0.0122	1	82
5 001–6 000	0.0308	6	195	0.0595	5	84	0.0090	1	111
G<=0	0.0541	2	37	0.0952	2	21	0.0000	0	16
G>0	0.0253	4	158	0.0476	3	63	0.0105	1	95
6 001–7 000	0.0190	3	158	0.0606	2	33	0.0080	1	125
G<=0	0.0857	3	35	0.3333	2	6	0.0345	1	29
G>0	0.0000	0	123	0.0000	0	27	0.0000	0	96
7 001–	0.0015	1	679	0.0286	1	35	0.0000	0	644
G<=0	0.0000	0	120	0.0000	0	3	0.0000	0	117
G>0	0.0018	1	559	0.0313	1	32	0.0000	0	527
TOTAL	0.0213	88	4 126	0.0198	49	2481	0.0237	39	1 645
G<=0	0.0324	41	1 265	0.0240	21	874	0.0512	20	391
G>0	0.0164	47	2 861	0.0174	28	1607	0.0152	19	1 254

Key: 'Level' stands for per capita income, in 1985 purchasing power parity US$. PJK is the probability of transitions, TJK is their total number, N is the number of annual observations, PAD is the probability of transitions from authoritarianism to democracy and TAD their number, PDA is the probability of transitions from democracy to authoritarianism and TDA their number.

TABLE 3
CASES WHEN DEMOCRACY WAS OVERTHROWN (BY PER CAPITA INCOME AND THE PERPETUATORS)

Income	Number of transitions		
	Total	By incumbents	Not by incumbents
–1 000	17	10	7
1 001–3 000	29	12	17
3 001–6 055	9	1	8
6 066–	0	0	0
TOTAL	55	23	32

development, democracies are about equally likely to die at any age. Since democracies are much more likely to survive in wealthier countries, these findings indicate that the hazard rates uncorrected for income decline because countries develop, not because a sheer passage of time has a habituating effect. Thus, even if habituation to democracy generates a democratic culture, it is wealth that keeps democracies going, not culture.

As a glance at Table 2 indicates, economic factors do not have an equally strong effect on the survival of dictatorships and thus on transitions to democracy. The probability that a democracy is established increases as countries become wealthier but then declines again once they become wealthy enough. Economic crises have a weaker effect on the survival of dictatorships. Indeed, statistical analyses indicate that transitions to democracy are almost impossible to predict, even with the entire panopticum of observable factors, economic or cultural. Dictatorships just seem to run many risks and to die for a broad variety of reasons.

Yet even if economic factors play a more important role in making democracies survive than emerge, per capita income and its growth are sufficient to explain the dynamic of both political regimes. To test the predictive power of these factors, we revert to a computer experiment. Take each of the 135 countries for which we have data with its regime and its per capita income when first observed (1950 or the year of independence or the first year when economic data are available) and the observed rates of economic growth during the period until 1990 (or the last year for which economic data are available) and make countries change regimes according to their current level of income and their rates of growth, i.e. the probabilities portrayed in Table 2. Since these probabilities are assumed to be the same for any country that at a particular level of income experiences a particular rate of growth, the assumption is that culture does not affect the emergence and survival of democracy. Now generate

1,000 'histories' for each country and compare the patterns based on these assumptions with those actually observed. The simulated patterns reproduce the actual histories almost exactly: the correlation between the predicted and observed proportions of time each country spends under each regime is 0.91.

Hence, the evidence in favour of economic factors is overwhelming. No recourse to culture is necessary to reproduce the actually observed patterns of regime dynamics. True, one could still defend the culturalist view by claiming that some culture, say 'market culture', is what causes development in the first place and that the ultimate explanation is thus still cultural. That may well be, but this line of inquiry leads to infinite regress, since one could ask in turn what causes the 'market culture' to emerge, and so forth. Hence, we stop here.

Cultures, the democratic culture and democracy

Are particular, otherwise identifiable cultures, conducive or detrimental to the rise and durability of democratic institutions? The question is the following: Suppose we were to observe that, independently of their wealth and other factors, all countries with a high proportion of Protestants are democracies and no countries with a low proportion of Protestants are. We would then have prima facie evidence that, whatever the 'democratic culture' is, Protestantism furnishes its necessary ingredients. But note that if we fail to find such patterns, it may be for two distinct reasons: either because the rise and durability of democracy need not call for a particular set of cultural patterns or because, while democracy does have cultural requisites and cultural barriers, all cultures are, or at least can be made, compatible with these patterns.

We first discuss the issue of compatibility of particular cultures, in plural, with the democratic culture. Then we examine some empirical patterns.

Cultures and the democratic culture

Historically, the discussion of this topic revolved mainly around cultures identified by dominant religions. The idea of the primary causal force of religion is due to Max Weber's (1958 [1904–05]) argument that religiously motivated, ascetic 'calling' for accumulation of wealth was the key to the economic success of capitalism. Weber (p. 180) claimed that: 'One of the fundamental elements of the spirit of modern capitalism, and not only of that but of all modern culture: rational conduct on the basis of the idea of the calling, was born . . . from the spirit of Christian ascetism.' This 'spirit of capitalism, in the sense of a definite standard of life claiming ethical sanction . . .' (p. 58) was the principal explanation of the difference between Protestants (or at least the ascetics among them) and other religions with regard to economic conduct (p. 40).

Weber had next to nothing to say about the consequences of this spirit of capitalism for politics in general, and democracy (about which he had ambivalent and changing beliefs) in particular. There is one passage (p. 45) in *The Protestant Ethic and the Spirit of Capitalism* in which he cited Montesquieu to the effect that the English 'had progressed the farthest of all peoples of the world in three important things: in piety, in commerce, and in freedom', and then asked, perhaps rhetorically: 'Is it not possible that this commercial superiority and their adaptation to free political institutions are connected in some way with that record of piety which Montesquieu ascribes to them?' Yet he did not follow up this thought and, at the end of the text (p. 182), just announced that: 'The next task would be rather to show the significance of ascetic rationalism . . . for the content of practical social ethics, thus for types of organization and the functions of social groups from the conventicle to the State.' But here he stopped.

Yet the idea that Weber saw in Protestantism the wellspring of modern democracy is widespread among contemporary political scientists. In the most influential article on the conditions for democractic stability, Lipset (1959, p. 165) claimed that: 'It has been argued by Max Weber among others that the factors making for democracy in this area [north-western Europe and their English-speaking offsprings in America and Australasia] are a historically unique concatenation of elements, part of the complex which also produced capitalism in this area', since 'the emphasis within Protestantism on individual responsibility furthered the emergence of democratic values'.[15] In turn, Catholicism, in Lipset's (1960, pp. 72–3) view, was antithetical to democracy in pre-Second World War Europe and Latin America.

In his Presidential Address to the American Sociological Association, Lipset (1994, p. 5) attributed the origins of these views not to Weber but to Toqueville, again without indicating a specific text. Yet, Toqueville (1961, Vol. I, p. 427), referring to Irish immigrants, not only observed that 'Ces catholiques . . . forment la classe la plus républicaine et la plus démocratique qui soit aux Etats-Unis', but went on to conclude that 'on a tort de regarder la religion catholique comme un ennemi naturel de la démocratie', pointing in particular to the egalitarian features of Catholicism.

Catholicism is not the worst enemy of democracy: Islam and Confucianism hold the palm (Eisenstadt, 1968, pp. 25–7). Huntington (1993, p. 15) reported: 'No scholarly disagreement exists regarding the proposition that traditional Confucianism was either undemocratic or antidemocratic.' Similar views about Islam abound (Gellner, 1991, p. 506; Lewis, 1993, pp. 96–8).

Yet Lee Teng Hui (1997), the President of Taiwan, found in traditional Confucianism an emphasis on limited government that is essential to democracy. And in a systematic review of writings on Confucianism and democracy, Im (1997), as some others before him, finds a very mixed picture: on the one hand, Confucianism has no concept of civil society, no concept of individual rights (but instead

one of roles that people should perform), or of the rule of law but, on the other hand, it has deep traditions of limited government, recognizes the right of rebellion against rulers who deviate from the prescribed 'Way', is religiously tolerant, and anti-militaristic. Moreover, at least in Korea, a plurality of opinion, a public sphere, existed during the six centuries of the Chosun dynasty.

The discussion within and about Islam is even more complex. According to Esposito and Voll (1996), the three basic tenets of Islam lend themselves and have been subject to more or less anti-democratic interpretations. Thus, the principle of the Unity of God (*tawhid*), while requiring consistency with God's laws, can leave interpretation of them to every capable and qualified Muslim and need not be inconsistent with a system of government in which the executive 'is constituted by the general will of the Moslems who have also the right to depose it' (p. 24), or with 'an assembly whose members are the real representatives of the people' (p. 27). Similarily, the principle of God's representative on earth (*khilafah*) need not be interpreted in monarchical terms but can be extended to all men and women. Finally, the traditions of consultation, consensus and independent interpretative judgement can be used as arguments for or against democracy. And in fact, Eickelman and Piscatori (1996) show that such doctrinal interpretations have in the past served and now serve to justify quite different political arrangements.

There are several reasons to doubt that cultures, or civilizations, as Mazrui (1997, p. 118) prefers to think of Islam, furnish requisites for or constitute irremovable barriers to democracy. First, the arguments relating civilizations to democracy appear terribly *ex-post*: if many countries dominated by Protestants are democratic, we look for features of Protestantism that promote democracy; if no Muslim countries are democratic, obviously there must be something about Islam that is anti-democratic.

Eisenstadt (1968), for example, finds that the Indian civilization has what it takes but Confucianism and Islam do not, and one wonders what he would have found if China were democratic and India not.[16]

Secondly, one can find elements in every culture, Protestantism included, that appear compatible and others that seem incompatible with democracy. Protestant legitimation of economic inequality, not to speak of the very ethic of self-interest, offer a poor moral basis for living together and resolving conflicts in a peaceful way. Other cultures are authoritarian but egalitarian, hierarchical but respectful of the right of rebellion, communal but tolerant of diversity, and so forth. So one can pick and choose.[17]

Thirdly, each of the religious traditions has been historically compatible with a broad range of practical political arrangements. This range is not the same for different religious traditions, but broad enough in each case to demonstrate that these traditions are quite flexible with regard to the political arrangements with which they can be made compatible.

Finally, and most importantly, traditions are not given once and for all: they are continually invented and reinvented (Hobsbawm and Ranger, 1983), a point stressed by Eickelman and Piscatori (1996) in their analysis of Islam. In fact, the very analyses of the Confucian tradition cited above are best seen as attempts to invent a democratic Confucianism. Cultures are made of cloth but the fabric of culture drapes differently in the hands of different tailors.

This view was vigorously contested recently by Huntington (1993, p. 40). He began by observing that 'Western concepts differ fundamentally from those prevalent in other civilizations. Western ideas of individualism, liberalism, constitutionalism, human rights, equality, liberty, the rule of law, democracy, free markets, the separation of church and state, often have little resonance in Islamic, Confucian, Japanese, Hindu, Buddhist or Orthodox cultures'. And, he continued, 'Western efforts to propagate such ideas produce instead a reaction against "human rights imperialism" and a reaffirmation of indigeneous values, as can be seen in the support for religious fundamentalism by the younger generation of non-Western cultures'. It is difficult to guess on what bases one can arrive at this assertion. Most students of Islamic religious fundamentalism attribute its rise to the deteriorating economic conditions of the urban masses, not to 'human rights imperialism'; the rise of religious fundamentalism is limited to some countries within some cultural areas, and is prominent in the most 'Western' country of them all, the United States. But more importantly, the Cassandras of the impending *Kulturkampf* (also Fukuyama, 1995) would be well advised to look back before they plunge forward.

Contrary to Lipset, Almond and Verba, or Huntington (1984), who claimed that cultures that are consummatory in character are less favourable to democracy, Weber himself (in Gerth and Mills, 1958, pp. 337–8) thought that the political role of organized religions depends on their interests, not their content: 'The widely varying empirical stands which historical religions have taken in the face of political action have been determined by the entanglement of religious organizations in power interests and in struggles for power . . . by the usefulness and the use of religious organizations for the political taming of the masses and, especially, by the need of the powers-that-be for the religious consecration of their legitimacy.' In an exhaustive study of the rise of European Christian Democracy, Kalyvas (1996) showed that the relation between Catholicism and democracy followed strategic considerations of the Catholic Church. And in a daring comparison of nineteenth-century Belgian *ultramontane* Catholic fundamentalism and the contemporary Algerian Islamic fundamentalism, Kalyvas (1997) concluded that the different outcomes in these two countries were due to the organizational structure of the respective religions,

rather than to their cultural content. Linz and Stepan (1996, p. 453) came to the same conclusion with regard to the recent cases of democratization. Finally, Laitin (for the most recent summary, see 1995) examined in several contexts the role played by 'cultural entrepreneurs' in the dynamic of cultural change, providing extensive evidence that, while conflicts over culture can end in different outcomes, they are a matter of interests and strategies, not of any primordially given cultural contents. Thus, the claim that the anti-democratic proclivities of 'civilizations' are given once and for all hurls itself against historical experience. To go back to Mill, whom we cited above: 'People are more easily induced to do, and do more easily, what they are already used to; but people also learn to do things new to them.'

Empirical evidence

What, then, is the empirical evidence concerning the impact of religions on the dynamic of political regimes? Protestants, and Catholics, are more frequent in democracies; Moslems and others in dictatorships. But this prima facie observation does not suffice to establish a causal link. Even if one grants that democracy originated in Protestant countries, once it was established in these countries, the question is whether it can be transplanted and survive elsewhere. This is not a rhetorical question, as Lipset (1994, p. 5), citing Lewis (1993), seems to imply, but an empirical one. And the evidence relevant to this question is not whether at some moment, be it in 1950 or 1990, more Protestant than Catholic or Moslem countries are democratic, but whether democracy is more likely to emerge and to endure in Protestant countries. In technical terms, what this means is that the relevant evidence is historical and dynamic, rather than cross-sectional and static.

Hence, to test the importance of religions for regime dynamics, we calculated the impact of different variables on the probabilities that democracy will be established and that it will collapse. We

TABLE 4
RELIGIONS AND REGIME TRANSITIONS: DYNAMIC PROBIT MODEL

Log-likelihood	−355.9044
Restricted (Slopes=0) Log-L.	−2 685.421
Chi-squared (13)	4 659.033
Significance level	0.0000000

	Transitions to dictatorship			Transitions to democracy		
Variable	Coefficient	t-ratio	Prob|t|≥x	Coefficient	t-ratio	Prob|t|≥x
Constant	−0.53859	−5.676	0.00000	−2.46014	−11.762	0.00000
Income	−0.84880E−04	−3.935	0.00008	0.102732E−03	1.814	0.06961
Growth	−0.16626E−01	−2.942	0.00327	−0.222413E−01	−3.764	0.00017
Turnover	0.17583	1.938	0.05262	0.636220	3.585	0.00034
Catholic	0.83732E−03	0.781	0.43487	0.497148E−02	1.941	0.05221
Protestant	−0.84245E−03	−0.418	0.67630	−0.512016E−02	−0.962	0.33593
Muslim	0.18935E−02	1.360	0.17386	−0.186515E−02	−0.657	0.51107

Frequencies of actual and predicted outcomes.
Predicted outcome has maximum probability.

	Predicted		
Actual	DEM	DIC	Total
DEM	1 546	49	1 595
DIC	38	2 358	2 396
TOTAL	1 584	2 407	3 991

Key: Coefficients are partial derivatives of the respective probabilities with regard to the variables, evaluated at the mean. DEM represents democracy, and DIC dictatorship.

considered first the three variables that made our non-cultural model: per capita income, its rate of growth, and the rate of turnover of heads of government accumulated during the life of the regime.[18] As Table 4 shows, all these variables are statistically significant. The wealthier a democracy, the less likely it is to collapse; while wealthier dictatorships are somewhat more likely to collapse. Both regimes are much less likely to collapse if their economy grew during the preceding year. Democracies in which heads of government change more frequently are somewhat more likely to collapse, while dictatorships are much more likely to die under such conditions.

When added to this non-culturalist model, the frequency of the three religions for which we have data – Catholics, Protestants and Moslems – in the population of each country has no impact whatever on the durability of democracy and only Catholicism has some – negative – impact on the stability of dictatorships. Moreover, when other variables are introduced into the analysis – the colonial legacy, religious and ethnic heterogeneity, or the proportion

142

TABLE 5
ETHNOLINGUISTIC FRACTIONALIZATION AND REGIME TRANSITIONS: DYNAMIC PROBIT MODEL

Log-likelihood	−306.7057
Restricted (Slopes=0) Log-L.	−2 382.604
Chi-squared (13)	4 151.797
Significance level	0.0000000

Variable	Transitions to dictatorship			Transitions to democracy		
	Coefficient	t-ratio	Prob|t|≥x	Coefficient	t-ratio	Prob|t|≥x
Constant	−1.4462	−5.822	0.00000	−2.08905	−11.480	0.00000
Income	−0.22950E–03	−4.090	0.00004	0.11891E–03	1.567	0.11709
Growth	−0.43770E–01	−2.750	0.00596	−0.25457E–01	−3.565	0.00036
Turnover	0.53737	2.273	0.02305	0.53882	3.428	0.00061
Elf60	0.90067	2.517	0.01185	0.16581	2.390	0.01684
Newc	0.20553E–01	0.060	0.95183	−0.85350	−2.106	0.03517
Britcol	−0.47802	−1.402	0.16103	0.35732	0.303	0.76211

Frequencies of actual and predicted outcomes.
Predicted outcome has maximum probability.

Actual	Predicted		
	DEM	DIC	Total
DEM	1 475	43	1 518
DIC	36	1 924	1 960
TOTAL	1 511	1 967	3 478

Key: ELF60 stands for ethnolinguistic fractionalization, as of 1960. NEWC is a dummy variable, indicating that the country was not independent as of 1945. BRITCOL is a dummy variable indicating that it was a British colony. Coefficients are partial derivatives of the respective probabilities with regard to the variables, evaluated at the mean.

of countries in the world that are democracies during the particular year – none of the religions matter for anything.

To test the hypothesis about the impact of cultural heterogeneity, we used indices of ethnolinguistic and religious fractionalization.[19] Ethnoliguistic fractionalization makes democracies less likely to survive: this much confirms common wisdom. But, when the colonial legacy of a country is considered, it makes dictatorships less likely to survive as well. Hence, it seems that ethnolinguistic heterogeneity just makes political regimes less stable and, indeed, its effects on both regimes vanish when controlled for past political instability. Thus, the claim that common values are needed to support democracy reduces to the observation that regime transitions are more frequent in heterogeneous countries. In turn, religious heterogeneity has no effect on the stability of either regime.

This is scant evidence, but cultures just do not lend themselves to simple classifications. Hence, the opportunity for statistical analyses is limited. We

would have obviously liked to be able to classify cultures as hierarchical or egalitarian, universalistic and particularistic, religious and secular, consensual or conflictuous, and so on. But the evidence we do have does not support the claim that some cultures are incompatible with democracy. They seem to have little effect on whether democracy is established and none on whether it endures.

Re-assessing cultural relativism

A few years ago, one of us participated in a meeting concerned with the development of capital/labour relations in the Republic of Korea. As the discussion proceeded, it became clear to us, Westerners, that our Korean interlocutors could imagine only two possible states of the world: either 'harmony and co-operation' or outright war with no holds barred. The idea that conflicts can be regulated and thus limited seemed just unfathomable to them. It was not a part of their cultural repertoire.

All of us probably had such an experience at one time or another. Cultures are not the same and what people can imagine and are prepared to do is shaped by cultural understandings and habits. Yet cultures are also heterogeneous and malleable. Indeed, we could tell Koreans that Western Europeans had also thought not so long ago that free unions are incompatible with democracy and yet over the past forty years they enjoyed civil labour relations, with workers having the right to associate and strike, with minutely regulated collective-bargaining institutions, and with conflicts that ended in peaceful settlements. And while our evidence met with some doubt whether such a system could function in their country, our interlocutors also knew that sooner or later they would have to develop such a system.

Thus while the intuition that culture matters for the viability of democratic institutions is born from our everyday experience, we should not be surprised that systematic evidence in favour of the culturalist views is so weak. Historical comparisons of cultural traditions fail to identify which elements of culture are supposed to play the causal role and to specify what this causal role is. Answers to questions differ across societies but as evidence in favour of the causal role of culture they suffer from the same weaknesses. In turn, statistical evidence in favour of non-culturalist explanations of the viability of democratic institutions seems strong. Hence, there is little, if anything, that should lead us to believe that cultural obstacles to democracy are immovable. The 'Lee hypothesis', as Sen (1997) terms the pronouncements of Lee Kuan Yew, is just a thin veneer over his desire to hold on to power.

But suppose that the evidence had gone the other way, and that culturalist perspectives were vindicated by our review of evidence. The standard relativist argument is that cultural preferences should be respected because they are held and expressed by people whom we should respect (even if in fact they are typically expressed by those among them who speak on their behalf, perhaps not without a dose of self-interest). But the normative question is whether endogenous preferences can underlie moral judgements when they are not symmetrically informed. What we mean is this: suppose that without having the experience of regulated conflicts, Koreans justify paternalistic labour relations by evocations of 'harmony and co-operation'. Yet suppose that once they instituted a system of free collective bargaining they would discover not only that they can live with this system but that they prefer it to labour repression. Should we have respected their preference for 'harmony and co-operation'? To put it more generally, should one respect anti-democratic cultures that languish in societies that never had an experience of democracy?

This is not a rhetorical question, since well-meaning and reasonable people can disgree about the answer in specific contexts. But it points to a generic weakness of cultural relativism.

Notes

1.   Rousseau (1985 [1771, p. 1]) carried this view even further, arguing that each specific type of democratic institution can prosper only if it is compatible with the mores of a particular society. Even if his view of Poland was quite folkloric, his claim was general: 'One must know thoroughly the nation for which one is building; otherwise the final product, however excellent it may be in itself, will prove imperfect when it is acted upon – the more certainly if the nation is already formed, with its tastes, customs, prejudices and failings too deeply rooted to be stifled by new plantings.'

2.   Quotations from Montesquieu are cited in the text using abbreviations, e.g. *EL*, III, 1 denotes *De l'esprit des lois*, Book III, Chapter 1.

3.   Weingast assumes implicitly that the state is a potential threat to everyone: the possibility of a stable alliance between the state and particular classes is ruled out. As a result, he misinterprets his own conclusions when he says that citizens act out of a sense of 'duty' when they oppose the state. What kind of 'duty' is it that is driven only by self-interest?

4.   A new fashion among game theorists is to interpret culture as 'out-of-equilibrium' beliefs: beliefs about what would happen if something that never happens actually transpired. Suppose the bourgeoisie is considering whether to accede to workers' demands or to turn to the military with the request to suppress them. The bourgeoisie believes that the military would not suppress and, therefore, accedes to workers' demands. Hence, the belief that the military is non-political, an out-of-equilibrium belief, underlies democratic stability. Or suppose that workers believe that the military would suppress them if requested to do so by the bourgeoisie: then the bourgeoisie, knowing that workers would moderate their demands out of the fear of military intervention, would not turn to the military. Now it is workers' out-of-equilibrium belief that the military are prone to intervention that supports democracy. The problem with such explanations is that while equilibrium beliefs can be based on observations of past events, and can be thus updated rationally, out-of-equilibrium beliefs are completely arbitrary. Hence, 'culture' becomes just a name for the black box of beliefs. This does not seem to us a fruitful line of investigation.

5.   On the difficulties of this conception as a positive theory of action, see Dunn (1996, Chap. 4).

6.   Trust is the recent fashion of democratic theorists. But one might wonder if democratic citizens should trust their governments too much: should they not, instead, monitor what governments are doing and sanction them appropriately?

7.   Such a consensus may be 'overlapping' (Rawls, 1993) in the sense that the reasons people accept the particular institutional framework may be different among groups holding different 'fundamental' values.

8.   Eckstein (1961), as well as Eckstein and Gurr (1975), are among those who claim that democratic politics also require democratic value to permeate less inclusive social units such as families, communities or workplaces. For a contrary view, see Linz (1996).

9.   According to Wiarda (1981) the political systems of contemporary Latin America are the product of a political culture that is unique to the region and incompatible with democracy. This culture, which he calls the 'corporative model', follows directly from 'the Spanish colonial system of organicism, patrimonialism, manorialism, corporatism, and feudalism' (p. 39). When applied to particular countries, this approach leads to observations such as 'Dominican political culture historically has not been conducive to democratic rule. We consider this a very important factor. Dominican political culture, inherited from Spain, has been absolutist, élitist, hierarchical, corporatist, and authoritarian' (Wiarda, 1989, p. 450).

10.   For a technical reader, we need to raise a caveat. In most situations, there are several equilibria. One is 'war': the winner expects the loser to rebel, the loser expects the winner not to hold elections, and they fight it out. Another is dictatorship without a war: the dictator does not put down so much as provoke the opposition and the opposition finds that it is better off acquiescing to the dictatorship than fighting. Thus, a democratic equilibrium, if one exists, is just one of several, which means that Weingast (1997) is correct to emphasize the importance of co-ordination. Yet if the choice of equilibrium depends on economic development, then culture plays no role in this choice.

11.   Note that rates of time preference are fixed and exogenous in this story. These conclusions do not depend on the assumption that wealth makes people more patient.

12.   All the statistical results presented here are based on Przeworski et al. (in preparation). Published results include Przeworski et al. (1996) and Przeworski and Limongi (1997). The data cover 135 countries and a total of 4,126 years. Among them, there were 100 democracies which together lasted 1,645 years. All the income figures are expressed in 1985 purchasing power parity United States dollars.

13. These patterns are not random. A dynamic probit analysis in which transition probabilities are conditioned on per capita income predicts quite well the observed values. The coefficient on per capita income in survival analyses, in which the dependent variable is the logarithm of the duration, is positive and highly significant. See Przeworski and Limongi (1997).

14. Transitions to dictatorship are coded differently in Table 4 and in Table 3. In Table 3, regimes in which the incumbents perpetuated an *autogolpe* at any time during their tenure in office are classified as dictatorships throughout. In Table 2, such regimes are classified as democracies until the *autogolpe* occurred. Hence, the transitions in Table 4 include all those in Table 3 plus the transitions by incumbents. For details see Alvarez et al. (1996). Note that what we observe are the outcomes of conflicts rather than their initiation: hence, an inference is entailed in interpreting these results.

15. Lipset does not point to any specific text of Weber. Neither do Almond and Verba (1965 [1963], p. 8), who assert that 'the development of Protestantism, and in particular the nonconformist sects, *have been considered* vital to the development of stable political institutions in Britain, the Old Commonwealth, and the United States'. (Italics added.)

16. The *ex-post* method is even more apparent in cultural analyses of economic growth. See Sen (1997).

17. Thus Nathan and Shi (1993) find elements of democratic culture in China, while Gibson, Duch and Tedin (1992) discover them in Russia.

18. The proportion of legislative seats held by the largest party is not significant in statistical analyses.

19. Fractionalization indices measure the probability that two randomly chosen individuals do not belong to the same group. The index of ethnolingistic fractionalization is taken from Easterly and Levine (1997; from the Web). Their data set also contains indices measuring the percentage of the population not speaking the official and the most widely used language. These two indices have no effect on regime stability.

Bibliography

ALVAREZ, M.; CHEIBUB, J. A.; LIMONGI, F.; PRZEWORSKI, A. 1996. Classifying Political Regimes. *Journal of International Comparative Development*, No. 31, pp. 3–36.

BARRY, B. 1978. *Sociologists, Economists, and Democracy.* Chicago, University of Chicago Press.

COHEN, J. 1997. Procedure and Substance in Deliberative Democracy. In: J. Elster (ed.), *Democratic Deliberation.* New York, Cambridge University Press.

COLLINI, S.; WINCH, D.; BURROW, J. 1983. *That Noble Science of Politics.* Cambridge, Cambridge University Press.

DAHL, R. 1956. *A Preface to Democratic Theory.* Chicago, University of Chicago Press.

DUNN, J. 1992. Conclusion. In: J. Dunn (ed.), *Democracy: The Unfinished Journey,* pp. 239–66. Oxford, Oxford University Press.

——. 1996. *The History of Political Theory and Other Essays.* Cambridge, Cambridge University Press.

ECKSTEIN, H. 1961. *A Theory of Stable Democracy.* Princeton, New Jersey, Princeton University Center for International Studies.

ECKSTEIN, H.; GURR, T. R. 1975. *Patterns of Inquiry: A Structural Basis for Political Inquiry.* New York, Wiley.

EICKELMAN, D. F.; PISCATORI, J. 1996. *Muslim Politics.* Princeton, Princeton University Press.

EISENSTADT, S. N. 1968. The Protestant Ethic Theses in the Framework of Sociological Theory and Weber's Work. In: S. N. Eisenstadt (ed.), *The Protestant Ethic and Modernization: A Comparative View,* pp. 3–45. New York, Basic Books.

ESPOSITO, J. L.; VOLL, J. O. 1996. *Islam and Democracy.* New York, Oxford University Press.

FUKUYAMA, F. 1995. The Primacy of Culture. *Journal of Democracy,* No. 6.

GELLNER, E. 1991. Civil Society in Historical Context. *International Social Science Journal* (Paris, UNESCO), No. 129, pp. 495–510.

GERTH, H. H.; WRIGHT MILLS, C. (eds.). 1958. *From Max Weber: Essays in Sociology.* New York, Oxford University Press.

GIBSON, J. L.; DUCH, R. M.; TEDIN, K. L. 1992. Democratic Values and the Transformation of the Soviet Union. *Journal of Politics,* No. 54.

GRANATO, J.; INGLEHART, R.; LEBLANG, D. 1996. Cultural Values, Stable Democracy, and Economic Development: A Reply. *American Journal of Political Science,* No. 40, pp. 680–96.

HOBSBAWM, E.; RANGER, T. (eds.). 1983. *The Invention of Tradition.* Cambridge, Cambridge University Press.

HUNTINGTON, S. P. 1993. Democracy's Third Wave. In: L. Diamond and M. F. Plattner (eds.), *The Global Resurgence of Democracy,* pp. 3–25. Baltimore, Johns Hopkins Press.

IM, H. B. 1997. *The Compatibility of Confucianism and Democratic Civil Society in Korea.* (Paper presented at the IPSA XVIIth World Congress, Seoul, Republic of Korea, 17–21 August 1997.)

INGLEHART, R. 1990. *Culture Shift in Advanced Industrial Society.* Princeton, Princeton University Press.

JACKMAN, R. W.; MILLER, R. A. 1996. A Renaissance of Political Culture? *American Journal of Political Science,* No. 40, pp. 632–59.

KALYVAS, S. N. 1996. *The Rise of Christian Democracy in Europe.* Ithaca, Cornell University Press.

——. 1997. *Religion and Democratization: Belgium and Algeria.* (Paper presented at the Annual Meeting of the American Political Science Association, Washington, D.C., 28–31 August 1997.)

LAITIN, D. 1995. National Revivals and Violence. *Archives Européennes de Sociologie,* No. 36, pp. 3–43.

LASWELL, H. D. 1946. *Power and Personality.* New York.

LEWIS, B. 1993. Islam and Liberal Democracy. *Atlantic Monthly,* Vol. 271, No. 2, pp. 89–98.

LINZ, J. J.; STEPAN, A. 1996. *Problems of Democratic Transition and Consolidation.* Baltimore, John Hopkins.

LIPSET, S. M. 1959. Some Social Requisites of Democracy: Economic Development and Political Legitimacy. *American Political Science Review,* No. 53, pp. 69–105.

——. 1960. *Political Man.* Garden City, New York, Doubleday.

——. 1994. The Social Requisites of Democracy Revisited. *American Sociological Review,* No. 59, pp. 1–21.

MARAVALL, J. M. 1995. *Democracia y Democratas. Estudio 1995/65.* Madrid, Instituto Juan March de Estudios e Investigaciones.

MAZRUI, A. A. 1997. Islamic and Western Values. *Foreign Affairs,* Vol. 76, No. 5, pp. 118–32.

MILL, J. S. 1991. *Considerations on Representative Government.* Buffalo, New York, Prometheus Books (First published in 1861.)

MONTESQUIEU. 1995. *De l'esprit des lois.* Paris, Gallimard.

MULLER, E. N.; SELIGSON, M. A. 1994. Civil Culture and Democracy: The Question of Causal Relationships. *American Political Science Review,* No. 88, pp. 635–52.

NATHAN, A. J.; SHI, T. 1993. Cultural Requisites for Democracy in China: Findings from a Survey. *Dedalus,* No. 122.

NEUBAUER, D. E. 1967. Some Conditions of Democracy. *American Political Science Review,* No. 61, pp. 1002–9.

PRZEWORSKI, A. 1991. *Democracy and the Market.* New York, Cambridge University Press.

——. 1997. *Why Democracy Survives in Affluent Countries.* (Paper presented at the Annual Meeting of the American Political Science Association, San Francisco, 1997.)

PRZEWORSKI, A.; ALVAREZ, M.; CHEIBUB, J. A.; LIMONGI, F. 1996. What Makes Democracy Endure? *Journal of Democracy,* Vol. 7, No. 1, pp. 39–56.

——. (In preparation.) *Democracy and Development: Political Institutions and Economic Performance in the World, 1950–1990.*

PRZEWORSKI, A.; LIMONGI, F. 1997. Modernization: Theories and Facts. *World Politics,* No. 49, pp. 155–84.

RAWLS, J. 1993. The Domain of the Political and Overlapping Consensus. In: D. Copp, J. Hampton and J. E. Roemer (eds.), *The Idea of Democracy.* Cambridge, Cambridge University Press.

ROUSSEAU, J.-J. 1985. *The Government of Poland.* Indianapolis. Hackett. (First published in 1771.)

SCHMITTER, P. C.; KARL, T. L. 1991. What Democracy Is . . . and Is Not. *Journal of Democracy,* No. 2, pp. 75–88.

SEN, A. 1997. *Culture and Development: Global Perspectives and Constructive Criticism.* (Paper prepared for UNESCO's *World Culture Report 1998.*)

TOCQUEVILLE, A. DE. 1961. *De la démocratie en Amérique.* Paris, Gallimard.

VERSINI, L. 1995. Introduction. In: Montesquieu, *De l'esprit des lois,* pp. 9–64. Paris, Gallimard.

WEBER, M. 1958. *The Protestant Ethic and the Spirit of Capitalism.* New York, Charles Scribner's Sons. (First published in 1904–05.)

WEINGAST, B. R. 1997. Political Foundations of Democracy and the Rule of Law. *American Political Science Review,* No. 91, pp. 245–63.

WIARDA, H. J. 1981. *Corporatism and National Development in Latin America.* Boulder, Westview.

——. 1989. The Dominican Republic: Mirror Legacies of Democracy and Authoritarianism. In: L. Diamond, J. J. Linz and S. M. Lipset (eds.), *Democracy in Developing Countries: Latin America.* Boulder, Colorado, Lynne Rienner Publishers.

WIATR, J. J. 1979. The Civic Culture from a Marxist Sociological Perspective. In: G. A. Almond and S. Verba (eds.), *The Civic Culture Revisited,* pp. 103–23. Boston, Little, Brown & Co.

WINCH, D. 1978. *Adam Smith's Politics: An Essay in Historiographic Revision.* Cambridge, Cambridge University Press.

Chapter 9
Culture, ethics and globalization

Yoro K. Fall
Historian and philosopher; Former member,
World Commission on Culture and Development;
Director of the International Centre for Human
and Social Sciences, Beirut (Lebanon)

'Confusion emerges where cultural values are pitted against human rights. Everyone knows that cultural rights are relative but, in strictly philosophical terms, that view is more political than truly cultural.'

Ethical sedimentation

Contemporary ethical requirements are intricately linked to the current process of globalization in culture, communication and the economy. The relationship between culture and ethics would seem to be more evident and easier to clarify at first glance. The Universal Declaration of Human Rights and the regional legal instruments which are related to those rights or which provide them with an additional geographical basis in relation to the international system (which is more authentic in terms of the commitment of states to implement the principles of the Declaration), the lengthy process of ethical sedimentation that we have witnessed for several years on account of the combined progress of science and technology and, lastly, needs which have arisen from the raising of the intellectual, cultural and academic level of populations, all reveal very close links between ethics and culture. There is talk today of the rights of future generations and the ethics of science and technology, all of which converge on international declarations.

The Universal Declaration on the Human Genome and Human Rights provides for the first time in history a scientific definition of human rights. Whereas the Declaration on the Responsibility of Present Generations Towards Future Generations innovates by recognizing the rights of unborn persons.

Naturally, there may be a certain diversity in positions and it is already possible to classify them according to two major approaches: the first of these consists in stating that the Universal Declaration of Human Rights is quite adequate and that any attempt to extend its scope in the form of other declarations would entail a proliferation of declarations which would reduce the scope of the Universal Declaration; the second approach consists in saying that the very development of the world necessitates seeking an agreement on a number of principles within the international community, and all the more so in the face of new challenges put forward by the sciences, technology and the lightning pace of development in communication that has abolished space and time, and distance and duration. These principles are born out of the necessity to place such developments and new technologies at the service of humanity rather than that of the enslavement of human beings. The second approach is probably the more judicious.

The elaboration of the Universal Declaration of Human Rights was much more the result of the cristallization of various parameters which had emerged several centuries earlier – at least since the Age of Enlightenment – and which had gradually been fashioned through political strife in Europe itself, the Americas and the colonial world, and through the agents and repercussions of the struggle against Nazism and Fascism.

Another very important aspect of the links between culture and ethics is the fact that the principles of the said international instruments have now become present in all countries. Regardless of the positions of states, and whether or not they acknowledge that their populations should be able to enjoy such rights, there is no longer a single country in the world where organized groups of young people and women do not call for implementation of the principles of the Universal Declaration of Human Rights, thereby contributing to anchor in the daily experience of nations, and in their political and social aspirations, the implementation of principles to ensure that those defined in the Declaration are made effective.

Human rights as a universal achievement

This means that the development and dissemination of the principles of the Universal Declaration of Human Rights give substance to cultural life and involve innovators, artists, poets and writers, quite as much and often more so than lawyers who have contributed substantially to disseminating the principles of the Declaration.

Finally, this is all the more so when human rights are increasingly seen today as the indispensable basis for human existence, and in so far as the very legitimacy of the Declaration of Human Rights stems from the fact that every human being calls for, requires and claims the right to benefit from the principles of the Declaration on which the universality of human beings is based. Therefore, culture and ethics are bound together by close links, constantly renewed, developing substantially in the present-day world and likely to develop even further in the future. However, this has become combined with new phenomena through globalization. An admittedly long-standing process is involved, the cumulative effects of which are relatively recent, however; these imply the standardization of the whole range of production and marketing systems. The phenomena of standardization have developed in a world which is profoundly marked by diversity in economic policies according to the societies concerned. For example, the way a Japanese company operates is very different from that of a French one as each of the operating patterns is intricately linked to Japanese or French culture. The system of redistribution of wealth is also closely linked to cultures and values; the debate on equality and equity accurately reflects this phenomenon where there is a shift from the legal concept of equality to the economic concept of equity. It is this debate that calls for a degree of clarification.

The economy of the contemporary world is torn between the logic of standardization and homogenization and the logic of heterogeneousness. Here lies a source of conflicts. According to trade-union traditions, methods of social organization and the socio-economic traditions of countries, the phenomenon which manifests itself in the contrast between the homogenization and heterogeneousness of economic policies is a source of conflict. We can, therefore, expect to see social conflicts arise in many countries on accounts of this genuine economic and

technological change. Furthermore, the problems that we have to face today in the relationship between ethics and culture or between ethics and the economy have arisen in a context in which the notion of ethics has not yet been clarified.

Globalization itself lies at the heart of the complexity of phenomena facing humanity and society today in terms of ethics and the implementation and effectiveness of the principles enshrined in the Declaration of Human Rights, the instruments attached to it, the pacts and regional instruments and the new generation of human rights represented by the Declaration on the Human Genome, responsibility as regards present and future generations and, in certain instances, the Declaration on the Human Right to Peace.

Human rights and cultural values

The complexity of the very concept of ethics rightly calls for, within the heart of society and the development of peoples, the identification of a number of standards that need to be observed, more urgently than others, by societies and states.

In *Our Creative Diversity*, the World Commission on Culture and Development selected five major lines of emphasis, namely human rights and responsibilities, democracy and the elements of civil society, the protection of minorities, commitment to peaceful conflict-resolution and fair negotiation and, last but not least, equity within and between generations.[1]

It can be said, however, that these correspond to seeking only a minimum of values, principles and ethical standards. The debate or call for a solution is hampered by two obstacles: the first is linked to the debate on rights and values, while the second rests on the confusion between morality and ethics.

The first stumbling-block is the confusion between rights and values. The Universal Declaration of Human Rights and the very principles of human rights naturally have a cultural value, but they are cultural values in so far as they constitute values that are virtually universally valid, acceptable and proclaimed. In fact, every man and woman calls for the principles of the Universal Declaration of Human Rights to be applied to them. This represents the universal dimension which, as such, is a value in the mathematical sense of the term. These principles also have a value in so far as they correspond to principles in all cultures and societies. The universality of human rights and principles is therefore based on the fact that every man and woman acknowledges, claims and demands that those principles be applied to them.

Confusion emerges where cultural values are pitted against human rights. Everyone knows that cultural rights are relative but, in strictly philosophical terms, that view is more political than truly cultural.

The political stance emerges when a man or woman, whoever he or she may be, is asked whether he or she accepts that the principles should be applied to another man or woman. There is marked similarity between this stance and that which amounts to saying 'Human rights do not apply to us because our culture is this or that' or 'Human rights stem from Western culture'. It must be said, however, that Westerners are perhaps too eager to claim for themselves, or their country, authorship of human rights and to assert that the Universal Declaration of Human Rights is part of or even the very expression of their own culture. On the other hand, in the name of the values of their own people, political leaders from other parts of the world, those of non-Western countries in general, claim that these principles are linked to Western values which are culturally different from their own. In actual fact, the political, ideological and non-cultural stance comes to light as soon as these cultural values, which are supposed to be in a process of transition, are claimed to be absolute and, on the other hand, when the issue is to know whether or not the rights of minorities and women should be recognized, and so forth. In actual fact, it is the minorities themselves which should decide whether these principles are applicable to them or not. No minority will refuse such principles being applied to them. Similarly, women must make their position clear: no woman will refuse equality. The problem, therefore, is a confusion between a political decision – an ideological choice – and principles, in the name of so-called 'cultural values' which do not really exist.

This debate is by no means new in historical terms. It in fact originated before the Universal Declaration of Human Rights, as it dates back to the late eighteenth century. The arguments put forward today were largely to be found in the controversy on the application to slaves of the principles, standards and codes laid down or specified in the Declaration of the Rights of Man and of the Citizen proclaimed by the French Revolution. The debate continued between the advocates and opponents of slavery. The former persevered in asking whether slaves actually had a soul and whether or not they should be recognized, once they had been liberated, as men and citizens. The latter finally won the case and were able to secure the first abolition of slavery in France by the Convention.[2]

Two contradictory questions opposed the protagonists in the debate: 'What do we have in common?' and 'What common features do we share?'

The manner in which yesterday's arguments coincide with those of today is as symbolic and instructive as the coincidence of the 150th anniversary of the abolition of slavery with the 50th anniversary of the Universal Declaration of Human Rights. The logic underlying circumstances often coincides with the logic of choices.

Morals and ethics

The second confusion is that raised between morals and ethics. Morals are linked to the very definition of ethics. Moral principles are extremely diverse. As it happens, morals, historically speaking, have come to be increasingly connected with religion as human

society has developed. Therefore, the moral debate has also become a religious one and, as many religious phenomena do not lie beyond the scope of laws, between majorities and minorities, nor the ideological choices involved, it may be difficult to find the same moral values for all societies. Moral values are very diverse. A number of values are universal: 'Thou shalt not steal', for example; but there are societies where 'honourable theft' is part of the structuring of the human personality, and therefore morals. We can therefore think that moral values are admittedly absolute in nature and, as such, are fundamental for each culture.

Ethics are related to institutions and rights. The Universal Declaration of Human Rights and human rights accordingly stem from ethics even if no moral grounds can be adduced. Yet moral grounds are to be found everywhere, including science. From the point where, in the name of ethics, science itself does not fall outside this domain, morals, similarly, do not lie outside the realm of ethics as ethics are a profoundly human, secular construction in so far as they represent a conscious choice or plan and a legal endeavour in terms of the law. The confusion that exists between rights and values on the one hand and between morals and ethics on the other lie at the heart of the debate on universal ethics, that is to say, universal ethics based on recognition of human rights.

Effectiveness of human rights

In fact, the only major contemporary issue raised by ethics in the context of globalization is the effectiveness of human rights through the societies and cultures of all countries and all societies. We know that when human rights are effectively recognized, we can identify the foundations of a democratic society. However, the effectiveness of human rights, i.e.the reality of democracy – whether it be electoral procedure or the political management of democracy – is obviously linked to democratic culture, and it can only be achieved if

human rights are institutionalized, that is to say, if institutions and legislative regulatory legal machinery are set up, in order to ensure the effectiveness of human rights.

Observation of recent world phenomena suggests that violent conflicts arise out of the absence of institutions aimed at guaranteeing human rights. All too often, contemporary conflicts, of which violence is a major feature, can be solved once judicial institutions have been created. Evidence of this is to be found in the international tribunals: one has been created for Rwanda and another for the former Yugoslavia. These belong to the great tradition of international tribunals which began with the Nuremberg trials. For resolving such conflicts, human rights and the institutionalization of a state of law have become a necessity in political, economic and moral terms. Conversely, trends towards ethics do not eliminate moral trends. This can be perceived through the spectacular gestures of forgiveness and repentance – such as when a German head of state seeks forgiveness for Nazi crimes or when another head of state recognizes the responsibility of his country for the Sho'ah; or in South Africa, where an institution was set up for repentance and forgiveness. This involves the rehabilitation of moral principles in political life and international relations.

Other phenomena which have received great media attention also constitute an example. This is true of the death of Princess Diana which, by the way it is expressed, can be likened to a classical tragedy. Indeed, faced with the same event, men, women and young people throughout the world have had at the same time the same reactions, those of dismay and repulsion. Among the various interpretations that could be given to the event were the aspiration to love without frontiers in spite of religious differences, the tragic union of two individuals in death, the struggle for the recognition of women's rights, the struggle for the recognition of young people's rights, newly developing forces

seeking to display the role they have to play in contemporary society, the fight against anti-personnel mines and the commitment that is a token of the human conscience. This gives some measure of how massive a phenomenon it is, of very great social intensity in the claim for and the effectiveness for implementing human rights.

The logic of responsibility

It is the logic of rights that leads also to the logic of responsibility. This is shown by the increasing importance of public opinion as conveyed and expressed by civil society and the media, in its call for political, diplomatic, military or peaceful intervention in order to put an end to the violence in which conflicts of identity tend to develop or the massive violation of human rights. This was the case in Bosnia as, alas, it has now become the case in Algeria with the currents of intolerable slaughter. This applies as much to culture as to the economy. As cultures, societies and economic approaches are multiple, policies too have to be of a pluralistic nature. This accounts for their crucial importance in relationships between culture and development. Human rights, in simple terms, are also a question of responsibility, rights that are part of the responsibility of every individual and every state. Naturally, the logic of responsibility is intrinsically linked to the logic of rights because, in the social field, any right becomes a responsibility towards another human being. The necessity of living together transforms every right into a responsibility. The need to recognize and respect every individual's rights introduces the notion of responsibility towards others in the effectiveness and implementation of those rights. Conversely, we can see that insisting exclusively on responsibility does not necessarily lead to a logic of rights. Whereas the logic of rights entails, introduces and leads to that of responsibility. States are wholly responsible for ensuring the effectiveness of human rights in political, legal, institutional and jurisdictional terms.

These deeply rooted social phenomena represent the hidden side of globalization and introduce reflection on ethics into any thinking on globalization. That being so, they bring the cultural dimension into play in globalization since ethics have now become the most accomplished expression of cultural production and of the human conscience.

Notes

1.   World Commission on Culture and Development, *Our Creative Diversity*, Paris, UNESCO, 1995, pp. 40–6.
2.   C. Wanquet, *La France et la première abolition de l'esclavage 1794–1802*, Paris, Karthala, 1998.

Part Three
Creativity, markets and cultural policies

Introduction to Part Three

The closing years of the twentieth century have been marked by an increasingly rapid rate of globalization in world markets. As economic systems become more closely integrated, as financial markets transcend national boundaries and information exchange around the world becomes easier and faster, global markets have emerged for many of the goods and services that are bought and sold in every country every day by countless millions of people.

Although these rapid changes have expanded the range of choice available to citizens all over the world, they also bring with them a sense of insecurity. The cultural values which identify and link local, regional or national communities seem in danger of being overwhelmed by the relentless forces of the global market place. In these circumstances questions are raised as to how societies can manage the impacts of globalization such that local and national cultures, and the creativity that sustains them, are not damaged but rather are preserved and enhanced. This is a central task for cultural policy.

This Part of the report examines the ways in which cultural policy, whether in developed or developing countries, can be recontextualized and reformulated so that it will be able to meet the changing demands on it in the opening years of the new millennium. It looks particularly at the impact of global markets on creativity, on the emergence and development of the cultural industries, on cultural heritage, and on the protection of the rights of creators and of the public interest in the age of cyberculture. These chapters acknowledge a role for national (or regional or local) governments in representing the collective interests of their citizens, allowing us to speak of a cultural policy which can be directed at shaping and managing cultural change on behalf of those citizens.

Although the state (including both national and subnational governments) is the principal locus for cultural policy formulation, private initiatives may also be significant and indeed in some countries, such as the United States, may be of central

importance. In addition, independent organizations such as NGOs, artists' associations and so on, may be stakeholders in the process. In many countries, a shift towards the private sector in the balance of economic activity has been occurring in recent years, indicating the need for new partnerships between governments, corporations and communities, as the purely state-based intra-national policies of the past are replaced by broader trans-regional and multi-level approaches to cultural policy formulation.

In a rapidly changing world, there will be differences between countries and regions in the ways in which cultural policies can respond to the new challenges of the global market place. Canclini reports that in Latin America, for example, traditional forms in music and drama are using new media technologies to their advantage in producing new cultural products for export to the rest of the world. In post-communist Eastern Europe, according to Anastasyev, the fundamental economic and social changes of the last few years have redrawn the entire landscape in which cultural policy operates, whilst in Japan, as indicated by Watanabe, the cultural industries, especially the media, are emerging as a major economic sector, and notions of cultural development for culture's sake are increasingly difficult to maintain. This Part of the report describes four key aspects of cultural policy in the context of global change.

First, it may be suggested that, just as the arts lie at the core of the cultural sector, so too does the process of creativity lie at the centre of the arts. In a very real sense, then, cultural policy is about fostering creativity. But how does globalization affect the creative process? Perhaps there are opportunities here rather than threats. In music, in the visual arts, in literature, artists have responded to the stimuli provided by new technologies, new modes of communication and new aesthetic discourses. Stimpson and Bhabha, in fact, consider that the possibility can be entertained of a new notion of 'global creativity' drawing on a multiplicity of

cultural sources, utilizing new forms of communication, and reaching audiences far more diverse than has traditionally been the case.

Second, cultural policy is increasingly recognizing the economic importance of the cultural industries. These are industries which radiate outwards from the central role for the creative arts to embrace publishing, broadcasting, film and video, new media and so on. Some artists and others see the designation of the 'cultural industries' as indicating a subjugation of art to the market place, and a replacement of aesthetic values by commercial ones. But an alternative view is to see these processes as expanding the range of creative possibilities for artists, and as providing a means for gaining a clearer perspective on the role of culture in the economy. Cultural policy, then, can be linked with economic policy, in pursuit of the cultural as well as the economic objectives of society.

Cultural industries within national boundaries are being increasingly caught up in global market processes. Throsby proposes the example of music. Although in most countries a local music industry emerges at a certain stage of development, serving a domestic market with home-grown cultural messages conveyed in musical form, it is not long before the international music industry begins to have an impact, both on the type of music available for consumption and on the conditions of production of music by local individuals and groups. The dominance of transnational corporations in the music-recording industry is well-known, and even 'World Music', which has emerged as a distinct category incorporating the music of ethnic minorities, indigenous peoples and political movements, has been manipulated by the global music industry to its own advantage.

As the role of cultural industries becomes more sharply defined at both national and international levels, so the need to protect and reward creativity grows more urgent. Del Corral and Abada show that it is the central task of copyright law, enacted by domestic legislation and ratified by international treaty, to provide equitable remuneration to creative effort, and to ensure fair access by consumers to the products of that effort. There are many problems still in copyright enforcement in many parts of the world. Too frequently are creators of intellectual property in the cultural sphere denied their rightful recompense because of piracy and other infringements. In the age of new communications technologies, problems of copyright regulation are multiplied many times, and it is essential that more rapid progress be made, both within and between countries, in designing effective means of copyright protection in the digital era.

The third aspect of cultural policy to be considered is heritage. Cultural policy, in the words of Prott, in virtually all countries continues to have a major focus on the protection of cultural heritage, both tangible and intangible. Here again global market forces are having some significant impacts. Growth of trading relationships between countries brings with it greater opportunities for illicit trade in cultural property. Heritage management is being increasingly affected by transnational economic forces as new players (corporations, foundations, NGOs) enter the market place. Awareness is growing amongst international development and aid agencies of the impacts of development projects on cultural sites and on local cultural practice. Access to cultural heritage is changing too. Museum collections, states Vinson, are being digitized, enabling the functions of museums to be transformed to provide 'contact zones' between cultures, accessible to a vastly greater audience than in the past.

This leads us to the final aspect of cultural policy to be considered, namely its role in cyberculture. The information revolution has had economic, social, cultural and political ramifications whose eventual significance has yet to be fully understood. It also brings with it dangers of exacerbating economic, social and cultural inequality. Quéau reminds us that it is important in this context to identify the sphere of public interest in cyberspace, so that the rights of citizens can be protected. Cultural policies dealing explicitly with new communications technologies are appearing in some countries, but overall policy development in this area is still embryonic.

To sum up, a common thread running through the contributions to this Part of the report is the challenge to cultural policy presented by global economic change. It is argued that an inward-looking and defensive response to such change will be counter-productive. Rather, positive approaches are needed which look for new opportunities to harness change in pursuit of the cultural aspirations of society. Cultural policy must be seen not as resisting change but as managing it, in a context of global economic and cultural transformation.

Chapter 10
Cultural policy options in the context of globalization

Néstor García Canclini
Anthropologist and Head of the Programme of Studies
in Urban Culture, Autonomous Metropolitan University
of Mexico (UNAM) (Mexico)

'Cultural policies can no longer be approached as intranational policies implemented essentially by national governments.'

Democratization in the national perspective

This chapter attempts to understand how cultural policies can be revised in relation to the structural changes that have occurred in recent years in states, cultural markets and social movements. We shall confine the analysis to three changes: (a) the recomposition of national cultures through the advance of globalization and regional integration; (b) the predominance of the mass communication industries over traditional, local forms of production and circulation of culture, and (c) the new conditions generated by these changes for democratization and multicultural cohabitation.

In the first and second sections I shall present a description of the principal patterns of change. I shall then analyse some cultural policy options that have been developing in recent years, taking into account these end-of-century trends.

One way to focus the changes that have transpired in recent decades is to compare the lines of cultural policy thinking in the 1970s and 1980s with the current situation. In short, until a few years ago cultural policies were considered to mean all the action taken by the state, private institutions and community associations to orientate symbolic development, satisfy cultural needs within the nation and obtain a consensus around a form of order or

social change (Brunner, 1989; Fabrizio, 1982; Martín Barbero, 1995; Mattelart, 1991).

In the countries of Europe and Latin America, and in many African and Asian countries which have recently gained independence, nation-states were the main protagonists of cultural policies. States were considered responsible for the administration of the historic heritage, material and immaterial, from major monuments to manifestations of popular culture (language, music, traditional celebrations and dance), i.e. the distinctive features that differentiate one nation from another. The modern states achieved certain successes in unifying different ethnic groups and regions in a national heritage they more or less shared. In some countries this national cohesion hinged almost exclusively on the culture of the elite, of European origin, which the state endeavoured to transmit to the rest of the population through the school system. In others, like Mexico, Bolivia and Cuba, with different strategies, elements of popular culture were included in this policy. In this way many governments promoted the study and rehabilitation of archaeological sites and historic city centres, opened museums and produced publications designed to keep the memory of the past alive and disseminate it – all with a view to strengthening the common identity. Before the mass media and tourism, such measures succeeded in helping ethnic crafts, music and some regional knowledge to transcend their purely local dimension. In Mexico, for example, the joint dissemination of Tzotzil textiles, mural painting, Purepechan and Mixtec pottery and the Mayan pyramids formed a united iconographic repertory that was seen, inside and outside the country, as representative of Mexican culture.

Modern art (plastic arts, literature, music) and the mass media also received support from the state which owned radio stations and television channels, publishing houses and film production units. Even in countries where this was not the case, the arts and the mass media were studied and administered as part of the national culture. Avant-garde groups endeavouring to transcend the local context were identified with specific countries, as if national profiles served to define their projects of renovation: Russian constructivism, American pop art, Italian neo-realism, and the *nouveau roman* in France.

The cultural policy debate analysed whether the many groups, ethnic communities and regions were sufficiently represented in each national heritage, or whether states, in the organization and administration of their heritage, excessively reduced their local specificities to politico-cultural abstractions in the interest of social control or to legitimize a certain form of nationalism. There was also a controversy throughout the twentieth century over how to reconcile the traditional and the modern, how to disseminate cultural goods and messages in a more equitable manner and involve

different sectors in their creation and appropriation. The positions defended by the different policies over the decades were called 'statism', 'populism', 'nationalism', 'cultural democratization' and 'participative democracy' (Arantes, 1984; García Canclini, 1995; Vidal Beneyto, 1981). These terms expressed differences in cultural policies, but generally concurred in setting the debate within the national horizon and acknowledging the leading role played by the state.

In some countries, particularly the United States, private initiatives had always played an important part in the development of education and culture. Mainly, however, they promoted the arts and literature, through patronage and in keeping with the ideals of altruism and freedom to create in the fine arts. Of course the donors sought prestige and other, not necessarily symbolic, recompenses, while claiming to support creative artists out of pure generosity, for no other purpose than to foster spiritual development (Becker, 1988; Moulin, 1992). Private patronage of the arts gradually reorganized with the growth in purchasing power of the middle classes and the emergence of art markets and specific audiences, leading to the establishment of independent fields for the arts and literature (Becker, 1988; Bourdie, 1979). Foundations led by individuals or families sustained and continue to sustain the more costly activities or those least able to finance themselves (theatre, opera, biennial exhibitions), without their financial contributions affecting the independence of the artistic research. Sometimes this notion of patronage of the arts has influenced state policies (grants, subsidies), but in general it has been prevalent mainly in the private sector.

The third category of promoters of cultural policy is composed of independent organizations: associations of artists, communicators and cultural organizers, NGOs, neighbourhood organizations or groups representing so-called civil society. Their actions are almost always altruistic in terms of financial gain, and differ from patronage of the arts

because they are not motivated by the tastes of privileged individuals but by a collective conception of culture that links it with the aesthetic needs and practices of the receivers or users; their limited funds in relation to these needs, or the voluntary work they do, and the importance they generally attribute to local lifestyles mean that their policies focus on restricted areas. As José Vidal Beneyto (1981) has said, in these cases cultural policy 'aims more at the activities than at the works, more at participation in the process than at consumption of the product' (p. 128). This line of work gradually increased on every continent, especially in Africa, Asia and Latin America, with the processes of political and social democratization. It has been adopted by international organizations (UNESCO, OAS), and various foundations, and their cultural work undoubtedly favours the formation and organization of popular groups in defence of their rights to document their living conditions and their creativity. But these essentially local actions are no substitute today for the state; nor do they counterbalance the growing privatization of the public sector.

Deterritorialized cultures

These three sides of cultural policies still exist, and to a large extent their action continues to have meaning within national societies. A large proportion of production in crafts, arts and the media continues to express national cultural traditions, and circulates only within the country concerned. The visual arts, literature and increasingly the electronic media continue to fuel the imagination of each nation; they are the scene of consecration and communication for artists, expressions and signs of regional identities.

However, an increasing sector of cultural production is taking on an industrialized shape, circulating in transnational communication networks, being received by the consuming masses, who are learning to be the audiences of deterritorialized messages: what Brazilian anthropologist Renato Ortiz calls 'an international-

popular folklore'. These international communities of spectators reduce the importance of national differences. The younger generations in particular live their cultural practices in accordance with homogenized information and styles that are received by different societies independently of their political, religious or national context. Consumers from different social backgrounds are able to read the messages of a multi-locational imagination projected by television and advertising; Hollywood movie stars, pop stars, the works of famous painters, sports champions and politicians from different countries compose a repertory of ever available signs.

The changes that have occurred since the middle of the century, especially since the 1960s, may be resumed in the difference between internationalization and globalization. The internationalization of economies and cultures, which has marked the whole of the modern era, consists in opening the geographical frontiers of each society to messages and goods from other countries. A period of globalization, on the other hand, is marked by functional interaction between different economic activities and cultures, generated by a system with many centres, where speed in reaching other parts of the world and strategies for attracting audiences are more decisive than the inertia of local traditions (Appadurai, 1990; Arizpe, 1996; Castells, 1995; Hannerz, 1992; Ortiz, 1994).

This process is doubtless most apparent in the electronic communication networks. To a certain extent, however, it spans almost every area of cultural development, including the traditional arts and crafts. As a result, it redefines the roles of the various protagonists we have mentioned: states, private initiative and independent organizations.

To realize just how far we have come in only two decades we need only remember that twenty years ago one of the key dilemmas in cultural policies was the extent to which imported products and messages should be accepted, interaction with international trends in art and thinking should be

Cultural policies in post-Soviet Russia

During the 1980s, the perestroika process broke down much of the repressive climate which had surrounded the arts and culture in the former Soviet Union for many years. The changes were largely due to a discarding of obsolete ideologies and had little to do with economics. But the collapse of Communism and the transition from a state-controlled to a market economy turned the arts upside down almost overnight. The winds of economic change then blew sharply on the cultural sector.

Before 1992 publishers did not have to worry about the cost of paper, materials and printing facilities. Theatre administrators and directors did not need to worry about rent, the price of sets, electricity and so on. Librarians could order new books within their budgets without hesitation. Everything was controlled by the state, and so the state was responsible for financing all such cultural activity.

Many professional workers in the cultural sector were not prepared for the suddenness of the change, and the economic effects on the sector have been catastrophic. Although many theatres, publishing houses, film studios, museums, libraries and so on are still state property, subsidies have been either cut to a minimum or terminated altogether. Print runs of literary magazines have fallen from hundreds of thousands in the late 1980s to 10,000 or less now. For example, *The Urals*, one of the most reputable journals in Russia outside Moscow and St Petersburg, now has a circulation of only 1,600. *Theatre Monthly*, the only title in the country focused on the dramatic arts, has now ceased publication. Print-runs of books have been drastically reduced. The film industry is in ruins; the leading Russian studio, Mosfilm, which used to produce up to fifty films a year in the 1970s and 1980s, brought out only three films in 1997. Libraries have no money to maintain their holdings, and the administration of the Tretyakov Gallery, with its unique collection of Russian paintings and drawings, has twice had to reduce its security service.

Thus, whilst spiritual freedom may be an absolute value and an undisputed blessing, economic freedom, in the form of the free market, has proved to be a curse.

Yet the picture of the cultural sector in present-day Russia is not an entirely gloomy one. For instance, the number of private publishing houses is growing steadily,

encouraged and endogenous creation should be protected and promoted. African and Asian artists, whose countries were emerging from long periods of colonization, and Latin American artists who were endeavouring to keep up with the cosmopolitan modernization and at the same time the independent industrial development of their societies, felt new options opening up between the local and the remote. Some opted to integrate the innovations of the international avant-garde into their local cultures, while others believed that symbolic customs barriers should be set up to control the 'invasion' of foreign cultures and each nation should invest its resources in strengthening its own independent progress. These options, taken to their extreme, have become less viable because of the technological, economic and symbolic changes in cultural market structures. But the alternatives continue to have a certain echo in the present conditions. We shall now look at how processes are reorganizing in three fields: the plastic arts, literature and the communication industries.

The post-national visual arts

The visual arts began to be absorbed in the process of globalization in the 1980s, as the market for the works produced expanded, prices rose and exhibitions and auctions became the scene of heavy investment. A minority of artists, although they numbered several thousand among the forty or fifty countries that made up the international market,

and some of them are bringing out what may be termed serious literature. The theatre is slowly picking itself up. Some of the drama companies that first appeared with the dawn of perestroika are now coming of age; the most striking example of these is Oleg Takakov's Tabakerka, and some of the older theatres too, such as the Arts Theatre and the Sovremennik, are regaining public attention.

In fact, the process of transition has meant that the place of the state in subsidizing cultural projects is being taken over by various foundations, sponsors and patrons from abroad. For example, the Tabakerka company is generously supported by Incombank, one of the most respected of Russian financial institutions. Logovaz, a leading company in the Russian automobile industry, has been supporting the activities of the Triumpf Foundation which gives annual prizes for high achievements in Russian arts and letters. Another major financial group, Oneksim, has just signed an agreement with the Hermitage Museum in St Petersburg to finance an ambitious publishing programme. The contributions from outside the country of George Soros's 'Open Society' Institute are noteworthy, as is the 'Pushkin' programme inaugurated six years ago by the French Government to stimulate Russian translation of French literature.

Against this background, the cultural policies of the state look unimpressive, to say the least. True, the government has to look to countless urgent priorities elsewhere. It is true, too, that a democratic state in a free market system cannot be the sole, or even the main, patron of the arts. However, it should be said that the government is making an effort to support libraries, museums, theatres and publishers, and has taken several commendable initiatives in the field of culture, including the federal book-publishing programme and the recently launched state-owned TV channel called 'Culture'. But it is clear none the less that culture is fairly low in the order of state priorities.

Culture in Russia will of course survive. But it also needs certain facilities if it is to function normally. It remains for Russia to reconsider its priorities and to adapt cultural policies to the changes that have intervened in the economy since 1992.

Nickolay Anastasyev
Specialist in comparative literature, Professor of World Literature, Moscow State University (Russian Federation)

formed a system of rivals manipulated by galleries based in cities on different continents: Buenos Aires, London, Milan, New York, Paris, São Paulo and Tokyo. These galleries, allied with the main museums and international magazines, controlled the world market in a concentrated form. Towards the end of the 1980s, Sotheby's and Christie's accounted for almost three-quarters of the public sales of art. Although Sotheby's capital is predominantly American, giving the impression that the United States play a hegemonic role in the art market, the firm has auction houses in fourteen countries, and has opened offices in over a hundred countries on every continent (Moulin, 1994). Other firms, of lesser stature, also have multinational structures, giving their operations a financial and aesthetic versatility that enables them to react to movements, artists and audiences in different societies. The more or less simultaneous circulation of exhibitions, or at least of information about them, in museum networks in different countries and in international fairs and exhibitions in which the marks of individual countries have less and less importance, and the media impact of art events, have reduced the national character of creative productions.[1]

The traces of national artistic frameworks are still to be found in those countries which used their cultural policies to strengthen their national identities and mark their international diplomacy: France and the United Kingdom, which now account together for no more than 15% of all public operations on the world market, have lost some of their aesthetic leadership and organized fewer exhibitions in the 1990s. At the same time, the prosperity of the industrial countries of South-East Asia and the legislation through which they encourage public and private patronage of the arts has boosted the opening of museums in these countries, which acquire large quantities of works from Western and Asian countries alike. Japan, for example, in 1989 alone, imported almost 2 billion dollars' worth of works of art. And Hong Kong and Singapore have become centres of international art fairs and exhibitions which attract artists from all over the world.

It should be noted that the global reorganization of artistic development is not based on economic considerations alone. The fact that the art market no longer functions as a juxtaposition of national markets but has its own worldwide structure is important, but this reorganization of the market could not take place if the museums, publishers and academic circles which influence aesthetic values and the prestige of the artists and experts who consecrate them, did not also function on a global scale. The best-known critics and artists are not the product of a national context or a long stay in a major city, or a leading university or museum, but rather of the ability to move flexibly between numerous centres on every continent. Transfrontier relations are becoming more decisive than national representativity, and multicultural alliances more important than identification with a particular culture: it is to the artists, critics, galleries and museum experts who combine the local with the global that we might apply the term 'glocalize', coined by Japanese businessmen to denote the ductility of those who combine the distinctive features of the different cultures in which they are active with the new global culture, i.e. that which governs both the plastic arts and the iconography produced for circulation via the transnational

audiovisual and electronic communication media. In these conditions, cultural policies must consider the promotion both of national museums and of international exhibitions, and the relationship between their own national historic and artistic heritage and the global circuits on which the works are exhibited, traded and appreciated.

The publishing industry

One field in which the difficulties experienced by national cultural production and the complexity of its interactions with the transnational markets are particularly manifest is the production of books, magazines, comics and *fotonovelas*. I shall take as an example what is happening in the Latin American countries, particularly Mexico, and the reorganization of their ties with Europe and the United States.

Argentina and Mexico developed prosperous publishing industries in the twentieth century. Partly under their own economic and cultural steam and partly with the help of Spanish exiles, they published a profusion of works written in their own societies, in other Latin American countries and in Spain. They also published translations of works by numerous European and American authors and some Asian authors between 1940 and 1970. It was in this field that Latin America made a successful contribution in economic, literary and journalistic terms to the international circulation of cultural goods.

The decline of the region's economies over the last two decades and the simultaneous rise of Spain changed this picture. Publishing houses and bookshops closed and many newspapers and magazines went bankrupt or reduced their size in almost all the countries of Latin America. Some 400 publishing houses in Mexico went bankrupt from 1989 onwards, and among the survivors less than ten which are nationally owned publish more than fifty works per year (Citesa, Era, Esfinge, Fernández, Fondo de Cultura Económica, Limusa, Porrúa, Siglo XXI and Trillas). The global increase in

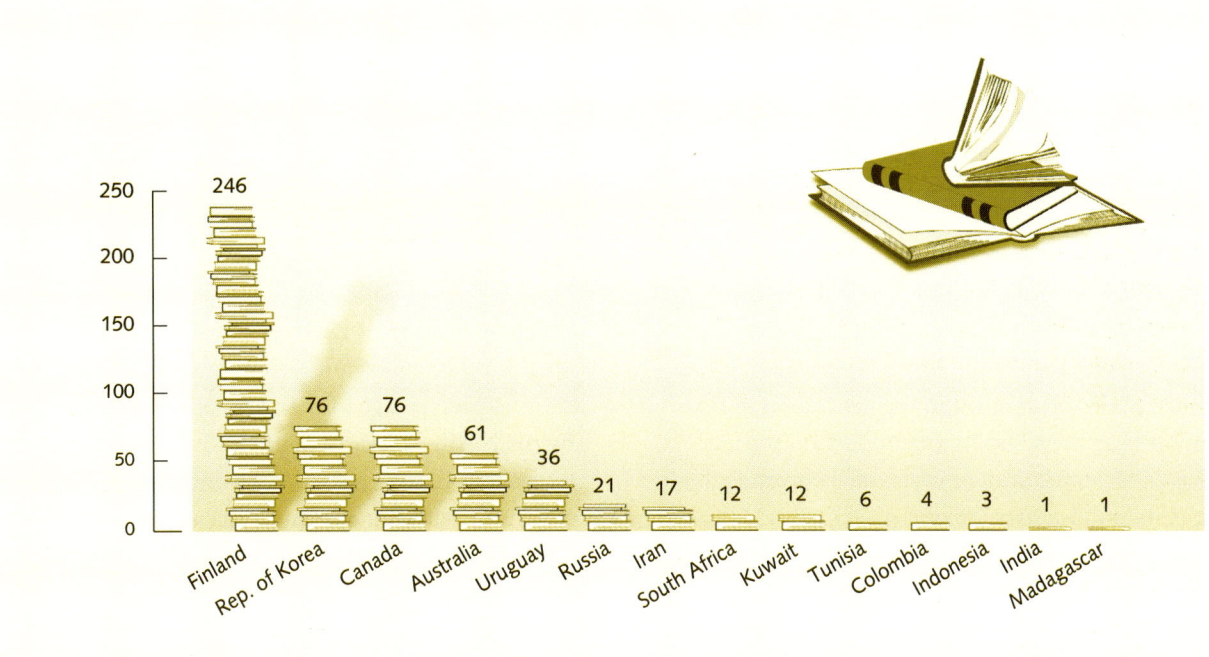

GRAPH 8
NUMBER OF BOOKS PUBLISHED PER 100,000 PERSONS
(1991–94)
Source: Statistical Table 1 in Part Seven of this report.

One or two countries have been selected for each region and the book publication rate per capita varies widely among regions but also within most regions. The rate for Uruguay is 9 times higher than for Colombia, Finland 12 times higher than Russia, South Africa 12 times higher than Madagascar, and the Islamic Republic of Iran 17 times higher than India. Industrial country rates as a whole are 8 times higher than developing countries, while the European rate is by far the highest.

the price of paper, compounded by the devaluation of the Mexican peso, is one of the reasons for this downturn. Others include the general fall-off in consumption as a result of the impoverishment of the middle and working classes and the transformation of books into simple consumer goods, depriving them of the customs and tax incentives they previously enjoyed.

Can the development of free trade help to revive publishing in Latin America? Strictly speaking, the liberalization of trade in this field began in Mexico twenty years ago. Spanish publishers in the main took advantage of this opening to sell their products on the Mexican market and to form associations with Mexican publishers or take them over. Because of the common language and cultural traditions, Spain still seems to be the commercial partner most likely to benefit in the future. Although the situation has become more complex with the 'Europeanization' of the Spanish publishing industry, several publishers in Madrid and Barcelona which had taken over Mexican publishers were themselves absorbed in the 1980s by publishers in other countries of Europe (Anaya acquired Alianza, Labor and Nueva Imagen, Mondadori took over Grijalbo, and Planeta absorbed Ariel and Seix Barral).

Changes were also brought about by the Free Trade Agreement between Mexico, the United States and Canada, which took effect in 1994. As I explained in greater detail in a recent book (García Canclini, 1996), several United States publishers, such as McGraw-Hill and Prentice Hall, have entered the Mexican market with dictionaries, secondary school and university text books and 'personal improvement' books. Some publishers believe that the future impact of the North American industry will be felt not so much in the generation of new publishing houses as in the production process: paper, machines and, as is already happening, high-quality publications (colour, glossy paper), areas in which they have the necessary infrastructures and skilled staff.

But other Mexican publishers who have cultivated relationships with the United States in recent years have a different outlook. There is reason to believe that the closer relationship between the American and Mexican publishing markets may lead to as many changes in the publishing market in the United States as in Mexico. The novel by Mexican author Laura Esquivel, *Como agua para chocolate*, sold over a million copies in English, plus 200,000 in Spanish, in the United States. Books by García Márquez, Carlos Fuentes and Julio Cortázar in Spanish are starting to sell in Price Club and other self-service stores in New York, California and Texas. It is not surprising, says Sealtiel Alatriste, director of the Spanish Santillana group in Mexico, that for the first time there is a market in the United States for Spanish-language authors and their rights. Just as the Latin music section has grown in size in Tower Record and other important chains, the best-selling titles of Spanish origin take pride of place alongside the best-sellers in English. Chicano writers attribute this success to the 'Latin phenomenon' which has been given frequent attention in *Time* and the *New York Book Review*: the initial successes of Sandra

Cisneros with *The House of Mango Street* and Oscar Hijuelos with *Los reyes del mambo traen canciones de amor*, which won the Pulitzer prize, has spread to other novels in recent years. The interaction between the mainstream and the marginal is becoming less straightforward, more complex than in the past. The 'Americanization' of Latin America is offset, to a certain extent, by the Latinization of the United States.

This does not mean, however, that the development gap or the uneven balance of resources between the two regions is levelling out. And while they take advantage of the new opportunities offered by the North American market, some observers, such as Sealtiel Alatriste, wonder what will happen if the American publishing industry decides to launch into full-scale competition with Mexico: their technology, production costs and computerized data banks 'will destroy the Mexican industry, which is not ready at this level'.

How are Mexican books faring in Latin America, their 'natural' market because of the language, the shared historical interests and the consumer patterns of the readers? Sales have decreased because of economic and political difficulties throughout the region. The only country where the government is determined to promote the publishing industry is Colombia: the Book Law enacted in 1993, exempting resident publishers from taxes for twenty years and guaranteeing the purchase of 20% of all their production by libraries, is boosting the development of a thriving publishing industry, with transnational capital and increasing export potential.

In these conditions the proposals of Cerlalc, the UNESCO organization for Latin American books, on the measures needed to strengthen exchanges within the region by something along the lines of a 'Latin American common market for books' remain valid: exempt inputs for the book sector from taxation (and in particular free transit for films with editorial content); encourage the importation of equipment for the graphic design industry; reduce costs through

large print-runs and more intra-regional co-productions; do away with customs barriers and other levies on the circulation of books; improve and cut the cost of transport (by air, sea and post); introduce incentives to export and credits for importing books; adhere fully to the international conventions on intellectual property rights; define national book policies, harmonize the corresponding legislation and create steering bodies on which the social and private interests in the publishing sector are represented.

Television, films and video: towards a multimedia culture

Much has been said and written about the 'death of the cinema', but the figures reveal that more films are seen nowadays than ever before. The difference is that nowadays people watch films at home, on the television or on tape. More than 13 million of Mexico's 20 million homes have television sets, and over 6 million have video recorders. There are some 9,500 video clubs throughout the country, including popular districts and rural areas. A similar expansion in the audiovisual entertainment sector is observed in the other countries of Latin America, although in some cases – the most noteworthy being Argentina – cable television is becoming the most prosperous growth area: at present 60% of homes there are cabled.

Generally speaking, Latin America is poorly placed where production for these new communication services is concerned. The export situation is even worse. Latin American countries broadcast more than 500,000 hours of television per year: in Colombia, Panama, Peru and Venezuela there is more than one video recorder for every three households with television sets, which is more than in Belgium (26.3%) or Italy (16.9%) (Roncagliolo, 1996). Latin America is underdeveloped in terms of domestic production for the electronic media, but not in terms of audiovisual consumption.

This imbalance between the low level of audiovisual production and the high level of consumption is reflected in the poor representation of the national or Latin American cultures on the small screen, and an overwhelming presence of entertainment and news made in the United States. But the extent of the imbalance varies from country to country. Like Rafael Roncagliolo, we must distinguish between the exporting countries and the importing countries. Only two, Brazil and Mexico, are 'part of the global economy of cultural goods, with giant audiovisual enterprises in Red Globo and Televisa respectively'.

Globo is basically an exporter of audiovisual products, and has placed Brazil in fourth place as a producer and third place as an exporter of audiovisual products, but it has not transnationalized its production; Televisa, on the other hand, acts as a genuine transnational corporation in the region, purchasing channels and internationalizing its production activities. (Roncagliolo, 1996)

Then there are a few 'incipient exporting countries', such as Argentina and Venezuela, and to a greater extent Colombia, Chile and Peru. As the same author says, these intermediate countries are in the second line when they attempt to accede to liberalization and integration. 'Their situation is ambiguous, since on the one hand they are in search of markets for their cultural production, and on the other they have to defend themselves against penetration not only by corporations from outside the region but also from the Latin American transnational corporations themselves, such as Televisa.'

The other countries are 'net importers', importing virtually all their programmes from the United States. Note, however, that even where domestic production is healthier, as in Brazil, Mexico and Argentina, more than 70% of films and series are imported from the United States, and American programmes occupy more than 50% of prime time. National production is devoted essentially to news programmes, covering current affairs, subjects of direct interest to the viewers, while a larger

TABLE 6
BREAKDOWN (HOURS) OF TELEVISION PROGRAMMES BROADCAST IN LATIN AMERICA AND THE CARIBBEAN
(BY COUNTRY OF ORIGIN)

	Own	National	Foreign	Total	Own	National	Foreign	Total
					(%)	(%)	(%)	(%)
Entertainment	1 134.3	848.3	2 285.4	4 268.0	26.58	19.88	53.55	100.00
News	600.6	276.6	18.9	896.1	67.02	30.87	2.11	100.00
Education/Culture	136.0	71.4	93.7	301.1	45.17	23.71	31.12	100.00
Religion	43.1	7.7	16.5	67.3	64.04	11.44	24.52	100.00
Others	101.5	42.2	12.5	156.2	64.98	27.02	8.00	100.00
TOTAL	2 015.5	1 246.2	2 427.0	5 688.7	35.43	21.91	42.66	100.00

Source: Mauricio Estrella, *Programación televisiva y radiofónica: Análisis de lo que se difunde en América Latina y el Caribe,* Quito, CIESPAL,
1993, Table 1.

proportion of imported products is found in the entertainment sector.

The imbalance between domestic production and the increasing consumption of imported programmes continues to grow as the 'conventional' mass media (radio, cinema, television) join the communication highways. In addition to this process of technological concentration, the monopolistic reorganization of the market is subordinating national circuits to transnational production and sales systems.

All this is important not only because of its cultural significance. The communication industries are among the most dynamic economic agents and the principal generators of investment and employment; so they are a key factor of development and multicultural exchanges. Knowing who will run these networks in the years to come is therefore a vital question. The audiovisual production of news and entertainment is mainly in the hands of the United States, while 70% of worldwide electronic consumer goods are controlled by Japanese firms.

While these two nations lead the field, however, the report by the World Commission on Culture and Development entitled *Our Creative Diversity* points

TABLE 7
FLOW OF TELEVISION PROGRAMMES TOWARDS
LATIN AMERICA AND THE CARIBBEAN

Country	Hours	%
United States	1 506.3	62.06
Latin America and the Caribbean	721.0	29.71
Europe	145.6	6.00
Asia	40.6	1.67
Others	13.05	0.56
TOTAL	2 427.0	100.00

Source: Mauricio Estrella, *Programación televisiva y radiofónica: Análisis de lo que se difunde en América Latina y el Caribe,* Quito, CIESPAL, 1993, Table 8.

out (p. 27) that British pop groups, Japanese cartoons, Venezuelan and Brazilian *telenovelas* and Kung Fu films made in Hong Kong also have worldwide audiences, and Indian films are widely screened in the Arab world. Be that as it may, most of the developing countries are in a disadvantageous position on the world market.

Even Europe is almost as ill-prepared as the peripheral nations to face this reorganization of culture around the media. Not only is the level of its production and technological innovation low, but only a few small countries – Belgium, Ireland, the Netherlands, Switzerland and the Scandinavian countries – have developed cable television. In France, Greece, Portugal and Spain cable only began to grow in the 1990s (Miège, 1993).

Recent European Community documents reveal an imbalance in its trade with the United States in the communication sector comparable to that of Latin America. The current deficit in this sector is $3,500 million. According to Miquel de Moragas, Europe's deficit in audiovisual consumption will grow from 23,000 million ecus in 1993 to 45,000 million in the year 2000. 'While Europe consumed 650,000 hours of television programmes in 1993, the figure will be 3,250,000 hours per year by the year 2000. But instead of the European industry, this spectacular growth looks set to benefit the United States, which sold Europe programmes to the value of 300 million dollars in 1984, rising to 3,600 million in 1992' (De Moragas, 1996).

The cultural changes brought on by the communication technologies, together with other internationalization and globalization trends in production and consumption, migration and tourism, are causing almost all societies to interact simultaneously. Until fifteen or twenty years ago, attempts were made to control the challenges of these flows of communication between societies by setting quotas for the air-time devoted to the broadcasting of foreign and domestic productions in each country: an obligation, for example, for

television channels to screen 50% of domestic films, or for radios to broadcast an equivalent percentage of domestic music.

These controls proved impractical for various reasons: (a) the deterritorialization of artistic production, which reduces its ties with any particular country (films, *telenovelas* and many musical shows are designed as co-productions between several countries and based on international urban cultural features), and (b) the technological facilities for broadcasting media messages all over the world, the rising cost of film- or record-making, which makes it difficult to recoup one's investment in a single country, and the monopolistic concentration of production and distribution in the hands of powerful multinational corporations.

As a result, in the 1990s certain European countries adopted other protective and promotional measures, not only for domestic but also for European productions. Spain introduced a law in December 1993, for example, based on production and distribution conditions in the region, requiring movie theatres in cities of over 125,000 inhabitants to screen 30% of European films. The law was amended when the Partido Popular came to power, but this progression from national to regional protective measures could be applied in other parts of the world. The promotion of regional markets for cultural goods is ineffective unless comparable protective measures are taken to protect distribution and consumption. Similarly, the measures should be applied not to each medium individually – different policies for television, films and other electronic media – but to the media as a whole, taking into account the multimedia reorganization of the audiovisual sector. This, of course, means co-ordinating and perhaps merging the bodies responsible for films, television, video and other communication sectors.

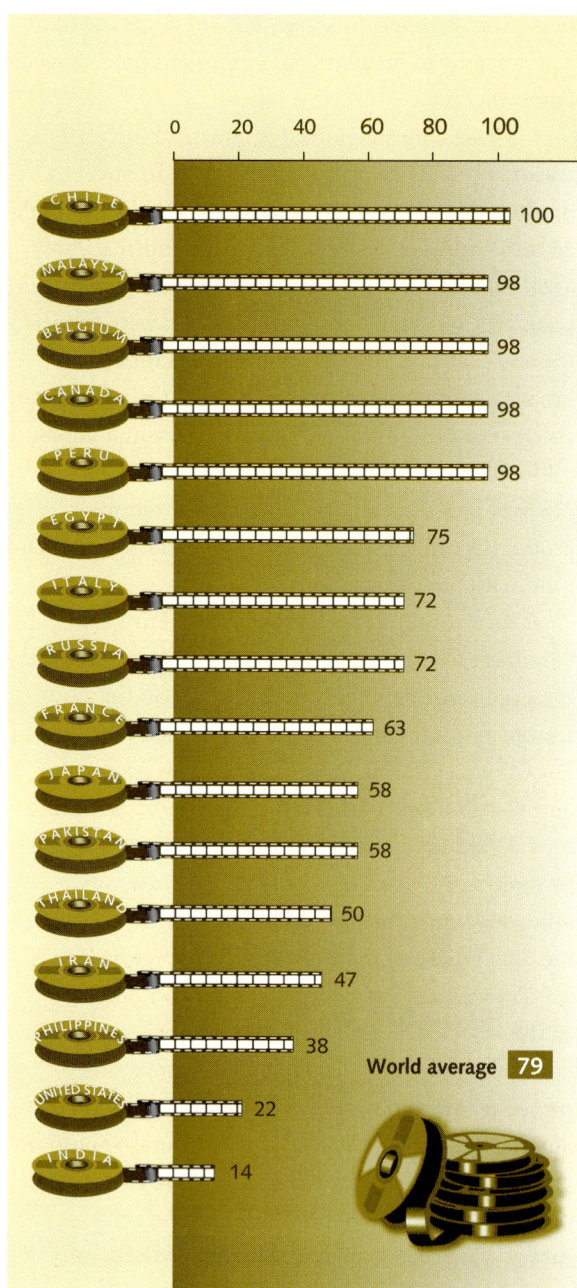

Source: Statistical Table 2(b) in Part Seven of this report.

**GRAPH 9
PERCENTAGE OF IMPORTS
IN TOTAL FILMS DISTRIBUTED
(1990–93)**

The United States film industry dominates the world market, yet has not conquered all domestic markets.

In some countries – even developing ones – a domestic film industry continues to enjoy a large share of the home market. India is the prime example of a country with a thriving domestic film industry. During this period it produced 840 films, while importing only 140.

In developing countries such as the Islamic Republic of Iran, Pakistan, the Philippines and Thailand the share of imported films too was also 50% or less. Among industrial countries, Japan's share of imported films (58%) was among the lowest.

The world average for imported films was 79%.

In the United States, the share was only 22%. It imported only 118 foreign films. By contrast, Canada imported 1,115. Not surprisingly, this number constituted 98% of the total films shown in the country.

Similarly high percentages of imported films are found in countries such as Belgium, Malaysia and Peru among many others.

End-of-century options

The analysis of these three fields shows that cultural policies can no longer be approached as intranational policies implemented essentially by national governments. At the same time, however, the complex interactions between the local, the national and the global mean that the globalization process cannot be considered merely in terms of the homogenization of the world's cultures. Nowadays any new approach to cultural policy must take at least two questions into account: the first is how many forms of homogenization are currently being developed by globalizing policies as they take on the different cultural production technologies and their communication circuits, and link up with the different communities of consumers? The second is how many artists, cultural middlemen and consumers is each of these transnational homogenization policies capable of incorporating, and how many will be left out?

We have already seen that globalization is proceeding amidst the asymmetrical interdependence of the world system. We must now add that in order to homogenize, it uses the historical multiculturality of societies and builds new forms of multiculturality. The same globalizing process that integrates also segregates and stratifies. Lawrence Grossberg wrote that globalization is a 'stratifying machine' that not only erases differences but reorganizes them to produce new stratifications or divisions linked less to territories than to market distribution.

In addition to the ethnic and regional differences within each nation there is now the stratification engendered by the unequal access of countries and their domestic sectors to the new communication media. The inequality between central and peripheral nations, and between economic and educational levels in each country, is giving rise to new forms of injustice. For large masses of people, inclusion in the global culture is limited because they have access only to the first

level of the audiovisual industries: the entertainment and information broadcast on free radio and television. The middle classes and some sections of the popular classes can update and refine their information by participating in the second stage of audiovisual communication, which includes cable television, environmental and health education and political information on video. But only businessmen, politicians and academics have access to interactive communication media, i.e. the third level, which includes the fax, electronic mail, satellite dishes and interactive information and games: from amateur video films to the building of international electronic networks of the horizontal type (Internet). Audiovisual consumption statistics reveal that approximately 90% of the population of Latin America have radio and television, 50 to 70% (depending on the country) have video recorders, but fewer than 10% have access to the technologies which provide the information necessary for decision-making and innovation (Brunner, Barrios and Catalán, 1989; García Canclini, 1995; Roncagliolo, 1996; World Commission on Culture and Development, 1995).

These macrosocial tendencies must be considered in the light of complexities and counter trends to which less attention is given: heterodox and horizontal uses of the Internet and videos, community radios and television channels, local production for cable, and so forth. It will be important for future cultural policies to include qualitative and quantitative studies of these experiences, with assessments where possible of their various effects. In view of the frequent use of these technologies by social movements, it is highly likely that new forms of citizenship, consumption and sociocultural interaction are taking shape in these interstitial practices.

In this process combining multidirectional globalization and local and regional market integration, cultural homogenization and heterogeneity, the peripheral countries need to try cultural policies that allow them to exploit their capacities and at the same time place themselves in a less disadvantageous position in relation to the central countries. In the last two decades, for example, the production of books, records and films in Latin America has declined, cinemas, bookshops, theatres and museums have closed their doors and programmes to support popular culture have been abandoned. What accounts for this? Cutbacks in public spending and private initiatives confront us with this contradiction: increased trade between the countries of Latin America and with the outside world is being promoted at a time when the continent is producing fewer books, films and records; and integration is being fostered at a time when Latin America has fewer cultural goods to trade and lower wages are causing mass consumption to decline.

Only transnational communication corporations like Televisa and Globo are increasing their investments, and only in those areas where they are sure to benefit (television, video and popular magazines). As Jesús Martín Barbero (1995) says:

In the 'lost decade' of the 1980s, the only industry in Latin America which developed was the communication industry. The number of television channels increased from 205 in 1970 to 1,459 in 1998, Brazil and Mexico acquired their own satellites, radio and television opened up worldwide links via satellite, data networks, satellite dishes and cable television sprang up and regional television channels developed. But all this growth was the work of market forces alone, with very little state intervention, for which there was little call and little possibility, i.e. leaving the public space without any real footing while increasing monopolistic concentrations.

Various national and regional strategies emerged from this contradictory situation. I shall examine one or two examples representative of tendencies which are very present in the debate and, as we shall see, are sometimes at the origin of innovative policies.

Entrenchment in one's own culture

In the face of the effects of economic and cultural opening, some countries have exalted local traditions and trusted in building alternatives to development based on the radical autonomy of the nation, religious movements, ethnic Indian groups or underprivileged popular minorities: this occurs in areas controlled by Islamic fundamentalism, evangelic fundamentalism in the United States, neo-Inca movements in the Andes and neo-Mexicanist and neo-Mayan groups in Guatemala. Without a doubt, there are cases of suffering inflicted from without on peripheral societies that cause them to overestimate their own resources, their particular ways of organizing society and power. But this position entails a number of difficulties when it comes to developing coherent policies.

At the end of the twentieth century, most ethnic groups and nations are economically, politically and culturally integrated in the modern era, or are experiencing processes of intense hybridization which have given them a complex heterogeneity. Even many ethnic groups with strong linguistic and social traditions have discovered the economic benefits in the course of this century of selling their farm produce and their crafts on the national and international markets, migrating to other regions and adopting modern knowledge, practices and entertainments. From a purely cultural and aesthetic point of view, various authors have drawn attention to the fact that the 'literal and isolated representations' of each entity tend to generate a repetitive art, as is seen in the stereotyped monotony of some Chicano and neo-Mexicanist art (Ramirez, 1994). The underestimation of craft work and naive art as opposed to 'real' art and technological innovations, the over-ritualization of traditional emblems and situations, may hold a passing fascination for new-age consumers or lovers of the picturesque, but locking oneself up in this solipsistic insistence on the 'self' can obstruct the formal innovation and the

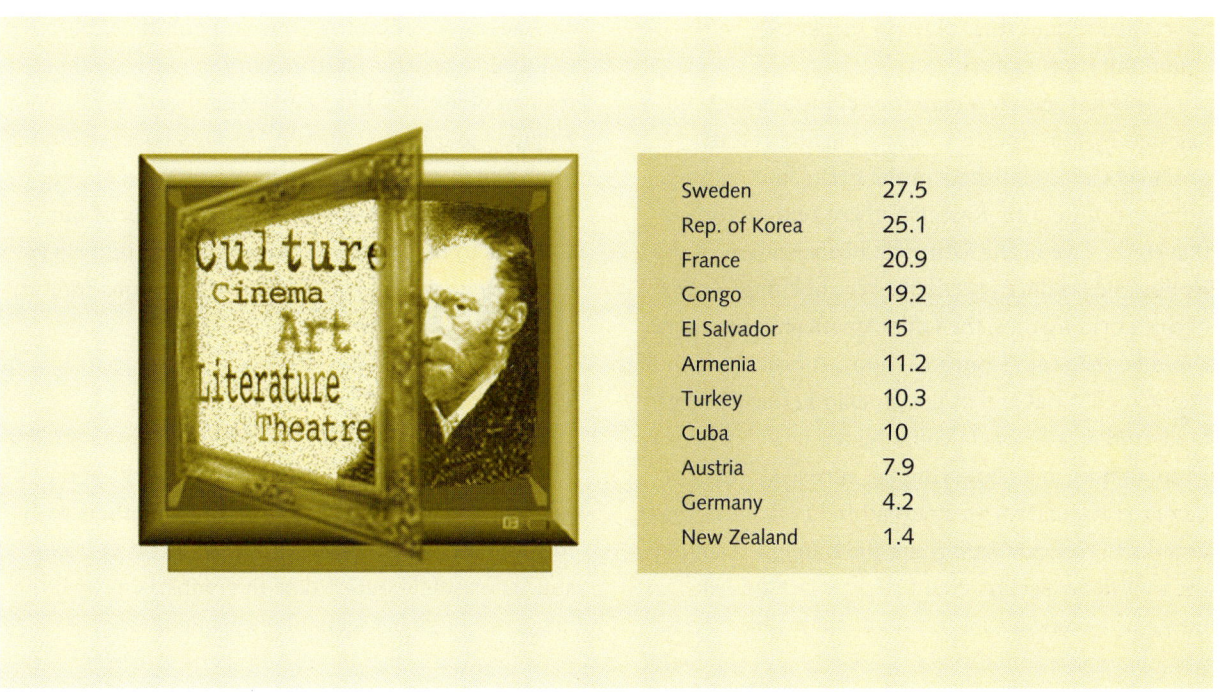

Sweden	27.5
Rep. of Korea	25.1
France	20.9
Congo	19.2
El Salvador	15
Armenia	11.2
Turkey	10.3
Cuba	10
Austria	7.9
Germany	4.2
New Zealand	1.4

GRAPH 10
CULTURAL TELEVISION PROGRAMMES: PERCENTAGE OF TOTAL PROGRAMMES (1989–94)

Source: Statistical Table 2 in Part Seven of this report.

One indication of how seriously a country regards culture is the share of cultural programmes on television. Differences in definition of what there are exist widely.

In industrial countries, cultural programmes constitute only one-tenth of programmes, although this percentage is considerably exceeded by France and Sweden where the share is over 20%. In New Zealand, by contrast, the percentage is less than 2%.

In developing countries, televisions are less common. However, in a significant number the share of cultural programmes is higher than the industrial-country average. In the Republic of Korea the proportion is 25%, in the Congo about 19% and in El Salvador 15%. Turkey's share of cultural programmes (10.3%) is more than twice that of Germany.

transcultural exchange so essential to creativity and critical thinking in a global society. In spite of the political, cultural and aesthetic qualities sometimes found in artists in these localist movements, the decisive question for cultural policy is: how does one move on from the separatist exaltation of difference, which in the long term perpetuates inequality and fosters discrimination, to the shared acknowledgement of the different and the heterogeneous in symbolic searchings capable of intercultural communication?

Export soap operas and folk music

Other uses are made of traditional creativity with a view to the financial gain which the interest they may arouse in other peoples may generate. The international success of Latin American *telenovelas*, ethnic or regional music and the dances of Africa, Asia and Latin America gives reason to believe that the exploitation of these cultural resources for entertainment could help the developing countries concerned to find their place in the global communication market.

It is not merely a matter of cultural policy inspired by film directors, television and record producers and publishers in the peripheral nations. European film critic Román Gubern said recently that in the face of the 'controlled Babelization of the Hollywood studios' and their overwhelming control of the world market, the Latin American soap opera could be the region's greatest hope. A prolongation of the printed serial and of post-romantic theatre, the modern-day soap opera could be the most fertile way of combining and conveying the surrealist, pre-modern imaginary with an urban-industrial imaginary. Thanks to this dramatic genre the symbolic capital of the traditional sectors could recover ground lost through the advance of transnational media culture. The demonstration of this is the success of the Latin American *telenovela* in 150 countries all over the world, and even its influence on the work of Pedro Almodovar, Spain's 'most international film director and the perpetuator of the absurd in the post-modern urban culture'. Why not expand this shared heritage of the Latin American countries through film and television co-productions, to make these nations more competitive in 'the post-Gutenbergian era'?

It is well-known that this aspect of culture is producing considerable economic benefits for Latin cultures on the global markets. But in addition to the purely economic results, there are also the cultural, aesthetic and political aspects to be considered. Some Latin American authors wonder what connections there are in Latin America between the massive success of the soap opera – not only in fiction but also in political and social news programmes, the 'neopopulism of the market' (Sarlo, 1994) which governs the media with its acritical vision of the ratings and the political populism that neutralizes criticism of the structures responsible for social injustice and organizes consensus from the heights of the charismatic power of authoritarian leaders. Are the aspirations of the peripheral societies in

exchanges with other regions and cultures to be reduced to recognition through the marvellous realism of authors like García Márquez, Laura Esquivel and Isabel Allende, through *telenovelas* and films which captivate by their picturesque quality and their magic? In short, is it the destiny of our societies to be content to perceive their conflicts as family dramas, and social affairs as relations forever bewitched by the feelings?

Globalization as an aesthetic organization of multiculturality

The countries of the so-called Third World find themselves faced on the international markets with this dual dilemma: their production is on the wane and increasingly out-of-date in comparison with the magnates of global technology, while their consumption is fast increasing. Latin America, with 9% of the world population, accounts for 0.8% of the world's cultural exports, while the European Union, with 7% of the world population, exports 37.5% and imports 43.6% of all cultural trade (Garretón, 1994).

The imbalance between production and consumption in the developing countries mentioned above results in scanty representation of national and regional cultures. The contrast is accentuated by the recent expansion of transnational American toll-free and cable television virtually all over Latin America, Africa and Asia. In Latin America the countries with the most powerful firms, with years of experience of exporting audiovisual products (Argentina, Brazil, Colombia, Chile, Mexico and Venezuela) have succeeded in negotiating exchange deals with CNN, MTV, TVE and other transnational groups which are unevenly balanced but which make some recognition of Latin American products possible on the transnational circuits.

These innovations merit close attention, because easy access to music on different continents, even from the peripheral societies, helps to bring discoveries from other cultures to the attention of composers, performers and audiences, and to merge

them with local traditions. The strategies of the major communication firms are encouraging us all, with their worldwide expansion, to interrelate with multicultural repertoires. In this interaction, some Latin American musicians, actors and directors are finding room to work. But the recording and reproduction technologies that bring these far-off styles to us also make them too readily commensurable by submitting them to stereotyped tastes: the drums of a samba school or a salsa band sound increasingly like the kettledrums of a symphony orchestra or the drums used in African or Indonesian religious music.

This generates misunderstandings, which José Jorge De Carvalho summarizes as follows:

The post-modern urban listener learns to receive as something familiar what is meant by its traditional creators or makers to be singular, original; and the run-of-the-mill listener in a traditional musical community has serious difficulties in appreciating the fundamentally ironic, allegorical or sham nature of the musical production generated by the contemporary mass media. In other words, instead of the ideal of mutual exegesis, of the hermeneutic fusion of musical horizons, what we now have to analyse increasingly frequently are situations of communicational incompatibility. (De Carvalho, 1995, p. 4)

However, these misunderstandings and this incompatibility are concealed with electronic wizardry. The equalizer can be seen not only as a device which balances the sounds of the instruments in a group in relation to the voices, but as a strategy for the aesthetic organization of globalization. Applied to intercultural differences, this ability to balance high-, medium- and low-pitched sounds, and different tracks, so that every sound can be heard in a harmonious whole, becomes an act of multicultural policy.

Invented to serve Western tastes, equalization becomes a process of tranquilizing hybridization, reducing the points of resistance of other musical aesthetics and resisting the challenges that different cultures present. Under the appearance of a friendly reconciliation between cultures, hides the pretence that we can be close to others without trying to hear

or understand them. Like hurried tourism, like so many transnational film superproductions, equalization is generally an attempt at monological acclimatization, at acoustic accommodation.

True, equalization has also served to restore the sounds of ancient, medieval and Renaissance music, to refine the recording of non-Western music and to experiment with acoustic effects and original sounds in the composing and performance of electronic, minimalist and random music. And you can always pull out the plug: since Eric Clapton recorded his *Unplugged* album, Sinead O'Connor, Neil Young and several Latin American musicians, including Gilberto Gil and Charly García, have reminded us that it is still possible to rediscover the modulations and subtleties of different styles. But the scope for resistance of this kind must be placed in the perspective of everything the transnational monopolies are doing to take control of these experiments in 'alternative' styles of music. A case in point is MTV's interest in broadcasting unplugged and other dissident music, which gives an idea of the complexity of the interactions between artists, middle men and audiences.

MTV is an eloquent example of how flexible global corporations can be in organizing the market in all its regional diversity. If this firm, which was founded as recently as 1989, manages to attract an audience of young people all over the world, it is because of its ability to combine all sorts of innovations: it subtly mixes every style and genre, from rebel rock to hedonistic melodies and 'standardized liberal thinking'; it fights for worthy causes (combating poverty, illiteracy, AIDS and pollution), proposing daily international exercises compatible with a modern, sensitive approach to everyday life. But at the same time, understanding the limitations of globalization, MTV set up five regional subsidiaries in less than five years, including two in Brazil and Miami, with staff from various countries in the region and spaces for local groups which to a certain extent counterbalance the eternal

Cultural policies in Japan

Aside from the protection of cultural policies, both tangible and intangible, Japanese cultural policy in the post-war period has focused on facilitating the creative activities of individual citizens, in stark contrast to the nation-oriented policies of pre-war governments which used culture as a means to achieve national goals. In more recent years this individualistic posture of the government towards cultural policy has been changing, partly due to a lessening of the fear among people concerning government intervention in creative activities. Although the cultural budget of the central government has been increasing only slowly, contributions by local governments and private donors have multiplied. This decentralization and diversification of support has alleviated considerably the fear among some people that public cultural policy may compromise freedom of creative expression.

Thus the Japanese Government now has a series of articulate cultural policies, including the 'Arts 21' policy that presents a long-term development plan for creative activities. The recent opening of the New National Theatre represents a direct involvement of the government in creative activities, and opens up a completely new dimension in the history of cultural policy in Japan.

Further, it is expected that, with the growth of the media industries, the cultural sector will soon develop into one of the largest sectors of the Japanese economy. Since the arts and culture make up a major part of the media programme, media policy will feature prominently in cultural policy development. The notion of cultural development merely for the sake of culture is increasingly difficult to maintain.

Democratization of culture is an important element in any consideration of cultural policy in Japan. Substantial progress has been made in giving people wider access to the arts and culture; the arts, once the domain of the privileged few, are now available to people from all walks of life wishing to enjoy them. Furthermore, efforts have been made to shift policy priorities from the dissemination of high culture in the big cities to the promotion of more indigenous cultures throughout the country as a whole. The recent law concerning the Promotion of Ainu Culture, and the move to construct a national theatre for Okinawa Kumiodori, are illustrations of the fact that Japanese cultural policy is paying increasing attention to the cultural traditions of minority groups and under-served localities.

And yet there remains in Japanese cultural policy

predominance of North American music. Can the hundreds of millions of teenagers and young people in the industrialized countries and in the Third World who follow MTV really be so easily reduced to and reconciled in this 'advertising medium of the future', as one analyst (Eudes, 1997) calls it, where the products advertised (Levis, Coca Cola, Reebok, Nike, Apple, IBM and Kodak) come from only three countries?

Strengthening endogenous production and intra-regional circulation

The three lines of cultural policy I have just analysed may be pertinent options for improving the representation of different sectors, if we elaborate on the questions we have left open. But no answer will be consistent if it is not accompanied by a revision of the roles of the protagonists we mentioned initially – states, firms and independent organizations – and of the links between them.

The convergence between these three forces must aim first and foremost to strengthen, update and expand the endogenous production of the peripheral countries, and the fluid circulation of these goods in these countries. An important step to reduce the imbalance between the central and peripheral countries is to increase investment in the renovation of technological infrastructures and in

an undeniable tendency to continue to give priority to arts and culture that reflect the lifestyle of educationally and culturally dominant groups in the big cities. Non-profit high arts are given preferential treatment in public financial support, none of the 120 members of the Japan Arts Academy represent popular, local or commercial arts, and only a few artists from outside the high arts have ever been awarded the Order of Cultural Merit.

Contemporary Japanese culture is a blending of ancient indigenous tradition, influenced by the civilization of the Asian continent and by Western culture which was introduced with the aim of modernizing the nation. These cultural currents have shaped and transformed each other, and today make up the multi-layered complex fabric that is modern Japanese culture.

It is only since the 1970s and 1980s that people have begun to grow aware of the need to develop the wealth of traditional cultures and indigenous local cultures in Japan. This trend has nothing to do with nationalistic sentiments, nor is it a return to narrow-minded fundamentalism. On the contrary, it represents a search for a cultural authenticity that will support a more spiritually satisfying life. Yet there are many people who still consider everything in Japanese culture that is associated with the accumulated tradition of the past to be a dead-weight.

Reflecting this ambivalence, the policy of the government tends to embrace both trends. It encourages the revival of local cultural identity and traditional culture. At the same time it strives for international cultural interchange in the belief that outside stimuli are essential for maintaining the cultural vitality of the nation.

The issue which Japanese cultural policy is facing today is more than that of the choice between foreign-influenced culture and indigenous culture, or between multiculturalism and cultural unity. In fact, Japan is endeavouring to create a hybrid culture, different both from its own tradition and from Western culture. It is looking to international exchange in cultural activity as a way of linking the local with the global. It remains to be seen whether Japan's experiment in creating a universal culture through international co-operation, while at the same time retaining and diversifying indigenous cultures of its own, will be successful.

Michihiro Watanabe
Cultural affairs specialist and Dean, Department of Music and Arts Administration, Showa University of Music, Atsugi (Japan)

technical training. Women and marginal (ethnic and regional) minorities must be included in the vocational training effort in balanced proportion. Also necessary is a revision of what is meant by public interest in the context of cultural policies.

It is essential, of course, to reverse the tendency simply to privatize cultural institutions and programmes. In many cases privatization does not consist, as is often claimed, in a transfer from the state to civil society, but in the transfer of the function of the state to the groups with the greatest national and transnational concentrations of capital. In order to find a new role for states in the present context, we shall have to reconsider their conception and functions as agents of the public interest, of the collective multicultural heritage. The presence of the state, considered as a democratic and plural space, is essential if cultural goods and research are not to be reduced to mere saleable commodities, essential for the defence of everything in the symbolic lives of our societies that cannot be commercialized, such as human rights, aesthetic innovations, and the collective construction of our history. In this respect, we need spaces like national museums, public art schools and art research and experimentation centres subsidized by the state, or by mixed systems in which governments, private firms and independent groups work together to guarantee that the interests and the needs of the masses in terms of information, recreation and experimentation are not sacrificed to profit.

Perhaps the time has come to overcome the dissociation and sometimes the oppositions between the activities of the state, private firms and independent organizations. Increasing awareness of the sociocultural influence and the economic potential of the cultural industries seems to have made conditions more suitable for the public and private sectors to work together to develop research programmes and co-operation policies focusing on the public interest on an international scale. In some cases the free trade and regional integration agreements that have been concluded or are in preparation between various countries provide a suitable context in which to develop similar initiatives in the field of culture and communication. These regional integration processes must be supported by international studies and cultural and educational policies to promote enhanced mutual understanding between the participating societies and the intelligent handling of the challenges raised by the new forms of multiculturality.

One important factor in achieving these objectives is that cultural policies should reconsider the brokering systems. Artistic and cultural production has always required middlemen to help it reach the public and give shape to the meaning of the pyramids and temples, of the paintings and musical works. But at a time of dense interaction between art and the mass media, and of transnational circulation of culture, between artists, craftsmen or writers and the end users of their work, there is a complex network of institutions (galleries, museums, publishers), financial support (banks, foundations, public and private sponsors) and professionals in the fields of literary criticism, communication, tourism and other related activities, all of whom influence the social meaning cultural goods come to assume. This web is not merely intranational; it involves international organizations and global systems of commercialization and aesthetic evaluation. This is evident in the art exhibitions designed to travel to numerous countries, which adapt to the cultures of the places they visit; the same applies to Western soap operas, the endings of which are changed for distribution in Asia, so as not to offend the morals of the Islamic societies there. Sometimes, however, intercultural negotiations are more secret and dependent on economic and political strategies. Some researchers (Ramírez, 1994; Yúdice, 1996) have demonstrated the links between free trade agreements and cultural diplomacy in the exhibitions promoted by Latin American and Asian countries in the Metropolitan Museum and the Pompidou Centre, with the participation of the state, major firms and renowned writers, in a joint effort to propose a vision of peripheral cultures which, through the fascination of their 'magical realism', manage to achieve recognition for their 'splendours' in the shrines of art and in political and economic operations on a global scale.

The increased anthropological and journalistic interest in the 'primitive' arts, the re-reading from an aesthetic viewpoint of works which, until recently, were stored away in ethnological museums (Clifford, 1995), and the spread of multiculturalism help to amplify and enhance the vision of the modern Western world. But the protests of artists in Africa, Asia and Latin America and the organization of counter-exhibitions, like those staged by the Chicanos and Indians in the United States show the need for further debate on how artists and creative peoples should participate in the dissemination and redefinition of their cultures, and for cultural policies that make this possible. By no means a minor problem in this respect is international trafficking in works of art and the regulation of the balance between the prices they fetch in auctions in the world's capital cities and the prices paid in peripheral countries to the producers or middlemen. The recent proliferation of new international fairs in Singapore (for the first time in 1993), the rise in sales in Taipei,

'Culture is about having a future'[2]

Young people face an uncertain future in Europe today, not least because of structural unemployment. The lack of opportunities for them to express their hopes, anxieties and opinions in meaningful ways also leads to alienation. The Phoenix Project is an intriguing attempt to confront the lack of engagement between different peoples, cultures and groups in society by facilitating a dialogue between young people and artists, intellectuals, scientists and decision-makers on problems younger generations face, such as the future of work and productive use of time. Initiated by Trans-Europe Halles, a European network of twenty-six independent cultural centres, the Phoenix Project brings together constituencies of peoples whose paths rarely cross, in an attempt to create sustainable relationships and to explore the possibilities of change through the arts.

The first action research initiative, for example, took place in Copenhagen in October 1996, during the Danish capital's celebrations as European City of Culture, when some 250 participants from all over Europe gathered to exchange experiences and ideas with the local community on what they saw as their future in a society that provides fewer and fewer opportunities for work. The subtext of the project was that, for young people, 'culture is about having a future'. A range of complementary projects are taking place in Trans-Europe Halles network centres across Europe. At the Noorderlight, Tilburg, in the Netherlands, for example, a multidisciplinary artwork by dancers, musicians and video-makers on the theme 'Working Overtime at the Factory' will be created through workshops with students, teachers, factory workers and unemployed

people. The City Arts Centre, Dublin, is investigating the question 'What's Work?' through the arts and changing nature of work practices in the South Inner City quarter of the Irish capital. 'Time Sailors' is a workshop organized at the Wuk, Vienna, with a group of unemployed young people and senior citizens to promote intergenerational understanding. A musical environment, including mime and visual arts, based on the history of work and use of time, is being created at the Junction, Cambridge, and in May 1997 in Retina, Ljubljana in Slovenia, as part of the City's European Cultural Month celebrations, a project on 'TV – the Drug of the Nation' examined the function of television and its multiple effects on society.

The aims of the Phoenix Project are ambitious and include: the use of arts and artists as a catalyst to facilitate a genuine exchange of views and experiences on the problems facing young people; the provision of impulses for new ideas and actions in support of social integration; the encouragement of openness towards other peoples and cultures among young people; the enrichment of young people's own culture and the promotion of solidarity and tolerance; the creation of artistic projects at cultural centres across Europe involving young people that will lead, among other things, to new approaches to working with disadvantaged young people. The Phoenix Project involves not only the cultural centres of Trans-Europe Halles, but also a range of European cultural networks and co-operation with the Fondation pour le progrès de l'Homme – the Paris-based group of philosophers and intellectuals – and Europe 99, Paris, a group involved in theoretical research headed by Edgar Morin.

European Task Force on Culture and Development (Council of Europe)

Tokyo and Hong Kong and the 'sliding' of large volumes of art from Eastern to Western Europe after the fall of the Berlin Wall show the broad geographic radius now suddenly faced with new problems of customs protection, intellectual property and non-commercial brokering (Moulin, 1994).

If this is what happens in the physical circulation of works of art, it is all the more necessary and difficult to develop cultural policies appropriate for the distribution of media messages and the use of information networks. Needless to say, the old forms of censorship or controls at national borders – however controversial they may be – have become quite useless in these days of satellites, optic fibres and the Internet. The global dimension of the problem evidently calls for supranational agreements and the determined participation of international and regional organizations in cultural policy research and agreements. One consequence is that training for civil servants, administrators and promoters in the cultural field must teach them to deal with a variety of situations in an international context, so that they are able to cope with the cultural, aesthetic, financial and political implications of transcultural brokering.

Relating cultural policies to the employment and educational needs of young people

There are some politicians and people in charge of economic and social programmes who continue to see art as a weekend activity. It is important that cultural policy designers bear in mind the importance of the production of cultural goods and messages in national economies and employment. In the United States, culture, especially audiovisual production and sales, accounts for 6% of Gross Domestic Product and employs 1.3 million people, which is more than mining, the police or forestry. In France in 1992 it accounted for 3.1% of GDP.

However, young people – who in many countries have become the main consumers of culture and communication – find little connection between cultural development and their basic needs, especially the increasingly difficult access to employment. In this connection a section from the Council of Europe's report *In from the Margins*, concerning one of the programmes active in this field, is of interest (see box on previous page).

Developing new regional cultural programmes and institutions

Intermediate channels exist between the weakening of national local cultures and globalization. The redistribution of power in culture and communication must not be seen as a simple opposition between these two extremes. On every continent there are groups of countries which have recently formed alliances to strengthen their regional economies in the competitive global market. Sometimes they confine themselves to reducing customs barriers to trade within the region. In other cases, particularly the European Union, they are developing integration measures which facilitate the free circulation not only of goods but also of people and information. They include joint educational programmes, policies to defend the common cultural heritage and what they call the 'European audiovisual space'. In an effort that respects the internal diversity of the region, they have built up forms of resistance and autonomous development in the face of the United States and Japan. The deep-rooted traditional role played by the public sector in Europe has enabled the Union not only to issue declarations and recommendations but to introduce binding regulations compelling the Member States to promote books and reading, defend authors' rights and develop the audiovisual sector.

The audiovisual sector is regarded as a priority. Although there is a trend, as on other continents, towards the privatization of public television, post and telecommunications firms, the Member States have agreed on common standards to foster the circulation of European programmes, setting minimum requirements for programme content and

limits on advertising for all the members to respect; programmes such as MEDIA, Eurimages and Eureka were set up to develop Europe's audiovisual industries, and promote high-definition television and common standards for satellite broadcasting. These policies not only defend the European identity but also take into account the important role played by the cultural industries in economic growth, job creation and the consolidation of more participative democratic societies. Without going into the details here, it must not be forgotten that the progress achieved in these cultural policies is based on extensive research on every dimension of culture, from the production and distribution economy to the habits and tastes of consumers, on a larger scale than in any other region. It contributes to the democratic and public debate on these programmes, in so far as the studies are not concerned only with costs, profits and ratings for the hermetic use of firms or government bureaucracies, but are published or readily available for consultation by all interested parties.

In other regions attempts at regional co-operation and co-operation between states, private firms and independent bodies are being made, the innovative value of which merits attention. The last example I shall refer to is the Mexico–United States Trusteeship for Culture. In 1991 the Rockefeller Foundation, the National Foundation for Culture and the Arts (a Mexican public body) and a bank institution, the Bancomer Cultural Foundation, also in Mexico, set up a joint body to 'enhance cultural exchange' between the two countries. Although there is a National Endowment for the Arts in the United States and a National Council for Culture and the Arts in Mexico, these bodies only support activities in their own countries. Throughout the twentieth century, however, geographical proximity and reciprocal interests led writers, plastic artists, film directors and scientists from one country to live and work now and then in the other. Then the expansion of radio, television and, more recently, electronic communication continued to develop intensive exchanges. The interaction has been unevenly balanced, in keeping with the different levels of economic and sociocultural development in the two countries. This uneven balance has been particularly manifest in other types of contact, with mass migration from Mexico to the United States, an area in which the differences and the difficulties between the two societies have led to conflicts with which we are all familiar. The importance of these encounters and separations has increased in the last fifteen years, since the economic opening of Mexico and the trend towards globalization have made exchanges between the two countries increasingly important.

Although the Free Trade Agreement between Canada, Mexico and the United States was designed solely as an economic instrument and not to regulate social or cultural relations, it has fostered mutual interest and communication between the societies, educational and scientific agreements and cultural exchanges. The Trusteeship is endeavouring to boost this process, granting financial support every year to bilateral projects concerning libraries, publications, music, dance, museums, visual arts, art in the media, theatre, cultural research and interdisciplinary studies. The 2,144 applications made from 1992 to 1996, 283 of which received support, demonstrate the great impact this initiative is making in two countries which, in spite of the intensity of the interactions between them, were not accustomed to working together on joint programmes, partly for want of cultural institutions to support them. A close look at the evolution over the years of this project and the criteria on the basis of which the Trusteeship distributes financial support,[3] reveals the difficulties experienced by many artists and institutions in developing programmes involving both nations, overcoming the stereotypes in their perception of the other society and relating their artistic and cultural actions to the habits in each country and their respective regions. When interviewed, artists and institutions which had received support agreed on the usefulness of these experiences in 'interactive co-operation' and the elaboration of the artistic imagination in everyday contacts with one another. They suggested that as well as distributing funds, the Trusteeship might organize workshops, symposia and other activities to promote awareness of one country's culture in the public sphere in the other and to help to study their differences in an intercultural light and to stimulate the 'ethnic- and community-based arts' and the multicultural reflection and research which the market and the conventional institutions ignore. It was interesting to see that these confrontations, as well as generating shared experiences between different cultures, encouraged work on the differences in the very conception of diversity. While civil society in the United States was built around the rights of the individual, starting in the Civil Rights Era, democratization has come to be understood in terms of the access (or lack of access) certain groups have, access which is conditional on what defines them as groups (race, ethnic origin, gender, sexual orientation, and so forth). 'Diversity' is also an important criterion in the administration of public goods in Mexico, but it is considered in a different light. In general it refers to differences of class, region and ethnic group (which means indigenous community in Mexico, in contrast with the multitude of ethno-racial definitions in the United States).

Another significant point arose in respect of what each society values in the art of the other. While Mexicans, and Latin Americans in general, see the United States as the centre of the most advanced positions in art and science, much of American society and many of its institutions tend to value Mexico's past, but are reluctant to consider Mexican art as something competitive in the modern era. The folk culture is seen as representative of Mexico. Many of the artists interviewed criticized the fact that the exhibition entitled 'Thirty Centuries of Splendour', Mexico's main international exhibition of the decade, presented in New York, San Antonio and

Los Angeles, went no further than the 1950s. Miriam Kayser, Director of International Relations of the National Council for Culture and the Arts, confirmed that in the United States, as in other regions, 'the battle horses are pre-Hispanic culture, Frida, Diego, Orozco and Siquieros'. The question of how to change this relegation of Mexico to the past and show off its modern creativity and cultural studies is an essential one if we are to overcome prejudice and foster deeper understanding between different national communities.

In brief, these last two references show concrete examples of how intra- and interregional policies can be developed, working on medium-range dilemmas within globalization. It would be useful for UNESCO and other international organizations to promote encounters, workshops and comparative studies to help the different regions to take advantage of innovations made elsewhere. This line of work would serve to transcend the limitations of purely national cultural policies. In some ways national policies could be strengthened through improved understanding of the (different) transformations afoot in the traditional arts, and the publishing and communication industries, for this would help them to find their creative place in keeping with the new demands of each of these scenarios. And as we advanced in this direction, perhaps cultural policies would no longer need to focus on self-defence and entrenchment in one's own traditions, and could set about creating new forms of inter- and multicultural co-operation in which national and foreign cultures developed side by side, in mutual enhancement.

Notes

1. At the 1993 Venice Biennial, where most of the fifty-six countries represented did not have their own pavilions, almost all the Latin American countries (Bolivia, Chile, Colombia, Costa Rica, Cuba, Ecuador, El Salvador, Mexico, Panama, Paraguay and Peru) exhibited in the Italian section. But this was of little account in an exhibition devoted, under the title 'Cardinal Points of Art', to showing that art nowadays is built on 'cultural nomadism'. It is as if the differences between Latin American countries did not count: the ideology of globalization and the post-modern idealization of nomadism erases contextual references.

2. Quoted from *In from the Margins*, a report prepared for the Council of Europe by the European Task Force on Culture and Development Cultural Committee, Strasbourg, 1996.

3. This information is based on the diagnosis and evaluation study (unpublished) of the Mexico–United States Trusteeship for Culture made by Néstor García Canclini and George Yúdice in 1996.

Bibliography

APPADURAI, A. 1990. Disjuncture and Difference in the Global Cultural Economy. In: M. Featherstone (ed.), *Global Culture: Nationalism, Globalization and Modernity*. London, Newbury Park, and New Delhi, Sage Publications.

ARANTES, A. A. (ed.). 1984. *Produzindo o passado: Estratégias de construção do património cultural*. São Paulo, Editora Brasiliense and CONDEPHAAT.

ARIZPE, L. (ed.). 1996. *The Cultural Dimensions of Global Change: An Anthropological Approach*. Paris, UNESCO Publishing.

BECKER, H. S. 1988. *Les mondes de l'art*. Paris, Flammarion.

BOURDIEU, P. 1979. *La distinction: Critique sociale du jugement*. Paris, Minuit.

BRUNNER, J. J.; BARRIOS, A.; CATALÁN, C. 1989. *Chile: Transformaciones culturales y modernidad*. Santiago, FLASCO.

CASTELLS, M. 1995. *La ciudad informacional*. Madrid, Alianza.

CLIFFORD, J. 1995. *Dilemas de la cultura*, Barcelona, Gedisa.

DE CARVALHO, J. J. 1995. *Hacia una etnografía de la sensibilidad musical contemporánea*. Brasilia, University of Brasilia, Department of Anthropology. (Série Antropologia.)

EUDES, Y. 1997. MTV: chaîne du rock et de la jeunesse: culture, idéologie et société. *Le Monde* (Paris), March.

FABRIZIO, C. 1982. *El desarrollo cultural en Europa: Experiencias regionales*. Paris, UNESCO.

GARCÍA CANCLINI, N. 1995. *Consumidores y ciudadanos: Conflictos multiculturales de la globalización*. Mexico City, Grijalbo.

——. (ed.). 1996. *Culturas en globalización: América Latina–Europa–Estados Unidos: Libre comercio e integración*. Caracas, Nueva Sociedad.

GARRETÓN, M. A. 1994. *Políticas, financiamiento e industrias culturales en América Latina y el Caribe*. (Paper presented at the third meeting of the UNESCO World Culture and Development Commission, San José, Costa Rica, 22–26 February 1994.)

GOLDBERG, D. T. (ed.). 1994. *Multiculturalism: A Critical Reader*. Oxford, United Kingdom, and Cambridge, Massachusetts, Blackwell.

GROSSBERG, L. 1997. Cultural Studies, Modern Logics and Theories of Globalization. In: A. McRobbie (ed.), *Back to Reality: Social Experience and Cultural Studies*. Manchester University Press.

GUBERN, R. 1997. *Pluralismo y comunidad de nuestras cinematografías*. (Contribution to the International Congress of the Spanish Language, Zacatecas, Mexico, April 1997, and published in *La Jornada* (Mexico City), 11 April 1997.)

HANNERZ, H. 1992. *Cultural Complexity: Studies in the Social Organization of Meaning*. New York, Columbia University Press.

MARTIN BARBERO, J. 1995. *Comunicación e imaginarios de la integración*. Cali, Taller de Comunicación.

MIÉGE, B. 1993. Les mouvements de longue durée de la communication en Europe de l'ouest. *Quaderni: La revue de la communication* (Paris), No. 19, Winter.

DE MORAGAS, M. 1996. Políticas culturales en Europa: entre las políticas de comunicación y el desarrollo tecnológico. In: N. García Canclini (ed.), *Culturas en globalización: América Latina–Europa–Estados Unidos: Libre comercio e integración*. Caracas, Nueva Sociedad.

MOULIN, R. 1992. *L'artiste, l'institution et le marché*. Paris, Flammarion,

——. 1994. Face à la mondialisation du marché de l'art. *Le Débat* (Paris, Gallimard), No. 80, May–June.

NIEBLA, G. G.; GARCÍA CANCLINI, N. (eds.). 1994. *La educación y la cultura ante el Tratado de Libre Comercio*, 2nd ed. Mexico City, Nexos-Nueva Imagen.

ORTÍZ, R. 1994. *Mundialição e cultura*. São Paulo, Brasilense.

RAMÍREZ, M. 1994. Between Two Waters: Image and Identity in Latin American Art. In: N. Tomassi, M. J. Jacob and I. Mesquita (eds.), *American Visions/Visiones de las Américas*. New York, American Council for the Arts and Allworth Press.

RONCAGLIOLO, R. 1996. La integración audiovisual en América Latina: Estados, empresas y productores independientes. In: N. García Canclini (ed.), *Culturas en globalización: América Latina–Europa–Estados Unidos: Libre comercio e integración*. Caracas, Nueva Sociedad.

SARLO, B. 1994. *Escenas de la vida posmoderna*. Buenos Aires, Ariel.

VIDAL BENEYTO, J. 1981. Hacia una fundamentación teórica de la política cultural. *REIS*, No. 16.

WORLD COMMISSION ON CULTURE AND DEVELOPMENT. 1995. *Our Creative Diversity: Report of the World Commission on Culture and Development*. Paris, UNESCO.

YUDICE, G. 1996. *El impacto cultural del Tratado de Libre Comercio norteamericano*. In: N. García Canclini (ed.), *Culturas en globalización: América Latina–Europa–Estados Unidos: Libre comercio e integración*. Caracas, Nueva Sociedad.

Chapter 11
Global creativity and the arts

Catharine R. Stimpson
Writer; Literary and cultural critic; Professor and Dean,
the Graduate School of Arts and Science, New York University
(United States)

Homi Bhabha
D.Phil. in English Literature; Chester D. Tripp Professor
in the Humanities, University of Chicago (United States)
and Visiting Professor in the Humanities,
University College, London (United Kingdom)

'. . . the phrase "global creativity" refers to a new historical phenomenon that has grave and lively consequences for the arts.'

The global and the international

Let us imagine two plausible scenes from late twentieth-century culture.[1]

The first shows a European information systems specialist for an international drug company. On a flight from London to Singapore, he debates whether he should watch an in-flight movie – tonight a Hollywood action movie about terrorism – or listen to music. Choosing the latter, he opens up his laptop computer with a compact disc (CD) player. Although he was the drummer in a rock band as a young man, he no longer performs. Music is now pleasure, relaxation, entertainment. Deciding what to play, he rummages among discs in his airline carry-on bag: a nineteenth-century Italian opera; a South African jazz group; a master of the Indian *sitar*; an anthology of music from around the world that includes a J. S. Bach chorale and Australian indigenous songs.

The second scene features a young Afro-Brazilian dancer on a bus, going to a rehearsal of the dance company to which she belongs and which presents the work of her cultures. The company is particularly excited because its director is negotiating for an appearance at an international dance festival in France that attracts critical and media attention. Among the items in her bag is a translation of a book about formal, abstract experiments in post-modern

choreography, especially those of an American, Merce Cunningham. She is also thinking to herself, with some amusement, about the advice of a friend in the computer business to create a personal Website that will carry professional information about her and display her charismatic dancing.

Although these scenes are imaginary, neither is an unrealistic example of the consumers and producers of global creativity in the late twentieth century. Each scene could easily happen. Neither could have happened before the Second World War in mid-century. There was music, but there were no CDs on which it could be played. There was dance, but there were no Websites that a dancer might use, let alone a young Afro-Brazilian woman.

In brief, the phrase 'global creativity' refers to a new historical phenomenon that has grave and lively consequences for the arts. Although global creativity follows and incorporates older work, it has an identity – at once promising and problematic – of its own. In part because of this newness, 'global creativity' is often uttered imprecisely and calls out for greater clarity of definition.

Although many artists explore space, for example sculptors and dancers, 'creativity' has a temporal dimension in that creative people, groups and organizations strive to make it new, to bring a *techne* into the world in time present. They are indebted to time past for ideas, forms, structures and practices. Very often, they want time future to be indebted to them. But creative work erupts or emerges in the present, its freshness to be sensed by measuring it against past achievements.

'Global' is a spatial term. A global creator can come from anywhere on earth, use a variety of materials from earth or space, speak to any place on earth. Modern colonialism was responsible for the first processes of globalization; post-colonialism reminds us of their displacing and disjunctive force. Global creators, with their ambitious reach and span, believe that human beings are *proximate* beings. That is, they exist within calling distance of each other, a location that reveals the differences between them but also the similarities. Figures in the multicultural Benetton ads (the domain of fantasy) or people in the equally diverse transit lounges of major airports (the domain of fact) are contemporary examples of the condition of proximity. The transit lounge itself is an aspect of the twentieth-century transportation systems that have so upgraded the possibilities of proximity by speeding up travel around the globe.

'Global' differs subtly but significantly from 'international'. The former asks us to think and act transnationally, or, to use a related term, as cosmopolitans. We are to move, move across, move beyond and above national borders as if we were as fluid and strong as the winds. The latter asks us to think and act as if each of us belonged to a nation that is both autonomous and related geographically, politically, economically or culturally to other nations. If globals strive to be independent of the nation-state, internationals both support the nation-state *and* connect it to other nation-states.

Obviously, pure globality has never existed. Nor does it exist today. For the local exerts its power, influence and attraction over creative people and organizations. In part, the form of the local is the nation-state. The most world-famous of movie stars, the most puissant of world moguls, the most travelled of world tourists all carry national passports. We commonly speak of the spirit of a nation, of national cultures, literatures and arts. Post-colonialism has sharpened the search for a national identity. New nations must develop one; older nations that have lost colonial empires must ask what they now are. What, for example, is Black Britain? In part, the form of the local is a region or an even more specific site. In some instances, the local spreads beyond a physical space and becomes a cultural geography, for example, panethnic formations.

One important characteristic of contemporary life that pulls against globality is the deliberate, well-meaning, well-documented effort by many parties to support national, regional and local cultures and by many artists to practise them. An Irish citizen might think of public and private devotion to the Gaelic language. The more vaunting rhetorics of globality and transnationality unfortunately obscure a conceptual and experiential reality, that is: we cannot refer adequately to 'the global' without referring to 'the local'. For example, technologies may have all sorts of global capacities, but the exercise of these capacities is limited by mundane and local things – like whether one is wired or whether one has access to political and economic goods. Evocations of globality can be as banal and misleading as evocations of 'universalism' in an unequal world. However, claims of globality, again like the claims to universality, remind us continually, if we wish to be reminded, of what does not fit into its grip, or, to change the metaphor, what

is outside its frame. The complexities of the connections and tensions among the global and local call out for creative ways of thinking. Ben Lee, the anthropologist, writes:

Local and transnational issues are being brought into closer and faster contact. . . . Our views of ourselves and others are increasingly intertwined, and no single site possesses either the intellectual or institutional resources to understand those processes affecting all of us. The interplay between local, national and transnational is producing a world in which dealing with local and domestic issues requires placing them in cross-national contexts, while understanding the 'emerging global order' requires greater cultural sensitivity to such problems elsewhere. From this interplay a paradox seems to emerge: there can be no understanding of the global without understanding it as the ways in which different 'local' sites are co-ordinated; yet there can be no understanding of any 'local' without understanding the global of which it is a part. The challenge is, however, from a given location, do we create forms of understanding that can grapple with both the situatedness of local knowledge and its more global implications?[2]

Even if there is no pure globality, much of the most vital creative talent in the late twentieth century is being spent on three global activities that are arguably so pervasive and influential that historians may use them to characterize these years. The first, obviously, is the creation of global economic and financial systems, and the second the creation of global information systems. The tensions between the global and the local provide one warning against any market or technophilic belief in the emancipatory force of these creations. One's cheque or e-mail can be sent anywhere, if one has the capacity for writing a cheque or sending an e-mail, but how easy would it be for a refugee or a gay partner to cross a border, a frontier or an immigration barrier? The third creation is of global entertainment systems that draw on sanitized news, movies, television programming and sports for content. It is no accident that two of the most

recognizable global celebrities are African-American sports figures: Muhammad Ali, the boxer, and Michael Jordan, the basketball player. Intersecting with each other, these three activities depend on post-Second World War technologies, professions and workers in order to function. Saskia Sassen, the sociologist and political economist, writes:

International finance became an immensely creative practice in the 1980s, with many new, often daring instruments invented and the creation of several new markets. For this to work required not only state of the art technological infrastructure and new types of expertise. It also required a very specific transnational subculture within which these innovations could circulate, be acceptable and be successful – that is bought. . . . These massive innovations entailed a very significant set of negotiations in view of what had been the dominant banking culture. And it entailed a rather dramatic increase in the number of very young and very smart professionals who had command over both the math and the computer/software knowledge required, and who at a far younger age than had been the case had significant control over vast amounts of capital.[3]

Global information and entertainment systems

These three activities have had major consequences for the arts. In general, the processes of globalization, in all their oscillations with the local, in all their unevenness, have become subject matter and themes for artists. The two scenarios with which we began could each be the beginning of a story or movie. More specifically, not only have global corporations become patrons of the arts; some – like hotel or restaurant chains – have commissioned buildings that replicate each other no matter where they are. The McDonald's arch is proof triumphant of the existence of a global architectural style. Not only do global information systems circulate information about the arts: the technologies behind them have become instruments of art-making. Computer-generated art is unthinkable without the computer, video art is unthinkable without video. Not only do global entertainment systems produce art, for example, the complexities of brilliant fashion photography. The popular media produce raw material for artists – such as the United States visual artist Cindy Sherman – to use, analyse, ironize, deconstruct and take apart. Artists have become our most incisive students of the muscle, excitement and triteness of media vogues and bazaars.

Together, global information and entertainment systems suffuse people with visual images and sound rather than with literature – in literate and partially literate societies alike. The heroes of action movies are more apt to spit bullets than to recite metrically intricate poetry. The popularity of World Music, the production and marketing of ethnic musics, beginning around 1980, is another case in point.[4] Helping to make this development possible is the fact that pictures and music travel more profitably across cultures than a text in Bengali or Norwegian or Spanish.

In part this happens because visual images and music appear to be immediately open to diverse audiences, an appearance that is, of course, an illusion. Visual signs, units of meaning, do not inspire the exact same interpretation – locally, nationally or globally. The statue of Lady Liberty in Tiananmen Square in Beijing in 1989 had one meaning to the Chinese students who built it, another to the Chinese political and military leaders who watched them do so, and still another to Americans seeing the statue on Cable News Network (CNN) and interpreting it as the triumph of American political ideas.[5] However, unlike a visual image or a piece of music, a natural language patently needs a translator if it is to reach someone for whom that language is alien. Literature – in a natural language or translation – is hardly impotent, desiccated, aimless or defeated. Moreover, both popular texts, such as photonovels, and foundational religious texts, such as the Bible and the Koran, exercise immense power in their domains.

Nevertheless, contemporary global systems have reduced the role of the writer as the creator of culture.

It is foolish to speak of a globally uniform artistic sensibility or practice. This is because of the richness and depth of the interplay among global, national, regional and local cultures; the great and often painful variance in the political and material situation of artists; the vital unpredictability and individuality of aesthetic choices that artists make as they work; and the diversity of beliefs about the purpose of art. Is art to discover and illuminate universal truths and beauty? Or is art to offer informative mimetic reflections of reality? Or is art to be the vehicle of the imagination? Or is art to serve God? Or is art to serve a political end? Or is art to serve a particular society by embodying its nature and aspirations? Or, on the contrary, is art to expose the vice, follies and corruption of a society? Or is art to express individual subjectivity, perceptions, feelings? Or is art to be therapeutic? Or is art to amuse and distract us? Or is art to explore art itself? Or is art to make money? To be a business or a tool of economic development? Each and every one of these beliefs, which have evolved through history, has its adherents today.

Yet, as artists participate in globality, even if sceptically, creative patterns are discernable. The first concerns the elemental question of who can be an artist. One of the great movements has been the insistence of members of previously silenced, marginalized or minority groups that they, too, will be artists; that they, too, will speak in the public sphere. Such groups define themselves in different, cross-cutting ways: as women, as racial or ethnic minorities, as a post-colonial people, or simply as artists, writers, performers. Some claims to the public sphere of art are made by artists who identify themselves as individuals, other claims are by artists who identify themselves as members of a creative community that sees itself as being at somewhat of an oblique angle to 'national' society. This

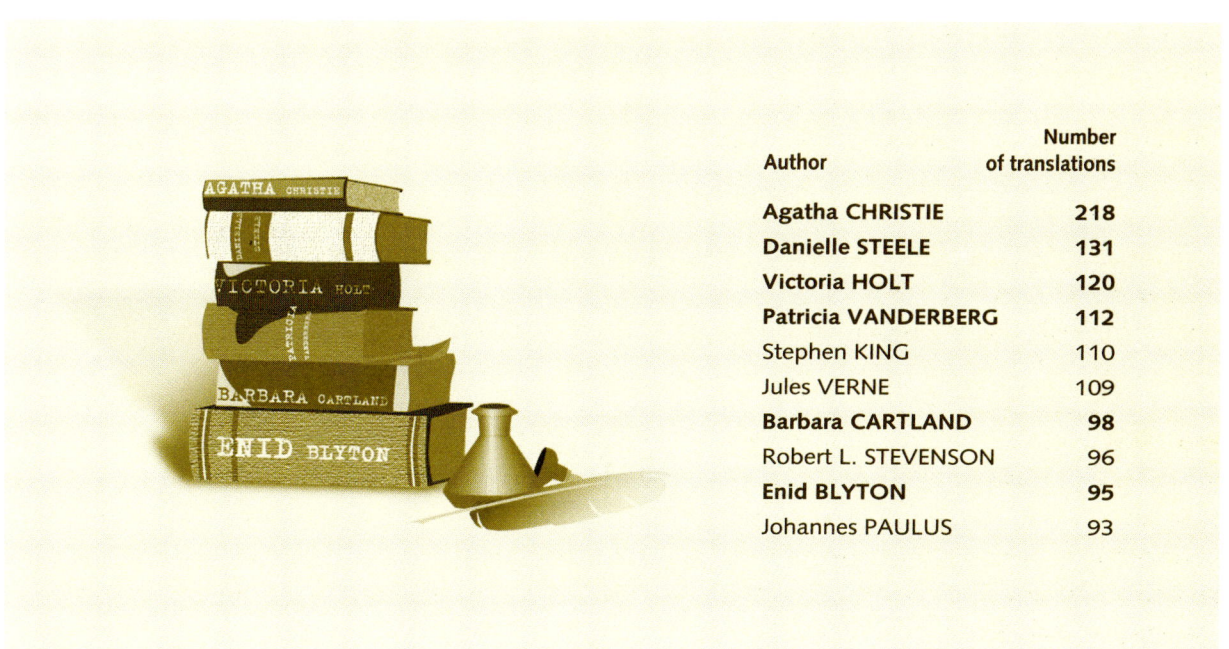

Author	Number of translations
Agatha CHRISTIE	**218**
Danielle STEELE	**131**
Victoria HOLT	**120**
Patricia VANDERBERG	**112**
Stephen KING	110
Jules VERNE	109
Barbara CARTLAND	**98**
Robert L. STEVENSON	96
Enid BLYTON	**95**
Johannes PAULUS	93

GRAPH 11
MOST-TRANSLATED AUTHORS
(1994)
Source: *Index Translationum*, 3rd cumulative ed., Paris, UNESCO, 1996.
Of the ten most-translated authors in 1994, the latest year for which comprehensive data are available, no less than six were women. Women authors have consistently headed the list of most-translated authors in the world.

minoritization is not victimage alone, but rather a way of registering and restructuring a sense of audience, accountability and representation on the grounds of a *habitus* or *mythos* that is not in keeping with consensuality or contractualism as a principle of communication.

Whether such artists act self-consciously as individuals or members of a creative community, the effects of their actions have been culturally significant: pressure on educators and cultural gate-keepers to be more open; the rise of extraordinary artistic talents, such as those of African or Indian women writers; and the dispersal of any centralized cultural authority. Ironically, this decentralization is occurring even as some states continue to act as censors and even as corporate ownership of technologies and the media is centralizing.

Multiple voices

The increase of remarkable voices has invigorated an interest in narrative and story-telling in a number of media.[6] Some stories are personal, belonging to the genre of autobiography. Some are collective, aspiring to the genre of the epic, which creative communities can produce. These people's stories bind a group by articulating an identity, history, future and purpose that the group can claim proudly. So doing, narrative gratifies a longing for a hearth and home. Significantly, in English, the Websites that present a cyberidentity are called 'home pages'. Woefully, the stories that create the identity of a people often create the identity of a non-people as well, an enemy, the barbarians, the infidels, a different and often lesser Other. When this happens, the people's story

GRAPH 12
**DISSEMINATING THE WORLD'S CULTURE THROUGH ITS LANGUAGES
(1994)**
Source: *Index Translationum*, 3rd cumulative ed., Paris, UNESCO, 1996.

At least ten titles were translated into and published in more than sixty languages in 1994. Overall, more than 220 languages were translated. These languages include the national languages of newly independent countries, national secondary languages (four from Spain alone) and historical ones. Of the remainder nearly half are non-European.

will justify violence against and contempt for the non-people.

In hope, personal or group stories are 'real' and say true things. In practice, the genre of the narrative or story-telling carries the seeds of the destruction of its veracity within it, whether the story-teller admits it or not. For a narrative, a story, is, after all, just that, a narrative, a story. Lacking the rugged credibility of science, it seeks to convince an audience to believe on the basis of rhetorical persuasiveness and/or the audience's will to believe.

The instability of narrative as a statement about identity and reality has become a global artistic theme. In addition, global systems of information give artists access to multiple and often conflicting accounts about people, places and things. Think of

the number of narratives that exist about Salman Rushdie's novel *Satanic Verses* (1988). There is the narrative of the novel itself; the narrative of the novelist about it; the narrative of the Islamic religious authorities that found it blasphemous, banned it, and declared a *fatwa* against the novelist; the narrative of the supporters of these religious authorities who burned the novel; and the narrative of the supporters of the novelist who defended his intellectual and artistic freedom.

These two cultural features – the instability of narratives, no matter how sincerely told; the pluralism of narratives, told from any number of perspectives – have helped to stimulate a global artistic mode known loosely as 'post-modernism'. It has several characteristics, not all of which may

appear simultaneously in a single piece or place. Thematically, artists are interested in power, relations of domination and dependence and escapes from them. A second major theme is performativity, the theory that our lives do not express primordial, natural givens. Rather, we construct our lives as we construct our group narratives – by performing them, acting out roles and gestures over and over again. This challenges anyone who vainly seeks a pure, unchanging, authentic, essential identity – be it based in a slab of land, an ethnicity or a nation.

Dramatically, artists may use their own bodies as the local site of performance. Often defiant of decorum, they offer their own flesh as the stage on and from which they will act and act out. Whether artists are playing with body art or not, their style is often fragmented, deploying pieces of images, sounds, objects and narratives. This fragmentation can lead to hybridity, the mixing of genres, media and elements from various periods, societies and cultures. Traditional distinctions, such as that between the arts and crafts, blur. The hybrid work of art is parallel to the hybrid social and psychological identity that mingles elements from various societies, cultures and families.[7]

Performativity, fragmentation and hybridity lead to a perpetually unsettled art, the meanings of which must constantly be negotiated by artists and audiences. Of these elements, hybridity is perhaps the most complex. It is not historically novel. For example, the English language consists of Celtic, Anglo-Saxon, Latin, French, Arabic, Sanskrit and other elements. However, the sheer number of global sources for the hybrid work of art, the ability to access them quickly, and the intensity of the desire to work with them all does seem new.

A lazy hybridity has its dangers. It can cannibalize images and ideas from many cultures without understanding them. This, added to the use of fragments, can create an art of surface but not of depth; an art that skims and samples but does not

explore; an art that synthesizes but does not invent. However, a vital hybridity revalues and translates cultural norms. For example, a dance work that derives from the gestural vocabulary of the Indian classical Kathak tradition transposed into a modern avant-garde choreography demands to be judged successful or meaningful as it performs a transition or transformation that seriously deforms both prescribed traditions. There is no perfected 'norm' of translation or appropriation possible, because such hybrid works contest the 'meaningfulness' of culture as being embodied in idealized modes of 'representation' or judgement or conduct. They also question the notion that criticism is only possible on the basis of an ideal aesthetic distance between the critic and the cultural object or objective.

Exploring new spaces

Let a tale of two paintings speak to this subject. One, Peter Blake's *The Meeting* or *Have a Nice Day, Mr Hockney*, an icon of English art and artists, hangs in the Tate Gallery in London. Two portly gentlemen greet each other, one resting on a cane, the other leaning on an outsized paintbrush. A third stands aside, his head bowed. A closer view reveals the trick in the *tableau vivant*: the staged meeting between the artists Peter Blake, David Hockney and Howard Hodgkin at Venice Beach, California, is a translation/transposition of Courbet's *The Meeting* or *Bonjour Monsieur Courbet* (1854). In the move from the Provençal landscape to Santa Monica, from realism to a kind of post-Pop/post-modernism, there is a recasting of the figure of the British artist in an international frame. Their studied poses, replicating the Courbet painting, recall a European painterly past that is surprisingly restaged in the midst of the southern California landscape of youth, lust and leisure that has largely been explored in the pictorial by David Hockney. It is this palimpsest of Courbet/Blake/Hockney – these interlocking landscapes – that argue for a 'tradition' of Western painting, while the West Coast ambience, the endless azure and lilac horizon looking out over the ocean has a marked 'pacific rim' light about it – there lies Asia, Australia. Viewed from the late 1990s, such light, such a landscape, almost seems as if the painting may have been a precursor to the technique of computerized image transfer.

There is an edginess about Blake's 'transnational' stage of both art history and cultural history that suggests that these very 'English artists' find themselves culturally or sexually or stylistically 'at home' in a liminal space, in-between traditions, histories, in an exploratory and innovative space between the national and the inter-national. It is this hybrid, culturally diverse landscape that makes visible the rough edges, the complex negotiations of aesthetic values that find themselves not only 'outside' the work in the social problems of its production, but 'inside' the work itself as its form and function. This art is of no less value because it takes the unresolved, ambivalent, even antagonistic and performs it in the work, showing up the struggle for translation. The second picture is by an Indian artist, Vivan Sundaram, who lives in Delhi but shows and works internationally. *People Come and Go* is just such a work of the cross-roads: awkwardly intersected picture-planes, edgy surfaces, a pointillist mottled light flooding one corner, while the other is treated in the flat, overframed illumination in the manner of Howard Hodgkin catching the heavy glare of Indian sunlight. The *mise en scène* is unmistakably 'Indian': a dhoti-kurta clad gentleman on the floor, with a laconic lavender-suited foreign figure in a pool of light behind him, seems oddly at home and out of place. It is indeed Howard Hodgkin himself, a Hodgkin-like canvas beside him, sitting in Baroda (western India) in the studio of his primitivist painter friend, Bhupen Khakar. Their interlocked gazes are fixed on a canvas that is turned away from us. What are they thinking? Where do those two very different visions meet – and necessarily part?

This is no simple celebration of cultural borders and boundaries collapsing before the transcendence of the artistic vision – an international coterie of the inspired. The title of the painting, *People Come and Go*, especially when spoken by a post-colonial artist from the Third World, is too ironic and informed to be either celebratory or nostalgic. The hybrid nature of the work – with its citations, imitations and especially its enigmatic, unreadable canvas that hits the eye-line at a peripheral angle – raises the issue of identity and cultural 'authenticity'. What both paintings demonstrate is the power of creativity that emerges when culture is seen not as the 'conserver' of identity, but as the crossroads for articulating different landscapes, histories, genres, styles of perceptions and performance.

Such work challenges secular judges, for example museums and universities. Projecting a vision of a museum responsive to a pluralistic and inclusive globalism, John G. Hanhardt writes:

The museum must redefine the notion of art as property and its valuation in a centralized market place of capitalized goods and ideas. The museum must be an open text of possibility, become a hybrid space and culture engaged in communication and technologies, through projects that constantly question its ends. In this way, the museum can redefine itself for the next millennium and contribute to the rethinking of art and culture.[8]

Perhaps even more strongly, such work confronts religious judges who perceive themselves to be final arbiters of truth and morality. Ironically, the identification with religious fundamentalisms – Christian, Islamic – is a way of refusing change while these fundamentalisms are themselves great global cultural phenomena. The global secularism that fundamentalisms disdain has yet fully to take account of their extent. The brevity of this comment about clashes and divisions between religious and secular systems must not mask their seriousness. The existence of the contest demonstrates one of the sharpest points of the art we have been describing: in

our global world, cultural authority is dispersed and struggles over truth, interpretation and meanings are inevitable. A profound question is whether we have a sufficiently strong global public space in which we can negotiate struggles without resorting to violence or accepting tyranny.

Let us end by evoking an example of the kind of art that is at stake. In an essay about African art, Salah M. Hassan analyses its assimilation of Western forms, ideas and materials. Among his exemplary artists is Houria Niati, an Algerian woman who spent part of her childhood in Algeria during the French occupation and the war for independence and later moved to the West to study art. Since 1979 she has lived in London. In Hassan's description, she is a serious, valuable example of artistic creativity in a global culture. She has had a double confrontation with the West as a colonial force and as a purveyor of Orientalized images of 'her country and people as fictionalized, exoticized'. From these encounters and her own 'complex background as a woman, an Algerian of Arabo-Berber heritage, and Islamic influences', she creates a hybrid but whole vision. Hassan writes:

Houria Niati takes on the genres of installation and conceptual art, redefines them in her own image, and recreates them in a new and totally unrecognizable fashion to those who claim to have invented them. In her live performances, which often accompany her installations, Niati brings together the visual and verbal expressive elements of her culture and makes them relevant to contemporary issues and concerns. Houria sings traditional Algerian songs as well as Andalusian *Sha'bi* and sometimes reads English translations of her own poetry. Houria also uses synthesizers, sound recording, and special light effects to create a theatrical-like atmosphere and a vibrant magical environment of sound, body movement and colour. . . . [Her installation] *There is Nothing Romantic About Bringing Water From the Fountain* [has] a sound track of female voices and of water [that accompanies] several huge painted jars. In addition, Niati installs plaster moulds of her bare feet in a circle placed on the center of the gallery's floor. . . . On the walls hang a series of old

photographs in the tradition of the French colonial postcards of Algeria. . . . Niati's installations force the viewer to see the truth about Western images of Algerian women as private fantasies of their creators and consumers. In confronting the oppression of women, Houria does not stop in the past or limit herself to her own society, but extends her concerns and reaches out to women on a global level.[9]

The scenarios about global culture with which this essay began are benign – a well-employed man travelling in an airplane who assumes he will land safely, a young woman travelling to a dance rehearsal who dreams of graceful movements as yet unborn. At best, the good cheer of these scenarios characterizes the experiences of only a portion of the citizens of global society. The essay could have as easily started with far more awful scenarios: one in which contemporary technology, if available, is an instrument of violence and surveillance; or one in which information, if it circulates, is about blood, fear and the precariousness of survival; or one in which global entertainment, if it is received, blows off the vibrancy and beauty of cultures for Hollywoodized, sensational blockbusters; or one in which negotiations, if they take place, are at the point of a gun. The arts emerge from and bear witness to humankind's divided capacities for pleasure and terror, shapeliness and chaos. The question as to which capacities will prove most enduring on this cybernetic old planet is beyond the ability of the arts – which can do so much – to prophesy.

Notes

1.   The following comments arise from a Round Table on 'Globalism and Global Creativity' that the Fellows Program of the MacArthur Foundation sponsored from 14 to 17 November 1996 in Chicago, Illinois, United States. We are grateful to the Foundation for its sponsorship. The participants were Arjun Appadurai, K. Anthony Appiah, Lourdes Arizpe, Alberta Arthurs, Roger Bartra, Homi Bhabha, Timothy Druckrey, John Hanhardt, Salah Hassan,

James Hung, Jane Kramer, Jaron Lanier, Ben Lee, Miya Masaoka, Martin Roberts, Saskia Sassen, Andre Schiffrin, Richard Sennett, Adele Simmons, Marcia Southwick, Catharine Stimpson, Mark Taylor, Jianying Zha, and Carol Burbank and Scott Nielsen from the Fellows Program staff. This chapter will cite individual participants where relevant, but the interpretation of the Round Table and other commentary on the subject is the responsibility of the authors.

2.   Ben Lee, *Peoples and Publics* (paper prepared for the MacArthur Round Table, dated 5 November 1996), p. 25.

3.   Saskia Sassen, *The Global Economy and Its Cultures* (paper prepared for the MacArthur Round Table, November 1996), p. 3.

4.   Martin Roberts' Round Table paper, *World Music: The Relocation of Culture*, treats the global use of the Javanese gamelan and gamelan music as a case-study of World Music.

5.   At the MacArthur Round Table, both K. Anthony Appiah and Ben Lee made this point.

6.   At the MacArthur Round Table, Richard Sennett stressed the importance of individuals being able to tell the story of their lives, including their work experiences.

7.   K. Anthony Appiah's model of 'rooted cosmopolitanism', which argues that each of us can have roots in a specific location and yet dwell in the world at large, is a sophisticated, appealing treatment of hybridity.

8.   John G. Hanhardt, *Acts of Enclosure: Touring the Ideological Space of the Art Museum* (MacArthur Round Table background paper), p. 47.

9.   Salah M. Hassan, *The Modernist Experience in African Art: Towards a Critical Understanding* (MacArthur Round Table background paper), pp. 20–1.

Chapter 12
The role of music in international trade and economic development

David Throsby
Professor of Economics, School of Economic
and Financial Studies, Macquarie University, Sydney
(Australia)

'. . . interpreting music as a commodity opens up the possibilities for extending music from being simply a form of cultural expression to being also a vehicle for economic empowerment . . .'

The structure of the music industry

Music is one of the most basic forms of human expression and as such it is a fundamental element of local, regional, national and international culture. At the same time music is an important commodity in economic terms: it comprises a significant item in consumers' leisure expenditure, it provides a livelihood for countless workers involved in its production and distribution, and it is a key component in the increasingly globalized media and communications industries. This chapter examines the structure and size of the world music industry, with particular emphasis on international trade in music and the role of music as a force in economic development.

The layout of this chapter is as follows. In order to analyse international movements in music, it is necessary to understand the economic structure of the music industry in national and international terms. Accordingly the first main section looks at the structure of the music industry and the nature of the goods and services produced and exchanged in the market place. In the next section we gather together what data can be gleaned on the size of the industry worldwide. We then consider the relationships between music and development, looking at the economic and cultural value that music generates in the development context, with some specific illustrations drawn from several countries. Finally, some conclusions are drawn.

Unlike most commodities which are readily definable in terms of a single physical good or a specific identifiable service, music output and trade take many forms. Music can be bought and sold as a physical product, for instance as sound recordings in various formats, or as published printed works such as musical scores. It can take the form of a service such as that provided by performing musicians before a live audience. But music can also be traded as rights, since it is ultimately a form of intellectual property,[1] and hence its use is controlled by rights to reproduce and disseminate it in various ways such as recording, live performance, broadcast, renting, transmission via cable or satellite, and so on (Muller, 1994; Vogel, 1994). In addition to all this, music-related trade occurs in commodities connected in some way with music, including musical instruments, merchandise such as that associated with famous recording groups, and consumer goods for the reproduction of music such as audio and hi-fi equipment.

It is thus apparent that the definition of the 'music industry' as a basis from which we might consider the extent and nature of trade flows will be problematical. Indeed, no single standard industry classification adequately encompasses the diversity of musical activity and commerce; rather, it is possible to identify several components or 'players' which taken together provide a comprehensive view of the whole area. Hence, we can identify the following primary participants: creative artists such as composers, songwriters and musical performers; agents, managers, promoters, etc., who act on behalf of artists; music publishers who publish original works in various forms; record companies which make and distribute records (LPs, cassettes, CDs, music videos); copyright collecting societies which administer the rights of artists, publishers and record companies; a variety of other service providers including studio owners, manufacturers, distributors, retailers, broadcasters, venue operators, ticket agents, etc.; users of music such as film-makers, multimedia producers, advertisers, etc.; and individual consumers who purchase a musical good or service (buying a record, attending a live performance, subscribing to a 'pay' diffusion service) or consume it free of charge (listening to broadcasts, background music, etc.).

Within music itself it is quite difficult to categorize different market segments corresponding to different musical genres, since the lines between even major musical forms such as jazz, folk, country and so on are blurred. There is, however, a

reasonably clear distinction between 'classical' music (which accounts for about 7% of the world sound-recording market) and the rest, comprising 'contemporary' or 'popular' music, but even here, in regard to music being written today, the dividing line is becoming increasingly difficult to draw.

It is important to understand the central role of copyright in the music market and in the international flows of music, deriving, as noted earlier, from the fact that the creative output of music exists in an intangible form, i.e. as intellectual property. Whilst this output may be physically embodied in a tangible product such as sheet music or an audio recording, the intrinsic value of the output lies in the underlying work itself, and also in the creative input of the performer in interpreting the work. It is the rights to exploit the creative work of the writer and/or performer that lie at the heart of the economic and legal processes involved within the music industry.

Although the basic purposes of copyright in all countries are, first, to provide a means for creators to control and benefit from the use of their work and, second, to allow reasonable public access to those works, the actual copyright laws in place in different countries differ quite significantly. Some countries have broadly defined rights which cover many types of usage, thus reducing the need for legislative amendments to meet changing circumstances such as the advent of new technologies. Others have more narrowly defined rights such that changing circumstances have to be reflected in changes in the law. The last few years have witnessed very rapid technological change in the means by which musical and other cultural products can be reproduced and disseminated. These developments have made it increasingly difficult for national copyright laws to be effective in protecting creators' rights, and the pace of change in legislation virtually everywhere has lagged far behind what has been required. As a result, the main countries which export intellectual property (principally the United

States) have moved to bring improved copyright protection directly within the ambit of trade forums and trade negotiations, through avenues such as TRIPS (the Trade Related Intellectual Property Rights protocol).

There seems little doubt that the growing strategic value of copyright in the international arena, the continuation of rapid technological change, and the expanding worldwide consumer demand for cultural products, will mean that the allocation and administration of rights will continue to dominate the agenda of the world music industry in the years ahead. The phenomenon of convergence, whereby the technologies for providing electronic consumer services in media, entertainment, communications and commercial activity are inexorably coming together, will have enormous implications for economic, social, political and cultural behaviour in the twenty-first century. In this environment the owners of rights in intellectual property will hold a potentially dominant position.

The global music industry and international trade in music

Ever since the emergence of the long-playing record in the 1950s, the music industry has been a 'global' phenomenon. In the last thirty to forty years, further technological developments – the music cassette, FM radio, the compact disc, digital audio tapes, and now on-line transmission – have continued to make it easier for music created in one part of the world to be heard in another. At the same time, increased concentration in the means of production and distribution of music has seen the world industry become dominated by a relatively small number of very large transnational conglomerates.

Components of the world music industry

The main components of the music industry when looked at in global terms are the publishing and the sound-recording sectors, and the corresponding copyright collecting societies.

The music publishing industry generates income in the form of copyright payments to the creative originators (composers and songwriters) and their publishers. A survey by the National Music Publishers' Association (NMPA) of the United States found that total reported music publishing revenues in 58 major world markets was $5.8 billion in 1994, comprising the following main components: public performance revenue (mainly derived from broadcasting): 44% of the total; mechanical royalties (royalties on sale of sound recordings): 31%; synchronization royalties (royalties from the use of music in film and video) and other reproduction revenue (royalties from background music, etc.): 11%; and print revenue (sheet music and other print sales): 9%.

The music publishing industry is split between Europe, Japan and the United States, the largest countries being the United States (21% of total world revenues in 1994), Japan (16%), Germany (15%), France (11%) and the United Kingdom (9%). Details of music publishing revenues worldwide are given in Table 8.

In global terms, the music publishing industry is quite concentrated with five major international publishers dominating the market, and with two of these (Warner–Chappell Music and EMI Music Publishing) having world market shares in excess of 20% each. In addition there are more than twenty significant international music publishing houses, some of which are affiliated with record companies. In fact, there has been a growing involvement of record companies in music publishing in recent years, as the importance of rights income in the music market increases.

The size of the sound-recording industry is measured by the volume and value of retail sales of records to consumers. Data from the International Federation of the Phonographic Industry (IFPI) indicate that the global value of reported retail sales in 1996 was almost $40 billion. More than 80% of the world market is controlled by the so-called 'Big

TABLE 8
WORLD REVENUES FROM MUSIC PUBLISHING ($ MILLION) (1994)

	United States	Japan	Germany	France	United Kingdom[1]	Other	World total
Public performance revenue							
Radio	184.1	102.2[2]	53.5	18.8	62.1	189.9	610.6
TV/cable/satellite	241.6	11.3	76.6	102.1	68.9	264.9	765.4
Live performance	149.5	152.5	171.5	176.4	120.9	440.0	1 214.5
Subtotal	575.2	265.9	301.6	297.2	251.8	898.8	2 590.5
Reproduction revenue							
Mechanical royalties	427.2	425.0	240.6	113.8	162.5	440.7	1 809.8
Synchronization royalties	51.9	125.4	147.9	72.2	5.6	56.3	459.3
Other	0.2	32.5	21.8	63.1	24.8	65.5	207.9
Subtotal	479.3	582.9	410.3	249.1	192.9	562.5	2 477.0
Distribution revenue							
Sheet music sales	1 87.3	17.5	1 16.2	47.0	51.9	1 15.3	5 35.2
Rental/lending rights	n.a.	56.5	9.7	n.a.	n.a.	2.7	68.9
Subtotal	187.3	74.0	125.8	47.0	51.9	118.1	604.1
Other	n.a.	n.a.	37.4	50.4	6.4	72.0	166.2
TOTAL	1 241.8	922.8	875.1	643.7	503.0	1 651.4	5 837.8

1. Including Ireland.
2. Including television.

Source: National Music Publishers' Association (NMPA) data.

Six' transnational corporations: Sony (Japan), Polygram (Netherlands), Warner (United States), BMG (Germany), Thorn–EMI (United Kingdom), and MCA (Japan). In addition there are a number of independent record producers, mostly nationally based and relatively small, but often catering to particular types or styles of music in defiance of the mass-market orientation of the majors. The size of the world music recording industry in 1995 is shown in Table 9. The dominance of Europe, Japan and the United States in the world market is readily apparent.

The collecting societies act to collect copyright revenue from users of music and to distribute it to appropriate rights-holders. Composers and performers may retain the copyright in their works or may assign it to a publisher or direct to a collecting society. Record companies generally own the copyright in the sound recordings they produce. When a work is performed, recorded, broadcast or used in any way, the appropriate collecting society will claim the fees on behalf of the artist, publisher and/or record company, and distribute the revenue to rights-holders after deducting administrative costs.

Growth and regional market shares

There has been a rapid growth in record sales over the last ten years. Between 1986 and 1996, retail sales value in current prices rose at a compound rate of just over 10% per annum, or around 7% per annum in real terms. The annual growth rate in the

TABLE 9
WORLD SALES OF MUSIC RECORDINGS (1995)[1]

	Sales value ($ million)	Sales volume (million units)	Value of sales/head ($/head)	Volume of sales/head (units/head)
North America				
Canada	1 113.1	77	39.19	2.7
United States	12 102.0	1 035	46.00	3.9
Subtotal	13 215.1	1 112	45.33	3.8
Central and South America				
Brazil	1 053.1	75	6.52	0.5
Mexico	299.0	61	3.30	0.7
Other	697.6	57	3.68	0.3
Subtotal	2 049.7	193	4.64	0.4
Europe				
France	2 391.8	134	41.17	2.3
Germany	3 269.6	223	40.32	2.8
Netherlands	716.5	39	46.53	2.5
United Kingdom	2 571.6	220	44.11	3.8
Other	4 447.2	385	10.68	0.9
Subtotal	13 396.7	1 000	21.26	1.6
Asia				
Japan	7 552.1	320	60.32	2.6
Other	2 068.2	683	0.77	0.3
Subtotal	9 620.3	1 003	3.43	0.4
Australasia	790.8	52	36.44	2.4
Africa	270.9	40	1.21	0.2
Middle East	345.9	92	2.39	0.6
WORLD TOTAL	39 689.4	3 491	8.70	0.8

1. Legitimate sales only, not including pirate sales.

Source: International Federation of Phonographic Industries (IFPI) data.

TABLE 10
TRENDS IN MUSIC RECORDING SALES (1986–96 AND FORECAST 2001)[1]

	1986	1991	1996[2]	2001[3]
World sales value ($ million at current prices)	14 000	26 506	39 766	61 098
World sales volume (million units)	1 800	2 393	3 382	5 276
Format shares (% by volume)				
Singles	21.4	10.8	11.5	n.a.
LPs	30.1	5.1	0.5	n.a.
Cassettes	42.4	52.2	34.5	n.a.
CDs	6.1	31.9	53.4	n.a.

1. Legitimate sales only, not including pirate sales.
2. Provisional data.
3. Forecast.

Source: Compiled from IFPI data.

volume of sales over this period was also about 7%, with a significant decline in the market share of vinyl records, matched by a huge increase in the sales of compact discs (see Table 10). Despite some slowing of the world market during the early 1990s, the industry forecasts are for continued growth into the new millennium. Music Business International's *World Report* for 1997 estimates that the compound annual growth rate will continue at around 10%, with world sales in the year 2001 of over $60 billion.

At the same time there have been some shifts in the geographical pattern of demand over recent years, with relatively slower growth in the traditional United States and Western European markets, and more rapid growth rates in Eastern Europe, Latin America, Asia and Africa/Middle East (see Table 11). In these circumstances some doubts have been expressed as to whether the traditional Anglo-American dominance of the world music market will be maintained in the years ahead (Frith, 1991; Boon et al., 1996).

Analysis of the per capita demand for music in different countries indicates that it is consumer incomes that principally determine the amounts spent by consumers on music recordings. A simple

TABLE 11
PERCENTAGE SHARE OF MUSIC RECORDING SALES,
(BY REGION, 1991, 1996 AND FORECAST 2001)[1]

	1991	1996	2001
Europe[2]	38.2	33.7	30.1
North America	34.4	33.2	28.2
Central and South America	2.4	6.3	7.3
Asia (excluding Japan)	3.2	5.7	11.6
Japan	18.8	17.0	18.6
Australasia	2.1	2.4	1.7
Africa/Middle East	0.5	1.7	2.1
Other	0.5	0.1	0.5
TOTAL	100.0	100.0	100.0

1. Shares of legitimate sales, by value.
2. Eastern Europe as a share of total Europe grew from 0.1% in 1991 to 4.5% in 1996, and is forecast to grow to 8.6% by 2001.

Source: Calculated from IFPI data.

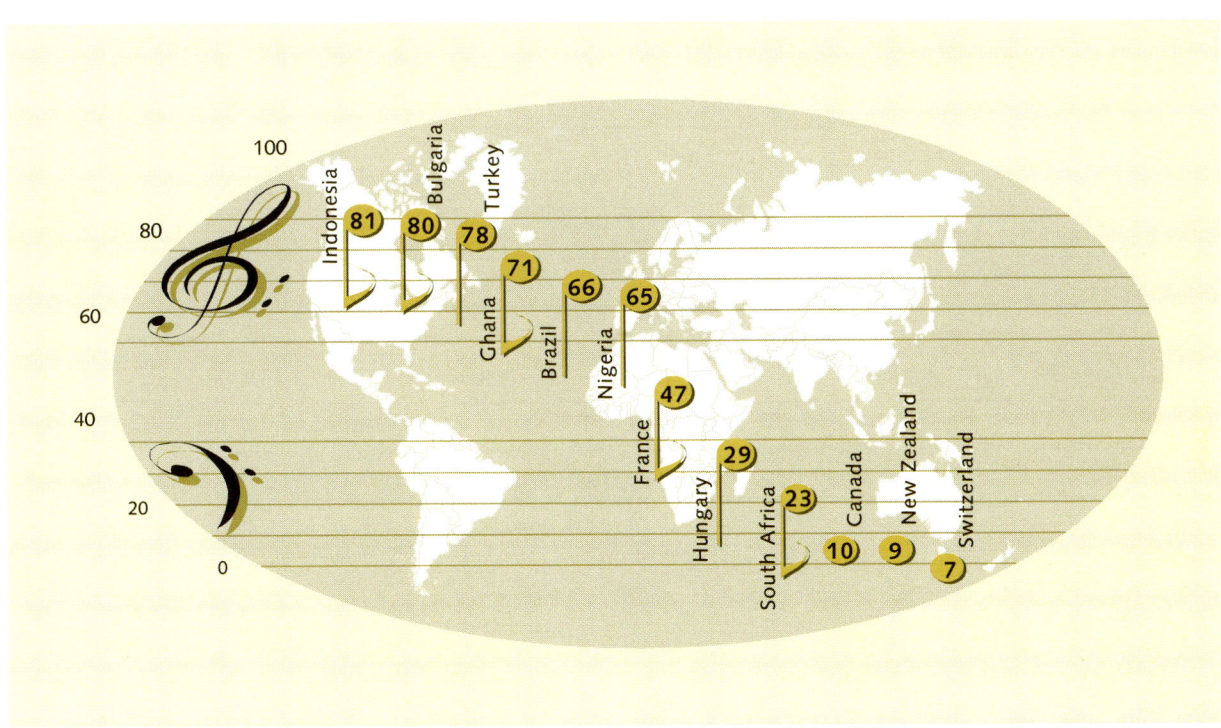

Graph 13
National popular music as a percentage of all popular music (1996)

Source: Statistical Table 3 in Part Seven of this report.

The music industry has become increasingly globalized. It is dominated by a few industrial countries and concentrated in a handful of companies. How has this affected national popular music?

Such music continues to dominate the market of many developing countries. International popular music enjoys only a minority share. In Indonesia the share of national popular music is 81%, in Turkey 78%, and in Brazil and Nigeria well over 60%.

The opposite appears to be the case in many industrial countries. In Switzerland, for example, the share of national popular music is only 7% and in Canada and New Zealand only 11%.

demand equation (see Annex) estimated for data across thirty-five countries in 1994 shows that although price differentials between countries do appear to exert some influence on demand, it is primarily per capita incomes that explain relative purchases. As might be expected, the level of piracy in a country also depresses legitimate sales per capita.

Piracy

When copyright regimes are lax or non-existent, it is a relatively easy matter for pirated copies of music recordings to find a market. Even in a country such as the United States, where copyright is strictly enforced, non-legitimate sales in 1995 amounted to about 27 million units, valued at $280 million. Worldwide pirate sales in that year amounted to over $2.1 billion, the principal problem areas being Eastern Europe, the Middle East, Asia, Africa and Latin America. Table 12 shows the eight major pirate markets in the world, ranked by value of pirate sales in 1995. In some countries, such as the Republic of Korea and Thailand, new copyright laws have recently been introduced, lowering levels of piracy dramatically; in other countries, however, the

TABLE 12
MAJOR MUSIC PIRACY MARKETS (1995)

	Value of sales[1]			Piracy as % of country's sales	Piracy as % of world pirate sales
	Legitimate	Pirate	Total		
Russia	224.3	363.1	587.4	61.8	16.9
United States	12 102.0	279.4	12 381.4	2.3	13.0
China	178.4	168.0	346.4	48.5	7.8
Italy	582.7	145.6	728.3	20.0	6.8
Brazil	1 053.1	118.8	1 171.9	10.1	5.5
Mexico	299.0	85.3	384.3	22.2	4.0
India	275.4	82.1	357.4	23.0	3.8
Pakistan	4.1	62.1	66.2	93.8	2.9
WORLD TOTAL	39 689.4	2 148.1	41 837.5	5.1	100.0

1. Expressed in millions of dollars.

Source: Calculated from IFPI data.

inadequacy or absence of a national law against piracy means that legal action cannot be taken against infringing copies, and music creators, publishers and record companies are denied a proper return.

Trade

Deriving a comprehensive statistical picture of the direction and magnitude of music flows between countries is especially difficult. Music trade is recorded in imports and exports of a physical product by countries, principally sound recordings ready for sale to consumers, but mostly records are not shipped in final form but in the form of masters which are then pressed locally for domestic retail distribution. In any case much of the trade, in the sense of payment for a musical product, occurs in the form of rights income flowing between countries. Thus it is difficult enough to evaluate the aggregate volumes and values of imports and exports of music

for a single country, let alone to compile a worldwide picture.

Notwithstanding these difficulties, we can illustrate the orders of magnitude involved for specific countries where data are available. We take the United Kingdom and Australia as examples, representing respectively a net exporter and a net importer of musical products. Table 13 compiles a statistical picture of international trade in music for the two countries for the years 1993 (United Kingdom) and 1991/92 (Australia). The preponderance of rights income in the total value of trade is apparent in these figures; for example, shipment of physical products accounted for only 5% of Australian musical exports and 30% of United Kingdom exports in the years under study, whereas more than half the music export incomes of both countries derived from royalty payments from abroad. In both countries there is strong interest in

TABLE 13
EXPORTS AND IMPORTS OF MUSICAL GOODS AND SERVICES: AUSTRALIA (1991/92)
AND THE UNITED KINGDOM (1993)

	Australia 1991/92 ($A million)			United Kingdom 1993 (£ million)		
	Exports	Imports	Balance	Exports	Imports	Balance
Visibles						
Records	4.4	70.7	–66.3	260.0	158.7	101.3
Musical instruments	1.6	68.9	–62.5	86.0	112.6	–26.6
Other	—	—	—	12.8	6.8	6.0
TOTAL VISIBLES	6.0	139.6	–133.6	358.8	278.1	80.7
Invisibles						
Royalty payments	79.3	150.6	–71.3	614.2	252.4	361.8
Live performance income/payments	20.0	40.0	–20.0	100.9	46.4	54.5
Other	16.8	3.5	13.3	84.0	10.0	74.0
TOTAL INVISIBLES	116.1	194.1	–78.0	799.1	308.8	490.3
TOTAL EXPORTS/IMPORTS	122.1	333.7	–211.6	1 157.9	586.9	571.0

Sources: For Australia: compiled from data in Price Waterhouse Economic Studies and Strategies Unit, *The Australian Music Industry: An Economic Profile* (Canberra, 1993), p. 53 ff., and Australian Bureau of Statistics, *Foreign Trade: Merchandise Exports* (Cat. 5434.0) and *Imports* (Cat. 5435.0). For the United Kingdom: A. Feist, *Overseas Earnings of the Music Industry*, London, British Invisibles, 1995.

expanding export markets for locally produced musical products. In Australia, for example, the promotion of Australian composers, songwriters and performers abroad is supported by an active export encouragement programme through the Australia Council (the Federal Government's arts funding agency), which is starting to tap into lucrative export markets, especially in the Asian region.

Music in economic development

The importance of music as a cornerstone of cultural life in developing countries is well understood (Wallis and Malm, 1984; Robinson et al., 1991; Nettl, 1997). The production of local popular music has grown from its roots in a long-established local culture, and has emerged in many countries in the developing world to become a significant economic industry through the wider spread of live music practice, local and national broadcasting, the

establishment of a domestic recording industry and eventually, for some participants, access to the international music market. Local popular music is not a static phenomenon remaining only in a specific local context, but a dynamic cultural practice 'linked to questions of mass communication, culture and democracy and away from the politics of a narrow-minded cultural nationalism' (Rutten, 1991, p. 295).

Music in the development process

In analysing the role of music in economic development, it is necessary to conceptualize music in economic terms in a manner that may be applicable at all levels from primitive through to advanced stages of development. Two interpretations of music as an economic phenomenon might be suggested.

First, music might be seen as a form of cultural

capital,[2] i.e. as a means of storage and transmission of cultural value. As such the sum total of the music of a community, a group, a nation, or indeed of humankind at large, can be seen as a major component of cultural heritage, which is passed from one generation to the next. Music as a capital asset can be increased by new investment and can deteriorate through neglect. Like other forms of capital, music is profoundly affected by technological change, in particular through the effects of technology on modes of production, distribution and consumption. As a capital asset, music has an economic value which can be measured using the usual economic yardsticks and which is additional to (but not independent from) its cultural value measured in whatever terms are appropriate within a cultural discourse.

Second, music can be seen in economic terms simply as a commodity, with the characteristics discussed earlier in this paper. That is, whilst music remains primarily a non-excludable public good, it can also be used as a means of commercial gain, if property rights over particular compositions and performances can be established and enforced. In the context of development, interpreting music as a commodity opens up the possibilities for extending music from being simply a form of cultural expression to being also a vehicle for economic empowerment, and thus provides the key to understanding the potential role for music in the economic development process.

Music as a means of entry to the modern sector

The process of economic development has been characterized within economics in a variety of ways (Todaro, 1994), generally entailing a shift in the balance of economic activity from the subsistence to the modern sectors. The production of music for economic gain can provide a relatively accessible avenue for individuals and groups to move into the cash economy. Many of the performance skills will already have been acquired, and capital requirements and barriers to entry are relatively low. Typically individuals or groups begin with live performance for payment, and, if they are successful and motivated, they may move into broadcasting or recording for the local market. In many countries throughout the developing world, small-scale recording companies have sprung up over the years, serving local broadcasting networks and retail outlets (Graham, 1988). Since there is often no effective copyright regime in force, the costs to users can be quite small, and of course this also means that the returns to composers and performers of the music are likely to be similarly constrained.

Eventually, however, the emerging local music industries of developing countries are affected by the international market, through two avenues. First, the production sector of the music industry in these countries becomes increasingly a target for the large transnational record companies. Second, consumers' demands for the sort of music that circulates internationally grows as such music becomes more readily available, as incomes rise, and as tastes change; thus the proportion of domestically produced music in a country's total music demand tends to decline as development proceeds. These observations are borne out by music industry data. At the smallest and least-developed end of the spectrum, a number of countries (including many in Africa) have too small a record market and too high a level of piracy to offer a viable economic return to international corporations; furthermore, the local music scene in such countries is often based more on other modes of production and distribution, such as live performance (Rutten, 1991, p. 298) and is thus less attractive to record companies. Larger developing countries, and those whose per capita incomes are increasing, gradually become integrated into the international music industry; the share of the domestic repertoire in total record sales (and the levels of piracy) tend to fall as more advanced stages of economic development are reached. Data from

Music Business International (1996, pp. 57–8) show that, amongst the approximately 70 countries participating in the international music market in 1994, about fifteen out of the twenty countries with the highest shares of domestic music in their record sales could be classed as developing countries, with an average piracy level of around 25%. By contrast, virtually all of the top twenty most international markets were developed countries, with piracy levels of less than 5%.

Thus, the expansion of music markets in developing countries themselves has primarily arisen from a growing consumption of European and American music in those countries; that is, the main flow in international trade in music has been from the developed to the developing world, not the other way around. As Negus (1992) notes:

The dominance of world markets by Anglo-American music and artists is reinforced by the way in which the American and British sales charts decisively influence the local policies of record companies and the decisions of radio programmers throughout the world . . . [T]he world markets for popular music have been constructed to provide a series of opportunities for British and American artists across the globe (pp. 10–11).

What then are the chances that artists and music styles from developing countries might break into world markets and hence might contribute to the local economy through the generation of export revenue?

Uptake of Third World music in the international market

Some local music genres have grown over time to dominate the international scene, beginning with jazz and moving on to rock'n'roll, rap, hiphop, reggae and other musical forms. Nevertheless, despite the apparently rapid uptake of musical style and fashion by the international recording industry, artists from the South have found it very difficult to be recorded and to gain exposure in the international market place. In most cases, music from the Third World has been brought to wider attention through the activities of independent record producers, standing somewhat apart from the major transnational companies. Over time, however, a number of successful independents have been absorbed by the majors, and although these firms may continue to produce some specialist music within the larger conglomerate, the scope for a truly independent channel for the development, marketing and promotion of new music and new artists from outside the mainstream is very limited.

Nevertheless, over the last decade the category known as 'World Music' has emerged in the West, representing a range of specific musical genres or styles originating in various parts of the world, including such musics as salsa from Cuba and Puerto Rico, zouk from the French Antilles, rembetika from Greece, raï from Algeria, qawwali from Pakistan and India, and many more (Broughton et al., 1994). World Music encompasses much popular and folk music of the Third World and of Eastern and Central Europe, and music of migrant, minority and indigenous communities. Although boundaries have sometimes become blurred when some Western recording artists have integrated elements of World Music into their own performance, a reasonably clear distinction can be maintained between World Music as it has evolved, and the mass of Western popular music produced for large-scale global consumption.

Despite its rapid growth, World Music remains a relatively small element in the total international music picture. As Mitchell (1996) notes:

In the context of the global economy of the popular music industry, the category of world music represents a very small subculture, predominantly produced, marketed and consumed in Europe and the United States, although usually commanding a vast groundswell of consumption in the musics' countries of origin, often through local audio cassette distribution networks (p. 52).

World Music:
the relocation of culture

The music of Indonesia, collectively known as gamelan music, is in many ways located at the intersection of World Music and ethnomusicology. While it may be regarded as a variety of World Music, a cultural commodity available at HMV and Tower Records, its ethnographic reality as a cultural practice in the world today extends well beyond this.

Gamelan music derives its name from the set of instruments on which it is played. A gamelan ensemble is a set of tuned percussion instruments, typically comprising gongs of various sizes, metallophones (similar to xylophones but with metal rather than wooden keys), drums and other instruments (violin, flutes and zither). Within Indonesia, gamelan music of various forms is played throughout the islands of Bali and Java. It is often said that gamelan music transcends class differences, having both a popular and a classical tradition. In village life, gamelan clubs continue to serve as a focal point for the local community; on the other hand, in the Javanese courts of the late eighteenth and nineteenth centuries, gamelan evolved into a highly developed and sophisticated musical form. In fact, it is likely that from the outset gamelan music was a transcultural music, a hybridized form of cultural production which in many ways anticipated the forms it has taken in the contemporary world.

The history of the Western encounter with gamelan music is usually told as a series of encounters with Western composers and its subsequent impact on their work. These composers range from Claude Debussy, through Colin McPhee, Benjamin Britten and Olivier Messaien, to John Cage, Lou Harrison and Steve Reich. Until the advent of World Music, gamelan music outside Indonesia was largely an academic phenomenon. It has been studied and performed in the music departments of Western universities since the 1960s at least. More recently, it has begun to attract larger audiences. Gamelan music is now taught and practised by a remarkably diverse community, circulating in a global network of arts festivals and concert tours. Indonesian gamelans are regular performers on the World Music circuit, while non-Indonesian gamelans perform at festivals in Bali and the Javanese city of Yogyakarta. There are currently over eighty gamelan ensembles based in the United States and Canada, and active groups in Australia, France, Germany, Japan, the Netherlands, New Zealand and the United Kingdom.

The commitment of American composers to gamelan music, and its performance by American musicians, provide an interesting case study in transculturation and the dilemmas which accompany it. On the one hand American composers rejected more or less from the outset the idea of merely imitating a putatively 'authentic' Javanese/Balinese gamelan music, adopting an aesthetic which freely acknowledges – even flaunts – the culturally impure, hybridized nature of their music. In its most overt form, this has involved writing music which combines gamelan instruments with Western ones, from clarinets to electric guitars. At the same time, from an ethnographic standpoint, performing gamelan music raises questions which extend beyond the solely musicological domain. Gamelan instruments in Indonesia are invested with magical properties and are the subject of elaborate rituals. Should Western musicians observe those rituals, even though they may not share the beliefs on which they are based ?

Within Indonesia, gamelan is no less of a transcultural affair than elsewhere in the world. Just as the globalization of gamelan music has changed the production and performance of that music in the world

at large, the impact of technological modernity, of Western popular music, and tourism within Indonesia have also changed gamelan music locally. Gamelan music in Indonesia today is a national cultural institution, continuing to serve its traditional purposes. At the same time it has been fully integrated into the modern Indonesian mediascape. Performances of gamelan music are regularly broadcast on Indonesian radio and television, and gamelan is ubiquitous in everyday media culture, from advertising to fashion shows. It also plays a key role in attracting foreign visitors to the country.

One way in which Western mass culture has inflected gamelan music is in the continuing hybridization of the music itself. Gamelan orchestras on Indonesian television, for example, sometimes include Western drum-kits or synthesizers. While Indonesian youth culture today is more focused on Indonesian hybridized pop musics such as jaipongan and dangdut, pop songs in these genres frequently include real or sampled gamelan music. Tourism has also played a role; gamelan orchestras today play in the large hotels of Yogyakarta and Bali, either as an accompaniment to dance performances or simply providing exotic music in the lobby. Finally, the recording of gamelan music is another area of transcultural encounter that has changed the nature of gamelan performance itself.

The production and consumption of gamelan music around the world today in many ways exemplifies the cultural contradictions of global post-modernity. In part, this production and consumption take place within the commercial circuits of global commodity culture, from World Music to tourist spectacle. What is striking here is how, within these commercial circuits, gamelan music is represented in exclusively local terms, as a uniquely Indonesian cultural form. Browsing through the 'Indonesia' section of the World Music department in any record store, one might easily conclude that gamelan music did not exist outside Indonesia. In a sense, this should cause little surprise: global capitalism and its associated culture industries depend on the construction of a cultural otherness that can be presented as the 'authentic' instance of a culture to consumers.

However, this commercial dimension of gamelan music in fact accounts for only a small part of its reality in the world today. In a sense, the World Music image of gamelan music is not a complete misrepresentation: within Indonesia, gamelan music still plays its traditional role as an everyday social practice within local communities. Yet if gamelan does exist in this traditional form, it also exists, as noted above, in increasingly modernized, hybridized and global forms. It is this global hybridized dimension of gamelan music that is ignored (perhaps even denied) by World Music through its exclusive focus on gamelan in its traditional, local forms – all the more ironic, given that the emergence of World Music itself is symptomatic of this process of globalization.

The dissonance of gamelan tuning and scales in relation to their Western counterparts serves as an apt metaphor for the irreducibility of gamelan music as a social practice either to the commercial dimension of the global music industry or to the cultural studies analyses of World Music. Rather than metaphorically try to retune it to fit these models, we would do better to listen more attentively to its musical and cultural dissonance, reflect on the limitations of our own scales of value and meaning, and recalibrate them accordingly.

Martin D. Roberts
Ph.D. in French Literature and Professor,
French Studies, Foreign Languages and Literatures
Program, Massachusetts Institute of Technology,
Cambridge (United States)

The emergence of World Music has been fuelled by the role of music in some parts of the world as a key element in political dissent (Sakolsky and Ho, 1995). In Bulgaria in the 1980s, for example, the government took action to suppress wedding music because it interpreted such music as a form of anti-state political expression (Rice, 1996). In Australia, indigenous music has grown from its traditional roots in the richness of Aboriginal civilization to become an important means of cultural expression in the contemporary struggle for land rights and political recognition (Breen, 1992; Mitchell, 1996, pp. 173–214). In these sorts of circumstances, music can become a powerful vehicle for political and hence economic empowerment and can generate wide international interest as much for its political as for its musical content.

For many musicians in the developing world, the prospect of breaking into the international music market, no matter how remote that prospect might be, is an attractive one, holding out as it does the lure of instant riches. The vast earnings of stars in the world musical circuit are well known (Tremlett, 1990). Yet very few artists can achieve such status when coming from outside of the mainstream. Even those from the Third World who do become established outside their own countries may not necessarily reap huge rewards. For example, the music of Cape Verde is known in many parts of the world through the work of Cesaria Evora, a powerful singer of the *morna* song form, a traditional mode of musical expression in these islands. Although she is the best-known Cape Verdean artist in Europe, it seems unlikely that her earnings would match those of the popular megastars on the international stage.

When musical styles from developing countries are taken up by the world music market, they are profoundly affected by a combination of cultural and economic forces which inevitably change them. Take, for example, the development of salsa. This is a music genre which grew out of Cuban and Puerto Rican music during the 1970s, and soon spread throughout Latin America and the Caribbean. Initially practised in New York, it has grown to become one of the most popular forms of World Music. It carries strong cultural messages involving the national identities of Cuba, Colombia, Puerto Rico, Venezuela and other countries of the region. It includes elements deriving from Afro-Catholic religious practice, and commands large audiences in the United States, Europe and elsewhere, as well as in its countries of origin. Much of it has been recorded and distributed by smaller independent record producers rather than by the major companies. But its uptake by an international audience has shifted it away from its portrayals of barrio life and its themes of Latino solidarity to a blander and more sentimental style. To some observers, the hard political edge has been lost as a result of economic and cultural pressures in catering to a mass market (Duany, 1988; Manuel, 1995).

Similarly, the diffusion of Algerian raï music in the West has disconnected it from its origins in the cabarets of Oran (Algeria's second largest city) and processed it into a significant component of World Music. Now, it is suggested, raï music stands at a crossroads:

What seems most striking at the present time is the increasing discrepancy between how raï is produced on the multinational level and how it is produced locally in Algeria, exemplified by the impermeability of the Algerian music market for foreign interests, by the West's advanced CD and studio technology, and by the political appropriation of raï artists in the West. (Schade-Poulsen, 1997, p. 81)

Thus, while raï music has been transformed in the international context, its capacity to act as a vehicle for expressing the concerns of an anti-establishment constituency in Algeria ('the young, the working class, the unemployed, the illiterate, the dispossessed, the fed-up') is threatened (Morgan and Kidel, 1994, p. 132).

It is apparent, then, that whilst music can be a

significant contributor to economic life in developing countries as an important industry in the domestic economy, its role cannot be assessed without reference to the impacts on it of the global music industry, which becomes inexorably a more and more significant force as development proceeds. It may be, as Hannerz (1991, pp. 119–20) suggests, that local entrepreneurs can continue to carve out niche markets in local popular cultural forms, including music, in defiance of the global dominance, and may even be able to draw on the 'global flow of culture' to use new technologies, organizational forms and modes of expression in this process. But in the end the economic influences of the world music market on the structure, conduct and performance of the domestic music industries of developing economies cannot be overlooked.

Strengthening copyright mechanisms

This chapter has identified the economic role of music in terms of a construction of music as cultural capital or as a commodity that can be bought and sold. As such, music has an economic value which is separate from, though not independent of, its cultural value. The production and consumption of music thus provides a basis for defining the music industry both in national terms as a major component of the cultural sector in a given country, and in international terms as an important element in the global economy.

In the process of cultural development, widely interpreted, music plays a key role, as a language of communication, as a means of storage and transmission of cultural value, as a vehicle for political and social comment and dissent, and as a source of economic empowerment. We have discussed the economic opportunities that music may open up for individuals and communities in developing countries. But it must be borne in mind that it is often difficult to disentangle economic from political, social and cultural considerations in analysing the development process.

Inevitably, any discussion of national music industries must take account of the overwhelming influence which the world music market exerts on production, distribution and consumption of music in virtually every country of the world. The globalization of music has seen a dominating role played by the publishing and sound-recording industries centred in the United States, Europe and Japan, with a handful of transnational corporations gaining an every-growing control over the market. In these circumstances, the scope for independent artists and music producers, especially from the developing world, to gain a share of the market is severely constrained. Nevertheless, some local musical genres and styles have been taken up on the international circuit, establishing a means for cultural interchange and diffusion. Indeed it has been pointed out that the international music industry can 'boast a more multicultural, multiracial and multinational array of stars than the film industry' (Alleyne, 1995, p. 48). Whilst this has led to some substantial economic rewards for some individuals and for some developing economies, the diffusion of local music into the world sphere has frequently occurred without any payment whatsoever accruing to the originators of the music; for example, Harry Belafonte made millions of dollars from songs whose composers – traditional Jamaican, Trinidadian and Barbadian artists – made nothing.

Thus, it is apparent that a stronger copyright regime will be important in dealing with the problem of piracy and in ensuring appropriate rewards to musical creators, not just in developing countries but throughout the world. As we have noted here, the development of more effective copyright mechanisms in the future will be especially important in an age of digital processing and on-line transmission.

Annex: Demand for music recordings

Data on the value of music sales per head of population in 1994 in various countries can be used to estimate a cross-section demand function for music, with explanatory variables of price and income, measured respectively by average dealer prices for CD albums (United States dollars per unit) and per capita Gross Domestic Product in (also in dollars). The effect of piracy levels on per capita legitimate sales can also be estimated, where piracy is measured as each country's proportion of pirate to total value of record sales.

Using statistics from the Music Business International's *World Report* for 1996 covering thirty-five countries, and with D = demand, p = price, y = income and z = piracy, as defined above, the following function can be obtained (t - statistics in parentheses):

$$\log D = 1.1548 - 0.2429 \log p + 1.0265 \log y - 0.1214 \log z$$
$$\quad\;\; (0.96) \quad\; (-0.55) \qquad\quad (15.41) \qquad\quad (-1.69)$$

Adjusted R2 = 0.9235

F = 137.74

n = 35

This equation shows a highly significant income elasticity of just greater than 1, indicating that expenditure on music per head increases slightly more than proportionately with income as development proceeds, and a negative but non-significant price elasticity showing a relatively low level of price responsiveness. A 10% increase in a country's level of piracy reduces the value of legitimate sales per head by about 1.2%, other things being equal.

Notes

1.   In economic terms, music, once published or performed, becomes a public good, potentially available to everyone without their being obliged to pay – that is, until property rights can be established.

2.   The concept of cultural capital, as an addition to the phenomena of physical, human and natural capital familiar in economics, is discussed in Throsby (1997).

Bibliography

ALLEYNE, M. D. 1995. *International Power and International Communication*. London, Macmillan.

BOON, A. et al. 1996. Complete Control? Judicial and Practical Approaches to the Negotiation of Commercial Music Contracts. *International Journal of the Sociology of Law*, Vol. 24, No. 2, June, pp. 89–115.

BREEN, M. 1992. Desert Dreams, Media and Interventions in Reality: Australian Aboriginal Music. In: Reebee Garofalo (ed.), *Rockin' the Boat: Mass Music and Mass Movements*, pp. 149–70. Boston. South End Press.

BROUGHTON, S. et al. (eds.). 1994. *World Music: The Rough Guide*. London, Rough Guides Ltd.

DUANY, J. 1988. Popular Music in Puerto Rico: Towards an Anthropology of Salsa. *Latin American Music Review*, Vol. 5, No. 2, pp. 186–216.

FRITH, S. 1991. Anglo-America and its Discontents. *Cultural Studies*, Vol. 5, No. 3, October, pp. 263–9.

GRAHAM, R. 1988. *The Da Capo Guide to Contemporary African Music*. New York, Da Capo Press.

HANNERZ, U. 1991. Scenarios for Peripheral Cultures. In: A. D. King (ed.), *Culture, Globalization and the World System: Contemporary Conditions for the Representation of Identity*, pp. 107–28. London, Macmillan Education.

MANUEL, P. 1995. Latin Music in the New World Order: Salsa and Beyond. In: Sakolsky and Ho (eds.), *Sounding Off! Music as Subversion/Resistance/ Revolution*, pp. 277–86. New York, Autonomedia.

MITCHELL, T. 1996. *Popular Music and Local Identity*. London, Leicester University Press.

MORGAN, A.; KIDEL, M. 1994. Thursday Night Fever: Algeria's Happiest Hour. In: S. Broughton et al. (eds.), *World Music: The Rough Guide,* pp. 126–34, London, Rough Guides Ltd.

MULLER, P. 1994. *The Music Business: A Legal Perspective*. Westport, Quorum Books.

MUSIC BUSINESS INTERNATIONAL. 1996, 1997. *World Report.* London, MBI.

NEGUS, K. 1992. *Producing Pop: Culture and Conflict in the Popular Music Industry.* London, Edward Arnold.

NETTL, B. 1997. Studying Musics of the World's Cultures. In: B. Nettl et al., *Excursions in World Music*, 2nd ed., pp. 1–13. Upper Saddle River, Prentice-Hall.

RICE, T. 1996. The Dialectic of Economics and Aesthetics in Bulgarian Music. In: M. Slobin (ed.), *Retuning Culture: Musical Changes in Central and Eastern Europe*, pp. 176–99. Durham, Duke University Press.

ROBINSON, D. C. et al. 1991. *Music at the Margins: Popular Music and Global Diversity.* Newbury Park, Sage Publications.

RUTTEN, P. 1991. Local Popular Music on the National and International Markets. *Cultural Studies*, Vol. 5, No. 3, October, pp. 294–305.

SAKOLSKY, R.; HO, F. W. (eds.). 1995. *Sounding Off! Music as Subversion/Resistance/ Revolution.* New York, Autonomedia.

SCHADE-POULSEN, M. 1997. Which World? On the Diffusion of Algerian Raï to the West. In: K. F. Olwig and K. Hastrup, *Siting Culture: the Shifting Anthropological Object*, pp. 59–85. London, Routledge.

SHORE, L. K. 1983. *The Crossroads of Business and Music: A Study of the Music Industry in the United States and Internationally.* Ann Arbor, University Microfilms International.

THROSBY, D. 1997. Sustainability and Culture: Some Theoretical Issues. *European Journal of Cultural Policy*, Vol. 3.

TODARO, M. P. 1994. *Economic Development.* New York, Longmans.

TREMLETT, G. 1990. *Rock Gold: The Music Millionaires.* London, Unwin Hyman.

VOGEL, H. L. 1994. *Entertainment Industry Economics: A Guide for Financial Analysis.* 3rd ed. Cambridge, Cambridge University Press.

WALLIS, R.; MALM, K. 1984. *Big Sounds from Small Peoples: The Music Industry in Small Countries.* New York, Pendragon Press.

Chapter 13
Cultural and economic development through copyright in the information society

Milágros del Corral
Librarian and copyright expert;
Director of the Division of Creativity, Cultural Industries
and Copyright and of the Publishing Office, UNESCO

Salah Abada
Copyright expert specialized in the developing world;
Founder of the Organisation Nationale du Droit d'Auteur
(ONDA) (Algeria);
Chief of the Creativity and Copyright Section, UNESCO

'How are we to market, licence and enforce rights on the Internet, or CD-ROMs and on machines not yet built?'

What is copyright all about?

The need to ensure the protection of intellectual creation through specific legal provisions derives from its intangible character. As recently noted by Jacques Delors, former President of the Commission of the European Community, 'culture is not an ordinary commodity and should not be dealt with as if it were on a par with refrigerators or cars'.

Indeed, a work is the property of its author, but it is also true that, once the work has been made public by whatever means, the author will not be able to control its subsequent uses if they are unauthorized. The problem began with the development of the reproduction technology (the 'Gutenberg galaxy') and was aggravated more recently with the advent of communication and electronic transmission technologies (the cybergalaxy). In other words, the author or creator will not be able to control the exploitation of his/her intellectual work without the existence of an adequate legal protection.

Intellectual property rights find their justification in the safeguarding of the interests of authors, including literary and artistic authors and performers, but also other creators such as inventors and researchers. Intellectual property has two branches: industrial property (patents, utility models, industrial designs, trademarks, etc.), mainly applying to the exploitation of new intellectual developments such as manufactured products, and copyright, intended to protect intellectual works in the fields of literature, science and art. Broadly speaking, the main difference between them is that industrial property protects the ideas of the objective world (laws of nature) which may be discovered by anybody, at any time, even simultaneously, whereas copyright protects the individual form of expression. Under copyright, the same ideas may be described or represented by different authors; all of these descriptions or representations will be different and original (e.g. several plastic artists will represent differently the same model using the same materials) and all of them will be equally protected, regardless of their value or merit.

Because of this radical difference between industrial property and copyright, the subject matter of industrial property has to be recognized by the state by means of proof of novelty, establishment of priority, registration and deposit, and only then be

vested in a given person. On the other hand, copyright ownership is initially and automatically vested in the author upon creation of the work since it is impossible for two identical versions of the same work to be created by different persons.[1]

However, industrial property and copyright[2] have some common objectives:

• they guarantee to those who dedicate their talents and efforts to a creative activity the appropriate remuneration based on the uses that others may make of the results of their intellectual work. Every work, in fact, deserves remuneration and there is no valid reason to exclude intellectual work;

• they regulate human, economic and social relations through an equitable distribution of resulting benefits. Many actors are involved in the creative process and in its dissemination and, no doubt, several and sometimes contradictory interests come into play here;

• they directly encourage individual creativity and indirectly promote development in every country or society precisely because creativity is the most equally distributed 'natural resource' and not at all the exclusive patrimony of a 'happy few'. In the words of Federico Mayor, Director-General of UNESCO, addressing the General Conference of UNESCO at its twenty-ninth session in 1997: 'As far as creativity, imagination and inventiveness are concerned, there is no difference between developed countries and less-developed countries, between men and women, between the élite and marginalized groups.'

Unlike other properties, the intellectual creation of an author is not of an absolute nature; it is limited in both extent and duration in order to achieve a fair balance between the private interests of the author and the public interest. Indeed the Universal Declaration of Human Rights devotes its Article 27.2 to the right every human being enjoys to the protection of his/her moral and material interests related to the scientific, literary and artistic works

he/she has created. At the same time Article 27.1 recognizes the right of every person to access to culture, education, information and scientific research. This delicate balance is reflected in national laws governing intellectual property by limiting protection in time and by providing for a set of cases where a published work may be freely used by the public in certain circumstances. We are faced with one of the so-called cultural rights which is twofold and must remain so whatever the technological environment may be, if we are to respect the Universal Declaration of Human Rights.

Copyright: a cultural issue of strategic importance for development

If the great majority of industrialized countries dispose of a rich cultural heritage and profitably exploit this heritage, it is largely due to the fact that they have, at an early stage, assigned appropriate copyright protection to their creators and artists, in particular in inter-state exchange. Some of them have even gone so far as to include special provisions in their constitution (e.g. the United States Constitution stipulates that 'Congress shall have power to promote the progress of science and useful arts by securing for limited times to authors and inventors the exclusive right to their respective writings and discoveries').

Regretfully, many developing countries have not yet developed a co-ordinated copyright policy, are still without the appropriate infrastructures and suffer from an endemic shortage of qualified personnel to ensure copyright enforcement. More concerned with the short-term, they concentrate on exporting non-value-added raw materials and often neglect their own potential to export creative intangibles and cultural products.

Assisting developing countries in redressing this situation through the adoption of national and regional strategies and policies aimed to protect and promote their nationals' individual creativity, and conducive to the development of endogenous cultural industries, has become a strategic issue for the international community and a key element for democratization, cultural pluralism and the strengthening of national identities.

In other words, countries which have recognized the strategic importance of creation, copyright and cultural industries and which have accordingly taken appropriate measures, now enjoy a privileged position at the international level, both in economic terms and in cultural penetration through exports. Conversely, countries which have neglected to support their cultural industries for reasons of an ideological, political, short-term economical or even cultural nature, are now confronted with the dilemma of having to accept the 'invasion' of foreign cultural products and contents, with serious implications (endangered endogenous cultural identity, heavy royalty payments) or of having to build protection barriers, thereby contributing to a hazardous state of economic and cultural isolationism.

Copyright constitutes the sole valid encouragement for creators in a market economy as well as a common foundation for cultural industries. The existence and enforcement of adequate copyright protection and a country's adhesion to the major international copyright conventions are a significant way not only to protect national authors, to stop the brain-drain and to encourage national creativity, as is generally acknowledged, but also to allow cultural industries to develop at national and international levels.

Management of rights and negotiation of intangibles subject to increasingly sophisticated licensing systems, contracts and agreements are becoming important for every country, both in economic and cultural terms. Are developing countries properly aware of the potential that national creativity may have for their economic welfare and cultural expansion? Even where copyright protection has formally been enacted, how many developing countries ensure that their human resources are well-acquainted with the specifics of managing rights?

As a result of close co-operation between WIPO[3] and UNESCO, at 1 December 1997, there were 125 States Parties to the Berne Convention and 97 to the Universal Copyright Convention (UCC) of 1952, a large majority of states being now party to both. In total, some 120 states are party to the international system of copyright protection, and only 60 states, mainly the least-developed and small island states, do not yet participate in this system.

The decisive role of the collective administration of rights in copyright enforcement deserves particular attention. In fact, collecting societies have over the years become the most efficient infrastructure for the perception and distribution of rights since the individual author is unable to control the various uses of his/her works, forbid unauthorized use or estimate what is due for a given communication or performance. Collecting societies are also helpful for users who do not wish to have to go to the trouble of identifying individual right-holders, and can find out if a given work is still protected or already in the public domain, and undertake multiple negotiations with individuals.

Sometimes organized by categories (musical works, dramatic works, plastic works, audiovisual works, etc.), by modalities of exploitation (mechanical execution, reprographic rights, etc.) or, in other cases, administering a global national 'repertoire', collecting societies are internationally represented by the International Confederation of Authors and Composers' Societies (CISAC). They maintain close links and contractual agreements allowing mutual representation of 'repertoires' on the basis of a 'clearing-house regime' and develop blanket tariffs for particular modalities of exploitation. Thus, interested users in a given country will only need to contact the appropriate national collecting society in order to clear the rights for the works (whether national or foreign) which it is intended to exploit.

Because of the critical role of collective administration in the efficient exercise of rights and

because of their increasingly important turnover, collecting societies are usually regulated by national laws and often subject to governmental tutelage. The de facto monopoly exercised by collecting societies vis-à-vis anti-trust legislation has been questioned in some countries but it is also true that this kind of monopoly is in the interest of users and makes possible the smooth exercise of rights in a market economy. Without the existence of efficient collecting societies this exercise has proved to have been seriously hampered.

Contemporary developments of copyright and neighbouring rights

Scientific and technical progress has had a great impact on the evolution of copyright since it has brought into existence various new technical means for the communication of protected works to the public, allowing dissemination on an international scale: photography, sound recordings, cinematography, radio and television broadcasting, video and CDs have progressively become new vehicles for the dissemination of protected creations, generated new categories of protectable works and allowed the development of new and influential cultural industries, with the consequent increase in chances of the democratization of culture.

The 1960s introduced the transmission of protected works through different 'generations' of satellites. The consolidation of satellite technology through direct satellite broadcasting in the 1980s ensured the cable distribution of audiovisual programmes – and thus, of protected works – to paying subscribers and later generated new cable-originated programmes. The new supports – recorded music and film – could be multiplied and put on sale or rented to the public. There were also crucial inventions in terms of equipment: photocopying machines and audio and video recorders becoming familiar to the ordinary citizen in many countries. Revisions of the international copyright system, adoptions of new treaties and updating of national

legislations have accompanied technological development in the present century in order to cope with the successive new challenges and to fight increasing possibilities of 'piracy' by refocusing the delicate balance of interests between authors, performers and producers, copyright-owners and the public, industrialized and developing countries.

If scientific and technical progress has considerably increased the possibilities for production and dissemination of works of the mind, it has also created situations which have caused economic losses, not only to authors, but also to performers. With the development of the phonogram industry, cinematography, radio and television broadcasting, performers (singers, musicians, actors) began to gain notoriety while at the same time losing opportunities for live performance, jobs and economic benefits; they therefore claimed appropriate legal protection at the national and international levels. Simultaneously, the emerging phonogram industries and broadcasting organizations themselves learned the negative impact of piracy (unauthorized reproduction, rental, re-broadcasting, etc.) and began to suffer important economic losses. It became evident that the production of phonograms and broadcasts required considerable investment, skill, effort and time which justified their request for protection.

It is therefore not surprising that all three – performers, producers and broadcasters – became beneficiaries of a new instrument adopted in Rome in 1961 under the joint aegis of ILO, UNESCO and WIPO: the International Convention for the Protection of Performers, Producers of Phonograms and Broadcasting Organizations, known as the Rome Convention. Though none of the three beneficiaries felt entirely satisfied with the legal solutions offered by the Convention for the protection of its interests, the Rome Convention was undoubtedly a great step forward at the international level. It is presently ratified by fifty-five states and continues to have a considerable impact on national legislations.

In view of the constant erosion of the interests of performers and phonogram producers owing to the development of ever more performance reproduction techniques, the Rome Convention was soon supplemented by another international instrument, adopted in 1971 in Geneva: the Convention for the Protection of Producers of Phonograms against Unauthorized Duplication of their Phonograms, usually known as the Phonogram Convention. The choice of means to ensure protection to phonogram producers is left to the states and includes granting copyright or other specific rights under unfair competition law, as well as penal sanctions. The reference to copyright in this context is not accidental since in a number of states, in accordance with common law legal tradition, sound recordings are protected under copyright laws and not under specific, neighbouring rights as is the case in the states which have adopted the *droit d'auteur* system.

Understanding and settling the problems raised by new technology has not been and is not always an easy matter in the copyright field. Representatives of creators and the cultural industries have had to prove that they have suffered severe economic damage, and governments and legislators had not only to evaluate those losses in cultural and economic terms, but also to see to the public interest, bearing in mind that, as a general rule, the purpose of any copyright amendment must be to encourage creativity and the production of intellectual goods without hampering their dissemination or public access to them – in other words, to restore the balance between legitimate private and public interests, once there is evidence that such a balance has been broken by the generalization of a new technology.

The international struggle for copyright enforcement

While looking for a more efficient mechanism to ensure the enforcement of intellectual property laws, the Uruguay Round, at the initiative of the United States, decided to include the trade of intangibles (industrial property and copyright) together with services in the fields of competence of the General Agreement on Tariffs and Trade (GATT), traditionally limited to the trade of material goods. The origins of such a proposal are to be found in the economic importance of the 'content industries'[4] together with the increasing export capacities of a number of developing countries in terms of manufactured goods, which led the recognition and appreciation of the comparative advantage that intellectual 'goods' represented for industrialized countries. Market liberalization for the benefit of products coming from developing countries should therefore imply in exchange a stronger protection of intellectual property in the framework of a restructured global market. On the other hand, the positive results obtained bilaterally by the United States in the repression of piracy in several countries of South-East Asia through the application of the United States Trade Act and its Arts. 301 and 'super-301', were undoubtedly also instrumental in that decision, and all the more so when those results were compared with those of the existing international copyright and neighbouring rights conventions of the United Nations system (WIPO, UNESCO and ILO) where enforcement is based on a 'gentleman's agreement' rather than on efficient mechanisms of arbitration.

The United States initiative to include intellectual property as a new trade booster in the multilateral negotiations of GATT was finally supported, although for different reasons, both by industrialized and developing countries regardless of the opinion of most copyright experts, clearly opposed to the idea of considering intellectual works as trade commodities in spite of their cultural and spiritual value.

The Marrakesh Act, adopted in December 1993 by 117 States, decided on the establishment of the World Trade Organization (WTO) as a permanent organization within the Bretton Woods Group (World Bank and International Monetary Fund) in

succession to the former GATT. The Marrakesh Act was ratified in April 1994 and WTO assumed its functions in the trade not only of goods, but also of services and intellectual property rights (included in the TRIPS (Trade Related Aspects of Intellectual Property) Agreement by providing an integrated arbitration mechanism in case of differences among states.

It is, however, interesting to note that, although TRIPS takes the substantial provisions of the Berne Convention (as revised in 1971) as a standard for copyright protection and makes extensive use of the WIPO/UNESCO guiding principles on the implication of new technologies, the respect of moral rights, included in Art. 6 of the Berne Convention, is not compulsory under this treaty which otherwise includes computer programs as protected literary work and lays the foundations to protect original databases under copyright. Furthermore, the Rome Convention is also the standard for the protection of neighbouring rights under TRIPS.

New copyright challenges

A major impact on copyright was felt around 1967 with the popularization of computers, microprocessors and silicone chips, often considered as a second revolution only comparable in importance and scope to the invention of printing. For the first time electronic storage and retrieval of pre-existing protected works appeared to be as easy as a children's game, raising the question of its liability with regard to copyright. Computers were now being used for the creation of musical compositions, translations and so forth. For the first time, too, a new category of intellectual works appeared – computer programs – whose creative nature could not be denied but which did not appear to be readily assimilable to literary or artistic works.

Various studies and international discussions conducted jointly by UNESCO and WIPO from the end of the 1960s until the middle of the 1980s gradually led to a consensus: the reproduction right

already granted to authors under national laws and international conventions should be applied with regard to the electronic storage and retrieval of protected works since it involves their reproduction. The question of copyright ownership in computer-assisted works was also resolved without major problems by applying the already existing copyright principles. The issue of the protectability and the law applicable to computer programs (patents, copyright or *sui generis* protection) appeared to be more complicated but, under pressure from software producers, a consensus was finally reached in favour of copyright protection whereby computer programs were assimilated to a literary work albeit in the face of reticence from some copyright experts at that time. Computer programs have since been protected under copyright by national laws and international conventions. The European Union confirmed this approach by the adoption of a Council Directive which became obligatory for the Member States as of 1991. The same principle was explicitly included in the above-mentioned TRIPS Agreement and, later on, in the WIPO Treaty on Copyright adopted in December 1996.

Jumping into cyberspace

The technological challenge is far from being resolved in the field of copyright and neighbouring rights. The convergence of telecommunications, computer technology, broadcasting (including satellite broadcasting) cable distribution and digital compression techniques have allowed information to be communicated at high speed over a variety of wired and wireless networks practically everywhere. Moreover, intelligent interfaces and interactive hypertext facilities in information products and services provide tailor-made access by users. This combination and interaction of technologies is giving birth to new products and services based on imaging, video, advanced voice- and audio-processing, automated data retrieval, messaging and data banks which already are and will increasingly become

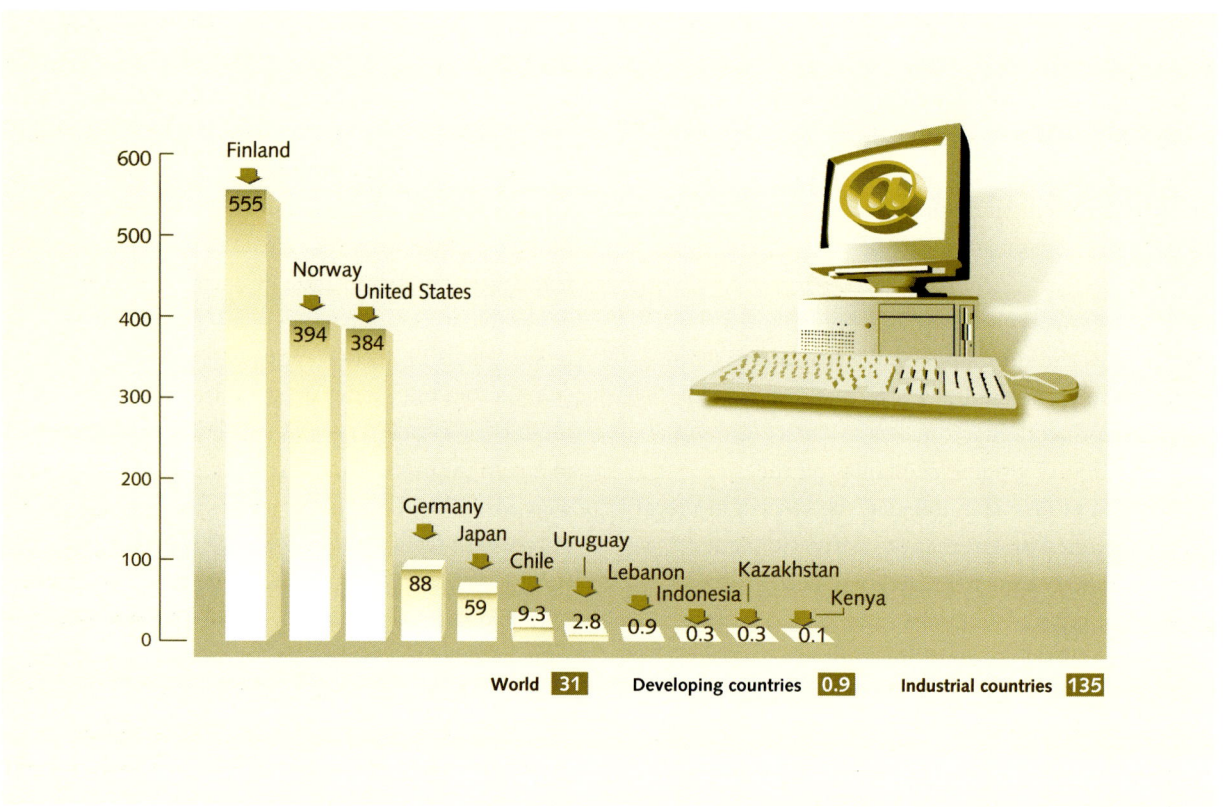

GRAPH 14
INTERNET HOSTS PER 10,000 PERSONS
(1996–97)
Source: Statistical Table 10(b) in Part Seven of this report.
A great gap between the industrial and developing countries relates to the use of the Internet: while industrial countries
have 135 Internet hosts per 10,000 people, developing countries have only 0.9. Among industrial countries, Finland has
the most: 555. At the other extreme are developing countries such as Kenya (0.1) and Kazakhstan (0.3).

accessible through a set of interconnected and
interoperable networks, progressively linking all
parts of the world in a single system with the virtual
elimination of space and time constraints. With the
digitalization of sounds and images, not only literary
works but also musical and audiovisual creations and
performances can be transmitted via electronic
networks, and the creation of multimedia data banks
for interactive use on demand has already been tested.

No doubt, the Internet is the forerunner of the
announced global information infrastructure.
Dramatic reductions in computer costs, the

launching of the Net-TVS or Net-computers and the
availability of inexpensive optic-fibre cable will do
the rest to enable us to jump into the global
information society on the threshold of the twenty-
first century. And, one might ask, in this changing
digital environment, is there still room for copyright?
How best to protect creators in the era of
cyberculture? Do traditional methods of production
and distribution of various categories of intellectual
works have any future? Will a new approach to
rights management allow us to re-establish a fair
balance between so many new and conflicting

interests? How are we to market, licence and enforce rights on the Internet, on CD-ROMs and on machines not yet built?

Several analysts agree that this fantastic new technological tool will be neither useful nor cost-effective if the contents circulating through it do not comply with consumer interests or the specific requirements of different societies. Favouring cultural pluralism and the open participation of all in this new modality of intercultural dialogue of the 'global village' appears to be the major challenge. On the superhighways, cultural or economic equality must be ensured both at the 'entry' (plurality of contents) and at the 'exit' (possibilities of access). Only if they are accessible to all – irrespective of race, nationality, gender, place of residence, occupation or social status – can the information superhighways be instrumental in achieving truly people-centred development.

Once the technological problems have been overcome and the liberalization of telecommunications has occurred, content will certainly become the major concern. This is why large multinational enterprises that wish to play a significant role in the future development of the information superhighways are already implementing vertical strategies aiming to 'control' content or, in other words, copyright. The acquisition of 'traditional' cultural industries (publishing houses, printed media, film productions, TV stations, cable networks, etc.) by powerful multinational consortia has recently become news. Concentration is, more than ever before, the keyword.

All these technological developments, however positive they may be, threaten to seriously erode the protection of copyright and neighbouring rights in this new technological environment. Although partly resolved by the two new WIPO Treaties[5] adopted in December 1996, the situation is far from satisfactory. The absence of a physical support opens up new possibilities to easily modify a work at no cost and without the author's consent; for the same reasons,

electronic piracy could become even more abusive than that experienced by copyright and neighbouring rights' holders with more traditional reproduction techniques. As Ralph Oman recently stated: 'In this new environment, every plugged-in consumer is a potential author, a potential publisher and a potential infringer, all at once at different times.'

On the other hand, most of the main actors in the global information infrastructure are completely alien to the traditional cultural industries and consequently to the copyright notion. As newcomers to the media arena from a large variety of industrial fields – telecommunication, electronics and diverse services – mainly attracted by the promises of a new eldorado, their strategy is to convert as many subscribers as possible to their new services allowing free access to the increasingly valuable contents transmitted on the networks to paying subscribers. To this end, they do not hesitate, at best, to stress the growing irrelevance of traditional copyright in cyberspace and, at worst, to proclaim the end of the copyright road.

Moreover, the historical origins of the Internet also play in favour of the access to free-of-charge contents. The academic and research community was particularly mobilized in December 1996 against the adoption of another WIPO Treaty intended to introduce *sui generis* protection to producers of databases which do not satisfy the original selection and arrangement criteria for copyright protection. Those database producers had already succeeded in obtaining such protection at the European level, based on the right to authorize 'extractions' from their context but the attempt to introduce *sui generis* protection at the international level failed at the WIPO Forum due to strong opposition to this protection on the part of scientific circles. Librarians, scientists and researchers felt that the introduction of this protection against unauthorized extraction would hamper educators' and scientists' access to scientific databanks and the scientific exchanges of information at national and international levels. An important movement is under way in favour of public-domain information and the 'copyleft' approach is promoted as a fashionable cyber-slogan based on a play on words which, in the opinion of creators, does not sound completely innocent.

Under present conditions, were technology, economic forces and civil society, for the sake of modernity, seen to jointly conspire against creativity and actively contribute to the erosion of its legal protection, then authors and creators would at first glance appear to be confronted with a serious dilemma: to either abandon their exclusive right to their works transmitted through networks – and then the question of the funding of creative activities would take a step back to pre-printing times – or avoid the network in order to escape its risks – in which case literary, scientific and artistic creativity would be constrained to the limits of traditional support to the prejudice of cultural development. Similarly, 'traditional' cultural industries might see their sun setting, with serious social and labour implications in an increasingly plugged-in society.

A matter of urgency

We remain, however, convinced that developments in the field of digital technology, rather than being a revolution, in fact represent an evolution which originated in the 1960s. We, accordingly, call for the urgent modification of the traditional norms of copyright protection to the new electronic environment.

One of the main achievements of the WIPO Diplomatic Conference of December 1996 was the recognition, under the Treaty on Copyright, of the author's right of communication to the public which was extended to digital transmission, thereby enlarging the copyright notion of public. The status of the protection of temporary reproduction (downloading for browsing purposes) in the digital environment remains to be clarified. The Treaty does not contain any reference to the right of reproduction. The Diplomatic Conference was

unable to reach an agreement in this matter and the statement clarifying the significance of Article 9 of the Berne Convention concerning this question was not unanimously adopted. A weak point in the recognition of the right was, however, the failure to identify who is liable to it since the agreed statement states that 'the mere provision of physical facilities for enabling or making a communication does not in itself amount to communication', thus liberating, for instance, service-providers from copyright liability.

In view of the development by copyright-owners of various technical means permitting the exercise of rights in the digital context (codes, inscriptions, 'watermarks', tattooing and so on), the Treaty on Copyright obliges states to provide adequate protection and effective legal remedies against the 'circumvention' of those means. Such remedies must also be provided against any person who commits illicit acts with regard to rights-management information allowing the identification of authors, works and other copyright-owners and including appropriate information about the terms and conditions of the use of the work. Analogous provisions are contained in the WIPO Treaty on Performances and Phonograms. This Treaty has improved the protection of performers' and phonogram-producers' rights, as recognized by the Rome Convention. It has also recognized the moral rights of performers. However, this protection does not apply to audiovisual performances although the exploitation of these performances is becoming particularly important in the multimedia age.

As this short review of the new WIPO Treaties shows, very modest steps forward have been taken so far. Authors, performers, cultural industries, collecting societies, Net operators, educators, librarians, scientists and consumers, governments, legislators and concerned international organizations have still a long way to go until a satisfactory copyright framework for cyberspace is achieved in a spirit of mutual understanding. This huge and urgent task must necessarily be accompanied by a major

effort towards educating consumers, particularly the younger generation, to respect those who put their creative talents to work for the scientific and cultural benefit of the community as a whole.

There is obviously a role for UNESCO to play in contributing to the development of the above-mentioned new principles and rules for copyright protection in the digital environment; in assisting states in the formulation of efficient copyright policies that ensure a fair balance between existing private and public interests; in encouraging the design of appropriate mechanisms for rights identification and management; in actively promoting copyright teaching at the university level as well as public awareness of the need to respect copyright and neighbouring rights in cyberspace too; and in facilitating information exchanges among specialists at the international level.

Support for creativity as a true locomotive for cultural and economic development is inconceivable nowadays without a clear commitment in favour of creators and cultural industries. Currently the best antidote against cultural standardization is the creation, production and worldwide circulation of as many varieties of cultural goods as possible so as to ensure a pluralistic cultural offer on the part of all communications media including the information superhighways. The ultimate goal is, however, to build a better world for all: a democratic global village presided over by justice and tolerance, where technologies are at the service of human beings and where 'our creative diversity' is protected, respected and recognized.

Notes

1.　For purely historical reasons, the copyright laws of some countries still require the fulfilment of obligatory formalities such as registration and deposit of works. Optional formalities are, however, generally practised in order to facilitate the burden of proof requirement in conflicts brought to court.

2.　At the United Nations level, industrial property and copyright have traditionally been dealt with by the World Intellectual Property Organization (WIPO) and, more recently, by the World Trade Organization (WTO). Because of its intellectual and ethical mandate, copyright also falls within the province of the United Nations Educational, Scientific and Cultural Organization (UNESCO) and has been part of its programme since the Organization was founded.

3.　The World Intellectual Property Organization based in Geneva was created in 1967 as an agency of the United Nations System.

4.　At the beginning of the 1990s, tertiary activities (services) represented 50% of the GNP of the European Community and 60% of its employment. Due to the existence of an international legal framework, it represented only 20% of its world trade. On the other hand, copyright industries come in second place in United States world exports, immediately after the aeronautic industry and considerably ahead of the automobile industry.

5.　The Treaty on Copyright and the Treaty on Performances and Phonograms adopted under the aegis of WIPO in December 1996.

Bibliography

GENERAL WORKS

COLOMBET, C. 1997. *Grands principes du droit d'auteur et des droits voisins dans le monde. Approche de droit comparé.* 2nd ed. Paris, Litec/Éditions UNESCO. Also published in Spanish (3rd ed., Madrid, Ediciones UNESCO/CINDOC, 1997).

LIPSZYC, D. 1997. *Droit d'auteur et droits voisins.* Paris, Éditions UNESCO, 901 pp. Also published in Spanish (Buenos Aires, Ediciones UNESCO/CERLALC/Zavalia, 1993, 933 pp.).

UNESCO. 1981. *The ABC of Copyright.* Paris, UNESCO. Also published in Arabic, Bengali, Chinese, Dutch, French, Hindi, Hungarian, Japanese, Korean, Portuguese, Russian, Spanish and Turkish.

COPYRIGHT AND DEVELOPMENT

ABADA, S. 1982. Le droit d'auteur, facteur de développement culturel. UNESCO *Bulletin du droit d'auteur,* Vol. 16, No. 2.

ALI-KHAN, S. 1996. The Role of Copyright in the Cultural and Economic Development of Developing Countries: The Asian Experience. *Copyright Bulletin,* Vol. 30, No. 4, pp. 3–31.

CORRAL, M. DEL. 1982. *Propiedad intelectual.* Madrid, Presidencia del Gobierno, 124 pp.

——. 1990. Copyright in Spain. In: M.B. Nimmer and P.E. Geller (eds.), *International Copyright Law and Practice,* New York, Matthew Bender Times Mirror Books, Vol. 2, 59 pp.

HUMMEL, M. 1990. The Economic Importance of Copyright. *Copyright Bulletin,* Vol. 24, No. 2, pp. 14–22.

FREITAS, D. DE. 1992. Piracy of Intellectual Property and the Measures Needed to Counter It. *Copyright Bulletin,* Vol. 26, No. 3, pp. 7–18.

GRAVILOV, E. P. 1987. World-wide Significance of the Universal Copyright Convention. *Copyright Bulletin,* Vol. 21, No. 3, pp. 26–31.

KÉRÉVER, A. 1991. Should the Rome Convention Be Revised and, If So, Is This the Right Moment? *Copyright Bulletin,* Vol. 25, No. 4, pp. 5–16.

——. 1994. The Protection of Copyright and Neighbouring Rights in the TRIPS Agreement Signed in Marrakesh. *Copyright Bulletin,* Vol. 28, No. 4, pp. 3–13.

LARREA, R.; GABRIEL, E. 1991. GATT, Intellectual Property Rights and the Developing Countries. *Copyright Bulletin,* Vol. 25, No. 3, pp. 4–10.

OLSSON, H. A. 1986. The Economic Impact of Copyright. *IPA Heidelberg Symposium.* Munich, Schweitzer Verlag.

ULMER, E. 1980. *Urheberrecht and Verlagsrecht.* 3rd ed. Berlin, Springer.

COPYRIGHT IN THE DIGITAL ENVIRONMENT

ABADA, S. 1989. La transmission par satellite, la distribution par câble et le droit d'auteur. Le *Droit d'Auteur* (OMPI), No. 10, October, pp. 307–17.

——. 1997. Les perspectives de la protection sui generis internationale de bases de données et les besoins de la communauté scientifique. *Congrès International du Centre du Droit de l'Information et de la Communication.* Brussels, Université Libre de Bruxelles.

CLARK, C. 1997. The Copyright Environment for the Publisher in the Digital World. *UNESCO International Symposium on Copyight and Communication in the Information Society.* Paris, UNESCO Publishing.

CORNISH, G.P. (ed.). 1997. Copyright. *IFLA Journal,* Vol. 23, No. 4.

CORRAL, M. DEL. 1982. La propiedad intelectual de las bases de datos. *Rev. Esp. de Docum. Cientif.,* Vol. 5, No. 3, pp. 245–66.

——. 1983. Data bases and intellectual property. *Copyright Bulletin,* Vol. 17, No. 4, pp. 8–15.

——. 1986. New Technologies, New Copyright? *IPA Heidelberg Symposium.* Munich, Schweitzer Verlag.

——. 1987. Le droit d'auteur et les bases de données: sujet d'étude ou d'inquiétude? *Le Droit d'Auteur* (OMPI), Vol. 100, No. 5, pp. 166–70.

——. 1987. *Data Bases and Copyright. Is There a Role for RROs?* Amsterdam, STM Publications.

——. 1990. Computer Programs and Computer Uses. *Regional Forum on Impact of Emerging Technologies on the Law of Intellectual Property,* pp. 69–83. Geneva, WIPO.

DREIER, T. 1996. Summary of the Debates of Panel II (International Symposium on Copyright and Communication in the Information Society). *Copyright Bulletin,* Vol. 30, No. 2, pp. 27–35.

——. 1997. *Copyright Law and Digital Exploitation of Works. The Current Copyright Landscape in the Age of the Internet and Multimedia.* Bonn, Friedrich-Ebert Stiftung/IPCC, and London, The Publishers Association.

GELLER, P. E. 1997. Conflict of Laws in Cyberspace: International Copyright. *Copyright Bulletin,* Vol. 31, No. 1, pp. 3–13.

HUET, J. 1998. *Quelle culture dans le cyberespace et quels droits intellectuels pour cette cyberculture?* (Report for the UNESCO Stockholm Conference, 30 March to 2 April 1998.)

IPA. 1995. The Future is Already Here: Publishers and New Technologies. *Third International Copyright Symposium.* Turin, CEDAM.

KÉRÉVER, A. 1996. Intellectual Property: Determination of the Law Applicable to Digitized Transmissions. *Copyright Bulletin,* Vol. 30, No. 2, pp. 13–23.

——. 1997. Problems Involved in the Adaptation of the Right of Reproduction and the Right of Communication to the Public in the Digital Multimedia Environment. *Copyright Bulletin,* Vol. 31, No. 2, pp. 4–24.

LUCAS, A. 1977. New Technology and Its Effects on Copyright and Related Rights. *UNESCO International Symposium on Copyright and Communication in the Information Society.* Paris, UNESCO Publishing.

LYONS, P. 1997. Managing Access to Digital Information: Some Basic Terminology Issues. *Congrès UNESCO sur l'Infoéthique, Monte Carlo, 1997.*

MILLÉ, A. 1996. The Effect of Digital Technology on the Rules for the Protection on Copyright and Neighbouring Rights and the Need to Harmonize National Legislation and the International Protection of Intellectual Works. *UNESCO Committee of Experts of Latin America, the Caribbean and Canada on Communication and Copyright in the Information Society.* Bogotá.

——. 1997. The Legal Status of Multimedia Works and Data Bases. *UNESCO International Symposium on Copyright and Communication in the Information Society.* Paris, UNESCO Publishing.

OMAN, R. In press. *The Need for Shared Liability on the Internet.*

RISHER, C. A. 1993. Copyright and New Technology: A Challenge for Book Publishers. *Copyright Bulletin,* Vol. 27, No. 3, pp. 4–12.

ROSLER, D. 1995. The European Union's Proposed Directive for the Legal Protection of Databases: A New Threat to Free Flow of Information? *High Technology Law Journal,* Vol. 10, pp. 105 ff.

SAMUELSON, P. 1997. Author's Rights in Cyberspace: Are New International Rules Needed? *UNESCO International Symposium on Copyright and Communication in the Information Society.* Paris, UNESCO Publishing.

TRUDEL, P. 1997. Responsabilités dans le cadre de l'infrastructure globale de l'information. *UNESCO International Symposium on Copyright and Communication in the Information Society.* Paris, UNESCO Publishing.

UNESCO. 1997. *UNESCO International Symposium on Copyright and Communication in the Information Society.* Paris, UNESCO Publishing.

——. 1997. *World Communication Report: The Media and the Challenge of the New Technologies.* Paris, UNESCO Publishing.

——. 1997. *World Information Report 1997/98.* Paris, UNESCO Publishing.

VANDOREN, P.; LECRENIER, S. 1997. The Nature and Scope of Adaptation Required for Protecting Copyright. *UNESCO International Symposium on Copyright and Communication in the Information Society.* Paris, UNESCO Publishing.

WIPO. 1993. *Worldwide Symposium on the Impact of Digital Technology on Copyright and Neighbouring Rights.* Geneva, WIPO.

——. 1994. *Worldwide Symposium on the Future of Copyright and Neighbouring Rights* (Paris, Musée du Louvre, June 1994).

COLLECTIVE ADMINISTRATION OF RIGHTS

ABADA, S. 1985. La gestion collective des droits d'auteur dans les pays en voie de développement. *Le droit d'auteur* (OMPI), September, pp. 227–85.

BAUTISTA, E. 1997. The Advantages of Collective Rights Management for Authors and Other Rights Holders in the Digital Environment. *International UNESCO Symposium on Copyright and Communication in the Information Society.* Paris, UNESCO Publishing.

CORRAL, M. DEL. 1987–88. Collective Administration of Rights: Wave of the Future. *Rights,* Vol. 1, No. 4, pp. 12–13.

Chapter 14
International standards for cultural heritage

Lyndel V. Prott
Jurist; Chief, International Standards Section,
Division of Cultural Heritage, UNESCO

'. . . norm-creation at the international level designed to protect the cultural heritage must be oriented to the wisdom of normative systems the world over.'

Standard-making and preserving diversity

'Respect diversity'. 'Apply international standards'. The seeming paradox can be resolved. UNESCO's activity over fifty years has been to define the best professional practice in the preservation of humanity's cultural heritage so that its diversity can be respected and preserved. What is common to the desert city of Shibam (Yemen), the colonial centre of Havana, Angra do Heroismo in the Azores, the historic part of Quebec city, St Petersburg and Kyoto? Culturally, they are as different as they could well be. But UNESCO's Recommendation concerning the Safeguarding and Contemporary Role of Historic Areas (1976) points out what they share: like all old cities they can be disfigured by the installation of poles, pylons, electricity and telephone cables, television aerials, large-scale advertising signs and the introduction of new buildings whose height, colours, materials and forms destroy the harmony of their traditional appearance. The Recommendation, in short, points out the ubiquity of elements of modernization which can unmake, very quickly, a unique cultural heritage, often by an accumulation of individual decisions. International conventions, recommendations and guidelines have been developed not only to help states further their international collaboration but also to adopt national legislation, administrative practices and policies.

They can thus prevent damage to, and minimize deterioration of, the great cultural achievements that are known and loved all over the world, as well as those of the small local communities, endangered languages and cultural practices which make up the rich inheritance of the human species.

What is the 'cultural heritage'?

The most visible element of the cultural heritage is the tangible heritage. It comprises immovables such as monuments, buildings, archaeological and other sites, historic complexes and those 'natural' elements such as trees, caves, lakes, mountains and others which embody culturally significant traditions as well as movables including artworks of every kind and of every sort of material, objects of

archaeological importance and those representing skills, perhaps vanished, and objects of daily life such as utensils, clothing and weapons. To these must be added the intangible heritage comprising intellectual heritage: creations of the mind such as literature, scientific and philosophical theories, religion, rituals and music as well as patterns of behaviour and knowledge embodied in skills, oral history, music and dance. Physical evidence of these may be preserved in writing, musical scores, photographic images or computer databases, but a performance itself, or historic evolutions of particular styles of presentation or interpretation are not always so preserved: significant developments are currently taking place in the law as to the protection of the integrity of creative ideas and as to rights of performance. Finally a significant component of the heritage relating to all the others mentioned is information: how a musical instrument was used, on what occasion and by whom, adds a great deal to our understanding of the human context from which it comes. Handing on this kind of information is as important as handing on the tangible object to which it relates.

Although genetic structures, human or other biological, are often now discussed as 'heritage', they are not 'cultural heritage': their preservation, use and development, as well as their legal protection, raise different, though very important, issues and require different techniques for management. They are not therefore included here.

Standards for the preservation of cultural heritage

No student of social history over the last 100 years could fail to note the growth of concern for the preservation of cultural heritage. The pace of technological change has increased dramatically – from fifty years over a range of key technologies in 1900 to about fifteen years in the 1950s to around three years in the informatics world of today. The information revolution and the globalized economy pose threats to heritage more immediate and widespread than any prior period, except for the menace of war. There is a desire to keep heritage – the physical world which we have known and can therefore give us a sense of continuity – as a familiar base on which to relate to the tide of innovation sweeping over us. As expressed by Stewart Brand,[1] as the bits go quicker, we want the atoms to go slower. We need to preserve some real world in the midst of the virtual world. So endemic is this passion to preserve that an English commentator has described the 'heritage industry' as an 'obsession'.[2]

Threats to the cultural heritage from the massive public-works projects made possible by modern engineering can affect any region. China's Three Gorges Dam will inundate 403 square miles (1,045 km^2) of territory, cause the loss of 800 known cultural sites (archaeological sites, early settlements and towns and villages that have been occupied for centuries) and, by the year 2008 when it becomes operational, force the displacement of over a million people. The Aswan Dam is another well-known case. The Yugoslav authorities resited a proposed dam which was within twelve miles of the World Heritage site of Studenica monastery when experts pointed out that the increase in humidity would lead to the destruction of fragile frescoes. Road and airport construction, mining and industrial development, hydrological work and land reclamation, urbanization and town planning projects, slum clearance and modernization of old city centres, as well as changes in land use, can all swiftly bring about enormous damage to or total loss of important parts of the heritage. This concern, particularly strong after the rescue of the Nubian monuments from the encroaching waters of the Aswan Dam, was reflected in an important international legal standard adopted by UNESCO in 1968, the Recommendation concerning the Preservation of Cultural Property Endangered by Public or Private Works.

This Recommendation is an example of how UNESCO responds with standard-setting instruments to threats to the cultural heritage. Such conventions and recommendations are based on the best professional practice of the day to ensure the care and preservation of the cultural heritage. In providing rules showing how to respond to threats to the cultural heritage they assist national governments to be more aware of this important human treasury and provide principles on which to base national legislation, which will, of course, take into account particular factors related to the uniqueness of the various heritages within the country. The recommendations also provide support to citizens in their efforts against inappropriate developments. They help establish networks of cultural professionals who can compare their successes and less successful procedures and thus increase the possibility of saving heritage which might otherwise be doomed.

UNESCO has prepared four multilateral treaties to enhance the protection of the tangible cultural heritage. They are the Convention for the Protection of Cultural Property in the Event of Armed Conflict (The Hague Convention) (1954) and its Protocol, the UNESCO Convention on the Means of Prohibiting and Preventing the Illicit Import, Export and Transfer of Ownership of Cultural Property (1970) and the Convention concerning the Protection of the World Cultural and Natural Heritage (1972). Between them, these instruments, applicable to cultural heritage in every region, provide a code of protective rules: in conflict (Hague Convention) and in peacetime (1970 Convention for movables, 1972 Convention for immovables). Like human rights instruments they set standards for proper management everywhere. The recommendations for the protection of cultural heritage, like the Recommendations of UNESCO in other areas, are adopted by the General Conference and provide a basis for national activities.[3] There is a constitutional obligation for Member States to transmit a standard-making recommendation to the appropriate national authorities for implementation and to report on such

implementation, or on the reasons why this cannot be made effective.[4] The recommendations often have a profound influence even though they are not reciprocally binding instruments between states. A good example is the Recommendation on International Principles Applicable to Archaeological Excavations (1956) which has become the standard adopted in most national legislation on the subject.

Participation in UNESCO conventions[5]

While information is only partial about the implementation of recommendations, it is possible to measure the commitment of states in different regions of the world to the rules embodied in the conventions. The World Heritage Convention has received very wide participation from all parts of the world and, judging only by numbers of participants, must be regarded as one of the world's most successful conventions. The other two conventions have an interesting pattern of participation. Eastern and Western Europe are the most active in the Hague Convention and Protocol, while Latin American, Asian and African States are to the fore in the 1970 Convention.

In the case of the Hague Convention and its Protocol, it is evident from the history of its drafting that its major proponents were the European states which had just emerged from a particularly devastating conflict and were recovering amid the shattered remnants of their tangible heritage. Ten American countries already had a convention on the topic in place (the 'Roerich Pact').[6] And many African and Asian States were not independent members of the international community in 1954. But these reasons, effective in their day, are no justification for non-adherence today. When the Director-General of UNESCO speaks on behalf of States Parties to a convention, he obviously speaks with more weight when as many states as possible of the international community are parties. The Hague Convention has ninety States Parties. Although the immediate impetus to the Convention came from

Europe, starting with the Peace Conferences of 1899 and 1907, followed by the devastation of war, the Convention represents existing traditions of humanitarian conduct of war that can be found in very many civilizations; indeed, some of them, such as the Muslim tradition, have had stricter rules on humanitarian behaviour in warfare for far longer than European countries.[7] The Convention, therefore, speaks not for, nor to, one geographical region, but represents the ideals of civilized humanity everywhere. This is shown by the promptitude with which some states, such as those of Central Asia (Kyrgyzstan, Kazakhstan, Tajikistan and Uzbekistan), became parties as soon as they were independently active in the international arena.

The 1970 Convention on Illicit Traffic grew out of particular concerns of newly independent states for the loss of their heritage. Much had been lost in colonial times, but losses were (and are) still occurring from looting of sites and theft. The issue of important cultural heritage taken in colonial times is controversial, and the holding states were unwilling to enter any international agreement on that topic, but there was agreement that some kind of instrument could be developed to restrain the excesses of illicit traffic for the future. A Recommendation on the Means of Prohibiting and Preventing the Illicit Export, Import and Transfer of Ownership of Cultural Property was adopted in 1964 and set out the steps which Member States should take at the national level to curb illicit traffic.

Are there some reasons why states from some areas such as Africa and Asia are consistently less active in participating in instruments for the protection of cultural heritage, while states from others such as North America, Europe and the Arab world, are much better represented? A thorough answer to this question would have to be based on an examination of regional participation in international instruments generally. One view might be that the states best-represented come from cultures where legalism is a strong political philosophy: making rules is their primary method of solving conflicts of interest both at the social and at the international level.[8] But it is certainly true that treaty-making has become a primary engine of settling conflicting interests at the international level and that states that are reluctant to engage in it lose the opportunity of advancing and securing their interests in a way that is regarded as binding on many powerful states.

Implementation of conventions

Participation in these international instruments is one measure of a government's activity in the protection of the heritage; but participation and implementation are not necessarily the same thing. Some governments act in accordance with the principles of an instrument, while not associating themselves as Parties: such is the case, for example, of the United States and the United Kingdom, which, though both are active in the negotiation of the Hague Convention and Protocol, have so far not become Parties, even though their military manuals incorporate the Convention's principles. Both states issued instructions to their armed forces during the Gulf intervention to avoid religious and historical monuments. Such reluctance to joining the instruments is regrettable, as it suggests to other countries that are not aware of the practice of non-joining states that there is less agreement on the principles than is in fact the case.

Then there are states which join the legal instruments but do not do much (or in some cases, anything) to implement them. How can their effort be judged? There are certain markers to compliance. Reports are periodically requested, as provided in the Hague and illicit traffic Conventions, on implementation. The Secretariat produces these reports and from these some interesting facts emerge. Seven sets of reports were published for the Hague Convention between 1962 and 1995. Of the ninety States Parties to this Convention, only fifty-two have ever provided reports, and only about twenty have provided substantial reports. There are eighty-seven States Parties to the Convention on Illicit Traffic of 1970. Three reports have been published, and only forty-six States have ever reported. Other tests for implementation can be considered: has a state implemented legislation to comply with the convention? Has it translated it into its national and local languages? Does it have an implementing authority? A resolution passed at the time of the adoption of the Hague Convention proposed that each State set up a co-ordinating committee to represent the different government bodies involved (Ministries of Culture, Defence and Civil Affairs) but only seven states have made reference to such a Committee and it is not clear whether all of these are still active.

In the case of the World Heritage Convention, a system of monitoring of sites has been started and is being adjusted to the needs of the World Heritage Committee to assess the maintenance of sites. This is particularly important since inscription on the World Heritage List often brings increased dangers to the site: pressures of tourist overuse, commercialization and development which can even threaten the very values for which the site was inscribed.

It is evident that the degree of compliance also has to be related to the size and resources of the state concerned. A small island state with a public service limited in size may find even the provision of the report a burden on its resources. The fact that some conventions give a degree of detail that is impossible for them to comply with should not be judged a reason for them not to participate at all. Of the thirty-six states which are not party to any of the UNESCO Conventions on protection of the cultural heritage, twenty are very small states with limited bureaucratic resources. Two others are very recently independent, another three suffering from current or intermittent internecine strife. Sixteen of the thirty-eight states are among the least-developed countries in the world. This interesting statistic shows that the other twenty-two least-developed states have managed nonetheless to become party to at least one

of the conventions. There are bigger and more prosperous states which, even though they are party to one or more of the conventions, have not regularly reported and which do not appear to have taken the action required to comply with the instrument concerned. In assessing the effectiveness of these instruments, account has to be taken of the relative resources of the states. The efforts sometimes made by states with little in the way of resources to apply the international instruments concerned must be applauded, when some of the bigger and more prosperous states do less.

Of course, there may also be factors of more general philosophical import influencing the rate of implementation. States which regard legal instruments as fundamental dictates of their conduct tend not to become party to a convention at all unless they are sure that they are going to be able to implement it thoroughly: the example of the United Kingdom and the United States in respect of the Hague Convention is here relevant. Many states with strong legalistic traditions will not adopt any international legal instrument which has implications for their own internal law until after they have passed legislation to ensure its compatibility with the obligations of the conventions. Some other states, once they have accepted the principles of an instrument, feel able to accede, but, since law does not generally have such a fundamental place in their culture, may be dilatory about adopting and enforcing the necessary internal rules to ensure immediate and effective implementation. This takes the discussion into areas of political philosophy and social and cultural attitudes that are beyond the scope of this chapter. Such a possible difference of views has relevance not only for the Hague Convention, but also for the Convention on Illicit Traffic and the Protocol to the Hague Convention, both of which require a State Party to seize an object shown to have been illicitly taken from a country (by illicit export or theft), thereby calling for new appropriate enabling legislation in the country of location.

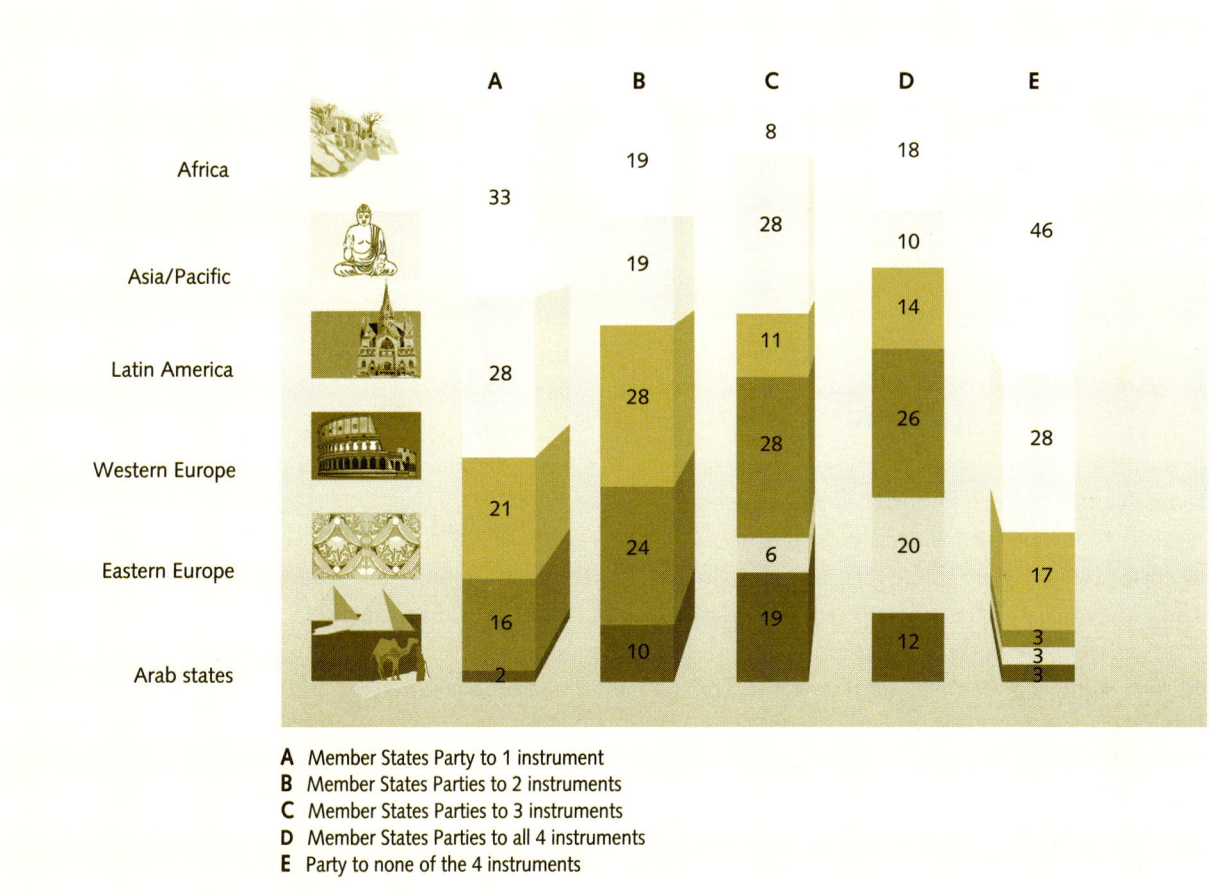

	A	B	C	D	E
Africa	33	19	8	18	
Asia/Pacific		19	28	10	46
Latin America	28	28	11	14	
Western Europe	21	24	28	26	28
Eastern Europe	16	10	6	20	17
Arab states	2		19	12	3 3 3

A Member States Party to 1 instrument
B Member States Parties to 2 instruments
C Member States Parties to 3 instruments
D Member States Parties to all 4 instruments
E Party to none of the 4 instruments

GRAPH 15
PARTIES TO UNESCO WORLD HERITAGE CONVENTIONS
(1997)

Global concepts of heritage

UNESCO's protective norms have been developed in such a way that they can be applied universally (although, of course, with some adaptation to local elements). Its universalist task in developing standards is paralleled by other universalist trends in discussions of heritage and also by globalization of the economy and threats of worldwide import.

Globalist concepts of heritage have now been adopted into legal discourse with the use of terms such as 'the cultural heritage of all mankind',[9] the 'world cultural and natural heritage[10] and the 'common heritage of mankind'.[11] Lowenthal has described the development of the idea of personal inheritance into that of communal heritage.[12] Recently, however, we have accepted the global unity of the natural heritage: it affects all humankind and all that we do affects it, as every other human being on the planet. And the language of cultural heritage concern has likewise taken on global dimensions.

The precise legal implications of terms such as 'common cultural heritage', 'world cultural heritage' and similar phrases are not yet clear, although their use in legal instruments makes it imperative to explore the subject. One commentator has suggested that the protection of national cultural property as part of the 'heritage of all mankind', as enshrined in the Preamble to the Hague Convention, is radically different from the obligation of every state to respect 'its own cultural heritage and that of all nations' in the Preamble to the UNESCO Convention on Illicit Traffic of 1970.[13] But there is no necessary opposition between these two principles. Common sense dictates that prevention of damage to cultural heritage is, in the first instance, most practically performed by the state where that heritage is located. The 1970 and 1972 Conventions recognize that not all states can adequately support the safeguarding of all their significant heritage: for that reason both Conventions enlist international co-operation to support them. More sensitive issues arise where local peoples do not see themselves as the true and empowered inheritors of the past around them. However, sensitization to the past and partnership with these people is more efficacious and ethical than any direct effort by the international community which did not concern them. Local communities must be involved.[14] The importance of this for the post-war rescue and revalidation of the cultural heritage of Lebanon has, for example, been stressed as essential if what remains of that heritage, so damaged by war and looting, is to survive.[15] And it is an important task for UNESCO to show that the heritage left by preceding or extinct civilizations and even by enemies is to be valued for all humanity and handed on, as intact as possible, to succeeding generations.

A recent systematic study of the concepts of 'heritage of mankind', 'world heritage' and 'common heritage' as used in UNESCO instruments reaches the conclusion that these concepts are by no means precise, although in course of development.[16] It also shows the great diversity of scholarly interpretations of them. For example, the idiosyncratic view that, since cultural objects are part of the 'cultural heritage of all mankind', this justifies broadening international trade in them to the benefit of museums, collectors and dealers[17] is found to be a surprising twist to the generally accepted view that such heritage should be managed in the public interest and for transmission to future generations.[18] But despite its uncertainties and divergent interpretations the broadening use of the concept 'cultural heritage of humanity' is considered to be a significant indication of general acceptance of the development of globally applicable rules defining the duty to protect.[19]

The global economy

Globalization of the economy has clearly changed heritage management. Market forces are penetrating to formerly remote areas of the world; trade opens up, as do the possibilities of illicit traffic. A recent case of illicit traffic showed that a collection of paintings stolen in Ireland was connected to a drug syndicate (the theft was engineered to assist in financing a drug deal) and involved transactions of a British citizen in Turkey, France, Belgium and Germany.[20]

Local heritage may find itself transported beyond its frontiers in ways unimaginable a few generations ago. Thus the Bolivian folktune 'El Condor Pasa' was popularized by Simon and Garfunkel, two popular music singers from the United States, and became part of the international repertoire of popular music played, thanks to the mobility of cassette tapes and players, in the furthest cities and most isolated places of the world.

Management of the heritage now also involves multinational and foreign businesses.

The same multinationals finance restoration in Prague and Peru, using techniques devised in Rome and London . . . Swedish, Japanese and German firms built the 'living' Shona village and replica of Old Bulawayo at Zimbabwe's Heritage Centre. Under the aegis of national patrimony looms a multinational enterprise.[21]

The globalization of business may be seen as directly increasing homogeneity: the facilities required to attract tourists include hotels, often those of multinational companies, where little but the colour scheme may change from country to country.

In 1974 the Egyptian Government signed a contract with South Pacific Hotels Ltd, a Canadian company, for a major development around the pyramids which would have included golf courses and swimming pools. The project was stopped when ecologists pointed out that the resulting increase in humidity could seriously damage monuments which had only survived the centuries because of aridity. Golf courses and swimming pools have become a global resort feature, no matter into what environment they have to fit. Cable cars are installed at the Great Wall of China at Si Matai and in the Cairns Rainforest (on the World Heritage List as the West Tropics of Queensland) and are planned for the World Heritage site of Machu Picchu. Helicopter flights are made over Machu Picchu and the Iguazu Falls and even over the painted churches of Romania – all World Heritage sites. 'Sound and light' installations are being installed on monumental sites everywhere; a lighting company advertises in the *World Heritage Review*.

The global dimension of trade can have other serious impacts on culture. Steiner describes how the main trade in African artefacts heads towards Europe. The preference for 'old' objects has led to the artificial ageing of new artefacts and the neglect of new developments in the artistic tradition. The lively carving of figures representing Europeans, for example, was long ignored in favour of traditional forms, thus limiting the range of styles.[22] The same dilemma faces Australian Aborigines – should they continue the painting on bark of traditional images, or should younger artists, exposed to wider cultural influences, use new techniques and materials to show old themes, or old techniques and materials to show new ones? Global market forces may reduce creative development by making certain forms of art

unsaleable. But it may also promote it by providing a market where none previously existed: the growth of Inuit stone carving is an example of a new form of artistic expression essentially undertaken to supply exotic markets. The now highly prized Australian Aboriginal art of the Western Desert is the flourishing of an ancient artistic tradition in new media: ephemeral designs originally made in sand first made permanent on hard materials and now immortalized in every sort of modern medium.

The efficiency of the publishing and entertainment industries ensures that music and film reach all corners of the world, and the huge English-speaking market ensures that its consequently lower-priced products can be dumped on overseas markets. Small linguistic communities, for whom movie production may not be economically feasible at all without some government support, feel their cultures under threat. Those who do not need government support because market forces in their own countries have already drawn a profit from domestic distribution in a very large linguistic market, want untrammelled export for their products, while those who do need such support struggle to preserve a place in the market for their more highly priced goods. A recent example of this battle is the inclusion (championed by France but much contested in the United States) of a special exception to cover cultural goods in the new international trade agreement. A major dilemma for the coming decades is between the drive to create ever bigger markets for mass media and the desire to retain cultural particularity.

The question arises as to how international standards should take account of these developments.

Defending diversity

Awareness of the impact of globalization of the economy on heritage also stimulates the defence of diversity. In the music business, societies exist to collect royalties for the performance of music for distribution to composers. These societies are organized on a national basis. However, by international agreement, they collect and distribute royalties in respect of performances in their countries for foreign composers. The ubiquity of music in airports, shopping malls, elevator and public waiting areas of any kind, is based more and more on programmed sequences of standard types from certain basic repertoires (chosen by the managers of those sites to suit, as best they can judge, the wishes of those using them). Changes are coming to the collecting societies:

Attitudes have gradually evolved and European authors' societies have become particularly aware of their responsibilities in relation to the cultural communities to which they belong. The more widespread domination of the international repertoire has dangerous implications for both regional and local culture and even threatens its very existence. The societies have therefore realized that they must move away from their cold managerial role and involve themselves in safeguarding their cultural heritage.[23]

However, an insistence on the use, or too high a percentage of the use, of national music may constrain national heritage. If market forces push in one direction, over-reaction can create other problems. Clearly a balance has to be found.

At the same time, globalization of communication may also facilitate protective mechanisms. Commercial databases of stolen cultural property, such as Art Loss Register, are open to registrations and searches from anywhere in the world. Recently a number of such databases – commercial and police – met to consider transfer of information between them,[24] and a consortium of international organizations and interest groups is in the course of adopting a standard form of core data, dubbed the 'Object ID' which will uniquely identify an object and facilitate its recovery,[25] providing also a standard for the exchange of data as more and more heritage managers connect to the international network.

An outstanding example of the use of global developments to defend diversity was the appearance at UNESCO Headquarters in Paris, in June 1997, of Ngarinyin elders from the remote Kimberley area of Australia, to reveal to the international community the spiritual meaning of certain of the rock art at their sacred sites. Excluded from their traditional areas about thirty years ago, their rights to these sites were recognized by a decision of the Australian High Court in 1992.[26] A change of government, however, has led to the threat of legislation to reverse this decision. The elders decided to put their case to the world community so that the importance of these sites in their culture and their mythological and artistic value should be appreciated in order to mobilize support for their continued access to and care of these traditional sites. For specialists in rock art from other continents, this provided an unprecedented glimpse of a living culture still related to this ancient art; and for the Aboriginals, a chance to have professional support from the international community for continued access to the sites.

The place of international standards

The development of global standards of protection for the cultural heritage can counter some of the worst effects that globalization of the economy may have on the cultural heritage. Yet it is not without anomalies.

This globalizing trend is recent, because only lately have all the world's peoples begun to be seen as similarly entitled to and jointly accountable for a global heritage. And global agendas are still viewed with intense suspicion, because they are recognizably rooted in chauvinist and imperial self-regard. These ideas stem above all from Europeans who rate their own national heritage as so superior it *ought* to be global.[27]

Early programmes of conservation of the monumental ruins at Great Zimbabwe were, it is noted, 'undertaken in a colonial context in which the local communities were not seen as relevant because this particular aspect of their cultural heritage was seen as not belonging to them'.[28]

In the development of standards, at least in the early days, Western heritage was the touchstone. A good example is the Venice Charter: the International Charter for the Conservation and Restoration of Monuments and Sites (1966) which was itself based on an earlier document called the Athens Charter adopted by a conference in 1931. Its principles are built into the criteria for the inscription of sites on the World Heritage List which has established criteria of authenticity. This test, strictly applied, forbids reconstruction: anastylosis[29] is as far as restoration should go. Such a test is clearly appropriate for the stone and brick buildings of which the Western authors of the text were thinking. But consider the very different traditions of Asia. In China, the most important buildings, the imperial palaces, for example, were built of wood, and if the test were applied strictly, few of them would pass. The Ise shrine in Japan has been rebuilt every twenty years to ensure its good condition: a strict tradition of proportion and of maintenance of form has ensured that the temple probably retains the appearance it had five centuries ago. Is it any less authentic? The practice, it should be noted also has the effect of ensuring the survival of outdated techniques of many traditional crafts.[30]

Doubts as to the reality of a proclaimed universalism are particularly apparent in respect of the movable cultural heritage.

In the course of their colonial exploits the European powers acquired global heritage and then came to construe their spoils of conquest as global stewardship.[31] The concept of global patrimony thus derives from an era of conquest that leaves much of it in a few privileged hands. The legacy of mankind ends up in the Louvre and the British Museum but is absent from Samoa and Somalia. Universalism endows the haves at others' expense. Few British connoisseurs, dismayed by the 1986 sale to Japan of Newcastle University's collection of Pacific tribal art, spared a moment's thought for Micronesians who could not afford to buy back any of the items fashioned by their own forebears.[32]

True universalism would ensure equal accessibility to the cultural heritage for all regions. It is apparent that it is easier today for someone from North America or Europe to visit New Guinea than for a Sepik villager to study Sepik art in one of the great 'universal' museums of the West. An African has noted that it is not just African culture which is missing from Africa: in the whole of black Africa there is not a single museum of Oriental art, a good gallery of modern impressionist or other art, and fields such as Greek sculpture, Aztec pottery and Slav silverware are completely unknown to African peoples.[33] A remedy has been suggested:

What objects from (say) Fiji, and not desired by Fiji, could be 'returned' from London to Rio de Janeiro? And what objects from Brazil now in Rio could be dispatched to London, and to Fiji? At one level . . . consideration of the return of cultural property implies also non-return. Equally, it raises the question of its return to 'culture at large' from temporary isolation within the museums of the Western world.[34]

Of course, the ability and desire of peoples to perceive cross-culturally varies, but exposure to other cultures by the increasingly penetrative media and the invasion of foreign enterprise inevitably influences local culture, without necessarily, indeed seldom, giving a view of the best that the exotic culture can provide.

Framing international standards

Present International Law developed over the last 300 years, for historic reasons, from the legal traditions of the European region, without taking into account other regional traditions which had existed or did exist at the same time. However, better understanding of other normative systems can now raise interesting questions. Some of them appear to have useful mechanisms which enhance the protection of cultural property more than those familiar in the existing system. Two examples may make this point.

International standards: an African perspective

The events of the Second World War and the post-colonial cultural revival in Africa and other Third World countries provided the catalyst for the beginning of the formulation of international standards for the protection of cultural heritage. The 1954 Hague Convention for the Protection of Cultural Property in the Event of Armed Conflict was the first international instrument accepted worldwide that focuses exclusively on the protection of cultural heritage. From an African perspective, with regard to the Convention, a parallel can be drawn between two African countries, namely, the Democratic Republic of the Congo and Nigeria.

When the Belgian Congo (later Zaire, and now the Democratic Republic of the Congo) became a sovereign country, it had almost no museums. As a result of Belgium's hasty decolonization and the strife that followed, most of the country's private museums still in operation could not defend themselves against pillage and other incidents which occurred during the first period of the country's independence. In the absence of civil government there was not much scope to claim protection from the Hague Convention of 1954, although Zaire became a Party to both Convention and Protocol in April 1961.

In the case of Nigeria, the situation was somewhat different. Although it had been a State Party to both instruments since 1961, it refused UNESCO's offer to moderate parties in conflict during the civil war (1967–70). The Nigerian Government provided official documents certifying the scrupulous observance of the Convention. However, soon after the civil war, national reports began to appear on losses of cultural objects and illicit traffic.

It can therefore be concluded that in the case of Africa the failure to implement the first international instrument for the protection of cultural heritage was due either to ignorance or to a false sense of national pride which led to negative results with regard to heritage preservation.

An interesting comparison can be made for Africa between the implementation of the Corollary of the Convention on International Trade in Endangered Species of 1973, and the Corollary of the Clandestine Narcotics Trade. Indeed, there are many similarities between the art trade and the hard-drug trade.

Art trade and the art market can be described as operating along illicit and mostly ignored paths, in the same way as clandestine narcotics traffic operates. And often the trade in cultural property is regarded as the most important illegal trade after the drug trade. It can be argued that though the West takes measures to combat the illicit drug trade, it has resisted the globalization of measures to combat the illicit trade in cultural objects. Can it, therefore, be said that because the industrialized countries are the beneficiaries of the traffic in cultural objects, they are indifferent to the plight of Third World countries? Yet, in the case of Africa, illicit traffic in cultural objects constitutes as great a menace to its well-being as the illicit trade in drugs. Its destructive effect on society is greater than the consumption of hard drugs, since it revives Africa's past emotional background of historical plundering and the negative outcome of efforts to recover stolen art treasures through foreign justice courts.

The latter phenomenon is due to the complex issue of conflicting laws and problems in the enforcement of foreign penal statutes. The absence of African cases being brought before the Intergovernmental Committee for Promoting the Return of Cultural Property to its Countries of Origin or its Restitution in Case of Illicit Appropriation is evidence confirming this pervasive lack of confidence in judicial procedures and legal instruments in general.

However, the development of national professionalism in African cultural heritage institutions offers concrete signs of hope for the future of African heritage, for example through the increase of long-term partnerships with conservation institutions and training programmes for African museum personnel. A major attainment can be found in the ICCROM project for building a cadre of trained Africans so that in a few years 90% of the ICCROM teaching staff would be African. Furthermore, the AFRICOM programme, the West African Museums Project, and the Foundation for African Archaeology are part of the significant emergence of a declared national policy aiming at empowering African cultural institutions in the long run for better management of cultural heritage.

Folarin Shyllon
Jurist; Dean, Faculty of Law, University of Ibadan (Nigeria)

There has been discussion for many years about the best way to ensure the protection of traditional knowledge – botanical, medical, folklore and other – of tribal peoples. One suggestion made is to include it in the protection system of the international agreements relating to copyright. But copyright was developed as a printer's perquisite in seventeenth-century England – is it really the best model for this completely different set of issues? Why not take terminology from one of the concepts of the many tribal systems which need to have such rights recognized and develop it as an international concept with its own special elements?[35] For that matter, is 'right' the best word at all? Many traditional communities think in terms of the obligations of the human community to the earth and the other species on it. Perhaps that idea may be the beginning of a new normative framework for the preservation of heritage.

The second example concerns the procedures for defence of the heritage. UNESCO Conventions and Recommendations presume the primary responsibility of governmental units for the protection of heritage. But what if these units do not act? In some legal systems, a heritage item may itself be endowed with legal personality which enables it to undertake legal proceedings. In the Hindu system of law, for example, an idol may sue – a system of legal personality recognized by the English court[36] and made use of by India in litigation pursued in London;[37] another suit commenced in the United States in the name of the idol itself on the ground of 'unjust imprisonment'.[38] In parts of Western Africa (Ghana, Nigeria), a 'stool' or 'skin' is a legal entity recognized by customary law as representing a particular tribal group and may sue. Application of rules such as these could be very useful for groups seeking the return of communally important cultural property, especially in cases in which the courts of the country where the property is now located are unfamiliar or uncomfortable with the kind of communal rules applicable to the property concerned.

These examples perhaps indicate that not only the substance, but also the methodology, of norm-creation at the international level designed to protect the cultural heritage must be oriented to the wisdom of normative systems the world over.

Heritage and the enrichment of human life

If globalization of the economy and communication gives unprecedented access to the cultures of other societies, it has the ability to widen human capacity by giving additional choices to communities and individuals. The point of concern is to try to ensure that the choices available enrich human life. Access to other cultures is an opportunity for a richer culture to develop: exposure to new arts and new levels of performance, as well as adoption or adaptation of new techniques, may stimulate greater creativity and raise standards. It may also lead to an impoverishment by the abandonment of traditional forms of creativity, the adoption of less-sophisticated techniques and the lowering of standards.

The choice between the better and the worse is not inevitably linked to economic dominance. Much has to do with self-confidence, pride in the achievements of a culture together with a curiosity and respect for other cultures which enable the artist or craftsman to be stimulated by them without losing respect for her or his own culture. For that reason globalization must be accompanied by respect for diversity. Loss of confidence in one's own culture, alienation of young people from the traditions of their communities, deprive human beings of the range of choices which might have been theirs if, equipped with a justified pride in the achievements of their own culture, they freely choose elements of others.[39]

The development of global legal standards has a part to play in ensuring that these choices are not pre-empted. The World Heritage Convention brought together two diverse traditions of the Western world: care of monuments and buildings and care of national parks. Indeed, the Convention itself started

out as two separate draft instruments, proposed by
two separate institutions and devised by two different
groups of specialists. Although these two drafts were
subsequently brought together under the aegis of
UNESCO in one international instrument, its
application continued to be separate with distinct
criteria for cultural and natural sites and different
advisory bodies (respectively the International
Council on Monuments and Sites – ICOMOS – and
the International Union for Conservation of Nature
and Natural Resources – IUCN) to evaluate the sites
against those criteria. In most traditional
communities a sharp distinction is not made between
the cultural and the natural: every part of nature is
endowed with spiritual force (good or bad) and every
myth is attached to nature. The site of Uluru in
central Australia and Tongariro in New Zealand were
both nominated and inscribed as natural sites. These
sites were sacred to Australian Aboriginals and Maori
people respectively: for them it was even offensive to
regard these sites as worthy of inscription as heritage
of universal value merely by virtue of their scientific
interest because of the integrity of their ecological
systems. Gradually these ideas were communicated
to the World Heritage Committee, which responded
first by accepting 'mixed' sites, and more recently by
developing the concept of 'cultural landscapes'.[40]

The concept of 'heritage' itself has been
broadened. One benevolent effect of global attention
to cultural traditions has been a broadening of the
concept of cultural heritage. Heritage concepts in the
West were long associated with monuments and
movables – the tangible cultural heritage. Indeed, the
early discussions all focused on *cultural property*, a
specifically Western concept.[41] In the early period of
colonization and Western expansion many peoples
were regarded as having no culture, since its primary
form of representation in the countries of the
colonizers was not recognizable in these newly
dominated areas. (Where they were, as in Benin,
China or Ethiopia, they were quickly pillaged.)
Where the culture was dominated by the intangible

culture, such as the performing arts, rituals or music,
it was discounted. This at last is being taken into
account in forums like UNESCO which has
developed legal standards applying to artists, has a
Recommendation on Folklore and has issued
Guidelines on 'living cultural treasures'.

Our Cultural Diversity is all about maximizing
choices to enhance human potential. Respect for
diversity will help ensure that the choices are real
ones and not the result of alienation from and
rejection of cultural traditions of value, distrust of
other cultures or deprivation of access. Global
standards for the protection of the cultural heritage,
by ensuring the preservation of the best of the past
and supporting the creativity of the present
generation, help people everywhere to enjoy and be
inspired by the cultural wealth of humankind. States
wishing that inheritance to live for succeeding
generations will participate actively in making and
applying the best standards of care to ensure its
survival.

Notes

1.   Meeting on 'Protecting Cultural Objects in the
Global Information Society' organized by the Getty
Information Institute, Amsterdam, 27–28 May 1997.
2.   H. Hewison, *The Heritage Industry*, 1987, p. 11.
3.   Listed in Note 5 below.
4.   Discussed in L. V. Prott and P. J. O'Keefe, *Law and the
Cultural Heritage. Vol.1: Discovery and Excavation*, pp. 75–9.
5.   List of UNESCO Conventions and Recommendations
for the protection of cultural heritage: Hague Convention
for the Protection of Cultural Property in the Event of
Armed Conflict (1954); Convention on the Means of
Prohibiting and Preventing the Illicit Import, Export and
Transfer of Ownership of Cultural Property (1970);
Convention concerning the Protection of the World
Cultural and Natural Heritage (1972); Recommendation on
International Principles Applicable to Archaeological
Excavations (1956); Recommendation concerning the most
Effective Means of Rendering Museums Accessible to
Everyone (1960); Recommendation concerning the
Safeguarding of the Beauty and Character of Landscapes
and Sites (1962); Recommendation on the Means of

Prohibiting and Preventing the Illicit Export, Import and Transfer of Ownership of Cultural Property (1964); Recommendation concerning the Preservation of Cultural Property Endangered by Public or Private Works (1968); Recommendation concerning the Protection, at National Level, of the Cultural and Natural Heritage (1972); Recommendation concerning the International Exchange of Cultural Property (1976); Recommendation concerning the Safeguarding and Contemporary Role of Historic Areas (1976); Recommendation for the Protection of Movable Cultural Property (1978); Recommendation for the Safeguarding and Preservation of Moving Images (1980); Recommendation on the Safeguarding of Traditional Culture and Folklore.

6.   Treaty on the Protection of Artistic and Scientific Institutions and Historic Monuments (1935).

7.   L. V. Prott, 'Cultural Heritage as Part of International Humanitarian Law', *Proceedings of the Regional Seminar on the Implementation of International Humanitarian Law and on Cultural Heritage Law*, Geneva, ICRC, 1996, pp. 25–6. (Conference organized by UNESCO/ICRC in Tashkent, 25–29 September 1995.)

8.   For a classic analysis along these lines in respect of states of 'Western' cultural origin, and the resulting implications for international affairs, see L. Shklar, *Legalism*, 1960.

9.   Preamble to the UNESCO Convention for the Protection of Cultural Property in the Event of Armed Conflict (The Hague Convention), 1954.

10.   Convention on the Protection of the World Cultural and Natural Heritage, 1972.

11.   A. Monden and G. Wils, 'Art Objects as Common Heritage of Mankind', *Revue belge de droit international*, No. 19, 1986, p. 327; A. Strati, 'The Implication of Common Heritage Concepts in the Quest for Cultural Objects and the Dialogue between North and South', *ASIL Proceedings*, 1995, pp. 439, 442; B. Genius-Devine, *Bedeutung und Grenzen des Erbes der Menschheit im völkerrechtlichen Kulturgüterschutz*, 1996.

12.   D. Lowenthal, *Possessed by the Past: The Heritage Crusade and the Spoils of History*, 1996, pp. 55–74.

13.   J. Merryman, 'Two Ways of Thinking about Cultural Property', *American Journal of International Law*, No. 80, 1986, p. 831.

14.   'Principles for Partnership in Cross-Cultural Human Sciences: Research with a Particular View to Archaeology', developed by an international conference under the leadership of the Swiss Academy of Humanities and Social Sciences, 28 September to 1 October 1994 at Rüschlikon in Switzerland and published in B. Sitter-Liver and C. Uehlinger (eds.), *Partnership in Archaeology*, Fribourg, University Press, 1997, makes clear the necessity to work with local communities on all scientific projects affecting cultural property of concern to them.

15.   H. Seeden, 'Archaeology and the Public in Lebanon: Developments Since 1986', in P. G. Stone and B. L. Molyneaux (eds.), *Heritage, Museums and Education*, 1995.

16.   Genius-Devine, op. cit., pp. 334–5.

17.   J. Merryman, 'International Art Law: From Cultural Nationalism to a Common Cultural Heritage', *New York University Journal of International Law and Politics*, No. 757, 1982–1983; see also the work cited in note 12.

18.   Genius-Devine, op.cit., pp. 406–7.

19.   Ibid., pp. 445–53.

20.   *The Art Newspaper*, Vol. 7, No. 66, February 1997, pp. 1 and 3.

21.   Example given by Lowenthal, op. cit. The project has been criticized as a distortion of the historic site in W. Ndoro and G. Pwiti, 'Marketing the Past: the "Shona village" at Great Zimbabwe', *Conservation and Management of Archaeological Sites*, No. 2, 1997, pp. 3–8.

22.   C. B. Steiner, *African Art in Transit*, 1994, pp. 148–54.

23.   J. Corbet, 'Authors' Societies in Europe' in D. Peeperkorn and C. van Rij (eds.), *Collecting Societies in the Music Business*, Apeldoorn, Maklu, 1989, pp. 22 and 25.

24.   Technical Meeting on Access to Data Bases on Stolen Cultural Objects, Prague, 4–6 November 1997, organized by UNESCO and the Czech National Commission for UNESCO with the support of the Getty Information Institute.

25.   Co-ordinated by the Getty Information Institute and discussed at the meeting cited in note 1. The co-operating bodies were UNESCO, ICOM, INTERPOL, Council of Europe, the Organization for Security and Co-operation in Europe (OSCE), representatives of dealers, insurers, appraisers, national police forces and cultural services.

26.   *Mabo and others* v. *State of Queensland* [No. 2] 175 CLR 1 (Australia).

27.   Lowenthal, op.cit., p. 239.

28.   G. Pwiti, 'Taking African Cultural Heritage Management into the Twenty-first Century: Zimbabwe's Masterplan for Cultural Heritage Management', *African Archaeological Review*, No. 14, 1997, p. 81.

29.   Replacement of a fallen element (such as a column) in its original position where this is evident and not speculative.

30.   K. E. Larsen, *Architectural Preservation in Japan* (ICOMOS International Wood Committee, Trondheim), 1994, pp. 12–18.

31.   Lowenthal, op.cit., pp. 240–2.

32.   Ibid.

33.   H. Abranches, *Report on the Situation in Africa.* Report submitted to the Intergovernmental Committee for Promoting the Return of Cultural Property to its Countries of Origin or its Restitution in Case of Illicit Appropriation. 1983. (UNESCO doc. CLT/83/CONF.216./3.)

34.   P. Gathercole, 'Recording Ethonographic Collections: The Debate on the Return of Cultural Property', *Museum,* No. 187, 1986, pp. 191–2.

35.   P. J. O'Keefe, *Intellectual Property. Cultural Property. Cultural Heritage. Do These Further Indigenous Interests?* (Paper presented at the First International Conference on the Cultural and Intellectual Property Rights of Indigenous Peoples, Protection of the Treasures of our Ancestors, New Zealand, Whakatane, 12–18 June 1993.)

36.   *Mullick* v. *Mullick* LR LII Indian Appeals 245.

37.   *Union of India* v. *Bumper Development Corporation Ltd* (unreported decision, Queens Bench Division, United Kingdom, 17 February 1988).

38.   *Union of India* v. *The Norton Simon Foundation* (U.S. District Court, Southern District of New York, 74 Cir. 5331; U.S. District Court, Central District of California, Case No. CV 74-3581-RJK).

39.   D. Walcott, 'The Antilles: Fragments of Epic Memory' (Nobel Prize Lecture, 7 December 1992, published in *The Nobel Prizes 1992,* Stockholm, Nobel Foundation, 1993, pp. 143–54.)

40.   *Operational Guidelines for the Implementation of the World Heritage Convention,* UNESCO, 1997, paras. 35–42. (UNESCO doc. WHC-97/WS/1.)

41.   L. V. Prott, and P. J. O'Keefe, ' "Cultural Heritage" or "Cultural Property" ', *International Journal of Cultural Property,* No. 1, 1992, pp. 307–20.

Chapter 15
Heritage and cyberculture: what cultural content for what cyberculture?

Isabelle Vinson
Archaeologist;
Alumna, École Nationale du Patrimoine (France),
Programme Specialist, UNESCO

'The great diversity of multimedia producers in the educational and cultural fields, and the youthfulness of the market are extremely conducive to cultural encounters.'

The culture of the virtual

The civilization of the late twentieth century is commonly called the 'information civilization' (McLuhan, 1967). Following in the wake of the 'book civilization',[1] this new civilization is based on the intensive use, in all economic, social and cultural activities, of the science of information processing, the technology of electronic communication networks and one tool in particular: the computer. Here we shall be looking not so much at cyberculture,[2] the culture of the computer, as at the presence of culture in the new media (Web sites and CD-ROMs), i.e. their cultural, and more specifically, their heritage content.

Why have we chosen this approach? Because for the protagonists most present in the network world, who are in fact its theorists, the meaning of cyberculture is narrow, subject to the use of the medium itself, so that only what appears on the networks and is created for the networks, especially the Web, is considered to constitute and represent cyberculture. This leads us to assimilate cyberculture with the culture of the virtual.

But what common idea do ordinary people, the general public, have of the network phenomenon and the way networks are used in social relations? What vision do they have of the possibilities they offer and how do they see their impact on their everyday lives?

It should be noted at the outset that information technology, especially the Internet[3] and the Web,[4] has the potential to change the world and human relations, and that cyberspace, the space in which these new relationships take place, generates changes in our conception of space/time, our modes of representation and our languages. But for the purposes of this chapter, we shall consider that this space, often called the 'second world', that of the networks and related technologies (multimedia, 3-D imaging, virtual reality) is not yet a world which has fully developed its own laws, those of a hybrid and complex world, and that no social usage has yet been definitively established. The current frantic rush to theorize about it is a form of 'epistemological aspiration' which partly deprives it of social recognition, and therefore of informed acceptance and collective construction. The 'second world' is first and foremost a new and powerful means of communicating with and getting to know otherness as it exists and as it is defined by our real world. We shall therefore concentrate here on cultural testimonies and their transfer on the networks, in order to gain a better insight into issues involved in the development of the cultural dimension of the networks and the conditions for their integration into our societies.

When it comes to drawing up a report on the subject, there is also a difficulty inherent in the subject itself, for the relatively recent character of large-scale public use of the networks, the place occupied by politics in the debate, the trend-setting impact of speculation, the vast magnitude of the effects we are told all this will have on our lives in the future all give writings on the subject an impassioned, dogmatic flavour, be they for or against. The lack of historical perspective means that approaches waver between strict descriptions of projects and examples and critical analysis. And, finally, most of the examples mentioned here are the fruit of European activities, mainly in France because of the specificity of France's position, often criticized for contrasting with that of the United States, the main player in the network field, in the cultural sphere but also in the documentation used by the author.

The place of the cultural heritage in network content: nature and problems

Cultural institutions, and particularly museums, were quick to realize the advantages that lay in using the new communication technologies to facilitate their scientific work and enhance the scope of their contact with the public. Today they enjoy a 'first occupant bonus' in the cultural nooks and crannies of cyberspace, a bonus dear to network economists

that guarantees their permanent presence. The large number of Web sites devoted to national museums bears this out, even if many provide only succinct information on access to their collections. Actual ability to use the networks to disseminate knowledge is geared to two things: the setting-up of digital image banks and of scientific data banks.

Building up digital memory: image banks and scientific data banks

Since the spread of the new communication technologies, one of the main concerns of cultural institutions and major information consortia has been to digitalize their image heritage. In 1993 public authorities were worried by rumours that Microsoft intended to purchase digital rights to the works in the Hermitage Museum in Saint Petersburg. Then came the announcement of the failure of negotiations for the rights to France's museum heritage. Finally, in 1995, Corbis, a firm founded by Microsoft,[5] purchased the world's largest photographic archives, the Bettman collection, comprising 16 million images. Alliances between the public and private spheres are inevitable because of the cost of digitalizing all the works in the cultural heritage in order to provide on-line access to the world's memory. But it is also a major potential source of income from copyrights. In practice the digitalization by resource-owners of their collections requires substantial investment, restricting the budget available for other activities. Because of this heavy investment[6] it cannot be envisaged at present to provide access to data free of charge.

Digitalizing images is considered the first step towards disseminating cultural resources, and is one of the main priorities of major cultural institutions today; but what about small museums and what we consider to be minor collections? This is a serious problem when it comes to representing cultural diversity on the networks, and for low-income countries in their efforts to harness their past and their memory. There is a risk that the less-developed

countries will be obliged to part-trade their cultural heritage for access to the technology. It is essential that heritage resources should be disseminated by servers established in their country of origin, both to make sure that these countries reap the benefits of the income generated by the cultural industries and to protect their essential meaning as emitted and modified by and within the community to whose memory they belong. Too many Web sites devoted to cultural heritage merely offer a succession of poor images with no caption, or with one caption for a series of photographs.[7] The risk here is that of developing not a multicultural vision of the world but a tourist-like vision reducing diversity to the picturesque and the anecdotal.

It is therefore important that all scientific resources should be made available on the networks in the same way as images. From the time of its opening and the programming of its activities at the end of the 1980s, the Gare d'Orsay Museum of nineteenth-century French art set about computerizing its collections and setting up data banks accessible to the public on the museum's premises. This programme was reviewed in the early 1990s and the main database, which today comprises 60,000 of the 70,000 works in the museum's collections, is now for internal and scientific use only. The scientific quality of the content, under the control of the experts in charge of the collections, has come to take pride of place over its dissemination to the general public, an ambition which has been put off until the new millennium. We give this example, not to criticize a backward-looking attitude towards the networks in France, but because it illustrates a situation which is virtually worldwide. It has become apparent that the cultural enhancement of the networks with high-quality images and texts is a complex process largely dependent on the age of the heritage institutions concerned, the nature of the collections in their possession and, to a lesser extent, whether or not they are accustomed to working in partnership with other institutions, nationally or internationally. The rather ethnographic (or at least historically fairly recent) and scientific nature of the North American collections, coupled with the fact that the cultural institutions are often privately run, facilitates the on-line dissemination of their content. The European heritage, particularly in France and Italy, is essentially artistic, and as a result access to the work and knowledge are more closely linked. It is therefore logical that North America should have much more experience of the on-line dissemination of museum content than Europe. Advantage should be taken of this in formulating specific policies concerning heritage on the networks.

Simulation and knowledge revolution

There is a tendency today in the debate on the networks and the Web to ignore the new media on which content is disseminated, such as CD-ROMs[8] and in the near future DVD-ROMs.[9] And yet, because of the still only average power of the equipment sold to the general public, the real multimedia and hypermedia[10] revolution, i.e. the cognitive prolongation of the new communication technologies, is taking place thanks to off-line cultural products. Museums have been a driving force in the production of these tools, creating a distinctive multimedia market in France where art and culture products account for 15 to 18% of the market, compared with about 10% on average internationally, and they have played a non-negligible part in the birth of a new cultural industry, called the 'edutainment' industry, which has met with an extremely positive welcome in schools, both in North America and Europe. This neologism well illustrates the change afoot in the field of knowledge, introducing the notion of play or entertainment into education. The bitter pill of education is wrapped in the sweet coating of entertainment. One illustration of the repercussion of edutainment on producers of knowledge is one of the latest CD-ROMs produced by the French National Museum Group: a police investigation set in the chateau of Versailles during the reign of Louis XIV. The atmosphere of the chateau at the end of the seventeenth century, entirely reconstituted in synthesis imagery – providing a setting in which the viewer moves about in virtual reality and in real time – drew the following comment from the curator responsible for the scientific supervision of the project: 'For the first time you really see how Versailles functioned, like never before. It is unbelievable. After twenty years' work on Versailles, what I see on the screen is better than anything I ever dreamed possible. Even more beautiful.'

More than the networks, off-line products in the heritage field are developing interesting experiments with new relationships between different media and different disciplines (music, painting, literature).[11] For the time being these products are more accomplished and more complete than anything available on the network sites. They help to erase the differences between thinking based on 'the analytical, the linear and discipline, and thinking based on synthesis, complementarity and multidisciplinarity'.[12] Thanks to their great data-handling capacity, they make it possible to combine several disciplines, cross-references and decompartmentalize knowledge. Multimedia virtual reality is a powerful means of explaining complex phenomena in the sciences, and how geography and history relate, offering a tangible representation of abstract phenomena. Modelling and simulation bring the most complex phenomena, from the very origins of human evolution, within reach of all, demystifying the hierarchization of learning and the possession of knowledge. In this respect, and in the prospect of the content of CD-ROMs going on-line, off-line cultural products are contributing to the development of new means of transmitting, sharing and appropriating knowledge.

At the beginning of 1997 the Corbis company published a cultural CD-ROM about Leonardo da Vinci and the Leicester Codex.[13] The personality of Leonardo da Vinci symbolizes the union, so coveted

today, of art and science. The price is relatively high, but the distributor had the astute idea of producing a presentation disc about the CD-ROM showing how to use the Codescope (or virtual magnifying glass) software specially created to make it possible to read the text from left to right, as Leonardo wrote it, and in the user's own language. This floppy disc was distributed free to schools and colleges in France, and is an example of how a limited but coherent part of the rich but costly content of a commercial product can be widely distributed.

With the support of public cultural institutions, the edutainment industry, one of the most promising paths to the true democratization of knowledge, should develop a multitude of 'by-products' based on commercial reference products designed for distribution on preferential terms with a view to creating new consumer habits, encouraging the use of new communication technologies, contributing to the variety of cultural contents on the market, and helping to make the learning revolution a process in which everybody participates.

Creating new knowledge

Like any new means of expression, multimedia technologies have found a following, and the new skills they call on are no longer limited, as with paper, to mastery of the subject and quality of expression. They require a feel for multimedia construction and navigation, for finding one's way in an arborescence, and for the relationship between image and writing. A French CD-ROM for children called *Lulu's World* was designed and developed from start to finish by the father of a young girl for her education, based on his observations of her development. Today it is an international best-seller in multimedia publishing.[14] A certain category of multimedia authors, out of passion for their subject and for the tool, put a lifetime's experience into the making of a work. In so doing, they express their talent, the infinite resources of creativity and a personal, non-static perception of the history of

civilizations, based on a system of comparison and contextualization. They concentrate their whole vision of the world in a single work. Running parallel with the catalogues built up by the publishing industries, these works are a reflection not of the patient work of a historian or a researcher, but of that of self-taught persons who are helping to invent a new way of organizing knowledge and addressing subjects generally considered to be the preserve of scientists. The days of stable knowledge are no doubt over, because of the numerous and varied factors left to individual inventiveness, in addition to the presentation of the subject.

The great diversity of multimedia producers in the educational and cultural fields, and the youthfulness of the market are extremely conducive to cultural encounters. Interestingly, the greatest sales of the *Lulu's World* were recorded in Japan, in spite of a graphic style and narrative spirit unfamiliar to the Japanese public.[15] These factors encourage the diversification of pedagogic practices, which must cater for the new sociocultural conditions of cultural mixing, particularly in urban cultures.

The possible disruption of established hierarchies

The Web should help to integrate certain marginal forms of creation into the realm of the arts. There are numerous Web sites on the art of graffiti.[16] They give coherence and strength to an art form linked to an urban environment (like the networks themselves) which enjoys little, if any, recognition on the part of the critics and institutions: there are twice as many documents on the Web devoted to graffiti art as to Jean-Michel Basquiat.[17] It is no easy matter to open a museum of graffiti, as much of the meaning of graffiti derives from their urban environment. Web sites, on the other hand, can collect works from all over the world, build them into a corpus and disseminate them, i.e. fulfil very much the same purposes as a museum, including that (albeit criticized) of 'labelling' artistic creations.

This reveals an interesting aspect of art on the networks, where the ratio of presence to social recognition tends to be the reverse of that in traditional publications. Young artists and fans of art forms which are under-represented in the traditional media have 'taken over' the networks to make them their favourite means of dissemination, occupying niches which only the networks can offer them. The explanation and validation of the hypothesis, based on detailed analysis of the sociocultural profile of site creators, the hosts that house them and their capacity to renew content and information, which is a sign of the vitality of a site and the use made of it, have yet to be confirmed, but in the long run the everyday frequentation of artistic fringe movements by young generations of 'Internauts' could disrupt the established hierarchies in art and the process of social recognition, for the sole benefit of the use made of them.[18]

Some authors go even further, seeing the networks as a new 'place of art', where relations with the public are different and influence artistic practices themselves. The use of network technologies in the creative process and for the dissemination of contemporary works opens up the vast debate of 'why and how' art exists, which is not a new question[19] or one that is peculiar to the networks, but one linked rather in our opinion to a state of interrogation in the Western world vis-à-vis the image and the different means of representing reality through art.[20]

It should be made clear here that the artistic challenge of the networks (in the generic sense of art encompassing heritage) is doubtless to be first and foremost a powerful cultural mediator and to make the manifestations of creativity intelligible to as many people as possible, in as clear and suitable a framework as possible (i.e. images must be accompanied by critical comment and a scientific apparatus that provide a genuine pedagogic approach to art on the networks). For this reason we cannot accept the detachment of scientific and historical commentary from the images concerned, or allow

Minority heritage: a priority for the networks

Another equally important aspect of cultural heritage on the networks is that of the cultures of indigenous populations in their material and immaterial dimensions, sometimes the world's oldest living cultures. Their cultural features are linked to their land, how they exploit it and the relations they develop with the natural environment: this applies to the indigenous peoples of America (the Amazonian Indians), of Africa (the Bushmen of the Kalahari, the Pygmies), the Aborigenes of Australia and the reindeer herdsmen of Siberia. The struggle to keep or recuperate their land is therefore a veritable fight for cultural survival. Built on the notion of identity, the Web sites of indigenous populations are often instruments for the political and humanitarian support of endangered cultures. The networks help to federate efforts to defend their rights, making them more effective.[21] To what extent does better awareness of the heritage of autochthonous societies help to understand, and therefore to peacefully settle, the conflicts kindled by recent history? It revives the long-term memory of the indigenous peoples: their quest for recognition of their fundamental rights has visible cultural foundations, while once their fundamental rights are taken for granted, the redefinition of national identities including their indigenous components draws on all these cultural manifestations, as in Australia today.[22] Having regard to this particular aspect of heritage, the networks, and through them the public scientific institutions, have an essential role to play in linking the present to the past for societies 'without history'. For a century now communication technologies have been used to conserve the heritage of living cultures, through films and recordings, by studying the fundamental structures and patterns of the oral traditions and lifestyles of autochthonous populations: the arrival of the networks must lead to their dissemination and renewed use.

This unprecedented recording of oral cultures and the creation of data banks should permit living oral cultures to escape the confines of specialized publications and the picturesque, and find new uses in the powerful functional outlets of the media. At the same time, through the creation of appropriate pedagogic sites and programmes, they should help to improve our knowledge of otherness.

There are already some stimulating experiments in this field. A site on the Canadian Schoolnet network establishes the link between the contemporary works of Inuit artists and the memories, legends and myths recounted by the elders in recorded interviews, to clarify certain aspects of the traditional life of the Arctic Inuits.[23] It was developed thanks to a partnership between the Library of the Canadian Ministry of Indian and Northern Affairs and two schools, including an Inuit school. The interview data were collected as part of a project conducted by a branch of the Science Research Institute of the Northeast Territories, designed not only to preserve traditional knowledge and cultural points of view, but above all to transmit them to future generations, in the Inuit tradition, using the most modern technologies.

Transfers to the networks of data banks on immaterial heritages should be among the priorities defined in the context of multilateral programmes by regions (Africa, America, Asia, Europe, Pacific), using the resources of the oldest scientific institutions in each region (research institutes, ethnographic and anthropological museums, etc.). The library of the University of York, which is linked to all the major libraries of Canada, houses a site with a wealth of material on video and film, available for educational use, on all questions concerning the autochthonous populations of North America, including political aspects (particularly the conflict in 1900 between the Mohawks and Quebec and the federal governments), administrative documents concerning their rights, but also the literary works which these cultures have inspired, their music, and more practically, their hunting techniques.

Isabelle Vinson
Archaeologist; Alumna, École Nationale du Patrimoine
(France), Programme Specialist, UNESCO

technology to be used to serve or accelerate the delocalization of the sources. Delocalization should operate in favour of dissemination, not serve to accentuate the already strong decontextualization of heritage resources.

Towards a pluralist universe?

We are currently witnessing the reconstruction of a universe encompassing multiple environments, a universality in which the notion of culture has replaced that of civilization.[24] The disruption of cultural hierarchies is already, at least conceptually, an acknowledged on-going phenomenon. Thanks to the networks, the prospect of the acceleration of this disruption of the hierarchies, and therefore of the general framework of references and values, carries the promise of enrichment and enlargement of the representation of our societies through the cultural heritage. The broad and integrating anthropological conception of the heritage which has emerged in recent decades should be accentuated by the properties of the networks (connection power, hypertext, low cost, constant evolution) which favour the integration of related fields such as the performing arts, traditional arts, crafts, oral traditions, into the cultural heritage and into the mental conception of the representation of the world. 'The material heritage can be interpreted only in the light of the underlying immaterial riches.'[25] These words are the foundation, for the societies of the future, of a new relationship with their cultural heritage. The networks must be among the new tools that contribute to the emergence of new modes of accounting for the 'rich and varied heritage which exists around the world',[26] especially if all the actors concerned by the transfer of the contents of the cultural heritage agree to establish three types of programme which we consider deserve priority: the transfer of minority heritage, material and immaterial, on the networks; the organization of content; and the development of virtual museums with their community prolongations/the development of sites/main reference sites.

Heritage, identity and better understanding of the present

In recent decades the cultural heritage has crystallized around itself a large share of the notion of identity, to which at the same time, by the play of cultural policies, a leading role in cultural expression has been attributed. Analysed through the converging prism of identities, the cultural heritage became synonymous with having roots in a territory, in customs and habits. The speed of reaction the networks provide must be used to increase the number of initiatives in favour of better understanding of the present, in particular in the face of contemporary events and dramas. The heritages of countries rocked by civil war disseminated in museums and foundations around the world (like former Yugoslavia or Afghanistan) must be used immediately to create sites linked with others devoted to the protection of human rights,[27] in order to enlighten the present – in the eighteenth-century philosophical sense of the term – and counterbalance the purely passion-based, vindictive use of heritage with reason and sense. Thus far the networks have not responded sufficiently to the opportunities offered by the technological possibilities of linking identity-forming modes of expression with the rich and vast cultural background in all its complexity.

Another example which illustrates an aspect of strategy specific to the networks is that of the craze among the Western public for Cesaria Evora, the singer from Cape Verde, whose records are also sold on the Web. Cape Verde is a multicultural society, a mixture of African, Portuguese and Brazilian cultures, whose history and musical and language traditions were and are little known, in spite of this recent wave of popularity. The speed and virtually zero cost of the development and transfer of information over the networks should have made it possible to take this opportunity to present the country's full cultural heritage and history through a link-up with the record retailer's site. Only in this

Cyberculture and infoethics

A cyberculture is emerging. It accompanies the development of the Internet, of the cyberspace and of new techniques of representation, including digital images, virtual reality, televirtuality, virtual communities, and so forth. The emergence of this new culture is linked to the process of globalization and its concomitant cultural, social and political changes. It is based on intellectual patterns, methods of social appropriations and artistic practices that are very different from those we are familiar with. Navigating in information and knowledge landscapes, working in virtual working groups, and interacting in virtual worlds are bringing about many forms of innovative behaviour and will certainly have tremendous social and cultural consequences.

The dematerialization of the economy, coupled with the delocalization of enterprises, institutions and political powers, is having dramatic consequences on social structures, leading on the one hand to exclusion, ghettos and unemployment, and, on the other, generating new intellectual groupings and new kinds of social solidarity. New patterns of social behaviour are emerging through new types of productivity. Deterritorialization, intrinsically linked to the ubiquitous nature of cyberspace, is introducing a new world order, entailing the erosion of national identities and loss of sovereignty of states. By its very nature, the cyberspace is multi-, trans- and supra-national. Henceforth the delocalization and disintermediation of economies are dissociating the 'real' world of nations from the 'virtual' world of speculation and money transactions on the Internet without any political or social regulations. The various national legal systems and their multiple contradictions do not povide for counterbalancing this development. However, not only legal frameworks, but also the relationship between the state and the market and between public and private interests need to be newly defined.

The cultural, socio-economic and political revolution now occurring has not yet generated a genuine culture capable of meeting the profound aspirations of global citizens and providing the intellectual models and instruments for a better understanding of the information society. What is destined to become cyberculture is today not much more than a technological and informational maelstrom.

The problem is one of knowing how the new culture can contribute to the creation of a new global forum for public, democratic debate on new ethical values – i.e. 'infoethics' – in the information society. The way will passing fads sparked off by the cultural industries themselves contribute to better knowledge of cultural contexts, so that the expression of culture is not severed from the environment from which it arose.

Cultural pluralism on the networks should be defended by devising strategies in co-ordination with all the cultural industries together, particularly those which target the younger generations (the record, film and dance industries), but not with a view to expanding market shares as is the case of most music sites at present. Increasing the consumption of cultural products must not be the objective of cultural policies revised in part to allow for the explosion of new technologies and means of dissemination. Their objective must be to establish complementary uses of the media according to their characteristics, in order to take into account history and the store of different means of access to knowledge and cultural expression.

Content organization and the rings of knowledge[28]

The slow pace at which cultural heritage content is being organized and federated in Europe, unlike the case in North America, leaves the field wide open for

debate calls for a public area open to participation in political discussion by all citizens, while giving the widest possible access to information, being a fundamental human right. Freedom of expression implies free access to information, particularly information in the public domain which will become a key element in the struggle against poverty, ignorance and social exclusion.

Yet the public domain is increasingly subject to privatization. Governments must counterbalance this development. If every nation makes the documentary and patrimonial information stored in its public libraries, archives and museums accessible to its own citizens, a gigantic virtual library open to the global citizen will have been created. But this cannot be done unless states establish national policies to promote their public heritage for educational and cultural purposes. Multilingualism and cultural diversity depend on the capacity of states to invest in this undertaking for the benefit of all citizens. Co-ordinated national strategies in this area will have an incalculable multiplier effect. *The essential challenge is to create awareness of the immensely rich collective property that constitutes a global public domain of information.*

The commercialization of any form of social interaction weakens the 'res publica' and the

philosophical and ethical values attaching to it. The search for virtue, which in Greek philosophy is conceived as a thing eminently public, is in peril of becoming a purely private affair. The emerging new culture should confront this development and be in a position to offer the global society instead a system of moral principles that are appropriate to the global information society while yet based on the central values of equality, freedom and human dignity. This is the new 'infoethics'.

The cyberculture will guide us on the road to building the society of the twenty-first century with new forms of human solidarity adapted to an increasingly interdependent world. At the very heart of cyberculture therefore lies a profoundly ethical challenge. It will not be enough merely to define a code of conduct for the Internet or to regularize electronic commerce. What is called for is a democratic debate on the future of global society and which attracts the broadest possible participation. The new culture we are now building has the awesome task of civilizing globalization in order to build today the utopias of tomorrow.

Philippe Quéau
Telecommunication engineer; Expert in new information and communication technologies; Director, Division of Information and Informatics, UNESCO

individual initiatives,[29] for galleries of aficionados in direct line with André Malraux's 'imaginary museum', which finds its justification in delectation. However, this space left to the private sphere raises the question of ease of access, the educational use of the networks, but above all, the general sense of content use. The lack of organization of cultural content may lead, in the event of increasing use of the networks both at school and in the home, to a weakening of cultural ties because of the multiplication of forms of cultural expression and consequently of the ties which federate social communities, whose cohesion is both a refuge and a necessary counterbalance to

the destabilization generated by the globalization process, for 'the brutal opening of our societies makes closer social relations necessary'.[30] Furthermore, if 'the international dissemination of cultural processes is at least as important as that of economic processes', to quote Marshall Sahlins,[31] we must take extra care to favour and develop their power of cohesion by dissemination on the networks in the context of the emergence of a world society. The past is impossible to decipher without reference marks, and at present the networks, and the Web in particular, provide too few of these. In order not to be completely severed from their social context, or 'dehumanized', to use a stronger image, the cultural contents present on the networks must be strongly and clearly organized.

What do we mean by content organization? Essentially two things: clarity and rapid access to the resource, and the development of new knowledge-sharing patterns.

Cultural content should take its place in a structure, a hierarchized architecture of information that takes into account the differences of scale between the national, regional and local levels, uses extremely powerful central servers and is housed in conventional knowledge dissemination centres such as libraries, archives, museums[32] and universities, which guarantee the quality of the content. Museums in the United States are the most advanced in terms of organizing the structure of cultural heritage content, and they have anticipated its consequences for the understanding and sharing of the meaning of the cultural heritage. Eleanor E. Fink, Director at the Getty Information Institute, writes 'we realize the value of information architecture in the effective integration of cultural heritage resources. By information architecture I mean the science of organizing information, based on the patterns inherent in data. It makes possible structures or maps of information that allow people to find their personal paths to knowledge'.[33] Numerous initiatives on the new means of knowledge-sharing are organized around conventional centres of knowledge. In Philadelphia, the Franklin Institute Science Museum got together with several local museums and a number of schools to build an information network on the Internet called Science Learning Network.[34] It provides elementary schools with easier access to the scientific information sources of the participating museums, enabling them to develop learning programmes based on a variety of high-quality data sources. This context is necessary for the educational use by schools of cultural content on the networks, so that children can situate themselves and what they learn about in a broader context, enriching

their experience of life.[35] It is best if the virtual places where resources are shared are the same as in reality, thereby strongly affirming the public nature of educational resources and their accessibility to all, as well as optimizing established educational habits. There should also be co-ordination between public and private initiatives.[36]

It is necessary too to develop powerful search engines, 'wise' tools oriented towards certain priority contents. This must be an essential concern of public authorities, research institutes and universities, and the role of the leading IP groups should be restricted.[37] To achieve this, free resources, with no rights, i.e. those developed by research institutes and universities, which make up a sort of indivisible human birthright, a common good, should be promoted by the public authorities and disseminated at least as extensively as private resources.

The development of powerful search engines, finely tuned and adapted to educational uses on the networks, and the implementation of multilingual automatic translation systems[38] which computer researchers are currently experimenting,[39] together with the development of security for their commercial use, are certainly the most important technological challenges of the coming years in cyberspace.

Another aspect of content organization is that of increasing the number of levels of access to information in order to encourage the multicultural approach. Indian researcher Ranjit Makkuni[40] is working on the production of learning models favouring multicultural dialogue by exploring creative processes. He reads the different meanings contained in a work, namely the Gita-Govinda, a twelfth-century Indian poem, multiplies the levels of access to information, enabling the user to reread the information as a function of the information already acquired. Three levels of information – narrative, interpretative (text, image, sound and motion) and reflective – are developed, providing personalized access to knowledge.

This research with a view to developing models for new means of sharing knowledge should be the basis of the notion of 'literacy' developed in the network world. Only then will the new technologies effectively provide 'a better understanding of the real'.[41]

Building new relations

We must bear in mind the theoretical nature of many of the analyses developed here, because of the very heterogeneous practices on the networks today. But whatever forms it takes, the role of the museums in building cyberculture is fundamental, because of the transfer of quality cultural content and the development of its democratic utilization. They are the key actors in the preservation and enhancement of cultural diversity in the new information society. They are real places which must accommodate the most powerful servers in each country disseminating cultural resources. They must be in constant liaison with the universities and make the link with the younger generations through their mission of information and dissemination of knowledge acquired through research, and their public service mission. At a time when everybody can produce and disseminate information, not only the museums, archives and libraries, but all the public and semi-public heritage and cultural institutions become the best guarantee of the quality of the information disseminated and the most widely recognized authorities in a space which must be devoted to sharing.

The still indeterminate nature of cyberspace is an opportunity for our societies of tomorrow. It provides an opportunity to build new relations by placing the extraordinary switching power of a new tool at the service of the complexity of our times. One can only hope that everybody will feel concerned and take part in the great debate on the future of human relations.

Notes

1.   Name given by Lucien Febvre to the modern era that followed the Renaissance.
2.   Definition given by Mark Dery in *Vitesse virtuelle: La cyberculture aujourd'hui*, Abbeville Press, 1997. (Coll. Tempo.)
3.   Defined by Joël de Rosnay as an integrated system for resource sharing on the networks.
4.   The World Wide Web: a user-friendly interface invented in 1991 by Tim Berners-Lee.
5.   Corbis was founded in 1989 by Bill Gates, founder and CEO of Microsoft. Its purpose is to become the world's leading supplier of digital images. Before acquiring the Bettman collection it possessed almost 1 million digital images.
6.   In 1997 the French National Audiovisual Institute (INA) invested 12% of its annual operating budget in digitalizing its resources as part of its commercial strategy.
7.   See http://www.archivision.com
8.   CD-ROM: compact-disc read-only memory.
9.   DVD-ROM: digital video disc read-only memory.
10.   Multimedia and hypermedia consist in providing still and moving pictures, sound and text simultaneously, in interactive mode.
11.   Three triptychs devoted to a painter, a poet and a musician and to the real and subjective links between their works were published by Arborescence in 1995 in France: *Monet–Verlaine–Debussy*, *Gauguin–Baudelaire–Tchaikovsky* and *Matisse–Aragon–Prokofiev*.
12.   See Joël de Rosnay, 'Les mutations de la science', *Le Monde de l'éducation, de la culture et de la formation*, February 1997.
13.   A manuscript by Leonardo da Vinci, acquired by the founder and CEO of Microsoft in 1994.
14.   In April 1997, one year after it went on the market, it had already been published in 23 countries and in 13 languages.
15.   In April 1997 according to *Le Monde de l'éducation, de la culture et de la formation*, 80,000 copies had been sold in Japan and 10,000 in France.
16.   See http://www.artcrimes.gatech.edu
17.   A Web search done in September 1997, in English and French, using the Altavista search engine, revealed 645 documents on the art of graffiti and 314 on Jean-Michel Basquiat.
18.   We have purposely avoided referring here to the artistic movements which are very closely linked to cyberspace, from techno music to the exthropians, which is

not the subject of this chapter. Mark Dery addresses the subject in his book *Vitesse virtuelle: La cyberculture aujourd'hui,* op. cit.

19. This moment can be compared with the period between the end of the Middle Ages and the beginning of the Renaissance in the West, when the figure of the artist as an individual emerged and gained social recognition.

20. One can draw a parallel between the public début of the Internet in France, when it and cyberculture in general were rejected by the French elite, and the extremely virulent debate on contemporary art that took place in 1992. Together these two events illustrate not the effects of the former on the latter but rather two aspects of a deeper crisis unrelated to the advent of the new communication technologies.

21. See http://survival.w

22. Simultaneously with research on a convention of reconciliation with the Aborigenes – the Supreme Court of Australia acknowledged their indigenous title in 1992 – the contemporary art museum of Sydney opened its collections to Aboriginal works, through agreements with the Aborigine community. See *Les nouvelles de l'Icom,* No. 4, 1997.

23. See site http://www.schoolnet.ca/collections/cape_dorset

24. See Hélé Béji, *L'imposture culturelle,* Stock, 1997, chaps. 7 and 8.

25. Amadou Hampâté Bâ, 'The Cultural Heritage at the Service of Development', *Our Creative Diversity,* Paris, UNESCO, 1995.

26. Hampâté Bâ, op. cit.

27. See that of the Human Rights Watch or http://www.sas.upenn.edu/African_studies/

28. Reference to a European programme under the fifth Draft Programme.

29. The very first appearance on the Web of works from the Louvre Museum was the work of young computer buff Nicolas Pioche. See also the site at http://sgwww.epfl.ch/BERGER/

30. Daniel Cohen in *Richesse du monde, pauvreté des nations,* Flammarion, 1997, p. 98.

31. Marshall Sahlins, 'Une culture mondiale fragmentée', *Our Creative Diversity,* Paris, UNESCO, 1995.

32. See the article by Cary Karp, ICOM activity co-ordinator on the Internet, on the efforts made by museums to facilitate access to their resources on the Internet by setting up a specific higher level facility (.org), in *Nouvelles de l'ICOM,* No. 3, 1997.

33. Eleanor E. Fink, *Sharing Cultural Entitlements in the Digital Age: Are we Building a Garden of Eden or a Patch of*

Weeds?, http://www.gii.getty.edu. There are a great many North American examples to illustrate both experiments by museums to develop an architecture of information on the Web and participation in efforts to develop new learnings. See the contribution by Deborah Seid Howes (Metropolitan Museum of Art, New York), in *Connecting with Classrooms through Computers* (ICHIM, Paris, 3–5 September 1997), and the numerous sites listed. Without underestimating the quality of these North American experiments, it should be remembered that these models are perfectly adapted to the environment in which they were created.

34. See http://www.sln.org

35. See the very convincing American site http://www.ref.desk.com/culture, an electronic encyclopedia for children.

36. In France there are three types of educational resource sites: *public,* which are run by the ministries (see the Ministry of Education site at http://www.education.gouv.fr); *private,* like those of the major textbook publishers, for example (see the Hachette site at http://www.Hachette.net/junior/); or *individual* (the best-known one was developed by a teacher, at http://www.imaginet.fr/momes.).

37. Software suppliers are currently studying what they call 'push' technologies which select which information available on the Web to push towards the user, depending on his or her areas of interest.

38. 200 countries are represented on the Internet. 70% of the sites surveyed in January 1997 were in English (compared with 90% in 1996). Among the three language groups which are growing in importance, Germanic languages (German, Dutch and north European languages) represent 11%, Romance languages (French, Spanish, Portuguese and Italian) 9%, and Japanese 5%. Source: *Le Monde,* 10 May 1997.

39. Military in origin, like the Internet, the oldest automatic translation systems were born in the United States. The SYSTRAN system, the world's most widely used automatic translation system, proposes the first on-line translation service of the pages of the Web. Today, Canada, France and Japan are engaged in research in which the economic stakes are proportional to the expansion of the networks. Source: *Le Monde,* 10 May 1997.

40. Contribution at the ICHIM international meeting at the Louvre Museum in Paris in 1997.

41. Philippe Quéau, *Note sur les implications socio-culturelles, les enjeux économiques des nouvelles technologies, et leurs incidences sur la création artistique,* p. 2 (personal communication).

Part Four
Public opinion and global ethics

Introduction to Part Four

This part of the report gives expression to *vox populi*. Mainly based on public opinion polls, it is an echo of thousands of voices answering questions about values and issues in about a third of the world's countries containing about half of the world's population.

No special poll was designed for this report but instead data from previous surveys were used. Some of them are quite old, dating from the beginning of the decade, and others are more recent. Though attitudes on some issues may vary over a relatively short period, for instance in the Western world in the 1970s, public opinion concerning values in general seems to change rather slowly. So dramatic differences would not necessarily be expected were a new survey to be conducted today. A new world survey on values may be held in 1999, with results becoming available by the year 2000.

The lack of representativeness in space is more of an obstacle than that in time. Certain areas in the world have been covered by public-opinion pollsters more intensively than others. The African continent and the Islamic world are still largely *terra incognita* in terms of research available for this report. It would be a considerable advance of knowledge if public opinion research from these areas would liberate them from their status as 'zones of silence'.

The methodological difficulties that discourage some critics from using opinion polls for scientific or policy purposes are varied. The cross-national interpretation of results coming from different cultures and languages remains especially difficult. Yet opinion polls are increasingly studied and used, especially in democratic societies. After all, however uncertain we may feel about what exactly we are hearing, we are listening to the confused, muted, garbled noises of *vox populi*. The voice of 'authority' is represented in this report quite amply by academics and politicians, universities and international institutions, and conferences and books reported on, but such articulate voices should not be allowed to silence what is coming to us from public opinion. It may be said of public-opinion polls what

has often been said of democracy itself, that it is a poor system but that there is none better. So the sceptical tone of the researcher audible in the following pages accompanies an attitude of humility. If some answers seem to be unexpected or difficult to interpret, they are the replies of thousands of human beings trying to answer difficult questions.

A few remarks may highlight some of the results.

The variety of opinions within countries stands out clearly. No values seem to be supported homogeneously. There are no uniform 'yes' or 'no' countries, but always majorities and minorities, always differences of degree in the frequencies with which certain opinions are held. Indeed, the whole concept of the identity of large entities like countries or continents seems more a matter of degree in which certain opinions are held than of the fundamental incompatibility of cultures. Public opinion overlaps frontiers. It should caution policy-makers against assuming a homogeneous unity for public opinion or imposing it.

Second, differences of gender do not seem to play a strong role in accounting for differences in public opinion around the world. In general within countries, males and females, husbands and wives seem to be far more in agreement about a series of important values than in disagreement.

On the other hand, it seems that being young or old does make a difference. In our dynamic world it is not surprising that the younger generation should have different experiences and approaches. Since young people tend to carry over some of their values and habits into later life, it is most important to analyse public opinion by age groups.

Another and not unexpected result is the importance of education. The level of education seems to be the single most important variable after income in explaining attitudes, including positive attitudes towards some of the values promoted by *Our Creative Diversity* and the present report. In general it is the uneducated, low-income strata that are most distrustful and intolerant in society.

Chapter 16
Public opinion and global ethics: a descriptive study of existing survey data

Adriaan van der Staay
Social scientist; Director of the Social and Cultural
Planning Office, The Hague (Netherlands)
and Professor Extraordinary in Cultural Policies
and Cultural Criticism, Rotterdam University (Netherlands)
(Research by Jos Becker and Johan Verweij, Social
and Cultural Planning Office)

'As for our chief concern – cultural diversity and unity – we can conclude that international value patterns are not rigidly compartmentalized.'

Introduction

Global ethics

The need for a global ethics is one of the central issues in the report *Our Creative Diversity* by the World Commission on Culture and Development. In the first chapter of the report we read:

Co-operation between different people with different interests and from different cultures will be facilitated and conflict kept within acceptable and even constructive limits, if participants can see themselves as being bound and motivated by shared commitments. It is, therefore, imperative to look for a core of shared ethical values and principles. (World Commission on Culture and Development, 1995, p. 34)

It is this search for shared ethical values and principles that motivates the analysis we present here. The World Commission has explored this domain in a more or less conceptual manner, without pretending to research empirically the way values and principles are shared. It was pointed out that cultures are not mutually exclusive, and that they may be differentiated within themselves. Also, their values are not fixed, but may evolve under new circumstances. In its search for indicators of shared principles and values, the World Commission predominantly cited authoritative and normative sources, such as the Universal Declaration of Human Rights.

That is a scientifically valid approach. Indeed, some studies confine themselves to describing policy documents – national or international. The research presented in the present chapter goes beyond this top-down approach. It seeks to discover what we know about such values and principles at the level of public opinion, as recorded by asking samples of the population about preferences for values and moral principles. This is basically a bottom-up approach, which tries to gauge the conceptual matters referred to above – in particular the universality and differentiation of values and principles – as expressed by ordinary people, that is, the general public.

Given the importance of values and principles in policy discourse, the empirical study of them leaves much to be desired. In sociology and anthropology the term 'values' is often used to denote shared cultural standards. In economics it refers to exchange value (price) or value in use (utility). The growing interest some thirty years ago

in the study of values (Myrdal) has not led to the expected upsurge in empirical insight (Hechter, Nadel and Michod, 1993). The present renewed interest seems to be driven by dissatisfaction among economists (Sen, Simon and others) and by the acute awareness among other social scientists (such as Etzioni and Inglehart) of major shifts in value orientations in present society.

In view of this imbalance between the importance of the subject in theory and the lack of conclusive empirical research in many areas, a theoretically unpretentious approach, as we intend to take here, is both necessary and advisable. The definition of value should be as simple and clear as possible. Moreover, the data used have been gathered not within the framework of our specific research design, but rather in different circumstances and for other purposes, as if to echo the cautionary remarks in the world report, *Our Creative Diversity,* cited earlier. In essence, this is one of the first reviews of the available data on a world scale.

The definition of values should leave open the origins of a possible global ethics. Have people evolved common attitudes and standards as a result of common experiences, or have they taken on attitudes and standards by imitating others? Does the diffusion and readaptation of attitudes and standards proceed by an invention of new values or by an exclusion of values from a set of pre-existing ones? Are values linked together into a common framework or are they fundamentally dissociated and in conflict? These matters will be discussed in other chapters, but will not be solved here. Ours is a very limited aim. How are values distributed in the world as recorded through the method of public-opinion research? Some values will be more universally recognized than others, some will be more specific to regions or groups. A longitudinal approach in a more specific research design may help answer the appeal of the World Commission to look for a core of shared ethical values and principles.

In the remainder of this Introduction we will discuss the phenomenon of globalization, provide a definition of values and outline the questions we wish to answer.

Globalization

We see globalization as a process in which ideas and behaviours are disseminated on a grand scale. We conceive this scale as being worldwide, or at least as encompassing large geographical areas. In debates about the subject, globalization is seen primarily from an economic or a cultural point of view. We will concentrate our efforts here on the cultural dimension of the process. Globalization in the economic sense is often seen as the dispersion of economic efforts and business activities from the industrialized countries to other parts of the world. The immense social impact of this process need hardly be stressed. Our intentions in writing this report, however, are directed mainly at the cultural dimension. The influence of travel, migration and mass media intensifies communication between various parts of the world. We presume that the denser international communication becomes, the more ideas and beliefs a given country will adopt from other cultures or, stated differently, the more important the process of cultural transmission will be.

This point of view can scarcely be called original. But it does provide an easily comprehensible starting-point for further considerations. The process of cultural transmission has been under way for some time. In her celebrated study *Male and Female,* Margaret Mead (1950) predicted that anthropologists would soon run into difficulties in studying non-Western lifestyles. Since transmission has now been going on for an extended period, at least the most general consequences of this 'cultural movement' should meanwhile have become clearly visible in today's world.

Cultural homogeneity is one obvious consequence, but it is not the only one that is conceivable. Cultural diversity could also be an outcome of transmission. In various parts of the

A search for common values

Call for Universal Values. The closing decade of the twentieth century is witness to a rising demand for common values. Against the backdrop of the positivistic abstinence on questions of value and of relativism of values of the preceding decades, there is a search for universal values and principles that could serve as the basis for peaceful and productive interaction among nations and societies, prevention of conflicts and crises, and collective efforts towards peace and prosperity.

UNESCO Universal Ethics Project. In a series of two UNESCO Universal Ethics Project meetings held in Paris and Naples in March and December 1997, the task of the project was defined as one of identifying a common substratum of values that would make economically, socially and culturally viable coexistence possible on a worldwide scale. The problem is one of identifying a minimum of common ethical values and principles that are valid across cultures and societies and that would help humanity deal with global problems in the immediate future. Several important points of agreement emerged in the course of two meetings attended by some thirty eminent philosophers, theologians, social

scientists and politicians who have been at the forefront of the search for common values representing many of the major cultural and religious traditions. The first of these agreements is of a methodological nature, which nevertheless contains important substantive implications. It was agreed that the ethical principles which would form the core of universal ethics should be ascertained 'reflectively and empirically'. The methodological approach to universal common values begins with an empirical search for values and principles widely held and factually recognized in diverse cultures and religions. Here philosophy must work in close co-operation with sociology of morals, cultural anthropology and other social sciences.

At the same time, a reflective method is an indispensable complement to the empirical approach. The task of identifying values and principles needed to deal with the problems of human survival and prospering is one that requires a search beyond the empirical. It should be possible to 'derive' in some sense ethical values and principles that are seen to be necessary in relation to the problems to be solved. This 'transcendental' approach requires not only that the goals be clearly set, but also that they should be clearly understood. Clear understanding of the nature of the changes that are

world, new ways of life and new modes of thought are being taken on with relative ease. In other areas, such adoption meets certain obstacles, such as extremely traditional thinking or the absence of the technical means needed to successfully absorb 'new' elements of culture. In some cases, national pride or pride in local cultural heritage fuels people's unwillingness to accept 'foreign' cultural elements as their own. This 'subcultural' factor can be identified in a generalized form: the idea that it is imperative to sustain an original or traditional cultural identity in a world seen as developing towards cultural unity.

Values

We consider values to be ideas about what is desirable in society. This may be a desirable state of affairs, for instance adequate housing for the population or a good state of public health. It can also refer to desirable ways of thinking and behaving. For an idea to be a value it must be widely shared by individuals. It must be very general in nature, and thus sufficiently abstract to be applied to a wide range of practical situations. In this respect, values differ from norms, which apply to more specific situations. Not all values are valid for the

occurring in the life-world of humanity, including globalization and fragmentation, must precede or at least accompany any realistic search for common universal values.

Human Rights. Another important point of agreement concerning universal ethics concerns its relationship to the existing documents on universal rights, values and norms, such as the Universal Declaration of Human Rights. The Declaration of Human Rights, which celebrates its fiftieth anniversary this year, today enjoys an acceptance across cultures wider than ever before, and it is clear that universal ethics, whatever form it may eventually come to take, cannot be intended to supplant the existing rights documents. It should rather be able to show how cross-culturally embedded the core rights of the Declaration are.

While the human rights documents are presented as legal documents, it is neither possible nor desirable to formulate universal ethics as an ethical legislation at the level of international law. It should not, indeed cannot, be understood as an attempt to impose a code of morals on diverse cultures, with some organized form of enforcement. The sole source of its authority should be the relevance and persuasiveness of the values and principles themselves for the tasks of human survival and flourishing. Some 'one-issue' NGOs have shown how this may be possible.

The final point of agreement is the importance of the idea of universality in this age of diversity. Given the fact of diversity in culture and value as something given and respected, the problem of how the very notion of universality should be understood must be confronted resolutely. One need not adopt a suspicious attitude to all universalistic projects. The traditional notion of universality as something given once and for all is now generally recognized as calling for further assessment. Many vigorous attempts are being made today to recognize and integrate diversity and relativity within a universal framework. Bringing clarity to this age-old question must therefore be one of the desiderata of the search for common universal values. Recognition and respect of diversity need not lead to a relativism of values and principles. It is in the spirit of this belief that the search for common values must be carried on in order to come to successful fruition.

Yersu Kim
Professor of Philosophy, Seoul National University;
Director, Division of Philosophy and Ethics, UNESCO

whole of society. Those that are valid are commonly called universals. Values applying to certain areas only, for instance medical ethics, are called particulars. We concern ourselves here exclusively with universals.

Values serve as guidelines for policy, thought and behaviour. They can also be used as standards to judge particular instances of these phenomena. This version of the value concept is very common in sociology, in the work of Parsons, for instance. As for the use of the concept in actual analysis, a few remarks are in order.

First, although values are widely shared, they need not be shared to the same degree by all categories of a population. The same may apply to different countries located in the same cultural sphere, for instance that of north-western Europe. An analysis of values should always take differentiations between population categories, and if possible cross-national differences, into account.

Second, when data are gathered by surveys, people's values are ideally equated with their opinions about 'what ought to be'. Many survey questions conform to this model, but it is possible to draw conclusions from other types of questions as well. A question about perceived satisfaction, for instance, reflects a respondent's judgement about an existing situation. Low satisfaction on an issue like housing can be taken to signify a value that remains largely unrealized.

Third, values reflect thinking. People often behave in conformity with their values. However, behaviour can also differ from what one would expect on the basis of an individual's values. Someone may report certain positive values, but their actual behaviour may be inconsistent with them, due perhaps to necessity or certain inhibitions. Socially negative thinking may also be reported, while actual behaviour is not as bad as one would anticipate. Hence, knowledge of values in a given culture reflects what people think is important, but not their actual behaviour.

Defining the problem

The report *Our Creative Diversity* (World Commission on Culture and Development, 1995, pp. 40–6) proposes five principles as the core of a new global ethics: (1) human rights and responsibilities; (2) democracy and the elements of civil society; (3) the protection of minorities; (4) commitment to peaceful conflict resolution and fair negotiation; and (5) equity within and between generations.

Opinions about these subjects are represented to varying degrees in cross-national survey research. We have derived the sectional divisions of this chapter from a tentative review of the available data. We will first examine opinions on several matters that are vital to people's well-being. We will then look at people's attitudes towards the political system and at the position of minorities. These topics are related to the first three areas of global ethics as distinguished in *Our Creative Diversity*:

• Essential needs: people's opinions on aspects of their life situation, such as satisfaction with housing, clothing, food, income and health.

• Politics: ideas about human rights, the functioning of democracy and the degree of political involvement.

• Tolerance towards minorities and the upholding of minority rights.

No data could be found about the fourth ethical pillar, i.e. commitment to peaceful conflict-resolution and fair negotiation. We have instead substituted a topic that received considerable attention in Chapter 5 of *Our Creative Diversity*: the position of women in society. In sociological theory, women are usually defined as a minority, but this defies common sense, since women constitute about half of any given population. We therefore treat the social position of women as a topic separate from minority rights, immediately following our discussion of ideas about minorities in general:

• Gender issues and women's emancipation (marriage and sexuality are included in this topic).

Concern about the quality of the natural environment (destruction of the rain forest, global warming, loss of ozone, loss of species, and other such issues) have made people more aware of growing global interdependence, since certain environmental problems can no longer be solved at a national level (Beck, 1992). The fifth ethical pillar in *Our Creative Diversity* – equity within and between generations – explicitly refers to this concern for the environment: 'The basic principle of intergenerational equity says that present generations must take care of and use the environment and cultural and natural resources for the benefit of all members of present and future generations.' (World Commission on Culture and Development, 1995, p. 46). We have therefore included the following category:

• Awareness of environmental problems.

Consistent with the importance assigned to shared values in *Our Creative Diversity*, and in the general perspective of globalization and its consequences, we have made cultural unity and diversity a focal point in our analysis. For each of the areas examined we will attempt to answer the following question:

• To what extent does similar thinking prevail in various countries or larger regions of the world with

regard to topics addressed by the *World Culture Report*, and to what extent do countries or geographical regions diverge in this respect?

A note on the analysis

Our analysis provides a fairly extensive description of relevant data, primarily, though not exclusively, from the viewpoint of unity and diversity. We consider cultural unity or cultural diversity to be reflected in agreement or disagreement between the populations of countries or larger regions on opinion questions. For example, we assess how close together the various countries' scores are on a certain type of satisfaction.

The word 'unity' sounds absolute. It cannot be expected, of course, that the publics in a large number of very diverse countries will completely agree about anything. 'Unity' conveys a stronger meaning than it can possibly carry in practice. Despite this drawback we have decided to use it for the sake of convenience. It forms a clear antithesis with 'diversity', a contrast that would disappear if words like 'unanimity' were to be used.

We should point out beforehand that rigorous statistical testing cannot reasonably be applied to the measure of agreement. The statistical means for such testing are available, and are even fairly simple. The standard deviation of a distribution shows how close the individual scores are to its mean. If a distribution consists of the scores of countries on a given variable, then the standard deviation would suggest to what degree the countries are alike. However, the data are not always suited for the systematic comparison of standard deviations. They are derived from different surveys, and those surveys used different selections of countries. If one selection contains a sizeable number of countries with extreme scores, that affects the level of the standard deviation. The Gallup research that we base some of our conclusions on contains eighteen countries, and the *World Values Survey 1990–1993* forty-two. Many of the poorer and smaller countries are represented in the latter. Standard deviations are comparable only within the same research. Between different studies they are not comparable, or they should at least be used with great care.

Despite this limitation we have based our conclusions on the standard deviations, nearly always within the bounds of one and the same survey. With respect to this procedure some remarks need to be made, which might only be meaningful to statistical experts. In some cases the value of the standard deviation is dependent on the value of the mean. If the mean for an opinion, calculated over a series of countries, is extremely low, for instance 10% or 20%, the standard deviation cannot be high. Generally the scores of the individual countries are compressed at the end of the percentual scale. If the mean is extremely high, say 80% or 90%, the same curtailment of the standard deviation occurs at the other end of the scale. In both cases one would suppose unity to exist, but this conclusion would be based on a statistical artefact only. In Table 26a,* for instance, the proposition that it is better to be unhappily married than it is not to be married at all is affirmed by small numbers of respondents in most of the countries. The general mean for this affirmation is 8%. The corresponding standard deviation is also small, its value being 8.1. More diversity than is indicated here could, however, be possible, seeing some of the scores, notably those for the Philippines, Bulgaria and Spain.

In order to avoid this type of meaningless conclusion, we expressed the scores of the individual countries in the form of so-called logits and used these in calculating the standard deviation. In this way the percentual scale from 1 to 100 was transformed into a scale ranging from $+\infty$ to $-\infty$, thereby avoiding 'bottom and ceiling' effects and allowing for the calculation of the standard deviation without being influenced by the value of the mean.

* To aid comparison, Tables 18–29 have been grouped together in Appendix A (pp. 278–302).

In the case of the example concerning the opinion on marriage, the value of the standard deviation changes to the high level of .41 and diversity is much larger than originally appeared to be the case. The effects on the transformation into logits are, by the way, not always as dramatic.

The means of the percentage distributions are of importance for ascertaining the general level of opinion between the countries in question. Normal standard deviations and those in logits are both shown, but conclusions on diversity and unity can strictly speaking only be derived from the standard deviations expressed in logits.

On the whole, the standard deviations expressed as logits range between .30 and .40. A value lower than .30 is taken to indicate unity, and one higher than .40 shows diversity. Clear-cut cases of unity and diversity are rare. Some attention is therefore given to the levels of the percentages. A middle value of the standard deviations together with rather high or low percentage levels is taken to be an instance of unity, since a majority in most countries is found to hold a certain opinion.

As the number of countries is rather large (up to forty-two), it is sometimes necessary to aggregate countries into larger geographical regions (also referred to here as continents). Otherwise, the tables showing differences by gender, age or educational attainment would become too bulky to be read with ease. Grouping countries into larger geographical regions carries the added advantage of more or less neutralizing any idiosyncrasies in one particular country's data. After some preliminary analysis we decided to proceed rather conventionally. We categorized countries as North America, Western Europe, Eastern Europe, Middle East, Central and South America, Asia, Oceania and Africa. We came to the conclusion that treating Europe as one whole would be unwise. Western and Eastern Europe should be seen as separate entities in any case. It is important to remember that, in the research we had at our disposal, Middle East (Israel or Saudi Arabia),

Oceania (mainly Australia) and Africa (mainly South Africa and Nigeria) are represented by only a few countries. Despite this scanty coverage, we decided to use the results anyway.

An analysis of larger parts of the world poses the problem of weighting. Countries differ in size. One could weight the results per country by the size of its population. Data from Belgium, for instance, then carry less weight than those from the United Kingdom. Although this is a reasonable solution to the problem of unequal population sizes, it has the disadvantage of giving primacy to the results from large countries. Within Western Europe the general picture would be dominated by a few of the larger countries like France and Germany. Worldwide the United States, China and India would cast their shadow over the whole picture. Especially in matters regarding culture, this would be far from ideal, because cultural influence need not be related to population size. We have therefore assigned each country equal weight in our calculations.

Sometimes we offer the reader findings at two levels of analysis. In cases where we had original survey data at our disposal, we were able to differentiate the results by certain personal characteristics of the respondent, such as gender, age or education. If we had only published tables to work with that were arranged by country, we performed calculations with the countries as units of analysis. It will be clear to those well-versed in statistics that the explained variance of an analysis at the individual level will be much lower than that of an analysis performed on countries or on still larger geographical regions.

Results

Essential needs

Satisfaction

Tables 18, 19a and 19b offer general insights into how satisfied people are with various aspects of their lives in different countries or parts of the world. The

data are drawn from Gallup and the *World Values Survey 1990–1993*.

In most countries, people value separate aspects of their lives more positively than their personal life as a whole (Table 18).[1] They are most satisfied with their family or home life (81%), followed by certain basic necessities such as health, clothing and housing. They are least content with their economic well-being as measured by education (63%), job (62%), financial situation (58%) and standard of living (53%) (Tables 18 and 19a).

In North America, Western Europe and Central and South America, satisfaction with home life and with life as a whole is higher than in Eastern Europe, Asia and Africa (Table 19b). Dissatisfaction with the working of democracy is a fairly general phenomenon. Only in such diverse places as North America, Germany, Iceland, Costa Rica and Thailand does a majority of the population – in this case 50% or more – appear satisfied with the democratic system (Table 18). In some countries the public may entertain very different ideas about what constitutes democracy.

Among the results of the *World Values Survey 1990–1993*, the low level of trust in one's fellow human beings (33%) is striking (Table 19a). Only in the Scandinavian countries (Denmark, Norway, Sweden, Finland), the Netherlands, Canada and China do more than 50% of the population believe

most other people can be trusted. The degree of 'trust' appears to be at a much lower level in Brazil, Turkey, Slovenia, Nigeria and France. The results for other sources of satisfaction correspond roughly to those of Gallup in Table 18. In comparing Tables 18 and 19a one should bear in mind that the surveys used differently formulated questions. Gallup asked, for instance, about satisfaction with health, while the *World Values Survey 1990–1993* asked whether respondents consider themselves to be in good health. Furthermore, the sample of countries is not the same.

How much agreement is there between countries where satisfaction with different aspects of life is concerned? It is difficult to formulate clear expectations concerning this question. In Chapter 1 of this report Rao mentions global convergence in patterns of consuming goods and services. The author also stresses convergence in national economic systems. In view of these growing similarities some unity in satisfaction about aspects of the life situation might be expected. Still according to Rao, the distribution of wealth between countries and regions remains uneven. This fact could give rise to differences in satisfaction. So it remains to be seen whether unity or difference prevails.

Table 14 shows the standard deviations calculated on logits, together with the means in percentages.

TABLE 14
MEANS AND STANDARD DEVIATIONS (LOGITS) FOR VARIOUS MEASURES OF SATISFACTION (1995)

	Health	Job	Democ-racy	Housing	Commu-nity	Edu-cation	Family life	Personal life in general	Living standard	Clothing	Food
Mean percentage satisfied	75	62	41	74	72	63	81	61	53	74	71
Standard deviation, logit	.25	.27	.29	.30	.30	.30	.32	.39	.39	.40	.46

Source: *People's Satisfaction with Their Lives and Government* (International Gallup Poll Report, 1995).

Satisfaction with two of life's basic necessities, clothing and food, shows a fairly high rate of diversity. The same applies to opinions about standard of living and satisfaction with life in general. As we indicated earlier, the level of satisfaction with personal life and standard of living is on the low side. Satisfaction with clothing and food is more or less what would be expected. (About three-quarters of any population commonly reports being satisfied with various items.) We can conclude that rather large differences between countries lie hidden behind this general picture.

A certain degree of unity can be discerned in the areas of health, working life and perception of democracy. The standard deviations are relatively low. The most striking case is that of democracy, where dissatisfaction (41% satisfied) is conspicuously high. Unity may also be present in the tendency to distrust other people. The standard deviations in Table 19a do not differ markedly from one another; in logit values they hover around .32, which could be considered a middle level.[2] People's trust in others proves extremely low, however. Since the differences between countries are not high, the conclusion that unity exists is warranted.

This raises the question of how the high satisfaction with community relates to the critical view of democracy. It should be borne in mind that the researchers asked for a judgement on 'your community as a place to live in'. This question encompasses various aspects of life, not only the political one. As soon as this aspect is introduced views seem to become more negative.

The other results in Table 18 and Table 14 are not very straightforward. The standard deviations as well as the means are at a middle level. All that can be concluded is that countries tend to differ in how satisfied their populations are with certain basic requirements of material well-being and with their lives in general, and that agreement exists on criticism of democracy, on 'social distrust' and on health.

The task of finding at least some explanation

for the regularities remains, and it is by no means an easy one. The general drift of the conclusion is clear, but if there are wide differences of opinion on economic matters, why is that not the case where housing is concerned? Why are countries rather similar in their satisfaction with health? Certainly the substantive conditions differ widely amongst nations. One explanation for these and other irregularities could be that health and housing are near to a person's personality. It is a basic psychological tendency to deny circumstances that form a threat to one's own personality. This process of reducing cognitive dissonance might then be responsible for the high satisfaction and small differences between countries.

Rather than basing the explanation on a universal psychological mechanism, one could focus on country-specific results. The verdict on clothing and food is especially unfavourable in China and Taiwan. That could reflect a real dissatisfaction with daily life in these countries, but it could also be a sign of high and unfulfilled expectations. According to Gallup (*People's Satisfaction . . .*, p. 19), the low percentages could be explained by a tendency in these countries to avoid extreme standpoints, whereby most people choose the middle position of 'neither satisfied nor dissatisfied'. All such explanations have their drawbacks. Besides, they all seem equally valid, making the argument uneconomical. One explanatory factor does seem of paramount importance, however. Perhaps not surprisingly, it is national income.

The present economic conditions in a country are strongly associated with the three measures of satisfaction in the *World Values Survey 1990–1993* (Table 19a). Per capita GNP,[3] corrected for differences in purchasing power, correlates at .84 with financial satisfaction (see Graph 16), at .76 with life as a whole and at .64 with home life. It can be concluded that economic well-being and subjective well-being are intertwined: in rich countries people are more satisfied with their lives than those in poor

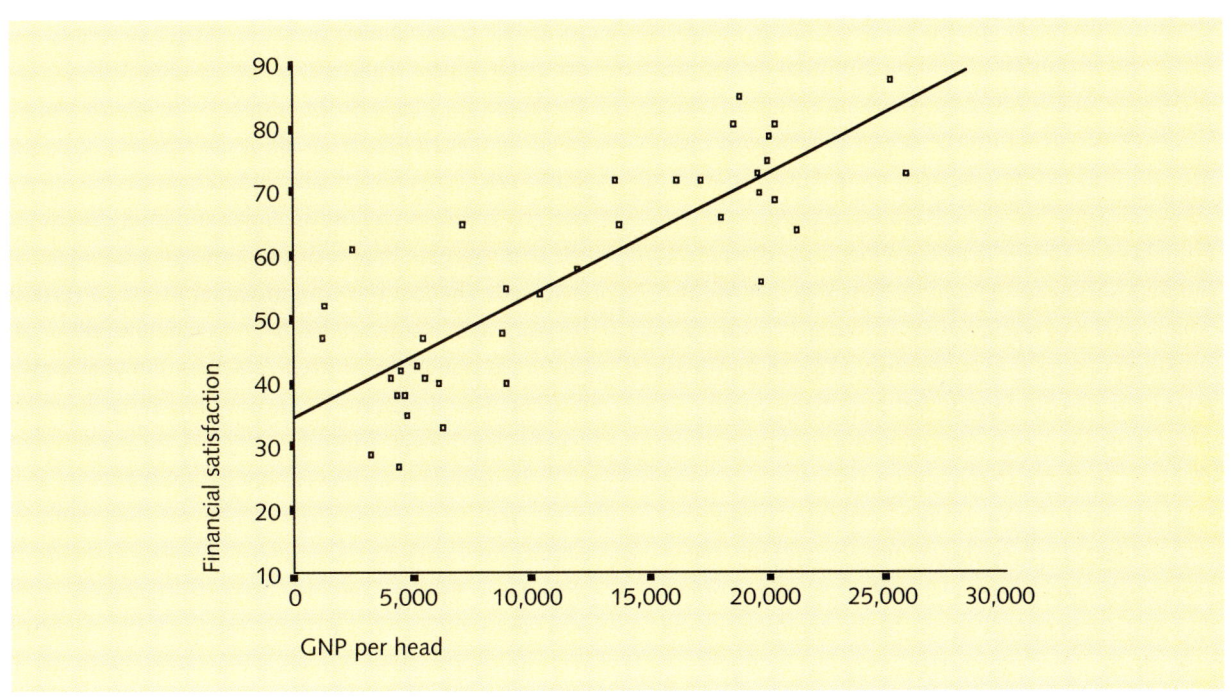

GRAPH 16
PERCENTAGE SATISFIED WITH FINANCIAL SITUATION BY PPP ESTIMATE OF GNP PER CAPITA (1994)

countries. As Veenhoven has shown (1994), happiness is not a fixed social construction unrelated to living conditions.[4]

Though spread fairly evenly over richer and poorer countries, the negative view of democracy nevertheless appears to be fostered by a low national income.[5] It may be that populations fault the political system for the poor performance of a national economy. This generally seems to confirm Przeworski's view that economic factors are conditioning the life expectancy of the democratic process. On the other hand one has not to subscribe fully to his conclusion about the relative unimportance of cultural traditions for democracy.

The policy study *Institutions, Values, Norms and Growth* by the Dutch Forum for Economic Research (NYFER) also utilizes data from the *World Values Survey 1990–1993*. The authors explore the connections between economic variables and value orientations. They conclude among others that economic growth is influenced by culture, although the direction of causality remains difficult to establish (NYFER, 1996, p. 31). Especially mutual trust and tolerance appear to contribute to economic growth in prosperous OECD countries (NYFER, 1996, pp. 21–6, 65).

The findings presented thus far have been based on comparisons between countries or geographical regions. How do categories of individuals respond to the questions? An approach via the scores of individuals constitutes a different level of analysis. The data are no longer treated as aggregated at the level of countries. This approach is possible only for the data taken from the *World Values Survey 1990–1993*, where we had the original survey at our disposal (see Table 19a).

The items from Table 19a were analysed simultaneously in terms of gender, age, income and education.[6] Trust in other people was found to be influenced mainly by education, followed by income and age. Gender proved an irrelevant factor. In most countries, highly educated people, people with high incomes, and older people put more trust in their fellow humans than do less educated people, individuals with low incomes and younger people.[7] The four socio-demographic factors together fail to explain much of the variance. Between 1% and 7% is explained in almost every country (12% in Northern Ireland). This could mean that personality characteristics, which could not be taken into account, are major explanatory variables.

Age is by far the strongest predictor of people's state of health, followed by education and income. Compared to young people, only small proportions of older people describe their health as good or very good. State of health is better explained by the background variables than trust in other people, from 5% to 15% in most of the countries involved (22% in Denmark).

The importance of the economic factor found at the aggregated level again shows up at the individual level. Income proves the most important micro variable associated with the three satisfaction items: in all countries but Sweden, people with a high income are more satisfied with their life in general, their home life and their financial situation than people with a low income. Age is the second most important variable influencing the three items, with old people generally more satisfied than young people.[8] In some countries, however, the Republic of Korea and Austria in particular, this relationship is reversed. In contrast to financial satisfaction, life satisfaction and satisfaction with home life are explained only weakly by the four socio-demographic variables (on average between 1% to 6%). For satisfaction with the financial situation, the explained variance generally varied between 5% and 15%, but it was around 25% in South Africa, Poland, Slovenia, Bulgaria and Romania.

The four socio-demographic variables are incapable of explaining the differences between the six geographical regions as given in Table 19b. Geographical region still has one of the largest and most significant effects on all of the items in Table 19b.[9] This means that any differences between the geographical regions are apparently not due to the demographic composition of the populations involved. The fact that an individual lives in a certain location and is surrounded by a specific overall culture is important in itself. We would further argue that our classification of countries into certain regions has proven fruitful.

In general it can be concluded that:
•   countries tend to differ in how satisfied their populations are with certain basic requirements of material well-being and also with life in general;
•   these differences are explained to a high degree by differences in the countries' material wealth;
•   agreement, or some measure of unity, exists when it comes to criticism of democracy and 'social distrust' and to satisfaction with family life;
•   criticism of democracy, while obviously fostered by failures of the system itself, may also result from people blaming the political system for poor national economic performance;
•   an individual's gender has little connection with the amount of satisfaction he/she experiences, while age, education and personal income have some connection, varying according to the type of satisfaction analysed;
•   the part of the world individuals inhabit is also of influence on their level of satisfaction.

Optimism and pessimism

Do publics in various countries view today's world as better, worse or the same as the world their parents grew up in? Will the world be better, worse or the same for the next generation (Table 20)?

Feelings about the quality of the present are mixed. When the answers of the publics from seventeen nations are taken together we see that 43% think of today's world as better than that of the past,

while 14% regard the state of the world as unchanged and 38% see the present as worse than the past. Some signs of diversity can be detected in the opinions. This disagreement does not show itself convincingly in the standard deviations. They have about the same values for 'better' or 'worse', whether expressed in logits or not. However, in seven countries the percentage of people regarding the state of today's world as worse exceeds the percentage with an optimistic view. These countries can be classified as generally pessimistic. In ten countries the opposite applies. In these countries, particularly Japan, Taiwan and Spain, the opinion climate can be characterized as optimistic. Since there are similar numbers of optimistic and pessimistic countries, one might be justified in speaking of cultural diversity in how the present is judged in the light of the past.

Diversity is certainly absent where the outlook on the future is concerned. Pessimism reigns about the future world. This can be concluded straight away from the total scores. In all countries taken together, 52% think the world will deteriorate and only 24% think the opposite. In nearly all countries the idea that the future will be worse has more supporters than the belief that the situation will get better. Only in several Asian countries (India, Taiwan and Thailand) is the group of people with a favourable view of the future larger than the pessimistic group (Table 20). Pessimism with respect to the future should therefore be deemed a universal phenomenon.

A few countries can be singled out as enduringly pessimistic, meaning that both the present and the future are seen in a negative light. Nearly all are found in the Western hemisphere, namely Canada, the United States, the United Kingdom, Costa Rica, Mexico and Venezuela. This proximity in location could be a coincidence. Outside the so-called Western world, India is enduringly optimistic.

It can be concluded from the foregoing that: (a)

cultural diversity exists in the assessment of the present, and (b) pessimism about the world's future is virtually universal.

Values to be taught to children

The values that an older generation thinks important enough to teach to the coming generation offer some insight into what constitutes the core of cultures.[10] These values can be taken as forming part of the cultural heritage. In the *World Values Survey 1990–1993* respondents were asked to specify five virtues (out of a choice of eleven) that they believed most important for children to learn at home (Table 21a). Since the table (showing the initial results for about forty countries) might be difficult to read, a small excerpt can serve as an illustration. Some 75% of the Canadians cited good manners as one of the five most important things to be taught to children, and 44% rated independence as such. Some scores are exceedingly low. Only a few per cent of the Scandinavian publics feel hard work to be important. In judging such low percentages one should bear in mind that the respondents were asked to name only the five most important values out of eleven. The Danish score means that 2% classified hard work as such, and 98% gave it a lower ranking. What rank that is – sixth, eleventh or in between – is unknown.

On the basis of the mean scores, calculated over all the countries, goals for upbringing tend to fall rather naturally into distinct groups according to their popularity:[11]

• The group of values with the highest acclaim involves the acquisition of good social behaviour, concern for others, or even good citizenship. Good manners (which 76% consider most important), feeling of responsibility (73%) and tolerance and respect for other people (71%) make up this category.

• The values independence (46%) and hard work (46%) may be taken to represent individual achievement.

• Thrift (36%), determination (34%) and obedience (33%) can be regarded as expressions of the more fundamental value of self-discipline.

• The last category is the most difficult to interpret. It concerns unselfishness (27%), religious faith (26%) and imagination (20%). To some extent the category bears the stamp of the realization or unfolding of the self/self-development. Imagination or creativity certainly does. Religious faith might be seen as a possibility to realize one's own personality in relation to a higher reality. Unselfishness or altruism does not seem to fit very well under this heading. The reader would have been justified in expecting this value to be a part of the first category, good social behaviour.

From the ranking of values it might be concluded that, on a very broad geographical scale, acceptable social behaviour is viewed as the most important thing to teach a new generation. It carries even more weight than values that foster high individual achievement. These in turn are more important than self-discipline. Altruism and self-development bring up the rear. The remaining virtues, even religious faith, tend perhaps to be regarded as luxuries.

Some details concerning the opinions prevailing in large geographical regions are worth mentioning (Table 21b). The continents do not differ significantly in how good manners, independence, determination and unselfishness are valued.[12] The

same is true of responsibility and obedience, if the two African countries are left out of consideration.[13] The most important difference with respect to tolerance is that between Asia (61%) and Eastern Europe (66%) on one side, and Western Europe (76%) on the other. Imagination has the strongest appeal in Central and South America (27%) and Western Europe (25%). Thrift is valued most in Eastern Europe (48%) and Asia (42%). Hard work is seen as unimportant in Western Europe (25%), especially in Scandinavia, as well as in Central and South America – but as exceedingly important in Eastern Europe (74%) (see also Table 21a). Eastern Europe is a society with an overriding interest in the reconstruction of its economic potential. Religious faith is least popular in Western Europe (22%), Eastern Europe (16%) and Asia (22%), but is seen as an important goal for upbringing in Africa (64%).

Table 15, based on Table 21a and containing the mean scores in percentages and the standard deviations in logits, offers some insight into the agreement amongst nations.

There is considerable agreement that tolerance should be an important value; it has the lowest standard deviation in Table 15. Countries also agree that determination (or perseverance) and thrift are relatively unimportant. Considering the mean scores and the rather low standard deviations, the same can be said of obedience, unselfishness, and especially of imagination or creativity.

TABLE 15
MEANS AND STANDARD DEVIATIONS (LOGITS) FOR VARIOUS VALUES TO BE TAUGHT TO CHILDREN (1993)

	Tolerance	Determination	Thrift	Obedience	Imagination	Responsibility	Unselfishness	Good manners	Independence	Religious faith	Hard work
Mean percentage, first five	71	35	36	33	20	73	27	76	46	26	46
Standard deviation, logit	.20	.21	.28	.30	.31	.31	.35	.39	.41	.48	.71

Source: *World Values Survey 1990–1993.*

At the opposite end of the scale of agreement we find hard work. Countries clearly disagree on its value (this finding is heavily influenced by the climate of opinion in Eastern Europe). The same applies to religious faith and independence. Religious faith is generally seen as unimportant, but certainly not all countries concur with this view. The continents are similar with regard to independence, but countries clearly disagree on this value.[14] It is seen as unimportant in, for example, France, Portugal, Czechoslovakia (former), Romania, Brazil, India and Turkey but as exceedingly important in West Germany, Denmark, Hungary, Lithuania, China and Japan (Table 21a).

Responsibility and good manners take a position somewhere in the middle of the range. They are considered important values, and the standard deviations are neither large nor small. Independence is seen as relatively unimportant, but disagreement is fairly high.

All in all, we cannot claim the results to be very clear. Tolerance is a value to be taught to children on whose importance public opinion in most countries agrees. These findings point to a general climate in which, by means of education (Touraine), a compromise between equality and difference or between 'we' and 'the others' (Todorov, 1989) could be achieved.

Hard work encounters the highest possible disagreement. Social obligations might be in contrast with individual achievement. As for the other values, various more or less subtle distinctions are found.

Countries and larger geographical regions differ in the size of the families living there. It is conceivable that bringing up children in a small family poses different problems from those in a large family. To gain insight into this, we correlated the scores of countries with the average family sizes there between 1980 and 1990 (Goldstone, 1998, data for thirty-two countries available). This structural, country-specific variable proved unimportant for most of the educational values. However, in countries where large families predominate, stronger emphasis is put on good manners (r = .38) and obedience (r = .39), and less emphasis on independence (r = –.37) and tolerance (–.37). Probably, good manners and obedience favour the smooth functioning of a large family, while independence – in large families possibly seen as self-will – does not. Showing patience and goodwill towards other members of the family might be especially necessary if the family is large. For this reason one might have expected tolerance to be more highly regarded in large families than proved to be the case. In this case the results are unclear. In passing it should be mentioned that average family size correlated strongest with religious faith (r = .50, p < .01). This comes as no surprise, because religious parents are reputed to have large families.

Men and women play different roles in raising children, so that differences in their attitudes towards upbringing are to be expected. For six large geographical regions the data were differentiated by the gender of the respondents. Contrary to our expectations, however, this trait proved a relatively unimportant determinant of the values throughout the world (Table 21c).[15] In all geographical regions, differences in the thinking of men and women turned out small, as shown by the generally low level of the Cramer's V coefficient. Working hard and having religious faith were partial exceptions.[16] In Western Europe as well as in Central and South America and Africa, women consider educating children in a religious faith a more important goal than men do. This finding seems rather persistent in survey research and may be linked to a division of labour in families, whereby it is primarily the mother or wife who is charged with the religious aspect of life. In North America and Africa the achievement motive seems to be supported more by men than by women, with men putting more stress on hard work than women do.[17]

This lack of findings may surprise the reader, since gender is often believed to be a major explanation for differences in attitudes and behaviour. Indeed it is in some cases, as when health problems or the use of time is involved. But it appears far less important when it comes to opinions on values. That the categories of men and women are socially extremely heterogeneous is no doubt of significant influence: poor and rich, young and old, illiterate and well-educated women or men are all part of the same category. It is not to be expected that such extremely mixed categories will differ distinctly in their ways of thinking.

Indications of the values into which a new generation is being socialized are critical for a deeper understanding of culture. It is therefore regrettable that our initial review of accessible data yields results that were not altogether clear. It can, however, be concluded that:

•   values predisposing the individual towards acceptable social behaviour are considered most important;

•   unselfishness, religious faith and imagination are seen as least important, and

•   values relating to achievement and self-restraint take an intermediate position.

As to unity and diversity it can be concluded that:

•   countries agree on the importance of tolerance;

•   countries agree to varying extents on the relative lack of importance of determination, thrift and imagination;

•   hard work and religious faith find relatively low favour in the eyes of the overall public, but countries disagree on the importance of these values;

•   this disagreement is influenced in part by the strong emphasis on hard work and the weak emphasis on religion in Eastern Europe, and to a lesser degree in Asia as well.

It can further be concluded that:

•   family size and the gender of respondents have less to do with values than one might suppose.

Some political matters

Tables 22a, 22b and 22c show data on the degree of approval of the human rights movement, on the level of political interest and on the degree to which people identify with various geographical locations, ranging from their home town to the world in general.

About half of the total population approves of the human rights movement (58%) or shows a reasonably high level of political interest (51%). Identification with one's home town is the strongest (40%). Smaller numbers identify with a province (19%) or with their country as a whole (29%).[18] Identification with a continent (4%) or with the world (7%) is rare.

Cultural unity is clearly to be found in people's identification with their home town. The standard deviation in logits is .19, with all coefficients ranging around .33. We also conclude that countries are more or less united in the weak ties their citizens feel with their continent or the world, given the low mean percentages on these items. Some countries show a clearly localist orientation. Among these are Norway, Sweden and Russia. The people of the Republic of Korea, Argentina, Poland and Japan appear most markedly oriented towards their country as a whole.

Diversity seems to be the rule for the remaining opinions. A review of the results for human rights and political interest lends support to this thesis. In 31 of the 42 countries studied, over 50% of the population strongly approves of the human rights movement (Table 22a). The percentage is highest in Africa (76%) and Central and South America (70%), and lowest in Asia[19] (45%) (Table 22b).[20] In six countries, substantial numbers of people failed to answer the question (Japan 22%, India 34%, China 22%, Lithuania 18%, Latvia 15% and Estonia 24%). This could mean the subject is too sensitive to be talked about or that this concept of a human rights movement has little meaning in certain cultures.

In about half the countries involved, less than 50% of those interviewed say they are very or

somewhat interested in politics. On average, political interest is highest in Eastern Europe (60%) and lowest in Central & South America (38%) (Table 22b).[21] The high political interest in Eastern Europe is not accompanied by much trust in the government and the political system (Alwin, Gornev and Khakhulina, 1995, p. 126), although large proportions of the people in these post-Communist societies do feel the current system is better or even much better than the old regime (Rose, 1995, p. 464–9). Research in 1993–94 in fourteen Eastern European societies shows that people feel freer to decide for themselves whether or not to practise a religion (85%), join an organization (84%), say what they think (81%), take an interest in politics (75%) and travel and live where they want (68%). The fear of being unlawfully arrested presents a less favourable picture. On average 59% do not fear such an occurrence.[22]

Generally speaking, the human rights movement is supported by the more highly educated parts of various populations. This is certainly the case in North America: the more education respondents have, the more strongly they approve of the human rights movement (Table 22c). In Western Europe and Asia the most highly educated also give their support, and the low and middle educational levels somewhat less. In the African countries the movement is most strongly supported by people with a middle-range education. Educational level is of no consequence in Eastern Europe and Central and South America.[23]

It can be concluded that:

• countries differ in their approval of the human rights movement;

• approval for this movement is a disputed issue, given that the separation point between strong and weak support is found at about 50%;

• the human rights movement is primarily, but not exclusively, supported by the highly educated;

• major differences also exist in political interest; and

• cultural unity can be found only in peoples' fairly strong attachment to their home town and in their lack of strong attachment to geographical entities at the supranational level.

Some aspects of tolerance

We have seen that tolerance is the most important value that people wish children to be taught. The results shown in Tables 23a, 23b and 23c seem to confirm this conclusion. Only 17% of the publics in various countries say they do not want immigrants or people of another race as neighbours. Higher percentages would not like to live near people suffering from AIDS (44%) or near homosexuals (48%). The labour market seems to be the greatest stumbling block for tolerant thinking. In the event of high unemployment, 70% want jobs given to their compatriots rather than to immigrants. Such a restriction does not apply to the people with disabilities, for only 20% want them excluded from the labour market when unemployment was high (Table 23a). These findings highlight the importance of Touraine's remarks about the complementarity of equality in the labour market with the demand of adaptation of cultural identities as a policy.

This partially rosy picture could be deceptive, however. The way the questions were formulated could have been of influence. Respondents were to indicate what people they would definitely not accept as neighbours. Only two answers were possible, yes or no. Experience with other types of questions has shown that the choice of more than two answers uncovers more indications of negative feelings. In a 1995 Dutch survey, for instance, it was asked what attitude one would take if people from another race would move in as neighbours. Only 2% said they would resist, but 21% would consider it a less agreeable situation, while another 21% thought their attitude would depend on the kind of people their new neighbours turned out to be. Only 56% reported no objection at all. This result reveals an unwillingness to answer the question in a bluntly negative way. It shows moreover that negative feelings towards other races can be found amongst 23% to 42% of the Dutch population.

As to the questions on the labour market, we should point out that the statement on exclusion of the disabled was awkwardly formulated: 'It is *unfair* to give work to handicapped people when able-bodied people *can't* find jobs' (our italics). The statement contains a double negation, which is always difficult to understand. As might be expected, considerable numbers of people failed to answer the question (see Appendix C). The answer categories were again only 'yes' or 'no'. For these reasons the figures should be approached with some caution, and they should definitely not be taken as absolute indications for the level of tolerance.

Cultural diversity manifests itself most clearly in the cases of the rejection of homosexuals and people with AIDS. The standard deviations in logits are around .50, with all the other coefficients ranging between .30 and .40. Tolerance towards these categories is highest in North America and Western Europe and lowest in Eastern Europe, Asia and Nigeria (Table 23b). As for cultural unity, one might say that the countries are reasonably united in a desire to reserve scarce jobs for their own inhabitants, thereby excluding foreigners. In nearly all countries, 65% or more express this opinion.

A more general picture emerges if we construct an 'index of intolerance' consisting of four of the six items (Table 23a).[24] People in Eastern Europe, with the exception of the former East Germany, tend to be the most intolerant. Tolerance is highest in North America and Western Europe, and particularly in Denmark, the Netherlands and Sweden. Asia can be divided into two parts: tolerance is quite high in Japan and in the Republic of Korea and very low in China, India and Turkey (Table 23a). In the NYFER study a tolerance index was created and it appeared that the higher the level of expenditure on social protection in a country, the higher the level of tolerance (1996, pp. 39, 62).

A confrontation of the rankings of some countries on the tolerance index with the valuation of tolerance as measured by 'values to be taught to children' shows contradictions in some cultures. Some countries, like Sweden and the Netherlands, think tolerance an important value in education. These countries also rank low on intolerance to categories like foreign workers, homosexuals and people with AIDS. Other countries like Belarus, Russia, Slovenia and Nigeria think tolerance important as a value to be taught but do not seem to extend this feeling towards the categories just mentioned.

Does tolerance increase or decrease with age? We investigated this question for the four items of the 'intolerance index' (Table 23c). Age is most relevant in Western Europe, North America and Africa (Cramer's V ≥ .07). In the former two regions, older people are generally less tolerant than young people, but in Nigeria it is the young who are lacking in tolerance. People of different age groups diverge most in their opinions about homosexuals as neighbours. In Western Europe and Central and South America, intolerance increases with age. In North America, Asia and Africa middle-aged people are the most tolerant and older people above 55 years least tolerant (Table 23c). On the other three items, young and middle-aged people are more tolerant than older ones.[25]

All in all, we can conclude that:
•   people are more inclined (though on the basis of rather unsatisfactory survey questions) to reject homosexuals and people with AIDS as neighbours than to reject ethnic minorities;
•   countries are in disagreement on their attitudes towards the former two categories;
•   countries agree in their predominant wish to reserve scarce jobs for their own citizens; and
•   younger people show more tolerant thinking than older people.

Gender issues and women's emancipation

Status of women in society

In all countries of the Gallup research taken together, 53% believe that society favours men over women, 34% see no difference between their social positions, and only 9% believe women are better off. India is to some degree an exception (Table 24). In Western Europe and North America, large majorities feel that society favours men over women (72% and 69%), and in Central America the smallest group of people hold this opinion (33%). Within that region – in contrast to people in North America (21%), Western Europe (20%) and South America (24%) – most people (52%) feel women and men are treated equally.

Although a certain pessimism about women's status seems to reign in the general climate of opinion, the way this status is evolving is viewed in a more favourable light: 60% regard women's position as having improved in the past five years (Table 24). Opinions on the social differential between men and women are about equally divided. The standard deviations in logits have about the same values for 'men worse off', 'women worse off' and 'no difference', ranging from .30 to .33. It may be justified to conclude that cultural unity prevails in the belief that society favours women over men, because in all countries except India, only small minorities agree with this statement.

Optimism about how women's status has evolved is very marked, but countries diverge on this issue (the standard deviation in logits is quite high at .50). It is especially here that cultural diversity can be discerned. It is heavily determined, however, by the Eastern European countries, where only 15% see women's chances as having improved. In other regions this percentage stands at 63% to 78% (Table 24).[26]

It can be concluded that:
* men are generally thought to be treated better by society than women, or at least equally;
* countries diverge on this subject, but more

divergence is found in perceptions of how women's position has changed in recent years;
* this divergence is largely determined by the East European countries where relatively few people perceive improvement; and
* the beliefs about the relative social positions of men and women are characterized overall by a certain cultural diversity.

Women in the labour market

The climate of opinion concerning women in paid work is not very clear. Overall, 74% agree with the statement that both men and women should contribute to household income,[27] whilst 35% feel scarce jobs should be reserved for men (Table 25a). However, fairly high percentages also endorse the statements that children are likely to suffer if their mother is in paid employment (69%), that all a woman wants from life is a home and children (64%), and that being a housewife is just as fulfilling as working for pay (59%). Thus, the principle of married women doing paid work, even if they are mothers, appears widely accepted, while at the same time serious, traditionally perceived disadvantages of this way of life are affirmed. This combination of opinions suggests that paid work for married women is still a controversial issue.

The standard deviations in logits are about the same for all the statements, ranging between .30 and .40. Since the percentages affirming or denying the statements are rather extreme, one might be justified in postulating cultural unity. Broad agreement exists in endorsing paid employment for women, as well as in acknowledging its traditionally perceived drawbacks. In most countries, majorities feel that children suffer if their mothers work (Table 25a), but this idea is less popular in North America (52%), Africa (53%) and Western Europe (61%) than it is in Eastern Europe (77%), Asia (77%) and Central and South America (78%) (Table 25b). The view that being a housewife is as fulfilling as working for pay is subscribed to by more than half the respondents

TABLE 16

AFFIRMATION OF TRADITIONAL STATEMENTS ON MARRIAGE AND DIVORCE (1994)

	Marriage if children	Stay together if children	Marriage for financial security	Always stay together	Marriage to have children	Bad marriage better than no marriage
Mean score in percentages	61	27	30	10	33	8
Standard deviation in logits	.25	.29	.29	.31	.41	.41

Source: International Social Survey Programme (ISSP), 1994.

on all continents, but it is endorsed most in North America (68%) and least in Africa (50%) and Western Europe (54%) (Table 25b). In North America (45%) and Western Europe (49%), people are less likely to argue that women prefer a home and children above work than they are in Central and South America (68%), Asia (77%), Eastern Europe (78%) and Nigeria (85%) (Table 25b).

Opinions about the position of women in the labour market are unrelated to the prevailing labour force participation rates for women (Goldstone, 1998). Countries with the most liberal views on this issue boast no higher shares of working women (and vice versa). Overall correlations were extremely weak, for a large part due to the East European countries, which are characterized by a high percentage of working women but also by a 'traditional' point of view.

It will come as no surprise that men are somewhat more traditional in their views on women in paid work and its effects on family life than women are (Table 25c). This is especially the case on the issues of whether men have more right to scarce jobs than women and whether children suffer if their mothers work. With respect to the other questions, differences are marginal (Table 25c).

It can be concluded that:
• a measure of cultural unity comes to light with regard to the relationship between paid work and married women;

• the principle of paid work for married women is widely accepted;
• some traditional ideas on disadvantages to marriages and children still exist as well;
• views on paid work for married women have probably not yet fully crystallized; and
• female labour force participation rates and the gender of respondents are not strongly related to these values.

Marriage and sexuality

Although marriage and sexuality can be regarded as topics in their own right, there are advantages to treating them under the heading of gender relations, because traditional and liberal views on marriage and sexuality bear upon various aspects of the relations between men and women.

Table 16 shows the affirmative responses to six traditional statements on marriage and divorce (mean scores in percentages, standard deviations in logits). The table is based on Table 26a, and the data were derived from International Social Survey Programme (ISSP) research.

The picture presented by Table 16 is not particularly traditional. Overall, 61% feel couples should marry if they plan to have children, but much smaller percentages believe the main purpose of marriage is procreation (33%), that financial security is a major advantage of getting married (30%), or

that a bad marriage is better than none at all (8%). Divorce appears widely accepted. Only 10% feel married couples should always stay together, and 27% believe people should not divorce if their children are young enough to live with the family.

Agreement on these issues predominates in the results in Table 16. The standard deviations are not very large on most statements, such as the need to be married for the benefit of children and the association between marriage and financial security. More diversity can be seen with regard to divorce and the belief that children are the only goal of marriage.

On the whole, the main differences between traditionalism and liberalism appear between Eastern Europe and Asia on one side, and Oceania, North America and Western Europe on the other. The value attached to procreation as the main purpose of marriage indicates the nature of this difference. In North America procreation is deemed important by 13%, in Oceania by 17% and in Western Europe by 24%. These low percentages contrast with those in Asia (46%), Israel (49%) and Eastern Europe (51%). Traditional thinking in matters of marriage is clearly concentrated in the latter regions (Table 26b). The more traditional view of marriage gains strength with age. Younger people express more liberal opinions than older people whatever the issue. The watershed is around age 55. The relationship between age and attitudes towards marriage is strongest in Western Europe, Eastern Europe and Oceania (Table 26c). Age differences are most pronounced on the question of whether people who want children should marry

$(.09 \leq V \leq .34)$. This is also the only issue for which the effect of age is stronger than the effect of continent.[28]

It can be concluded that:
- ideas concerning marriage are rather liberal and are strongly related to the age of the respondents;
- the opinion that people ought to marry when they want children is a possible exception;
- the interests of children are generally a key reason behind more or less traditional answers;
- a gap exists between the less liberal opinions of people in Asia and Eastern Europe and the more liberal opinions in Oceania, North America and Western Europe; and
- cultural unity nevertheless seems the rule, though slightly less so in the case of divorce.

Sexual morality

Sexual freedom is not accepted without restrictions (Tables 17 and 27a). Though only 23% of the respondents reject sexual intercourse before marriage,[29] 82% take an unfavourable attitude towards extramarital affairs. The general conception behind these figures may be that people need not marry, but that they should be serious about fidelity if they do. The attitude towards teenagers having sexual intercourse before 16 is decidedly negative, with 73% rejecting it. Homosexual relationships between adults are rejected by 58%.

A measure of cultural unity can be detected in this partly restrained attitude to sexual behaviour. The standard deviations are close to .30 with the

TABLE 17
OPINIONS ON SEXUAL FREEDOM IN STANDARD DEVIATIONS (LOGITS) AND IN MEAN PERCENTAGES (1994)

	No sex in early teens	No extramarital affairs	No homosexual relations	No sex before marriage
Mean percentage	73	82	58	23
Standard deviation in logit	.32	.34	.36	.45

Source: *People's Satisfaction with Their Lives and Government* (International Gallup Poll Report, 1995).

exception of that for sexual intercourse before marriage, which rises to .45 (Table 17).

Comparison of the scores of geographical regions shows that on many issues the people in Asia are the most 'traditional' in their attitudes to sexual morality (Table 27b) and marriage (Table 26b). This result is largely due to the Philippines. The exceptional position of the Philippines has been underlined by a cross-national study of college students in eleven countries, which found weaker associations between love and marriage in the Philippines (and in some other Asian countries such as Pakistan and Thailand) than in countries like England, the United States and Brazil (Levine et al., 1995).

The cross-national rates of acceptance of homosexuality do not appear linked to specific regions (Table 27b). The attitudes are reasonably favourable in countries like Canada, former West Germany, the Netherlands, the Czech Republic and former East Germany but rather negative in countries such as the United States, Northern Ireland, Hungary and Japan (Table 27a). Though a certain degree of liberalism in sexuality seems to be fairly widespread tolerance for homosexuality is not yet common. Touraine may be overstating the Western experience in this respect.

It can be concluded that:

• sexual freedom is supported most strongly in the case of intercourse before marriage;

• other attitudes towards sexual freedom reflect some restraint;

• fidelity in marriage is considered important; and

• some measure of cultural unity seems to exist.

Environment

The environment is not at the front of people's minds, although it is certainly felt to be important. Only 14% of the respondents mention the environment spontaneously when asked to list their country's major social problems (Table 28a). None the less, 49% of the respondents consider environmental problems 'very serious'. They are more likely to perceive such problems at the world level (70%) than at their national level (45%), and even less as threats to their own local community (33%). This result seems to confirm the differences in local and global perceptions as mentioned by Leach.

The tendency for people to regard environmental problems as distant from the area they actually inhabit is well documented (Becker et al., 1996, p. 37–8). Individuals are probably reluctant to face up to problems that constitute a personal threat, and therefore project them as far away as possible. This may be one particular instance of a general psychological tendency, the reduction of cognitive dissonance.

Consistent with the perceived international nature of environmental problems, 78% of the respondents believe international agencies should receive funding to combat pollution, and 67% feel such agencies should have the power to enforce regulations (Table 28a). International institutions are supported most strongly in Western and Eastern Europe, and enthusiasm is lowest in Central and South America (Table 28b).

Countries differ in their citizens' assessment of national environmental problems. For example, 21% in Finland versus 67% in West Germany and the Republic of Korea regard these as very serious (Table 28a). Curiously, the percentages citing the environment as the foremost problem and those judging environmental problems as very serious are negatively correlated (r = –.26). In West Germany and Eastern European countries, environmental problems are seldom spontaneously mentioned amongst the major national dilemmas, but when specifically asked, the publics still rate them as very serious (Table 28b). This incongruity is difficult to explain. Possibly other problems like unemployment and poverty are considered so urgent that they come to mind first. This need not preclude a gloomy view on the environment being revealed by further questioning.

Although in most countries people view the

quality of the local environment more positively than they do the environmental situation in the world (Table 28a), the levels of such assessments differ. In Eastern Europe and Asia, high proportions rate quality at the local and national level as 'bad', in contrast with North America and Western Europe (Table 28b). Differences are less pronounced with respect to the world environmental situation, with the greatest optimism in Nigeria and Asia. The other parts of the world scarcely differ in this respect (Table 28b).

The present quality of the environment is estimated as good to fair by 75%, and by 25% as poor (Table 29). Beneath the surface of such relative optimism, some pessimism is discernable, since 56% believe the quality of the environment has worsened in the past ten years. Only 23% see improvement during that period, and 20% think the environment remained stable. Saudi Arabia is the only country where the group that feels environmental quality has improved in the past ten years is larger than the group thinking it is worse (Table 29). An overwhelming majority there also rates the quality of the national environment as 'good'. Saudi Arabia is an exception perhaps 'because of the rapid development which has taken place there in just the last twenty years' (Worcester and Corrado, 1991, p. 13). In Africa, too, people are quite optimistic about recent developments. An average of 36% on that continent feel the quality has improved, against 7% in Western Europe, 10% in Hungary and 13% in Central and South America (Table 29).

Cultural unity prevails the most where the role of international agencies is concerned. The standard deviations in logits are .20 (for 'money') and .15 (for 'having authority'). Unity is also considerable around the viewpoint that environmental problems are very serious (.26). However, since diversity in the spontaneous mentioning of the environment is so great (.57), no firm conclusions can be drawn. Ideas about the severity of environmental problems at the national level likewise diverge, with a standard

deviation of .47. There is relative concurrence in the generally pessimistic view of environmental trends in the recent past (standard deviation .21).

Are opinions about the environment influenced by a country's economic situation? It appears that the per capita GNP (corrected for differences in purchasing power) only correlates significantly with the verdict on environmental quality. In richer countries, fewer people rate the quality of their local and national environment as 'bad' (r = –.62 and r = –.52), but more people are likely to think the world environment is in a sorry state (r = .67) (Table 28a). Neither the tendency to spontaneously cite environmental problems as urgent nor the tendency to feel international agencies should address such problems is significantly related to a country's economic development.

It can be concluded that:
•   people tend to be aware of environmental problems, but they do not often mention them spontaneously, probably because other problems such as the economy or unemployment compete for the public's attention;
•   people tend to situate environmental problems at the supranational level and to look to that level for the solutions;
•   rich countries regard their national environments as favourable; and
•   a good deal of diversity exists, except on the role of international agencies and the belief that the environment was better off ten years ago.

Conclusions

This chapter is about global ethics and shared value commitments. The authors of *Our Creative Diversity* consider communal values to be a potential basis for international co-operation, and at least as a means for the containment or prevention of conflicts.

Against this conceptual and normative approach we have placed an empirical analysis of public opinion in various countries. We presumed these opinions to be indicators of values –

understood as standards for the correct way of behaving and thinking. Our data were derived from existing research: the *World Values Survey 1990–1993,* the International Social Survey Programme, and Gallup and MORI research.

With *Our Creative Diversity* as our point of departure, we delineated fields of interest. We asked whether similar thinking prevailed in various countries and larger regions of the world on issues relevant to the *World Culture Report,* and to what extent countries or geographical regions diverged in their thinking on such issues. This question refers to the degrees to which cultural unity or cultural diversity can be observed to exist. We caution that these concepts should not be given too absolute a meaning. Unity, for example, should be regarded as 'a fairly high degree of unanimity or homogeneity concerning issues of culture'. In a diverse world, no absolute agreement is to be expected.

Basically our conclusions are based on the opinions people hold all over the world. We would like to stress in advance, however, that although the research we had at our disposal did prove useful, its completeness left something to be desired. The research coverage of certain parts of the world, for instance the Islamic and African countries, was unsatisfactory. Some important concepts were not fully covered, or not addressed at all, by survey questions. Incomplete as our data was, extensive analysis still proved possible.

As for our chief concern – cultural diversity and unity – we can conclude that international value patterns are not rigidly compartmentalized. We used the statistical measure of the standard deviation in logit values. Middle-range deviations between .30 and .40 were the rule for the cultural values we were able to consider. Researchers cannot expect all of their readers to be knowledgeable about statistics, so let us phrase our principal conclusion in a different way. No statements on values could be found that were completely accepted by inhabitants of one geographical region and categorically rejected by the citizens of another. We were also unable to identify values that were completely accepted in all regions. We only succeeded in pinpointing some values that were fairly generally held (unity) and other values that countries rather clearly disagreed upon (diversity). In all other instances, we can only maintain that where unity cannot be claimed to exist, an impressive diversity is absent in any case. The general picture is that of a rather broad dispersion of values that might be interpreted as a stage in an evolution towards further cultural unification. How far this unification will proceed cannot be determined at present.

At the end of each section of our data analysis, we gave a summary of conclusions. We will refrain from repeating these here. Instead we will offer the reader an overview of our main conclusions.

In view of the widespread publicity on hunger in the world and the incidence of civil wars, natural disasters and their consequences, we think it remarkable that a rather high level of satisfaction with housing, clothing and nutrition seems to predominate in our data. On this point, however, diversity is also rather high. Countries with a remarkably high level of contentment contrast with countries where satisfaction is low. As the degree of satisfaction with material aspects of life is linked to a nation's level of income, the results of our survey largely reflect the way wealth is distributed over different parts of the world.

As regards the non-material aspects of life, a high level of satisfaction with family life can be juxtaposed to a rather low level of trust in one's fellow human beings. Both these findings show a fair measure of agreement between countries. They suggest that most societies do not succeed in creating a climate of 'social comfort', but that the closed micro-environment of the family offers a safe haven amidst an outside world that is not hospitable in every respect.

Countries vary on the measure in which their publics believe social progress has been achieved. In

a reasonably large number of countries, the general publics are convinced that today's world is better than that of their parents' youth, but for many countries the reverse is true. At the same time, a certain pessimism on the future of the coming generation is a general phenomenon, present even in wealthy nations. Countries are therefore united to a considerable degree in their gloom about the next generation's future. The reason for this pessimism is not clear.

Irrespective of the extent to which democracy is institutionalized, dissatisfaction prevails about the way it is functioning. This is a case of unity between peoples. Although the people questioned probably held wide-ranging notions of what constitutes democracy, it could be inferred with at least some plausibility that a democratic ideal of some sort is widely endorsed in the abstract. Furthermore, one could argue that this ideal is so highly regarded that the objective situation inevitably falls short of expectations. This disparity could explain the rather general dissatisfaction with the workings of the democratic system. The data also provide some indications, however, of a tendency to blame political systems for a nation's poor economic performance.

Dissatisfaction with democracy may just be a reflection of a general climate of opinion. It is not clear to us whether the unease with this aspect of the political situation has important consequences. Approval for human rights movements is clearly not absent, but countries vary greatly in this respect. The same is true of interest in politics.

An orientation towards one's home town, a province or department, a nation or the world is regarded here as a part of the domain of politics. Here localism seems to be the rule. People identify strongest with their home town and to a somewhat lesser degree with the nation. Identification with a continent or with the world plays a decidedly lesser role. This regularity is to be found in virtually all countries in the survey.

The values considered important enough to be taught to children constitute a major part of cultural heritage. These are the values to be transmitted to a new generation. A clear case of cultural unity is found in the importance attached to tolerance and respect for others. Countries tend to agree that this value is very important. They also widely concur on the relative unimportance of determination or perseverance and imagination. A social characteristic conducive to the smooth functioning of society is thus given precedence over achievement and creativeness. There is disagreement or diversity on the importance of hard work. Countries faced with the task of building up their economies tend to stress this value, countries with a fairly long history of wealth do not.

Despite the high regard in which tolerance is held, not all social groups are gladly accepted as neighbours. The resistance towards people suffering from AIDS and towards homosexuals is stronger than that towards various migrant groups. It must be noted, however, that the way some questions on this issue were formulated probably produced an unduly favourable picture of the attitude towards foreigners.

The situation in the labour market appears to be a stumbling block for the equitable treatment of foreigners. Most people feel that when jobs are scarce, the available work should be reserved for their own nationals, thus excluding foreigners from the labour market. Nationality or ethnic origin appears to be the deciding criterion, because such exclusion applies far less to the disabled. In the case of homosexuals and people with AIDS, countries disagree in their judgements, but are united in their tendency to exclude foreigners from the labour market.

Women's emancipation is generally viewed as desirable. Most countries are agreed on the idea that society favours men over women, but they also regard the social position of women as improving over time. The principle of married women being allowed to do paid work is widely accepted. Even the idea that men and women have equal rights to scarce jobs is no novelty anymore. Ideas about women's participation in paid work seem to have not yet taken definite shape, because rather traditional objections to their working outside the home are also widely voiced: the children would suffer, being a housewife could be just as fulfilling as working for pay and – to top it all – all women want is a home and children. This ambiguous cultural situation is widely prevalent. Only in a few countries are the scales tipped in favour of a clean-cut traditional or liberal viewpoint. Indecision about the desirability of women's work seems to be one more instance of cultural unity.

Liberal standpoints on marriage are fairly common among the countries. The view that it is better to be unhappily married than not to be married at all is regarded with scepticism. Sexual intercourse before marriage is only regarded as wrong by a minority in most countries. (Obviously the fact that only a few Islamic countries were represented in the research has its bearing on this finding.) The idea of divorce is accepted to a certain degree, but the level of acceptance varies widely amongst the countries. The acknowledgement that divorce is at least possible does not constitute a strange phenomenon in most societies, however. The importance of an official marriage is stressed if an unmarried couple has children or wants to have them. An idea that children ought to be protected from various potentially harmful influences could be at work here, given the strong prevalence of the opinion that children suffer discomfort if their mother is in paid work.

The objections to sexual intercourse before marriage are weak in most countries. However, approval is fairly generally withheld from sexual intercourse outside marriage or, put colloquially, 'having a bit on the side'. The idea could be that people need not marry and need not stay together forever, but that they should take the attendant responsibilities seriously if they do.

People tend to be aware of environmental problems, but these are not often amongst the ones they mention spontaneously, probably because other problems like economic ones or unemployment compete for the public's attention. Opinions are influenced by a country's wealth. Rich countries are more inclined to regard the state of their national environment as favourable than poor countries are. As rich countries have access to more effective means to combat pollution, the actual state of the environment is probably mirrored in the survey results. People are inclined to situate environmental problems at the supra-national level. They often rate the quality of their own immediate surroundings as acceptable, and locate the problems at the national level or on an even more remote geographical scale. They look to the international level for solutions. A certain diversity exists in the opinions about the environment, except in the responsibility assigned to international agencies and the belief that the environment was in a better state ten years ago.

In reviewing our inferences, we arrive at a tentative description of the world climate of public opinion, which we might also call the prevailing 'cultural mood'. In most countries, people do not seem to experience the social climate and their relationships with others as wholly favourable. When individuals look beyond the boundaries of the intimate family circle, the surrounding society is regarded with a good measure of distrust.

Some ideals seem widespread:
• the ideal of democracy, though not accompanied by a truly universal endorsement of human rights;
• the ideal of tolerance is upheld, though only partially applied to foreigners (not in the labour market) and though not encompassing all minorities, such as homosexuals;
• a localistic orientation to one's own home town or, to a lesser degree, to the nation;
• the idea of women's emancipation;
• the acceptance of paid work by married women, though traditionally perceived drawbacks are still emphasized;
• a fairly liberal view on marriage with some emphasis on marital fidelity; and

- the desire to protect children from harm.

It can be added that the environment is considered a problem, but to a far lesser degree than specialists in the field and environmentalists regard as necessary.

It could be argued that this description is rather positive in tone, and that actual behaviour in most of these areas presents a far less pretty picture. This is doubtless the case, but our view is that this is a very common constraint on the study of public opinion. Other parts of this report that deal with behaviour should furnish the reader with the necessary corrections.

As to cultural diversity, opinions are divided on the quality of material well-being, on the situation of today's world, and on the value of hard work or economic effort. On politics, diversity exists in the differing degrees of political interest and, as noted earlier, in the support for the human rights movement. The principle of divorce is accepted to varying degrees. Judgements on the present quality of the environment also differ for various countries.

Some of our results can be singled out with reference to the ideal of conviviability (Arizpe and Borofsky), one of the main themes in this report. Conviviability is seen as the ability of people to live together harmoniously notwithstanding their different identities or conceptions of the good life.

It should first be observed that conceptions of the good life are not so different as one might suppose. All over the world people want a reasonable standard of material well-being and a satisfactory family life. The quality of the place they live in – be it a city or a village – is important to them. Their basic needs are relatively simple and are directed towards the most immediate aspects of their life situation. Our data offer little support for the view that these needs are very different in different parts of the world. One supposes that meeting those needs and demands will contribute to social harmony.

Apart from these primary needs one finds that certain standards for decent social behaviour and the

idea of tolerance are broadly subscribed to. Tolerance, however, is not extended to all categories of people in all situations. In this matter there seems to exist a considerable discrepancy between ideal and practice.

Unfavourable to the ideal of conviviability is the prevalence of distrust. In our findings many people seem united in their opinion that other people are not to be trusted. Or put less strongly, that one should take some care in dealing with others. We took this to mean that societies do not universally succeed in creating conviviability. Furthermore, the political guarantee for conviviability, i.e. democracy, appears frequently to be the object of misgivings.

So that conviviability is not universally guaranteed by the state of public opinion. This desirable state of affairs may be enhanced by taking account of:
- the fulfilment and the equitable distribution of the basic conditions for well-being;
- the protection by civil society and the government of special categories of the population, e.g. foreigners;
- the prevalence of distrust and the need of confidence building measures; and
- the need to better integrate the political system of democracy into public opinion.

We would like to end our analysis with an observation on the importance of national income or wealth.[30] This factor influences people's views on economic well-being, on politics and on the present state of the environment in predictable ways. The greater the wealth, the more positive the assessments. Great accumulations of national wealth do not, however, appear to motivate economic effort. Countries faced with the task of building up their economic systems are most likely to value 'hard work'; wealthy countries do so to a far lesser degree. This finding may give rise to some caution on the future of wealthy nations or the effects of deep monetary crises on public opinion.

Appendix A (Tables 18 to 29)

TABLE 18
PERCENTAGE VERY OR SOMEWHAT SATISFIED WITH: THE WAY DEMOCRACY WORKS, THEIR PERSONAL LIFE;
PERCENTAGE VERY OR SOMEWHAT SATISFIED WITH ASPECTS OF LIFE: FAMILY LIFE, HEALTH, CLOTHING,
HOUSING, COMMUNITY, FOOD, EDUCATION, JOB, STANDARD OF LIVING (1995, 18 COUNTRIES)

Country	Democracy	Personal life	Family life	Health	Clothing	Housing	Community	Food	Education	Job	Living standard
North America											
Canada	62	86	92	90	90	91	91	94	86	76	86
United States	64	83	90	86	92	90	86	95	77	73	75
Western Europe											
France	43	64	86	79	82	83	82	87	60	69	46
Germany	55	84	89	77	92	84	76	79	79	79	83
United Kingdom	40	66	88	81	82	74	72	89	75	49	58
Iceland	54	87	92	84	77	86	82	—	60	81	60
Spain	31	41	87	69	77	77	77	77	54	56	47
Eastern Europe											
Hungary	17	21	78	55	57	63	71	65	57	53	17
Central America											
Costa Rica	52	63	—	77	78	76	78	78	60	67	62
Dominican Republic	40	52	83	73	61	59	68	60	60	57	42
Mexico	17	36	84	82	67	76	74	66	72	71	44
South America											
Chile	43	65	88	76	80	77	77	82	74	67	61
Venezuela	28	62	91	87	82	81	72	68	81	73	54
Asia											
China	—	51	45	62	21	45	37	23	27	35	22
India	32	52	77	65	78	74	67	47	65	50	46
Japan	35	60	74	69	77	62	76	79	60	55	51
Taiwan	25	42	57	51	51	49	36	44	32	35	29
Thailand	54	80	81	80	88	81	76	81	63	76	72
MEAN	41	61	81	75	74	74	72	71	63	62	53
STD. DEV.	14.6	18.8	12.8	10.9	17.5	13.2	14.3	19.2	15.5	14.2	19.1

Source: *People's Satisfaction with Their Lives and Government* (International Gallup Poll Report, 1995).

TABLE 19(A)
PERCENTAGE[1] BELIEVING THAT MOST PEOPLE CAN BE TRUSTED; PERCENTAGE SATISFIED (6–10) WITH: HOME LIFE, LIFE AS A WHOLE, FINANCIAL SITUATION; PERCENTAGE DESCRIBING THEIR HEALTH AS GOOD OR VERY GOOD (1990–93, 42 COUNTRIES)

Country	Trust in people	Home life satisfaction	Life satisfaction	Financial satisfaction	Good health
North America					
Canada	51	93	90	79	80
United States	49	91	87	73	79
Western Europe					
France	21	82	72	56	66
Great Britain	42	89	84	66	75
West Germany	31	83	80	73	56
Italy	35	87	83	81	60
Netherlands	52	95	93	85	74
Denmark	56	94	90	75	78
Belgium	31	91	87	81	72
Spain	32	87	80	65	56
Ireland	47	94	88	72	82
Northern Ireland	43	96	91	73	77
Norway	61	91	87	69	75
Sweden	60	93	89	72	80
Iceland	42	91	91	63	74
Finland	60	86	86	72	76
Portugal	21	88	77	58	44
Austria	28	63	72	70	62
Switzerland	27	92	92	88	81
Eastern Europe					
Hungary	24	80	56	40	31
Poland	31	90	70	41	38
Czechoslovakia (ex-)	28	78	64	40	44
East Germany	22	82	73	57	55
Bulgaria	29	61	40	27	51
Slovenia	16	77	62	33	43
Romania	16	73	57	41	47
Lithuania	31	61	54	–	43
Latvia	19	54	51	29	32
Estonia	28	61	60	42	36
Belarus	25	64	46	38	27
Russia	36	65	43	38	26
Central America					
Mexico	30	84	82	65	69
South America					
Chile	22	89	81	55	54
Brazil	7	86	75	47	69
Argentina	23	84	79	48	60

TABLE 19(A) – *cont.*

Country	Trust in people	Home life satisfaction	Life satisfaction	Financial satisfaction	Good health
Asia					
China	60	85	78	61	59
India	31	65	55	52	50
Japan	38	82	75	64	44
Republic of Korea	34	76	71	54	–
Turkey	10	65	60	35	60
Africa					
South Africa	27	67	60	43	68
Nigeria	21	77	65	47	80
MEAN	33	81	73	58	59
STD. DEV.	14.0	11.7	14.8	16.6	16.8

1. Including people who did not answer or without opinion.

Source: *World Values Survey 1990–1993.*

TABLE 19(B)
PERCENTAGE BELIEVING THAT MOST PEOPLE CAN BE TRUSTED; PERCENTAGE SATISFIED WITH HOME LIFE,
LIFE AS A WHOLE AND THE FINANCIAL SITUATION; PERCENTAGE DESCRIBING THEIR HEALTH AS
GOOD OR VERY GOOD (1990–93, 6 GEOGRAPHICAL REGIONS)

Geographical region	Trust in people	Home life satisfaction	Life satisfaction	Financial satisfaction	Good health
North America	50	92	89	76	80
Western Europe	41	88	85	72	70
Eastern Europe	25	71	56	39	39
Central and South America	21	86	79	54	63
Asia	35	75	68	53	53
Africa	24	72	63	45	74
Means are equal[1]	no	no	no	no	no

1. One-way analysis of variance with country as unit of analysis (f<.05, ranges = btukey).

Source: *World Values Survey 1990–1993.*

TABLE 20
HOW IS THE WORLD YOU LIVE IN TODAY COMPARED TO THE WORLD YOUR PARENTS GREW UP IN?;
HOW IS THE WORLD THE NEXT GENERATION WILL LIVE IN COMPARED TO THE WORLD YOU LIVE IN TODAY?
(1995, 17 COUNTRIES)

Country	Better	Same	World today worse	Diff.[1]	Better	Same	World future worse	Diff.[1]
North America								
Canada	35	16	46	−11	16	15	64	−48
United States	35	10	52	−17	23	14	60	−37
Western Europe								
France	43	16	40	3	21	21	56	−35
Germany	46	24	25	21	9	17	70	−61
United Kingdom	36	9	45	−9	13	13	63	−50
Iceland	43	28	24	19	20	42	31	−11
Spain	66	10	18	48	32	10	39	−7
Eastern Europe								
Hungary	44	17	34	10	22	14	48	−26
Central America								
Costa Rica	28	18	50	−22	15	15	64	−49
Dominican Republic	48	4	43	5	24	4	60	−36
Mexico	27	19	49	−22	19	14	59	−40
South America								
Chile	44	15	37	7	31	14	50	−19
Venezuela	16	8	74	−58	10	6	78	−68
Asia								
India	51	17	30	21	44	12	32	12
Japan	60	13	23	37	15	22	58	−43
Taiwan	78	8	10	68	46	9	21	25
Thailand	39	4	52	−13	46	3	37	9
MEAN	43	14	38		24	14	52	
STD. DEV.	14.9	6.6	15.7		12.0	8.8	15.5	

1. Diff. = % better − % worse.

Source: *People's Satisfaction with Their Lives and Government* (International Gallup Poll Report, 1995).

TABLE 21(A)
PERCENTAGE CONSIDERING ELEVEN QUALITIES ESPECIALLY IMPORTANT TO TEACH CHILDREN AT HOME
(1990–93, 40 COUNTRIES)

Country	Good manners	Respon-sibility	Toler-ance	Indepen-dence	Hard work	Thrift	Deter-mination	Obe-dience	Unself-ishness	Religious faith	Imagi-nation
North America											
Canada	75	75	80	44	35	21	38	28	42	31	23
United States	78	71	72	53	49	28	36	38	37	54	27
Western Europe											
France	53	72	78	27	53	36	39	53	40	13	23
Great Britain	89	48	79	43	29	26	31	39	57	19	18
West Germany	67	85	77	73	15	45	49	22	8	20	32
Italy	74	84	69	34	23	25	31	30	42	36	18
Netherlands	80	85	86	50	15	28	31	32	23	14	22
Denmark	66	86	81	81	2	19	30	20	50	9	37
Belgium	72	72	69	36	36	36	39	37	28	16	18
Spain	81	77	73	36	39	22	22	43	8	25	37
Ireland	75	61	76	43	28	22	26	35	53	57	14
Northern Ireland	95	38	80	37	29	25	18	56	49	44	14
Norway	77	90	64	86	7	22	33	31	10	14	31
Sweden	78	89	91	36	5	48	33	25	29	6	40
Finland	82	83	79	57	6	38	38	25	21	13	26
Portugal	82	77	69	24	67	31	23	45	28	26	20
Austria	78	85	66	63	14	55	39	25	7	23	24
Switzerland	59	77	77	42	36	42	0	20	37	24	30
Eastern Europe											
Hungary	77	66	62	70	70	49	12	45	26	24	9
Czechoslovakia (ex-)	86	65	64	21	85	48	42	28	38	15	7
East Germany	67	84	74	67	16	58	54	24	9	16	28
Bulgaria	72	68	52	62	91	39	41	19	22	11	16
Slovenia	89	71	75	33	32	58	42	40	33	21	10
Romania	92	56	56	24	71	37	40	20	20	43	17
Lithuania	35	72	57	81	92	37	34	25	33	21	6
Latvia	53	75	70	73	91	46	40	15	16	9	11
Estonia	74	76	70	43	92	35	51	19	25	3	13
Belarus	71	82	80	31	80	53	40	23	27	6	7
Russia	56	69	70	28	93	63	40	29	25	8	11
Central America											
Mexico	73	77	64	47	23	33	37	45	11	40	31
South America											
Chile	90	88	79	31	12	29	31	52	8	54	32
Brazil	77	72	66	27	52	29	26	41	28	46	12
Argentina	78	80	78	43	53	15	29	32	5	28	31

TABLE 21(A) – *cont.*

Country	Good manners	Respon- sibility	Toler- ance	Indepen- dence	Hard work	Thrift	Deter- mination	Obe- dience	Unself- ishness	Religious faith	Imagi- nation
Asia											
China	52	67	63	86	60	51	50	10	30	2	29
India	94	58	56	30	66	29	21	58	30	38	21
Japan	83	84	60	65	31	40	59	10	44	7	24
Republic of Korea	93	91	55	54	64	53	31	18	11	19	6
Turkey	92	66	69	19	73	36	20	31	28	44	23
Africa											
South Africa	81	45	61	16	30	17	28	42	20	50	8
Nigeria	98	33	76	16	79	7	20	75	19	77	4
MEAN	76	73	71	46	46	36	34	33	27	26	20
STD. DEV.	13.5	13.9	9.1	20.2	28.8	13.4	11.6	14.0	13.8	17.6	9.8

Source: *World Values Survey 1990–1993*.

TABLE 21(B)
PERCENTAGE CONSIDERING ELEVEN QUALITIES ESPECIALLY IMPORTANT TO TEACH CHILDREN AT HOME (1990–93, 6 GEOGRAPHICAL REGIONS)

Geographical region	Good manners	Respon- sibility	Toler- ance	Indepen- dence	Hard work	Thrift	Deter- mination	Obe- dience	Unself- ishness	Religious faith	Imagi- nation
North America	77	73	76	49	42	25	37	33	40	43	25
Western Europe	76	76	76	48	25	33	30	34	31	22	25
Eastern Europe	70	71	66	48	74	48	40	26	25	16	12
Central and South America	80	79	72	37	35	27	31	43	13	42	27
Asia	83	73	61	51	59	42	36	25	29	22	21
Africa	90	39	69	16	55	12	24	59	20	64	6
Means are equal[1]	yes	no	no	yes	no	no	yes	no	yes	no	no

1. One-way analysis of variance with country as unit of analysis (f<.05, ranges = btukey).

Source: *World Values Survey 1990–1993*.

TABLE 21(C)
PERCENTAGE CONSIDERING ELEVEN QUALITIES ESPECIALLY IMPORTANT TO TEACH CHILDREN AT HOME (BY GENDER 1990–93, 6 GEOGRAPHICAL REGIONS)

Geographical region	Good manners	Respon-sibility	Toler-ance	Indepen-dence	Hard work	Thrift	Deter-mination	Obe-dience	Unself-ishness	Religious faith	Imagi-nation
North America											
Men	77	70	75	44	48	26	37	32	40	40	26
Women	76	76	77	52	36	24	36	34	40	45	24
V	.01	.06	.03	.08	.12	.03	.02	.01	.00	.05	.02
Western Europe											
Men	74	76	74	47	28	32	33	33	30	19	27
Women	77	75	77	49	23	33	28	35	31	25	24
V	.03	.00	.05	.02	.06	.01	.05	.02	.02	.07	.03
Eastern Europe											
Men	68	71	64	51	74	46	44	25	24	14	15
Women	72	72	69	46	74	49	36	27	25	18	11
V	.04	.01	.05	.05	.00	.04	.08	.02	.01	.05	.06
Central and South America											
Men	80	79	70	36	36	28	33	41	13	38	29
Women	80	80	73	38	34	25	29	44	13	47	24
V	.00	.02	.03	.02	.02	.04	.05	.03	.01	.09	.06
Asia											
Men	81	75	60	54	59	41	37	24	28	20	21
Women	84	71	61	48	58	43	35	27	29	24	20
V	.04	.05	.01	.05	.01	.01	.02	.04	.02	.04	.01
Africa											
Men	90	39	69	16	59	13	24	63	18	58	6
Women	88	38	69	16	49	11	24	54	21	68	6
V	.04	.02	.01	.00	.11	.02	.00	.10	.03	.10	.01

Source: *World Values Survey 1990–1993.*

TABLE 22(A)
PERCENTAGE[1] STRONGLY APPROVING THE HUMAN RIGHTS MOVEMENT; PERCENTAGE VERY AND SOMEWHAT INTERESTED IN POLITICS; GEOGRAPHIC REGION WITH WHICH ONE IDENTIFIES (1990–93, 42 COUNTRIES)

Country	Human rights movement	Political interest	Identification				
			Town	Province	Country[2]	Continent[3]	World
North America							
Canada	56	58	31	16	40	3	10
United States	49	60	38	12	30	4	17
Western Europe							
France	60	38	41	14	28	8	10
Great Britain	40	49	40	17	32	3	10
West Germany	50	69	35	30	14	5	6
Italy	66	34	38	10	27	7	18
Netherlands	57	62	42	8	35	5	9
Denmark	49	54	52	22	22	2	2
Belgium	51	30	47	14	22	7	10
Spain	68	25	45	17	30	1	7
Ireland	62	37	44	14	37	3	3
Northern Ireland	30	34	48	23	22	1	6
Norway	64	72	69	13	14	1	2
Sweden	57	47	56	13	25	3	3
Iceland	64	47	41	6	48	1	5
Finland	52	48	33	12	41	5	9
Portugal	77	31	40	19	27	4	10
Austria	53	54	35	32	27	4	3
Switzerland	58	66	51	20	17	4	8
Eastern Europe							
Hungary	60	52	58	6	27	6	3
Poland	72	49	29	12	52	4	2
Czechoslovakia (ex-)	61	—	32	24	32	6	7
East Germany	63	85	25	27	9	5	4
Bulgaria	76	73	51	9	30	4	7
Slovenia	67	58	46	9	42	2	2
Romania	71	18	48	15	32	2	3
Lithuania	34	74	25	66	3	1	4
Latvia	41	79	34	55	6	1	4
Estonia	21	60	31	56	8	1	3
Belarus	76	—	52	30	12	1	5
Russia	66	53	31	22	11	16	19
Central America							
Mexico	60	38	38	16	28	8	10
South America							
Chile	74	37	33	15	40	5	8
Brazil	83	46	37	11	30	2	20
Argentina	64	30	28	3	58	1	10

TABLE 22(A) – *cont.*

Country	Human rights movement	Political interest	Identification				
			Town	Province	Country[2]	Continent[3]	World
Asia							
China	23	63	41	16	39	2	3
India	36	31	47	16	30	1	6
Japan	39	62	36	18	43	1	2
Republic of Korea	71	73	18	24	58	—	—
Turkey	57	48	34	12	46	1	8
Africa							
South Africa	68	57	38	18	33	7	5
Nigeria	83	33	40	12	31	9	8
MEAN	58	51	40	19	29	4	7
STD. DEV.	15.1	16.2	9.9	13.0	13.3	3.0	4.7

1. Including people who did not answer or without an opinion.
2. In Russia, 'country' referred to Russia as a whole whereas 'the continent' referred to Europe (instead of Europe, 1% identified with the Soviet Union as a whole).
3. In Chile and Brazil 'the continent' referred to Latin America, in Argentina 'the continent' referred to Europe.

Source: *World Values Survey 1990–1993*.

TABLE 22(B)
PERCENTAGE STRONGLY APPROVING THE HUMAN RIGHTS MOVEMENT; PERCENTAGE INTERESTED IN POLITICS;
PERCENTAGE IDENTIFYING WITH HOME TOWN, PROVINCE OR COUNTRY
(1990–93, 6 GEOGRAPHICAL REGIONS)

Geographical region	Human rights movement	Political interest	Identification		
			Town	Province	Country
North America	53	59	35	14	35
Western Europe	56	47	45	17	28
Eastern Europe	59	60	39	28	22
Central and South America	70	38	34	11	39
Asia	45	55	35	17	43
Africa	76	45	39	15	32
Means are equal[1]	yes	yes	yes	yes	no

1. One-way analysis of variance with country as unit of analysis (f<.05, ranges = btukey).

Source: *World Values Survey 1990–1993*.

TABLE 22(c)
PERCENTAGE STRONGLY APPROVING THE HUMAN RIGHTS MOVEMENT BY EDUCATION (1990–93, 6 GEOGRAPHICAL REGIONS)

Geographical region	Low education	Middle education	High education	Cramer's V
North America	45	50	59	.10
Western Europe	54	53	62	.08
Eastern Europe	58	60	58	.02
Central and South America	71	68	71	.02
Asia	40	36	49	.11
Africa	73	79	73	.07

Source: *World Values Survey 1990–1993.*

TABLE 23(A)
RANK ORDER ON 'INTOLERANCE SCALE'[1]; PERCENTAGE NOT WANTING THE FOLLOWING GROUPS OF PEOPLE AS NEIGHBOURS: PEOPLE OF A DIFFERENT RACE, IMMIGRANTS/FOREIGN WORKERS, PEOPLE WHO HAVE AIDS, HOMOSEXUALS; PERCENTAGE AGREEING THAT SCARCE JOBS SHOULD BE GIVEN TO AUTOCHTHONS OVER IMMIGRANTS; PERCENTAGE[2] AGREEING THAT IT IS UNFAIR TO GIVE WORK TO HANDICAPPED PEOPLE WHEN ABLE-BODIED PEOPLE CANNOT FIND JOBS (1990–93, 42 COUNTRIES)

Country	Rank order intolerance	Neighbour				Jobs autochthons	Jobs disabled
		Race	Immigrant	AIDS	Homosexual		
North America							
Canada	34	5	6	21	30	53	8
United States	32	10	10	28	38	52	10
Western Europe							
France	33	9	13	15	24	63	9
Great Britain	35	9	12	23	31	51	7
West Germany	25	10	16	29	34	62	14
Italy	22	10	12	39	33	68	17
Netherlands	38	7	8	14	10	32	11
Denmark	37	7	12	9	12	53	8
Belgium	24	17	21	24	24	65	15
Spain	18	10	9	35	30	77	20
Ireland	27	6	5	35	33	69	9
Northern Ireland	31	7	7	28	48	62	6
Norway	36	12	16	25	20	59	6
Sweden	39	7	9	18	18	35	5
Iceland	28	8	8	18	20	87	5
Finland	30	25	5	24	25	71	5
Portugal	15	15	10	44	50	88	23
Austria	20	8	20	32	43	77	16
Switzerland	—	2	2	—	—	—	—
Eastern Europe							
Hungary	13	23	22	66	75	87	23
Poland	—	—	—	—	—	67	38
Czechoslovakia (ex-)	7	31	34	64	59	88	30
East Germany	23	12	19	20	34	69	15
Bulgaria	2	39	34	63	68	87	41
Slovenia	6	40	40	41	43	79	35
Romania	3	28	30	66	75	75	37
Lithuania	1	20	15	78	87	92	52
Latvia	12	13	31	65	78	80	27
Estonia	14	19	17	63	73	82	25
Belarus	9	17	17	73	79	56	37
Russia	5	10	11	69	82	63	39
Central America							
Mexico	16	17	18	57	60	83	22
South America							
Chile	17	11	12	41	58	83	21
Brazil	19	5	4	24	30	82	19
Argentina	29	3	2	32	39	60	10

TABLE 23(A) – *cont.*

Country	Rank order intolerance	Neighbour				Jobs autochthons	Jobs disabled
		Race	Immigrant	AIDS	Homosexual		
Asia							
China	11	13	13	78	74	62	34
India	8	44	48	93	91	85	22
Japan	26	11	17	77	69	65	6
Republic of Korea	21	58	53	4	4	72	14
Turkey	10	34	28	89	92	75	25
Africa							
South Africa	—	—	—	—	—	74	22
Nigeria	4	34	28	76	73	80	34
MEAN		17	17	44	48	70	20
STD. DEV.		12.8	12.1	24.7	25.2	14.1	12.2

1. Factor scale; combination of 'neighbour: race', 'neighbour: homosexual', 'jobs autochthons', 'jobs disabled'.
2. Including people who did not answer or without an opinion.

Source: *World Values Survey 1990–1993.*

TABLE 23(B)
PERCENTAGE NOT WANTING THE FOLLOWING GROUPS OF PEOPLE AS NEIGHBOURS: PEOPLE OF A DIFFERENT RACE, IMMIGRANTS/FOREIGN WORKERS, PEOPLE WHO HAVE AIDS, HOMOSEXUALS; PERCENTAGE AGREEING THAT SCARCE JOBS SHOULD BE GIVEN TO AUTOCHTHONS OVER IMMIGRANTS; PERCENTAGE AGREEING THAT IT IS UNFAIR TO GIVE WORK TO HANDICAPPED PEOPLE WHEN ABLE-BODIED PEOPLE CANNOT FIND JOBS (1990–93, 6 GEOGRAPHICAL REGIONS)

Geographical region	Neighbour				Jobs autochthons	Jobs disabled
	Race	Immigrant	AIDS	Homosexual		
North America	8	8	25	34	53	9
Western Europe	10	11	26	28	64	11
Eastern Europe	23	25	61	68	77	33
Central and South America	9	9	39	47	77	18
Asia	32	32	68	66	71	20
Africa	34	28	76	73	77	28
Means are equal[1]	no	no	no	no	no	no

1. One-way analysis of variance with country as unit of analysis (f<.05, ranges = btukey).

Source: *World Values Survey 1990–1993.*

TABLE 23(c)
PERCENTAGE NOT WANTING PEOPLE OF A DIFFERENT RACE OR HOMOSEXUALS AS NEIGHBOURS; PERCENTAGE AGREEING THAT SCARCE JOBS SHOULD BE GIVEN TO AUTOCHTHONS OVER IMMIGRANTS; PERCENTAGE AGREEING THAT IT IS UNFAIR TO GIVE WORK TO HANDICAPPED PEOPLE WHEN ABLE-BODIED PEOPLE CANNOT FIND JOBS (BY AGE, 1990–93, 6 GEOGRAPHICAL REGIONS)

Geographical region	Neighbour race	Neighbour homosexual	Jobs autochthons	Jobs disabled
North America				
18–30	7	35	49	8
31–55	6	30	51	8
>55	9	40	58	12
V	.04	.09	.07	.07
Western Europe				
18–30	7	21	58	9
31–55	9	25	61	9
>55	15	40	74	17
V	.11	.17	.13	.11
Eastern Europe				
18–30	20	66	75	32
31–55	22	69	76	32
>55	28	70	81	37
V	.07	.04	.06	.05
Central and South America				
18–30	9	43	77	17
31–55	8	47	77	17
>55	10	54	75	21
V	.02	.08	.02	.04
Asia				
18–30	30	65	68	21
31–55	32	64	74	20
>55	34	73	75	19
V	.03	.07	.07	.02
Africa				
18–30	36	77	77	32
31–55	32	66	78	25
>55	19	78	72	19
V	.09	.12	.04	.09

Source: *World Values Survey 1990–1993.*

TABLE 24
PERCENTAGE SHARING THE OPINION THAT SOCIETY FAVOURS WOMEN OVER MEN, MEN OVER WOMEN
OR MEN AND WOMEN EQUALLY; PERCENTAGE THINKING THAT THE POSITION OF WOMEN HAS IMPROVED
IN THE PAST FIVE YEARS (1995, 22 COUNTRIES)

Country	Women > men	Society favours both sexes equally	Men > women	Improved position
North America				
Canada	7	24	65	70
United States	7	18	73	70
Western Europe				
France	2	23	74	60
Germany	4	16	76	68
United Kingdom	5	18	72	68
Iceland	4	16	76	51
Spain	7	25	64	77
Eastern Europe				
Hungary	11	39	43	18
Estonia	7	38	43	18
Latvia	4	44	33	10
Lithuania	7	38	48	12
Central America				
Honduras	8	57	26	56
Panama	13	51	35	62
El Salvador	11	63	22	55
Mexico	10	38	50	77
South America				
Chile	17	16	64	71
Colombia	12	32	54	78
Asia				
China	4	53	40	77
India	31	38	29	72
Japan	8	10	78	74
Taiwan	3	42	50	79
Thailand	7	52	42	89
MEAN	9	34	53	60
STD. DEV.	6.2	15.4	18.0	23.5

Source: *Gender and Society: Status and Stereotypes* (International Gallup Poll Report, 1996).

TABLE 25(A)
PERCENTAGE AGREEING THAT MEN HAVE MORE RIGHT TO SCARCE JOBS THAN WOMEN; PERCENTAGE AGREEING (STRONGLY AGREE + AGREE) THAT: PRE-SCHOOL CHILDREN WILL SUFFER IF THEIR MOTHERS ARE WORKING, WHAT MOST WOMEN REALLY WANT IS A HOME AND CHILDREN[1], BEING A HOUSEWIFE IS JUST AS FULFILLING AS WORKING FOR PAY[1], THAT BOTH THE HUSBAND AND WIFE SHOULD CONTRIBUTE TO HOUSEHOLD INCOME[1] (1990–93, 41 COUNTRIES)

Country	Scarce jobs to men	Children will suffer	Women want home	Housewife is fulfilling	Both contribute to income
North America					
Canada	19	53	40	66	66
United States	23	51	50	69	65
Western Europe					
France	33	65	61	53	77
Great Britain	34	55	42	54	67
West Germany	31	84	42	45	55
Italy	35	75	60	47	77
Netherlands	23	61	35	48	29
Denmark	11	32	23	49	67
Belgium	38	61	53	57	62
Spain	31	56	50	53	76
Ireland	36	53	56	69	68
Northern Ireland	34	44	51	67	81
Norway	16	46	46	50	72
Sweden	8	74	—	52	85
Iceland	6	52	67	65	66
Finland	15	52	37	47	72
Portugal	34	84	59	46	96
Austria	50	83	54	57	66
Eastern Europe					
Hungary	42	70	72	71	80
Poland	55	—	—	—	—
Czechoslovakia (ex-)	55	78	93	39	87
East Germany	31	79	45	31	84
Bulgaria	46	76	85	83	80
Slovenia	29	67	70	55	91
Romania	42	58	78	45	88
Lithuania	66	90	93	81	71
Latvia	34	92	82	56	69
Estonia	45	91	80	67	77
Belarus	38	81	78	79	81
Russia	42	69	86	82	78
Central America					
Mexico	23	78	59	64	80

TABLE 25(A) – *cont.*

Country	Scarce jobs to men	Children will suffer	Women want home	Housewife is fulfilling	Both contribute to income
South America					
Chile	37	82	75	71	86
Brazil	38	75	71	59	93
Argentina	24	78	69	55	75
Asia					
China	37	62	75	83	93
India	54	95	89	42	74
Japan	34	70	65	63	31
Republic of Korea	42	72	70	66	59
Turkey	51	85	84	74	81
Africa					
South Africa	45	—	—	—	—
Nigeria	47	53	85	50	93
MEAN	35	69	64	59	74
STD. DEV.	13.3	15.1	17.9	13.1	14.5

1. Including people who did not answer or without an opinion.

Source: *World Values Survey 1990–1993.*

TABLE 25(B)
PERCENTAGE AGREEING THAT MEN HAVE MORE RIGHT TO SCARCE JOBS THAN WOMEN; PERCENTAGE AGREEING THAT: PRE-SCHOOL CHILDREN WILL SUFFER IF THEIR MOTHERS ARE WORKING, WHAT MOST WOMEN REALLY WANT IS A HOME AND CHILDREN, BEING A HOUSEWIFE IS JUST AS FULFILLING AS WORKING FOR PAY, THAT BOTH THE HUSBAND AND WIFE SHOULD CONTRIBUTE TO HOUSEHOLD INCOME (1990–93, 6 GEOGRAPHICAL REGIONS)

Geographical region	Scarce jobs to men	Children will suffer	Women want home	Housewife is fulfilling	Both contribute to income
North America	21	52	45	68	66
Western Europe	27	61	49	54	70
Eastern Europe	44	77	78	63	80
Central and South America	31	78	68	62	84
Asia	44	77	77	66	68
Africa	46	53	85	50	93
Means are equal[1]	no	no	no	yes	yes

1. One-way analysis of variance with country as unit of analysis (f<.05, ranges = btukey).

Source: *World Values Survey 1990–1993.*

TABLE 25(C)
PERCENTAGE AGREEING THAT MEN HAVE MORE RIGHT TO SCARCE JOBS THAN WOMEN; PERCENTAGE
AGREEING THAT: PRE-SCHOOL CHILDREN WILL SUFFER IF THEIR MOTHERS ARE WORKING, WHAT MOST
WOMEN REALLY WANT IS A HOME AND CHILDREN, BEING A HOUSEWIFE IS JUST AS FULFILLING AS WORKING
FOR PAY, THAT BOTH THE HUSBAND AND WIFE SHOULD CONTRIBUTE TO HOUSEHOLD INCOME
(BY GENDER, 1990–93, 6 GEOGRAPHICAL REGIONS)

Geographical region	Scarce jobs to men	Children will suffer	Women want home	Housewife is fulfilling	Both contribute to income
North America					
Men	21	57	44	64	64
Women	21	47	45	71	67
V	.01	.10	.01	.07	.04
Western Europe					
Men	27	65	50	52	68
Women	27	57	49	55	71
V	.01	.09	.01	.03	.03
Eastern Europe					
Men	48	77	79	65	79
Women	40	78	78	61	82
V	.08	.02	.01	.04	.04
Central and South America					
Men	33	79	71	64	80
Women	28	77	66	61	87
V	.05	.02	.05	.03	.10
Asia					
Men	49	77	76	68	66
Women	39	77	76	64	69
V	.10	.01	.00	.04	.04
Africa					
Men	52	58	87	47	95
Women	39	47	83	53	91
V	.14	.10	.06	.06	.07

Source: *World Values Survey 1990–1993.*

TABLE 26(A)
PERCENTAGE AGREEING (STRONGLY AGREE + AGREE) THAT: THE MAIN ADVANTAGE OF MARRIAGE IS
FINANCIAL SECURITY[1], THE MAIN PURPOSE OF MARRIAGE IS TO HAVE CHILDREN[1], IT IS BETTER TO HAVE A
BAD MARRIAGE THAN NO MARRIAGE AT ALL, PEOPLE WHO WANT CHILDREN OUGHT TO GET MARRIED,
PARENTS SHOULD STAY TOGETHER IF THEY HAVE CHILDREN[1], A MARRIED COUPLE SHOULD ALSO STAY
TOGETHER IF THERE ARE NO CHILDREN[1] (1994, 24 COUNTRIES)

Country	Marriage financial security	Marriage to have children	Bad marriage over no marriage	Marriage if children	Stay together if children	Always stay together
North America						
Canada	9	12	3	49	10	4
United States	17	13	3	73	14	7
Western Europe						
Great Britain	21	17	2	58	21	5
West Germany	37	23	3	64	20	7
Italy	18	39	5	61	39	11
Netherlands	16	14	2	32	10	4
Spain	32	34	15	52	29	11
Ireland	25	28	7	72	34	10
Northern Ireland	20	20	3	71	25	9
Norway	20	24	2	55	23	6
Sweden	22	12	4	40	20	4
Austria	43	27	5	58	23	8
Eastern Europe						
Hungary	48	66	11	55	28	8
Poland	37	45	11	77	59	23
Czech Republic	35	55	6	71	30	5
East Germany	44	19	2	45	16	4
Bulgaria	50	71	30	77	—	14
Slovenia	34	47	8	40	25	6
Russia	52	55	13	53	27	8
Asia						
Japan	41	18	10	62	57	29
Philippines	52	74	32	83	44	34
Middle East						
Israel	26	49	12	74	27	8
Oceania						
Australia	16	22	3	71	21	5
New Zealand	15	12	2	60	13	4
MEAN	30	33	8	61	27	10
STD. DEV.	13.3	19.9	8.1	13.3	13.0	7.9

1. Including people who did not answer or who couldn't choose/didn't know.

Source: ISSP, 1994.

TABLE 26(b)

PERCENTAGE AGREEING THAT: THE MAIN ADVANTAGE OF MARRIAGE IS FINANCIAL SECURITY, THE MAIN PURPOSE OF MARRIAGE IS TO HAVE CHILDREN, IT IS BETTER TO HAVE A BAD MARRIAGE THAN NO MARRIAGE AT ALL, PEOPLE WHO WANT CHILDREN OUGHT TO GET MARRIED, PARENTS SHOULD STAY TOGETHER IF THEY HAVE CHILDREN, A MARRIED COUPLE SHOULD ALSO STAY TOGETHER IF THERE ARE NO CHILDREN (1994, 6 GEOGRAPHICAL REGIONS)

Geographical region	Marriage financial security	Marriage to have children	Bad marriage over no marriage	Marriage if children	Stay together if children	Always stay together
North America	13	13	3	61	12	6
Western Europe	25	24	5	56	24	8
Eastern Europe	43	51	12	60	31	10
Asia	47	46	21	73	51	32
Middle East	26	49	12	74	27	8
Oceania	16	17	3	66	17	5
Means are equal[1]	no	no	yes	yes	no	no

1. One-way analysis of variance with country as unit of analysis (f<.05, ranges = btukey).

Source: ISSP, 1994.

TABLE 26(C)
PERCENTAGE AGREEING THAT: THE MAIN ADVANTAGE OF MARRIAGE IS FINANCIAL SECURITY, THE MAIN
PURPOSE OF MARRIAGE IS TO HAVE CHILDREN, IT IS BETTER TO HAVE A BAD MARRIAGE THAN NO MARRIAGE
AT ALL, PEOPLE WHO WANT CHILDREN OUGHT TO GET MARRIED, PARENTS SHOULD STAY TOGETHER IF THEY
HAVE CHILDREN, A MARRIED COUPLE SHOULD ALSO STAY TOGETHER IF THERE ARE NO CHILDREN
(BY AGE, 1994, 6 GEOGRAPHICAL REGIONS)

Geographical region	Marriage financial security	Marriage to have children	Bad marriage over no marriage	Marriage if children	Stay together if children	Always stay together
North America						
15–30	13	10	3	42	10	6
31–55	11	12	2	59	10	5
>55	16	17	6	82	17	8
V	.06	.08	.10	.29	.09	.07
Western Europe						
15–30	17	15	3	37	15	5
31–55	21	20	4	52	21	6
>55	40	38	8	83	40	13
V	.21	.21	.09	.34	.23	.12
Eastern Europe						
15–30	30	39	7	45	25	7
31–55	41	50	10	55	26	8
>55	57	63	18	80	45	16
V	.20	.18	.14	.27	.18	.13
Asia						
15–30	42	46	21	68	46	28
31–55	43	46	21	71	46	28
>55	59	47	25	83	67	43
V	.14	.01	.04	.13	.17	.13
Middle East						
15–30	19	47	9	69	21	7
31–55	29	47	12	76	26	7
>55	29	59	17	80	39	12
V	.10	.10	.09	.09	.14	.07
Oceania						
15–30	10	9	1	41	8	4
31–55	11	14	2	61	12	3
>55	26	27	4	86	30	7
V	.20	.18	.09	.33	.24	.07

Source: ISSP, 1994.

TABLE 27(A)
PERCENTAGE THINKING[1] IT IS WRONG (ALWAYS WRONG + ALMOST ALWAYS WRONG) IF: A MAN AND
WOMAN HAVE SEXUAL RELATIONS BEFORE MARRIAGE, A MAN AND WOMAN HAVE SEXUAL RELATIONS IN
THEIR EARLY TEENS, A MARRIED PERSON HAS SEXUAL RELATIONS WITH OTHER PEOPLE, TWO ADULTS OF THE
SAME SEX HAVE SEXUAL RELATIONS (1994, 24 COUNTRIES)

Country	No sex before marriage	No sex in early teens	No extramarital affairs	No homosexual relations
North America				
Canada	18	66	81	37
United States	37	84	92	67
Western Europe				
Great Britain	14	82	87	54
West Germany	6	47	72	39
Italy	25	76	78	67
Netherlands	9	67	86	20
Spain	27	73	86	48
Ireland	39	90	88	62
Northern Ireland	35	90	91	76
Norway	10	75	93	44
Sweden	5	52	90	50
Austria	12	65	88	58
Eastern Europe				
Hungary	26	62	80	86
Poland	23	82	82	74
Czech Republic	11	77	67	34
East Germany	3	39	75	43
Bulgaria	31	74	61	70
Slovenia	5	62	73	61
Russia	26	68	55	57
Asia				
Japan	38	86	85	76
Philippines	77	92	98	93
Middle East				
Israel	25	78	87	61
Oceania				
Australia	21	79	82	59
New Zealand	22	84	90	53
MEAN	23	73	82	58
STD. DEV.	16.0	13.7	10.4	17.1

1. Including people who couldn't choose/didn't know.

Source: ISSP, 1994.

TABLE 27(B)
PERCENTAGE THINKING IT IS WRONG IF: A MAN AND WOMAN HAVE SEXUAL RELATIONS BEFORE MARRIAGE,
A MAN AND WOMAN HAVE SEXUAL RELATIONS IN THEIR EARLY TEENS, A MARRIED PERSON HAS SEXUAL
RELATIONS WITH OTHER PEOPLE, TWO ADULTS OF THE SAME SEX HAVE SEXUAL RELATIONS
(1994, 6 GEOGRAPHICAL REGIONS)

Geographical region	No sex before marriage	No sex in early teens	No extramarital affairs	No homosexual relations
North America	28	75	87	52
Western Europe	18	72	86	52
Eastern Europe	18	66	70	61
Asia	58	89	92	85
Middle East	25	78	87	61
Oceania	22	82	86	56
Means are equal[1]	no	yes	no	yes

1. One-way analysis of variance with country as unit of analysis (f<.05, ranges = btukey).

Source: ISSP, 1994.

TABLE 28(A)
PERCENTAGE MENTIONING THE ENVIRONMENT AS A MOST IMPORTANT PROBLEM; PERCENTAGE CONSIDERING
ENVIRONMENTAL PROBLEMS IN THEIR COUNTRY AS VERY SERIOUS; PERCENTAGE RATING THE QUALITY
OF THE ENVIRONMENT IN THE LOCAL COMMUNITY, THE NATION AND THE WORLD AS VERY OR FAIRLY BAD;
PERCENTAGE STRONGLY OR SOMEWHAT FAVOURING THE GOVERNMENT CONTRIBUTING MONEY TO AN
INTERNATIONAL AGENCY TO WORK ON SOLVING GLOBAL ENVIRONMENTAL PROBLEMS; PERCENTAGE
STRONGLY OR SOMEWHAT FAVOURING AN INTERNATIONAL AGENCY HAVING THE AUTHORITY TO INFLUENCE
THE GOVERNMENT'S POLICY IN ENVIRONMENTALLY IMPORTANT AREAS (1992, 24 COUNTRIES)

Country	Environment important problem	Environment very serious problem	Bad quality			Money to international agency	Authority to international agency
			Comm.	Nation	World		
North America							
Canada	10	53	18	28	79	77	70
United States	11	51	28	45	66	74	63
Western Europe							
West Germany	9	67	22	42	86	82	78
Great Britain	3	36	27	36	76	89	73
Netherlands	39	27	24	45	84	89	75
Switzerland	20	63	21	27	86	79	71
Ireland	39	32	10	14	73	79	70
Portugal	25	51	30	39	75	83	74
Denmark	13	26	12	18	92	78	52
Finland	28	21	13	13	73	90	74
Norway	7	40	10	12	88	83	65
Eastern Europe							
Hungary	1	52	48	72	71	84	72
Poland	1	66	71	88	73	78	70
Russia	9	62	69	88	66	79	76
Central America							
Mexico	29	66	31	56	70	77	61
South America							
Chile	20	56	41	68	88	68	54
Brazil	2	50	41	49	64	56	62
Uruguay	3	44	28	37	74	61	54
Asia							
India	21	51	44	52	42	75	57
Japan	12	42	31	52	73	78	65
Republic of Korea	9	67	57	74	65	83	74
Philippines	2	37	28	52	58	75	64
Turkey	18	61	44	42	45	74	60
Africa							
Nigeria	1	45	34	38	24	73	70
MEAN	14	49	33	45	70	78	67
STD. DEV.	11.6	13.8	16.8	21.6	15.9	8.0	7.6

Source: *Health of the Planet* (International Gallup Poll Report, 1993). (See Dunlap et al., 1993.)

TABLE 28(B)
PERCENTAGE MENTIONING THE ENVIRONMENT AS A MOST IMPORTANT PROBLEM; PERCENTAGE CONSIDERING
ENVIRONMENTAL PROBLEMS IN THEIR COUNTRY AS VERY SERIOUS; PERCENTAGE RATING THE QUALITY
OF THE ENVIRONMENT IN THE LOCAL COMMUNITY, THE NATION AND THE WORLD AS VERY OR FAIRLY BAD;
PERCENTAGE STRONGLY OR SOMEWHAT FAVOURING THE GOVERNMENT CONTRIBUTING MONEY TO AN
INTERNATIONAL AGENCY TO WORK ON SOLVING GLOBAL ENVIRONMENTAL PROBLEMS; PERCENTAGE
STRONGLY OR SOMEWHAT FAVOURING AN INTERNATIONAL AGENCY HAVING THE AUTHORITY TO INFLUENCE
THE GOVERNMENT'S POLICY IN ENVIRONMENTALLY IMPORTANT AREAS (1992, 6 GEOGRAPHICAL REGIONS)

Geographical region	Environment important problem	Environment very serious problem	Bad quality			Money to international agency	Authority to international agency
			Comm.	Nation	World		
North America	11	52	23	37	73	76	67
Western Europe	20	40	19	27	81	84	70
Eastern Europe	4	60	63	83	70	80	73
Central and South America	14	54	35	53	74	66	58
Asia	12	52	41	54	57	77	64
Africa	1	45	34	38	24	73	70
Means are equal[1]	yes	yes	no	no	no	no	no

1. One-way analysis of variance with country as unit of analysis (f<.05, ranges = btukey).

Source: *Health of the Planet* (International Gallup Poll Report, 1993).

TABLE 29
PERCENTAGE RATING THE ENVIRONMENT IN THE COUNTRY AS: GOOD (EXCELLENT + PRETTY GOOD), FAIR, POOR; PERCENTAGE RATING THE ENVIRONMENT IN THE LAST TEN YEARS AS: BETTER, THE SAME, WORSE (1988–89, 16 COUNTRIES)

Country	Environment			Last 10 years		
	Good	Fair	Poor	Better	Same	Worse
North America						
United States	36	44	20	—	—	—
Western Europe						
West Germany	15	55	31	7	33	60
Norway	43	43	1	37	29	64
Eastern Europe						
Hungary	8	49	42	10	20	69
Central America						
Mexico	14	34	52	12	28	61
Jamaica	24	56	21	15	18	67
South America						
Brazil	18	53	30	16	31	53
Argentina	36	46	19	10	13	77
Asia						
China	14	53	33	36	15	49
India	15	55	30	20	16	64
Japan	17	56	27	28	33	39
Africa						
Nigeria	27	46	27	47	7	47
Kenya	42	52	4	41	14	46
Senegal	12	56	31	15	24	63
Zimbabwe	42	51	8	41	17	42
Middle East						
Saudi Arabia[1]	63	31	5	47	9	43
MEAN	27	49	25	23	20	56
STD. DEV.	15.4	7.7	13.1	15.0	8.6	11.5

1. Interviews were only conducted with men (due to cultural and religious considerations).

Source: MORI Social Research Institute (Worcester and Corrado, 1991), SCP calculation.

Appendix B.
Wording of questions in Tables 18 to 29

Table 18

• How satisfied are you with the way democracy works in this country? Are you very satisfied, somewhat satisfied, neither satisfied nor dissatisfied, somewhat dissatisfied, or very dissatisfied?

• Overall, how satisfied are you with the way things are going in your personal life today? Are you very satisfied, somewhat satisfied, neither satisfied nor dissatisfied, somewhat dissatisfied, or very dissatisfied?

• How satisfied are you with the following aspects of your life? For each one please tell me if you are very satisfied, somewhat satisfied, neither satisfied nor dissatisfied, somewhat dissatisfied, or very dissatisfied?: – Your standard of living, all the things you can buy and do; – Your job or the work you do; – Your family life; – Your clothing; – Your current housing; – The amount and quality of food you get; – Your community as a place to live in; – Your personal health; – Your education.

Table 19a

• Generally speaking, would you say that most people can be trusted or that you can't be too careful in dealing with people?: – Most people can be trusted, – Can't be too careful.

• All things considered, how satisfied are you with your life as a whole these days?: 1 – Dissatisfied, 10 – Satisfied.

• How satisfied are you with the financial situation of your household?: 1 – Dissatisfied, 10 – Satisfied.

• Overall, how satisfied or dissatisfied are you with your home life?: 1 – Dissatisfied, 10 – Satisfied.

• All in all, how would you describe your state of health these days? Would you say it is: – Very good, – Good, – Fair, – Poor, – Very Poor.

Table 20

• Do you think the world you live in today is better, the same, or worse than the world your parents grew up in?

• Do you think the world the next generation of children live in will be better, the same, or worse than the world you live in today?

Table 21a

• Here is a list of qualities which children can be encouraged to learn at home. Which, if any, do you consider to be especially important? Please choose up to five: – Good manners; – Feeling of responsibility; – Tolerance and respect for other people; – Independence; – Hard work; – Thrift, saving money and things; – Determination, perseverance; – Obedience; – Unselfishness; – Religious faith; – Imagination.

Table 22a

• There are a number of groups and movements looking for public support. For each of the following movements which I read out, can you tell me whether you approve or disapprove of this movement? Human rights movement (at home or abroad): – Strongly approve, – Somewhat approve, – Somewhat disapprove, – Strongly disapprove.

• How interested would you say you are in politics?: – Very interested, – Somewhat interested, – Not very interested, – Not at all interested.[31]

• Which of these geographical groups would you say you belong to first of all?: 1. The town where you live; 2. The State or province in which you live; 3. Your country as a whole (France, Nigeria, etc. as a whole); 4. The continent in which you live (stated as 'Europe', 'Asia', etc.); 5. The world as a whole.[32]

Table 23a

• On this list are various groups of people. Could you please sort out any that you would not like to have as neighbours? People of a different race,

Immigrants/foreign workers, People who have AIDS, Homosexuals: – Mentioned, – Not mentioned.

• When jobs are scarce, employers should give priority to British (countries other than U.K.: please substitute your nationality!) people over immigrants: – Agree, – Disagree, – Neither.

• It is unfair to give work to handicapped people when able-bodied people can't find jobs: – Agree, – Disagree, – Neither.

Table 24

• Do you think that in this country, society generally favours men and women equally, or does it favour women over men, or men over women?

• In the past five years, do you think the position of women compared to men in this country has improved, worsened, or remained the same?

Table 25a

• When jobs are scarce, men have more right to a job than women: – Agree, – Disagree, – Neither.

• People talk about the changing roles of men and women today. For each of the following statements I read out, can you tell me how much you agree with each (strongly agree, agree, disagree, strongly disagree): A pre-school child is likely to suffer if his or her mother works; A job is all right but what most women really want is a home and children; Being a housewife is just as fulfilling as working for pay; Both the husband and wife should contribute to household income.

Table 26a

• The main advantage of marriage is that it gives financial security: – Strongly agree, – Agree, – Neither agree nor disagree, – Disagree, – Strongly disagree.

• The main purpose of marriage these days is to have children.

• It is better to have a bad marriage than no marriage at all.

• People who want children ought to get married.

• When there are children in the family, parents should stay together even if they don't get along.

• Even when there are no children, a married couple should stay together even if they don't get along.

Table 27a[33]

• Do you think it is wrong or not wrong if a man and a woman have sexual relations before marriage?: – Always wrong, – Almost always wrong, – Wrong only sometimes, – Not wrong at all.

• What if they are in their early teens, say under 16 years old, in that case is it . . .?

• What about a married person having sexual relations with someone other than his or her husband or wife, is it . . .?

• And what about sexual relations between two adults of the same sex, is it . . .?

Table 28a

• What do you think is the most important problem facing our nation today? (open-ended: environmental problems).[34]

• I'm going to read a list of issues and problems currently facing many countries. For each one, please tell me how serious a problem you consider it to be in our nation – very serious, somewhat serious, not very serious, or not at all serious? (environmental issues).

• When we say environment, we mean your surroundings – both the natural environment – the air, water, land and plants and animals – as well as buildings, streets and the like. Overall, how would you rate the quality of the environment in our nation, – very good, fairly good, fairly bad, or very bad? In your local community? In the world as a whole?

• Would you favour or oppose our government contributing money to an international agency to work on solving global environmental problems – strongly favour, somewhat favour, somewhat oppose, or strongly oppose?

• Would you favour or oppose giving an international agency the authority to influence our government's policy in environmentally important areas – strongly favour, somewhat favour, somewhat oppose, or strongly oppose?

Table 29[35]

• How would you rate the environment in this country?: – Excellent, – Pretty good, – Fair, – Poor, – Not sure.

• Do you feel that the environment where you live has become better or worse in the last ten years, or has it stayed about the same?: – Better, – Worse, – Stayed the same, – Not sure.

Appendix C.
Survey information

General remarks

World Values Survey 1990–1993

The valid percentages are presented (excluding people answering 'don't know' or giving no answer at all), except for (we considered 10% missing values as critical limit):

Table 19a – 'trust in people': more than 10% missing values – West Germany (17.8), East Germany (12.6), Switzerland (38.6) and Austria (10.9); in sixteen countries between 5% and 10%.

Table 22a – 'human rights movement': more than 10% missing values – Japan (22.2), India (34.3), China (21.5), Lithuania (17.8), Latvia (15.1) and Estonia (23.6); between 5% and 10% missing values – in thirteen countries, among others West Germany, Belgium, Austria, Spain, Portugal and Northern Ireland.

Table 23a – 'jobs disabled': more than 10% missing values – West Germany (11.7), Japan (17.9), Bulgaria (10.2), Austria (12.3), Latvia (20.8), Estonia (15.0) and Russia (10.0); in eleven other countries between 5% and 10% missing values. Discrimination of disabled people might not be a real topic in many countries.

Table 25a – 'what most women really want is a home and children': more than 10% missing values – France (10.1), West Germany (16.5), Netherlands (10.8), Belgium (12.5), Spain (11.2), Japan (19.8), Finland (11.6) and Austria (12.3); in seventeen countries between 5% and 10% missing values. So, in many countries a large proportion of the population did not answer this question. This might be due to the ambiguous meaning of this item. Subscription of this item might refer to a 'conservative' view on the role of woman in society and at the labour market, but it is also conceivable that 'progressive' people think that what many working mothers really want is a home and children.

Table 25a – 'being a housewife is just as fulfilling as working for pay': more than 10% missing values – France (12.1), West Germany (17.5), Austria (10.1), the Netherlands (10.5), Denmark (11.4), Sweden (16.0), Finland (12.1), Belgium (14.6), Spain (12.1), Japan (24.6), Argentina (10.5), India (13.1), Slovenia (12.8) and Latvia (15.1); in thirteen countries between 5% and 10% missing values. Again, the interpretation of this item might lead to confusion. It is conceivable that 'progressive' persons agree with this item, because they do not wish that women who would rather stay at home should feel obliged to go to work.

Table 25a – 'disagreeing that both the husband and wife should contribute to household income': more than 10% missing values – West Germany (13.9), Austria (10.3), Japan (33.6) and Latvia (10.7); in eight countries between 5% and 10% missing values.

International Social Survey Programme, 1994

For four of the six items in Table 26a, people who did not answer and people who couldn't choose/didn't know an answer are included while calculating the percentages:

• 'marriage financial security': more than 10% missing values – Poland (10.7) and Bulgaria (10.9); between 5% and 10% missing values – West Germany, Norway, Sweden, Spain, Slovenia and Russia.

• 'marriage to have children': more than 10% missing values – Poland (10.3) and Sweden (11.3); between 5% and 10% missing values – West Germany, Norway, Sweden and Russia.

• 'stay together if children': more than 10% missing values – Poland (11.7) and Russia (11.5); between 5% and 10% missing values – West Germany, Sweden, Spain, Northern Ireland, Ireland, United States, Austria and East Germany.

• 'always stay together': more than 10% missing values – Poland (15.1), Bulgaria (17.2), Russia (10.3); between 5% and 10% missing values – West Germany, Sweden, Spain, United States and East Germany.

For all variables in Table 27a, people who did not answer the questions are excluded and those who couldn't choose/didn't know an answer are included while calculating the percentages. It appeared that in at least half of the countries involved, between 5% and 30% of the population scored a missing value. These high percentages were largely due to the high number of people answering 'Can't choose, don't know'. We explain this by the fact that, in contrast with the items from Table 26a, no middle category was offered to express uncertainty with respect to these highly sensitive questions about sexual attitudes.

Detailed survey information

Gallup 1993

Source: Dunlap et al. (1993).
Year: Conducted from January to March 1992.
Number of countries: 24.
Survey method: Face-to-face interviews.
Sample size: About 1,000 in each country; exception: India (4,984).
Representativeness: Representative national samples, except for India where findings were based on a representative national sample of the adult population residing in non-rural areas.
Age of the respondents: Adult population.

Gallup 1995

Source: International Gallup Poll Report (*People's Satisfaction with Their Lives and Government*, 1995).
Year: Conducted in April/May 1995, in China between May and September 1994.
Number of countries: 18 countries (covering half of the world population) in which the Gallup Organization has a national polling office.
Survey method: Sometimes telephone polls, other times in-person surveys.
Sample size: About 1,000 in each country; exceptions: Venezuela (501) and China (3,429).
Representativeness: National samples except for: (a) Chile, Venezuela, India and Mexico (only the urban population); (b) India (the sample was further restricted to people in middle-class (or higher) neighbourhoods); (c) Spain (16+, no data for Ceuta, Melilla and Canary Islands); (d) China (excluding Tibet).
Sampling error: Between ±2% to 5%.

Gallup 1996

Source: International Gallup Poll Report (*Gender and Society: Status and Stereotypes*, 1996).
Year: Conducted from August to November 1995.
Number of countries: 22 countries (covering 53.3% of the world population) in which Gallup currently operates as a wholly owned subsidiary and/or joint venture company (for Estonia and Latvia data were donated by SAAR and Baltic Data House, respectively, under the auspices of Gallup's Lithuanian subsidiary).
Sample size: Typically 1,000 or more interviews.
Representativeness: Representative nationwide sampling of the adult population.
Age of the respondents: 18 years and over.
Sampling error: ±3%.

World Values Survey 1990–1993

Source: World Values Study Group. *World Values Survey, 1981–1984* and *1990–1993* (computer file). ICPSR version. Ann Arbor, Michigan, Institute for Social Research (producer), 1994. Ann Arbor, Michigan, Inter-university Consortium for Political and Social Research (distributor), 1994.

Year: Most surveys were carried out from March 1990 to January 1991, except in: Switzerland (November 1988 to February 1989), Poland (November/December 1989), Argentina (February to April 1991), Brazil (October 1991 to January 1992), Slovenia (February 1992) and Romania (Spring 1993).

Number of countries: 42 countries, representing almost 70% of the world population (we excluded the sample of the Moscow area). Fieldwork was carried out by professional survey research organizations in all countries except the Republic of Korea and Turkey (interviewing by university students).

Survey method: Personal face-to-face interviews.

Sample size: Mostly about 1,000 in each country; exceptions: Northern Ireland (304); Finland (588); Iceland (702); West Germany, Italy, Spain, United States, Canada, Brazil and Russia (around 2,000); Belgium, Spain, South Africa and India (around 3,000).

Sampling method: Both national random (in most cases stratified multi-stage random sampling) and quota sampling (assigned on the basis of sex, age, occupation and region) were used.

Non-response: Most of the participating institutes did not report response rates. Available information about response rates: Norway, Sweden and Denmark around 71%, Japan 62%, Slovenia 87% and Czechoslovakia (ex-) 96%.

Representativeness: Representative national samples were interviewed in all cases except for: (a) Chile and Argentina (in both countries the sample only covers the (urbanized) central portion of the country, where a majority of the population is concentrated (63% in Chile, 70% in Argentina) and which has above-average incomes); (b) India, Nigeria and China (the samples from these countries undersampled the illiterate portion of the population and oversampled the urban areas and the more educated strata).

Weighting: One should use the weight factor (V376) for 15 of the 42 countries involved in this study, to correct for internal sampling deficiencies. In the United States and South Africa minority races were over-represented; in Switzerland the sample over-represents the French-speaking and Italian-speaking groups. The samples of India, China and Nigeria have been weighted to correct for the under-representation of the rural and illiterate segments of the population, although this compensates imperfectly. In various other countries, such as Great Britain, West Germany, Brazil, Canada and Russia, the weight factor corrects for deviations from national parameters in age and education (in most countries (except Italy) the highly educated are oversampled).

Sampling error: The surveys from low-income countries have larger error margins than those from high income countries. The quality of the sample varies from one society to another, since both available funding and survey research infrastructure are limited in many of the societies included here. In some countries one does not have as much experience with nationwide surveys as in advanced industrial societies (in Belarus this was the first one ever executed). In other countries it is difficult to interview illiterate people and people living in geographically inaccessible areas, or there is a lack of an administrative infrastructure (for example in Nigeria).

Age of the respondents: Adults 18 and over.

MORI

Source: Worcester and Corrado (1991).

Year: Fieldwork was conducted throughout 1988 and the first half of 1989.

Number of countries: 16.

Survey method: Telephone or face-to-face interviews.

Sample size: About 400 to 600 in each country; exceptions: Jamaica, Kenya, Senegal and Zimbabwe (300); Norway (1,006) and the United States (1,253).

Representativeness: The samples were designed to be representative of the population. However, in most developing countries the sample was limited to major metropolitan areas and urban centres because of the difficulty of surveying rural populations.

Age of the respondents: 16 years and over.

International Social Survey Programme, 1994: Family and Changing Gender Roles – II

Source: The data utilized in this chapter were documented and made available by the Zentralarchiv für Empirische Sozialforschung (Cologne). The data for the 'ISSP' were collected by independent institutions in each country. Neither the original collectors nor the Zentralarchiv bear any responsibility for the analyses or interpretation presented here.

Year: In 18 countries fieldwork took place in 1994, except in: Slovenia (October/November 1993), Canada (February 1993 to March 1994), Australia (December 1993 to October 1994), the Netherlands (October 1994 to January 1995), Bulgaria (March 1995) and Austria (December 1995 to January 1996).

Number of countries: 24.

Survey method: Personal face-to-face interviews in 12 countries, personal self-completion questionnaires in 8 countries, postal self-completion questionnaires in 3 countries (Australia, New Zealand and Norway), a combined postal survey and telephone interview in one country (Sweden).

Sample size: In 13 countries about 1,000–1,200, otherwise: Northern Ireland (647), Canada, the United States, Hungary and Poland (around 1,500), Australia (1,779), the Netherlands, Russia and Norway (around 2,000), West Germany (2,324) and Spain (2,494).

Sampling method: National (multi-stage) simple random, stratified or cluster sampling.

Non-response: Response rates vary between 60% and 90% (total completed ISSP questionnaires received/total eligible in scope sample). There was a very high response in Australia (94%) and Spain (99%) and a very low response in West Germany (53%), East Germany (55%) and Great Britain (56%). For seven countries, there was no information available.

Representativeness: Representative samples, exceptions: (a) Israel (only Jewish population surveyed); (b) Spain (Ceuta and Melilla are excluded).

Weighting: To obtain representative data one must use the weight factor in the following 11 countries: Bulgaria, Poland, Hungary, Russia, Philippines, Austria, Italy, Great Britain, Northern Ireland, Canada and Sweden. The weighting-factor (V315) is based on variables such as age, sex, education and province and/or corrects for features of the used sampling method.

Age of the respondents: In most countries 18 years and over, exceptions: Austria (15+), Japan (16+), Sweden (18–74) and Norway (16–79). No information available for 9 of the 24 countries.

Notes

1.   A factor analysis (PAF, listwise deletion of cases) with countries as units of analysis showed that the nine aspects of life listed in Table 18 constitute one dimension (81.1% explained variance).

2.   If the standard deviations are calculated on the set of countries represented in both the Gallup survey and the World Values Survey, the differences between these statistical measures remain rather small. The standard deviation for 'trust' remains somewhere in the middle of the spectrum.

3.   These data were derived from Goldstone (1997): (a) no data were available for Taiwan, Northern Ireland, East Germany or Iceland; (b) we used his score for Germany for West Germany; (c) we used his score for the Czech Republic for Czechoslovakia; (d) the figure for Costa Rica is for 1995.

4.   Economic affluence is the strongest predictor of average happiness. Other relevant factors are social equality between women and men and access to education (Veenhoven, 1991, pp. 10–11; 1994, pp. 130–6).

5.   The standardized regression coefficient (beta) of opinion about democracy on national income is .51 (significant at the 5% level).

6.   We used multiple classification analysis in the cases of trust in other people and satisfaction with health, and regression analysis in the cases of home life satisfaction, life satisfaction and financial satisfaction. In the multiple classification analyses, trust in other people and satisfaction with health were coded as dichotomous variables (see Table 19a). Age (exact years) was recoded into three groups: (1) 18–30; (2) 31–55; (3) 56 and older. Level of education was measured by the age at which the respondent left school (with missing data for Switzerland and the Republic of Korea). We recoded the data as: (1) low: completed formal education at age 15 or earlier; (2) middle: completed education at 16 to 19; (3) high: completed education at 21 or older. Income was measured on a 10-point scale (with missing data for Iceland) and we recoded the data as: (1) low: 1–3; (2) middle: 4–6; (3) high: 7–10. In the regression analyses, the original 10-point scales of the three satisfaction items were entered. We also used the original codes on the questionnaire for age (missing data for Brazil, where only five age groups were distinguished), education (missing data for Turkey, where only three groups were distinguished) and income.

7.   The effect of education on trust was negative in Austria, and the effect of income on trust was negative in Sweden and Nigeria.

8.   Gender was relevant only with respect to home satisfaction. In five countries, women were significantly more satisfied with their home lives than men (Japan, India, Republic of Korea, Turkey, Nigeria), while in eight countries women were significantly less satisfied (Great Britain, Spain, Belgium, Brazil, Czechoslovakia, Estonia, Lithuania, Russia).

9.   In the regression analyses, geographical area was introduced as a dummy variable, with Central and South America as the reference category.

10.   Iceland and Poland were excluded from the analyses. In Iceland ten of the eleven qualities were chosen by 50% or more of the population, and in Poland none of the values was chosen by more than 50%. These results suggest that either these publics misunderstood the question (not picking five out of eleven items but rating each item separately) or that some coding error was made in processing the data.

11.   We also applied the statistical technique of factor analysis – PAF with two fixed factors, varimax rotation – to the data (with the countries in Table 21a as units of analysis). We found no place for unselfishness, while responsibility could be placed in more than one group of variables. It proved reasonably feasible to divide the remaining values into two distinct groups. In the first, good manners, religious faith and obedience had a negative statistical value, and independence, determination and thrift had a positive one. This group could be interpreted as 'individualism versus conformism'. In the other group, imagination and tolerance had a positive value and hard work a negative one. In this case we might discern a dimension of 'non-materialism versus materialism', or 'artistic endeavour, intuition and inspiration versus effort'.

12.   The hypothesis that all means are equal is not rejected (one-way analysis of variance with the countries as units of analysis, ranges = btukey).

13.   Africa takes an exceptional position in many respects. Compared to the other five continents, good manners, obedience and religious faith are rated there as most important, while responsibility, independence, thrift, determination and imagination are least unimportant.

14.   If the African countries are left out of consideration, differences within the continents are larger than differences between the continents (the within groups mean squares was greater than the between groups mean squares).

15.   The statistic V (Cramer's V) is a measure of the strength of the relationship between two variables. A V-value of .07 or higher is considered to be statistically meaningful (due to the high number of cases for each

continent, nearly any value of Cramer's V is statistically significant).

16.   Gender and continent explain respectively 8% and 17% of the variance of these two variables. For the other educational values this percentage lies between 1% and 4% (multiple classification analyses on all data aggregated with individuals as units of analysis). For all eleven goals, continent was found to be a more important variable than gender. The effect of gender varies over the continents (only in the case of tolerance and unselfishness was the interaction effect between gender and continent insignificant).

17.   Three other effects of gender were found. In North America, men regard independence as less important than women. In Eastern Europe men put more emphasis on determination than women, and in Africa men consider obedience more important than women do.

18.   In the Baltic states, people belong first of all to the province or region they live in (Table 22a). Inhabitants of these countries probably interpreted `country' as the Soviet Union. In former East Germany also a sixth category was offered which was chosen by the largest group of people: 29% identified most of all with `The Federal Republic and DDR together'. In former West Germany, this category was only chosen by 9%.

19.   The question of whether global ethics exist that are valid throughout the world can be well recognized in the debate on human rights and the position of East and South-East Asia. Some people claim there are human rights that are universally valid 'because they define us as human beings' (Neier, 1997, p. 23). Others argue that no universal consensus is possible because the definition of such rights is culturally determined (Kausikan, 1997, pp. 11, 20).

20.   The geographical areas did not differ significantly (one-way analysis of variance with the geographical areas as units of analysis, ranges = btukey).

21.   Again, these geographical distinctions do not significantly differ.

22.   This percentage is above 70% in Bulgaria, Romania, the Czech Republic and Poland and under 40% in Belarus and Russia (Rose, 1995, p. 469).

23.   Education and continent both have significant effects on the approval of the human rights movement (with continent more important than education), but they explain only 3% of its variance (multiple classification analyses on all data aggregated with the individual as unit of analyses). The effect of education varies over the continents (a significant interaction effect).

24.   A factor analysis (PAF, listwise deletion of cases) with countries as units of analysis showed that the items 'neighbour different race', 'neighbour homosexual', 'jobs autochthons' and 'jobs disabled' constitute one dimension (51.5% explained variance). Rejection of immigrants as neighbours was omitted because it correlated at .90 with rejection of people of a different race as neighbours. Similarly, the rejection of people with AIDS as neighbours correlated at .96 with the rejection of homosexuals. This 'intolerance index' is a reliable scale (Cronbach's alpha = .75).

25.   Both age and continent have significant main and interaction effects on all four items in Table 23c, with continent more important than age in all cases (multiple classification analyses on all data aggregated with individuals as units of analysis). They explain 15% of the rejection of homosexuals as neighbours, 3% of the desire to give job priority to natives above immigrants, and 6% of the other two items.

26.   If Eastern Europe is excluded, the overall mean increases to 70% and the standard deviation shrinks to 9.8%.

27.   Two countries have diverging scores on this item: Japan and the Netherlands (Table 25a). The low percentage in Japan (31%) is explained by the very large group which did not answer this question: 33.6% (see Appendix C). The low percentage found in the Netherlands (29%) is more difficult to explain. Maybe the word 'should' has a too compulsory connotation for the individualized Dutch. Another explanation might lie in the small number of working females in this country compared to other European nations; women in the Netherlands predominantly work part-time (OECD, 1996, pp. 186–92; SCP, 1996, p. 97).

28.   Age and continent have significant main and interaction effects on all of the items. With the exception of 'marriage if children', continent is always more important than age (multiple classification analyses on all data aggregated with the individuals as units of analysis). The proportion of explained variance varies from 5% to 12%.

29.   If Asia is omitted for 'no sex before marriage', the standard deviation of Table 27a drops from 16.0% to 10.9%.

30.   As we remarked earlier, the interconnections between economic variables and some values are more fully explored by the study *Institutions, Values, Norms and Growth* (NYFER, 1996).

31.   In the Swiss survey one asked about interest in community politics. Czechoslovakia was deleted because all respondents answered very or somewhat interested.

32. It is not clear to us which continent they referred to in East European countries (Europe or the Soviet Union). In Switzerland the category 'town' consisted of: the commune where you grew up, the commune where you now live, the canton where you grew up and the canton where you now live.

33. In Austria one could answer: – Not right at all, – (Rather) not all right, – (Rather) all right, – Totally all right. In Spain a fifth category was also offered: 'It depends'. This category was excluded from the analyses (only about 5% or less choose this answer).

34. In Poland one asked: How much attention do you give to environmental problems?

35. The figures presented by Worcester and Corrado (1991, p. 14) were recalculated because we interpreted the category 'not sure' as missing value (nearly always less than 5%).

Bibliography

ALWIN, D. F.; GORNEV, G.; KHAKHULINA, L. 1995. Comparative Referential Structures, System Legitimacy, and Justice Sentiments: An International Comparison. In: J. R. Kluegel, D. S. Mason and B. Wegener (eds.), *Social Justice and Political Change: Public Opinion in Capitalist and Post-Communist States*. New York, Aldine de Gruyter.

BECK, U. 1992. *Risk Society: Towards a New Modernity*. London, Sage.

BECKER, J. W.; VAN DEN BROEK, A.; DEKKER, P.; NAS, M. 1996. *Publieke opinie en milieu: Een verkenning van het sociale draagvlak voor het milieubeleid op grond van survey-gegevens*. Rijswijk, SCP.

DUNLAP, R. E.; GALLUP JR., G. H.; GALLUP, A. M. 1993. *Health of the Planet:. Results of a 1992 International Environmental Opinion Survey of Citizens in 24 Nations*. Princeton, The George H. Gallup International Institute.

——.1998. *Gender and Society: Status and Stereotypes* (International Gallup Poll Report, 1996). Princeton, The Gallup Organization.

GOLDSTONE, L. 1998. Statistical Tables and Culture. Indicators. *World Culture Report 1998*. UNESCO Publishing.

HECHTER M.; NADEL, L.; MICHOD, R. E. (eds.). 1993. *The Origin of Values*. New York, Aldine De Gruyter.

KAUSIKAN, B. 1977. Asian Versus 'Universal' Human Rights. *The Responsive Community*, Vol. 7, No. 3, pp. 9–21.

LEVINE, R.; SATO, S.; HASHIMOTO, T.; VERMA, J. 1995. Love and Marriage in Eleven Cultures. *Journal of Cross-Cultural Psychology*, Vol. 26, No. 5, pp. 554–71.

MEAD, M. 1950. *Male and Female: A Study of the Sexes in a Changing World*. Harmondsworth, Penguin Books.

NEIER, A. 1997. Asia's Unacceptable Standard. *The Responsive Community*, Vol. 7, No. 3, pp. 22–30.

NYFER. 1996. *Institutions, Values, Norms and Growth*. Breukelen, NYFER Forum for Economic Research.

OECD. 1996. *Employment Outlook*. Paris, OECD.

People's Satisfaction with Their Lives and Government. (International Gallup Poll Report, 1995). Princeton, The Gallup Organization.

ROSE, R. 1995. Freedom as a Fundamental Value. *International Social Science Journal* (Paris, UNESCO), Vol. 47, No. 145, pp. 457–71.

SCP. 1996. *Sociaal en cultureel rapport*. The Hague, VUGA.

TODOROV, T. 1989. *Nous et les autres: La réflexion francaise sur la diversité humaine*. Paris, Éditions du Seuil.

VEENHOVEN, R. 1991. Is Happiness Relative? *Social Indicators Research*, Vol. 24, pp. 1–34.

——. 1994. Is Happiness a Trait? Tests of the Theory that a Better Society Does Not Make People Any Happier. *Social Indicators Research*, Vol. 32, pp. 101–60.

WORCESTER, R. M.; CORRADO, M. 1991. Attitudes to the Environment – A North/South Analysis. (Paper prepared for the UNESCO International Forum on Environment and Development: Problems and Prospects for Sustainable Development.) London, MORI.

WORLD COMMISSION ON CULTURE AND DEVELOPMENT. 1995. *Our Creative Diversity: Report of the World Commission on Culture and Development*. Paris, UNESCO.

Part Five
Methodology:
building
cultural indicators

Introduction to Part Five

This part of the report deals with the conceptual basis of cultural indicators of human well-being. Directly or indirectly, all three chapter in this section address several basic questions that arise naturally in the context of such indicators. First, what exactly do we mean by 'cultural aspects of life in a society'? Second, what is the purpose of constructing cultural indicators, and, given the purpose, what indicators should one choose ? Lastly, should one try to aggregate these indicators so as to have only a few broad indicators, or, possibly, to construct a single overall composite index? These are some of the themes that run throughout the analyses of the three authors, Sen, McKinley and Pattanaik, in this part. While their conclusions are sometimes similar, they also differ in many ways.

The definition of culture

Before one can construct cultural indicators, it is necessary to have at least a tentative definition of culture. Both McKinley and Pattanaik settle for rather broad notions of culture. For McKinley, culture refers to 'the way that people live together, interact, and co-operate – together with how they justify such interactions through a system of beliefs, values and norms'. For Pattanaik, the cultural determinants of human well-being include political and social factors (e.g. participation in communal and political life and immunity from discrimination) as well as intellectual and aesthetic factors.

The purpose

Cultural indicators of human well-being can serve different purposes. First, there is the purely descriptive purpose. Like any indicator, cultural indicators give information about societies, which may be interesting even when one is not trying to evaluate the cultures of these societies from any normative point of view. When one lists, for various countries, the number of films produced in a year or the number of televisions per thousand persons, for instance, one is not necessarily concluding that a

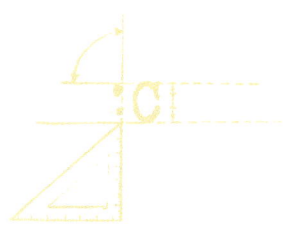

higher number of films or a higher number of televisions represents a better or a worse state of affairs. Cultural indicators may also have an evaluative purpose involving explicit or implicit normative criteria, and all three authors in this part take an explicitly evaluative approach. McKinley's central concern is with indicators based on 'universally accepted ethical standards that can distinguish cultures that hamper human development from those that foster it'. Pattanaik seeks to identify indicators that measure the achievements of a society with respect to the cultural determinants of human well-being. Sen's evaluative approach focuses on 'capabilities . . . which help distinct persons to pursue separate . . . objectives and achieve diverse functionings'. Given this emphasis on the capabilities of people, Sen argues for a human rights orientation in the choice of indicators.

The choice of indicators

The choice of indictors is obviously determined by the purposes which the indicators are intended to serve. Given the similarity between the normative criteria underlying the analyses of McKinley and of Pattanaik, it is not surprising that many of the factors (e.g. personal security, absence of discrimination on grounds of race, gender, age or sexual orientation, creativity), which they seek to capture through indicators are similar. There are, however, significant differences. For example, for McKinley, communication among people ('cultural dialogue') is an end in itself, and he devises several indicators to capture this end, but it does not figure as a basic 'functioning' in Pattanaik's analysis.

Aggregation

To what extent should one seek to aggregate the multitude of cultural indicators? Aggregation is not an all-or-nothing affair. Some amount of aggregation is desirable so as to avoid the lack of focus and coherence that may result from a very large number of separate indicators. The question is how far such

aggregation should proceed. Aggregation (one may argue) is valid only if there is a strong correlation between the components of an indicator. But in that case any one of the indicators is sufficient and aggregation is unnecessary. If, on the other hand, correlation between different indicators is low, one would wish to know, for many purposes, why this is so and therefore separate them. Separation permits one to investigate the relationship between different indicators, e.g. freedom and crime or democracy and tolerance of minorities or diversity and the number of patents registered (as an index of technological innovation). It can therefore be argued that aggregation is either unnecessary or undesirable.

The principal two arguments for a composite index are: (1) that it shows up the shortcomings of alternative single indexes, such as GNP, which have a powerful grip on the popular imagination although showing the same defects as the proposed new composite index, and (2) that it highlights certain features for policy-makers, journalists and the public in a form easily and quickly grasped.

Sen forcefully argues against a single composite cultural indicator. He feels that, given that cultures of different countries differ radically, and, even within the same culture, the different aspects of culture, such as music, fine arts and poetry, represent very different types of cultural products, an aggregate indicator of culture cannot but be misleading. In contrast, Pattanaik argues that it is useful to have an aggregate composite index in addition to the partial indicators. Such an aggregate indicator, he argues, will seek to measure the contribution made by the cultural 'functionings' to human well-being, rather than the aesthetic value of the culture. McKinley does not opt for a single composite index, but the type of partial aggregation that he carries out does allow for combining very diverse indicators, such as the sale of music albums per capita, annual cinema attendance per capita and television sets per head of the population.

As is clear from our brief comments above, the

three chapters often differ in their approaches to cultural indicators of human well-being. However, there is one point that clearly emerges from all these chapters: whatever approach it is decided to follow, we need more data than are available now before we can construct a satisfactory set of cultural indicators of well-being. Future progress in this area will depend as much on the compilation of more factual information as on further exploration of the conceptual foundations of cultural indicators of human well-being. As the box on pages 336–7, based on a paper by Barry Haydon, shows, several countries have already initiated serious and systematic attempts to extend the range of statistical information on culture. However, much more needs to be done in this direction before we can hope to have a reasonably comprehensive set of cultural indicators of well-being for different countries.

Chapter 17
Culture, freedom and independence

Amartya Sen
Economist and philosopher; Master, Trinity College,
Cambridge (United Kingdom)

'Equity in cultural as well as economic opportunities can be profoundly important in a globalizing world.'

The cultural side of human life

Dedicated development experts, keen on feeding the hungry and banishing economic poverty, are often impatient with what they take to be premature focusing on culture in a world of manifold material deprivation. How can you (so the argument runs) talk about culture – poetry or music or painting – while people succumb to starvation or undernutrition or easily preventable disease? The motivation behind this criticism cannot be dismissed, but the artificially separatist – and stage-wise – view of progress is unreal and unsustainable. Even economics cannot work, as Adam Smith noted, without understanding the role of 'moral sentiments', and Bertold Brecht's note of cynicism in his *Threepenny Opera*, 'Food comes first, then morals', is more a statement of despair than of an advocated priority.

Culture does not exist independently of material concerns, nor does it stand patiently waiting its turn behind them. The decision to launch the *World Culture Report* can be seen as an important step towards affirming a valuational commitment and providing an informed understanding of the depths and coverage of the cultural side of human life. There are, however, two types of problems that an initiative of this kind can face: determined opposition and uncritical acceptance. The former may come from 'practical' minds concerned with

sorting out the material world 'first'. I shall not return in this chapter to these 'one-thing-at-a-time' exponents, beyond quoting an old Bengali saying: 'the woman who cooks tasty food may also like, after all, to arrange her hair elegantly'. I am more concerned with the dangers of uncritical acceptance. I should add that the world of cultural indexes – and indicators of aggregate cultural achievements and scalar measures of irreducibly complex *n*-tuples – worries me almost as much. That is the subject of this chapter.

Some concerns and dangers

I shall begin by listing some grounds for scepticism.

The fact of heterogeneity. Culture is not just one thing, but a generic name for a diverse set of activities and pursuits. Even within the same country different people may have very disparate views of cultural achievements. And cultures vary radically between different countries and between distinct historical traditions and heritages. How can the search for one set of indices of cultural achievement be anything but counter-productive in the totally diversified world in which we live?

The importance of uniqueness. Going further than the need to recognize heterogeneity, it is necessary to see the importance of each culture as a unique tradition. In a world constantly bombarded by the 'imperialism' of the culture of the Western metropolis (the reference here tends to be more to MTV and Kentucky Fried Chicken than to Shakespeare or Aristotle), surely what is needed is to strengthen resistance rather than look for uniform indicators of international cultural comparison?

The dangers of aggregation. Even within a given culture can be found diverse parts of this capacious field. For one thing, music differs from fine arts, poetry from dance, and sculpture from drama. To look for an aggregate indicator of cultural achievement or progress (as has been recommended from time to time) cannot but be misleading. How can we even consider having any general index, on the lines of such indicators as the Human Development Index?

Heterogeneity and enabling conditions

The concern with heterogeneity is certainly legitimate. Any attempt at evaluation – even at reporting – has to take note of this basic fact. After taking on board this elementary wisdom (i.e. avoiding looking for indicators that only work for one culture and not for another), there is, however, need for some constructive assertion as well.

As John Rawls noted in proposing concentration on the 'primary goods' in the 'Difference Principle' as part of his theory of 'justice as fairness', there is more uniformity in the enabling conditions that are helpful for all than in the distinct achievements that different persons respectively value.[1] Primary goods are general-purpose resources that help people to achieve their respective ends (diverse though these may be).

While Rawls concentrated on the means of achievement, we can go further and look for the capabilities that are sustained by different means and which help distinct persons to pursue separate – and possibly dissimilar – objectives and achieve diverse functionings.[2] For example, literacy and numeracy are useful not just in one culture but in nearly every culture. So is the freedom to read what one likes and write as one pleases.

In this focus on enabling conditions and capabilities, there is no presumption that everybody sees culture in the same way. It does not involve any denial of the existence of heterogeneities in the world. We value different things, yet still have use for similar abilities. Even a Charles Darwin may complain: 'I have tried lately to read Shakespeare and found it so intolerably dull that it nauseated me'.[3] But both Shakespeare and Darwin had made good use, in their own ways, of the skills of reading and writing – the basic capabilities that *inter alia* helped to sustain their respective pursuits.

The same applies to the Taliban scholars, even though they may see no need to extend these skills to others, in other words women or men of the 'lower orders'. In reporting on the cultural state of the world, an interest in – and concern with – all people can be combined with the valuation of basic capabilities that can help all, even though a privileged few – who make energetic use of these skills – may choose to deny others the benefit that accrues from them.

The heterogeneity of cultural forms and values has to be accepted, but even after accepting this, there will be room for valuing certain basic enabling powers and opportunities. There is a case for concentrating particularly on these basic capabilities in reporting on the state and progress of culture in the world. They would have to be supplemented, of course, by information on more specific achievements (taking note of the need to have a wide enough coverage of attainments of diverse types), but the critical necessity of elementary powers to pursue

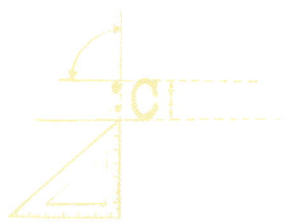

different manifestations of culture must be firmly reflected. This is bound to have something of a human rights orientation, but that is a necessary part of appreciating the nature of the exercise involved.

Uniqueness, conservation and interdependence

That the culture of each country has certain unique features goes without saying. It is quite likely that we may not be able to do justice to the uniqueness of each of the diverse cultures of the world. This fact should not be overlooked. However, such failures do not invalidate the positive achievements of a comparative analysis. Certain aspects *are* comparable, and whatever uniqueness there may be in each culture, certain things are shared. The fact that a framework cannot deliver some things should not be seen as a valid reason for denying the value of what it can deliver.

The threat to native cultures in the globalizing world of today is, to a considerable extent, inescapable. The one solution that is not really within reach is that of stopping globalization of trade and economies, since the forces of economic exchange and the division of labour are hard to resist in a competitive world. This is a problem, yet there is a good side to it, since global trade and commerce can bring – as Adam Smith foresaw – economic prosperity for every nation. But there can be losers as well as gainers, even if the net aggregate figures move up rather than down. In the context of economic disparities, the appropriate response has to include opportunities for the retraining and acquiring of new skills (for people who would be otherwise displaced), in addition to providing 'social safety-nets' (in the form of social security and other supportive arrangements) for those whose interests are harmed – at least in the short run – by the globalizing changes.

This class of response will to some extent work for the cultural side as well. Skill in computer use and the harvesting of the Internet and similar facilities not only transform economic possibilities, but also the lives of those who are influenced by such technical change. Again, this is not necessarily regrettable. There remain, however, two problems (one of which is shared with the world of economics).

The world of modern communication and interchange requires basic education and training. While some countries in the world have made excellent progress in this area (countries in East Asia and South-East Asia are good examples), others, such as those in South Asia and Africa, have tended to lag behind.[4] Equity in cultural as well as economic opportunities can be profoundly important in a globalizing world. This is a shared challenge for the economic and the cultural world.

The second issue is somewhat different. When economic adjustment occurs, few tears are shed for the shelved production methods and technology. In the case of culture, however, this is not the case. The demise of old ways of living can cause anguish, as well as cultural nostalgia. It is something like old species of animals becoming extinct – the existence of hardier species that are better able to cope may not be consolation enough.

This is an issue of some seriousness, but it is up to society to determine what, if anything, it wants to do to preserve old forms of living, even at considerable economic cost. Ways of life can often be preserved if society so decides; it is a matter of balancing the cost of such preservation against the value that society attaches to the objects and lifestyles preserved. There is, of course, no ready formula for this cost-benefit analysis, but what is crucial for a rational assessment of such choices is the opportunity for people to participate in public discussions on the subject. This brings us back to the perspective of capabilities: that different sections of society (and not just the well-heeled) should be able to contribute to the decisions regarding what to preserve and what to let go. There is no compulsion to preserve departing lifestyles that are costly, but people should be entitled to take part in these social decisions if they so choose. This is further reason for attaching importance to such elementary capabilities as reading and writing (through basic education), being well-informed and well-briefed (through a free media) and having realistic chances of participating freely (through elections, referendums and the existence of civil rights). Human rights in the broadest sense are part of this exercise too.

On top of these basic observations, it is also necessary to note that cross-cultural communication and appreciation need not necessarily be unsatisfactory – or a matter of shame and disgrace. We indeed have the capacity to enjoy things that have originated elsewhere, and cultural nationalism or chauvinism can be quite debilitating as an approach to living.

Just as there may be a danger in ignoring the uniqueness of cultures, there is also the possibility of being deceived by the presumption of ubiquitous insularity. Indeed, it is important to recognize that there are more interrelations and more cross-cultural influences in the world than is sometimes acknowledged. Indeed, the assertion of 'national tradition' often hides the history of outside influence. For example, chilli may be an essential part of Indian cooking as we understand it, but it is also a fact that it was unknown in India until the Portuguese brought it there. Hot curries are not any less Indian for that reason. Nor is there anything particularly shady in the fact that – given the popularity of Indian food in Britain today – the tourist board there describes curry as 'authentic' British fare.

My point is not to argue against the importance of each culture's uniqueness, but rather to plead in favour of the need for some sophistication in understanding cross-cultural influences as well as our basic ability to enjoy products of other cultures and other lands. We must not lose our capacity to understand each other and to enjoy the cultural products of different countries in the passionate advocacy of 'respect for uniqueness'.

Limits of aggregation

Aggregation can lead to confusion, since diverse objects do not become identical by the mere fact of evaluative aggregation. We may put apples and oranges together to get an index of the fruits we have, but, in the end, we still have a basket of mixed rather than of homogeneous fruits. Any aggregation, any indexing, is of necessity a compromise; and as the purpose changes, so must the nature of the aggregation exercise.

This is an important reason for approaching aggregation with caution. Information in a non-aggregated form can be both instructive and attractive. Basic information may be used towards a variety of ends, but no *one* aggregate index of cultural achievement could possibly serve all the purposes.

This is not to deny that within each field some aggregation will inevitably be involved: for example, in reporting on cultural and educational achievements in specific areas. But what is important is discriminating use of aggregation. Everyone is aware that some aggregation – some loss of information – is inevitable for practical purposes. A map of a country that is the same size as the country would not be very useful – the exercise necessarily involves the loss of some information. This does not, however, mean that we must go the whole hog and finish up with one single index of cultural achievement or, for that matter, one index of human rights fulfilment. Manageability and usefulness need not call for anything so radical.

Different responses

The different lines of critique I have considered in this chapter call for different responses. First, the recognition of heterogeneity is important, but equally so is the need for making use of commonalities in the form of the shared importance of capabilities. They indicate a case for focusing on enabling conditions and human rights to basic capabilities.

Second, the challenges of globalization must be taken seriously, but they too point to the need for equity in the development of human capabilities in political participation as well as in economic performance.

Third, the dangers of over-aggregation must be kept firmly in view. This, however, is no argument for not practising selective aggregation in particular fields, although the merits of any 'sweeping aggregation' over all forms of culture – or even over all forms of human rights – should be seriously questioned.

Finally, while recognizing the unique value of culture, we should not neglect the importance of communication and the pervasive fact of cultural interdependence. Treasuring one's culture should not be confused with the celebration of insularity.

Notes

1.　J. Rawls, *A Theory of Justice*, Cambridge, Massachusetts, Harvard University Press, 1971.

2.　On this, see: A. Sen, *Commodities and Capabilities*, Amsterdam, North-Holland, 1985; K. Griffin and J. Knight (eds.), *Human Development and the International Development Strategies for the 1990s*, London, Macmillan, 1990; M. Nussbaum and A. Sen (eds.), *The Quality of Life*, Oxford, Clarendon Press, 1993; M. Desai, *Poverty, Famine and Economic Development*, Aldershot, Edward Elgar, 1994.

3.　C. Darwin, *Autobiography*, edited by G. De Beer, London, 1974, p. 83.

4.　In India, half the adult population, including two-thirds of the adult women, are still illiterate, even though the country sends nearly six times as many persons to the university as does China. On inequalities in Indian education and social opportunities generally – and the effect that they have on economic development and on India's efforts to participate in globalized economic arrangements – see my book written jointly with J. Drèze, *India: Economic Development and Social Opportunity*, Delhi, Oxford University Press, 1995.

Chapter 18
Measuring the contribution of culture to human well-being: cultural indicators of development

Terry McKinley
Human Development Economist, United Nations
Development Programme (UNDP),
Bureau for Development Policy, Social Development
and Poverty Elimination Division, New York
(United States)

'Our starting assumption is that the ultimate test of a particular culture is whether it fosters an expansion of human capabilities and choice.'

Definitions

In this part, we attempt to identify cultural indicators of development. In order to do so, we need to first clarify what we mean by both culture and development. Our definition of culture is fairly broad: the way that people live together, interact and co-operate – together with how they justify such interactions through a system of beliefs, values and norms. In this definition, culture is a descriptive term, not a normative one.

Development introduces a normative dimension. For us, the term denotes human development. Our indicators are meant to examine human development from a 'cultural perspective', i.e. with particular focus on how people's quality of life is determined by how they are able to live together and the value systems that animate their interactions.

We are taking an explicitly ethical position: our concern is not only that a people's culture enables them to live together, but also that it enables them to live together *well*. What we seek are universally accepted ethical standards that can distinguish cultures that hamper human development from those that foster it. This is not an easy task. And it is not easy to identify indicators that embody such standards.

Our starting assumption is that the ultimate test of a particular culture is whether it fosters an expansion of human capabilities and choice. Such an evaluation could encompass a number of important dimensions. We propose to highlight three: cultural freedom, creativity and cultural dialogue.

Data availability

The above considerations can help us choose appropriate indicators, but there are two major stumbling blocks: devising meaningful indicators and finding data. In many cases, quantitative variables may be inadequate to evaluate the qualitative conditions we seek to identify. Also, data are sparse on social indicators with a significant cultural content. Many 'cultural indicators' currently being collected are based on a restricted definition of culture and are thus unnecessarily narrow.

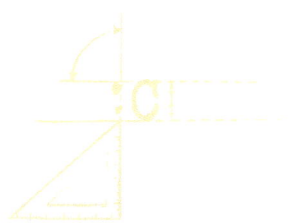

In what follows, we will attempt to provide examples of various cultural indicators of development. For some countries we are able to present data and do illustrative rankings. For many of the cultural dimensions of human development, however, data simply do not exist. One reason is that these dimensions have not been considered important. Hopefully, the publication of this first *World Culture Report* and our current efforts in the area of indicators can spur greater efforts in future.

Indicators of cultural freedom

Our first set of cultural indicators of human development is intended to register cultural freedom, which includes group rights, such as linguistic rights for minorities, and individual human rights, such as freedom of expression. Qualitative indicators are usually employed to capture such rights.

A prominent example of a composite index of such indicators is the Political Freedom Index in the 1991 *Human Development Report*. As a point of reference in discussing indicators we use a paper by Meghnad Desai, *Measuring Political Freedom* (1992), which was written as a background document for the *Human Development Report,* as our point of reference in discussing indicators of cultural freedom. In this paper, Desai categorizes freedom into five equally weighted clusters: (1) integrity of the self or personal security; (2) rule of law; (3) political participation; (4) freedom of expression; and (5) equality before the law.

Method of aggregation

Desai proposes that a small group of evaluators examine the evidence for conditions of political freedom in each country, place this evidence within its appropriate historical context, and rate the country's performance on a scale of 0–100 for each cluster. Desai's Political Freedom Index would then be a simple arithmetic average of the scores for the five clusters. Countries are classified as having 'high political freedom' (a score of 75–100), 'reasonable political freedom' (50–75), 'modest political freedom' (25–50), or 'low political freedom' (0–25).

An alternative to adding together the scores for the five clusters would be to group countries according to each of the five clusters and then add together the five ranks instead of the five scores. A recent example of this method is found in Partha Dasgupta's *An Inquiry into Well-Being and Deprivation* (1993), in which he combines indicators of civil and political liberties with human development indicators. This kind of approach gives less weight to particular scores since a range of scores could conceivably correspond to the same rank.

Whether five ranks or five scores are averaged together, the result could be used simply to place each country in one of several categories – such as 'high', 'above-average', 'modest', or 'low' political freedom. Such an approach could make meaningful distinctions between countries without giving the misleading impression of precision implied by a complete ordering of countries. We would propose following such an approach to construct a composite index of cultural freedom. But what should be included in such an index?

What to include

Of the five clusters proposed by Desai for the Political Freedom Index, we would recommend including three in a Cultural Freedom Index: integrity of the self, freedom of expression, and equality before the law.

Integrity of the self is concerned with the most basic and non-controversial human freedoms, such as freedom from torture and arbitrary arrest. While certain countries might contest the value of multiparty elections or an independent judiciary, surely none would claim the right to torture its citizens based on its own cultural values.

With regard to freedom of expression, groups should have the right to express their own cultural values. This would imply lack of censorship of books, plays, art, the press, television, radio and films.

Equality before the law implies lack of discrimination based on belonging to a group identified by such dimensions as race, ethnicity, religion, class or gender. Non-discrimination is a fundamental right that allows the exercise of all other rights and is particularly important for minority ethnic or indigenous groups.

A fourth cluster that would be especially relevant for a Cultural Freedom Index could be based on the right of self-determination. Explicit expressions of the four clusters of cultural freedoms can be found in the International Bill of Human Rights (United Nations, 1948), the International Covenant on Economic, Social and Cultural Rights (United Nations, 1966) and the Declaration on the Rights of Persons Belonging to National or Ethnic, Religious and Linguistic Minorities (United Nations, 1992):

Integrity of self

•   Are people free from arbitrary arrest, detention or exile and from torture and cruel, inhuman or degrading treatment or punishment?

•   Are people free from arbitrary interference with their privacy, family, home or correspondence?

Non-discrimination

•   Is everyone entitled without any discrimination to equal protection of the law, without regard for race, colour, sex, language, religion, political or other opinion, national or social origin, property, birth or other status?

Freedom of thought and expression

•   Does everyone have the right to freedom of thought, conscience and religion?

•   Does everyone have the right to freedom of opinion and expression, including the freedom indispensable for scientific research and creative activity?

•   Does everyone have the right freely to participate in the cultural life of their community, to enjoy the arts and share in scientific advancement and its benefits?

Right of self-determination

•   Do all people have the right of self-determination; and are they able freely to determine their political status and pursue their economic, social and cultural development?

•   Is the existence of national or ethnic, cultural, religious and linguistic minorities protected within the territories of the nation state, and are conditions encouraged for the promotion of their identity, such as developing their own culture, language, religion, traditions and customs?

•   Do members of minorities have adequate opportunities to learn their mother tongue and to have instruction in it?

•   Do states take measures in the field of education to encourage knowledge of the history, traditions, language and culture of the minorities residing within their territories?

With regard to each of these four clusters, the performance of countries could be evaluated on a scale of 0–10, and then the four scores could be averaged together with equal weight to derive a Cultural Freedom Index. Given the inevitable controversy that would be associated with such an index, careful consideration would have to be given to the quality of the data used for indicators and how judgements are made on the performance of countries.

Indicators of creativity

While a Cultural Freedom Index could indicate whether society respects and allows basic human freedoms of belief, thought and expression, a Creativity Index could indicate whether society actively encourages people to express themselves in creative and innovative ways and make a contribution to their society on such a basis.

Creativity can be measured either in terms of

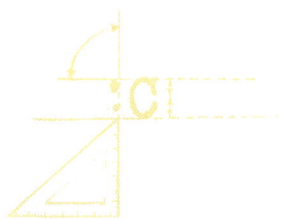

the opportunities that society provides its citizens with, such as access to the means for expression, or in terms of creative outcomes, e.g. plays, books, works of art. Measuring outcomes is preferable because it focuses on people's achievements, and is usually conclusive evidence of being afforded opportunities. But such measures are not always feasible.

Creativity expresses itself in complex ways. The creative outcomes may be social as well as individual. Creativity can be a collective phenomenon as well as an individual one.

Creativity can also characterize many forms of human activity – social, political and economic as well as cultural (in the narrow sense of the word). Just as culture is often mistakenly defined as a distinct and self-contained sphere of human activity, creativity is customarily identified exclusively with artistic or intellectual production. However, it is a much broader phenomenon that can shape activities in industry and business, in government and civil society. It is also the basis of the rapid pace of technological change that is dramatically reshaping whole societies and altering how nations and peoples relate to one another.

Creativity is usually identified with leisure activity, not with work. The productive members of society have to generate enough of a surplus to support a strata of artists, musicians, novelists, poets and other creative people whose works and performances people can enjoy in their 'free' time. Creativity is not usually thought of as a desirable characteristic of work itself, but it should be.

In constructing indicators of creativity, we can start with its manifestations in what are conventionally regarded as explicitly 'creative' spheres of activity – literature, music and performing arts, visual arts, crafts and design, and films and videos. However, where data are available, we should strive to supplement these indicators with others reflecting broader manifestations of creativity – in research and development, in business, in government and in civil society.

If we take conventionally defined 'cultural objects and activities' as an initial focus, we would recommend attaching priority to the 'production' of such objects, less priority to people's 'participation' in cultural activities, and the least priority to people's 'consumption' of cultural objects and enjoyment of cultural activities. Conceptually, participation is often difficult to distinguish from either production or consumption.

As additional information, we would want to know how many people are involved in the 'production' of cultural objects and activities. Only a minority of people may be able to support themselves completely through their creative activity; the relative size of this minority is an important barometer of creativity in a society, but it is not the only measure. Many people may also produce cultural goods for income only on a part-time basis. We should also include 'amateurs' – people who take up cultural activities for their own enjoyment or recreation rather than for income.

There is also the problem that many cultural products are now mass-produced. The creative process generates the prototype, but no creativity is invested in its reproduction. This implies that we would need to seek information on the volume of 'creations', not on the volume of cultural products as such.

All of the above considerations demonstrate that creativity is difficult to identify as a distinct, measurable phenomenon. Much of the data that we need do not exist. The data that are available are mostly based on the conventional notion of culture as a separate sphere of activities. Our illustrations have to rely on these available data.

For much of the currently available data on cultural activities, we could categorize the information in the ways described below.

Expenditures on cultural products and activities

The magnitude of expenditures on cultural products and services can be a useful beginning to gauge the

TABLE 30
PUBLICATION OF BOOKS

Country	Copies of books published (per 100 people) 1991–94	Book titles published (per 100,000 people) 1991–94	Combined rank (book copies and book titles)
1. Argentina	143	26	1.5
2. Malaysia	88	21	3.0
3. Sri Lanka	86	16	4.0
4. Uruguay	62	36	4.0
5. Jordan	113	7	5.0
6. Brazil	65	13	5.5
7. Azerbaijan	74	5	7.5
8. Cuba	42	9	8.0
9. Mongolia	40	12	8.0
10. Armenia	47	6	8.5
11. Colombia	31	4	11.0
12. Eritrea	12	3	12.5
13. Mauritius	8	4	12.5
14. Uganda	12	2	13.5
15. Tunisia	1	6	14.0
16. Gambia	3	2	15.5
17. Malawi	2	3	15.5
18. Morocco	5	1	16.5
19. Trinidad and Tobago	2	2	16.5
20. Lao People's Dem. Rep.	3	1	17.0
21. Algeria	2	1	18.0
22. Kenya	2	1	18.0
23. Madagascar	2	1	18.0
24. Benin	1	1	18.5
25. Oman	1	1	18.5

extent of support for creative activity. Although it is less important than the production of cultural goods and services, creativity cannot flourish without a demand or market for its products.

Creation of new products

Creation involves the generation of new products, services or activities. This could be measured in terms of the number of items generated or their monetary value. In either case, in order to convert the statistic into an indicator, the amount would have to be normalized at least by the size of the country's population. The most useful information would be the numbers of distinct creative items rather than the total number merchandised or their monetary value. For example, the number of new titles of books may be more valuable information than the total number sold or the revenue they generate.

Table 30 presents statistics on both the total number of copies published (per 100 people) and the number of new titles published (per 100,000 people). The twenty-five countries in the table are ranked according to each statistic, and then the two ranks are averaged. The third column shows this average.

Argentina has the highest average rank (1.5). Also ranking high are such Asian countries as Malaysia and Sri Lanka, as well as such other countries as Uruguay and Jordan. A number of sub-Saharan African countries, such as Benin, Madagascar and Kenya, rank low. The notable exceptions are Eritrea and Mauritius. Some middle-income Arab states, such as Oman and Algeria, also rank low.

Table 31 brings together information on how fifteen developing countries rank with regard to the sales of music albums per capita, annual cinema attendance per capita, and the kilos per capita of cultural paper consumed. The intent is to provide a more general picture of the performance of countries with regard to consumption of cultural goods and services. The fifteen countries were ranked

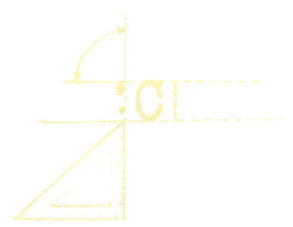

TABLE 31
CONSUMPTION OF CULTURAL GOODS AND SERVICES (MUSIC ALBUMS, FILMS, CULTURAL PAPER)

Country	Combined rank for the three items	GNP per capita (PPP$) 1995	GNP rank minus combined rank
1. Rep. of Korea	1.7	11 450	–0.7
2. Malaysia	2.7	9 020	0.3
3. Brazil	4.7	5 400	4.3
4. Mexico	5.7	6 400	–0.7
5. Venezuela	5.7	7 900	–1.7
6. Colombia	7.0	6 130	–1.0
7. Chile	7.3	9 520	–5.3
8. Costa Rica	7.7	5 850	–0.7
9. Guatemala	8.7	3 340	3.3
10. Ecuador	9.0	4 220	1.0
11. India	9.0	1 400	5.0
12. Turkey	9.0	5 580	–1.0
13. Egypt	11.7	3 820	–0.7
14. Zimbabwe	13.3	2 030	–0.3
15. Kenya	14.0	1 380	1.0

TABLE 32
PRODUCTION OF LONG FILMS

Country	Number of long films produced 1990–95	GNP per capita (PPP$) 1995
1. India	838	1 400
2. Philippines	456	2 850
3. United States	420	26 980
4. Japan	251	22 110
5. Thailand	194	7 540
6. China	154	2 920
7. France	141	21 030
8. Italy	96	19 870
9. Brazil	86	5 400
10. United Kingdom	78	19 260

somewhat different picture emerges when countries' GNP ranks are compared to their cultural-consumption ranks. India and Brazil show the biggest positive difference in rank, indicating that their population's consumption of cultural goods and services is at a higher level than would be expected given their income level. The opposite appears to be true of Chile.

Table 32 focuses on the top ten countries in terms of the number of long films that they produce. India is in first place by far, producing 838 films, despite being a low-income country. Also, other developing countries such as the Philippines, Thailand and China out-produce such richer industrial countries as France, Italy and the United Kingdom.

Number of people directly involved in creative activity

As already mentioned, an alternative way to begin gauging the extent of creative activity in society is to identify the number of people who engage in creative

independently with respect to each of the three indicators, and then the three ranks are averaged together for each country to provide an overall ranking. Column one provides the combined rank, column two the GNP per capita (PPP$) of each country, and column three the difference between each country's ranking according to GNP and its average rank with respect to music albums, cinema attendance and consumption of cultural paper.

Among the fifteen countries being compared, the Republic of Korea ranks first, followed closely by Malaysia. Two sub-Saharan African countries, Kenya and Zimbabwe, rank at the bottom. However, a activity: (a) those who do it as a profession, e.g. the number of painters, poets and performance artists; (b) those who engage in such activity only on a part-time basis, as a secondary source of income; and (c) the large numbers of people who engage in creative activity 'on their own time', as a leisure activity – e.g. amateur photographers, potters and dancers.

As suggested above, creative activity pervades society. Dynamic societies that can provide people with a high quality of life depend on a continual stream of creative activity. Ideally, indicators should be developed to reflect this broader spread of creativity. But the hallmarks of creativity in our broad sense are not easy to identify. One area in which the value of creativity is clearly recognized, however, is science and technology. Much information already exists, for example, on expenditures on research and development or on patents, and these could conceivably be used as proxy indicators of creative activity.

In other areas, such as people's creative contribution to developing new forms of governance and new civil-society organizations, much work would be needed to clarify concepts, develop indicators and gather the necessary information.

Indicators of cultural dialogue

To be able to live together well, people need to communicate and understand one another's culture. Communication is the basis of culture. It is also the basis of cultural interchange: it facilitates the functioning of any multi-ethnic, multi-cultural society.

Cultural diversity is of fundamental value, but what is most conducive to human development is a flourishing, *interactive diversity*, in which people of differing cultures are able to communicate their values, beliefs and traditions to one another in an atmosphere of mutual respect and learning. What is needed is communication based on genuine cultural

dialogue – an active effort on everyone's part to understand and appreciate other people's cultures.

In today's rapidly changing world, driven relentlessly by the so-called information revolution, people run the risk of becoming marginalized if they are not literate and do not have access to modern means of communication. Such means have tremendous potential to uphold and strengthen cultural diversity, but in fact they are often used to standardize cultural values, beliefs and lifestyles. This is why the concept of communication must be enriched to include authentic cultural communication – real dialogue among people of differing ethnic, religious and linguistic backgrounds.

If people are free to think and express themselves as they wish, if they are encouraged to employ their creative capabilities in different spheres of their life, and if they are able to communicate and learn from one another, the quality of their life is likely to be high. These are basic human needs, as important as the needs for food, clothing and shelter, although they may be less 'physical' or 'material'.

Freedom, creativity and communication are ends in themselves. Communication is an end in itself because it enhances the quality of human life – it expands human capabilities. Cultural dialogue has an added connotation: expanding people's ability to live together well – in the sense of being mutually enriched by learning from one another's culture.

People have the opportunity to communicate based either on their own abilities (such as literacy, general life skills or computer skills) or on the means or media to facilitate communication (such as newspapers, radios and telephones). In selecting indicators to reflect cultural dialogue, emphasis should be placed on people's abilities. In this respect, basic adult literacy would be an informative indicator. The value of such a variable is that it reflects an outcome, not an input; and that it reflects a human capability (an accumulated achievement, if you will), not the means to a capability.

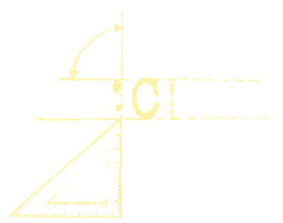

Adult literacy is a stock variable that registers a condition that arises as a result of activity over a number of years. It would be useful to supplement this indicator, which covers the whole adult population, with a measure that can reflect more recent efforts to educate people. One possibility is adult literacy for the age group 15–19.

What would be most promising is to be able to desegregate adult literacy by national, ethnic or indigenous group within nation-states. But such desegregated data are rare. Hopefully, in future, questions to elicit such information could be incorporated into national surveys as a standard practice.

Literacy and educational attainment

In order to reflect people's capabilities to communicate and learn from one another, a cluster of indicators could be constructed. Three indicators could be given equal weight in such a cluster: adult literacy (for the whole adult population), adult literacy for the age group 15–19, and mean years of schooling. The latter indicator has the disadvantage of recording the educational achievement only for the population aged 25 and older. An alternative formulation of the same information is the expected years of schooling, which is the average number of years of formal schooling that a child is expected to receive based on the calculation of the sum of the current age-specific gross enrolment ratios for primary, secondary and tertiary education. Whatever the formulation, such indicators do have the advantage of providing the full range of people's attainment. The assumption is that the more educated people are, the fuller and richer their communication.

The means of communication

A second cluster of indicators could contain information on the basic means of communication in society and people's access to these means. An important piece of information would be newspaper circulation per 100,000 people. This variable can give us a sense of whether people are indeed functionally literate. A capability such as literacy can decline with disuse. Newspapers remain an important means of communication in many countries, although in industrial countries such other media as television are pre-eminent, and such new media as the Internet are rapidly gaining ground.

Statistics of newspaper circulation should therefore be supplemented by those for other means of communication, such as televisions or radios per 1,000 people or telephone lines per 1,000 people. Also useful could be the number of post offices per 100,000 people or the number of letters posted per person. There is also relatively new information being gathered for many countries on personal computers or facsimile machines per 10,000 people and the number of mobile cellular telephone subscribers or Internet users per 10,000 people.

A number of these means of communication are luxury items, which either are used primarily by individuals with moderately high income or are concentrated in relatively rich countries. The higher the GNP per head of a country, the more prevalent such items are likely to be. For valid comparisons across countries, it would be advisable to normalize some of the above indicators by the country's GNP per head.

Also, gross per capita statistics, such as telephone lines per 1,000 people, do not give full information on people's access to such means of communication. It would be preferable to have a statistic that revealed, for instance, the percentage of the population that has a telephone, but such information would have to be supplied by specially designed questions in household surveys. Moreover, indicators for such means of communication as those listed above do not necessarily tell us much about the quality of the information being exchanged. In many countries, for example, the ownership of the major media is highly concentrated. These caveats should be kept in mind when comparing countries on the basis of the above indicators.

Diversity and dialogue

Ideally, a third cluster of indicators should go beyond people's capabilities for communication and the means at their disposal to focus on issues of cultural diversity and interaction. It would be valuable to know, for example, whether people are literate in

their own language as well as in the official national language (if the two differ). In addition, it would be useful to know whether people are literate in a lingua franca, such as French or English, for the purposes of international communication.

In this third cluster, countries could be evaluated on the linguistic abilities of their people. The assumption is that as people learn one another's languages, they would be better able to communicate

TABLE 33
EDUCATIONAL ATTAINMENT

Country	Overall score	Adult literacy rate (%) 1995	Young literacy rate (%) (age 15–19) 1995	Mean years of schooling (age 25+) 1992
1. Sri Lanka	0.803	90	93	7.2
2. Viet Nam	0.794	94	97	4.9
3. China	0.733	82	96	5.0
3. Indonesia	0.733	84	98	4.1
5. Bolivia	0.719	83	95	4.0
6. Brazil	0.707	83	90	4.0
7. Kenya	0.661	78	93	2.3
8. El Salvador	0.640	71	86	4.2
8. Iran	0.640	69	92	3.9
10. Tunisia	0.593	67	89	2.1
11. Egypt	0.505	56	70	3.0
12. Togo	0.467	52	72	1.6
13. India	0.460	52	64	2.4
14. Morocco	0.415	44	58	3.0
15. Sudan	0.411	46	67	0.8
16. Côte d'Ivoire	0.379	40	59	1.9
17. Bangladesh	0.333	38	44	2.0
18. Ethiopia	0.331	36	53	1.1
19. Mauritania	0.327	38	52	0.4
20. Nepal	0.273	28	39	2.1

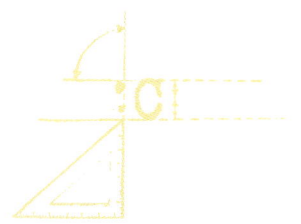

and more inclined to respect one another's culture. Statistics Canada provides information, for example, on people's knowledge of the two official languages, English and French, their mother tongue and the language they use at home. About two-thirds of the Canadian population speak English only, a little over 15% speak French only, and around 16% could conduct a conversation in either language. While English is the mother tongue of 61% of the population, it is used at home by 69% – but the difference is accounted for mainly by those whose mother tongue is not French.

If data were available, one indicator in this cluster could provide information on the circulation of newspapers in different languages. Another novel angle would be to record the extent of translations carried out in a country. The emphasis of this third cluster of indicators would not be on diversity per se, but on interactive diversity – on whether policies of cultural pluralism are being implemented that could be beneficial to all peoples, whether they be the majority or minority ethnic group within society.

There is very limited information for indicators that could reflect a population's linguistic abilities and the extent of interactive cultural pluralism in a society. In most countries, new surveys – or at least new survey questions – would have to be developed to gather such information. For the first two clusters of indicators, i.e., for literacy and educational attainment and for the means of communication, information is much more readily available.

Table 33 provides information on educational attainment and Table 34 provides information on means of communication. For the twenty countries listed in Table 33, three indicators are presented: adult literacy rate, young literacy rate (for ages 15–19) and mean years of schooling.

The index for educational attainment is constructed by giving ½ weight to adult literacy, ¼ weight to the young literacy rate and ¼ weight to mean years of schooling. For the two literacy rates, the maximum value is 100% and the minimum 0%;

TABLE 34
MEANS OF COMMUNICATION (NEWSPAPERS, TELEPHONE LINES, TVS AND COMPUTERS)

Country	Combined rank for the four means of communication	GNP per capita (PPP$) 1995	GNP rank minus combined rank
1. Rep. of Korea	1.75	11 450	1.25
2. Czech Republic	2.50	9 770	1.50
3. Hungary	4.25	6 410	5.75
4. Greece	5.25	11 710	–3.25
5. Portugal	6.50	12 670	–5.50
6. Trinidad and Tobago	6.75	8 160	1.25
7. Poland	7.25	5 400	5.75
8. Malaysia	7.75	9 020	–0.75
9. Chile	8.50	9 520	–3.50
10. Turkey	9.50	5 580	2.50
11. Saudi Arabia	10.50	9 480	–4.50
12. Colombia	13.25	6 130	–2.25
13. Thailand	13.25	7 540	–4.25
14. South Africa	13.75	5 030	1.25
15. Ecuador	14.75	4 220	1.25
16. Algeria	16.50	5 300	–2.50
17. Philippines	16.50	2 850	2.50
18. China	17.25	2 920	0.75
19. Mongolia	18.25	1 950	3.75
20. Nigeria	20.25	1 220	4.75
21. Sri Lanka	20.75	3 250	–3.75
22. Senegal	21.25	1 780	1.75
22. Zimbabwe	21.25	2 030	–0.25
24. Pakistan	21.75	2 230	–1.75
25. Uganda	24.75	1 470	–0.75

for mean years of schooling, the maximum value is 15 years and the minimum 0 years.

For such an index, Sri Lanka ranks first among the twenty countries, with a score of 0.803, followed closely by Viet Nam, with 0.794. China and Indonesia also rank high, followed somewhat by Bolivia and Brazil. Ranked last is Nepal, with a score of 0.273. Three countries have scores in the 0.30–0.35 range: Mauritania (0.327), Ethiopia (0.331) and Bangladesh (0.333).

The ranking in Table 34 (means of communication) is based on the average of the ranks of each country with respect to daily newspaper circulation per 1,000 people, main telephone lines per 1,000 people, TVs per 1,000 people and personal computers per 10,000 people. Column 1 is simply the arithmetic average of the four ranks. Column 2 presents the gross national product per head in purchasing power parity dollars for each. Column 3 presents the difference between the ranking of countries according to GNP per capita and their means of communication. A positive difference indicates that a country ranks higher with respect to its means of communication than with respect to its average income level.

Based on the combined rank with respect to the four means of communication, the Republic of Korea is first among the twenty-five countries – with an average rank of 1.75. It is followed closely by the Czech Republic and Hungary. Uganda ranks at the bottom, with an average rank of 24.75. The average ranks for Senegal, Zimbabwe and Pakistan are also below 20.

Among countries ranking higher with respect to its means of communication compared to its income level, Hungary and Poland do best (+5.75), followed by Mongolia (+3.75). Saudi Arabia, Portugal and Thailand also do relatively poorly.

Bibliography

DASGUPTA, P. 1993. *An Inquiry into Well-Being and Deprivation.* Oxford, Clarendon Press.

DESAI, M. 1992. *Measuring Political Freedom.* (Background document for the 1992 *Human Development Report.*) New York, Human Development Report Office, United Nations Development Programme.

STATISTICS CANADA. 1995. *Canada's Culture, Heritage and Identity: A Statistical Perspective.* Ottawa, Ministry of Industry.

STREETEN, P. 1996. *Life Expectancy as an Integrating Concept in Cultural Analysis.* (Note prepared for the Workshop on Cultural Indicators of Development, Royaumont Foundation, France, 4–7 January 1996.)

UNITED NATIONS. 1948. *The International Bill of Human Rights.* Resolution 217 A(III) of the General Assembly, 10 December 1948.

——. 1992. *Declaration on the Rights of Persons Belonging to National or Ethnic, Religious and Linguistic Minorities.* Resolution 47/135 of the General Assembly, 18 December, 1992.

——. 1996. *International Covenant on Economic, Social and Cultural Rights.* Resolution 2200 A (XXI) of the General Assembly, 16 December 1966.

UNITED NATIONS DEVELOPMENT PROGRAMME. 1991. *Human Development Report 1991.* New York, Oxford University Press.

Chapter 19
Cultural indicators of well-being: some conceptual issues

Prasanta Pattanaik
Professor of Economics, Department of Economics,
University of California, Riverside (United States)

'Whatever aggregation rule is chosen, however, it will involve parameters the values of which will depend on ethical judgements.'

Culture and human development

This part of the report examines some conceptual issues in the construction of cultural indicators of human development. In doing so we rely especially on the analytical framework provided by Amartya Sen's work (1985, 1987) on the standard of living. (Chakravarty (1995) provides a more formal treatment of some of the issues raised by Sen.) We argue that such indicators should seek to measure the contributions made to human well-being by the intellectual, aesthetic, social and political activities of people. Sen calls such activities people's 'functionings' or their 'doings' and 'beings'.

Before discussing our approach to cultural indicators of human development, we need to clarify some basic concepts. In the first place, what are indicators of human development? And, among this group of indicators, what can meaningfully be regarded as cultural indicators?

Some indicators are merely descriptive, e.g. the number of ethnic groups in a country. Indicators of human development are, however, evaluative. They could evaluate, for example, whether the level of human development of one ethnic group is higher than that of another. They could thus be used to rank ethnic groups – or whole countries, for that matter – on the basis of their average level of human well-being.

Every evaluation needs to be based on some normative standard. Human development indicators evaluate societies on the basis of their achievements with regard to direct components of human well-being. One could, of course, use other criteria, such as aesthetic norms, to evaluate the achievements of societies. For example, one might want to claim that the paintings in one historical era represent a higher level of artistic achievement than those of an earlier era, or that classical ballets represent a higher level of culture than folk dances. However, we are not concerned here with aesthetic judgements or with evaluating levels of culture.

We are concerned with evaluating societies' achievements with regard to human well-being, and, thus, we are interested in social, political, intellectual and aesthetic factors only to the extent that they are constituent components of such well-being. But how do we define this notion of well-being?

What is human well-being?

Traditionally, economists have regarded an individual's well-being as happiness or desire fulfilment and identified the command over commodities as the principal means to achieve such happiness. Amartya Sen has penetratingly criticized this approach for being subjective in so far as the degree of happiness depends on the accidental features of the individual's psychology.

As an alternative, Sen has proposed a more objective approach based on people's achievements with regard to essential activities or 'functionings', such as being adequately nourished, living in a society without feeling ashamed of one's station in life, having physical security, and so on. Sen then defines a person's freedom as the opportunity to choose from the set of all functioning bundles available to him/her.

Leaving aside the question of freedom for the moment, we adopt Sen's basic approach to human development. For us, the well-being of an individual depends on his/her achievements with respect to the different relevant functionings. Two basic issues arise here. First, is there a list of functionings that can be accepted by various peoples and cultures as being foundational or essential? In other words, can people agree on valuing certain fundamental goals for human activities? Second, if people can agree on the list of valued functionings, such as being adequately nourished or being literate and informed, how can the achievements along these various dimensions be aggregated into one summary measure? We believe that the first task, namely, identifying the fundamental goals, is much easier than agreeing on the relative weights to be attached to the various goals in order to assess people's total well-being.

The classification of functioning

We propose to classify people's functionings into three categories: (1) physical, (2) political and social, and (3) intellectual and aesthetic. Some of the important functionings in these categories are as follows:

(1) *Physical functionings:* (1a) expected length of life; (1b) adequate nourishment; (1c) shelter from the elements; (1d) absence of morbidity.

(2) *Political and social functionings:* (2a) personal security (in particular, security from invasive actions by the state and other agents); (2b) participation in communal and political life; (2c) immunity from discrimination on the ground of race, gender, age or sexual orientation; (2d) being able to live without shame about one's position in society.

(3) *Intellectual and aesthetic functionings:* (3a) having the intellectual ability to handle problems of life; (3b) intellectual fulfilment through contribution to human knowledge; (3c) aesthetic fulfilment through the expression of creative faculties or through participation in an aesthetic event.

This list is not meant to be exhaustive: it is illustrative only. However, given our approach, indicators of human development will essentially be indicators of a society's success in securing, for its members, valued functioning of the type listed above. It is worth emphasizing that we are concerned with measuring attributes that are perceived to be valuable in themselves as essential components of human well-being; we are not interested in them as means to achieve some other ends, nor are we interested in the causal factors that might have given rise to such attributes.

The general distinction between the three categories of functionings mentioned above is fairly clear. However, there are inevitable ambiguities in applying any such scheme. Thus a particular activity may contribute to functionings in more than one

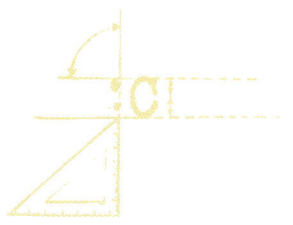

category. Singing in a choir, for instance, enables one to participate in the life of one's community as well as offering a creative activity that contributes to one's aesthetic life.

Also, some functionings may not fall neatly into one category or another. For example, personal security could be categorized as a physical functioning or as a social and political functioning. Additionally, it is obvious that some of the functionings are not easy to measure. For example, while 'the expression of one's creative faculties' has a fairly clear intuitive meaning, it is difficult to find an indicator that can adequately reflect it. In such a case, 'proxy' or 'surrogate' indicators might have to be used.

What is culture?

Now that we have discussed the nature of functionings, how do we define cultural functionings? This depends, of course, on how one defines culture. It is possible, for instance, to define culture very broadly to include virtually every aspect of the social, political, intellectual, religious and artistic life of a people – 'the customs, civilization and achievements of a particular time or people', which is a definition provided by the *Concise Oxford Dictionary* (1990).

In contrast to this broad definition, there is another, equally widely used, notion of culture that focuses only on the intellectual and aesthetic achievements of a people, i.e. 'the arts and other manifestations of human intellectual achievement regarded collectively', which is an alternative definition offered by the same dictionary.

The report of the World Commission on Culture and Development, *Our Creative Diversity*, certainly used culture in a much broader sense than as merely encompassed by 'human intellectual achievement'. Yet if we define culture too broadly, what is to distinguish cultural indicators from the general set of human development indicators? Should cultural indicators seek to reflect, for

example, 'physical' functioning such as life expectancy and adequate nourishment? Of course, in some ways, 'cultural' aspects of human life are inextricably interlinked with the 'physical' aspects. 'Cultural' attitudes might determine the diet of people, which, in turn, might significantly affect the level of nourishment (and, possibly, life expectancy); and recurring illness might seriously affect the schooling of children and, consequently, their intellectual development. But these facts, by themselves, do not seem to justify including indices of life expectancy and absence of morbidity as cultural indicators. The distinction between the 'cultural' and the 'physical' functionings is an intuitive one based on the nature of these functionings, rather than on the causal factors which affect our achievements in terms of these functionings.

In view of these considerations, we would recommend restricting the definition of 'cultural indicators' to cover only categories 2 and 3 of the functionings mentioned above – namely, political and social functionings and intellectual and aesthetic functionings.

Individual well-being and social well-being

Presumably, we want to use cultural indicators of human well-being to evaluate the achievements of societies, not just those of individuals. But what is the connection between social well-being and individual well-being? Traditional welfare economics assumes, for instance, that the well-being of a given society is determined by the levels of well-being of the individuals constituting it.

Given appropriate assumptions, one can have specific methods of aggregating the well-being of individuals to arrive at an assessment of the well-being of the society. However, to assess the individuals' well-being levels, we must have information about the achievements of each individual with respect to the different functionings

Cultural statistics within a developed statistical system (Australia and Canada)

The latest available data show that in 1995/96, the Australian Government spent over US$2,200 million funding cultural institutions and/or activities, while over US$4,000 million was spent by the Canadian Government in 1994/95. This means that expenditure per head was well over US$100 in each country. It is not surprising, therefore, that governments in Australia and Canada have tried to collect regular and reliable statistics on cultural sectors to ensure that the resources they are devoting to cultural activities are being used wisely.

The conceptual frameworks used by the Australian and Canadian statistical agencies for collecting and organizing information on these sectors are based essentially on *Framework for Culture Statistics* (FCS) published by UNESCO in 1986; the FCS approach has been to list the sectors of interest and then, in matrix form, highlight the data needs for various stages of the collection process (i.e. creation, production, distribution, consumption and preservation). Given this, the end-users of the information should be in no doubt as to what is (and what is not) included in the definition of culture. For the record, the nine FCS categories are : (1) cultural heritage; (2) printed matter and literature; (3) music; (4) performing arts; (5) audio media; (6) audiovisual media; (7) sociocultural activities; (8) sports and games; (9) environment and nature.

The Australian and Canadian statistical agencies have, in the main, similar ways of going about their business. However, there are significant differences in the manner in which they gather their cultural statistics. From the beginning Canada had sufficient funding to commence data gathering in its own right, while in Australia the tactic has been (of necessity) to influence the 'system' rather than independently collect information. Both approaches have distinct advantages – and, of course disadvantages – yet the two are very similar in the way they tackle their major tasks of ensuring that they are operating from a sound statistical framework.

An advantage of the Canadian method is that, within reason, the Culture Statistics Program can make important decisions concerning its data collections without necessarily worrying about how it integrates with the wider Statistics Canada statistical system.

On the other hand, one of the advantages of the

(recall that, in the Sen framework that we have adopted, it is the achieved functioning bundle of an individual that determines his/her well-being). What is more likely to be available is information on the proportion of the population that has achieved a certain level of any given functioning. Unfortunately, it is highly unlikely that we shall have such information.

Can we aggregate over these proportions? An example might clarify the situation. Suppose we have only two functionings: intellectual achievement (indicated by the number of books read) and the extent of aesthetic fulfilment (given by the number of concerts attended). Suppose that 90% of the population has read 10 books each in a given year, and 10% of the population has read none. Additionally, suppose that 20% of the population has attended 5 concerts each in the same year while 80% has attended none. However, we might not know what fraction of the population has read 10 books but attended no concerts, and so on. Yet, this latter information is what would be needed to do the standard calculation of the level of social well-being based on well-being of individuals.

The practical difficulties in collecting appropriate data present a formidable problem in the approach that proceeds first by aggregating the different components of an individual's well-being so

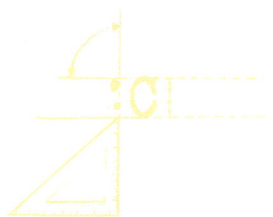

Australian system is that opportunities for influencing traditional collections arise where such collections would not normally have a cultural element. In addition, the very fact that the National Centre for Culture and Recreation Statistics does not have its own data collection programme has forced it to search existing databases for any relevant information.

The Statistics Canada programme consists of many surveys covering cultural industries and institutions (i.e. book publishing, film production, radio and television, sound recording and performing arts) as well as a survey of government agencies' expenditure on culture. In addition, surveys such as Time Use (including a supplement to measure cultural participation), and the detailed Cultural Labour Force Survey, help to paint a complete picture of cells in the cultural framework.In recent times, the Culture Statistics Program of Canada has also stepped up its efforts to improve the analysis of existing data: the biennial flagship publication, *Canada's Culture, Heritage and Identity: A Statistical Perspective*, and the quarterly magazine-style *Focus on Culture* testify to these efforts.

The cultural statistics programme in Australia can best be summarized as working within the wider statistical system in an effort to add items of interest to existing collection vehicles. The major items of interest are at the sectoral level, but some broader issues remain, such as documenting the size of the cultural sector as a persuasive argument in favour of the maintenance of government funding.

Nevertheless, as in the case of Canada, there is specific interest here in the economics of the cultural industries, i.e. how many businesses are operating and what is their employment, profit, value added, major sources of income, and main items of expenditure and production. At least one survey has been conducted of businesses and government organizations associated with book publishing, music, film and television production, distribution and exhibition, libraries, museums, sport and recreation and the arts, and more of such surveys are planned. In addition, special surveys of the activities of individual Australians have been conducted to determine how many attend various cultural venues (art galleries, museums, libraries, performing arts, etc.) and how many work in culture-related activities, be it as their main job, a second job or as a volunteer.

Barry Haydon
Statistician; Director, National Centre for Culture
and Recreation Statistics (NCCRS),
Australian Bureau of Statistics, Adelaide (Australia)

as to arrive at an assessment of the overall well-being of the individual, and then by aggregating the well-being levels of the different individuals in the society so as to arrive at an assessment of the well-being of the society as a whole. An additional consideration for not choosing such a method is that the various dimensions of social well-being are lost in the first stage of this two-stage aggregation procedure, since, in the first stage itself, the achievements of an individual in terms of the different functionings are combined to yield the level of the individual's overall well-being. Thus, such an approach does not serve our specific purpose of constructing cultural indicators of social well-being.

An alternative approach involves two steps: (1) for each separate functioning, we assess the social achievement by aggregating the different individual's achievements in terms of that functioning, and (2) we then aggregate the social achievements with respect to the different functioning in order to derive the total social achievement on all functionings. Certain strong assumptions are necessary to validate this approach. Also, the approach has certain drawbacks when one seeks to take into account inequalities when measuring social well-being. Inequalities among individuals with respect to certain functionings may increase, for example, but if the changes in inequality move in different directions, the level of individual well-being of each person, judging by his or her combination of functionings, could well remain the same. For example, if the inequality between two individuals in terms of both the number of books read and the numbers of concerts attended increases, but one person attends more concerts while the other reads more books, then each person's well-being may remain the same, if, in the case of one person, the increase in the number of books read compensates for the fewer number of concerts attended, and, in the case of the other person, the greater number of concerts attended compensates for the fewer books read.

The inclusion of freedom

As mentioned earlier, Amartya Sen regards individual freedom – defined as the range of opportunities open to the person – as an essential ingredient of the well-being of the individual. Yet, when freedom is defined in terms of the set of all bundles of functionings available to the person, it is not necessarily a matter of 'culture' per se. Some of the functioning (e.g. being well nourished) are not 'cultural' functionings. Moreover, one would need a formidable amount of data to map out the set of all available functioning bundles for each individual.

Nevertheless, it may be useful to capture at least those aspects of freedom in a society that could be categorized as 'negative freedoms', e.g. freedom of thought and expression, freedom to participate in the political process, immunity from invasive actions of the state, and so on. This is a more practical approach, but one that somewhat departs from Sen's notion of freedom as reflected in an individual's opportunity set, that is, the set of functioning bundles available to the individual.

Our restricted notion of freedom could be regarded as one of the basic functionings of an individual. For our present purposes, we categorize it as one of the political and social functionings along with dimensions such as personal security and being able to live without shame about one's position in society.

The construction of indicators

What are the cultural indicators of human development that could be chosen for the two categories of functionings that we have identified, namely, social and political functionings (including negative freedoms) and intellectual and aesthetic functionings? For the exercise to be tractable, we need to restrict our attention to a relatively small number of functionings that we consider to be crucial and that we can hope to capture through suitable indicators.

Indicators of intellectual and aesthetic functionings

For the category of intellectual and aesthetic functionings, we would suggest the following possible indicators: (1) an index of education; (2) an index of research; (3) an index of production of new books, journals, newspapers, etc.; (4) an index of production of music, dance, plays, operas, films, television programmes, paintings, and so on; (5) an index of consumption of books, journals, newspapers, and so on; and (6) an index of consumption of music, dance, plays, operas, films, television programmes, videos, museums, and so forth.

In the case of many of these indices, it would be difficult to maintain that the index under consideration is concerned only with intellectual or aesthetic functioning. For example, the production of books and journals could represent either literary output or the furthering of knowledge.

Several points are worth emphasizing here. The first is that, whatever indices are chosen for this category, they should cover the production as well as the consumption of aesthetic and intellectual products. An exclusive focus on consumption would neglect the important dimension of creativity. A second point is that the indicators must capture the wide range of cultural activities that often take place

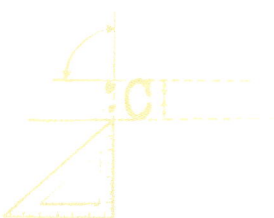

outside the organized 'cultural market' (e.g. dancing in tribal societies, choir music in churches, ritualistic wall paintings by housewives in rural India). The third point is that our concern here is not with aesthetic superiority or inferiority, but with human well-being. By this standard, the contribution of a tribal flautist's music may not be inferior to the sophisticated aesthetic contribution of classical music in a formal concert.

Two additional considerations also warrant mention. First, in the Workshop on Cultural Indicators of Development organized by UNESCO in January 1996, Paul Streeten introduced the idea of using time as the basis for several indicators. The analytical implications of this approach have not, unfortunately, been adequately explored in welfare economics. However, several of the indices that we recommend could in fact be usefully expressed in common time units. For example, the consumption of books, newspapers and journals could be measured by the time spent on such activity, as could the consumption of music, films, operas, and so on. Also, education could be measured in terms of the average number of years spent in schools and colleges.

In choosing indicators, we should also attempt to capture aspects of 'poverty' in terms of the attributes under consideration. As an example, we should adjust the average number of years of education of a population to take into account the incidence of illiteracy, which could be considered as a form of 'educational poverty'. Similarly, in constructing a time-based indicator of aesthetic functionings, we should make an adjustment to our indicator based on the proportion of the population that spends less than some stipulated minimum amount of time on the relevant activity.

Indicators of social and political functionings

While one could conceive of numerous indicators for social and political functionings, it seems prudent to concentrate on only a few key indicators directly reflecting some of the basic functionings. We would single out three areas for consideration: (1) violence, (2) discrimination and (3) political freedom, especially freedom of thought and expression and freedom to undertake political activities. An index of violence should include all types of violence, including ethnic violence and violent crimes. Also, a measure of discrimination should be broad enough to cover gender, race, religion, and so on.

Of the three areas we recommend, political freedom is likely to be the most elusive and the most controversial. We should rely as much as possible on quantitative information (such as the number of political prisoners, the incidence of state-induced violence against forces of opposition and the variety of recognized political parties). Any judgements that are made should be explicitly stated and based on 'precise' criteria.

Aggregation of indicators

Should the various indicators that we have proposed be aggregated to produce one composite cultural index of human development? Of course, aggregation need not be an all-or-nothing exercise. Various degrees of partial aggregation are possible.

Even without any aggregation, the cultural indicators will be useful in many ways, but the information conveyed by a large number of indices may lack intuitive focus and can often be confusing. Therefore, there is a need for some amount of aggregation which will replace a multitude of indices by a relatively small number of indicators. Should one go beyond this and try to construct a single composite index? Note that, if we decide to do so, we do not necessarily have to discard the partial indicators. Indeed, if one at all decides to go in for a single composite cultural index of human development, such a composite index should be introduced in addition to, rather than as a substitute of, the various partial indicators on which the composite index would need to be based. There is no doubt that throwing out the partial indicators and replacing them by a single composite index will be entirely unwise since it would involve an enormous loss of information. However, so long as all the constituent partial indicators are retained, a composite index may serve the useful function of promoting discussion and debate about the relative importance of the different dimensions involved in such an index.

It is sometimes objected that full aggregation does not make sense since very disparate things, such as the consumption of music, films, etc. are being combined. But our concept of human well-being, which every indicator is designed to reflect, provides the unifying analytical principle for aggregation. At the risk of emphasizing the obvious, it may be worth noting that, given the constraints imposed by scarce resources, societies often do weigh the benefit of devoting a certain amount of resources to, say, reducing violence in the society as against the benefits of devoting the same resources to, say, promoting classical music. The normative basis for such comparisons is usually provided by explicit or implicit judgements about individual and social well-being.

Another objection to a composite index is that there may be a low correlation among the indicators constituting it: indicators may move in opposite directions as we try to compare countries. The objection would be valid if our primary purpose were to determine why the individual indicators are moving in different directions. But our principal aim is to rank countries on the basis of their achievements with respect to cultural functionings, and for this purpose a lack of correlation among individual indicators is not particularly problematic.

A more complex issue is introduced by the fact that every rule for aggregating cultural indicators must directly or indirectly introduce judgements regarding the relative importance of the different indicators. No more than a partial ordering is likely from applying a weak rule such as the 'dominance principle' ('country A's achievement is higher than that of country B if A's achievement is at least as high as that of B for every indicator and strictly higher for some indicator'). Stronger rules for aggregation are necessary in order to achieve a more useful ranking. This is perhaps not an appropriate occasion for a detailed discussion of the structure of the different classes of plausible aggregation rules. Whatever aggregation rule is chosen, however, it will involve parameters the values of which will depend on ethical judgements. These judgements should be explicitly stated and sensitive analysis carried out to test the robustness of the results with respect to alternate values of the parameters.

Bibliography

CHAKRAVARTY, A. 1995. *The Concept and the Measurement of the Standard of Living.* (Ph. D. Dissertation, University of California, Riverside.)

SEN, A. 1985. *Commodities and Capabilities.* Amsterdam, North Holland.

——. 1987. *The Standard of Living.* Cambridge, Cambridge University Press.

WORLD COMMISSION ON CULTURE AND DEVELOPMENT. 1995. *Our Creative Diversity.* Paris, UNESCO.

Part Six
Implications
for policy

Recasting cultural policy

Globalization and growing international interdependence present new challenges and opportunities for culture and cultural policies throughout the world. These challenges are environmental, political, social, human and cultural (in the narrow sense). The analysis and evidence presented in the chapters of this first *World Culture Report* suggest that the role of culture will be seen to be of increasing importance in the discussion of development policies, especially of alternative approaches to development and its different styles. Culture is frequently invoked to explain both the successes and failures of development. For example, some have attributed the economic miracle of East Asian economies to Confucian culture and 'Asian values' and asserted that cultural diversity is not merely useful but essential for development. It has been established beyond doubt that the Protestant ethic is not the only source of thrift and hard work. At the same time, the recent turmoil in these economies has also been attributed to certain features of local cultures. Both positive and negative traits of economic development are said to be linked to culture. Neither view is fully persuasive. The discussion calls for a deeper analysis of the links between culture and development, as between culture and development crises. The chapters in this report point to key distinctions that should be made at the start of any such analysis.

Although we argue that diversity contributes to creativity, it is not enough to advocate diversity in the abstract. *Our Creative Diversity* (1995) set the scene, but our task now is to go beyond this and show precisely how diversity enhances economic success, social opportunity, political stability and conflict resolution, besides being valuable, beautiful and delightful in itself. The evidence suggests that democracy draws strength from certain cultural conditions. Yet it is by building democratic institutions that a more participatory culture evolves, and this in turn strengthens democracy. The direction of causality is mainly from social and political institutions to political values and practices.

The important evidence presented in this report that the existence of democratic institutions is not associated with culturally defined differences implies a clear signal: policy-makers cannot refuse democracy on the grounds of their own culture; they cannot use cultural traditions and features as an excuse for not institutionalizing participatory and democratic political structures of decision-making, open to diverse voices and interests. The countries that have weathered the recent Asian financial storm best are democracies, i.e. Japan, the Philippines and Taiwan. The Republic of Korea and Thailand are in the process of recovering. They have replaced their former corrupt regimes through democratic processes. Indonesia's disastrous road should put to rest any myth of 'Asian values' which hold that democracy and human rights are 'Western concepts' hostile to Asia and economic growth. A government that is not answerable to its people is not likely to have the institutions needed to impose discipline in order to overcome a financial crisis or embark on successful long-term development.

Cultural policies should be integrated with economic and political policies, so that national and local cultural values are recognized in the management of the economy. There is much room for experiment with creative forms of conflict resolution that foster equality instead of discrimination and conviviality instead of violence.

The growing risk of violent ethnic conflicts arising from the arrogant and intolerant assertion of cultural, indigenous, ethnic, racial, religious, linguistic or minority rights is apparent in many places. Several chapters in the present report demonstrate that isolating linguistic or cultural groups and 'drawing the borders in blood' reflects not only a misapprehension of the nature of culture and the evolution of history, but is doomed to fail in societies that are becoming increasingly interdependent and multicultural. Indigenous and culturally distinct groups, and ethnic, racial or religious sub-groups that demand rights to express and continue to develop their cultures, deserve to be supported, but their relationships with the wider societies, nations and world community in which they are embedded should also be recognized in thought and action. The cure for separatist, exclusive ethnicity is multicultural ethnicity. In the global system of cultural exchanges some cultures are disappearing. But as some forms of culture disappear, new forms appear locally. The disappearance of old cultural forms is entirely consistent with a rich variety of new forms of human life. Attitudes should be encouraged and laws and institutions established that recognize multiple voices and actors and provide ways of handling differences and plural, partial interpretations of the world. We should learn to value the variety of human forms of social and cultural life; and so long as these differences meet the constraints of a global ethics, in particular the respect for basic human rights, we should celebrate and rejoice in cultural variety.

Policy-makers have to rethink state, community and international institutions and policies to permit local populations to choose their languages, allegiances and ways of life, provided that the implementation of these choices is taken up by the local or micro-regional communities themselves. At the same time, institutions should be created that encourage a dialogue between leaders of different cultural groups to negotiate exchanges and promote better mutual understanding. Intercultural dialogue becomes a prime policy line of action which should be implemented according to local ways of management and organization. The important thing is that local communities and their administrative arrangements, and municipal, provincial and departmental or state governments should take on the main responsibility for this dialogue and ensure that no artificial walls are erected to stop the flow of intercultural discourse.

This is especially relevant for the young generations who, in their hearts and minds, are open to many cultures from which they take symbols, icons and customs that allow them to rejuvenate their traditions, thereby making them better adapted to the relentlessly changing conditions of a telecommunicated, globalized and shrunken world. Policies to encourage intercultural productions in the arts, especially by the young and by women, should be given priority. Women, where they are allowed to participate fully in social and cultural life, will contribute in large part to creating the new societies of the twenty-first century.

Cultural policy should look beyond a purely national emphasis and take, in addition, a broader, international, inter-regional and global perspective. New partnerships between governments, corporations, private voluntary associations and other stakeholders should be developed. The positive impact of globalization on local creativity, in that it opens up markets, should be identified and encouraged. The effects of global markets on local cultural industries, both good and bad, should be more clearly recognized, so that policy can protect and enhance their cultural and economic flowering.

Policies that favour the expression and development of cultural potential will also have repercussions on how people relate to their physical environment. Achieving environmental sustainability calls for democratization of expertise and participation of local communities. As is made clear in the final chapter, global problems give rise to pessimism on the part of the public, yet it is local problems that are their main concern. Cities, the most multicultural sites of the future, should evolve ways in which people who speak different languages and have different loyalties can live together in peace. Urban squalor, violence and crime are not the result of urbanization, but of inadequate incomes, unemployment, poor education, overcrowded housing, insecure tenure, homelessness and lack of social support.

City governments and municipalities can encourage peaceful and prosperous urban communities by strengthening their support for local initiatives. Apart from the necessary social services in health, education, housing, water and sanitation, they can encourage new expressions in art which enhance the dynamic of a local/global dialogue. Artists everywhere wish to express their personal and cultural identities, and in doing so they create global trends. The new site for the creation of art is the global market place. Policy-makers should ensure that artists are able to participate in the expanding global markets.

In Chapter 16 we hear the voices of people around the world who express their views directly. They are saying that they are moderately satisfied with their lives, and that they feel at ease in their families and local communities. They acknowledge progress, yet have fears about the future (unemployment, crime, drugs and the environment). They would like their children to be tolerant, yet feel very distrustful of the larger world. They are sympathetic to democracy, but critical of some of its results.

The analysis throughout this report shows that culture goes far beyond the field traditionally assigned to ministries of culture. Culture is indeed concerned with artistic creation and with ethnic and indigenous issues, but it also has social and political dimensions. It is relevant in designing and implementing models of economic development, constructing stable democracies, ensuring that diverse cultures can live together without violent conflict or war, and providing a sense of trust, partnership and solidarity that are necessary to any society in which people co-operate for their well-being. This calls for an education for world citizens who are rooted in their local culture, as well as for patriotic cosmopolitans who are loyal to their families, neighbours, local communities, countries and humankind in ever-wider concentric circles. Let us not forget that we are undermining the case for multicultural respect if we fail to place a greater respect for all human beings at the heart of education.

These processes can only be properly grasped by means of more and better data from a broader array of fields. And policy-makers should develop statistical and analytical capacities for analysing and monitoring such processes. A concerted effort should be made to develop an internationally agreed conceptual framework for cultural statistics with a broader interpretation of culture than the one currently in use. And within this framework, no attempt should be spared to fill the gaps in the available information.

Part Seven
Statistical Tables
and Culture
Indicators

Measuring culture: prospects and limits

Leo Goldstone
Statistician; Director, World Statistics Ltd, New York
(United States)

The indicators compiled, analysed and presented in this first *World Culture Report* have had to be drawn from material that was readily available. In many respects this has limited the depth and scope of the analysis. Many relevant cultural concerns are not reflected adequately through existing statistics and consequently are not included among the indicators in the report.

The Culture Indicators in the report do not pretend to measure world culture – the culture of the world is far more complex and multi-faceted. What the indicators do is to present those aspects of world culture that are readily measurable. However, one of the aims of the report is to start a process of broadening those measurable and reported aspects of world culture in the coming years so that subsequent reports will be able to present a more complete picture.

In addressing the question of what quantitative aspects of culture to emphasize and how to present them, one issue immediately arose. It became clear that the production and consumption of cultural goods that could be priced in the market was the area that was richest in indicators. Furthermore, the richer the country, the more cultural goods it usually produced and consumed. Not only did rich countries have more data, but they 'scored' higher in the area of producing and consuming cultural goods through market mechanisms.

One very powerful argument against trying to design a single cultural development index was that it would inevitably end up as a rich-country cultural achievement index and, apparently, the richer the country the more cultured it would appear, with a few inevitable exceptions. The other more important argument against a cultural achievement index was the fact that, in our view, culture is multi-faceted and cultural diversity should be nurtured. A monolithic single cultural development index would represent the antithesis of this view.

The challenge was how to introduce the multi-cultural aspects of all countries as a balance to the inevitable bias towards the rich countries in the cultural production and consumption market indicators. Those indicators had to stay, as they reflected an important and measurable part of world culture. The aim was to broaden the scope of the indicators so as to bring in cultural features that existed in all countries, could be provided by all countries, and could be presented in indicator tables.

These 'multi-cultural' features are found in the table on national public holidays, the table on heritage sites, and in the emphasis on the multi-cultural nature of the world, the movements among peoples: to study abroad, to tour abroad, to telephone abroad, and so forth. In all of these movements the names of the other countries involved are listed wherever possible so that the pattern of cultural human flows can be discerned. The tables on translations are multi-cultural by definition, particularly the table on translations by original language where 90 of the over 220 languages being translated are listed and quantified.

The last section on cultural context was also an attempt to broaden the cultural dimension, always asking and sometimes succeeding in replying to the question as to what were the contextual social and economic conditions which impinge on and materially affect cultural development and cultural diversity.

Many cultural concerns were omitted simply because there were too few countries with comparable reliable data. Some cultural elements were omitted because no satisfactory means of expressing them in tabular form have yet been developed. Other cultural issues could be adequately expressed in indicator terms but this would have required special purpose global inquiries for which there was not sufficient time for the purposes of this first report.

The more important cultural omissions make a formidable list. They include: cultural freedom; cultural discrimination; rights of and support to minority cultures; freedom of linguistic expression; freedom to travel; leading religions' freedom of worship and religious attendance; cultural tolerance; ethnicity; official languages, leading spoken languages and dialects; cultural education; cultural participation; cultural prizes; art galleries; music performances; professional arts and crafts; cultural industries and cultural labour force; artists, writers, musicians; the condition of the artist; intellectual property and copyright; taxes and tax allowances on cultural goods and services; cultural export controls; cost of paperback books and similar basic instruments of cultural diffusion compared to

average income; public and private expenditure on culture and cultural heritage; parks, gardens and nature reserves; heritage institutions; professional and non-professional sports and games; cable TV and videos; magazines and comic books; leisure-time use; food and drink traditions and practices, and so on. It is hoped that many of these cultural concerns will be addressed in some quantitative form in future editions of the *World Culture Report*.

Turning to the indicators that have been included in the tables of the report, many that were available often had an inadequate coverage and were lacking in timeliness. As many as one-third of the nearly 200 data items in the indicator tables were not readily available in some comparable form for at least half of the 150 countries with a population of more than 1 million which are listed in the main tables. It was sometimes necessary to go back to the 1980s just to include a respectable number of countries for some indicators. There is a great need to ask questions more frequently.

All this illustrates the crippling lack of basic indicators of culture among UNESCO Member States, and, as might be expected, this lack is greatest in the poorest countries. Among the indicators presented in the report that are missing for so many countries are some very important cultural ones: number of copies of books produced; registered public-library users; number of books in public libraries; cultural radio and television programmes; all the indicators on recorded music; all the indicators on performing arts; all the indicators on archives; museum personnel; all the indicators in the two tables on cultural trade; the trend data on book titles; the trend data on cinema attendance; the trend data on foreign visitors; all the indicators on translations and books in foreign languages; the major countries of origin of foreign students, and so forth.

Just reading this list tells the story. It is hoped that for future reports many missing countries will be able to provide the relevant cultural information about themselves so that the coverage of the indicators

becomes more representative. In this respect, the 1986 UNESCO Framework for Culture Statistics might be used by Member States as a starting point and it would also be very useful to revise this Framework to take into account the rapid cultural changes that have taken place in the last ten years.

Official government data received and standardized by the responsible United Nations agencies or other international and professional organizations were used wherever possible. In cases where there were no reliable official figures, estimates made by the responsible agency were used if available. In some cases the indicators have been obtained directly from the responsible international or professional organizations. In other cases the indicators have been specially developed by World Statistics Ltd for the *World Culture Report* based upon data received from these organizations. The location of each indicator with its source and nature is shown in the index of Culture Indicators on pages 485–7.

In addition to availability, coverage and source, there is the issue of reliability. The indicators in the report are based on data obtained from nearly twenty international and professional sources. Indicators developed from such a large number of sources will have a wide range of data availability, particularly in the case of the first global report of this nature.

Some cultural indicators, such as radios and televisions per inhabitant, are reliable and fairly comprehensive as are many of the indicators found in the tables of the last part on the cultural context. Other cultural indicators, like the indicators on cultural trade, are also reliable but, unfortunately, have a limited coverage. On the other hand, some cultural indicators, like cultural radio and television programmes, are only broad approximations, not necessarily comparable among countries, and with limited coverage.

We would very much welcome comments, suggestions and criticisms concerning the indicators and their presentation so that we can improve them for the next *World Culture Report*.

List of Statistical Tables and Culture Indicators

Cultural activities

TABLE 1: NEWSPAPERS, BOOKS AND LIBRARIES

- Daily newspapers
- Copies of books produced
- Book titles published
- Cultural paper consumed
- Public library users
- Public library books

TABLES 2 AND 2B: RADIO, TELEVISION AND CINEMA

- Radios
- Televisions
- Radios per televisions
- Cultural radio programmes
- Cultural television programmes
- Cinema attendance
- Films produced
- Films imported
- Imported films as percentage of total

TABLE 3: RECORDED MUSIC

- Sales
- Type of music
- Piracy
- Tax rates
- CD players

TABLE 4: PERFORMING ARTS

- Attendance at performing arts
- Foreign tours
- Establishments
- Performances and attendance

TABLE 5: ARCHIVES AND MUSEUMS

- Archives in metres
- User visits
- Visits per personnel
- Museums attendance
- Attendance per personnel

Cultural practices and heritage

TABLES 6 AND 6B: NATIONAL PUBLIC HOLIDAYS

- Number of public holidays
- Dates

TABLE 7: WORLD HERITAGE SITES

- Properties in the World Heritage List by type
- Tentative list
- Endangered heritage sites

Cultural trade and communication

TABLE 8: TRADE IN CULTURAL GOODS

- Books and pamphlets
- Newspapers and periodicals
- Music and related goods
- Visual arts
- Cinema and photography
- Radio and television

TABLE 9: INTERNATIONAL TOURISM

- Arrivals of foreign visitors
- Two major countries of origin
- Receipts from international tourism
- Departures of nationals abroad
- Two major countries of destination
- Expenditures abroad

TABLES 10 AND 10B: COMMUNICATION AND NEW TECHNOLOGY

- Post offices
- Letter post items
- Items sent abroad
- Telephones
- International telephone calls
- Leading international partners
- Cellular telephones
- Fax machines
- Personal computers
- Internet hosts

Cultural trends

TABLE 11: BOOKS
- Copies of books produced
- Book titles published
- Public-library books

TABLE 12: NEWSPAPERS AND CULTURAL PAPER
- Daily newspapers
- Cultural paper consumed

TABLE 13: RADIO AND TELEVISION
- Radios
- Televisions
- Radios per televisions

TABLE 14: CINEMA
- Cinema attendance
- Films produced
- Films imported

TABLE 15: COMMUNICATIONS AND TRAVEL
- Telephones
- Arrivals of foreign visitors

TABLE 16: CULTURAL TRADE
- Total cultural trade
- Cultural trade per capita
- Cultural trade as percentage of GNP
- Cultural exports

Ratification of conventions

TABLE 17: RATIFICATION OF CULTURAL CONVENTIONS
- Protection of the world heritage
- Protection of cultural property in the event of armed conflict
- Prevention of illicit import, export and transfer of ownership of cultural property

TABLE 18: RATIFICATION OF HUMAN RIGHTS CONVENTIONS
- Economic, social and cultural
- Civil and political
- Racial discrimination
- Discrimination against women
- Genocide
- Rights of the child
- Torture
- Refugees

Translations

TABLE 19: TRANSLATIONS AND BOOKS IN FOREIGN LANGUAGES

- Number of translations
- Two leading languages translated
- Titles published in foreign languages
- Multilingual publications

TABLE 20: TRANSLATIONS BY ORIGINAL LANGUAGE

- Number of translations
- Two leading languages into which translated

TABLE 21: MOST FREQUENTLY TRANSLATED AUTHORS

- Name of authors
- Associated country
- Number of translations
- Number of countries translating

Cultural context

TABLE 22: EDUCATION

- Primary net enrolment ratio
- Secondary gross enrolment ratio
- Tertiary gross enrolment ratio
- Public expenditure on education as percentage of GNP

TABLE 23: THIRD-LEVEL EDUCATION ABROAD

- Students abroad
- Two leading countries of study
- Foreign students
- Two leading countries of origin
- Foreign students as percentage of students abroad

TABLE 24: HUMAN CAPITAL

- Adult literacy rate
- Young adult literacy rate
- Mean years of schooling

TABLE 25: DEMOGRAPHY AND HEALTH

- Total population
- Urban population
- Life expectancy
- Female age at first marriage
- Family size
- Fertility rate
- Fertility in young women
- Contraceptive prevalence
- Maternal mortality rate

TABLE 26: MIGRATION AND REFUGEES

- Number of international migrants
- Percent female
- Foreign-born as percentage of population
- Remittances from abroad
- Refugees by country of origin
- Refugees by country of asylum

TABLE 27: ECONOMIC

- GNP per capita in United States dollars
- GNP per capita in international dollars (PPP)
- Ratios of household income share
- Labour-force participation rate

TABLE 28: ENVIRONMENT

- Land area
- Population density
- Nationally protected areas
- Forest area
- Deforestation

TABLE 29: RATIFICATION OF CULTURAL CONVENTIONS AND HERITAGE SITES (LESS-POPULOUS MEMBER STATES)

TABLE 30: REGIONAL AGGREGATES OF CULTURE INDICATORS

Table symbols

-	None or not ratifying.
..	Not available.
(.)	Less than half the unit shown.
1990-93	A dash between two years indicates that the data refer to any one of the years in the period shown.
1990/93	A slash between two years indicates an average for all the years in the period shown.
Note	The indicator tables consist of the 150 countries and territories with a population of 1 million or more; for reasons of space the names of certain regions and countries have had to be abbreviated. Unless otherwise stated the regional aggregates found at the end of each table and in Table 30 are the appropriately weighted values for each group (see the list of regions and countries for the composition of each group). Where the summary measure is a total, the letter T appears in the column.

TABLE 1
CULTURAL ACTIVITIES: NEWSPAPERS, BOOKS AND LIBRARIES

Country	Daily newspapers (daily circulation per thousand people)	Number of copies of books produced (per 100 people)	Book titles published (per 100,000 people)	Cultural paper a) consumed (Kilos per person)	Registered public library users (per 100 people)	Number of books in public libraries (per 100 people)
	1994	1991-94	1991-94	1994	1989-94	1989-94
Sub-Saharan Africa						
Angola	11	..	..	(.)	..	..
Benin	1	1	1	(.)	(.)	1
Botswana	31	..	11	..	..	..
Burkina Faso	1	..	..	..	..	..
Burundi	3	..	..	..	(.)	..
Cameroon	6	..	..	1	..	..
C.A.R.	1	..	..	..	..	..
Chad	(.)	..	..	..	..	..
Congo	8	..	..	(.)	1	1
Côte d' Ivoire	15	..	..	1	..	..
Eritrea	..	12	3	..	..	..
Ethiopia	2	1	(.)	(.)	(.)	(.)
Gabon	28	..	..	1	..	..
Gambia	1	3	2	(.)	..	9
Ghana	18	..	(.)	(.)	(.)	10
Guinea	..	..	..	..	..	(.)
Guinea-Bissau	6	..	..	1	..	..
Kenya	17	2	1	2	..	..
Lesotho	7	..	..	..	(.)	1
Liberia	16	..	..	(.)	..	..
Madagascar	4	2	1	(.)	..	..
Malawi	3	2	3	(.)	(.)	2
Mali	4	..	..	(.)	..	..
Mauritania	1	..	..	(.)	..	1
Mauritius	112	8	4	11	1	..
Mozambique	8	..	..	(.)	..	..
Namibia	100	..	13	..	..	..
Niger	(.)	(.)	(.)	(.)	..	..
Nigeria	17	..	2	1	(.)	1
Rwanda	(.)	..	..	(.)	..	..
Senegal	6	..	..	1	(.)	(.)
Sierra Leone	5	..	..	(.)	..	..
Somalia	1	..	..	(.)	..	..
South Africa	31	93	12	20	..	39
Sudan	24	..	..	(.)	..	..
Tanzania	12	..	..	1	..	..
Togo	2	..	..	(.)	(.)	2
Uganda	2	12	2	(.)	(.)	(.)
Zaire	3	1	(.)	(.)	..	..
Zambia	13	..	..	(.)	..	..
Zimbabwe	17	..	2	2	1	10
Arab States						
Algeria	51	2	1	3	..	..
Egypt	43	..	6	5	(.)	11
Iraq	26	..	..	2	..	..
Jordan	47	113	7	7	..	4
Kuwait	387	..	12	29	..	17

Country	Daily newspapers (daily circulation per thousand people)	Number of copies of books produced (per 100 people)	Book titles published (per 100,000 people)	Cultural paper a) consumed (Kilos per person)	Registered public library users (per 100 people)	Number of books in public libraries (per 100 people)
	1994	1991-94	1991-94	1994	1989-94	1989-94
Lebanon	110	..	..	17	..	..
Libya	13	..	..	1	..	..
Morocco	15	5	1	3	..	..
Oman	29	1	1	7	..	..
Saudi Arabia	58	..	..	6	..	4
Syria	19	..	4	3	..	..
Tunisia	45	1	6	7	..	28
U.A.E.	136	213	12	46	..	..
Yemen, Rep.	15	..	..	1	..	..
South Central Asia						
Afghanistan	10	8	(.)	(.)	..	..
Armenia	23	47	6	..	29	397
Azerbaijan	28	74	5	..	40	..
Bangladesh	6	..	..	1	..	1
Bhutan	..	..	..	..	..	..
Georgia	..	21	6	..	46	..
India	31	..	1	2	..	..
Iran	17	42	17	3	..	5
Kazakhstan	..	..	17	..	39	..
Kyrgyz Rep.	12	42	7	..	..	..
Nepal	7	..	..	..	..	..
Pakistan	21	1	(.)	1	(.)	(.)
Sri Lanka	25	86	16	5	1	3
Tajikistan	14	44	4	..	..	..
Turkey	118	..	8	6	..	15
Turkmenistan	..	150	13	..	..	..
Uzbekistan	6	197	6	..	..	..
East Asia						
China	23	..	9	8	1	26
Hong Kong	735	..	..	159	26	69
Japan	576	253	28	106	13	129
Korea, Dem.	226	..	..	(.)	..	..
Korea, Rep.	394	360	76	37	69	19
Mongolia	81	40	12	(.)	..	..
Southeast Asia and Oceania						
Australia	257	..	61	87	..	171
Cambodia	..	..	..	..	..	..
Indonesia	24	..	3	4	..	..
Lao PDR	3	3	1	(.)	..	..
Malaysia	139	88	21	27	7	41
Myanmar	22	..	8	(.)	..	..
New Zealand	239	..	..	54	..	..
P.N.G.	15	..	3	1	1	4
Philippines	62	..	2	5	2	9
Singapore	301	..	..	137	..	..
Thailand	46	..	13	11	..	..
Vietnam	8	115	7	1	..	18

Country	Daily newspapers (daily circulation per thousand people) 1994	Number of copies of books produced (per 100 people) 1991-94	Book titles published (per 100,000 people) 1991-94	Cultural paper a) consumed (Kilos per person) 1994	Registered public library users (per 100 people) 1989-94	Number of books in public libraries (per 100 people) 1989-94
Latin America and the Caribbean						
Argentina	135	143	26	18	..	..
Bolivia	67	..	..	2	..	..
Brazil	45	65	13	11	..	..
Chile	99	14	13	16	16	8
Colombia	42	31	4	10	..	5
Costa Rica	88	..	29	11	9	10
Cuba	119	42	9	1	2	48
Dom. Rep.	34	..	..	5	..	..
Ecuador	70	(.)	(.)	6	..	1
El Salvador	49	..	..	7	(.)	1
Guatemala	23	..	..	5	..	..
Haiti	6	..	..	(.)	..	..
Honduras	42	1	(.)	3	..	..
Jamaica	65	..	..	7	28	47
Mexico	115	..	..	11	..	36
Nicaragua	32	..	..	2	..	..
Panama	61	..	..	7	..	..
Paraguay	41	..	3	7	..	..
Peru	85	..	9	9	..	25
Trinidad	186	2	2	11	..	..
Uruguay	235	62	36	14	..	..
Venezuela	206	39	18	13	60	25
North America						
Canada	166	..	76	96	..	209
U.S.A.	218	..	20	143	..	..
Europe						
Albania	53	118	12	4	7	127
Austria	298	..	99	72	12	102
Belarus	174	..	32	..	41	..
Belgium	316	..	138	105	17	294
Bosnia	146	..	..	..	..	..
Bulgaria	212	509	71	5	16	..
Croatia	50	..	56	12	..	96
Czech Rep.	296	..	91	18	11	366
Denmark	308	..	230	75	..	625
Estonia	..	..	154	13	23	..
Finland	468	..	246	166	47	712
France	234	..	78	79	8	154
Germany	313	..	86	103	11	158
Greece	153	..	39	34	..	71
Hungary	169	..	98	18	16	489
Ireland	154	..	..	54	22	309
Israel	271	178	85	48	..	..
Italy	100	507	58	63	1	48
Latvia	233	433	68	17	..	..
Lithuania	134	..	78	2	..	..

Country	Daily newspapers (daily circulation per thousand people)	Number of copies of books produced (per 100 people)	Book titles published (per 100,000 people)	Cultural paper a) consumed (Kilos per person)	Registered public library users (per 100 people)	Number of books in public libraries (per 100 people)
	1994	1991-94	1991-94	1994	1989-94	1989-94
Macedonia, FYR	25	139	32	7	..	130
Moldova	24	136	18	..	29	428
Netherlands	329	..	221	93	29	271
Norway	596	..	159	98	..	462
Poland	140	256	28	12	17	353
Portugal	41	272	68	33	6	39
Romania	299	221	16	4	9	204
Russia	122	400	21	5	42	597
Slovakia	244	116	66	13	14	372
Slovenia	203	..	146	..	19	264
Spain	102	461	113	51	1	76
Sweden	460	..	158	94	..	513
Switzerland	371	..	219	122	5	395
Ukraine	50	169	10	..	42	..
U.K.	344	..	148	104	57	223
Yugoslavia	83	113	27	..	..	146

Region	Daily newspapers (daily circulation per thousand people)	Number of copies of books produced (per 100 people)	Book titles published (per 100,000 people)	Cultural paper a) consumed (Kilos per person)	Registered public library users (per 100 people)	Number of books in public libraries (per 100 people)
	1994	1991-94	1991-94	1994	1989-94	1989-94
World	97	..	18	21	..	..
Developing	43	..	7	6	..	..
Industrial	297	..	54	83	22	304
Dev exc India / China	..	..	8	7	..	..
Ind exc USA / Russia	..	..	73	76	18	246
Sub-Saharan Africa	10	..	..	2	..	..
Arab States	44	96	4	5	..	..
South Central Asia	29	37	3	2	..	46
East Asia	89	..	13	18	4	35
Southeast Asia / Oc	45	..	8	9	..	..
Latin Am / Carib	80	..	13	10	..	..
North America	213	..	26	138	..	..
Europe	278	368	70	53	24	342

a) Newsprint, other printing and writing paper.

TABLE 2
CULTURAL ACTIVITIES: RADIO, TELEVISION AND CINEMA

Country	Radios (per thousand people)	Televisions (per thousand people)	Radios per Televisions	Cultural radio programmes (% of total programmes)	Cultural television programmes (% of total programmes)
	1995	1995	1995	1989-94	1989-94
Sub-Saharan Africa					
Angola	34	7.4	4.6	..	..
Benin	92	5.9	15.6	1.1	..
Botswana	131	19	6.9	3.3	..
Burkina Faso	28	5.7	4.9	12.6	8.3
Burundi	68	2.0	34.0	2.1	8.0
Cameroon	152	24	6.3	..	..
Central African Rep.	75	4.9	15.3	..	..
Chad	248	1.4	177.1	5.4	10.6
Congo	116	7.7	15.1	6.4	19.2
Côte d' Ivoire	153	62	2.5	5.1	4.9
Eritrea	87	0.3	290.0	..	..
Ethiopia	193	4.4	43.9	5.2	0.2
Gabon	181	47	3.9	..	..
Gambia	164	3.2	51.3	..	..
Ghana	231	92	2.5	1.1	0.7
Guinea	44	8.8	5.0	..	..
Guinea-Bissau	42	..	..	..	..
Kenya	96	18	5.3	..	..
Lesotho	37	12	3.1	..	..
Liberia	318	26	12.2	..	..
Madagascar	192	20	9.6	25.8	4.8
Malawi	256	..	..	9.3	..
Mali	46	1.9	24.2	..	..
Mauritania	150	25	6.0	..	..
Mauritius	367	222	1.7	..	..
Mozambique	38	3.5	10.9	16.1	5.2
Namibia	140	25	5.6	..	..
Niger	68	11	6.2	10.0	16.0
Nigeria	197	55	3.6	..	..
Rwanda	101	1.0	101.0	..	..
Senegal	120	38	3.2	5.7	6.3
Sierra Leone	250	12	20.8	..	..
Somalia	42	13	3.2	..	..
South Africa	316	109	2.9	..	..
Sudan	270	84	3.2	10.5	10.0
Tanzania	28	2.3	12.2	..	9.7
Togo	215	12	17.9	..	4.2
Uganda	117	13	9.0	..	..
Zaire	98	2.2	44.5	20.2	2.2
Zambia	99	32	3.1	..	..
Zimbabwe	89	29	3.1	1.6	..
Arab States					
Algeria	238	89	2.7	..	..
Egypt	312	110	2.8	18.9	..
Iraq	224	80	2.8	2.6	..
Jordan	251	80	3.1	..	..
Kuwait	473	370	1.3	8.5	13.7

Country	Radios (per thousand people) 1995	Televisions (per thousand people) 1995	Radios per Televisions 1995	Cultural radio programmes (% of total programmes) 1989-94	Cultural television programmes (% of total programmes) 1989-94
Lebanon	891	366	2.4	..	..
Libya	231	102	2.3	..	..
Morocco	226	94	2.4	..	..
Oman	580	657	0.9	18.5	12.6
Saudi Arabia	291	257	1.1	..	2.5
Syria	264	67	3.9	..	..
Tunisia	200	89	2.2	..	..
Unit. Arab. Emirates	271	104	2.6	17	9.5
Yemen Rep.	43	28	1.5	5.6	11.7
South Central Asia					
Afghanistan	132	10	13.2	5.2	..
Armenia	..	224	..	15.8	11.2
Azerbaijan	20	33	0.6	..	..
Bangladesh	47	5.9	8.0	..	5.3
Bhutan	17	5.7	3.0	..	..
Georgia	..	..	..	..	7.8
India	81	51	1.6	..	8.1
Iran	228	63	3.6	30.5	16.2
Kazakhstan	384	256	1.5	..	..
Kyrgyz Rep.	114	34	3.4	..	..
Nepal	36	5.1	7.1	8.2	..
Pakistan	92	20	4.6	1.2	3.6
Sri Lanka	206	51	4.0	17.3	0.3
Tajikistan	171	..	..	..	..
Turkey	164	189	0.9	2.1	10.3
Turkmenistan	81	180	0.5	..	..
Uzbekistan	81	191	0.4	..	..
East Asia					
China	185	205	0.9	..	..
Hong Kong	668	286	2.3	..	..
Japan	916	684	1.3	..	..
Korea, Dem.	136	48	2.8	..	..
Korea, Rep.	1,024	334	3.1	35.5	25.1
Mongolia	134	45	3.0	..	..
Southeast Asia and Oceania					
Australia	1,304	495	2.6	1.6	0.1
Cambodia	112	8.5	13.2	..	..
Indonesia	149	66	2.3	..	..
Lao PDR	129	9.0	14.3	..	..
Malaysia	432	164	2.6	..	..
Myanmar	89	5.1	17.5	..	..
New Zealand	997	514	1.9	2.3	1.4
Papua New Guinea	77	3.5	22.0	..	..
Philippinas	147	49	3.0	..	..
Singapore	601	361	1.7	..	..
Thailand	189	189	1.0	..	..
Vietnam	106	43	2.5	..	..

Country	Radios (per thousand people)	Televisions (per thousand people)	Radios per Televisions	Cultural radio programmes (% of total programmes)	Cultural television programmes (% of total programmes)
	1995	1995	1995	1989-94	1989-94
Latin America and the Caribbean					
Argentina	676	219	3.1	10.5	5.3
Bolivia	672	115	5.8	0.2	..
Brazil	399	220	1.8	..	..
Chile	348	215	1.6	6.1	..
Colombia	564	117	4.8	..	7.1
Costa Rica	263	143	1.8	..	..
Cuba	351	228	1.5	23.7	9.8
Dominican Rep.	176	93	1.9	..	..
Ecuador	332	96	3.5	..	..
El Salvador	459	..	..	8.0	15.0
Guatemala	71	56	1.3	..	..
Haiti	53	4.8	11.0	..	..
Honduras	409	88	4.6	..	..
Jamaica	438	162	2.7	..	..
Mexico	263	219	1.2	..	..
Nicaragua	280	73	3.8	..	..
Panama	228	170	1.3	..	..
Paraguay	180	93	1.9	..	..
Peru	259	106	2.4	..	..
Trinidad	505	322	1.6	..	..
Uruguay	609	235	2.6	..	..
Venezuela	458	169	2.7	..	..
North America					
Canada	1,053	714	1.5	..	0.4
United States	2,093	805	2.6	..	..
Europe					
Albania	207	103	2.0	22.5	5.8
Austria	620	497	1.2	19.3	7.9
Belarus	285	227	1.3	4.9	5.0
Belgium	790	454	1.7	3.0	6.4
Bosnia	235	94	2.5	..	..
Bulgaria	471	378	1.2	3.9	3.5
Croatia	266	255	1.0	2.6	4.1
Czech Rep.	638	482	1.3	5.2	14.8
Denmark	1,034	574	1.8	16.6	13.2
Estonia	491	383	1.3	9.4	7.2
Finland	1,008	519	1.9	0.3	5.7
France	895	589	1.5	5.5	20.9
Germany	944	554	1.7	..	4.2
Greece	430	220	2.0	1.5	4.0
Hungary	643	433	1.5	4.7	7.7
Ireland	649	409	1.6	1.5	4.2
Israel	489	290	1.7	..	..
Italy	822	446	1.8	34.9	16.2
Latvia	678	477	1.4	..	..
Lithuania	401	415	1.0	..	..

Country	Radios (per thousand people)	Televisions (per thousand people)	Radios per Televisions	Cultural radio programmes (% of total programmes)	Cultural television programmes (% of total programmes)
	1995	1995	1995	1989-94	1989-94
Macedonia, FYR	183	167	1.1	0.3	2.1
Moldova	699	273	2.6	10.3	2.5
Netherlands	937	497	1.9	..	12.7
Norway	808	433	1.9	6.2	8.7
Poland	454	311	1.5	12.6	8.9
Portugal	245	326	0.8	25.1	0.8
Romania	211	220	1.0	7.2	12.2
Russia	340	377	0.9	..	..
Slovakia	570	476	1.2	1.8	..
Slovenia	384	327	1.2	1.2	3.7
Spain	314	404	0.8	..	5.5
Sweden	882	478	1.8	5.4	27.5
Switzerland	851	419	2.0	5.0	7.2
Ukraine	812	339	2.4	..	..
United Kingdom	1,433	448	3.2	..	..
Yugoslavia	141	190	0.7	4.2	2.5

Region	Radios (per thousand people)	Televisions (per thousand people)	Radios per Televisions	Cultural radio programmes (% of total programmes)	Cultural television programmes (% of total programmes)
	1995	1995	1995	1989-94	1989-94
World	362	204	1.8	..	..
Developing	185	115	1.6	..	..
Industrial	1,005	527	1.9	..	..
Dev exc India / China	225	92	2.4	..	..
Ind exc USA / Russia	800	469	1.7	..	..
Sub-Saharan Africa	169	33	5.1	..	..
Arab States	251	109	2.3	..	..
South Central Asia	96	53	1.8	..	..
East Asia	277	249	1.1	..	..
Southeast Asia / Oc	201	91	2.2	..	..
Latin Am / Carib	387	192	2.0	..	..
North America	1,990	796	2.5	..	..
Europe	672	416	1.6	..	..

TABLE 2B
CULTURAL ACTIVITIES: RADIO, TELEVISION AND CINEMA (CONT.)

Country	Annual cinema attendances (per person)	Number of long films produced	Number of long films imported	Imported long films (as % of total films distributed)
	1990-95	1990-95	1990-95	1990-95
Sub-Saharan Africa				
Angola	0.4	..	108	..
Benin	0.1	..	219	..
Botswana	..	..	..	..
Burkina Faso	0.7	..	..	..
Burundi	(.)	..	..	..
Cameroon	..	2	..	..
Central African Rep.	..	..	..	..
Chad	..	..	..	..
Congo	..	..	43	..
Côte d' Ivoire	0.5	2	86	98
Eritrea	..	..	..	..
Ethiopia	..	1	133	99
Gabon	1.6	..	55	..
Gambia	..	..	..	..
Ghana	0.3	..	..	..
Guinea	0.7	1	394	100
Guinea-Bissau	..	..	..	..
Kenya	0.2	..	364	..
Lesotho	..	..	..	..
Liberia	..	..	..	..
Madagascar	(.)	..	19	..
Malawi	..	..	124	..
Mali	..	3	..	..
Mauritania	..	..	..	..
Mauritius	0.7	1	50	98
Mozambique	0.3	..	..	..
Namibia	..	..	..	..
Niger	..	..	..	..
Nigeria	..	..	..	..
Rwanda	..	..	..	..
Senegal	..	..	..	..
Sierra Leone	..	..	..	..
Somalia	..	..	..	..
South Africa	..	..	..	..
Sudan	..	1	104	99
Tanzania	0.1	..	71	..
Togo	..	..	520	..
Uganda	..	..	..	..
Zaire	..	..	..	..
Zambia	..	..	..	..
Zimbabwe	0.2	..	215	..
Arab States				
Algeria	0.9	3	..	..
Egypt	0.3	72	220	75
Iraq	..	1	..	..
Jordan	(.)	..	271	..
Kuwait	0.5	..	..	..

Country	Annual cinema attendances (per person)	Number of long films produced	Number of long films imported	Imported long films (as % of total films distributed)
	1990-95	1990-95	1990-95	1990-95
Lebanon	..	5	277	98
Libya	..	..	..	..
Morocco	0.7	4	393	99
Oman	..	..	96	..
Saudi Arabia	..	..	..	..
Syria	0.3	2	122	98
Tunisia	..	..	50	..
Unit. Arab.Emirates	..	..	428	..
Yemen Rep.	..	..	..	..
South Central Asia				
Afghanistan	..	3	33	92
Armenia	..	3	28	90
Azerbaijan	0.3	4	3	43
Bangladesh	0.3	77	..	..
Bhutan	..	..	..	..
Georgia	..	5	39	89
India	5.0	838	141	14
Iran	0.4	62	54	47
Kazakhstan	0.4	10	51	84
Kyrgyz Rep.	0.1	..	65	..
Nepal	..	..	..	..
Pakistan	..	64	89	58
Sri Lanka	1.5	58	61	51
Tajikistan	0.1	1	66	99
Turkey	0.3	39	131	77
Turkmenistan	..	..	..	..
Uzbekistan	1.3	10	53	84
East Asia				
China	..	154	..	..
Hong Kong	4.6	315	177	36
Japan	1.1	251	352	58
Korea, Dem.	..	..	..	..
Korea, Rep.	1.3	63	347	85
Mongolia	9.5	..	..	..
Southeast Asia and Oceania				
Australia	3.9	18	239	93
Cambodia	..	..	..	..
Indonesia	..	27	..	..
Lao PDR	(.)	..	112	..
Malaysia	2.0	12	518	98
Myanmar	..	..	..	..
New Zealand	3.9	4	124	97
Papua New Guinea	..	..	..	..
Philippinas	..	456	280	38
Singapore	..	..	..	..
Thailand	..	194	191	50
Vietnam	3.8	..	..	..

Country	Annual cinema attendances (per person)	Number of long films produced	Number of long films imported	Imported long films (as % of total films distributed)
	1990-95	1990-95	1990-95	1990-95
Latin America and the Caribbean				
Argentina	0.5	16	200	93
Bolivia	0.3	4	149	97
Brazil	0.7	86	..	..
Chile	0.6	1	220	100
Colombia	1.3	3	418	99
Costa Rica	0.5	..	49	..
Cuba	2.2	6	22	79
Dominican Rep.	..	..	..	..
Ecuador	0.6	2	203	99
El Salvador	..	..	200	..
Guatemala	0.9	..	..	..
Haiti	..	..	..	..
Honduras	..	..	..	..
Jamaica	..	..	..	..
Mexico	0.7	53	268	83
Nicaragua	..	..	..	..
Panama	..	..	..	..
Paraguay	..	..	..	..
Peru	..	5	211	98
Trinidad	..	..	50	..
Uruguay	..	..	..	..
Venezuela	0.9	4	171	98
North America				
Canada	2.8	22	1,115	98
United States	3.9	420	118	22
Europe				
Albania	1.0	11	9	45
Austria	1.5	22	219	91
Belarus	1.2	2	235	99
Belgium	1.9	8	477	98
Bosnia	..	..	..	..
Bulgaria	0.6	11	134	92
Croatia	0.8	3	33	92
Czech Rep.	0.9	22	109	83
Denmark	1.7	12	150	93
Estonia	0.7	3	85	97
Finland	1.1	8	131	94
France	2.2	141	235	63
Germany	1.5	63	197	76
Greece	1.0	25	148	86
Hungary	1.4	12	80	87
Ireland	2.7	17	137	89
Israel	1.8	15	152	91
Italy	1.6	96	247	72
Latvia	0.4	2	..	..
Lithuania	0.2	3	70	96

Country	Annual cinema attendances (per person)	Number of long films produced	Number of long films imported	Imported long films (as % of total films distributed)
	1990-95	1990-95	1990-95	1990-95
Macedonia, FYR	0.1	2	25	93
Moldova	0.3	6	108	95
Netherlands	1.0	16	173	92
Norway	2.7	15	171	92
Poland	0.4	20	126	86
Portugal	0.8	13	195	94
Romania	0.7	9	101	92
Russia	0.9	46	118	72
Slovakia	1.1	4	121	97
Slovenia	1.5	2	96	98
Spain	2.4	59	346	85
Sweden	1.7	32	203	86
Switzerland	2.2	37	359	91
Ukraine	0.6	6	164	96
United Kingdom	2.0	78	240	77
Yugoslavia	0.2	8	44	85

Region	Annual cinema attendances (per person)	Number of long films produced	Number of long films imported	Imported long films (as % of total films distributed)
	1990-95	1990-95	1990-95	1990-95
		T	T	
World	2.4	4,250	16,350	79
Developing	2.7	2,670	8,960	77
Industrial	2.0	1,580	7,390	82
Dev exc India / China	0.8	..	..	..
Ind exc USA / Russia	1.5	..	..	..
Sub-Saharan Africa	..	..	..	..
Arab States	..	..	1,860	..
South Central Asia	3.8	1,170	810	41
East Asia	1.4	780	880	53
Southeast Asia / Oc	..	..	1,460	..
Latin Am / Carib	..	..	..	..
North America	3.8	440	1,230	74
Europe	1.3	830	5,440	87

TABLE 3
CULTURAL ACTIVITIES: RECORDED MUSIC a)

Country	Unit Sales Retail value (US$ per capita)	Distribution by type of music			Piracy (%)	Combined tax rates c) (%)	CD players (Per 100 households)
		Domestic popular (%)	International popular (%)	Classical (%)			
	1996	1996	1996	1996	1995	1995	1996
Sub-Saharan Africa							
Angola	..	..	..	..	..	..	..
Benin	..	..	..	..	..	..	..
Botswana	..	..	..	..	..	..	..
Burkina Faso	..	..	..	..	..	..	..
Burundi	..	..	..	..	..	..	..
Cameroon	..	..	..	..	..	..	..
C.A.R.	..	..	..	..	..	..	..
Chad	..	..	..	..	..	..	..
Congo	..	..	..	..	..	..	..
Côte d' Ivoire	..	..	..	..	..	..	..
Eritrea	..	..	..	..	..	..	..
Ethiopia	..	..	..	..	..	..	..
Gabon	..	..	..	..	..	..	..
Gambia	..	..	..	..	..	..	..
Ghana	1.0	71	29	(.)	2	..	..
Guinea	..	..	..	..	..	..	..
Guinea-Bissau	..	..	..	..	..	..	..
Kenya	0.1	47	52	1	92	55	1
Lesotho	..	..	..	..	..	..	..
Liberia	..	..	..	..	..	..	..
Madagascar	..	..	..	..	..	..	..
Malawi	..	..	..	..	..	..	..
Mali	..	..	..	..	..	..	..
Mauritania	..	..	..	..	..	..	..
Mauritius	..	..	..	..	..	..	..
Mozambique	..	..	..	..	..	..	..
Namibia	..	..	..	..	..	..	..
Niger	..	..	..	..	..	..	..
Nigeria	0.1	65	35	(.)	45	35	2
Rwanda	..	..	..	..	..	..	..
Senegal	..	..	..	..	..	..	..
Sierra Leone	..	..	..	..	..	..	..
Somalia	..	..	..	..	..	..	..
South Africa	5.1	23	71	3	20	40	4
Sudan	..	..	..	..	..	..	..
Tanzania	..	..	..	..	..	..	..
Togo	..	..	..	..	..	..	..
Uganda	..	..	..	..	..	..	..
Zaire	..	..	..	..	..	..	..
Zambia	..	..	..	..	..	..	..
Zimbabwe	0.3	60	39	1	11	20	..
Arab States							
Algeria	..	..	..	..	..	..	..
Egypt	0.4	83 d)	17	(.)	25	..	(.)
Iraq	..	..	..	..	..	..	..
Jordan	..	..	..	..	..	..	..
Kuwait	..	..	..	..	..	..	..

Country	Unit Sales Retail value (US$ per capita)	Distribution by type of music			Piracy (%)	Combined tax rates c) (%)	CD players (Per 100 households)
		Domestic popular (%)	International popular (%)	Classical (%)			
	1996	1996	1996	1996	1995	1995	1996
Lebanon	..	..	..	..	..	..	..
Libya	..	..	..	..	..	..	..
Morocco	..	..	..	..	..	..	..
Oman	..	..	..	..	..	..	..
Saudi Arabia	5.4	59 d)	41	(.)	43	12	17
Syria	..	..	..	..	..	..	..
Tunisia	..	..	..	..	..	..	..
U.A.E.	23.6	17 d)	73	12 e)	..	4	38
Yemen, Rep.	..	..	..	..	..	..	..
South Central Asia							
Afghanistan	..	..	..	..	..	..	..
Armenia	..	..	..	..	..	..	..
Azerbaijan	..	..	..	..	..	..	..
Bangladesh	..	..	..	..	..	..	..
Bhutan	..	..	..	..	..	..	..
Georgia	..	..	..	..	..	..	..
India	0.3	95	5	(.)	30	..	(.)
Iran	..	..	..	..	..	..	..
Kazalhstan	..	..	..	..	..	..	..
Kyrgyz Rep.	..	..	..	..	..	..	..
Nepal	..	..	..	..	..	..	..
Pakistan	0.1	88	12	(.)	94	15	(.)
Sri Lanka	..	..	..	..	..	..	..
Tajikistan	..	..	..	..	..	..	..
Turkey	2.6	79	21	(.)	32	15	..
Turkmenistan	..	..	..	..	..	..	..
Uzbekistan	..	..	..	..	..	..	..
East Asia							
China	0.1	95 d)	4	1	54	32	7
Hong Kong	28.0	55	37	8	13	0	78
Japan	53.3	73	..	..	..	3	72
Korea, Dem.	..	..	..	..	..	..	..
Korea, Rep.	11.6	53	36	11	18	18	68
Mongolia	..	..	..	..	..	..	..
Southeast Asia and Oceania							
Australia	44.7	12	83	5	4	22	62
Cambodia	..	..	..	..	..	..	..
Indonesia	..	81	19	(.)	9	10	..
Lao PDR	..	..	..	..	..	..	..
Malaysia	5.0	51 d)	47	2	16	33	18
Myanmar	..	..	..	..	..	..	..
New Zealand	34.5	9	85	6	..	13	63
P.N.G.	..	..	..	..	..	..	..
Philippines	0.1	35	60	5	22	40	2
Singapore	27.1	36 d)	59	5	9	3	60
Thailand	3.1	80	19	1	13	37	10
Vietnam	..	..	..	..	..	..	..

Country	Unit Sales Retail value (US$ per capita)	Distribution by type of music			Piracy (%)	Combined tax rates c) (%)	CD players (Per 100 households)
		Domestic popular (%)	International popular (%)	Classical (%)			
	1996	1996	1996	1996	1995	1995	1996
Latin America and the Caribbean							
Argentina	9.6	72 d)	25	3	17	32	45
Bolivia	0.8	53 d)	43	4	87	26	25
Brazil	8.6	66	33	1	45	31	20
Chile	6.3	57 d)	39	4	14	18	10
Colombia	8.3	68 d)	30	2	15	31	30
Costa Rica	2.5	70 d)	25	5	19	12	..
Cuba	..	..	..	..	..	..	..
Dom. Rep.	..	..	..	..	..	..	..
Ecuador	0.7	75 d)	20	5	75	10	..
El Salvador	0.5	70 d)	25	5	84	12	..
Guatemala	0.6	70 d)	25	5	46	12	..
Haiti	..	..	..	..	..	..	..
Honduras	0.4	70 d)	25	5	80	12	..
Jamaica	..	..	..	..	..	..	..
Mexico	4.4	58 d)	40	2	54	15	18
Nicaragua	0.1	70 d)	25	5	94	12	..
Panama	1.8	70 d)	25	5	58	12	..
Paraguay	2.8	85 d)	14	1	72	10	2
Peru	1.1	54 d)	45	1	83	33	3
Trinidad	..	..	..	..	..	..	..
Uruguay	7.4	30	65	5	19	32	2
Venezuela	1.9	83 d)	15	2	25	13	12
North America							
Canada	37.4	10	85	5	3	13	53
U.S.A.	46.8	..	..	3	3	5	67
Europe							
Albania	..	..	..	..	..	..	..
Austria	51.3	10	82	8	2	40	70
Belarus	..	..	..	..	..	..	..
Belgium	44.0	15	79	6	4	21	85
Bosnia	..	..	..	..	..	..	..
Bulgaria	0.2	80	20	(.)	80	..	..
Croatia	..	..	..	..	..	..	..
Czech Rep.	9.1	38	55	7	6	24	24
Denmark	58.8	34	62	4	1	25	100
Estonia	..	..	..	..	..	..	..
Finland	28.8	41	49	10	2	24	68
France	39.8	47	45	8	3	21	103
Germany	39.2	40	50	10	3	15	86
Greece	12.3	59	38	3	26	18	30
Hungary	7.4	29	58	13	23	51	20
Ireland	23.8	19	78	3	5	21	..
Israel	14.7	33	60	7	14	26	30
Italy	11.0	54	41	5	33	16	39
Latvia	5.1	67 d)	29	4	54	19	6
Lithuania	..	..	..	..	..	..	..

Country	Unit Sales Retail value (US$ per capita)	Distribution by type of music			Piracy (%)	Combined tax rates c) (%)	CD players (Per 100 households)
		Domestic popular (%)	International popular (%)	Classical (%)			
	1996	1996	1996	1996	1995	1995	1996
Macedonia, FYR	..	..	..	..	..	..	..
Moldova	..	..	..	..	..	..	..
Netherlands	42.7	23	68	9	6	18	95
Norway	61.0	24	71	5	4	23	123
Poland	2.9	31	64	5	22	32	18
Portugal	16.0	22	72	6	..	21	37
Romania	0.6	65	20	15	85	35	5
Russia	1.5	85	12	3	73	45	4
Slovakia	2.5	42	52	6	8	39	13
Slovenia	..	..	..	..	..	..	23
Spain	14.9	36	56	8	2	16	50
Sweden	45.7	29	67	4	3	25	105
Switzerland	56.7	7	83	10	4	..	108
Ukraine	..	..	..	..	..	..	..
U.K.	46.5	51	42	7	1	18	140
Yugoslavia	..	..	..	..	..	..	..

Region	Unit Sales Retail value (US$ Percapita)	Distribution by type of music			Piracy (%)	Combined tax rates c) (%)	CD players (Per 100 households)
		Domestic popular (%)	International popular (%)	Classical (%)			
	1996	1996	1996	1996	1995	1995	1996
World	..	..	..	..	..	..	..
Developing	..	..	..	..	..	..	..
Industrial	32.2	51	44	5	20	18	60
Dev exc India/ China	..	..	..	..	..	..	..
Ind exc USA / Russia	33.2	42	51	7	14	18	70
Sub-Sah Africa	..	..	..	..	..	..	..
Arab States	..	..	..	..	..	..	..
South Central Asia	..	..	..	..	..	..	..
East Asia	5.3	93	5	2	53	29	..
Southeast Asia / Oc	7.6	66	32	2	12	22	..
Latin Am / Carib	6.0	65 d)	33	2	45	24	..
North America	45.9	..	..	3	3	6	67
Europe	21.3	52	42	6	29	28	55

a) Including CD's, MC's, Singles and LP's.
b) 3 singles equals 1 album.
c) Including sales taxes, international import taxes and additional special taxes.
d) Including Regional popular.
e) Indian music.

TABLE 4
CULTURAL ACTIVITIES: PERFORMING ARTS

Country	Performing arts companies		Performing arts establishments		
	Annual attendance per thousand people	Foreign tours a)	Number per million people	Performances per establishment	Annual attendance per thousand people
	1980-85	1980-85	1980-85	1980-85	1980-85
Sub-Saharan Africa					
Angola	6	8	0.4	..	..
Benin	..	..	..	..	..
Botswana	..	..	..	..	..
Burkina Faso	..	..	3.2	..	..
Burundi	..	7	..	6	6
Cameroon	..	..	..	..	..
C.A.R.	..	..	..	..	..
Chad	..	4	0.9	..	..
Congo	..	8	0.6	..	..
Côte d' Ivoire	..	..	..	..	..
Eritrea	..	..	..	..	..
Ethiopia	22	5	0.1	105	8
Gabon	..	..	..	..	..
Gambia	..	..	..	..	..
Ghana	..	..	0.7	..	..
Guinea	..	..	..	..	..
Guinea-Bissau	..	..	..	11	208
Kenya	..	..	..	..	..
Lesotho	..	..	..	..	..
Liberia	..	..	..	..	..
Madagascar	7	8	0.3	..	..
Malawi	..	..	0.7	..	..
Mali	..	..	..	..	..
Mauritania	..	..	..	..	..
Mauritius	36	7	6.0	..	..
Mozambique	..	..	..	..	..
Namibia	..	..	..	..	..
Niger	..	..	..	..	..
Nigeria	..	..	..	..	..
Rwanda	11	1	0.9	..	..
Senegal	..	..	..	..	..
Sierra Leone	..	..	..	..	..
Somalia	..	..	..	..	..
South Africa	..	..	..	..	..
Sudan	..	..	..	..	..
Tanzania	..	..	..	..	..
Togo	..	..	..	..	..
Uganda	..	..	..	..	..
Zaire	8	7	0.1		
Zambia	..	..	..	..	..
Zimbabwe	..	..	..	..	..
Arab States					
Algeria	..	..	..	..	..
Egypt	..	..	..	..	..
Iraq	16	13	10.2	..	..
Jordan	62	10	1.7	..	..
Kuwait	..	18	2.1	..	..

Country	Performing arts companies		Performing arts establishments		
	Annual attendance per thousand people	Foreign tours a)	Number per million people	Performances per establishment	Annual attendance per thousand people
	1980-85	1980-85	1980-85	1980-85	1980-85
Lebanon	..	..	..	..	..
Libya	53	..	4.7	..	..
Morocco	..	..	..	..	..
Oman	..	2	..	..	..
Saudi Arabia	2	..	..	..	..
Syria	7	..	1.0	33	7
Tunisia	..	..	3.4	..	..
U.A.E.	..	..	18.0	3	45
Yemen, Rep.	..	..	..	..	..
South Central Asia					
Afghanistan	..	..	..	..	..
Armenia	..	..	..	..	..
Azerbaijan	..	..	..	..	..
Bangladesh	..	..	..	..	..
Bhutan	..	..	..	..	..
Georgia	..	..	..	..	..
India	..	..	..	..	..
Iran	..	..	0.5	..	..
Kazalkstan	..	..	..	..	..
Kyrgyz Rep.	..	..	..	..	..
Nepal	..	..	..	..	..
Pakistan	2	3	0.1	..	..
Sri Lanka	41	13	1.5	..	..
Tajikistan	..	..	..	..	..
Turkey	44	..	0.7	84	21
Turkmenistan	..	..	..	..	..
Uzbekistan	57	9	2.6	114	58
East Asia					
China	72	104	1.8	126	..
Hong Kong	..	..	0.8	..	..
Japan	..	141	0.8	237	..
Korea, Dem.	..	..	..	..	..
Korea, Rep.	..	..	..	..	..
Mongolia	..	..	..	..	..
Southeast Asia and Oceania					
Australia	..	..	..	..	..
Cambodia	..	..	..	..	..
Indonesia	14	19	0.1	5	..
Lao PDR	..	..	..	..	..
Malaysia	..	61	..	..	..
Myanmar	..	..	..	..	..
New Zealand	..	..	..	..	..
P.N.G.	..	..	2.3	..	..
Philippines	3	14	0.1	..	..
Singapore	269	22	..	..	..
Thailand	..	..	..	..	..
Vietnam	..	..	..	..	..

Country	Performing arts companies		Performing arts establishments		
	Annual attendance per thousand people	Foreign tours a)	Number per million people	Performances per establishment	Annual attendance per thousand people
	1980-85	1980-85	1980-85	1980-85	1980-85
Latin America and the Caribbean					
Argentina	3	3	..	..	..
Bolivia	..	..	2.4	..	..
Brazil	..	..	2.1	73	89
Chile	79	..	1.8	..	79
Colombia	3	9	..	..	..
Costa Rica	..	..	3.9	..	..
Cuba	..	..	4.3	171	153
Dom. Rep.	13	6	0.4	..	..
Ecuador	..	..	9.4	..	..
El Salvador	76	11	1.3	58	..
Guatemala	..	..	0.1	..	..
Haiti	..	..	..	..	..
Honduras	..	..	..	..	..
Jamaica	134	7	..	..	..
Mexico	25	3	0.2	208	25
Nicaragua	..	..	0.4	..	..
Panama	..	..	0.5	..	..
Paraguay	..	..	..	..	..
Peru	..	..	1.6	5	..
Trinidad	..	..	..	..	..
Uruguay	..	..	..	..	..
Venezuela	..	..	..	..	..
North America					
Canada	385	..	..	..	..
U.S.A.	..	..	8.6	..	..
Europe					
Albania	321	8	4.8	126	187
Austria	..	..	4.8	..	271
Belarus	..	..	1.7	..	..
Belgium	144	..	3.0	..	..
Bosnia	..	..	..	..	..
Bulgaria	..	..	6.5	..	..
Croatia	..	..	..	..	..
Czech Rep.	..	..	..	..	..
Denmark	547	..	7.3	291	543
Estonia	..	..	..	..	..
Finland	545	28	12.0	182	522
France	..	..	..	..	..
Germany	503	..	5.8	..	..
Greece	205	..	..	..	..
Hungary	664	..	5.1	238	562
Ireland	..	..	4.1	..	..
Israel	..	..	..	..	..
Italy	229	..	0.3	..	..
Latvia	..	..	..	..	..
Lithuania	..	..	..	..	..

Country	Performing arts companies		Performing arts establishments		
	Annual attendance per thousand people	Foreign tours a)	Number per million people	Performances per establishment	Annual attendance per thousand people
	1980-85	1980-85	1980-85	1980-85	1980-85
Macedonia, FYR	..	..	..	..	..
Moldova	..	..	..	..	..
Netherlands	235	..	..	..	..
Norway	281	..	2.4	310	78
Poland	609	..	3.3	..	..
Portugal	61	..	3.8	79	50
Romania	649	..	..	..	..
Russia	..	..	..	..	..
Slovakia	..	..	..	..	..
Slovenia	..	..	..	..	..
Spain	..	..	8.0	..	..
Sweden	453	70	5.4	..	..
Switzerland	518	..	10.6	188	518
Ukraine	..	..	1.6	..	413
U.K.	..	..	7.2	..	..
Yugoslavia	..	..	..	..	..

a) Including tours abroad and visiting foreign companies.

TABLE 5
CULTURAL ACTIVITIES: ARCHIVES AND MUSEUMS

Country	Conventional archives (metres per thousand people)	Annual archive user visits		Annual museum attendances (per 100 people)	Annual daily museum attendance per museum personnel
		per 10,000 people	per archive personnel		
	1982-88	1982-88	1982-88	1988-94	1988-94
Sub-Saharan Africa					
Angola	..	..	..	..	..
Benin	0.1	..	..	(.)	1
Botswana	0.2	..	730	3	1
Burkina Faso	..	..	..	3	124
Burundi	0.1	0.4	27	(.)	2
Cameroon	0.3	..	..	..	..
Central African Rep.	..	0.9	45	(.)	2
Chad	..	0.1	13	..	..
Congo	0.1	..	..	..	..
Côte d' Ivoire	..	..	..	..	..
Eritrea	..	..	..	9	58
Ethiopia	(.)	..	..	(.)	1
Gabon	1.4	..	..	..	..
Gambia	..	..	..	..	..
Ghana	0.2	0.5	4	..	..
Guinea	..	..	3	..	..
Guinea-Bissau	..	..	..	(.)	(.)
Kenya	0.2	0.8	12	..	..
Lesotho	..	..	..	..	..
Liberia	..	..	..	..	..
Madagascar	..	..	..	1	14
Malawi	..	..	..	1	4
Mali	0.1	2.1	200	(.)	1
Mauritania	..	..	..	..	..
Mauritius	1.7	15.0	82	32	33
Mozambique	1.6	..	..	..	..
Namibia	..	..	..	..	..
Niger	..	..	..	5	17
Nigeria	..	..	..	(.)	(.)
Rwanda	..	0.3	29	..	..
Senegal	1.3	..	..	..	..
Sierra Leone	1.4	..	..	..	..
Somalia	..	..	..	..	..
South Africa	..	..	..	..	..
Sudan	..	..	..	..	..
Tanzania	..	(.)	5	(.)	1
Togo	..	..	..	..	..
Uganda	..	..	..	..	..
Zaire	..	0.2	23	..	..
Zambia	0.2	5.3	123	2	4
Zimbabwe	0.4	4.6	58	1	1
Arab States					
Algeria	..	..	..	..	..
Egypt	..	..	..	7	7
Iraq	..	..	..	2	..
Jordan	..	..	..	11	18
Kuwait	..	..	..	20	5

Country	Conventional archives (metres per thousand people) 1982-88	Annual archive user visits		Annual museum attendances (per 100 people) 1988-94	Annual daily museum attendance per museum personnel 1988-94
		per 10,000 people 1982-88	per archive personnel 1982-88		
Lebanon	1.1	1.2	21	..	..
Libya	..	..	..	..	..
Morocco	..	..	..	1	9
Oman	..	..	..	1	3
Saudi Arabia	..	..	..	..	..
Syria	..	..	..	8	14
Tunisia	0.5	0.5	56	..	..
Unit.Arab Emirates	..	..	..	..	..
Yemen, Rep.	..	..	..	..	..
South Central Asia					
Afghanistan	..	..	..	..	..
Armenia	..	..	..	8	1
Azerbaijan	..	..	..	31	4
Bangladesh	(.)	(.)	9	(.)	2
Bhutan	..	..	..	..	..
Georgia	..	..	..	..	..
India	(.)	0.1	19	(.)	4
Iran	..	..	..	3	..
Kazakhstan	..	..	..	..	..
Kyrgyz Rep.	..	..	..	..	..
Nepal	..	..	..	..	..
Pakistan	..	..	..	..	..
Sri Lanka	0.7	3.3	44	..	..
Tajikistan	..	..	..	..	..
Turkey	..	..	..	11	6
Turkmenistan	..	..	..	..	..
Uzbekistan	..	..	..	13	..
East Asia					
China	..	10.5	..	..	..
Hong Kong	1.1	2.7	43	..	..
Japan	0.5	7.8	372	59	31
Korea, Dem.	..	..	..	..	..
Korea, Rep.	0.2	0.6	22	..	..
Mongolia	..	..	..	..	..
Southeast Asia and Oceania					
Australia	23.3	4.7	22	102	..
Cambodia	..	..	..	..	..
Indonesia	0.1	(.)	1	2	6
Lao PDR	..	..	..	..	..
Malaysia	..	13.1	7	13	34
Myanmar	..	..	..	..	..
New Zealand	4.9	7.1	125	9	2
Papua New Guinea	..	..	..	..	..
Philippines	..	..	..	2	6
Singapore	0.6	..	..	..	..
Thailand	0.1	0.1	13	3	6
Vietnam	0.7	..	..	..	..

Country	Conventional archives (metres per thousand people)	Annual archive user visits		Annual museum attendances (per 100 people)	Annual daily museum attendance per museum personnel
		per 10,000 people	per archive personnel		
	1982-88	1982-88	1982-88	1988-94	1988-94
Latin America and the Caribbean					
Argentina	0.3	2.5	148	..	..
Bolivia	..	..	..	..	..
Brazil	(.)	0.1	5	..	..
Chile	1.2	6.5	260	5	9
Colombia	0.1	..	..	..	..
Costa Rica	2.1	6.1	31	22	7
Cuba	2.2	2.2	18	61	7
Dominican Rep.	..	..	..	..	..
Ecuador	..	..	..	..	..
El Salvador	..	..	..	..	..
Guatemala	..	..	..	..	..
Haiti	0.3	..	..	1	..
Honduras	..	..	..	..	..
Jamaica	4.9	2.7	27	..	..
Mexico	0.3	1.1	29	11	20
Nicaragua	0.1	..	..	..	..
Panama	..	..	..	3	3
Paraguay	..	..	..	..	..
Peru	0.6	..	..	..	..
Trinidad	..	..	..	..	..
Uruguay	..	..	..	13	4
Venezuela	..	..	..	..	..
North America					
Canada	18.2	..	..	94	10
United States	1.7	8.3	115	..	..
Europe					
Albania	..	..	..	..	..
Austria	28.3	41.7	123	228	..
Belarus	..	..	..	26	4
Belgium	15.8	61.4	437	24	16
Bosnia	..	..	..	..	..
Bulgaria	..	..	..	41	4
Croatia	..	..	..	12	2
Czech Rep.	..	..	..	88	6
Denmark	46.9	135.4	281	215	..
Estonia	..	..	..	53	2
Finland	27.0	124.7	304	72	10
France	36.3	116.1	319	24	21
Germany	..	..	..	115	..
Greece	..	..	..	23	5
Hungary	17.9	30.6	42	72	5
Ireland	6.4	17.4	156	..	..
Israel	3.2	10.4	102	..	..
Italy	22.6	43.3	..	70	8
Latvia	..	..	..	50	2
Lithuania	..	..	..	34	2

Country	Conventional archives (metres per thousand people)	Annual archive user visits		Annual museum attendances (per 100 people)	Annual daily museum attendance per museum personnel
		per 10,000 people	per archive personnel		
	1982-88	1982-88	1982-88	1988-94	1988-94
Macedonia, FYR	..	..	..	10	1
Moldova	..	..	..	15	3
Netherlands	..	74.5	397	149	12
Norway	0.8	2.6	191	191	9
Poland	...	9.4	35	41	..
Portugal	..	..	..	51	8
Romania	..	..	..	29	2
Russia	..	..	..	54	6
Slovakia	..	..	..	53	5
Slovenia	..	..	..	90	7
Spain	7.3	..	..	73	17
Sweden	..	..	130	212	14
Switzerland	19.4	49.6	271	126	18
Ukraine	..	..	..	29	5
United Kingdom	..	..	233	..	..
Yugoslavia	..	..	..	18	3

Region	Conventional archives (metres per thousand	Annual archive user visits		Annual attendances (per 100 people)	Annual attendance per museum
		per 10,000 people	per archive personnel		
	1982-88	1982-88	1982-88	1988-94	1988-94
World	..	..	..	..	..
Developing	..	..	..	..	..
Industrial	..	..	..	66	13
Dev exc India / China	..	..	..	..	..
Ind exc USA / Russia	..	..	..	69	15
Sub-Saharan Africa	..	..	..	..	..
Arab States	..	..	..	5	9
South Central Asia	..	..	..	..	..
East Asia	0.4	9.9	..	..	..
Southeast Asia / Oc	..	..	..	8	..
Latin Am / Carib	0.3	..	..	..	..
North America	3.3	8.3	115	..	..
Europe	..	..	..	65	9

TABLE 6
NATIONAL PUBLIC HOLIDAYS (1997)

Country	Year	Jan	Feb	Mar	Apr	May	June
Sub-Saharan Africa							
Angola	11	1.4	4.11	8.26		1	
Benin	12	1	9	31	18	1.8.19	
Botswana	13	1.2		28.29.31		1.8	
Burkina Faso	16	1.3	9	8.31	18	1.8	
Burundi	10	1	5			1.8	
Cameroon	10	1	9.11	28	18	1.8.20	
C.A.R.	11	1		29.31		1.8.19	
Chad	12	1	9	31	18	1.26	
Congo	9	1		31		1.8.19	10
Côte d' Ivoire	12	1	9	31	18	1.8.19	
Eritrea							
Ethiopia	13	7.19	9	21	18.25.27	1.5.28	
Gabon	13	1	10.11.12	28.31		1.8.19	
Gambia	13	1	9.10.18	28	18.19	1.17	
Ghana	11	1	9	6.28.31	18	1	4
Guinea	10	1	9	31	3.18	1	
Guinea-Bissau	10	1.20	9	8	13	1	
Kenya	12	1	9	28.31		1	1.2
Lesotho	11	1		11.28.31	4	1.8	
Liberia	15	1	11	12.14.15.28	11		
Madagascar	12	1		28.29.31		1.8.19	26
Malawi	11	1.15		3.28.31		1	14
Mali	12	1.20	9	26	7.20	1.25	
Mauritania	8	1	9		18	1.8.25	
Mauritius	14	1.2.23	7.8.10	7.12	8	1	
Mozambique	9	1	3		7	1	25
Namibia	14	1		21.28.31		1.4.5.8.25.26	
Niger	9	1	9		18.24	1	
Nigeria	12	1	9.10	28.31	18.19	1	
Rwanda	11	1	9		7	1	
Senegal	14	1	9	30.31	4.18	1.8.17.19	
Sierra Leone	10	1	9	28.31	18.27.28		
Somalia	10	1	9.10		18.19	1	
South Africa	13	1		21.28.31	27.28	1	16
Sudan	9	1	9		7.18	8	30
Tanzania	17	1.12.13	9.10	28.31	18.26	1	
Togo	12	1	9	31	18.27	1.8.15	21
Uganda	14	1.26	9.10	8.28.31	18	1	3.9
Zaire	10	1.4		1			24.30
Zambia	13	1		12.28.29.31		1.25.26	
Zimbabwe	12	1		28.29.31	18	1.25.26	
Arab States							
Algeria	11	1	9.10		18	1.2.17	19
Egypt	14	7	9		16.17.20.25.27.28	1.8	
Iraq	19	1.6	8.9.10.11.12	21	17.18.19.20.21	1.8.17	
Jordan	20	1	9.10.11.12		18.18.20.21.22.27	1.8.25	10
Kuwait	15	1	9.10.11.12.25.26		18.19.20.21.22	8	

Country	Year	Jan	Feb	Mar	Apr	May	June
Lebanon	20	1	9.10.11	28.31	18.19.20.25.28	1.6.8.17	
Libya	12		9.10.11	2	18.19.20.21		11
Morocco	16	1.11	9.10	3	18.19	1.8.23	
Oman	12		9.10.11		18.19.20	8	
Saudi Arabia	10		9.10.11.12.13		18.19.20.21.22		
Syria	15	1	9.10.11	8.21.30	17.18.27	6.8	
Tunisia	12	1	9	20.21	9.18	1	17
U.A.E.	13	1	9.10.11		16.18.19.20	8	
Yemen, Rep.	18		9.10.11.12		18.19.20.21.22	1.8.22	
South Central Asia							
Afghanistan	11	11	9	21	18.26.27	1.17	
Armenia	11	1.2.6			7.24	9.28	
Azerbaijan	12	1.27		8.21	18	9.17.28	
Bangladesh	24		7.8.9.10.11.21	26	14.18.19.20.21	1.8	
Bhutan	17		8.9		17	2	2.15
Georgia	10	1		3	9.15	9.26	
India	11	1.26	9	31		1	
Iran	24		9.10.11	5.19.21.22.23.24	1.12.18.26	16.17.28	4.5.6
Kazalkstan	9	1.2		8.22		1.9	
Kyrgyz Rep.	8	1.7		8.21		1.5.9	
Nepal	16	11.29	12.18	7.8.9.23	7.13.16.17	15	
Pakistan	20	11	7.9.10.11	23	18.19.20	1.8.9	
Sri Lanka	23	14.23	4.9.21	23.28	13.14.22	1.21.22	20
Tajikistan	6	1	9	21.22			
Turkey	12	1	9.10.11	18.19.20.21.23		19	
Turkmenistan	10	1.12	9.16	8.21	18	9.18	
Uzbekistan							
East Asia							
China	9	1	6.7.8.9.10			1	
Hong Kong	16	1	6.7.8	28.29.30			
Japan	20	1.2.3.15	11	21	29	3.4.5	
Korea, Dem.							
Korea, Rep.	17	1.2	7.8.9	1	5	5.14	6
Mongolia	8	1	7.8.9				1
Southeast Asia and Oceania							
Australia	10	1.27		28.29.31	25		9
Cambodia							
Indonesia	12	1	9.10	28	8.18	8.22	
Lao PDR	..	..	..	..	..		..
Malaysia	14	1	7.8.9.10			1.8.21	7
Myanmar	18	4.9	12	2.23.27	13.14.15.16.17	1.21	
New Zealand	10	1.2	6	26.31	25		2
P.N.G.	10	1		28.29.31			9
Philippines	12	1		27.28	9	1	12
Singapore	12	1	7.8.9.10	28	18	1.21	
Thailand	16	1	9.21		7.14.15	1.5.20	
Vietnam							

Country	Year	Jan	Feb	Mar	Apr	May	June
Latin America and the Caribbean							
Argentina	13	1		27.28		1.25	9.16
Bolivia	10	1	11	28		1.29	
Brazil	19	1	10.11.12	27.28.29	21	1.29	
Chile	16	1		28.29		1.21.29	29
Colombia	20	1.6	12	24.27.28.30		1.2	2.9.30
Costa Rica	14	1		27.28	11	1	
Cuba	20	1.28	24	8.13	16.19	1.17	
Dom. Rep.	11	1.6.21.26	27	28		1.29	
Ecuador	11	1	10.11	27.28		1.24	
El Salvador	13	1		26.27.28		1	
Guatemala	20	1		26.27.28.29		1.9.10	30
Haiti	12	1.2	11	28		1.18	
Honduras	11	1		27.28	14	1	
Jamaica	9	1	12	28.31		23	
Mexico	16	1	5	21.27.28		1.5	
Nicaragua	9	1		27.28		1	
Panama	18	1.9	10.11.12	27.28.29		1	
Paraguay	11	1		1.27.28		1.15	12
Peru	12	1		27.28		1	29
Trinidad	12	1	10.11	28.31		29.30	19
Uruguay	15	1.6	11.12	27.28	19	1.18	19
Venezuela	19	1.6	10.11	19.27.28	19	1.12	2.24
North America							
Canada	11	1		28.31		19	
U.S.A.	10	1.20	17			26	
Europe							
Albania	12	1.11	9	22.24.30.31	27.28	1	
Austria	11	1.6		31		1.6.19.29	
Belarus	12	1.7		8.15.31	23.28	1.9	
Belgium	13	1		31		1.8.9.19	
Bosnia	5	1				1	
Bulgaria	9	1		3	25.28	1.24	
Croatia	11	1.6		31		1.30	22
Czech Rep.	10	1		31		1.8	
Denmark	11	1		27.28.31	25	8.19	5
Estonia	10	1	24	28.30		1.18	23.24
Finland	13	1.6		27.28.31		1.8	20
France	13	1		29.31		1.8.19	
Germany	12	1	10.12	28.31		1.18.19	
Greece	12	1.6		10.25	25.28	1	16
Hungary	9	1		15.31		1.19	
Ireland	11	1		17.28.31		5	2
Israel	24	1.23		20.24	22.28	4.11.12.25	4.11
Italy	13	1		31	25	1	29
Latvia	9	1		28		1	23.24
Lithuania	8	1	16	30.31			

Country	Year	Jan	Feb	Mar	Apr	May	June
Macedonia, FYR	5	1				1	
Moldova	12	1.7.8		8	27.28	1.4.5.9	
Netherlands	9	1		28.31	30	5.8.19	
Norway	13	1		26.27.28.31		1.8.17.19	
Poland	10	1		31		1.3.29	
Portugal	16	1	11	27.28	25	1.8.29	10
Romania	7	1.2			27.28		
Russia	12	1.2.7		8.10	1	1.2.9	12
Slovakia	14	1.6		28.31		1.8	
Slovenia	13	1.2	8	31	27	1.2	25
Spain	12	1.6		27.28.29		1	
Sweden	14	1.6		28.31		1.8.19	20.21
Switzerland	13	1.2		28.31		8.19.29	
Ukraine	14	1.7		8.10	27.28	1.2.9	16.26
U.K.	8	1		28.31		5.26	
Yugoslavia	11	1.2.7		28	28	1.2	

Region	Year	Jan	Feb	Mar	Apr	May	June
World	12.2	1.3	1.1	1.6	1.2	1.8	0.4
Developing	12.1	1.3	1.1	1.7	1.1	1.9	0.4
Industrial	12.4	1.3	1.3	1.6	1.3	1.7	0.5
Dev exc India / China	12.0	1.3	1.0	1.7	1.0	1.9	0.4
Ind exc USA / Russia	12.5	1.4	1.4	1.6	1.3	1.6	0.5
Sub-Saharan Africa	11.0	1.3	0.9	1.5	0.9	2.0	0.3
Arab States	11.4	1.4	1.0	1.9	0.9	2.1	0.4
South Central Asia	12.9	1.4	1.4	1.8	1.4	1.8	0.6
East Asia	12.5	1.0	1.5	1.3	1.8	1.8	0.3
Southeast Asia / Oc	10.7	1.4	1.3	1.7	0.9	1.7	0.3
Latin Am / Carib	14.4	1.2	1.1	1.8	1.3	1.7	0.4
North America	10.5	1.5	0.5	1.0	0.0	1.0	0.0
Europe	12.5	1.4	1.4	1.5	1.4	1.6	0.5

TABLE 6B
NATIONAL PUBLIC HOLIDAYS (CONT.)

Country	July	Aug	Sept	Oct	Nov	Dec
Sub-Saharan Africa						
Angola			17		2.11	25
Benin	17	1.15			1	25
Botswana	1.21.22		30			25.26
Burkina Faso	17	4.5.15		15	1	11.25
Burundi	1	15		13.21	1	25
Cameroon		15				25
C.A.R.		13.15			1	1.25
Chad	17	11			1.28	1.25
Congo		15			1	25
Côte d' Ivoire	17	7.15			1	25
Eritrea						
Ethiopia	17		11.27			
Gabon		15.16			1	25
Gambia	17.22	15				25
Ghana						5.25.26
Guinea	17	15		2		25
Guinea-Bissau		3	24		14	25
Kenya				10.20		12.25.26
Lesotho	17			4		25.26
Liberia	25.26	24.25			6.28.29	25
Madagascar		15			1	25.31
Malawi	6			14		25.26
Mali	17.28		22			25
Mauritania	17				28	
Mauritius			6	31	1	25
Mozambique			7.25		10	25
Namibia		26				10.25.26
Niger	17	3				18.25
Nigeria	17			1		25.26
Rwanda	1.4	15	25	1	1	25
Senegal	17	15			1	25
Sierra Leone	17					25.26
Somalia	1.17			21.22		
South Africa		9	24			16.25.26
Sudan	17					3.25
Tanzania	7.17.18	8				9.25.26
Togo		15			1	25
Uganda				9		25.26
Zaire		1		12.27	17	25
Zambia	7.8	4		24		25
Zimbabwe		11.12				25.26
Arab States						
Algeria	5.17				1	
Egypt	1.17.23			6		
Iraq	14.17	8				
Jordan	17	11			14.28	25
Kuwait	17				28	

Country	July	Aug	Sept	Oct	Nov	Dec
Lebanon	17	15			1.22	25
Libya	17.23		1			
Morocco	9.17	14.20			6.18	
Oman	17				18.19.28	31
Saudi Arabia						
Syria	17			6		25
Tunisia	17.25	13			7	
U.A.E.	17	8			28	2
Yemen, Rep.	7.17		26	14	28.30	
South Central Asia						
Afghanistan	17.22	19				
Armenia	5		21			7.31
Australia				6		25.26
Azerbaijan				9.18	17	31
Bangladesh	1.17	18.23		10	7	16.25.28.31
Bhutan	8.15		22	7.11.12.13	11.12.13	17
Georgia		15.28		14	23	
India		15	30	2.21	12	25
Iran	4.23				14.28	16
Kazalkstan		30		25		16
Kyrgyz Rep.		31				
Nepal			8		8	29
Pakistan	1.17	14	6.11		9	25.31
Sri Lanka	17.19	18	16	15.30	14	13.25
Tajikistan			9		6	
Turkey		30		29		
Turkmenistan				27		
East Asia						
Uzbekistan						
China				1.2		
Hong Kong	1.2	18	17	1.2.10		25.26
Japan	20.21		15.23	10	3.23.24	23.31
Korea, Dem.						
Korea, Rep.	17	15	15.16.17	3		25
Southeast Asia and Oceania						
Mongolia	10					8.25
Cambodia						
Indonesia	17	17			28	25
Lao PDR						
Malaysia	17	31	1	30		25
Myanmar	19			16	14.24	25
New Zealand				27		25.26
P.N.G.	18.23		16			25.26
Philippines		27			1.30	25.30.31
Singapore		9		31		25
Thailand	1.21	12		23		5.10.31
Vietnam						

Country	July	Aug	Sept	Oct	Nov	Dec
Latin America and the Caribbean						
Argentina	9	18		12		8.25.31
Bolivia		6			1.2.3	25
Brazil			7	12	1.2.15	18.24.25.31
Chile		15	11.18.19	12	1	8.25.31
Colombia	20	7.18		13	3.17	8.25
Costa Rica	25	2.25	15	12		25.29.30.31
Cuba	25.26.27.30	12		8.10.28	27	2.7
Dom. Rep.		16	24			25
Ecuador		10			2.3	25
El Salvador		4.5.6	15		2	25.30.31
Guatemala	1	15	16	12.13.20.31	1	24.25.31
Haiti		15		17	1.18	5.25
Honduras			15	3.12.13.21		25
Jamaica	4			20		25.26
Mexico			1.15.16		2.20	12.24.25.31
Nicaragua	19	1.10	15			25
Panama		15			3.4.10.28	8.24.25.31
Paraguay		15	29			8.25
Peru	28.29	30		8	1	8.25
Trinidad		1.31				25.26
Uruguay	18	25		12	2	25
Venezuela	5.24	18		12	1	8.25
North America						
Canada	1	4	1	13	11	25.26
U.S.A.	4		1	13	11.17	25
Europe						
Albania					28	25
Austria		15				8.24.25.26
Belarus	27				2	25
Belgium	21	15			1.3.11	25.26
Bosnia	4.27				25	
Bulgaria						24.25.26
Croatia		5.15			1	25.26
Czech Rep.	5.6			28		24.25.26
Denmark						24.25.26
Estonia						25.26
Finland						6.24.25.26.31
France	14	15			1.10.11	24.25
Germany						24.25.26.31
Greece		15		28		25.26
Hungary		20		23		25.26
Ireland		4		27		25.26.29
Israel	22	12	2.3.5.11.16.23.28		6	24.31
Italy		14.15				7.8.24.25.26.31
Latvia					18	25.26.31
Lithuania	6				1	25.26

Country	July	Aug	Sept	Oct	Nov	Dec
Macedonia, FYR		2	8	11		
Moldova		27.31				
Netherlands						25.26
Norway						24.25.26.31
Poland		15			1.11	25.26
Portugal		15		5	1	1.8.24.25
Romania						1.25.26
Russia					7	12
Slovakia	5	29	1.15		1	24.25.26
Slovenia		15		31	1	25.26
Spain		15		12	1	6.8.25
Sweden					1	24.25.26.31
Switzerland		1.15			1	24.25.26
Ukraine		24.25			7	
U.K.		25				25.26
Yugoslavia	4.7				29.30	

Region	July	Aug	Sept	Oct	Nov	Dec
World	0.7	0.7	0.4	0.5	0.7	1.6
Developing	0.8	0.8	0.4	0.6	0.8	1.4
Industrial	0.4	0.6	0.3	0.3	0.7	2.3
Dev exc India / China	0.9	0.8	0.4	0.6	0.8	1.4
Ind exc USA / Russia	0.4	0.7	0.3	0.3	0.6	2.4
Sub-Saharan Africa	0.8	0.8	0.3	0.4	0.6	1.5
Arab States	1.5	0.5	0.1	0.2	1.1	0.4
South Central Asia	0.8	0.6	0.5	0.9	0.8	1.1
East Asia	0.8	0.3	1.0	1.2	0.5	0.8
Southeast Asia / Oc	0.7	0.4	0.2	0.4	0.4	1.3
Latin Am / Carib	0.7	1.3	0.6	1.0	1.1	2.3
North America	1.0	0.5	1.0	1.0	1.5	1.5
Europe	0.3	0.7	0.3	0.2	0.7	2.4

TABLE 7
WORLD HERITAGE SITES

Country	Properties included in the World Heritage list				Tentative list of world heritage properties	Endangered heritage sites	
	Cultural	Natural	Combined	Total		World heritage committee	World monument fund
	1997	1997	1997	1997	1997	1997	1996
Sub-Saharan Africa							
Angola	-	-	-	-	-	-	-
Benin	1	-	-	1	-	1	1
Botswana	-	-	-	-	-	-	-
Burkina Faso	-	-	-	-	4	-	-
Burundi	-	-	-	-	-	-	-
Cameroon	-	1	-	1	-	-	-
C.A.R.	-	1	-	1	-	-	-
Chad	-	-	-	-	-	-	-
Congo	-	-	-	-	-	-	-
Côte d' Ivoire	-	3	-	3	-	1	-
Eritrea	-	-	-	-	-	-	-
Ethiopia	6	1	-	7	-	1	-
Gabon	-	-	-	-	-	-	-
Gambia	-	-	-	-	3	-	-
Ghana	2	-	-	2	-	-	-
Guinea	-	1	-	1	-	1	-
Guinea-Bissau	-	-	-	-	-	-	-
Kenya	-	-	-	-	-	-	-
Lesotho	-	-	-	-	-	-	-
Liberia	-	-	-	-	-	-	-
Madagascar	-	1	-	1	-	-	-
Malawi	-	1	-	1	-	-	-
Mali	2	-	1	3	-	1	1
Mauritania	1	1	-	2	4	-	-
Mauritius	-	-	-	-	-	-	-
Mozambique	1	-	-	1	-	-	1
Namibia	-	-	-	-	-	-	-
Niger	-	2	-	2	-	1	-
Nigeria	-	-	-	-	8	-	-
Rwanda	-	-	-	-	-	-	-
Senegal	1	2	-	3	-	-	-
Sierra Leone	-	-	-	-	-	-	-
Somalia	-	-	-	-	-	-	-
South Africa	-	-	-	-	-	-	-
Sudan	-	-	-	-	-	-	-
Tanzania	1	4	-	5	-	-	1
Togo	-	-	-	-	-	-	-
Uganda	-	2	-	2	-	-	-
Zaire	-	5	-	5	-	2	-
Zambia	-	1	-	1	-	-	-
Zimbabwe	2	2	-	4	-	-	1
Arab States							
Algeria	6	-	1	7	-	-	-
Egypt	5	-	-	5	14	-	1
Iraq	1	-	-	1	-	-	-
Jordan	2	-	-	2	-	1	1
Kuwait	-	-	-	-	-	-	-

Country	Properties included in the World Heritage list				Tentative list of world heritage properties	Endangered heritage sites	
	Cultural	Natural	Combined	Total		World heritage committee	World monument fund
	1997	1997	1997	1997	1997	1997	1996
Lebanon	4	-	-	4	-	-	1
Libya	5	-	-	5	10	-	-
Morocco	4	-	-	4	14	-	2
Oman	2	1	-	3	5	1	-
Saudi Arabia	-	-	-	-	-	-	-
Syria	4	-	-	4	-	-	-
Tunisia	6	1	-	7	1	1	-
U.A.E.	-	-	-	-	-	-	-
Yemen, Rep.	3	-	-	3	-	-	-
South Central Asia							
Afghanistan	-	-	-	-	-	-	-
Armenia	1	-	-	1	7	-	-
Azerbaijan	-	-	-	-	-	-	-
Bangladesh	2	-	-	2	-	-	-
Bhutan	-	-	-	-	-	-	-
Georgia	3	-	-	3	9	-	1
India	16	5	-	21	-	1	2
Iran	3	-	-	3	-	-	-
Kazalkstan	-	-	-	-	-	-	-
Kyrgyz Rep.	-	-	-	-	-	-	-
Nepal	1	2	-	3	-	-	2
Pakistan	5	-	-	5	-	-	1
Sri Lanka	6	1	-	7	-	-	-
Tajikistan	-	-	-	-	-	-	-
Turkey	6	-	2	8	-	-	3
Turkmenistan	-	-	-	-	-	-	-
Uzbekistan	2	-	-	2	21	-	-
East Asia							
China	10	3	3	16	55	-	3
Hong Kong	-	-	-	-	-	-	-
Japan	6	2	-	8	11	-	-
Korea, Dem.	-	-	-	-	-	-	-
Korea, Rep.	3	-	-	3	10	-	-
Mongolia	-	-	-	-	-	-	1
Southeast Asia and Oceania							
Australia	7	-	4	11	1	-	-
Cambodia	1	-	-	1	11	1	1
Indonesia	3	2	-	5	17	-	1
Lao PDR	1	-	-	1	4	-	1
Malaysia	-	-	-	-	-	-	-
Myanmar	-	-	-	-	-	-	-
New Zealand	-	1	1	2	2	-	-
P.N.G.	-	-	-	-	3	-	-
Philippines	2	1	-	3	12	-	1
Singapore	-	-	-	-	-	-	-
Thailand	3	1	-	4	-	-	1
Vietnam	1	1	-	2	-	-	2

Country	Properties included in the World Heritage list				Tentative list of world heritage properties	Endangered heritage sites	
	Cultural	Natural	Combined	Total		World heritage committee	World monument fund
	1997	1997	1997	1997	1997	1997	1996
Latin America and the Caribbean							
Argentina	1	2	-	3	3	-	1
Bolivia	3	-	-	3	-	-	-
Brazil	7	1	-	8	10	-	1
Chile	1	-	-	1	3	-	3
Colombia	4	1	-	5	10	-	-
Costa Rica	-	1	-	1	1	-	-
Cuba	2	-	-	2	3	-	1
Dom. Rep.	1	-	-	1	-	-	-
Ecuador	1	2	-	3	-	1	1
El Salvador	1	-	-	1	7	-	-
Guatemala	2	-	1	3	-	-	-
Haiti	1	-	-	1	-	-	
Honduras	1	1	-	2	-	1	-
Jamaica	-	-	-	-	-	-	-
Mexico	14	2	-	16	29	-	4
Nicaragua	-	-	-	-	6	-	-
Panama	1	2	-	3	5	-	-
Paraguay	1	-	-	1	3	-	-
Peru	5	2	2	9	3	1	2
Trinidad	-	-	-	-	-	-	-
Uruguay	1	-	-	1	2	-	-
Venezuela	1	1	-	2	-	-	-
North America							
Canada	5	7	-	12	13	-	-
U.S.A.	8	12	-	20	82	2	7
Europe							
Albania	1	-	-	1	-	-	1
Austria	2	-	-	2	17	-	2
Belarus	-	1	-	1	-	-	-
Belgium	-	-	-	-	-	-	1
Bosnia	-	-	-	-	-	-	1
Bulgaria	7	2	-	9	12	1	2
Croatia	2	1	-	3	9	2	4
Czech Rep.	6	-	-	6	8	-	2
Denmark	2	-	-	2	10	-	-
Estonia	-	-	-	-	5	-	-
Finland	4	-	-	4	11	-	-
France	21	1	-	22	21	-	2
Germany	18	1	-	19	11	-	1
Greece	12	-	2	14	6	-	1
Hungary	3	1	-	4	8	-	1
Ireland	2	-	-	2	4	-	1
Israel	-	-	-	-	-	-	2
Italy	17	-	-	17	64	-	11
Latvia	-	-	-	-	6	-	1
Lithuania	1	-	-	1	3	-	-

Country	Properties included in the World Heritage list				Tentative list of world heritage properties	Endangered heritage sites	
	Cultural	Natural	Combined	Total		World heritage committee	World monument fund
	1997	1997	1997	1997	1997	1997	1996
Macedonia, FYR	-	-	1	1	-	-	-
Moldova	-	-	-	-	-	-	-
Netherlands	2	-	-	2	19	-	-
Norway	4	-	-	4	-	-	1
Poland	5	1	-	6	11	1	3
Portugal	8	-	-	8	1	-	1
Romania	3	1	-	4	20	-	2
Russia	8	3	-	11	4	-	3
Slovakia	3	1	-	4	14	-	-
Slovenia	-	1	-	1	3	-	-
Spain	21	2	-	23	52	-	1
Sweden	7	-	1	8	9	-	-
Switzerland	3	-	-	3	-	-	-
Ukraine	1	-	-	1	8	-	1
U.K.	12	4	-	16	37	-	-
Yugoslavia	3	1	-	4	11	1	1

Region	Properties included in the World Heritage list				Tentative list of world heritage properties	Endangered heritage sites	
	Cultural	Natural	Combined	Total		World heritage committee	World monument fund
	1997	1997	1997	1997	1997	1997	1996
	T	T	T	T	T	T	T
World	380	104	19	503	790	23	96
Developing	176	61	10	247	297	16	43
Industrial	204	43	9	256	493	7	53
Dev exc India / China	150	53	7	210	242	15	38
Ind exc USA / Russia	188	28	9	225	407	5	43
Sub-Saharan Africa	17	28	1	46	19	8	5
Arab States	42	2	1	45	44	3	5
South Central Asia	45	8	2	55	37	1	9
East Asia	19	5	3	27	76	..	4
Southeast Asia / Oc	18	6	5	29	50	1	7
Latin Am / Carib	48	15	3	66	85	3	13
North America	13	19	..	32	95	2	7
Europe	178	21	4	203	384	5	46

TABLE 8
TRADE a) IN CULTURAL GOODS

Country	Books and pamphlets (%) 1990-94	Newspapers and periodicals (%) 1990-94	Music related goods (%) 1991	Visual arts (%) 1991	Cinema and photography (%) 1991	Radio + television (%) 1991
Sub-Saharan Africa						
Angola	..	..	..	..	..	..
Benin	..	..	..	..	..	..
Botswana	..	..	..	..	..	..
Burkina Faso	..	..	..	..	..	..
Burundi	..	..	..	..	..	..
Cameroon	74.5	7.9	3.2	0.1	11.1	3.2
Central African Rep.	..	..	..	..	..	..
Chad	..	..	..	..	..	..
Congo	..	..	..	..	..	..
Côte d' Ivoire	..	..	..	..	..	..
Eritrea	..	..	..	..	..	..
Ethiopia	..	..	..	..	..	..
Gabon	..	..	..	..	..	..
Gambia	..	..	..	..	..	..
Ghana	..	..	..	..	..	..
Guinea	..	..	..	..	..	..
Guinea-Bissau	..	..	..	..	..	..
Kenya	33.2	5.6	11.1	0.6	21.7	27.8
Lesotho	..	..	..	..	..	..
Liberia	..	..	..	..	..	..
Madagascar	28.2	14.1	28.2	1.3	..	28.2
Malawi	..	..	..	..	..	..
Mali	..	..	..	..	..	..
Mauritania	..	..	..	..	..	..
Mauritius	21.6	6.5	28.1	0.4	19.5	23.8
Mozambique	..	..	..	..	..	..
Namibia	..	..	..	..	..	..
Niger	..	..	..	..	..	..
Nigeria	..	..	..	..	..	..
Rwanda	..	..	..	..	..	..
Senegal	46.7	..	9.3	1.9	23.4	18.7
Sierra Leone	..	..	..	..	..	..
Somalia	..	..	..	..	..	..
South Africa	..	..	..	..	..	..
Sudan	..	..	..	..	..	..
Tanzania	..	..	..	..	..	..
Togo	..	..	..	..	..	..
Uganda	..	..	..	..	..	..
Zaire	..	..	..	..	..	..
Zambia	..	..	..	..	..	..
Zimbabwe	..	..	..	..	..	..
Arab States						
Algeria	..	..	..	..	..	..
Egypt	21.4	10.1	20.2	1.6	46.7	..
Iraq	..	..	..	..	..	..
Jordan	34.6	0.2	..	2.0	21.2	42.0
Kuwait	..	..	..	..	..	..

Country	Books and pamphlets (%) 1990-94	Newspapers and periodicals (%) 1990-94	Music related goods (%) 1991	Visual arts (%) 1991	Cinema and photography (%) 1991	Radio + television (%) 1991
Lebanon	..	..	..	..	..	..
Libya	..	..	..	..	..	..
Morocco	31.6	5.1	24.0	0.1	22.8	16.4
Oman	3.7	2.5	32.1	..	18.5	43.2
Saudi Arabia	..	..	..	..	..	..
Syria	..	..	..	..	..	..
Tunisia	21.4	9.2	20.0	0.2	24.6	24.6
Unit.Arab Emirates	..	..	..	..	..	..
Yemen, Rep.	..	..	..	..	..	..
South Central Asia						
Afghanistan	..	..	..	..	..	..
Armenia	..	..	..	..	..	..
Azerbaijan	..	..	..	..	..	..
Bangladesh	..	..	..	..	..	..
Bhutan	..	..	..	..	..	..
Georgia	..	..	..	..	..	..
India	17.8	3.5	19.7	0.2	30.8	28.0
Iran	..	..	..	..	..	..
Kazakhstan	..	..	..	..	..	..
Kyrgyz Rep.	..	..	..	..	..	..
Nepal	..	..	..	..	..	..
Pakistan	9.3	3.1	11.6	..	20.9	55.1
Sri Lanka	..	..	..	..	..	..
Tajikistan	..	..	..	..	..	..
Turkey	9.1	2.2	19.6	(.)	16.8	52.3
Turkmenistan	..	..	..	..	..	..
Uzbekistan	..	..	..	..	..	..
East Asia						
China	4.3	0.5	30.9	0.3	11.7	52.3
Hong Kong b)	6.1	0.9	30.0	0.4	17.7	44.9
Japan	1.6	0.8	48.4	3.7	22.7	22.8
Korea, Dem.	..	..	..	..	..	..
Korea, Rep.	1.4	0.5	45.7	1.2	8.5	42.7
Mongolia	..	..	..	..	..	..
Southeast Asia and Oceania						
Australia	26.7	11.3	47.1	2.5	..	12.4
Cambodia	..	..	..	..	..	..
Indonesia	0.5	0.3	2.2	0.1	5.6	91.3
Lao PDR	..	..	..	..	..	..
Malaysia	3.2	0.4	28.8	0.1	14.8	52.7
Myanmar	..	..	..	..	..	..
New Zealand	21.7	12.1	28.4	1.2	14.7	21.9
Papua New Guinea	..	..	..	..	..	..
Philippines	1.1	0.3	1.7	..	2.2	94.7
Singapore	4.9	0.7	34.9	0.2	10.2	49.1
Thailand	0.3	0.1	5.1	0.1	1.5	92.9
Vietnam	..	..	..	..	..	..

Country	Books and pamphlets (%) 1990-94	Newspapers and periodicals (%) 1990-94	Music related goods (%) 1991	Visual arts (%) 1991	Cinema and photography (%) 1991	Radio + television (%) 1991
Latin America and the Caribbean						
Argentina	16.2	7.5	21.0	0.1	19.5	35.7
Bolivia	..	..	..	..	..	..
Brazil	7.8	4.6	14.5	(.)	31.0	42.1
Chile	17.7	11.4	21.4	0.1	16.4	33.0
Colombia	57.7	16.4	10.9	1.1	13.9	..
Costa Rica	40.7	4.7	15.6	10.9	12.5	15.6
Cuba	..	..	..	..	..	..
Dominican Rep.	..	..	..	..	..	..
Ecuador	56.2	6.8	6.8	0.1	..	30.1
El Salvador	..	..	..	..	..	..
Guatemala	..	..	..	..	..	..
Haiti	..	..	..	..	..	..
Honduras	..	..	..	..	..	..
Jamaica	54.3	13.6	9.0	0.5	18.1	4.5
Mexico	21.3	5.8	28.2	1.2	18.2	25.3
Nicaragua	..	..	..	..	..	..
Panama	16.4	7.5	25.4	..	16.4	34.3
Paraguay	..	..	..	..	..	..
Peru	..	..	..	..	..	..
Trinidad	33.6	3.4	20.1	0.7	12.1	30.1
Uruguay	0.4	3.6	60.9	1.4	33.7	..
Venezuela	3.2	1.5	4.4	0.5	56.6	33.8
North America						
Canada	17.5	12.0	26.7	1.9	12.9	29.0
United States b)	9.2	3.3	38.7	7.3	18.1	23.4
Europe						
Albania	..	..	..	..	..	..
Austria	9.4	7.7	21.9	0.8	10.3	49.9
Belarus	..	..	..	..	..	..
Belgium	16.3	11.3	31.1	5.9	16.4	19.0
Bosnia	..	..	..	..	..	..
Bulgaria	..	..	..	..	..	..
Croatia	..	..	..	..	..	..
Czech Rep.	..	..	..	..	..	..
Denmark	8.0	3.0	23.0	1.3	8.3	56.4
Estonia	..	..	..	..	..	..
Finland	8.5	10.5	25.7	1.1	12.7	41.5
France	7.9	5.3	26.1	5.6	18.8	36.3
Germany	7.7	6.7	36.9	5.4	2.3	41.0
Greece	10.7	10.2	25.6	0.5	17.5	35.5
Hungary	..	..	..	..	..	..
Ireland	5.6	4.0	63.2	0.7	4.1	22.4
Israel	0.7	0.1	2.6	0.4	1.5	94.7
Italy	9.1	4.7	24.2	4.3	20.1	37.6
Latvia	..	..	..	..	..	..
Lithuania	..	..	..	..	..	..

Country	Books and pamphlets (%)	Newspapers and periodicals (%)	Music related goods (%)	Visual arts (%)	Cinema and photography (%)	Radio + television (%)
	1990-94	1990-94	1991	1991	1991	1991
Macedonia, FYR	..	..	..	..	..	..
Moldova	..	..	..	..	..	..
Netherlands	8.1	3.4	42.3	3.5	21.3	21.4
Norway	12.4	4.3	34.6	2.8	16.7	29.2
Poland	..	..	..	..	..	..
Portugal	5.4	4.6	18.9	0.2	9.6	61.3
Romania	7.5	1.2	19.6	..	2.6	69.1
Russia	..	..	..	..	..	..
Slovakia	..	..	..	..	..	..
Slovenia	..	..	..	..	..	..
Spain	11.2	4.3	19.4	2.9	11.9	50.3
Sweden	7.5	3.0	18.7	3.2	11.4	56.2
Switzerland	11.7	6.8	17.7	20.0	11.6	32.2
Ukraine	..	..	..	..	..	..
United Kingdom	9.7	2.7	18.3	14.3	14.3	40.7
Yugoslavia	..	..	..	..	..	..

Region	Books and pamphlets (%)	Newspapers and periodicals (%)	Music related goods (%)	Visual arts (%)	Cinema and photography (%)	Radio + television (%)
	1990-94	1990-94	1991	1991	1991	1991
World	..	..	..	..	..	..
Developing	..	..	..	..	..	..
Industrial	8.2	4.2	31.9	6.3	14.8	34.6
Dev exc India / China	..	..	..	..	..	..
Ind exc USA / Russia	8.0	4.4	30.3	6.1	14.0	37.2
Sub-Saharan Africa	..	..	..	..	..	..
Arab States	..	..	..	..	..	..
South Central Asia	..	..	..	..	..	..
East Asia	2.5	0.7	44.0	2.5	19.0	31.3
Southeast Asia / Oc	3.6	1.1	17.4	0.2	5.8	72.1
Latin Am / Carib	21.1	8.3	20.7	1.0	20.9	28.0
North America	10.6	4.7	36.8	6.4	17.2	24.3
Europe	9.3	5.1	27.5	6.0	13.0	39.1

a) Exports plus imports.
b) Not excluding re-exports.

TABLE 9
INTERNATIONAL TOURISM

Country	Arrivals of foreign visitors (per 100 inhabitant)	Main countries of origin		International tourism receipts (US$ per visitor)	Departures of nationals abroad (per 100 people)	Main countries of destination		International tourism expenditures abroad (US$ per national abroad)
		First country	Second country			First country	Second country	
	1996	1995	1995	1996	1996	1995	1995	1996
Sub-Saharan Africa								
Angola	0.2	Zaire	Congo	..	0.1	Brazil	Spain	..
Benin	2.7	..	..	197	0.3	Côte d' Ivoire	Togo	278
Botswana	58	South Africa	Zimbabwe	..	24	South Africa	Zambia	406
Burkina Faso	0.6	France	Cote D' Ivore	491	0.2	Côte d' Ivoire	Togo	1,304
Burundi	0.5	..	..	30	(.)	China	Russia	..
Cameroon	0.7	USA	UK	..	0.1	Côte d' Ivoire	Spain	..
Central African Rep	0.2	..	..	..	0.1	Côte d' Ivoire	Spain	..
Chad	0.3	France	..	..	(.)	Russia	Spain	..
Congo	1.3	France	..	..	0.8	Zaire	Côte d' Ivoire	1,857
Côte d' Ivoire	1.5	France	Burkina Faso	434	0.3	Ghana	Burkina Faso	..
Eritrea	..	..	..	..	..	..	..	..
Ethiopia	0.1	USA	Italy	1,438	(.)	India	Egypt	2,083
Gabon	12	..	..	..	0.5	Côte d' Ivoire	Congo	..
Gambia	8.2	UK	..	244	0.3	Spain	Hong Kong	..
Ghana	1.7	Nigeria	UK	802	0.1	USA	Côte d' Ivoire	1,400
Guinea	1.3	..	..	..	0.2	Côte d' Ivoire	Burkina Faso	1,750
Guinea-Bissau	..	..	..	..	0.2	Spain	Hong Kong	..
Kenya	2.7	Germany	UK	677	0.4	Tanzania	India	1,324
Lesotho	5.4	South Africa	UK	176	53	South Africa	Botswana	34
Liberia	..	..	..	..	0.4	Ghana	Russia	..
Madagascar	0.5	France	Germany	792	0.1	Reunion	Mauritius	..
Malawi	1.0	Mozambique	Zambia	..	0.5	South Africa	Zambia	301
Mali	0.4	France	Switzerland	455	0.3	Côte d' Ivoire	Burkina Faso	1,833
Mauritania	..	..	..	..	0.7	Tunisia	Morocco	1,188
Mauritius	40	France	South Africa	1,087	6.0	Reunion	Singapore	2,409
Mozambique	..	..	..	..	1.4	South Africa	Zimbabwe	..
Namibia	..	..	..	..	14	South Africa	Hong Kong	385
Niger	0.1	France	USA	2,429	0.2	Burkina Faso	Ghana	1,235
Nigeria	0.2	Niger	Benin	..	0.1	UK	Ghana	993
Rwanda	(.)	..	..	..	(.)	Russia	Hong Kong	..
Senegal	3.5	France	Italy	507	0.3	Côte d' Ivoire	Spain	2,679
Sierra Leone	0.3	UK	France	714	0.1	Hong Kong	China	154
Somalia	0.2	..	..	..	0.1	U.A.E.	Egypt	..
South Africa	11	Lesotho	Zimbabwe	269	2.8	Zimbabwe	UK	1,530
Sudan	0.1	..	..	..	0.3	Egypt	Syria	538
Tanzania	1.1	Kenya	UK	988	0.1	Zambia	India	..
Togo	0.7	France	Burkina Faso	296	0.5	Ghana	Côte d' Ivoire	1,190
Uganda	1.1	..	..	..	(.)	Hong Kong	India	..
Zaire	0.1	Congo	Belgium	200	0.1	Zambia	Belgium	294
Zambia	2.1	Zimbabwe	UK	349	7.5	Zimbabwe	South Africa	94
Zimbabwe	14	Zambia	South Africa	141	10	South Africa	Botswana	95
Arab States								
Algeria	0.2	France	Tunisia	231	4.8	Tunisia	Spain	93
Egypt	5.9	Germany	Israel	928	0.2	UK	Syria	..
Iraq	2.0	Jordan	Syria	..	0.2	Turkey	Russia	..
Jordan	20	Egypt	Syria	698	5.1	Israel	Syria	1,511
Kuwait	4.3	..	..	..	11	Egypt	Jordan	..

Country	Arrivals of foreign visitors (per 100 inhabitant)	Main countries of origin		International tourism receipts (US$ per visitor)	Departures of nationals abroad (per 100 people)	Main countries of destination		International tourism expenditures abroad (US$ per national abroad)
		First country	Second country			First country	Second country	
	1996	1995	1995	1996	1996	1995	1995	1996
Lebanon	14	Jordan	France	1,702	6.4	Syria	Israel	..
Libya	1.5	Turkey	UK	192	15	Tunisia	Egypt	2,222
Morocco	10	France	Spain	514	3.8	Spain	Tunisia	301
Oman	15	..	..	294	1.7	India	Jordan	1,270
Saudi Arabia	18	..	..	390	4.7	Jordan	Egypt	..
Syria	5.7	Lebanon	Jordan	1,813	1.0	Egypt	Turkey	2,702
Tunisia	43	Algeria	Germany	373	1.0	Morroco	Algeria	2,758
Unit.Arab Emirates	49	UK	India	..	7.9	Egypt	Thailand	..
Yemen, Rep.	0.2	Germany	France	1,147	0.5	Egypt	India	1,056
South Central Asia								
Afghanistan	(.)	..	..	..	0.3	Pakistan	India	19
Armenia	..	..	..	..	9.7	Russia	Iran	..
Azerbaijan	..	..	..	..	4.4	Russia	Iran	212
Bangladesh	0.1	India	UK	140	0.4	India	Thailand	515
Bhutan	0.2	Japan	USA	..	0.1	Nepal	Hong Kong	..
Georgia	..	..	..	..	9.5	Russia	Iran	..
India	0.2	UK	Bangladesh	1,323	0.1	Singapore	UK	565
Iran	0.7	Pakistan	Russia	362	0.2	Syria	U.A.E.	..
Kazakhstan	..	..	..	..	1.5	Russia	China	..
Kyrgyz Rep.	..	..	..	..	1.9	Russia	China	70
Nepal	1.9	India	Germany	322	0.4	India	Hong Kong	1,447
Pakistan	0.3	UK	USA	296	0.2	UK	U.A.E.	1,435
Sri Lanka	2.3	Germany	UK	417	1.1	India	Singapore	907
Tajikistan	..	..	..	..	1.1	Russia	Iran	..
Turkey	13	Germany	Russia	824	2.3	Bulgaria	Romania	644
Turkmenistan	..	..	..	..	1.1	Russia	Iran	..
Uzbekistan	..	..	..	..	0.3	Russia	Iran	..
East Asia								
China	2.1	Japan	Korea Dem.	403	0.3	Hong Kong	Russia	1,029
Hong Kong	192	China	Japan	957	42	Thailand	Singapore	..
Japan	1.6	Korea Rep.	USA	1,796	8.7	USA	Hong Kong	3,377
Korea, Dem.	0.5	..	..	..	0.5	China	Russia	..
Korea, Rep.	8.5	Japan	USA	1,655	4.0	Japan	USA	2,104
Mongolia	6.0	..	..	..	17	China	Russia	46
Southeast Asia and Oceania								
Australia	23	Japan	New Zealand	1,983	12	UK	USA	2,102
Cambodia	2.0	China	Japan	256	0.1	China	Hong Kong	1,333
Indonesia	2.3	Singapore	Malaysia	1,265	0.9	Singapore	Malaysia	1,251
Lao PDR	6.3	Thailand	Vietnam	161	(.)	China	Russia	..
Malaysia	39	Singapore	Thailand	569	14	Thailand	Singapore	653
Myanmar	0.1	Japan	Thailand	1,176	0.2	Singapore	China	316
New Zealand	42	Australia	USA	1,766	26	Australia	USA	1,365
Papua New Guinea	0.7	Australia	USA	2,067	1.1	Australia	N. Zealand	1,531
Philippines	3.0	USA	Japan	1,358	1.3	Hong Kong	China	463
Singapore	200	Japan	Indonesia	1,424	199	Malaysia	Indonesia	769
Thailand	12	Malaysia	Japan	1,194	2.4	Malaysia	Hong Kong	2,454
Vietnam	1.9	China	France	62	0.1	Thailand	China	..

Country	Arrivals of foreign visitors (per 100 inhabitant)	Main countries of origin		International tourism receipts (US$ per visitor)	Departures of nationals abroad (per 100 people)	Main countries of destination		International tourism expenditures abroad (US$ per national abroad)
		First country	Second country			First country	Second country	
	1996	1995	1995	1996	1996	1995	1995	1996
Latin America and the Caribbean								
Argentina	12	Uruguay	Chile	1,064	11	Uruguay	Brazil	553
Bolivia	2.5	Peru	USA	865	5.2	Argentina	Chile	482
Brazil	1.5	Argentina	USA	995	1.3	USA	Argentina	497
Chile	11	Argentina	Peru	615	6.4	Argentina	USA	856
Colombia	5.6	USA	..	..	1.4	USA	Ecuador	1,634
Costa Rica	23	USA	Nicaragua	840	6.9	USA	Nicaragua	1,333
Cuba	7.9	Canada	Germany	1,590	0.3	Spain	USA	..
Dominican Rep.	26	..	..	890	2.8	USA	Spain	395
Ecuador	4.2	Colombia	USA	525	1.3	USA	Panama	1,599
El Salvador	3.0	USA	Guatemala	450	4.7	Guatemala	USA	269
Guatemala	4.9	USA	El Salvador	559	3.3	Belize	USA	491
Haiti	1.8	USA	Canada	637	1.0	USA	Panama	500
Honduras	4.5	USA	El Salvador	..	3.5	Nicaragua	USA	284
Jamaica	46	USA	UK	971	10	USA	Canada	567
Mexico	24	USA	Canada	317	9.4	USA	France	369
Nicaragua	5.3	Honduras	USA	266	4.0	Costa Rica	USA	234
Panama	8.3	USA	Colombia	1,588	5.4	USA	Costa Rica	908
Paraguay	6.6	Argentina	Brazil	753	10	Argentina	Brazil	469
Peru	2.2	USA	Chile	1,039	1.7	Chile	USA	749
Trinidad	16	USA	Canada	346	13	USA	Venezuela	473
Uruguay	69	Argentina	Brazil	279	50	Argentina	Brazil	147
Venezuela	2.8	USA	Netherlands	1,353	3.2	USA	Spain	2,634
North America								
Canada	59	USA	UK	503	56	USA	UK	626
United States	17	Canada	Mexico	1,415	15	Mexico	Canada	1,088
Europe								
Albania	0.5	Italy	USA	444	0.8	Bulgaria	Macedonia	138
Austria	208	Germany	Italy	907	120	Czech Rep.	Hungary	1,213
Belarus	..	..	..	..	29	Poland	Russia	..
Belgium	56	UK	France	1,047	42	Spain	UK	2,178
Bosnia	..	..	..	..	2.0	Croatia	Slovenia	..
Bulgaria	40	Yugoslavia	Turkey	132	13	Romania	Hungary	226
Croatia	53	Italy	Austria	..	17	Hungary	Slovenia	1,017
Czech Rep.	167	..	..	..	11	Poland	Slovakia	1,430
Denmark	35	Germany	Sweden	2,248	53	France	Germany	1,561
Estonia	23	..	..	..	17	Russia	Finland	409
Finland	18	Germany	Sweden	2,073	39	Russia	Spain	1,211
France	106	Germany	Netherlands	459	18	Spain	UK	1,567
Germany	18	Netherlands	USA	874	55	France	Austria	1,120
Greece	93	Germany	UK	434	9.6	Cyprus	Bulgaria	1,303
Hungary	205	Germany	Romania	108	20	Czech Rep.	Austria	537
Ireland	132	UK	USA	365	73	UK	Spain	770
Israel	42	USA	Germany	1,340	20	Egypt	UK	2,931
Italy	62	Switzerland	France	770	17	France	Spain	1,263
Latvia	..	..	..	..	4.2	Russia	Lithuania	231
Lithuania	2.5	Russia	Germany	..	37	Poland	Russia	100

Country	Arrivals of foreign visitors (per 100 inhabitant)	Main countries of origin		International tourism receipts (US$ per visitor)	Departures of nationals abroad (per 100 people)	Main countries of destination		International tourism expenditures abroad (US$ per national abroad)
		First country	Second country			First country	Second country	
	1996	1995	1995	1996	1996	1995	1995	1996
Macedonia, FYR	4.3	Yugoslavia	Bulgaria	213	1.3	Slovenia	Russia	926
Moldova	..	..	..	..	4.0	Russia	Romania	281
Netherlands	43	Germany	UK	878	83	France	Spain	894
Norway	68	Germany	Denmark	859	43	Sweden	UK	2,297
Poland	50	Germany	Czech Rep.	360	12	Czech Rep.	Russia	1,211
Portugal	101	Spain	UK	430	21	Spain	France	1,073
Romania	18	Moldova	Bulgaria	126	18	Hungary	Bulgaria	169
Russia	6.5	Ukraine	Finland	534	2.8	Poland	Hungary	2,780
Slovakia	11	Czech Rep.	Germany	1,127	3.8	Poland	Austria	1,618
Slovenia	27	Italy	Germany	2,359	39	Hungary	Croatia	551
Spain	104	France	Portugal	688	26	Portugal	France	436
Sweden	29	Germany	Norway	1,495	37	France	Spain	1,684
Switzerland	154	Germany	USA	891	102	France	Spain	1,044
Ukraine	..	..	..	..	14	Poland	Hungary	..
United Kingdom	44	USA	France	791	47	France	Spain	903
Yugoslavia	0.5	Russia	Greece	860	20	Hungary	Russia	..

Region	Arrivals of foreign visitors (per 100 inhabitant)	International tourism receipts (US$ per visitor)	Departures of nationals abroad (per 100 people)	International tourism expenditures abroad (US$ per national abroad)
	1996	1996	1996	1996
World	10	829	5.6	1,060
Developing	3.4	782	1.3	919
Industrial	40	1,007	22	1,580
Dev exc India / China	5.5	759	2.4	1,025
Ind exc USA / Russia	50	947	28	1,515
Sub-Saharan Africa	2.0	699	1.0	1,225
Arab States	8.4	750	2.5	1,066
South Central Asia	0.8	1,016	0.4	662
East Asia	3.1	570	1.4	1,271
Southeast Asia / Oc	6.3	1,064	3.3	1,198
Latin Am / Carib	9.5	823	4.6	715
North America	21	1,324	19	1,042
Europe	50	672	26	1,469

TABLE 10
COMMUNICATION AND NEW TECHNOLOGY

Country	Post offices (per 100,000 people)	Letter post items		Main telephone lines	International telephone calls	
		(per person)	(per person sent abroad)	(per thousand people)	(minutes per person)	Major international partner
	1994-95	1994-95	1995	1995	1995	1995
Sub-Saharan Africa						
Angola	1	(.)	0.1	6	2	..
Benin	3	1	0.6	5	1	France
Botswana	14	22	1.4	41	20	South Africa
Burkina Faso	..	..	..	3	1	..
Burundi	(.)	1	0.4	3	(.)	Belgium
Cameroon	2	..	0.1	5	2	USA
Central African Rep.	1	..	..	2	1	France
Chad	1	1	0.2	1	(.)	France
Congo	4	(.)	0.3	8	2	..
Côte d' Ivoire	3	3	0.5	8	2	..
Eritrea	1	(.)	0.1	5	(.)	..
Ethiopia	1	(.)	0.1	3	(.)	..
Gabon	5	1	0.3	31	15	..
Gambia	..	..	..	18	4	..
Ghana	6	4	1.7	4	1	..
Guinea	1	1	0.3	2	1	France
Guinea-Bissau	3	..	..	9	2	..
Kenya	4	22	2.3	9	1	UK
Lesotho	8	20	11.3	9	6	..
Liberia	..	..	..	2	1	..
Madagascar	6	3	0.3	2	(.)	..
Malawi	3	2	1.5	4	1	Botswana
Mali	1	(.)	0.1	2	1	France
Mauritania	3	(.)	0.1	4	2	..
Mauritius	9	30	8.6	131	18	France
Mozambique	3	(.)	(.)	3	1	..
Namibia	6	..	..	51	31	South Africa
Niger	1	(.)	(.)	2	(.)	..
Nigeria	3	5	2.1	4	1	..
Rwanda	..	..	..	2	(.)	..
Senegal	2	1	0.5	10	2	..
Sierra Leone	1	(.)	0.1	4	1	..
Somalia	..	..	..	2	..	..
South Africa	5	56	3.2	95	7	Namibia
Sudan	2	..	0.1	3	(.)	Saudi Arabia
Tanzania	2	1	0.2	3	(.)	..
Togo	1	1	0.4	5	2	France
Uganda	2	1	0.2	2	(.)	UK
Zaire	1	..	..	1	..	..
Zambia	2	1	0.2	8	1	USA
Zimbabwe	3	22	3.4	14	5	UK
Arab States						
Algeria	11	17	2.7	42	3	France
Egypt	6	4	1.5	46	2	Saudi Arabia
Iraq	..	..	..	33	..	..
Jordan	25	11	3.8	73	17	Saudi Arabia
Kuwait	4	23	17.3	230	76	Egypt

Country	Post offices (per 100,000 people)	Letter post items		Main telephone lines	International telephone calls	
		(per person)	(per person sent abroad)	(per thousand people)	(minutes per person)	Major international partner
	1994-95	1994-95	1995	1995	1995	1995
Lebanon	..	..	..	82	9	..
Libya	7	..	..	59	9	..
Morocco	5	8	1.0	43	5	France
Oman	4	..	..	77	25	..
Saudi Arabia	7	28	14.2	96	30	Egypt
Syria	5	1	0.2	63	4	Saudi Arabia
Tunisia	11	12	0.8	58	9	Italy
Unit.Arab Emirates	7	40	19.1	283	212	India
Yemen, Rep.	3	(.)	0.1	12	2	Saudi Arabia
South Central Asia						
Afghanistan	2	..	..	2	..	..
Armenia	..	..	..	156	14	Russia
Azerbaijan	25	1	0.1	85	4	..
Bangladesh	..	..	0.3	2	(.)	..
Bhutan	6	1	0.1	7	1	..
Georgia	..	..	..	96	(.)	..
India	17	15	0.2	13	(.)	Saudi Arabia
Iran	17	3	0.2	99	3	UAE
Kazakhstan	26	25	..	118	1	..
Kyrgyz Rep.	20	13	0.6	73	(.)	..
Nepal	14	4	0.8	4	1	..
Pakistan	11	2	0.3	16	1	Saudi Arabia
Sri Lanka	23	25	1.9	11	2	..
Tajikistan	13	1	0.2	45	(.)	Russia
Turkey	51	21	1.7	230	6	Germany
Turkmenistan	..	..	..	76	1	..
Uzbekistan	..	..	..	76	6	..
East Asia						
China	6	7	0.1	25	1	Hong Kong
Hong Kong	2	171	26.5	530	273	China
Japan	20	195	0.9	488	13	USA
Korea, Dem.	..	..	..	47	(.)	..
Korea, Rep.	8	77	0.6	415	12	USA
Mongolia	15	..	0.7	32	1	Russia
Southeast Asia and Oceania						
Australia	22	245	10.3	510	53	USA
Cambodia	(.)	(.)	0.3	1	1	..
Indonesia	4	8	0.2	17	1	Singapore
Lao PDR	3	(.)	0.1	4	(.)	..
Malaysia	7	51	5.2	166	18	Singapore
Myanmar	3	2	0.1	3	(.)	..
New Zealand	..	..	..	479	86	Australia
Papua New Guinea	..	..	..	10	5	..
Philippines	5	14	3.5	21	3	USA
Singapore	40	195	22.1	479	259	Malaysia
Thailand	7	21	1.8	59	4	Japan
Vietnam	..	..	..	11	(.)	..

Country	Post offices (per 100,000 people)	Letter post items		Main telephone lines	International telephone calls	
		(per person)	(per person sent abroad)	(per thousand people)	(minutes per person)	Major international partner
	1994-95	1994-95	1995	1995	1995	1995
Latin America and the Caribbean						
Argentina	17	..	..	160	4	Uruguay
Bolivia	2	1	1.0	35	2	Argentina
Brazil	7	35	0.2	75	2	USA
Chile	4	21	0.8	132	10	USA
Colombia	5	3	0.5	100	3	USA
Costa Rica	15	9	3.6	164	16	USA
Cuba	14	1	0.7	32	1	Mexico
Dominican Rep.	3	..	..	79	8	USA
Ecuador	2	1	0.4	61	3	USA
El Salvador	5	2	0.8	53	12	USA
Guatemala	5	7	3.0	27	3	El Salvador
Haiti	2	1	0.4	8	3	USA
Honduras	8	3	1.8	29	6	USA
Jamaica	32	21	7.7	116	22	Trinidad
Mexico	8	9	1.5	97	10	USA
Nicaragua	5	..	..	23	7	Costa Rica
Panama	13	2	1.0	114	15	Colombia
Paraguay	7	1	0.2	31	3	Argentina
Peru	3	(.)	0.2	47	3	USA
Trinidad	19	16	4.0	160	45	USA
Uruguay	9	3	0.8	196	16	Argentina
Venezuela	2	4	0.3	110	6	USA
North America						
Canada	64	..	..	600	100	USA
United States	19	684	2.5	627	60	Canada
Europe						
Albania	21	1	0.2	12	6	Italy
Austria	33	417	27.9	466	112	Germany
Belarus	37	..	0.2	190	13	Ukraine
Belgium	16	330	..	456	109	France
Bosnia	..	..	(.)	71	2	..
Bulgaria	43	..	..	306	10	..
Croatia	25	50	3.4	269	44	Germany
Czech Rep.	34	65	4.3	232	18	Germany
Denmark	24	337	2.5	613	101	Germany
Estonia	39	21	5.3	277	31	Finland
Finland	35	228	4.0	550	62	Sweden
France	29	413	6.1	563	48	Germany
Germany	21	228	4.8	495	64	Austria
Greece	12	..	..	494	44	Germany
Hungary	31	101	15.6	185	24	Germany
Ireland	54	142	17.8	367	114	UK
Israel	12	88	5.1	418	45	USA
Italy	25	97	2.7	434	33	Germany
Latvia	41	7	1.0	280	17	Russia
Lithuania	27	9	1.7	254	15	Russia

Country	Post offices (per 100,000 people)	Letter post items		Main telephone lines	International telephone calls	
		(per person)	(per person sent abroad)	(per thousand people)	(minutes per person)	Major international partner
	1994-95	1994-95	1995	1995	1995	1995
Macedonia, FYR	13	11	1.4	165	21	..
Moldova	30	12	1.0	131	15	Russia
Netherlands	13	..	..	525	94	Germany
Norway	55	489	9.8	558	99	Sweden
Poland	20	30	1.0	148	10	Germany
Portugal	67	103	6.0	362	10	France
Romania	23	8	0.6	131	4	Germany
Russia	31	..	..	170	2	Ukraine
Slovakia	33	95	0.5	208	11	..
Slovenia	26	127	5.4	309	51	Croatia
Spain	12	106	4.2	385	27	France
Sweden	20	501	9.9	681	108	Finland
Switzerland	52	..	..	623	247	Germany
Ukraine	32	10	0.7	157	..	Russia
United Kingdom	33	313	13.6	502	70	USA
Yugoslavia	..	..	..	192	20	Germany

Region	Post offices (per 100,000 people)	Letter post items		Main telephone lines	International telephone calls
		(per person)	(per person sent abroad)	(per thousand people)	(minutes per person)
	1994-95	1994-95	1995	1995	1995
World	13	71	1.3	137	11
Developing	9	12	0.7	44	3
Industrial	26	329	4.2	431	43
Dev exc India / China	8	14	1.2	81	5
Ind exc USA / Russia	27	185	4.9	411	45
Sub-Saharan Africa	3	9	1.2	11	2
Arab States	7	10	3.1	55	10
South Central Asia	18	13	0.3	32	1
East Asia	7	27	0.3	80	4
Southeast Asia / Oc	6	23	1.8	64	6
Latin Am / Carib	7	17	0.8	88	5
North America	23	684	2.5	623	64
Europe	28	180	5.7	337	38

TABLE 10B
COMMUNICATION AND NEW TECHNOLOGY (CONT.)

Country	Mobile cellular telephone subcribers (per 10.000 people)	Facsimile machines (per 10.000 people)	Personal computers (per 10.000 people)	Internet hosts (per 10.000 people)
	1995	1992-95	1995	1996-97
Sub-Saharan Africa				
Angola	2	..	..	(.)
Benin	2	2	..	(.)
Botswana	..	22	..	(.)
Burkina Faso	..	..	..	(.)
Burundi	1	(.)	..	..
Cameroon	2	..	..	(.)
Central African Rep.	..	1	..	(.)
Chad	..	(.)	..	..
Congo	..	(.)	..	..
Côte d' Ivoire	..	..	..	(.)
Eritrea	..	2	..	..
Ethiopia	..	(.)	..	(.)
Gabon	25	..	45	..
Gambia	13	6	..	..
Ghana	4	3	12	(.)
Guinea	1	(.)	2	(.)
Guinea-Bissau	..	5	..	..
Kenya	1	1	7	0.1
Lesotho	..	3	..	..
Liberia	..	..	..	..
Madagascar	..	..	..	(.)
Malawi	..	1	..	..
Mali	..	..	..	(.)
Mauritania	..	1	..	(.)
Mauritius	104	182	319	0.4
Mozambique	..	5	..	(.)
Namibia	23	..	..	0.5
Niger	..	(.)	..	(.)
Nigeria	1	..	41	(.)
Rwanda	..	1	..	..
Senegal	..	..	72	0.1
Sierra Leone	..	2	..	..
Somalia	..	..	..	..
South Africa	129	19	265	20
Sudan	..	2	..	..
Tanzania	1	1	..	(.)
Togo	..	3	..	..
Uganda	1	1	5	(.)
Zaire	2	1	..	..
Zambia	2	1	..	..
Zimbabwe	..	1	30	..
Arab States				
Algeria	2	3	30	(.)
Egypt	1	4	34	0.1
Iraq	..	..	..	..
Jordan	26	80	80	0.2
Kuwait	707	219	571	12

Country	Mobile cellular telephone subcribers (per 10.000 people)	Facsimile machines (per 10.000 people)	Personal computers (per 10.000 people)	Internet hosts (per 10.000 people)
	1995	1992-95	1995	1996-97
Lebanon	300	8	125	0.9
Libya	..	..	..	..
Morocco	11	3	17	0.1
Oman	37	8	..	(.)
Saudi Arabia	9	42	251	0.2
Syria	..	4	1	(.)
Tunisia	4	28	67	(.)
Unit.Arab Emirates	542	104	484	2.0
Yemen. Rep.	5	1	..	..
South Central Asia				
Afghanistan	..	..	..	..
Armenia	..	1	..	0.3
Azerbaijan	1	3	..	(.)
Bangladesh	..	(.)	..	..
Bhutan	..	..	..	..
Georgia	..	1	..	0.2
India	1	1	13	(.)
Iran	1	5	..	0.1
Kazakhstan	3	2	..	0.3
Kyrgyz Rep.	..	..	..	..
Nepal	..	(.)	..	(.)
Pakistan	3	1	12	(.)
Sri Lanka	28	1	11	0.1
Tajikistan	..	2	..	..
Turkey	70	16	125	2.1
Turkmenistan	2	..	..	..
Uzbekistan	..	1	..	(.)
East Asia				
China	2	(.)	22	0.1
Hong Kong	1,290	467	1,163	39
Japan	815	480	1,525	59
Korea. Dem.	..	1	..	..
Korea. Rep.	366	84	1,208	11
Mongolia	..	9	2	(.)
Southeast Asia and Oceania				
Australia	1,277	267	2,758	285
Cambodia	15	1	..	(.)
Indonesia	11	4	37	0.3
Lao PDR	1	1	..	(.)
Malaysia	434	29	397	4.2
Myanmar	..	(.)	..	..
New Zealand	1,080	186	2,227	236
Papua New Guinea	..	2	..	(.)
Philippines	73	5	114	0.5
Singapore	977	191	1,724	129
Thailand	185	10	153	1.1
Vietnam	2	2	4	..

Country	Mobile cellular telephone subcribers (per 10.000 people)	Facsimile machines (per 10.000 people)	Personal computers (per 10.000 people)	Internet hosts (per 10.000 people)
	1995	1992-95	1995	1996-97
Latin America and the Caribbean				
Argentina	99	22	246	2.7
Bolivia	10	..	..	0.2
Brazil	80	13	130	2.9
Chile	138	11	378	9.3
Colombia	71	28	162	1.4
Costa Rica	55	7	..	7.6
Cuba	2	(.)	..	(.)
Dominican Rep.	42	3	..	0.2
Ecuador	46	27	39	0.5
El Salvador	25	..	..	0.1
Guatemala	28	10	28	0.2
Haiti	..	..	..	..
Honduras	..	..	..	0.2
Jamaica	179	6	..	0.8
Mexico	70	20	261	3.3
Nicaragua	11	..	..	0.7
Panama	..	..	..	0.8
Paraguay	32	4	..	0.2
Peru	31	6	59	1.0
Trinidad	43	15	192	0.5
Uruguay	126	34	220	2.8
Venezuela	180	8	167	..
North America				
Canada	865	180	1,928	204
United States	1,284	539	3,280	384
Europe				
Albania	..	2	..	0.2
Austria	476	313	1,242	114
Belarus	6	9	..	0.1
Belgium	232	163	1,383	64
Bosnia	..	..	..	..
Bulgaria	25	18	215	2.7
Croatia	71	80	209	5.1
Czech Rep.	47	71	532	40
Denmark	1,573	481	2,705	204
Estonia	205	87	67	44
Finland	1,992	328	1,821	555
France	238	259	1,343	42
Germany	428	178	1,649	88
Greece	261	15	334	15
Hungary	259	44	392	29
Ireland	441	222	1,450	76
Israel	535	259	998	72
Italy	674	35	837	26
Latvia	60	3	79	12
Lithuania	40	10	65	3.6

Country	Mobile cellular telephone subcribers (per 10.000 people)	Facsimile machines (per 10.000 people)	Personal computers (per 10.000 people)	Internet hosts (per 10.000 people)
	1995	1992-95	1995	1996-97
Macedonia. FYR	..	9	..	0.4
Moldova	11	1	21	(.)
Netherlands	332	325	2,005	175
Norway	2,244	302	2,730	394
Poland	19	14	285	14
Portugal	344	36	605	26
Romania	4	9	53	1.2
Russia	6	3	177	2.2
Slovakia	23	84	410	10
Slovenia	136	78	477	50
Spain	241	55	816	28
Sweden	2,294	369	1,925	264
Switzerland	635	281	3,480	182
Ukraine	3	(.)	56	0.9
United Kingdom	980	308	1,862	101
Yugoslavia	..	1	118	..

Region	Mobile cellular telephone subcribers (per 10.000 people)	Facsimile machines (per 10.000 people)	Personal computers (per 10.000 people)	Internet hosts (per 10.000 people)
	1995	1992-95	1995	1996-97
World	164	58	..	31
Developing	27	5	..	0.9
Industrial	635	251	1,555	135
Dev exc India / China	59	11	..	1.9
Ind exc USA / Russia	525	197	1,204	72
Sub-Saharan Africa	..	4	..	..
Arab States	24	14	67	0.2
South Central Asia	5	2	..	0.1
East Asia	92	47	199	5.9
Southeast Asia / Oc	124	17	215	1.7
Latin Am / Carib	76	15	174	2.5
North America	1,242	503	3,146	366
Europe	330	107	860	48

TABLE 11
CULTURAL TRENDS: BOOKS

Country	Number of copies of books produced (per 100 people)		Annual rate of change	Number of book titles published (per 100,000 people)		Annual rate of change	Number of books in public libraries (per thousand people)		Annual rate of change
	1981-83	1991-94	81-3/91-4	1981-83	1991-94	81-3/91-4	1981-83	1991-94	81-3/91-4
Sub-Saharan Africa									
Angola	..	..		..	..	..	..	..	..
Benin	..	..	..	..	..	..	..	..	..
Botswana	..	..	..	..	..	..	..	..	..
Burkina Faso	..	..	..	..	..	..	..	..	..
Burundi	..	..	..	..	..	..	..	..	..
Cameroon	..	..	..	..	..	..	..	..	..
C.A.R.	..	..	..	..	..	..	..	..	..
Chad	..	..	..	..	..	..	..	..	..
Congo	..	..	..	..	..	..	3.2	0.6	-10.2
Côte d' Ivoire	..	..	..	..	..	..	..	..	..
Eritrea	..	..	..	..	..	..	..	..	..
Ethiopia	0.4	1.2	20.0	0.4	0.2	-6.3	..	..	..
Gabon	..	..	..	..	..	..	..	..	..
Gambia	..	..	..	..	..	..	10.5	8.5	-1.6
Ghana	..	..	..	0.1	0.2	10.0	8.7	9.5	0.8
Guinea	..	..	..	..	..	..	..	..	..
Guinea-Bissau	..	..	..	..	..	..	..	..	..
Kenya	1.3	1.8	3.8	1.3	0.9	-3.8	..	..	..
Lesotho	..	..	..	..	..	..	..	..	..
Liberia	..	..	..	..	..	..	..	..	..
Madagascar	10.3	2.2	-6.6	4.6	0.9	-7.3	..	..	..
Malawi	1.2	1.5	3.1	..	..	..	..	..	..
Mali	..	..	..	..	..	..	..	..	..
Mauritania	..	..	..	..	..	..	..	..	..
Mauritius	18	8.1	-4.6	8.0	3.9	-4.3	..	..	..
Mozambique	..	..	..	..	..	..	..	..	..
Namibia	..	..	..	..	..	..	..	..	..
Niger	0.1	0.1	0.0	..	..	..	..	..	..
Nigeria	..	..	..	2.3	1.5	-3.9	0.7	0.6	-1.2
Rwanda	..	..	..	..	..	..	..	..	..
Senegal	..	..	..	..	..	..	..	..	..
Sierra Leone	..	..	..	..	..	..	..	..	..
Somalia	..	..	..	..	..	..	..	..	..
South Africa	..	..	..	..	..	..	..	..	..
Sudan	..	..	..	..	..	..	..	..	..
Tanzania	..	..	..	..	..	..	..	..	..
Togo	..	..	..	..	..	..	..	..	..
Uganda	..	1.3	..	..	..	..	0.6	0.4	-2.8
Zaire	0.4	1.3	15.0	..	..	..	..	..	..
Zambia	..	..	..	..	..	..	..	..	..
Zimbabwe	..	..	..	7.5	2.2	-8.8	..	..	..
Arab States									
Algeria	6.9	1.8	-7.4	2.7	1.2	-5.1	..	..	..
Egypt	..	..	..	..	..	..	3.0	11	24.2
Iraq	..	..	..	..	..	..	..	..	..
Jordan	..	..	..	..	..	..	2.4	3.5	7.6
Kuwait	..	..	..	..	..	..	21	17	-1.6

Country	Number of copies of books produced (per 100 people)		Annual rate of change	Number of book titles published (per 100,000 people)		Annual rate of change	Number of books in public libraries (per thousand people)		Annual rate of change
	1981-83	1991-94	81-3/91-4	1981-83	1991-94	81-3/91-4	1981-83	1991-94	81-3/91-4
Lebanon	..	..	..	..	..	..	..	..	..
Libya	..	..	..	..	..	..	..	..	..
Morocco	..	..	..	..	..	..	..	..	..
Oman	..	..	..	..	..	..	..	..	..
Saudi Arabia	..	..	..	..	..	..	..	..	..
Syria	..	..	..	1.4	4.3	23.0	..	..	..
Tunisia	..	..	..	2.7	6.1	12.6	14	28	8.3
U.A.E.	159	213	3.4	8.4	12	4.3	..	..	..
Yemen, Rep.	..	..	..	..	..	..	..	..	..
South Central Asia									
Afghanistan	37	7.9	-8.7	..	..	..	..	..	..
Armenia	..	..	..	..	..	..	..	..	..
Azerbaijan	..	..	..	..	..	..	..	..	..
Bangladesh	..	..	..	..	..	..	..	..	..
Bhutan	..	..	..	..	..	..	..	..	..
Georgia	..	..	..	..	..	..	..	..	..
India	..	..	..	3.0	1.3	-4.7	..	..	..
Iran	..	..	..	7.6	17	11.2	5.6	5.3	-0.5
Kazalkstan	..	..	..	..	..	..	..	..	..
Kyrgyz Rep.	..	..	..	..	..	..	..	..	..
Nepal	..	..	..	..	..	..	..	..	..
Pakistan	1.5	0.6	-5.0	2.1	0.2	-7.0	0.1	0.4	25.0
Sri Lanka	119	86	-2.5	13	16	2.1	4.9	2.7	-3.7
Tajikistan	..	..	..	..	..	..	..	..	..
Turkey	..	..	..	15	7.5	-4.5	11	15	3.0
Turkmenistan	..	..	..	..	..	..	..	..	..
Uzbekistan	..	..	..	..	..	..	..	..	..
East Asia									
China	496	489	-0.1	3.2	8.5	15.1	..	..	..
Hong Kong	..	..	..	..	..	..	20	69	20.4
Japan	561	253	-5.5	37	28	-2.4	59	129	11.9
Korea, Dem.	..	..	..	..	..	..	..	..	..
Korea, Rep.	296	360	2.0	93	76	-1.7	3.7	19	29.5
Mongolia	29	40	2.2	51	12	-8.5	..	..	..
Southeast Asia and Oceania									
Australia	..	..	..	..	..	..	..	..	..
Cambodia	..	..	..	..	..	..	..	..	..
Indonesia	..	..	..	3.8	3.3	-1.5	..	..	..
Lao PDR	1.0	2.9	11.9	..	..	..	..	..	..
Malaysia	58	88	4.0	17	21	2.0	18	41	10.6
Myanmar	..	..	..	..	..	..	..	..	..
New Zealand	..	..	..	..	..	..	..	..	..
P.N.G.	..	..	..	..	..	..	..	..	..
Philippines	..	..	..	1.7	1.8	0.0	2.1	8.6	25.8
Singapore	..	..	..	..	..	..	..	..	..
Thailand	..	..	..	12	13	0.9	..	..	..
Vietnam	..	..	..	..	..	..	..	..	..

Country	Number of copies of books produced (per 100 people)		Annual rate of change	Number of book titles published (per 100,000 people)		Annual rate of change	Number of books in public libraries (per thousand people)		Annual rate of change
	1981-83	1991-94	81-3/91-4	1981-83	1991-94	81-3/91-4	1981-83	1991-94	81-3/91-4
Latin America and the Caribbean									
Argentina	52	143	14.6	15	26	6.7	..	..	..
Bolivia	..	..	..	..	..	..	..	..	..
Brazil	377	65	-6.9	16	13	-1.6	..	..	..
Chile	179	114	-4.5	12	13	0.9	5.2	8.0	4.5
Colombia	124	31	-9.4	29	4.1	-10.7	..	..	..
Costa Rica	..	..	..	..	..	..	2.4	9.7	38.0
Cuba	424	42	-8.2	20	8.5	-5.8	28	48	6.0
Dom. Rep.	..	..	..	..	..	..	..	..	..
Ecuador	..	..	..	..	..	..	..	..	..
El Salvador	..	..	..	..	..	..	..	..	..
Guatemala	..	..	..	..	..	..	..	..	..
Haiti	..	..	..	..	..	..	..	..	..
Honduras	..	..	..	..	..	..	..	..	..
Jamaica	..	..	..	..	..	..	52	47	-1.1
Mexico	..	..	..	..	..	..	3.6	36	69.2
Nicaragua	..	..	..	..	..	..	..	..	..
Panama	..	..	..	..	..	..	..	..	..
Paraguay	..	..	..	..	..	..	..	..	..
Peru	..	..	..	4.1	8.6	10.0	24	25	0.7
Trinidad	..	..	..	..	..	..	..	..	..
Uruguay	29	62	11.4	29	36	2.7	..	..	..
Venezuela	..	..	..	..	..	..	6.5	25	21.9
North America									
Canada	..	..	..	..	..	..	185	209	1.3
U.S.A.	..	..	..	34	20	-3.7	..	..	..
Europe									
Albania	244	118	-5.2	39	12	-8.7	214	127	-5.1
Austria	..	..	..	80	99	2.0	70	102	3.8
Belarus	496	775	5.1	34	32	-0.5	905	742	-1.5
Belgium	..	..	..	278	138	-6.3	245	294	2.0
Bosnia	..	..	..	..	..	..	..	..	..
Bulgaria	672	509	-2.2	55	71	2.6	552	680	1.9
Croatia	..	..	..	..	..	..			
Czech Rep.	..	..	..						
Denmark	..	..	..	185	230	2.2	576	625	0.7
Estonia	..	..	..	..	..	..	..	..	..
Finland	..	..	..	179	246	3.4	489	712	3.5
France	..	..	..	70	78	1.0	94	154	5.3
Germany	..	..	..	83	86	0.3	159	158	-0.1
Greece	..	..	..	..	..	..	..	..	..
Hungary	..	..	..	79	98	2.2	381	489	2.2
Ireland	..	..	..	..	..	..	218	309	3.8
Israel	299	178	-4.0	..	..	..	..	..	..
Italy	255	507	9.0	24	58	12.9	25	48	7.7
Latvia	..	..	..	..	..	..	..	..	..
Lithuania	..	..	..	..	..	..	..	..	..

Country	Number of copies of books produced (per 100 people)		Annual rate of change	Number of book titles published (per 100,000 people)		Annual rate of change	Number of books in public libraries (per thousand people)		Annual rate of change
	1981-83	1991-94	81-3/91-4	1981-83	1991-94	81-3/91-4	1981-83	1991-94	81-3/91-4
Macedonia, FYR	..	..	..	..	..	..	..	..	..
Moldova	..	..	..	..	..	..	..	..	..
Netherlands	..	..	..	95	221	12.1	217	271	2.1
Norway	..	..	..	135	159	1.6	344	462	2.9
Poland	548	256	-4.8	25	28	1.1	266	353	2.5
Portugal	591	272	-4.9	88	68	-2.1	54	39	-2.1
Romania	359	221	-3.2	30	16	-3.9	270	204	-1.9
Russia	..	..	..	..	..	..	..	..	..
Slovakia	..	..	..	..	..	..	..	..	..
Slovenia	..	..	..	..	..	..	..	..	..
Spain	727	461	-3.0	86	113	2.6	31	76	12.1
Sweden	..	..	..	97	158	5.7	470	513	0.7
Switzerland	..	..	..	137	219	5.0	..	..	..
Ukraine	306	169	-4.5	18	10	-4.4	742	772	0.3
U.K.	..	..	..	85	148	6.7	233	223	-0.3
Yugoslavia	..	..	..	..	..	..	..	..	..

Region	Number of copies of books produced (per 100 people)		Annual rate of change	Number of book titles published (per 100,000 people)		Annual rate of change	Number of books in public libraries (per thousand people)		Annual rate of change
	1981-83	1991-94	81-3/91-4	1981-83	1991-94	81-3/91-4	1981-83	1991-94	81-3/91-4
World	..	..	..	..	..	..	..	..	..
Developing	..	..	..	..	..	..	..	..	..
Industrial	..	..	..	49	54	1.0	..	..	..
Dev exc India / China	..	..	..	..	..	..	..	..	..
Ind exc USA / Russia	..	..	..	..	..	..	..	..	..
Sub-Saharan Africa	..	..	..	..	..	..	..	..	..
Arab States	..	..	..	..	..	..	..	..	..
South Central Asia	..	..	..	..	..	..	..	..	..
East Asia	..	..	..	10	13	3.0	..	..	..
Southeast Asia / Oc	..	..	..	..	..	..	..	..	..
Latin Am / Carib	..	..	..	..	..	..	..	..	..
North America	..	..	..	..	..	..	..	..	..
Europe	..	..	..	56	70	2.5	..	..	..

T ABLE 12
C ULTURAL TRENDS: NEWSPAPERS AND CULTURAL PAPER

Country	Daily newspapers (daily circulation per thousand people)		Annual rate of change	Cultural paper a) consumed (kilos per person)		Annual rate of change
	1980	1994	1980/94	1980	1994	1980/94
Sub-Saharan Africa						
Angola	20	11	-3.8	0.6	0.2	-5.1
Benin	..	..	..	..	..	..
Botswana	21	31	4.0	..	..	..
Burkina Faso	..	..	..	..	..	..
Burundi	..	..	..	..	..	..
Cameroon	8	6	-2.1	0.5	0.5	0.0
C.A.R.	..	..	..	..	..	..
Chad	..	..	..	..	..	..
Congo	..	..	..	..	..	..
Côte d' Ivoire	10	15	4.2	0.6	0.8	2.6
Eritrea	..	..	..	..	..	..
Ethiopia	..	..	..	..	..	..
Gabon	22	28	2.3	..	..	..
Gambia	..	..	..	..	..	..
Ghana	47	18	-5.1	0.5	0.4	-1.5
Guinea	..	..	..	..	..	..
Guinea-Bissau	8	6	-2.1	..	..	..
Kenya	13	17	2.6	1.2	2.1	5.8
Lesotho	33	7	-6.6	..	..	..
Liberia	6	16	13.9	..	..	..
Madagascar	6	4	-2.8	0.5	0.4	-1.5
Malawi	..	..	..	..	..	..
Mali	..	..	..	..	..	..
Mauritania	..	..	..	..	..	..
Mauritius	83	112	2.9	2.2	11	30.8
Mozambique	4	8	8.3	0.5	0.1	-6.2
Namibia	..	..	..	..	..	..
Niger	..	..	..	..	..	..
Nigeria	15	17	1.1	1.0	0.6	-3.1
Rwanda	..	..	..	..	..	..
Senegal	6	6	0.0	0.5	0.6	1.5
Sierra Leone	..	..	..	..	..	..
Somalia	..	..	..	..	..	..
South Africa	48	31	-3.0	14	20	3.3
Sudan	6	24	25.0	..	..	..
Tanzania	11	12	0.8	0.6	0.6	0.0
Togo	6	2	-5.6	..	..	..
Uganda	..	..	..	..	..	..
Zaire	..	..	..	0.1	0.2	7.7
Zambia	19	13	-2.6	1.6	0.3	-6.3
Zimbabwe	19	17	-0.9	3.4	2.1	-2.9
Arab States						
Algeria	24	51	9.4	2.2	2.9	2.4
Egypt	39	43	0.9	4.3	5.0	1.3
Iraq	26	26	0.0	..	..	..
Jordan	23	47	8.7	3.3	6.8	8.2
Kuwait	222	387	6.2	30	29	-0.3

Country	Daily newspapers (daily circulation per thousand people)		Annual rate of change	Cultural paper a) consumed (kilos per person)		Annual rate of change
	1980	1994	1980/94	1980	1994	1980/94
Lebanon	109	110	0.1	15	17	1.0
Libya	18	13	-2.3	..	..	..
Morocco	14	15	0.6	1.7	2.9	5.4
Oman	..	..	..	..	..	..
Saudi Arabia	36	58	5.1	6.1	6.0	-0.1
Syria	13	19	3.8	3.9	2.5	-2.8
Tunisia	43	45	0.4	5.4	7.3	2.7
U.A.E.	149	136	-0.7	..	..	..
Yemen, Rep.	13	15	1.3	0.2	0.5	11.5
South Central Asia						
Afghanistan	6	10	5.6	..	..	..
Armenia	..	..	..	..	..	..
Azerbaijan	..	..	..	..	..	..
Bangladesh	3	6	8.3	0.5	1.1	9.2
Bhutan	..	..	..	..	..	..
Georgia	..	..	..	..	..	..
India	21	31	4.0	1.2	1.8	3.8
Iran	25	17	-2.7	2.3	2.6	1.0
Kazakhstan	..	..	..	..	..	..
Kyrgyz Rep.	..	..	..	..	..	..
Nepal	8	7	-1.0	..	..	..
Pakistan	12	21	6.3	1.0	1.2	1.5
Sri Lanka	30	25	-1.4	2.4	4.9	8.0
Tajikistan	..	..	..	..	..	..
Turkey	56	118	9.2	5.2	6.0	1.2
Turkmenistan	..	..	..	..	..	..
Uzbekistan	..	..	..	..	..	..
East Asia						
China	34	23	-2.7	2.3	7.8	18.4
Hong Kong	715	735	0.2	37	159	25.4
Japan	567	576	0.1	57	106	6.6
Korea, Dem.	219	226	0.3	0.2	0.4	7.7
Korea, Rep.	210	394	7.3	12	37	16.0
Mongolia	106	81	-2.0	..	..	..
Southeast Asia and Oceania						
Australia	323	257	-1.7	64	87	2.8
Cambodia	..	..	..	..	..	..
Indonesia	15	24	5.0	1.4	4.3	15.9
Lao PDR	4	3	-2.1	..	..	..
Malaysia	59	139	11.3	9.3	27	14.2
Myanmar	10	22	10.0	0.6	0.4	-2.6
New Zealand	333	239	-2.4	44	54	1.7
P.N.G.	9	15	5.6	..	..	..
Philippines	41	62	4.3	3.5	5.0	3.3
Singapore	286	301	0.4	45	137	15.7
Thailand	57	46	-1.6	3.7	11	15.2
Vietnam	10	8	-1.7	0.5	1.4	13.8

Country	Daily newspapers (daily circulation per thousand people)		Annual rate of change	Cultural paper a) consumed (kilos per person)		Annual rate of change
	1980	1994	1980/94	1980	1994	1980/94
Latin America and the Caribbean						
Argentina	142	135	-0.4	16	18	1.0
Bolivia	42	67	5.0	2.2	2.0	-0.7
Brazil	45	45	0.0	8.9	11.4	2.2
Chile	..	..	..	10	16	4.6
Colombia	53	42	-1.7	6.3	10	4.5
Costa Rica	110	88	-1.7	8.6	11	2.1
Cuba	108	119	0.8	8.1	1.4	-6.4
Dom. Rep.	39	34	-1.1	6.7	4.9	-2.1
Ecuador	70	70	0.0	7.0	6.0	-1.1
El Salvador	64	49	-2.0	4.0	6.6	5.0
Guatemala	29	23	-1.7	3.4	4.8	3.2
Haiti	7	6	-1.2	..	..	..
Honduras	59	42	-2.4	3.3	3.0	-0.7
Jamaica	51	65	2.3	4.9	6.9	3.1
Mexico	124	115	-0.6	12	11	-0.8
Nicaragua	49	32	..	1.7	1.5	-0.9
Panama	56	61	0.7	3.8	7.2	6.9
Paraguay	51	41	-1.6	4.4	6.7	4.0
Peru	81	85	0.4	4.7	8.9	6.9
Trinidad	143	186	2.5	8.6	11	2.1
Uruguay	240	235	-0.2	13	14	0.6
Venezuela	195	206	0.5	16	13	-1.4
North America						
Canada	221	166	-2.1	77	96	1.9
U.S.A.	273	218	-1.7	110	143	2.3
Europe						
Albania	54	53	-0.2	..	..	..
Austria	351	298	-1.3	33	72	9.1
Belarus	243	174	-2.4	..	..	..
Belgium	232	316	3.0	69	105	4.0
Bosnia	..	..	..	..	..	..
Bulgaria	253	212	-1.4	10	4.5	-4.3
Croatia	..	..	..	..	..	..
Czech Rep.	..	..	..	..	..	..
Denmark	366	308	-1.3	67	75	0.9
Estonia	..	..	..	..	..	..
Finland	505	468	-0.6	88	166	6.8
France	192	234	1.8	50	79	4.5
Germany	859	313	-5.3	..	..	..
Greece	120	153	2.3	14	34	11.0
Hungary	247	169	-2.6	18	18	0.0
Ireland	229	154	-2.7	29	54	6.6
Israel	258	271	0.4	22	48	9.1
Italy	85	100	1.5	35	63	6.2
Latvia	..	..	..	..	..	..
Lithuania	..	..	..	..	..	..

Country	Daily newspapers (daily circulation per thousand people)		Annual rate of change	Cultural paper a) consumed (kilos per person)		Annual rate of change
	1980	1994	1980/94	1980	1994	1980/94
Macedonia, FYR	..	..	..	..	..	..
Moldova	..	..	..	..	..	..
Netherlands	326	329	0.1	81	93	1.1
Norway	463	596	2.4	55	98	6.0
Poland	236	140	-3.4	10	12	1.5
Portugal	49	41	-1.4	11	33	15.4
Romania	181	299	5.4	6.3	4.0	-2.8
Russia	..	..	..	..	..	..
Slovakia	..	..	..	..	..	..
Slovenia	..	..	..	..	..	..
Spain	93	102	0.8	24	51	8.7
Sweden	528	460	-1.1	98	94	-0.3
Switzerland	393	371	-0.5	91	122	2.6
Ukraine	..	..	..	..	..	..
U.K.	417	344	-1.5	54	104	7.1
Yugoslavia	..	..	..	..	..	..

Region	Daily newspapers (daily circulation per thousand people)		Annual rate of change	Cultural paper a) consumed (kilos per person)		Annual rate of change
	1980	1994	1980/94	1980	1994	1980/94
World	86	97	0.9	14	21	4.3
Developing	36	43	1.3	3.0	6.0	7.4
Industrial	251	297	1.2	59	83	3.1
Dev exc India / China	..	..	..	4.3	6.8	4.3
Ind exc USA / Russia	..	..	..	46	76	5.1
Sub-Saharan Africa	12	10	-1.4	..	..	..
Arab States	27	44	5.2	3.8	4.5	1.3
South Central Asia	20	29	3.8	..	..	..
East Asia	92	89	-0.2	7.5	18	10.6
Southeast Asia / Oc	39	45	1.3	5.0	9	6.2
Latin Am / Carib	83	80	-0.3	9.4	10	0.5
North America	268	213	-1.7	107	138	2.3
Europe	242	278	1.2	33	53	4.7

a) Newsprint, other printing and writing paper.

TABLE 13
CULTURAL TRENDS: RADIO AND TELEVISION

Country	Radios (per thousand people)		Annual rate of change	Televisions (per thousand people)		Annual rate of change	Radios per televisions	
	1980	1995	1980/95	1980	1995	1980/95	1980	1995
Sub-Saharan Africa								
Angola	21	34	4.8	4.3	7.4	5.5	4.9	4.6
Benin	66	92	3.0	1.4	5.9	24.7	47.1	15.6
Botswana	83	131	4.4	..	..	..	..	..
Burkina Faso	18	28	3.7	2.9	5.7	7.4	6.2	4.9
Burundi	39	68	5.0	..	..	..	..	..
Cameroon	88	152	5.6	..	..	..	..	..
C.A.R.	52	75	2.9	0.3	4.9	117.9	173.3	15.3
Chad	168	248	3.7	..	..	..	..	..
Congo	60	116	7.2	2.2	7.7	19.2	27.3	15.1
Côte d' Ivoire	122	153	2.0	38	62	4.2	3.2	2.5
Eritrea	..	..	..	..	..	..	..	..
Ethiopia	82	193	9.0	0.8	4.4	34.6	102.5	43.9
Gabon	130	181	3.0	12	47	19.4	10.8	3.9
Gambia	114	164	3.4	..	..	..	..	..
Ghana	158	231	3.6	5.3	92	125.8	29.8	2.5
Guinea	30	44	3.6	1.3	8.8	44.4	23.1	5.0
Guinea-Bissau	31	42	2.7	..	..	..	..	..
Kenya	39	96	11.2	3.7	18	25.8	10.5	5.3
Lesotho	25	37	3.7	..	..	..	..	..
Liberia	179	318	6.0	11	26	10.5	16.3	12.2
Madagascar	177	192	0.6	5.0	20	20.0	35.4	9.6
Malawi	42	256	34.0	..	..	..	..	..
Mali	15	46	15.9	..	..	..	..	..
Mauritania	97	150	3.6	..	..	..	..	..
Mauritius	269	367	2.8	95	222	10.3	2.8	1.7
Mozambique	21	38	5.4	0.2	3.5	126.9	105.0	10.9
Namibia	..	..	..	4.9	25	31.6	..	..
Niger	45	68	3.4	0.9	11	86.3	50.0	6.2
Nigeria	97	197	7.9	7.6	55	48.0	12.8	3.6
Rwanda	34	101	15.2	..	..	..	..	..
Senegal	65	120	6.5	1.4	38	201.1	46.4	3.2
Sierra Leone	139	250	6.1	6.2	12	6.2	22.4	20.8
Somalia	17	42	11.3	..	..	..	..	..
South Africa	274	316	1.2	69	109	4.5	4.0	2.9
Sudan	187	270	3.0	43	84	7.3	4.3	3.2
Tanzania	16	28	5.8	0.4	2.3	36.5	40.0	12.2
Togo	203	215	0.5	3.8	12	14.4	53.4	17.9
Uganda	30	117	19.3	5.5	13	9.1	5.5	9.0
Zaire	56	98	5.0	0.4	2.2	34.6	140.0	44.5
Zambia	24	99	20.8	10	32	16.9	2.4	3.1
Zimbabwe	34	89	12.4	10	29	14.6	3.4	3.1
Arab States								
Algeria	197	238	1.6	52	89	5.5	3.8	2.7
Egypt	137	312	9.8	32	110	16.3	4.3	2.8
Iraq	161	224	3.0	50	80	4.6	3.2	2.8
Jordan	188	251	2.6	59	80	2.7	3.2	3.1
Kuwait	284	473	5.1	257	370	3.4	1.1	1.3

Country	Radios (per thousand people)		Annual rate of change	Televisions (per thousand people)		Annual rate of change	Radios per televisions	
	1980	1995	1980/95	1980	1995	1980/95	1980	1995
Lebanon	749	891	1.5	281	366	2.3	2.7	2.4
Libya	66	231	19.2	61	102	4.5	1.1	2.3
Morocco	155	226	3.5	46	94	8.0	3.4	2.4
Oman	272	580	8.7	32	657	150.2	8.5	0.9
Saudi Arabia	260	291	0.9	219	257	1.3	1.2	1.1
Syria	195	264	2.7	44	67	3.5	4.4	3.9
Tunisia	157	200	2.1	47	89	6.9	3.3	2.2
U.A.E.	236	271	1.1	88	104	1.4	2.7	2.6
Yemen, Rep.	32	43	2.3	6.9	28	23.5	4.6	1.5
South Central Asia								
Afghanistan	75	132	5.1	2.8	10	19.8	26.8	13.2
Armenia	..	..	..	..	..	..	..	..
Azerbaijan	..	..	..	..	..	..	..	..
Bangladesh	17	47	11.8	0.9	5.9	37.0	18.9	8.0
Bhutan	6	17	13.1	..	..	..	..	..
Georgia	..	..	..	..	..	..	..	..
India	38	81	8.7	4.4	51	70.6	8.6	1.6
Iran	163	228	2.7	51	63	1.8	3.2	3.6
Kazakhstan	..	..	..	..	..	..	..	..
Kyrgyz Rep.	..	..	..	..	..	..	..	..
Nepal	21	36	4.8	..	..	..	..	..
Pakistan	64	92	3.4	11	20	6.3	5.8	4.6
Sri Lanka	98	206	7.3	2.4	51	135.0	40.8	4.0
Tajikistan	..	..	..	..	..	..	..	..
Turkey	113	164	3.5	79	189	9.3	1.4	0.9
Turkmenistan	..	..	..	..	..	..	..	..
Uzbekistan	..	..	..	..	..	..	..	..
East Asia								
China	55	185	18.2	9.0	205	145.2	6.1	0.9
Hong Kong	506	668	2.5	221	286	2.0	2.3	2.3
Japan	678	916	2.7	539	684	1.8	1.3	1.3
Korea, Dem.	82	136	4.4	7.1	48	44.3	11.5	2.8
Korea, Rep.	525	1,024	7.3	165	334	6.8	3.2	3.1
Mongolia	96	134	3.0	3.4	45	94.1	28.2	3.0
Southeast Asia and Oceania								
Australia	1,098	1,304	1.4	384	495	1.9	2.9	2.6
Cambodia	92	112	1.4	5.4	8.5	4.4	17.0	13.2
Indonesia	99	149	3.4	20	66	17.7	5.0	2.3
Lao PDR	109	129	1.2	..	..	..	..	..
Malaysia	411	432	0.3	87	164	5.9	4.7	2.6
Myanmar	23	89	19.1	..	..	..	..	..
New Zealand	885	997	1.0	332	514	4.2	2.7	1.9
P.N.G.	58	77	2.5	..	..	..	..	..
Philippines	43	147	16.1	22	49	9.4	2.0	3.0
Singapore	373	601	4.1	311	361	1.2	1.2	1.7
Thailand	140	189	2.3	21	189	61.5	6.7	1.0
Vietnam	93	106	1.1	..	..	..	..	..

Country	Radios (per thousand people)		Annual rate of change	Televisions (per thousand people)		Annual rate of change	Radios per televisions	
	1980	1995	1980/95	1980	1995	1980/95	1980	1995
Latin America and the Caribbean								
Argentina	427	676	4.5	183	219	1.5	2.3	3.1
Bolivia	523	672	2.2	56	115	8.1	9.3	5.8
Brazil	313	399	2.1	124	220	6.0	2.5	1.8
Chile	292	348	1.5	110	215	6.4	2.7	1.6
Colombia	124	564	27.3	85	117	2.9	1.5	4.8
Costa Rica	83	263	16.7	68	143	8.5	1.2	1.8
Cuba	300	351	1.3	131	228	4.9	2.3	1.5
Dom. Rep.	158	176	0.9	70	93	2.5	2.3	1.9
Ecuador	305	332	0.7	63	96	4.0	4.8	3.5
El Salvador	343	450	2.6	..	..	..	..	..
Guatemala	51	71	3.0	25	56	8.3	2.0	1.3
Haiti	20	53	11.0	3.0	4.8	4.6	6.7	11.0
Honduras	140	409	14.8	18	88	25.9	7.8	4.6
Jamaica	375	438	1.3	80	162	7.9	4.7	2.7
Mexico	134	263	7.4	57	219	18.9	2.4	1.2
Nicaragua	239	280	1.3	57	73	2.2	4.2	3.8
Panama	154	228	3.7	115	170	3.7	1.3	1.3
Paraguay	112	180	4.7	22	93	24.8	5.1	1.9
Peru	159	259	4.8	52	106	8.0	3.1	2.4
Trinidad	277	505	6.3	194	322	4.4	1.4	1.6
Uruguay	559	609	0.7	126	235	6.7	4.4	2.6
Venezuela	391	458	1.3	113	169	3.3	3.5	2.7
North America								
Canada	721	1,053	3.5	432	714	4.4	1.7	1.5
U.S.A.	1,996	2,093	0.4	684	805	1.2	2.9	2.6
Europe								
Albania	150	207	2.9	36	103	12.4	4.2	2.0
Austria	507	620	1.7	391	497	2.1	1.3	1.2
Belarus	223	285	1.9	218	227	0.3	1.0	1.3
Belgium	731	790	0.6	387	454	1.2	1.9	1.7
Bosnia	..	..	..	..	..	..	..	..
Bulgaria	395	471	1.5	243	378	4.3	1.6	1.2
Croatia	..	..	..	..	..	..	..	..
Czech Rep.	..	..	..	..	..	..	..	..
Denmark	927	1,034	0.9	498	574	1.2	1.9	1.8
Estonia	..	..	..	..	..	..	..	..
Finland	837	1,008	1.6	414	519	1.7	2.0	1.9
France	741	895	1.6	353	589	4.5	2.1	1.5
Germany	774	944	1.7	464	554	1.3	1.7	1.7
Greece	343	430	2.0	171	220	1.9	2.0	2.0
Hungary	499	643	2.2	310	433	2.6	1.6	1.5
Ireland	375	649	5.6	231	409	5.1	1.6	1.6
Israel	245	489	7.7	232	290	1.7	1.1	1.7
Italy	602	822	2.8	390	446	1.0	1.5	1.8
Latvia	..	..	..	..	..	..	..	..
Lithuania	..	..	..	..	..	..	..	..

Country	Radios (per thousand people)		Annual rate of change	Televisions (per thousand people)		Annual rate of change	Radios per televisions	
	1980	1995	1980/95	1980	1995	1980/95	1980	1995
Macedonia, FYR	..	..	..	..	..	..	..	..
Moldova	..	..	..	..	..	..	..	..
Netherlands	650	937	3.4	399	497	1.9	1.6	1.9
Norway	661	808	1.7	350	433	1.6	1.9	1.9
Poland	298	454	4.0	246	311	2.0	1.2	1.5
Portugal	170	245	3.4	158	326	7.1	1.1	0.8
Romania	177	211	1.5	184	220	1.5	1.0	1.0
Russia	..	..	..	..	..	..	..	..
Slovakia	..	..	..	..	..	..	..	..
Slovenia	..	..	..	..	..	..	..	..
Spain	258	314	1.7	253	404	4.0	1.0	0.8
Sweden	842	882	0.4	461	478	0.2	1.8	1.8
Switzerland	813	851	0.4	364	419	1.0	2.2	2.0
Ukraine	579	812	3.1	255	339	2.5	2.3	2.4
U.K.	950	1,433	3.9	401	448	0.8	2.4	3.2
Yugoslavia	..	..	..	..	..	..	..	..

Region	Radios (per thousand people)		Annual rate of change	Televisions (per thousand people)		Annual rate of change	Radios per televisions	
	1980	1995	1980/95	1980	1995	1980/95	1980	1995
World	294	362	1.7	126	204	4.4	2.3	1.8
Developing	97	185	6.5	26	115	24.5	3.7	1.6
Industrial	878	1,005	1.0	424	527	1.7	2.1	1.9
Dev exc India / China	145	225	3.9	47	92	6.8	3.1	2.4
Ind exc USA / Russia	605	800	2.3	346	469	2.5	1.7	1.7
Sub-Saharan Africa	92	169	6.0	12	33	12.5	7.7	5.1
Arab States	164	251	3.8	55	109	7.0	3.0	2.3
South Central Asia	52	96	6.0	12	53	24.4	4.3	1.8
East Asia	127	277	8.4	61	249	21.9	2.1	1.1
Southeast Asia / Oc	143	201	2.9	38	91	10.0	3.8	2.2
Latin Am / Carib	260	387	3.5	99	192	6.7	2.6	2.0
North America	1,869	1,990	0.5	659	796	1.5	2.8	2.5
Europe	603	672	0.8	350	416	1.3	1.7	1.6

TABLE 14
CULTURAL TRENDS: CINEMA

Country	Annual cinema attendances (per person)		Annual rate of change	Number of long films produced		Annual rate of change	Number of long films imported		Annual rate of change
	1980-83	1990-95	80-3 / 90-5	1980-83	1990-95	80-3 / 90-5	1980-83	1990-95	80-3 / 90-5
Sub-Saharan Africa									
Angola	0.9	0.4	-9.3	..	..	..	186	108	-5.2
Benin	0.3	0.1	-3.9	..	..	..	..	..	..
Botswana	..	..	..	..	..	..	..	..	..
Burkina Faso	0.6	0.7	2.8	..	..	..	..	..	..
Burundi	..	..	..	..	..	..	..	..	..
Cameroon	..	..	..	3	2	-6.7	..	..	..
C.A.R.	..	..	..	..	..	..	..	..	..
Chad	..	..	..	..	..	..	..	..	..
Congo	..	..	..	..	..	..	..	..	..
Côte d' Ivoire	0.9	0.5	-3.2	2	2	0.0	..	..	..
Eritrea	..	..	..	..	..	..	..	..	..
Ethiopia	..	..	..	..	..	..	211	133	-4.6
Gabon	2.2	1.6	-1.5	..	..	..	..	..	..
Gambia	..	..	..	..	..	..	..	..	..
Ghana	..	..	..	..	..	..	..	..	..
Guinea	..	..	..	1	1	0.0	..	..	..
Guinea-Bissau	..	..	..	..	..	..	..	..	..
Kenya	0.6	0.2	-4.2	..	..	..	142	364	9.8
Lesotho	..	..	..	..	..	..	..	..	..
Liberia	..	..	..	..	..	..	..	..	..
Madagascar	..	..	..	..	..	..	..	..	..
Malawi	..	..	..	..	..	..	..	..	..
Mali	..	..	..	..	..	..	..	..	..
Mauritania	..	..	..	..	..	..	..	..	..
Mauritius	..	..	..	2	1	-3.8	321	50	-8.4
Mozambique	..	..	..	..	..	..	..	..	..
Namibia	..	..	..	..	..	..	..	..	..
Niger	..	..	..	..	..	..	..	..	..
Nigeria	..	..	..	..	..	..	..	..	..
Rwanda	..	..	..	..	..	..	..	..	..
Senegal	..	..	..	..	..	..	..	..	..
Sierra Leone	..	..	..	..	..	..	..	..	..
Somalia	..	..	..	..	..	..	..	..	..
South Africa	..	..	..	..	..	..	..	..	..
Sudan	..	..	..	1	1	0.0	137	104	-3.4
Tanzania	0.2	0.1	-5.0	..	..	..	162	71	-5.6
Togo	..	..	..	..	..	..	..	..	..
Uganda	..	..	..	..	..	..	..	..	..
Zaire	..	..	..	..	..	..	..	..	..
Zambia	..	..	..	..	..	..	..	..	..
Zimbabwe	..	..	..	..	..	..	..	..	..
Arab States									
Algeria	1.2	0.9	-4.2	2	3	5.6	..	..	..
Egypt	1.2	0.3	-6.4	90	72	-1.5	385	220	-3.3
Iraq	..	..	..	2	1	-10.0	..	..	..
Jordan	..	..	..	..	..	..	438	271	-5.9
Kuwait	..	..	..	..	..	..	..	..	..

Country	Annual cinema attendances (per person)		Annual rate of change	Number of long films produced		Annual rate of change	Number of long films imported		Annual rate of change
	1980-83	1990-95	80-3 / 90-5	1980-83	1990-95	80-3 / 90-5	1980-83	1990-95	80-3 / 90-5
Lebanon	..	..	..	6	5	-0.7	..	..	..
Libya	..	..	..	..	..	..	..	..	..
Morocco	1.8	0.7	-6.1	12	4	-6.7	302	393	3.0
Oman	..	..	..	..	..	..	..	..	..
Saudi Arabia	..	..	..	..	..	..	..	..	..
Syria	1.6	0.3	-8.1	1	2	7.7	149	122	-1.8
Tunisia	..	..	..	..	..	..	230	50	-4.6
U.A.E.	..	..	..	..	..	..	..	..	..
Yemen, Rep.	..	..	..	..	..	..	..	..	..
South Central Asia									
Afghanistan	..	..	..	2	3	10.0	41	33	-3.3
Armenia	..	..	..	..	..	..	..	..	..
Azerbaijan	..	..	..	..	..	..	..	..	..
Bangladesh	..	..	..	..	..	..	..	..	..
Bhutan	..	..	..	..	..	..	..	..	..
Georgia	..	..	..	..	..	..	..	..	..
India	6.8	5.0	-2.6	741	838	1.3	190	141	-2.6
Iran	4.2	0.4	-7.5	..	..	..	95	54	-4.3
Kazakhstan	..	..	..	..	..	..	..	..	..
Kyrgyz Rep.	..	..	..	..	..	..	..	..	..
Nepal	..	..	..	..	..	..	..	..	..
Pakistan	..	..	..	82	64	-2.2	81	89	1.0
Sri Lanka	2.7	1.5	-4.4	33	58	7.6	151	61	-6.0
Tajikistan	..	..	..	..	..	..	..	..	..
Turkey	1.4	0.3	-6.5	74	39	-3.9	..	..	..
Turkmenistan	..	..	..	..	..	..	..	..	..
Uzbekistan	..	..	..	..	..	..	..	..	..
East Asia									
China	..	..	..	82	154	6.8	..	..	..
Hong Kong	..	..	..	141	315	12.3	..	..	..
Japan	1.3	1.1	-1.3	320	251	-1.8	199	352	6.4
Korea, Dem.	..	..	..	..	..	..	..	..	..
Korea, Rep.	..	..	..	91	63	-3.1	26	347	123.5
Mongolia	..	..	..	..	..	..	..	..	..
Southeast Asia and Oceania									
Australia	..	..	..	10	18	8.0	900	239	-7.3
Cambodia	..	..	..	..	..	..	..	..	..
Indonesia	..	..	..	76	27	-6.4	..	..	..
Lao PDR	..	..	..	..	..	..	78	112	4.4
Malaysia	2.7	2.0	-2	13	12	-0.8	1,045	518	-8.4
Myanmar	..	..	..	..	..	..	..	..	..
New Zealand	..	..	..	9	4	-5.1	..	..	..
P.N.G.	..	..	..	..	..	..	..	..	..
Philippines	..	..	..	..	..	..	589	280	-3.5
Singapore	..	..	..	..	..	..	..	..	..
Thailand	..	..	..	120	194	6.2	260	191	-2.7
Vietnam	5.2	3.8	-3.0	..	..	..	604	171	-6.0

Country	Annual cinema attendances (per person)		Annual rate of change	Number of long films produced		Annual rate of change	Number of long films imported		Annual rate of change
	1980-83	1990-95	80-3 / 90-5	1980-83	1990-95	80-3 / 90-5	1980-83	1990-95	80-3 / 90-5
Latin America and the Caribbean									
Argentina	1.7	0.5	-8.8	27	16	-4.1	205	200	-0.4
Bolivia	5.7	0.3	-6.8	..	..	..	394	149	-4.4
Brazil	..	..	..	103	86	-3.3	..	..	..
Chile	1.0	0.6	-4.0	..	..	..	..	..	..
Colombia	2.4	1.3	-9.2	9	3	-6.7	363	418	2.5
Costa Rica	0.9	0.5	-3.2	..	..	..	..	..	..
Cuba	8.7	2.2	-7.5	8	6	-2.5	133	22	-8.3
Dom. Rep.	..	..		..	..		..	..	..
Ecuador	5.6	0.6	-5.3	..	..		..	..	..
El Salvador	..	..		..	..		..	..	..
Guatemala	1.3	0.9	-5.1	..	..	..	..	..	..
Haiti	..	..	..	..	..	..	..	..	..
Honduras	..	..	..	..	..	..	..	..	..
Jamaica	..	..	..	..	..	..	..	..	..
Mexico	..	..	..	105	53	-5.0	309	268	-1.3
Nicaragua	..	..	..	..	..	..	..	..	..
Panama	..	..	..	..	..	..	..	..	..
Paraguay	..	..	..	..	..	..	..	..	..
Peru	..	..	..	1	5	40.0	707	211	-8.8
Trinidad	..	..	..	..	..	..	..	..	..
Uruguay	..	..	..	..	..	..	..	..	..
Venezuela	4.7	0.9	-6.7	12	4	-5.1	..	..	..
North America									
Canada	4.0	2.8	-3.8	32	22	-2.6	468	1,115	17.3
U.S.A.	4.5	3.9	-1.1	396	420	0.5	..	..	..
Europe									
Albania	..	..		..	..	..	7	9	1.8
Austria	2.4	1.5	-3.1	16	22	3.1	314	219	-2.5
Belarus	14.1	1.2	-9.8	..	..		..	..	..
Belgium	2.1	1.9	-0.8	14	8	-3.6	..	..	..
Bosnia	..	..	..	..	..		..	..	..
Bulgaria	10.6	0.6	-7.9	32	11	-5.5	164	134	-1.5
Croatia	..	..		..	..		..	..	..
Czech Rep.	..	..		..	..		..	..	..
Denmark	2.7	1.7	-3.1	11	12	0.8	233	150	-3.0
Estonia	..	..		..	..		..	..	..
Finland	1.9	1.1	-4.2	13	8	-3.2	212	131	-3.2
France	3.5	2.2	-3.1	131	141	0.6	241	235	-0.2
Germany	2.8	1.5	-3.9	99	63	-3.0	440	197	-4.6
Greece	..	..	..	47	25	-3.9	261	148	-3.6
Hungary	6.5	1.4	-6.5	25	12	-4.3	198	80	-5.0
Ireland	..	..		..	..		192	137	-2.4
Israel	6.6	1.8	-4.5	15	15	0.0	287	152	-4.7
Italy	2.9	1.6	-3.7	128	96	-2.1	275	247	-0.8
Latvia	..	..		..	..		..	..	..
Lithuania	..	..	..	..	..	..	..	..	..

Country	Annual cinema attendances (per person)		Annual rate of change	Number of long films produced		Annual rate of change	Number of long films imported		Annual rate of change
	1980-83	1990-95	80-3 / 90-5	1980-83	1990-95	80-3 / 90-5	1980-83	1990-95	80-3 / 90-5
Macedonia, FYR	..	..	..	..	..	..	..	..	..
Moldova	..	..	..	..	..	..	..	..	..
Netherlands	2.0	1.0	-4.2	7	16	10.7	332	173	-4.0
Norway	3.6	2.7	-2.1	8	15	7.3	284	171	-3.3
Poland	3.0	0.4	-7.2	35	20	-3.6	90	126	3.3
Portugal	3.1	0.8	-6.2	9	13	3.7	410	195	-4.4
Romania	9.6	0.7	-7.7	32	9	-6.0	113	101	-0.9
Russia	..	..	..	..	..	..	..	..	..
Slovakia	..	..	..	..	..	..	..	..	..
Slovenia	..	..	..	..	..	..	..	..	..
Spain	3.7	2.4	-3.5	99	59	-3.4	463	346	-2.1
Sweden	2.3	1.7	-2.2	15	32	9.4	318	203	-3.0
Switzerland	3.0	2.2	-2.2	22	37	5.7	466	359	-1.9
Ukraine	..	..	..	24	6	-3.9	129	164	1.7
U.K.	1.1	2.0	6.8	39	78	8.3	142	240	5.8
Yugoslavia	..	..	..	..	..	..	..	..	..

Region	Annual cinema attendances (per person)		Annual rate of change	Number of long films produced		Annual rate of change	Number of long films imported		Annual rate of change
	1980-83	1990-95	80-3 / 90-5	1980-83	1990-95	80-3 / 90-5	1980-83	1990-95	80-3 / 90-5
World	..	..	..	..	..	..	..	..	..
Developing	..	..	..	..	..	..	..	..	..
Industrial	3.1	2.0	-3.0	..	..	..	..	..	..
Dev exc India / China	..	..	..	..	..	..	..	..	..
Ind exc USA / Russia	..	..	..	..	..	..	..	..	..
Sub-Saharan Africa	..	..	..	..	..	..	..	..	..
Arab States	..	..	..	..	..	..	..	..	..
South Central Asia	..	..	..	..	..	..	..	..	..
East Asia	..	..	..	..	..	..	..	..	..
Southeast Asia / Oc	..	..	..	..	..	..	..	..	..
Latin Am / Carib	..	..	..	..	..	..	..	..	..
North America	4.5	3.8	-1.2	..	..	..	..	..	..
Europe	3.0	1.3	-4.7	..	..	..	..	..	..

TABLE 15
CULTURAL TRENDS: COMMUNICATION AND TRAVEL

Country	Main telephone lines (per thousand people)		Annual rate of change	Arrivals of foreign visitors (per thousand inhabitants)		Annual rate of change
	1980	1995	1980/95	1980	1996	1980/96
Sub-Saharan Africa						
Angola	..	..	..	..	..	..
Benin	..	..	..	..	..	..
Botswana	9	41	23.7	..	..	..
Burkina Faso	..	..	..	..	..	..
Burundi	..	..	..	..	..	..
Cameroon	..	..	..	..	..	..
Central African Rep.	..	..	..	..	..	..
Chad	..	..	..	..	..	..
Congo	..	..	..	..	..	..
Côte d' Ivoire	..	..	..	..	..	..
Eritrea	..	..	..	..	..	..
Ethiopia	..	..	..	..	..	..
Gabon	..	..	..	..	..	..
Gambia	..	..	..	..	..	..
Ghana	..	..	..	..	..	..
Guinea	..	..	..	..	..	..
Guinea-Bissau	..	..	..	..	..	..
Kenya	..	..	..	..	..	..
Lesotho	..	..	..	..	..	..
Liberia	..	..	..	..	..	..
Madagascar	..	..	..	..	..	..
Malawi	..	..	..	..	..	..
Mali	..	..	..	..	..	..
Mauritania	..	..	..	..	..	..
Mauritius	24	131	29.7	..	..	..
Mozambique	..	..	..	..	..	..
Namibia	..	..	..	..	..	..
Niger	..	..	..	..	..	..
Nigeria	..	..	..	..	..	..
Rwanda	..	..	..	..	..	..
Senegal	3	10	15.6	..	..	..
Sierra Leone	..	..	..	..	..	..
Somalia	..	..	..	..	..	..
South Africa	55	95	4.8	2.4	11	22.4
Sudan	..	..	..	..	..	..
Tanzania	..	..	..	..	..	..
Togo	..	..	..	..	..	..
Uganda	..	..	..	..	..	..
Zaire	..	..	..	..	..	..
Zambia	6	8	2.2	..	..	..
Zimbabwe	14	14	0.0	3.4	14	19.5
Arab States						
Algeria	17	42	9.8	5.1	0.2	-6.0
Egypt	..	..	..	2.9	5.9	6.5
Iraq	19	33	4.9	..	..	..
Jordan	..	..	..	..	..	..
Kuwait	114	230	6.8	..	..	..

Country	Main telephone lines (per thousand people)		Annual rate of change	Arrivals of foreign visitors (per thousand inhabitants)		Annual rate of change
	1980	1995	1980/95	1980	1996	1980/96
Lebanon	..	..	..	..	..	..
Libya	..	..	..	..	..	..
Morocco	9	43	25.2	7.3	10	2.3
Oman	13	77	32.8	..	..	..
Saudi Arabia	34	96	12.2	10	18	5.0
Syria	28	63	8.3	..	..	..
Tunisia	18	58	14.8	25	43	4.5
Unit.Arab Emirates	116	283	9.6	30	49	4.0
Yemen, Rep.	2	12	33.3	..	..	..
South Central Asia						
Afghanistan	..	..	..	..	..	..
Armenia	97	156	4.1	..	..	..
Azerbaijan	55	85	3.6	..	..	..
Bangladesh	..	..	..	..	..	..
Bhutan	..	..	..	..	..	..
Georgia	63	96	3.5	..	..	..
India	3	13	22.2	0.2	0.2	0.0
Iran	23	99	22.0	..	..	..
Kazakhstan	44	118	11.2	..	..	..
Kyrgyz Rep.	40	73	5.5	..	..	..
Nepal	..	..	..	..	..	..
Pakistan	4	16	20.0	..	..	..
Sri Lanka	4	11	11.7	..	..	..
Tajikistan	30	45	3.3	..	..	..
Turkey	26	230	52.3	2.1	13	32.4
Turkmenistan	38	76	6.7	..	..	..
Uzbekistan	36	76	7.4	..	..	..
East Asia						
China	2	25	76.7	0.4	2.1	26.6
Hong Kong	254	530	7.2	35	192	28.0
Japan	342	488	2.8	0.7	1.6	8.0
Korea, Dem.	..	..	..	..	..	..
Korea, Rep.	71	415	32.3	2.6	8.5	14.2
Mongolia	..	..	..	..	..	..
Southeast Asia and Oceania						
Australia	323	510	3.9	6.2	23	16.9
Cambodia	..	..	..	..	..	..
Indonesia	3	17	31.1	0.3	2.3	41.7
Lao PDR	..	..	..	..	..	..
Malaysia	29	166	31.5	7.5	39	26.3
Myanmar	..	..	..	..	..	..
New Zealand	361	479	2.2	15	42	11.3
Papua New Guinea	8	10	1.7	..	..	..
Philippines	9	21	8.9	2.0	3.0	3.1
Singapore	235	479	6.9	107	200	5.4
Thailand	8	59	42.5	4.0	12	12.5
Vietnam	..	..	..	..	..	..

Country	Main telephone lines (per thousand people)		Annual rate of change	Arrivals of foreign visitors (per thousand inhabitants)		Annual rate of change
	1980	1995	1980/95	1980	1996	1980/96
Latin America and the Caribbean						
Argentina	67	160	9.3	4.0	12	12.5
Bolivia	24	35	3.1	..	..	..
Brazil	40	75	5.8	1.0	1.5	3.1
Chile	33	132	20.0	3.8	11	11.8
Colombia	41	100	9.6	2.1	5.6	10.4
Costa Rica	69	164	9.2	..	..	..
Cuba	..	..	..	..	..	..
Dominican Rep.	19	79	21.1	6.7	26	18.0
Ecuador	28	61	7.9	..	..	..
El Salvador	15	53	16.9	..	..	..
Guatemala	12	27	8.3	..	..	..
Haiti	..	..	..	..	..	..
Honduras	8	29	17.5	..	..	..
Jamaica	25	116	24.3	19	46	8.9
Mexico	38	97	10.4	18	24	2.1
Nicaragua	11	23	7.3	..	..	..
Panama	65	114	5.0	..	..	..
Paraguay	16	31	6.3	..	..	..
Peru	18	47	10.7	..	..	..
Trinidad	40	160	20.0	..	..	..
Uruguay	75	196	10.8	37	69	5.4
Venezuela	54	116	7.7	..	..	..
North America						
Canada	415	600	3.0	52	59	0.8
United States	414	627	3.4	9.8	17	4.6
Europe						
Albania	10	12	1.3	..	..	..
Austria	290	466	4.0	183	208	0.9
Belarus	75	190	10.2	..	..	..
Belgium	248	456	5.6	18	56	13.2
Bosnia	..	..	..	..	..	..
Bulgaria	102	306	13.3	62	40	-2.2
Croatia	79	209	11.0	..	..	..
Czech Rep.	..	..	..	..	..	..
Denmark	434	613	2.7	19	35	5.3
Estonia	135	277	7.0	..	..	..
Finland	364	550	3.4	..	..	..
France	295	563	6.1	56	106	5.6
Germany	332	495	3.3	14	18	1.8
Greece	235	494	7.3	50	93	5.4
Hungary	58	185	14.6	88	205	8.3
Ireland	142	367	10.6	66	132	6.3
Israel	222	418	5.9	29	42	2.8
Italy	231	434	5.9	39	62	3.7
Latvia	161	280	4.9	..	..	..
Lithuania	115	254	8.1	..	..	..

Country	Main telephone lines (per thousand people)		Annual rate of change	Arrivals of foreign visitors (per thousand inhabitants)		Annual rate of change
	1980	1995	1980/95	1980	1996	1980/96
Macedonia, FYR	..	..	..	..	..	..
Moldova	..	..	..	..	..	..
Netherlands	346	525	3.4	20	43	7.2
Norway	293	556	6.0	31	68	7.5
Poland	55	148	11.3	16	50	13.3
Portugal	107	362	15.9	28	101	16.3
Romania	73	131	5.3	15	18	1.3
Russia	70	170	9.5	..	..	..
Slovakia	94	208	8.1	..	..	..
Slovenia	..	..	..	..	..	..
Spain	193	385	6.6	62	104	4.2
Sweden	580	681	1.2	..	..	..
Switzerland	444	623	2.7	140	154	0.6
Ukraine	76	157	7.1	..	..	..
United Kingdom	332	502	3.4	22	44	6.3
Yugoslavia	..	..	..	..	..	..

Region	Main telephone lines (per thousand people)		Annual rate of change	Arrivals of foreign visitors (per thousand inhabitants)		Annual rate of change
	1980	1995	1980/95	1980	1996	1980/96
World	74	137	5.7	..	..	..
Developing	12	44	17.9	..	..	..
Industrial	270	431	4.0	24	40	4.3
Dev exc India / China	26	81	13.8	..	..	..
Ind exc USA / Russia	258	411	4.0	30	50	4.2
Sub-Saharan Africa	..	..	..	..	..	..
Arab States	20	55	11.3	..	..	..
South Central Asia	8	32	21.1	..	..	..
East Asia	36	80	8.4	0.6	3.1	23.5
Southeast Asia / Oc	27	64	9.2	3.0	6.3	6.9
Latin Am / Carib	39	88	8.5	6.6	9.5	2.8
North America	414	623	3.4	14	21	3.2
Europe	194	337	4.9	38	50	2.0

TABLE 16
CULTURAL TRENDS: CULTURAL TRADE ª/

Country	Cultural Trade						Cultural exports as % of total cultural trade	
	US$ Mill.	US$ Mill.	US$ per capita	US$ per capita	As % of GNP	As % of GNP		
	1980	1991	1980	1991	1980	1991	1980	1991
Sub-Saharan Africa								
Angola	..	..	..	..	..	..	..	..
Benin	..	..	..	..	..	..	..	..
Botswana	..	..	..	..	..	..	..	..
Burkina Faso	..	..	..	..	..	..	..	..
Burundi	..	..	..	..	..	..	..	..
Cameroon	18	43	2	4	0.3	0.4	4.4	0.2
C.A.R.	..	..	..	..	..	..	..	..
Chad	..	..	..	..	..	..	..	..
Congo	..	..	..	..	..	..	..	..
Côte d' Ivoire	..	..	..	..	..	..	..	..
Eritrea	..	..	..	..	..	..	..	..
Ethiopia	6	87	(.)	(.)	0.1	0.1	1.6	0.1
Gabon	..	..	..	..	..	..	..	..
Gambia	..	..	..	..	..	..	..	..
Ghana	..	..	..	..	..	..	..	..
Guinea	..	..	..	..	..	..	..	..
Guinea-Bissau	..	..	..	..	..	..	..	..
Kenya	42	21	3	1	0.6	0.2	5.3	24.1
Lesotho	..	..	..	..	..	..	..	..
Liberia	..	..	..	..	..	..	..	..
Madagascar	12	9	1	1	0.4	0.3	0.9	11.1
Malawi	..	..	..	..	..	..	..	..
Mali	..	..	..	..	..	..	..	..
Mauritania	..	..	..	..	..	..	..	..
Mauritius	11	48	11	46	1.0	1.9	1.9	13.3
Mozambique	..	..	..	..	..	..	..	..
Namibia	..	..	..	..	..	..	..	..
Niger	..	..	..	..	..	..	..	..
Nigeria	..	..	..	..	..	..	..	..
Rwanda	..	..	..	..	..	..	..	..
Senegal	20	18	4	2	0.7	0.3	25.2	2.8
Sierra Leone	..	..	..	..	..	..	..	..
Somalia	..	..	..	..	..	..	..	..
South Africa	..	..	..	..	..	..	..	..
Sudan	..	..	..	..	..	..	..	..
Tanzania	..	..	..	..	..	..	..	..
Togo	3	8	1	2	0.3	0.5	3.0	7.5
Uganda	..	..	..	..	..	..	..	..
Zaire	..	..	..	..	..	..	..	..
Zambia	..	..	..	..	..	..	..	..
Zimbabwe	..	..	..	..	..	..	..	..
Arab States								
Algeria	80	258	4	10	0.2	0.5	0.3	2.4
Egypt	39	89	1	2	0.2	0.3	3.1	11.0
Iraq	..	..	..	..	..	..	..	..
Jordan	35	32	12	8	0.8	0.7	3.4	0.9
Kuwait	..	..	..	..	..	..	..	..

430

Country	Cultural Trade						Cultural exports as % of total cultural trade	
	US$ Mill.	US$ Mill.	US$ per capita	US$ per capita	As % of GNP	As % of GNP		
	1980	1991	1980	1991	1980	1991	1980	1991
Lebanon	..	..	..	..	..	..	..	..
Libya	..	..	..	..	..	..	..	..
Morocco	47	86	2	4	0.3	0.3	0.6	5.9
Oman	25	93	22	44	0.8	0.9	8.3	21.0
Saudi Arabia	..	..	..	..	..	..	..	..
Syrian	..	..	..	..	..	..	..	..
Tunisia	44	67	7	8	0.5	0.5	14.4	15.2
U.A.E.	..	..	..	..	..	..	..	..
Yemen, Rep.	..	..	..	..	..	..	..	..
South Central Asia								
Afghanistan	..	..	..	..	..	..	..	..
Armenia	..	..	..	..	..	..	..	..
Azerbaijan	..	..	..	..	..	..	..	..
Bangladesh	14	6	(.)	(.)	0.1	(.)	0.7	61.0
Bhutan	..	..	..	..	..	..	..	..
Georgia	..	..	..	..	..	..	..	..
India	18	259	(.)	(.)	(.)	0.1	41.9	41.8
Iran	..	..	..	..	..	..	..	..
Kazalhstan	..	..	..	..	..	..	..	..
Kyrgyz Rep.	..	..	..	..	..	..	..	..
Nepal	..	..	..	..	..	..	..	..
Pakistan	18	210	(.)	2	(.)	0.4	3.4	69.4
Sri Lanka	20	58	1	3	0.5	0.7	1.5	7.4
Tajikistan	..	..	..	..	..	..	..	..
Turkey	19	564	(.)	7	(.)	0.5	13.4	52.9
Turkmenistan	..	..	..	..	..	..	..	..
Uzbekistan	..	..	..	..	..	..	..	..
East Asia								
China	..	..	..	..	..	..	..	..
Hong Kong b/	2,167	8,774	430	1,529	8.3	11.2	56.5	17.6
Japan	13,404	29,941	115	242	1.2	0.9	92.4	82.1
Korea, Dem.	..	..	..	..	..	..	..	..
Korea, Rep.	1,263	7,554	33	176	1.4	2.7	75.6	83.2
Mongolia	..	..	..	..	..	..	..	..
Southeast Asia and Oceania								
Australia	1,042	2,353	72	139	0.9	0.8	12.1	12.4
Cambodia	..	..	..	..	..	..	..	..
Indonesia	139	416	1	2	0.2	0.4	5.9	49.7
Lao PDR	..	..	..	..	..	..	..	..
Malaysia	293	3,966	21	222	1.3	8.4	23.6	83.2
Myanmar	..	..	..	..	..	..	..	..
New Zealand	180	543	58	161	0.9	1.3	9.6	4.3
P.N.G.	..	..	..	..	..	..	..	..
Philippines	79	316	2	5	0.2	0.7	18.2	54.9
Singapore	1,968	9,570	815	6,173	17.9	24.4	61.6	55.2
Thailand	80	1,773	2	675	0.3	2.0	14.0	70.6
Vietnam	..	..	..	..	..	..	..	..

TABLE 17
RATIFICATION OF CULTURAL CONVENTIONS (1997)

Country	Protection of the world cultural and natural heritage	Protection of cultural property in the event of armed conflict		Means of prohibiting and preventing the the illicit import , export and transfer of ownership of cultural property
		Convention	Protocol	
Date of convention	1972	1954	1954	1970
Sub-Saharan Africa				
Angola	X	-	-	X
Benin	X	-	-	-
Botswana	-	-	-	-
Burkina Faso	X	X	X	X
Burundi	X	-	-	-
Cameroon	X	X	X	X
Central African Rep.	X	-	-	X
Chad	-	-	-	-
Congo	X	-	-	-
Côte d' Ivoire	X	X		X
Eritrea	-	-	-	-
Ethiopia	X	-	-	-
Gabon	X	X	X	-
Gambia	X	-	-	-
Ghana	X	X	X	-
Guinea	X	X	X	X
Guinea-Bissau	-	-	-	-
Kenya	X	-	-	-
Lesotho	-	-	-	-
Liberia	-	-	-	-
Madagascar	X	X	X	X
Malawi	X	-	-	-
Mali	X	X	X	X
Mauritania	X	-	-	X
Mauritius	X	-	-	X
Mozambique	X	-	-	-
Namibia	-	-	-	-
Niger	X	X	X	X
Nigeria	X	X	X	X
Rwanda	-	-	-	-
Senegal	X	X	X	X
Sierra Leone	-	-	-	-
Somalia	-	-	..	-
South Africa	-	-	..	-
Sudan	X	X	-	-
Tanzania	X	X	X	X
Togo	-	-	-	-
Uganda	X	-	-	-
Zaire	X	X	X	X
Zambia	X	-	-	X
Zimbabwe	X	-	-	-
Arab States				
Algeria	X	-	-	X
Egypt	X	X	X	X
Iraq	X	X	X	X
Jordan	X	X	X	X
Kuwait	-	X	X	X

Country	Protection of the world cultural and natural heritage	Protection of cultural property in the event of armed conflict		Means of prohibiting and preventing the the illicit import , export and transfer of ownership of cultural property
		Convention	Protocol	
Date of convention	1972	1954	1954	1970
Lebanon	X	X	X	X
Libya	X	X	X	X
Morocco	X	X	X	-
Oman	X	X	-	X
Saudi Arabia	X	X	-	X
Syria	X	X	X	X
Tunisia	X	X	X	X
Unit.Arab Emirates	-	-	-	-
Yemen, Rep.	X	X	X	-
South Central Asia				
Afghanistan	X	-	-	-
Armenia	X	X	X	X
Azerbaijan	X	X	X	-
Bangladesh	X	-	-	X
Bhutan	-	-	-	-
Georgia	X	X	X	X
India	X	X	X	X
Iran	X	X	X	X
Kazakhstan	X	-	-	-
Kyrgyz Rep.	X	X	-	X
Nepal	X	-	-	X
Pakistan	X	X	X	X
Sri Lanka	X	-	-	X
Tajikistan	X	X	X	X
Turkey	X	X	X	X
Turkmenistan	X	-	-	-
Uzbekistan	X	X	X	X
East Asia				
China	X	-	-	X
Hong Kong	-	-	-	-
Japan	X	-	-	-
Korea, Dem.	-	-	-	X
Korea, Rep.	X	-	-	X
Mongolia	X	X	-	X
Southeast Asia and Oceania				
Australia	X	X	-	X
Cambodia	X	X	X	X
Indonesia	X	X	X	-
Lao PDR	X	-	-	-
Malaysia	X	X	X	-
Myanmar	X	X	X	-
New Zealand	X	-	-	-
Papua New Guinea	X	-	-	-
Philippines	X	-	-	-
Singapore	-	-	-	-
Thailand	X	X	X	-
Vietnam	X	-	-	-

Country	Protection of the world cultural and natural heritage	Protection of cultural property in the event of armed conflict		Means of prohibiting and preventing the the illicit import , export and transfer of ownership of cultural property
		Convention	Protocol	
Date of convention	1972	1954	1954	1970
Latin America and the Caribbean				
Argentina	X	X	-	X
Bolivia	X	-	-	X
Brazil	X	X	X	X
Chile	X	-	-	-
Colombia	X	-	-	X
Costa Rica	X	-	-	X
Cuba	X	X	X	X
Dominican Rep	X	X	-	X
Ecuador	X	X	X	X
El Salvador	X	-	-	X
Guatemala	X	X	X	X
Haiti	X	-	-	-
Honduras	X	-	-	X
Jamaica	X	-	-	-
Mexico	X	X	X	X
Nicaragua	X	X	X	X
Panama	X	X	-	X
Paraguay	X	-	-	-
Peru	X	X	X	X
Trinidad	-	-	-	-
Uruguay	X	-	-	X
Venezuela	X	-	-	-
North America				
Canada	X	-	-	X
United States	X	-	-	X
Europe				
Albania	X	X	X	-
Austria	X	X	X	-
Belarus	X	X	X	X
Belgium	X	X	X	-
Bosnia	X	X	X	X
Bulgaria	X	X	X	X
Croatia	X	X	X	X
Czech Rep.	X	X	X	X
Denmark	X	-	-	-
Estonia	X	X	-	X
Finland	X	X	X	-
France	X	X	X	X
Germany	X	X	X	-
Greece	X	X	X	X
Hungary	X	X	X	X
Ireland	X	-	-	-
Israel	-	X	X	-
Italy	X	X	X	X
Latvia	X	-	-	-
Lithuania	X	-	-	-

Country	Protection of the world cultural and natural heritage	Protection of cultural property in the event of armed conflict		Means of prohibiting and preventing the the illicit import , export and transfer of ownership of cultural property
		Convention	Protocol	
Date of convention	1972	1954	1954	1970
Macedonia, FYR	-	-	-	-
Moldova	-	-	-	-
Netherlands	X	X	X	-
Norway	X	X	X	-
Poland	X	X	X	X
Portugal	X	-	-	X
Romania	X	X	X	X
Russia	X	X	X	X
Slovakia	X	X	X	X
Slovenia	X	X	X	X
Spain	X	X	X	X
Sweden	X	X	X	-
Switzerland	X	X	X	-
Ukraine	X	X	X	X
United Kingdom	X	-	-	-
Yugoslavia	X	X	X	X

Region	Protection of the world cultural and natural heritage		Protection of cultural property in the event of armed conflict				Means of prohibiting and preventing the the illicit import , export and transfer of ownership of cultural property	
			Convention		Protocol			
Date of convention	1972		1954		1954		1970	
	T	(%)	T	(%)	T	(%)	T	(%)
World	128	85	81	54	70	47	82	55
Developing	90	82	53	48	44	40	60	55
Industrial	38	95	28	70	26	65	22	55
Dev exc India / China	88	81	52	48	43	40	58	54
Ind exc USA / Russia	36	95	27	71	25	66	20	53
Sub-Saharan Africa	29	71	13	34	12	29	16	39
Arab States	16	84	18	89	15	79	14	74
South Central Asia	12	100	6	50	5	42	9	75
East Asia	4	67	1	17	0	0	4	67
Southeast Asia / Oc	11	92	6	50	5	42	2	17
Latin Am / Carib	21	95	10	45	7	32	16	73
North America	2	100	0	0	0	0	2	100
Europe	33	94	27	77	26	74	19	54

TABLE 18
RATIFICATION OF HUMAN RIGHTS CONVENTIONS

Country	Economic, social and cultural rights	Civil and political rigths	Elimination of all forms of racial discrimination	Elimination of all forms of discrimination against women	Prevention and punishment of the crime of genocide	Rights of the child	Torture and other cruel inhuman or degrading treatment or punishment	Status of refugees
Date of convention	1966	1966	1969	1979	1948	1989	1984	1954
Sub-Saharan Africa								
Angola	X	X	-	X	-	X	-	X
Benin	X	X	X	X	-	X	X	X
Botswana	-	-	X	-	-	X	-	X
Burkina Faso	-	-	X	X	X	X	-	X
Burundi	X	X	X	X	-	X	X	X
Cameroon	X	X	X	X	-	X	X	X
Central African Rep.	X	X	X	X	-	X	-	X
Chad	X	X	X	X	-	X	X	X
Congo	X	X	X	X	-	X	-	X
Côte d' Ivoire	X	X	X	X	X	X	X	X
Eritrea	-	-	-	X	-	X	-	-
Ethiopia	X	X	X	X	X	X	X	X
Gabon	X	X	X	X	X	X	X	X
Gambia	X	X	X	X	X	X	X	X
Ghana	-	-	X	X	X	X	-	X
Guinea	X	X	X	X	-	X	X	X
Guinea-Bissau	X	-	-	X	-	X	-	X
Kenya	X	X	-	X	-	X	-	X
Lesotho	X	X	X	X	X	X	-	X
Liberia	X	X	X	X	X	X	-	X
Madagascar	X	X	X	X	-	X	-	X
Malawi	X	X	-	X	-	X	-	X
Mali	X	X	X	X	X	X	-	X
Mauritania	-	-	X	-	-	X	-	X
Mauritius	X	X	X	X	-	X	X	-
Mozambique	-	X	X	-	X	X	-	X
Namibia	X	X	X	X	X	X	X	-
Niger	X	X	X	-	-	X	-	X
Nigeria	X	X	X	X	-	X	X	X
Rwanda	X	X	X	X	X	X	-	X
Senegal	X	X	X	X	X	X	X	X
Sierra Leone	-	-	X	X	-	X	X	X
Somalia	X	X	X	-	-	-	X	X
South Africa	X	X	X	X	-	X	X	-
Sudan	X	X	X	-	-	X	X	X
Tanzania	X	X	X	X	X	X	-	X
Togo	X	X	X	X	X	X	X	X
Uganda	X	X	X	X	X	X	X	X
Zaire	X	X	X	X	X	X	-	X
Zambia	X	X	X	X	-	X	-	X
Zimbabwe	X	X	X	X	X	X	-	X
Arab States								
Algeria	X	X	X	-	X	X	X	X
Egypt	X	X	X	X	X	X	X	X
Iraq	X	X	X	X	X	X	-	-
Jordan	X	X	X	X	X	X	X	-
Kuwait	-	-	X	X	X	X	-	-

Country	Economic, social and cultural rights	Civil and political rigths	Elimination of all forms of racial discrimination	Elimination of all forms of discrimination against women	Prevention and punishment of the crime of genocide	Rights of the child	Torture and other cruel inhuman or degrading treatment or punishment	Status of refugees
Date of convention	1966	1966	1969	1979	1948	1989	1984	1954
Lebanon	X	X	X	-	X	X	-	-
Libya	X	X	X	X	X	X	X	-
Morocco	X	X	X	X	X	X	X	X
Oman	-	-	-	-	-	-	-	-
Saudi Arabia	-	-	-	-	X	-	-	-
Syria	X	X	X	-	X	X	-	-
Tunisia	X	X	X	X	X	X	X	X
Unit.Arab Emirates	-	-	X	-	-	-	-	-
Yemen, Rep.	X	X	X	X	X	X	X	X
South Central Asia								
Afghanistan	X	X	X	X	X	X	X	-
Armenia	X	X	X	X	X	X	X	X
Azerbaijan	X	X	-	X	-	X	-	X
Bangladesh	-	-	X	X	-	X	-	-
Bhutan	..	..	X	X	..	X	..	..
Georgia	X	X	-	X	X	X	X	-
India	X	X	X	X	X	X	-	-
Iran	X	X	X	-	X	X	-	X
Kazakhstan	-	-	-	-	-	X	-	-
Kyrgyz Rep.	X	X	-	-	-	X	-	-
Nepal	X	X	X	X	X	X	X	-
Pakistan	-	-	X	-	X	X	-	-
Sri Lanka	X	X	X	X	X	X	X	-
Tajikistan	-	-	X	X	-	X	X	X
Turkey	-	-	X	X	X	X	X	X
Turkmenistan	-	-	X	-	-	X	-	-
Uzbekistan	X	X	X	X	-	X	X	-
East Asia								
China	-	-	X	X	X	X	X	X
Hong Kong	-	-	-	-	-	-	-	-
Japan	X	X	X	X	-	X	-	X
Korea, Dem.	X	X	-	-	X	X	-	-
Korea, Rep.	X	X	X	X	X	X	X	X
Mongolia	X	X	X	X	X	X	-	-
Southeast Asia and Oceania								
Australia	X	X	X	X	X	X	X	X
Cambodia	X	X	X	X	X	X	X	X
Indonesia	-	-	-	X	-	X	X	-
Lao PDR	-	-	X	X	X	X	-	-
Malaysia	-	-	-	X	X	X	-	-
Myanmar	-	-	-	-	X	X	-	-
New Zealand	X	X	X	X	X	X	X	X
Papua New Guinea	-	-	X	X	X	X	-	X
Philippines	X	X	X	X	X	X	X	X
Singapore	-	-	-	X	X	X	-	X
Thailand	-	-	-	X	-	X	-	-
Vietnam	X	X	X	X	X	X	-	-

Country	Economic, social and cultural rights	Civil and political rigths	Elimination of all forms of racial discrimination	Elimination of all forms of discrimination against women	Prevention and punishment of the crime of genocide	Rights of the child	Torture and other cruel inhuman or degrading treatment or punishment	Status of refugees
Date of convention	1966	1966	1969	1979	1948	1989	1984	1954
Latin America and the Caribbean								
Argentina	X	X	X	X	X	X	X	-
Bolivia	X	X	X	X	X	X	X	X
Brazil	X	X	X	X	X	X	X	X
Chile	X	X	X	X	X	X	X	X
Colombia	X	X	X	X	X	X	X	X
Costa Rica	X	X	X	X	X	X	X	X
Cuba	-	-	X	X	X	X	X	-
Dominican Rep.	X	X	X	X	X	X	X	X
Ecuador	X	X	X	X	X	X	X	X
El Salvador	X	X	X	X	X	X	-	X
Guatemala	X	X	X	X	X	X	X	X
Haiti	-	X	X	X	X	X	-	X
Honduras	X	X	-	X	X	X	-	X
Jamaica	X	X	X	X	X	X	-	X
Mexico	X	X	X	X	X	X	X	-
Nicaragua	X	X	X	X	X	X	X	X
Panama	X	X	X	X	X	X	X	X
Paraguay	X	X	-	X	X	X	X	X
Peru	X	X	X	X	X	X	X	X
Trinidad	X	X	X	X	-	X	-	-
Uruguay	X	X	X	X	X	X	X	X
Venezuela	X	X	X	X	X	X	X	-
North America								
Canada	X	X	X	X	X	X	X	X
United States	X	X	X	X	X	X	X	-
Europe								
Albania	X	X	X	X	X	X	X	X
Austria	X	X	X	X	X	X	X	X
Belarus	X	X	X	X	X	X	X	-
Belgium	X	X	X	X	X	X	X	X
Bosnia	X	X	X	X	X	X	X	X
Bulgaria	X	X	X	X	X	X	X	X
Croatia	X	X	X	X	X	X	X	X
Czech Rep.	X	X	X	X	X	X	X	X
Denmark	X	X	X	X	X	X	X	X
Estonia	X	X	X	X	X	X	X	-
Finland	X	X	X	X	X	X	X	X
France	X	X	X	X	X	X	X	X
Germany	X	X	X	X	X	X	X	X
Greece	X	-	X	X	X	X	X	X
Hungary	X	X	X	X	X	X	X	X
Ireland	X	X	X	X	X	X	X	X
Israel	X	X	X	X	X	X	X	X
Italy	X	X	X	X	X	X	X	X
Latvia	X	X	X	X	X	X	X	-
Lithuania	X	X	-	X	-	X	-	-

Country	Economic, social and cultural rights	Civil and political rigths	Elimination of all forms of racial discrimination	Elimination of all forms of discrimination against women	Prevention and punishment of the crime of genocide	Rights of the child	Torture and other cruel inhuman or degrading treatment or punishment	Status of refugees
Date of convention	1966	1966	1969	1979	1948	1989	1984	1954
Macedonia, FYR	X	X	X	X	-	X	X	-
Moldova	X	X	X	X	X	X	X	-
Netherlands	X	X	X	X	X	X	X	X
Norway	X	X	X	X	X	X	X	X
Poland	X	X	X	X	X	X	X	X
Portugal	X	X	X	X	-	X	X	X
Romania	X	X	X	X	X	X	X	X
Russia	X	X	X	X	X	X	X	X
Slovakia	X	X	X	X	X	X	X	X
Slovenia	X	X	X	X	X	X	X	X
Spain	X	X	X	X	X	X	X	X
Sweden	X	X	X	X	X	X	X	X
Switzerland	X	X	X	X	-	X	X	X
Ukraine	X	X	X	X	X	X	X	-
United Kingdom	X	X	X	X	X	X	X	X
Yugoslavia	X	X	X	X	X	X	X	X

Region	Economic, social and cultural rights		Civil and political rigths		Elimination of all forms of racial discrimination		Elimination of all forms of discrimination against women		Prevention and punishment of the crime of genocide		Rights of the child		Torture and other cruel inhuman or degrading treatment or punishment		Status of refugees	
Date of convention	1966		1966		1969		1979		1948		1989		1984		1954	
	T	(%)	T	(%)	T	(%)	T	(%)	T	(%)	T	(%)	T	(%)	T	(%)
World	122	81	122	81	129	86	130	87	109	73	145	97	96	64	104	69
Developing	81	74	82	75	89	82	89	82	73	67	104	95	57	52	71	65
Industrial	41	100	40	98	40	98	41	100	36	88	41	100	39	95	33	80
Dev exc India / China	80	75	81	76	87	81	87	81	71	66	102	95	56	52	70	65
Ind exc USA / Russia	39	100	38	97	38	97	39	100	34	87	39	100	37	95	32	82
Sub-Saharan Africa	34	83	34	83	36	88	35	85	18	44	40	98	19	46	37	90
Arab States	10	71	10	71	12	86	8	57	12	86	11	79	7	50	5	36
South Central Asia	11	65	11	65	13	76	12	71	10	59	17	100	9	53	6	35
East Asia	4	67	4	67	4	67	4	67	4	67	5	83	2	33	3	50
Southeast Asia / Oc	5	42	5	42	7	58	11	92	10	83	12	100	5	42	6	50
Latin Am / Carib	20	91	21	95	20	91	22	100	21	95	22	100	17	77	17	77
North America	2	100	2	100	2	100	2	100	2	100	2	100	2	100	1	50
Europe	36	100	35	97	35	97	36	100	32	89	36	100	35	97	29	81

TABLE 19
TRANSLATIONS AND BOOKS IN FOREIGN LANGUAGES

Country of publication	Total translations published		Major language translated 1980		Major language translated 1994		Percentage of titles published in foreign languages	Percentage of titles published in two or more languages
	1980	1994	First language 1980	Second language 1980	First language 1994	Second language 1994	1991-93	1991-93
Sub-Saharan Africa								
Angola	11	..	French	English	..	..	..	..
Benin	..	..	..	..	..	..	..	..
Botswana	..	..	..	..	..	..	..	..
Burkina Faso	..	..	..	..	..	..	..	..
Burundi	..	..	..	..	..	..	..	..
Cameroon	..	..	..	..	..	..	..	..
Central African Rep.	..	..	..	..	..	..	..	..
Chad	..	..	..	..	..	..	..	..
Congo	2	..	..	..	..	..	..	..
Côte d' Ivoire	..	..	..	..	..	..	..	..
Eritrea	..	..	..	..	..	..	79.2	..
Ethiopia	..	..	..	..	..	..	14.2	..
Gabon	..	..	..	..	..	..	..	..
Gambia	..	..	..	..	..	..	9.5	..
Ghana	..	..	..	..	..	..	..	..
Guinea	..	..	..	..	..	..	..	..
Guinea-Bissau	..	..	..	..	..	..	..	..
Kenya	..	..	..	..	..	..	..	..
Lesotho	..	..	..	..	..	..	..	..
Liberia	..	..	..	..	..	..	..	..
Madagascar	13	7	French	English	English	French	3.5	2.8
Malawi	3	1	English	..	English	..	26.2	..
Mali	..	..	..	..	..	..	..	..
Mauritania	..	..	..	..	..	..	..	9.4
Mauritius	4	3	French	..	English	..	..	..
Mozambique	..	..	..	..	..	..	..	..
Namibia	..	11	..	..	Afrikaans	German	..	..
Niger	39	..	English	..	..	..	..	..
Nigeria	9	..	English	..	..	..	0.5	..
Rwanda	..	..	..	..	..	..	..	..
Senegal	..	..	..	..	..	..	..	..
Sierra Leone	..	..	..	..	..	..	..	..
Somalia	..	..	..	..	..	..	..	..
South Africa	..	..	..	..	..	..	6.8	5.7
Sudan	..	..	..	..	..	..	..	..
Tanzania	..	..	..	..	..	..	..	..
Togo	..	..	..	..	..	..	..	..
Uganda	..	..	..	..	..	..	..	..
Zaire	..	..	..	..	..	..	..	..
Zambia	..	..	..	..	..	..	..	..
Zimbabwe	..	..	..	..	..	..	..	..
Arab States								
Algeria	..	8	..	..	French	English	49.0	..
Egypt	123	..	English	French	..	..	10.7	..
Iraq	53	..	English	Arabic	..	..	..	..
Jordan	10	81	English	..	English	French	1.3	..
Kuwait	19	5	French	English	English	Russian	..	..

Country of publication	Total translations published		Major language translated 1980		Major language translated 1994		Percentage of titles published in foreign languages	Percentage of titles published In two or more languages
	1980	1994	First language 1980	Second language 1980	First language 1994	Second language 1994	1991-93	1991-93
Lebanon	10	22	French	..	French	English	..	..
Libya	4	..	French	..	..	..	..	..
Morocco	..	..	..	..	..	..	..	..
Oman	..	..	..	..	..	..	..	..
Saudi Arabia	2	24	English	..	English	German	..	..
Syria	44	114	French	English	French	English	..	..
Tunisia	7	9	..	..	Arabic	French	34.9	..
Unit.Arab Emirates	..	3	..	..	English	..	14.3	..
Yemen, Rep.	..	..	..	..	..	..	..	..
South Central Asia								
Afghanistan	..	..	..	..	..	..	..	..
Armenia	..	..	..	..	..	..	..	..
Azerbaijan	..	..	..	..	..	..	3.8	4.0
Bangladesh	..	..	..	..	English	..	..	..
Buthan	..	..	..	..	..	..	..	..
Georgia	..	..	..	..	..	..	..	..
India	685	223	English	Sanskrit	English	Sanskrit	..	..
Iran	7	..	English	..	..	..	..	..
Kazakhstan	..	..	..	..	..	..	..	..
Kyrgyz Rep.	..	3	..	..	Kirghiz	Tadzik	..	..
Nepal	..	..	..	..	..	..	..	..
Pakistan	79	34	English	Arabic	English	Arabic	5.2	..
Sri Lanka	30	56	English	Russian	English	German	45.9	24.7
Tajikistan	..	..	..	..	..	..	..	..
Turkey	684	322	English	French	English	French	4.3	0.8
Turkmenistan	..	..	..	..	..	..	..	..
Uzbekistan	..	..	..	..	..	..	16.9	0.1
East Asia								
China	..	..	..	..	..	..	..	..
Hong Kong	..	..	..	..	..	..	..	..
Japan	1,966	3,183	English	French	English	German	..	..
Korea, Dem.	..	..	..	..	..	..	0.2	0.0
Korea, Rep.	363	2,018	English	French	English	German	..	..
Mongolia	..	..	..	..	..	..	..	..
Southeast Asia and Oceania								
Australia	113	..	English	Classical	..	..	..	..
Cambodia	..	..	..	..	..	..	..	..
Indonesia	377	354	English	French	English	French	..	..
Lao PDR	..	..	..	..	..	..	17.2	..
Malaysia	331	343	English	Arabic	English	Arabic	40.0	4.1
Myanmar	47	..	English	Chinese	..	..	..	..
New Zealand	21	61	English	..	English	Samoan	..	..
Papua New Guinea	..	..	..	..	..	..	1.6	..
Philippines	29	4	English	Classical	Iloko	..	35.9	0.4
Singapore	70	..	English	Arabic	..	..	..	..
Thailand	95	108	English	Russian	English	Chinese	6.6	..
Vietnam	..	..	..	..	..	..	..	..

Country of publication	Total translations published		Major language translated 1980		Major language translated 1994		Percentage of titles published in foreign languages	Percentage of titles published In two or more languages
			First language	Second language	First language	Second language		
	1980	1994	1980	1980	1994	1994	1991-93	1991-93
Latin America and the Caribbean								
Argentina	248	1,009	English	French	English	French	0.3	..
Bolivia	..	..	..	..	..	..	..	..
Brazil	716	1,364	English	French	English	French	63.6	..
Chile	24	189	English	French	English	French	..	..
Colombia	48	72	English	French	English	Italian	..	..
Costa Rica	1	..	..	..	..	..	..	..
Cuba	..	18	..	..	Spanish	French	..	..
Dominican Rep.	1	..	..	..	..	..	..	..
Ecuador	1	..	..	..	..	..	..	..
El Salvador	..	..	..	..	..	..	..	..
Guatemala	..	..	..	..	..	..	..	..
Haiti	..	..	..	..	..	..	..	..
Honduras	..	..	..	..	..	..	..	..
Jamaica	..	..	..	..	..	..	..	..
Mexico	2,702	..	English	French	..	..	..	..
Nicaragua	..	..	..	..	..	..	..	..
Panama	9	8	English	..	English	French	..	..
Paraguay	..	..	..	..	..	..	0.7	..
Peru	19	7	English	..	Spanish	English	10.0	..
Trinidad	..	2	..	..	Spanish	French	..	..
Uruguay	11	14	English	French	English	..	..	..
Venezuela	15	4	French	English	English	Classical	..	..
North America								
Canada	360	718	English	French	English	French	2.2	13.6
United States	1,390	..	German	French	French	German	..	..
Europe								
Albania	173	44	Russian	French	English	French	43.3	0.3
Austria	327	327	English	French	English	German	6.5	1.7
Belarus	..	29	..	..	..	..	0.7	..
Belgium	1,149	..	English	German	English	Russian	9.7	3.4
Bosnia	..	..	..	..	..	..	..	..
Bulgaria	656	1,672	Russian	English	English	French	5.1	1.8
Croatia	..	460	..	..	English	Serbo-croat	8.1	0.4
Czech Rep.	..	2,463	..	..	German	English	10.6	3.4
Denmark	1,913	1,873	English	Swedish	English	Swedish	17.3	2.8
Estonia	..	533	..	..	English	Estonian	23.3	4.5
Finland	1,476	1,164	English	Swedish	English	Swedish	16.4	0.3
France	5,691	5,627	English	German	English	German	11.4	2.4
Germany	7,681	9,992	English	French	English	French	..	..
Greece	358	683	English	French	English	French	..	..
Hungary	1,121	1,383	French	English	French	English	5.9	0.7
Ireland	..	215	..	..	English	German	..	..
Israel	330	198	English	German	English	French	..	..
Italy	2,055	1,958	English	French	English	French	9.3	3.4
Latvia	..	..	..	..	..	..	20.6	..
Lithuania	..	562	..	..	English	French	13.1	0.6

Country of publication	Total translations published		Major language translated 1980		Major language translated 1994		Percentage of titles published in foreign languages	Percentage of titles published In two or more languages
	1980	1994	First language 1980	Second language 1980	First language 1994	Second language 1994	1991-93	1991-93
Macedonia, FYR	..	118	..	..	Macedonian	English	..	..
Moldova	..	92	..	..	Russian	Moldavian	23.4	6.5
Netherlands	1,846	4,243	English	German	English	German	18.5	..
Norway	1,175	1,153	English	Swedish	English	Swedish	13.7	..
Poland	883	2,358	English	Russian	English	German	5.1	0.3
Portugal	839	1,444	French	English	English	French	39.3	2.3
Romania	609	1,061	Hungarian	French	English	French	..	..
Russia	..	5,136	..	..	English	French	7.6	0.6
Slovakia	..	959	..	..	English	Czech	20.9	4.8
Slovenia	..	..	..	..	..	..	12.9	..
Spain	6,366	6,314	English	French	English	French	4.7	1.4
Sweden	2,189	2,188	English	Scandinavian	English	Scandinavian	18.3	3.0
Switzerland	811	972	English	German	English	German	17.7	..
Ukraine	..	363	..	..	English	French	10.3	7.2
United Kingdom	1,348	1,560	French	German	French	German	..	..
Yugoslavia	..	573	..	..	English	Serbo-Croat	20.0	9.5

Region of publication	Total translations published		Percentage of titles published in foreign languages	Percentage of titles published In two or more languages
	1980 T	1994 T	1991-93	1991-93
World	..	..	..	..
Developing	..	..	..	..
Industrial	..	..	11.0	3.0
Dev exc India / China	..	..	..	..
Ind exc USA / Russia	41,460	56,540	12.4	4.0
Sub-Saharan Africa	..	..	..	..
North Af / West Asia	270	..	..	..
South Central Asia	..	..	..	..
East Asia	..	..	..	..
Southeast Asia / Oc	1,080	..	..	..
Latin Am / Carib	3,800	..	..	..
North America	1,750	..	..	..
Europe	..	57,720	11.5	2.3

TABLE 20
TRANSLATIONS BY ORIGINAL LANGUAGE

Original language	Number of translations published *		Major languages into which translated 1980		Major languages into which translated 1994	
			First language 1980	Second language 1980	First language 1994	Second language 1994
	1980	1994				
Abhaz	15	2	..	..	Russian	..
Adygej	..	5	..	..	Russian	..
Afrikaans	..	16	..	..	Dutch	English
Albanian	118	20	English	French	French	German
Arabic	230	227	French	English	English	Russian
Aramaic	..	12	..	..	English	..
Armenian	54	13	Russian	English	French	English
Avarskij	..	6	..	..	Russian	..
Azerbaijani	47	2	Russian	German	Turkish	..
Baskir	18	10	..	..	Russian	..
Belorussian	98	12	Russian	English	Russian	English
Bengali	77	26	English	..	English	Hindi
Bosnian	..	24	..	..	German	Portuguese
Breton	..	7	..	..	French	English
Bulgarian	239	37	Russian	German	Russian	German
Catalan	27	344	Spanish	English	Spanish	French
Chinese	187	187	French	English	English	French
Cuvash	14	3	..	..	Russian	..
Czech	651	355	Slovak	German	Slovak	German
Danish	649	370	Swedish	German	English	German
Dutch	409	441	German	English	German	English
English	22,415	28,642	German	French	German	French
Middle English	..	4	..	..	English	..
Estonian	124	71	Russian	English	Russian	English
Euskera	..	76	..	..	Spanish	Catalan
Finnish	165	151	Swedish	English	English	Swedish
French	5,972	5,661	Spanish	German	Russian	German
Middle Old French	17	37	French	German	English	French
Frisian	..	8	..	..	Dutch	..
Gallegan	..	58	..	..	Spanish	Catalan
Georgian	71	6	Russian	German	Russian	English
German	4,823	4,667	English	French	Czech	English
Middle High German	20	25	German	..	German	Dutch
Classical Greek	458	444	German	Spanish	French	German
Modern Greek	86	62	English	German	French	Spanish
Hebrew	181	281	English	Spanish	English	German
Hindi	63	26	English	..	English	Russian
Hungarian	633	108	English	German	German	French
Icelandic	39	18	English	German	German	Danish
Indonesian	..	9	..	..	Dutch	English
Irish	..	13	..	..	English	German
Italian	1,476	1,494	Spanish	French	French	German
Jakut	..	6	..	..	Russian	..
Japanese	199	292	English	German	English	French
Kannada	..	7	..	..	English	Tamil

Original language	Number of translations published *		Major languages into which translated 1980		Major languages into which translated 1994	
			First language 1980	Second language 1980	First language 1994	Second language 1994
	1980	1994				
Karakalpa	..	9	..	..	..	..
Kazakh	66	3	Russian	..	Russian	Jakut
Kirghiz	68	3	Russian	German	Russian	..
Korean	21	26	French	English	French	Russian
Latin	537	444	German	French	German	Spanish
Latvian	77	10	Russian	..	Lithuanian	Belorussian
Lithuanian	99	54	Russian	..	English	Russian
Macedonian	36	59	..	..	Albanian	Turkish
Malay	31	2	..	..	Korean	..
Malayalam	..	9	..	..	Tamil	English
Marathi	26	6	..	..	..	..
Moldavian	45	27	Russian	..	Russian	English
Niuean	..	5	..	..	Tongan	..
Old Norse	..	6	..	..	German	..
Norwegian	358	237	Danish	Swedish	Danish	German
Occitan	23	10	French	..	French	..
Pali	..	12	..	..	German	English
Persian	96	63	English	French	German	English
Polish	608	319	German	English	Russian	English
Portuguese	198	264	Spanish	French	Spanish	French
Romanian	392	43	English	Hungarian	French	English
Russian	6,450	1,193	English	German	English	German
Old Russian	..	5	..	..	Russian	..
Samoan	..	15	..	..	Niuean	Tongan
Sanskrit	204	94	English	German	English	Russian
Serbo-Croatian	382	293	English	German	English	German
Slovak	148	78	Hungarian	Russian	Hungarian	Czech
Slovene	41	14	..	..	German	Lituanian
Spanish	851	1,708	French	German	English	French
Surinam Javanese	..	5	..	..	Dutch	..
Swedish	1,225	810	Danish	Norwegian	Danish	Norwegian
Tadzik	22	1	Russian	..	Jakut	..
Tamil	24	5	..	..	English	..
Tatar	32	13	Russian	..	Russian	..
Telugu	..	11	..	..	Tamil	English
Thai	..	5	..	..	German	English
Tibetan	14	46	German	English	English	French
Turkish	52	54	German	French	German	English
Turkman	30	1	..	..	Russian	..
Ukranian	158	22	Russian	English	Russian	German
Urdu	37	22	English	..	English	Hindi
Uzbek	64	7	Russian	..	Russian	Turkish
Valencian	..	25	..	..	Spanish	..
Vietnamese	11	13	..	..	English	French
Yiddish	69	38	English	Russian	German	Polish

* Not including 672 translations of over 130 languages with less than five entries in either year.

TABLE 21
MOST FREQUENTLY TRANSLATED AUTHORS [a]

Rank	Authors	Associated Country	Number of Translations	Number of countries translating	Rank	Authors	Associated Country	Number of Translations	Number of countries translating
1980	1980	1980	1980	1980	1994	1994	1994	1994	1994
1	Lenin V. I.	USSR	468	15	1	Christie A.	UK	218	21
2	The Bible	Palestine	232	48	2	Steel D.	USA	131	19
3	Christie A.	UK	189	20	3	The Bible	Palestine	126	20
4	Verne J.	France	172	21	4	Holt V.	UK	120	15
5	Blyton E.	UK	147	12	5	Vandenberg P.	..	112	2
6	Marx K.	Germany	136	20	6	King S.	USA	110	17
7	Cartland B.	UK	135	13	7	Verne J.	France	109	20
8	Engels F.	Germany	132	17	8	Cartland B.	UK	98	9
9	Shakespeare W.	UK	112	22	9	Stevenson R. L.	UK	96	18
10	Breznev L. I.	USSR	109	14	10	Blyton E.	UK	95	12
11	Grimm J.	Germany	103	14	11	Joannes Paulus II	Holy See	93	20
12	Goscinny R.	France	101	10	11	Shakespeare W.	UK	93	19
13	London J.	USA	93	20	13	Chase J. H.	UK	87	9
14	Andersen H. C.	Denmark	91	17	14	Dumas (Pere) A.	France	86	17
15	Twain M.	USA	88	21	15	Koontz D. R.	USA	84	17
16	Dostoevskij F. M.	Russia	85	16	16	Asimov I.	USA	78	15
17	Asimov I.	USA	82	17	17	May K.	Germany	67	8
17	Simenon G.	Belgium	82	21	18	Doyle A. C.	UK	66	18
19	Tolstoj L. N.	Russia	79	22	19	Brown S.	USA	64	11
20	Konsalik H. G.	Germany	72	10	19	Twain M.	USA	64	19
21	Buck P. S.	USA	70	13	21	Andersen H. C.	Denmark	62	18
21	Joannes Paulus II	Holy See	70	16	21	Ludlum R.	USA	62	16
23	Hemingway E.	USA	64	21	21	Simenon G.	Begium	62	10
24	Greene G.	UK	63	17	24	Dostoevskij F. M.	Russia	59	16
24	Stevenson R. L.	UK	63	19	25	Grimm J.	Germany	58	21
26	Hesse H.	Germany	62	13	26	Grimm W.	Germany	57	20
27	Robbins H.	USA	60	17	26	Sheldon S.	USA	57	18
28	Dickens C.	UK	59	14	28	Rendell R.	UK	55	11
28	Grover M.	USA	59	3	29	Lindgren A.	Sweden	54	14
28	Kolmogorov A. N.	USSR	59	1	29	London J.	USA	54	18
31	Maclean A.	UK	57	14	31	Grisham J.	USA	52	18
32	Masterson L.	Norway	55	5	32	Dickens C.	UK	51	20
33	Gardner E. S.	USA	54	11	32	Hesse H.	Germany	51	14
34	Tito J. B.	Yugoslavia	52	1	34	Gardner E. S.	USA	50	11
35	Cehov A. P.	Russia	51	24	35	Crichton M.	USA	49	11
36	Defoe D.	UK	50	17	35	Lindsey J.	USA	49	8
36	Dumas (Pere) A.	France	50	17	35	Maclean A.	UK	49	11
38	Lindgren A. E.	Sweden	49	16	38	Clark M. H.	UK	48	16
39	Balzac H. de	France	48	14	38	Forsyth F.	UK	48	17
39	Doyle A. C.	UK	48	14	38	Pilcher R.	UK	48	12

Rank	Authors	Associated Country	Number of Translations	Number of countries translating	Rank	Authors	Associated Country	Number of Translations	Number of countries translating
1980	1980	1980	1980	1980	1994	1994	1994	1994	1994
39	Singer I. B.	USA	48	12	41	Bradley M. Z.	USA	46	7
42	Uderzo A.	France	46	8	41	Kipling R.	UK	46	14
43	Peyo	Belgium	45	6	41	Peters E.	UK	46	9
43	Sartre J. P.	France	45	12	44	Le Carre J.	UK	45	17
43	Shaw I.	USA	45	18	44	Wilde O.	UK	45	11
46	Makarycev J. N.	Russia	44	1	46	Cook R.	USA	43	14
46	Pushkin A. S.	Russia	44	11	47	Collins J.	UK	42	11
46	Stratemeyer E. L.	USA	44	1	47	Steiner R.	Germany	42	15
49	De Villiers G.	France	43	6	49	Parker S.	UK	41	12
49	Miller H.	USA	43	9	50	Deveraux J.	USA	40	8
49	Poe E. A.	USA	43	11	50	Pratchett T.	UK	40	11
52	Homerus	Greece	42	13	50	Rajneesh B. S.	India	40	14
53	Caldwell T.	USA	41	6	50	Saint-Exupery A. de	France	40	14
53	Hoxha E.	Albania	41	4	50	Tolstoj L. N.	Russia	40	5
53	Platon	Greece	41	15	55	Benzoni J.	France	39	5
56	Cronin A. J.	UK	40	13	55	Garcia Marquez G.	Colombia	39	17
56	Gorkij M.	USSR	40	13	55	Nietzsche F. W.	Germany	39	16
56	Lobsang T. R	UK	40	7	58	Courths Mahler H.	Germany	38	6
59	Carroll L.	UK	39	10	58	Poe E. A.	USA	38	10
59	Fromm E.	USA	39	13	58	Robbins H.	USA	38	11
59	Mather A.	..	39	7	58	Stout R.	USA	38	8
59	Tolkien J. R.	UK	39	12	62	Dahl R.	UK	37	9
63	Cooper J. F.	USA	38	12	62	Follett K.	UK	37	16
63	Heyer G.	UK	38	6	62	Higgins J.	UK	37	16
63	Scott W.	UK	38	15	62	Woolf V.	UK	37	14
66	Stalin I. V.	USSR	38	5	66	Platon	Greece	36	12
66	Steiner R.	Germany	38	11	67	Montgomery L. M.	Canada	35	8
68	Nietzsche F. W.	Germany	37	9	67	Nabokov V.	Russia	35	12
69	Solohov M. A.	USSR	36	7	67	Van Lustbader E.	..	35	7
70	Carter N.	USA	35	4	67	Wood B.	UK	35	8
70	Freud S.	Austria	35	9	71	Camus A.	France	34	12
70	Garcia Marquez G	Colombia	35	19	71	Duras M.	France	34	15
70	Goethe J. W. Von	Germany	35	12	71	Hemingway E.	USA	34	9
70	McBain E.	USA	35	6	71	Queen E.	USA	34	11
70	Schultz C. M.	USA	35	8	75	Arabian Nights	Persia	33	11
70	Slaughter F. G.	USA	35	9	75	Calvino I.	Italy	33	8
77	Arabian Nights	Persia	34	5	75	Francis R. S.	UK	33	12
77	Klepinina Z. A.	Russia	34	1	75	Goscinny R.	France	33	7
77	Le Carre J.	UK	34	9	79	Kundera M.	Czech R.	32	9
77	Mann T.	Germany	34	13	79	Smith W. A.	UK	32	12

Rank	Authors	Associated Country	Number of Translations	Number of countries translating	Rank	Authors	Associated Country	Number of Translations	Number of countries translating
1980	1980	1980	1980	1980	1994	1994	1994	1994	1994
77	Moliere	France	34	16	81	Cehov A. P.	Russia	31	13
77	Morris M.	Belgium	34	4	81	Eco U.	Italy	31	12
77	Winspear V.	..	34	6	81	Tolkien J. R. R.	UK	31	11
77	West M. L.	Austria	34	9	84	Bradford B. T.	USA	30	14
85	Flaubert G.	France	33	16	84	Bukowski C.	USA	30	10
85	Perrault C.	France	33	10	84	Greene G.	UK	30	12
87	Gogol N. V.	Russia	32	13	84	Rice A.	USA	30	11
87	Huxley A.	UK	32	11	84	Vonnegut K.	USA	30	11
87	Wahloo P.	Sweden	32	8	84	Wallace E.	USA	30	7
90	Amado J.	Brazil	31	12	90	Auster P.	USA	29	10
90	Arthur R.	UK	31	4	90	Gordon N.	USA	29	11
90	Hodakov J. V.	Russia	31	1	90	Hay L. L.	USA	29	10
90	Kent L.	USA	31	3	90	Maugham W. S.	UK	29	13
90	Kipling R.	UK	31	9	90	Perrault C.	France	29	12
90	Shuttleworth C.	UK	31	1	90	Ross T.	USA	29	8
90	Werner L.	Denmark	31	3	96	Clarke A. C.	UK	28	10
97	Camus A.	France	30	14	96	Forbes C.	UK	28	5
97	Lem S.	Poland	30	11	96	Krentz J. A.	USA	28	6
97	Maupassant G. de	France	30	13	96	McBain E.	USA	28	11
97	Sjowall M.	Sweden	30	8	96	Zola E.	France	28	11
97	Vilenkin N. S.	Russia	30	1	101	Balzac H. de	France	27	12
97	Wolde G.	Sweden	30	5	101	Foster A. D.	USA	27	4
97	Woolf V.	UK	30	11	101	Goethe J. W. Von	Germany	27	10
104	Buhovcev B. B.	Russia	29	2	101	Highsmith P.	USA	27	13
104	Harper C.	..	29	1	101	Kafka F.	Austria	27	16
104	Holt V.	UK	29	29	101	Lewis C. S.	UK	27	11
104	Johns W. E.	UK	29	5	101	Maupassant G. de	France	27	11
104	Melville H.	USA	29	15	101	Yourcenar M.	France	27	10
104	Mjakisev G. J.	Russia	29	3	109	Andrews V. C.	USA	26	8
104	Steinbeck J.	USA	29	13	109	Auel J. M.	USA	26	9
111	Aristoteles	Greece	28	28	109	Castaneda C.	Mexico	26	10
111	Brecht B.	Germany	28	13	109	Flaubert G.	France	26	9
111	Conrad J.	UK	28	14	109	Homerus	Greece	26	11
111	Hampson A.	USA	28	6	109	Keneally T.	USA	26	13
111	Heinlein R. A.	USA	28	6	109	Macdonald J. R.	USA	26	6
111	Kafka F.	Austria	28	12	109	Miller H.	USA	26	12
111	Lawrence D. H.	UK	28	10	109	Morrison T.	USA	26	11
111	Nin A.	France	28	12	109	Saul J.	USA	26	7
111	Popov S. G.	Russia	28	2	119	Clancy T.	USA	25	11
111	Swift J.	UK	28	14	119	Conrad J.	UK	25	11

Rank	Authors	Associated Country	Number of Translations	Number of countries translating	Rank	Authors	Associated Country	Number of Translations	Number of countries translating
1980	1980	1980	1980	1980	1994	1994	1994	1994	1994
121	Farmer P J.	USA	27	6	119	Dailey J.	USA	25	12
121	Gilman G. G.	UK	27	3	119	Darcy E.	USA	25	8
121	Goodman L.	USA	27	6	119	Defoe D.	UK	25	14
121	Hugo V.	France	27	13	119	Du Maurier D.	UK	25	10
121	Keene C.	USA	27	6	119	Fielding J.	Canada	25	12
121	L´Amour L.	USA	27	7	119	George E.	UK	25	10
121	Moravia A.	Italy	27	12	119	Gookin D.	USA	25	12
121	Pendleton D.	USA	27	4	119	Jung C. G.	Austria	25	12
121	Sagan F.	France	27	8	119	Lamb C.	UK	25	7
121	Scarry R.	USA	27	7	119	Lawrence D. H.	UK	25	11
121	Srebnickij A. K.	Russia	27	1	119	Moliere	France	25	9
121	Wilde O.	UK	27	8	119	Norton A.	USA	25	5
133	Chandler R.	USA	26	8	119	Nostlinger C.	Germany	25	7
133	Collodi C.	Italy	26	10	119	Rodari G.	Italy	25	3
133	De Beauvoir S.	France	26	8	119	Sagan F.	France	25	12
133	Du Maurier D.	UK	26	9	119	Sartre J. P.	France	25	10
133	Fischer M. L.	Germany	26	4	119	Scott W.	UK	25	9
133	Hargreaves R.	..	26	4	119	Steinbeck J.	USA	25	10
133	Wallace E.	USA	26	6	119	Updike J.	USA	25	11
133	Wells H. G.	UK	26	12	119	Weis M.	..	25	8
141	Ajtmatov C.	USSR	25	5	119	Weldon F.	UK	25	10
141	Deighton L.	UK	25	9	119	Zweig S.	Austria	25	6
141	Fleming I.	UK	25	6					
141	Franquin A.	Belgium	25	4					
141	Hailey A.	UK	25	14					
141	Kardelj E.	Yugoslavia	25	3					
141	Leguin U. K.	USA	25	16					
141	Lewis C. S.	UK	25	11					
141	Maugham W. S.	UK	25	11					
141	Simmel J. M.	Germany	25	11					

a) Twenty five or more translations.

TABLE 22
EDUCATION

Country	Enrolment Ratios (%)					Public expenditure on education as % of GNP
	Primary (net)		Secondary (gross)		Tertiary (gross)	
	Boys	Girls	Boys	Girls		
	1995	1995	1991-94	1991-94	1991-94	1992-94
Sub-Saharan Africa						
Angola	49	31	14		1	..
Benin	68	41	17	7	2	5.4
Botswana	96	98	54	58	5	8.5
Burkina Faso	40	27	12	6	1	3.6
Burundi	64	44	8	5	1	3.8
Cameroon	88	68	32	22	3	3.1
Central African Rep.	83	47	17	6	2	2.8
Chad	46	25	13	3	1	2.2
Congo	70	68	..	..	..	8.3
Côte d' Ivoire	69	47	33	17	3	7.2
Eritrea	28	25	19	13	1	..
Ethiopia	32	9	11	10	1	6.4
Gabon	98	95	..	..	3	3.2
Gambia	64	46	25	13	1	2.7
Ghana	65	57	45	29	1	3.1
Guinea	55	27	18	6	2	2.2
Guinea-Bissau	55	45	10	2	1	..
Kenya	77	74	28	23	2	6.8
Lesotho	60	71	23	34	2	4.8
Liberia	..	..	..	..	3	..
Madagascar	56	63	14	14	4	1.9
Malawi	91	93	6	4	1	3.3
Mali	31	21	12	6	1	2.1
Mauritania	67	34	19	11	4	..
Mauritius	98	99	58	60	4	3.7
Mozambique	38	29	9	6	(.)	6.3
Namibia	88	95	57	69	8	8.7
Niger	48	17	9	5	..	3.1
Nigeria	67	52	33	28	3	1.3
Rwanda	35	37	11	9	1	3.7
Senegal	52	39	21	11	3	4.2
Sierra Leone	39	39	22	12	1	1.4
Somalia	21	4	9	5	2	0.5
South Africa	95	93	76	88	16	7.1
Sudan	43	37	24	19	3	..
Tanzania	55	51	6	5	..	5.0
Togo	79	57	34	12	3	6.1
Uganda	64	58	14	8	1	1.9
Zaire	59	53	33	15	2	1.0
Zambia	70	68	31	19	2	2.6
Zimbabwe	84	84	49	39	6	8.3
Arab States						
Algeria	99	91	66	58	11	5.6
Egypt	81	80	82	71	17	5.0
Iraq	95	85	53	34	13	4.0
Jordan	82	83	63	62	25	3.8
Kuwait	64	64	65	64	24	5.6

Country	Enrolment Ratios (%)					Public expenditure on education as % of GNP
	Primary (net)		Secondary (gross)		Tertiary (gross)	
	Boys	Girls	Boys	Girls		
	1995	1995	1991-94	1991-94	1991-94	1992-94
Lebanon	99	94	75	83	29	2.0
Libya	99	95	95	95	16	7.1
Morocco	79	59	40	29	10	5.4
Oman	74	71	67	61	5	4.5
Saudi Arabia	66	59	57	47	14	6.3
Syria	98	89	50	41	18	4.2
Tunisia	100	96	58	53	12	6.3
Unit.Arab Emirates	100	99	88	97	11	2.0
Yemen, Rep.	65	32	37	9	4	..
South Central Asia						
Afghanistan	42	14	32	11	2	..
Armenia	..	..	80	90	49	7.4
Azerbaijan	..	..	87	85	20	5.5
Bangladesh	89	78	25	13	4	2.3
Bhutan	60	15	7	2	..	2.8
Georgia	82	81	62	76	42	1.9
India	98	76	59	38	7	3.8
Iran	100	93	76	62	13	5.9
Kazakhstan	..	..	89	92	35	5.4
Kyrgyz Rep.	..	..	84	89	20	6.8
Nepal	80	46	47	24	5	2.9
Pakistan	36	25	33	17	3	2.7
Sri Lanka	100	100	71	79	6	3.2
Tajikistan	..	..	83	75	25	9.5
Turkey	92	87	76	50	20	3.3
Turkmenistan	..	..	..	..	22	7.9
Uzbekistan	..	..	99	87	32	..
East Asia						
China	97	95	60	51	4	2.6
Hong Kong	86	91	83	87	23	..
Japan	100	100	98	99	29	4.7
Korea, Dem.	..	..	..	..	..	..
Korea, Rep.	93	94	100	99	55	4.5
Mongolia	76	81	50	70	14	5.2
Southeast Asia and Oceania						
Australia	99	99	83	86	41	6.0
Cambodia	84	37	31	18	1	..
Indonesia	100	95	49	41	9	1.3
Lao PDR	77	67	31	19	2	2.3
Malaysia	97	81	58	64	10	5.3
Myanmar	98	85	30	30	5	2.4
New Zealand	99	98	100+	100+	60	7.3
Papua New Guinea	82	71	17	11	3	..
Philippines	97	95	80	81	27	2.4
Singapore	100	99	67	70	35	3.3
Thailand	94	65	50	49	21	3.8
Vietnam	97	78	42	39	3	..

Country	Enrolment Ratios (%)					Public expenditure on education as % of GNP
	Primary (net)		Secondary (gross)		Tertiary (gross)	
	Boys	Girls	Boys	Girls		
	1995	1995	1991-94	1991-94	1991-94	1992-94
Latin America and the Caribbean						
Argentina	99	89	66	70	36	3.8
Bolivia	97	93	40	34	22	2.7
Brazil	86	88	42	49	11	1.6
Chile	86	85	66	70	27	2.9
Colombia	96	65	59	70	18	3.7
Costa Rica	89	91	47	51	30	4.7
Cuba	99	100	70	79	14	6.6
Dominican Rep.	79	83	34	47	18	1.9
Ecuador	98	89	54	56	20	3.0
El Salvador	95	63	27	30	15	1.6
Guatemala	91	46	25	23	8	1.6
Haiti	52	21	22	21	1	1.4
Honduras	85	86	29	37	9	4.0
Jamaica	100	96	62	70	6	4.7
Mexico	99	99	57	58	14	5.8
Nicaragua	78	81	40	47	10	3.8
Panama	99	96	63	68	28	5.2
Paraguay	89	90	38	40	10	2.9
Peru	99	90	78	70	31	2.9
Trinidad	84	84	74	78	8	4.5
Uruguay	94	94	74	88	27	2.5
Venezuela	98	83	29	41	29	5.1
North America						
Canada	97	96	100+	100+	..	7.6
United States	99	100	98	97	80	5.5
Europe						
Albania	..	..	36	37	10	3.0
Austria	89	91	100+	100+	43	5.5
Belarus	98	95	92	97	42	6.1
Belgium	95	97	100+	100+	40	5.6
Bosnia	..	..	..	..	..	..
Bulgaria	80	79	68	72	34	4.5
Croatia	80	80	75	81	27	..
Czech Rep.	..	..	90	94	19	5.9
Denmark	97	98	100+	100+	45	8.5
Estonia	81	80	92	90	24	5.8
Finland	..	..	100+	100+	63	8.4
France	99	99	100+	100+	50	5.8
Germany	80	83	100+	100	36	4.8
Greece	93	94	99	96	43	3.0
Hungary	91	92	79	83	17	6.7
Ireland	89	90	100+	100+	36	6.4
Israel	..	..	83	89	34	6.0
Italy	..	..	81	82	37	5.2
Latvia	82	80	84	89	22	6.5
Lithuania	..	..	80	84	27	4.5

Country	Enrolment Ratios (%)					Public expenditure on education as % of GNP
	Primary (net)		Secondary (gross)		Tertiary (gross)	
	Boys	Girls	Boys	Girls		
	1995	1995	1991-94	1991-94	1991-94	1992-94
Macedonia, FYR	85	84	55	56	17	5.6
Moldova	..	..	71	74	30	5.5
Netherlands	92	96	100+	100+	47	5.5
Norway	99	99	100+	100+	54	9.2
Poland	96	96	95	96	28	5.5
Portugal	100	100	78	91	35	5.4
Romania	77	76	77	78	13	3.1
Russia	96	96	84	91	43	4.4
Slovakia	..	..	88	93	19	4.9
Slovenia	96	97	89	91	30	6.2
Spain	99	100	100+	100+	44	4.7
Sweden	100	100	99	100	40	8.4
Switzerland	93	95	93	89	31	5.6
Ukraine	..	..	88	95	46	6.1
United Kingdom	100	100	93	95	41	5.4
Yugoslavia	69	70	61	63	18	..

Region	Enrolment Ratios (%)					Public Educational expenditure as % of GNP
	Primary (net)		Secondary (gross)		Tertiary (gross)	
	Boys	Girls	Boys	Girls		
	1995	1995	1991-94	1991-94	1991-94	1991-94
World	90	82	61	54	16	5.1
Developing	89	79	53	43	9	3.6
Industrial	95	96	93	94	47	5.4
Dev exc India / China	80	71	47	42	12	3.8
Ind exc USA / Russia	94	94	93	94	36	5.3
Sub-Saharan Africa	60	49	27	22	3	5.4
Arab States	85	76	63	52	14	5.2
South Central Asia	90	71	56	38	8	3.6
East Asia	97	95	65	57	8	4.4
Southeast Asia / Oc	97	86	52	48	13	4.2
Latin Am / Carib	92	86	50	55	17	3.3
North America	99	100	98	97	80	5.7
Europe	93	93	90	93	39	5.4

TABLE 23
THIRD-LEVEL EDUCATION ABROAD

Country	Number of students abroad (thousands)	Major countries of study		Number of foreign students (thousands)	Major countries of origin		Foreign students as % of students abroad
		First country	Second country		First country	Second country	
	1992-95	1992-95	1992-95	1992-95	1992-95	1992-95	1992-95
Sub-Saharan Africa							
Angola	2.6	Portugal	Russia	..	..	..	..
Benin	1.9	France	Russia	0.7	..	..	37
Botswana	1.2	UK	USA	0.3	..	..	25
Burkina Faso	1.2	France	Morocco	0.4	..	..	33
Burundi	0.7	Belgium	Canada	0.4	..	..	57
Cameroon	7.9	France	USA	0.2	..	..	3
Central African Rep.	0.5	France	USA	0.2	..	..	40
Chad	0.6	France	Algeria	0.1	..	..	17
Congo	3.7	France	Ukraine	0.2	..	..	5
Côte d' Ivoire	3.7	France	USA	..	..	..	..
Eritrea	..	,,	,,	..	..	..	..
Ethiopia	4.6	USA	Germany	0.1	..	..	2
Gabon	1.7	France	Canada	0.4	..	..	24
Gambia	0.6	USA	UK	..	..	..	..
Ghana	3.4	USA	Germany	0.1	..	..	3
Guinea	1.2	France	Canada	0.1	..	..	8
Guinea-Bissau	0.5	Portugal	Russia	..	..	..	..
Kenya	4.8	USA	India	..	..	..	..
Lesotho	0.6	South Africa	UK	0.2	..	..	33
Liberia	0.5	USA	Germany	..	..	..	..
Madagascar	3.6	France	Russia	0.3	..	..	8
Malawi	0.8	USA	UK	(.)	..	..	..
Mali	1.7	France	Russia	..	..	..	..
Mauritania	2.2	France	Tunisia	0.5	..	..	23
Mauritius	1.8	France	UK	(.)	..	..	..
Mozambique	1.3	Portugal	Cuba	0.1	..	..	8
Namibia	..	South Africa	India	0.4	..	..	..
Niger	0.8	France	Canada	..	..	..	..
Nigeria	5.7	USA	UK	..	..	..	..
Rwanda	1.0	Belgium	France	0.3	..	..	30
Senegal	4.7	France	USA	1.9	..	..	40
Sierra Leone	0.8	USA	UK	.:	..	..	..
Somalia	1.1	Italy	USA	..	..	..	..
South Africa	3.1	USA	UK	12.6	Zimbabwe	..	406
Sudan	5.0	Egypt	Syria	0.8	..	..	16
Tanzania	2.1	USA	UK	..	..	..	..
Togo	1.6	France	USA	0.2	..	..	13
Uganda	1.4	USA	UK	..	..	..	..
Zaire	5.7	Belgium	France	..	..	..	..
Zambia	1.4	UK	USA	..	..	..	..
Zimbabwe	5.1	South Africa	Cuba	..	..	..	..
Arab States							
Algeria	22.0	France	Belgium	2.6	Palestine	Morocco	12
Egypt	5.6	USA	Germany	6.8	Palestine	Kuwait	121
Iraq	2.7	Jordan	Germany	..	..	..	..
Jordan	12.8	Syria	USA	8.1	Palestine	Yemen	63
Kuwait	4.0	USA	Egypt	2.6	Jordan	Palestine	65

Country	Number of students abroad (thousands)	Major countries of study		Number of foreign students (thousands)	Major countries of origin		Foreign students as % of students abroad
		First country	Second country		First country	Second country	
	1992-95	1992-95	1992-95	1992-95	1992-95	1992-95	1992-95
Lebanon	11.1	France	USA	..	..	..	..
Libya	1.8	UK	Egypt	..	..	..	..
Morocco	32.5	France	Belgium	3.6	Tunisia	Mauritania	11
Oman	1.8	USA	UK	..	..	..	..
Saudi Arabia	5.7	USA	UK	6.4	Yemen	Palestine	112
Syria	8.5	France	Russia	13.4	Palestine	Jordan	158
Tunisia	10.5	France	Marocco	2.7	Morocco	Mauritania	26
Unit.Arab Emirates	2.5	USA	UK	0.7	..	..	28
Yemen, Rep.	6.5	Syria	Saudi Arabia	1.0	..	..	15
South Central Asia							
Afghanistan	3.2	Russia	Germany	0.2	..	..	6
Armenia	2.5	Russia	Ukraine	..	..	..	..
Azerbaijan	4.5	Russia	Turkey	1.5	..	..	33
Bangladesh	5.4	USA	Japan	0.2	..	..	4
Bhutan	0.1	India	UK	..	..	..	..
Georgia	5.5	Russia	Ukraine	..	..	..	..
India	42.3	USA	Ukraine	12.8	Nepal	Kenya	30
Iran	27.7	Germany	USA	0.4	..	..	1
Kazakhstan	15.8	Russia	Turkey	1.6	Mongolia	Syria	10
Kyrgyz Rep.	3.0	Russia	Turkey	..	..	..	..
Nepal	2.1	India	USA	..	..	..	..
Pakistan	11.4	USA	UK	0.9	Afghanistan	Palestine	8
Sri Lanka	5.1	USA	India	0.1	..	..	2
Tajikistan	1.4	Russia	Ukraine	..	..	..	..
Turkey	30.4	Germany	USA	15.0	Cyprus	Azerbaijan	49
Turkmenistan	2.7	Turkey	Russia	..	..	..	..
Uzbekistan	5.3	Russia	Turkey	..	..	..	..
East Asia							
China	126.9	USA	Japan	22.8	Japan	Korea Rep.	18
Hong Kong	33.6	USA	Australia	1.0	China	UK	3
Japan	59.5	USA	China	45.1	China	Korea Rep.	76
Korea, Dem.	2.1	Philippines	Norway	..	..	..	..
Korea, Rep.	55.9	USA	Japan	1.9	Japan	USA	3
Mongolia	1.5	Russia	Kazaklustan	0.2	..	..	13
Southeast Asia and Oceania							
Australia	5.1	USA	New Zealand	42.4	Malaysia	Hong Kong	831
Cambodia	1.6	France	Russia	..	..	..	..
Indonesia	20.7	USA	Australia	..	Malaysia	Japan	,,
Lao PDR	1.0	France	Russia	0.1	..	..	10
Malaysia	35.8	USA	UK	..	..	..	..
Myanmar	0.7	USA	Japan	..	..	..	..
New Zealand	5.7	Australia	USA	4.5	Malaysia	Fiji	79
Papua New Guinea	0.6	Australia	New Zealand	..	..	..	..
Philippines	5.5	USA	Japan	4.9	Korea Dem.	Pakistan	89
Singapore	15.3	Australia	USA	..	..	..	..
Thailand	13.3	USA	Japan	..	..	..	..
Vietnam	5.1	Germany	France	..	..	..	..

Country	Number of students abroad (thousands)	Major countries of study		Number of foreign students (thousands)	Major countries of origin		Foreign students as % of students abroad
		First country	Second country		First country	Second country	
	1992-95	1992-95	1992-95	1992-95	1992-95	1992-95	1992-95
Latin America and the Caribbean							
Argentina	4.4	USA	Spain	12.7	Peru	Chile	289
Bolivia	3.2	Argentina	USA	..	..	..	..
Brazil	11.5	USA	France	..	..	..	..
Chile	4.6	Argentina	USA	0.6	..	..	13
Colombia	5.9	USA	France	..	..	..	..
Costa Rica	1.2	USA		..	..	..	..
Cuba	0.4	Spain	USA	4.8	Zimbabwe	Angola	1,200
Dominican Rep.	1.3	USA		..	..	..	..
Ecuador	2.2	USA	Cuba	..	..	..	..
El Salvador	1.1	USA		0.2	..	..	18
Guatemala	0.9	USA	..	..	..	..	..
Haiti	1.4	USA	France	..	..	..	..
Honduras	1.1	USA	..	0.5	..	..	45
Jamaica	3.4	USA	Canada	0.1	..	..	3
Mexico	10.8	USA	France	..	..	..	..
Nicaragua	1.3	USA	Cuba	0.1	..	..	8
Panama	1.9	USA	Spain	..	..	..	..
Paraguay	1.9	Argentina	USA	..	..	..	..
Peru	8.8	Argentina	USA	..	..	..	..
Trinidad	2.5	USA	Canada	0.1	..	..	4
Uruguay	2.2	Argentina	USA	..	..	..	..
Venezuela	6.1	USA	Spain	..	..	..	..
North America							
Canada	27.4	USA	UK	35.5	Hong Kong	China	130
United States	25.7	UK	Germany	449.7	China	Japan	1,750
Europe							
Albania	1.1	Italy	France	0.5	..	..	45
Austria	8.8	Germany	USA	23.9	Italy	Germany	272
Belarus	6.6	Russia	Poland	2.7	Cebanon	Syria	41
Belgium	6.2	France	UK	27.4	Italy	Morocco	442
Bosnia	1.5	Croatia	Turkey	..	..	..	..
Bulgaria	4.2	USA	France	8.1	Greece	Moldova	193
Croatia	0.9	Austria	USA	1.3	Italy	Slovenia	144
Czech Rep.	1.2	Germany	Holy See	2.8	Slovakia	Greece	233
Denmark	3.8	USA	Norway	7.6	Iran	Norway	200
Estonia	1.9	Russia	Finland	..	..	..	..
Finland	3.1	Swden	USA	2.3	China	Sweden	74
France	27.9	UK	USA	139.6	Morocco	Algeria	500
Germany	41.7	USA	UK	116.5	Turkey	Iran	279
Greece	40.4	Germany	Italy	1.5	..	..	4
Hungary	3.4	USA	Germany	6.3	Romania	Greece	185
Ireland	9.2	UK	USA	4.2	UK	USA	46
Israel	9.2	USA	Romania	..	..	..	..
Italy	31.1	Austria	Holy See	22.6	Greece	Germany	73
Latvia	1.1	Russia	USA	0.9	..	..	82
Lithuania	0.5	Russia	Poland	0.3	..	..	60

Country	Number of students abroad (thousands)	Major countries of study		Number of foreign students (thousands)	Major countries of origin		Foreign students as % of students abroad
		First country	Second country		First country	Second country	
	1992-95	1992-95	1992-95	1992-95	1992-95	1992-95	1992-95
Macedonia, FYR	0.5	Bulgaria	Turkey	0.5	..	..	100
Moldova	7.0	Romania	Russia	1.1	..	..	16
Netherlands	9.7	Germany	Belgium	11.4	Germany	Suriname	118
Norway	7.1	USA	UK	11.3	Iran	Sweden	159
Poland	8.2	Germany	USA	5.0	Ukraine	Lithuania	61
Portugal	7.3	France	Germany	3.6	Angola	Brazil	49
Romania	5.4	France	Hungary	11.9	Greece	Moldova	220
Russia	8.7	Ukraine	USA	73.2	Ukraine	Kazakhstan	841
Slovakia	1.1	Czech Rep.	Hungary	2.1	Czech Rep.	Greece	191
Slovenia	0.8	Austria	Romania	0.5	..	..	63
Spain	19.2	USA	France	12.6	Morocco	France	66
Sweden	7.6	USA	Norway	10.7	Finland	Norway	141
Switzerland	7.0	USA	Italy	25.3	Germany	Italy	361
Ukraine	19.5	Russia	Poland	18.3	Russia	Moldova	94
United Kingdom	21.9	USA	France	95.6	Germany	Ireland	437
Yugoslavia	5.3	Germany	Netherlands	1.1	Greece	Iran	21

Region	Number of students abroad (thousands)	Number of foreign students (thousands)	Foreign students as % of students abroad
	1992-95 T	1992-95 T	1992-95
World	1,250	1,380	110
Developing	790	150	19
Industrial	460	1,230	267
Dev exc India / China	620	120	19
Ind exc USA / Russia	430	710	165
Sub-Saharan Africa	90	20	22
Arab States	130	50	38
South Central Asia	170	30	18
East Asia	280	70	25
Southeast Asia / Oc	110	50	..
Latin Am / Carib	80	20	..
North America	50	490	980
Europe	340	650	191

TABLE 24
HUMAN CAPITAL

Country	Adult literacy rate (age 15+)			Young adult literacy rate (age 15-19)	Mean years of schooling (age 25+)		
	Total (%)	Male (%)	Female (%)	(%)	Total (years)	Male (years)	Female (years)
	1995	1995	1995	1995	1992	1992	1992
Sub-Saharan Africa							
Angola	41	49	32	..	1.5	2.0	1.0
Benin	37	49	26	49	0.7	1.1	0.3
Botswana	70	81	60	88	2.5	2.6	2.5
Burkina Faso	19	30	9	..	0.2	0.3	0.2
Burundi	35	49	23	55	0.4	0.7	0.3
Cameroon	63	75	52	..	1.6	2.6	0.8
Central African Rep.	60	69	52	..	1.1	1.6	0.5
Chad	48	62	35	..	0.3	0.5	0.2
Congo	75	83	67	94	2.1	3.1	1.1
Côte d' Ivoire	40	50	30	59	1.9	2.9	0.9
Eritrea	..	..	..	..	..	..	..
Ethiopia	36	46	25	53	1.1	1.5	0.7
Gabon	63	74	53	..	2.6	3.9	1.3
Gambia	39	53	25	..	0.6	0.9	0.2
Ghana	65	76	54	..	3.5	4.9	2.2
Guinea	36	50	22	..	0.9	1.5	0.3
Guinea-Bissau	55	68	43	68	0.4	0.7	0.1
Kenya	78	86	70	93	2.3	3.1	1.3
Lesotho	71	81	62	..	3.5	2.8	4.1
Liberia	38	54	22	54	2.1	3.3	0.8
Madagascar	..	..	..	..	2.2	2.6	1.7
Malawi	56	72	42	66	1.7	2.4	1.1
Mali	31	39	23	..	0.4	0.7	0.1
Mauritania	38	50	26	52	0.4	0.7	0.1
Mauritius	83	87	79	93	4.1	4.9	3.3
Mozambique	40	58	23	59	1.6	2.2	1.2
Namibia	..	..	..	90	1.7	..	..
Niger	14	21	7	22	0.2	0.4	0.2
Nigeria	57	67	47	..	1.2	1.7	0.5
Rwanda	61	70	52	78	1.1	1.5	0.5
Senegal	33	43	23	45	0.9	1.5	0.5
Sierra Leone	31	45	18	..	0.9	1.4	0.4
Somalia	..	..	..	..	0.3	0.5	0.2
South Africa	82	82	82	..	3.9	4.1	3.7
Sudan	46	58	35	67	0.8	1.0	0.5
Tanzania	68	79	57	..	2.0	2.8	1.3
Togo	52	67	37	72	1.6	2.4	0.8
Uganda	62	74	50	75	1.1	1.6	0.6
Zaire	77	87	68	..	1.6	2.4	0.8
Zambia	78	86	71	88	2.7	3.7	1.7
Zimbawe	85	90	80	95	3.1	4.5	1.8
Arab States							
Algeria	62	74	49	84	2.8	4.8	0.9
Egypt	56	64	39	70	3.0	4.2	1.7
Iraq	58	71	45	..	5.0	5.9	4.0
Jordan	87	93	79	98	5.0	6.0	4.0
Kuwait	79	82	75	94	5.5	6.1	4.8

Country	Adult literacy rate (age 15+)			Young adult literacy rate (age 15-19)	Mean years of schooling (age 25+)		
	Total (%)	Male (%)	Female (%)	(%)	Total (years)	Male (years)	Female (years)
	1995	1995	1995	1995	1992	1992	1992
Lebanon	92	95	90	..	4.4	5.3	3.5
Libya	76	88	63	96	3.5	5.7	1.4
Morocco	44	57	31	58	3.0	4.4	1.6
Oman	..	..	..	..	0.9	1.4	0.3
Saudi Arabia	63	72	50	..	3.9	6.3	1.6
Syria	71	86	56	86	4.2	5.2	3.1
Tunisia	67	79	55	89	2.1	3.1	1.2
Unit.Arab. Emirates	79	79	80	93	5.6	5.6	5.7
Yemen, Rep.	46	69	23	..	0.9	1.5	0.2
South Central Asia							
Afghanistan	32	47	15	..	0.9	1.6	0.2
Armenia	100	100	100	100	..	..	..
Azerbaijan	98	100	96	100	..	..	..
Bangladesh	38	49	26	44	2.0	3.1	0.9
Bhutan	42	56	28	..	0.3	0.5	0.2
Georgia	99	100	99	..	..	..	..
India	52	66	38	64	2.4	3.5	1.2
Iran	69	78	59	92	3.9	4.6	3.1
Kazakhstan	98	99	96	100	..	..	..
Kygyz Rep.	97	99	96	..	..	..	..
Nepal	28	41	14	39	2.1	3.2	1.0
Pakistan	38	50	24	46	1.9	2.9	0.7
Sri Lanka	90	93	87	93	7.2	8.0	6.3
Tajikistan	100	100	100	100	..	..	..
Turkey	82	92	72	94	3.6	4.9	2.4
Turkmenistan	100	100	100	100	..	..	..
Uzbekistan	100	100	100	100	..	..	..
East Asia							
China	82	90	73	96	5.0	6.3	3.8
Hong Kong	92	96	88	..	7.2	8.8	5.5
Japan	..	..	..	..	10.8	10.9	10.7
Korea, Dem.	..	..	..	..	6.0	7.4	4.6
Korea, Rep.	98	99	97	100	9.3	11.6	7.1
Mongolia	83	89	77	..	7.2	7.4	7.0
Southeast Asia and Oceania							
Australia	..	..	..	..	12.0	12.1	11.9
Cambodia	65	80	53	..	2.0	2.3	1.7
Indonesia	84	90	78	98	4.1	5.3	3.1
Lao PDR	57	69	44	..	2.9	3.6	2.1
Malaysia	84	89	78	94	5.6	5.9	5.2
Myanmar	83	89	78	88	2.5	3.0	2.1
New Zealand	..	..	..	..	10.7	10.5	10.9
Papau New Guinea	72	81	63	..	1.0	1.3	0.7
Philippines	95	95	94	97	7.6	8.0	7.2
Singapore	91	96	86	99	4.0	4.8	3.2
Thailand	94	96	92	99	3.9	4.4	3.4
Vietnam	94	96	91	97	4.9	6.2	3.6

Country	Adult literacy rate (age 15+)			Young adult literacy rate (age 15-19)	Mean years of schooling (age 25+)		
	Total (%)	Male (%)	Female (%)	(%)	Total (years)	Male (years)	Female (years)
	1995	1995	1995	1995	1992	1992	1992
Latin America and the Caribbean							
Argentina	96	96	96	98	9.2	9.0	9.5
Bolivia	83	91	76	95	4.0	5.0	3.0
Brazil	83	83	83	90	4.0	4.1	3.9
Chile	95	95	95	99	7.8	8.1	7.4
Colombia	91	91	91	95	7.5	7.3	7.7
Costa Rica	95	95	95	98	5.7	5.8	5.6
Cuba	96	96	95	100	8.0	7.9	8.1
Domincan Rep.	82	82	82	89	4.3	4.6	4.0
Ecuador	90	92	88	97	5.6	5.8	5.3
El Salvador	71	74	70	86	4.2	4.4	4.0
Guatemala	56	63	49	..	4.1	4.4	3.8
Haití	45	48	42	62	1.7	2.0	2.3
Honduras	73	73	73	..	4.0	4.1	3.8
Jamaica	85	81	89	90	5.3	5.3	5.2
Mexico	90	92	87	98	4.9	5.0	4.8
Nicaragua	66	65	67	..	4.5	4.3	4.7
Panama	91	91	90	96	6.8	6.6	7.0
Paraguay	92	94	91	96	4.9	5.2	4.6
Peru	89	95	83	97	6.5	7.3	5.8
Trinidad	98	99	97	100	8.4	8.4	8.5
Uruguay	97	97	98	99	8.1	7.7	8.6
Venezuela	91	92	90	96	6.5	6.6	6.4
North America							
Canada	..	..	..	..	12.2	12.4	12.0
United States	..	..	..	..	12.4	12.3	12.5
Europe							
Albania	..	..	..	..	6.2	7.2	5.2
Austria	..	..	..	..	11.4	12.0	10.8
Belarus	99	100	99	100	..	..	..
Belgium	..	..	..	..	11.2	11.2	11.2
Bosnia	..	..	..	..	..	..	..
Bulgaria	98	99	97	99	7.0	7.6	6.4
Croatia	97	99	95	100	..	..	..
Czech Rep.	..	..	..	..	..	..	..
Denmark	..	..	..	..	11.0	11.1	10.9
Estonia	100	100	100	100	..	..	..
Finland	..	..	..	..	10.9	11.0	10.8
France	..	..	..	..	12.0	11.9	12.1
Germany	..	..	..	..	11.6	12.2	11.1
Greece	97	98	95	100	7.0	7.4	6.6
Hungary	99	99	99	99	9.8	9.7	9.9
Ireland	..	..	..	..	8.9	8.8	9.0
Israel	95	97	93	99	10.2	11.1	9.2
Italy	98	99	97	100	7.5	7.6	7.5
Latvia	100	100	100	100	..	..	..
Lithuania	99	100	99	100	..	..	..

Country	Adult literacy rate (age 15+)			Young adult literacy rate (age 15-19)	Mean years of schooling (age 25+)		
	Total (%)	Male (%)	Female (%)	(%)	Total (years)	Male (years)	Female (years)
	1995	1995	1995	1995	1992	1992	1992
Macedonia, FYR	..	..	..	..	..	..	..
Moldova	99	98	100	100	..	..	..
Netherlands	..	..	..	..	11.1	10.9	11.4
Norway	..	..	..	..	12.1	12.2	11.9
Poland	100	100	100	100	8.2	8.5	7.8
Portugal	90	93	87	99	6.4	7.3	5.6
Romania	98	99	97	99	7.1	7.5	6.7
Russia	99	100	99	100	..	..	..
Slovakia	..	..	..	..	..	..	..
Slovenia	99	100	99	100	..	..	..
Spain	97	98	96	100	6.9	7.1	6.6
Sweden	..	..	..	..	11.4	11.4	11.4
Switzerland	..	..	..	..	11.6	12.0	11.2
Ukraine	99	98	99	100	..	..	..
United Kingdom	..	..	..	..	11.7	11.6	11.8
Yugoslavia	98	99	97	100	..	..	..

Region	Adult literacy rate (age 15+)			Young adult literacy rate (age 15-19)	Mean years of schooling (age 25+)		
	Total (%)	Male (%)	Female (%)	(%)	Total (years)	Male (years)	Female (years)
	1995	1995	1995	1995	1992	1992	1992
World	..	..	..	..	4.9	5.8	4.1
Developing	70	79	62	82	3.7	4.7	2.8
Industrial	..	..	..	..	10.8	10.9	10.7
Dev exc India / China	71	78	64	81	3.6	4.3	2.8
Ind exc USA / Russia	..	..	..	..	10.2	10.4	10.0
Sub-Saharan Africa	57	67	47	66	1.6	2.2	1.0
Arab States	57	68	44	76	3.2	4.6	1.9
South Central Asia	54	66	41	65	2.5	3.5	1.3
East Asia	83	90	74	..	5.7	6.9	4.5
Southeast Asia / Oc	87	91	83	97	4.8	5.7	4.1
Latin Am / Carib	87	88	86	94	5.4	5.5	5.3
North America	..	..	..	..	12.4	12.3	12.5
Europe	..	..	..	..	9.8	10.0	9.6

TABLE 25
DEMOGRAPHY AND HEALTH

Country	Population (millions)	Urban population (as % of total population)	Life expectancy at birth (years)	Average female age at first marriage	Average family size	Total fertility rate	Fertility in young women. Number of births to a thousand women from age 15 to 19	Contraceptive prevalence rate (% of females 15-45)	Maternal mortality rate (per 100,000 live births)
	1996	1994	1995	1980-90	1980-90	1995	1991 to 1996	1990-94	1993
Sub-Saharan Africa									
Angola	11.2	36	46	17.9	..	7.2	1,180	..	1,500
Benin	5.6	41	54	18.3	5.4	6.3	720	9	2,500
Botswana	1.5	30	54	26.4	4.8	4.8	500	33	220
Burkina Faso	10.8	25	46	17.4	6.2	7.1	785	8	940
Burundi	6.2	7	45	21.9	5.2	6.8	300	9	1,330
Cameroon	13.6	44	55	18.8	5.2	5.7	705	16	510
C.A.R.	3.3	39	48	17.3	5.1	5.3	735	15	650
Chad	6.5	21	47	16.5	..	5.9	960	..	1,590
Congo	2.7	58	51	19.6	5.3	6.3	730	..	890
Côte d' Ivoire	14.0	43	52	18.9	..	5.7	755	11	820
Eritrea	3.3	17	50	..	..	5.8	700	8	1,400
Ethiopia	58.2	13	47	17.5	..	7.0	845	4	1,530
Gabon	1.1	49	54	17.7	..	5.0	795	..	440
Gambia	1.1	25	45	..	3.4	5.6	855	12	1,050
Ghana	17.8	36	56	19.4	4.8	5.7	615	20	740
Guinea	7.5	29	44	16.0	6.7	7.0	1,205	2	1,600
Guinea-Bissau	1.1	22	43	18.3	..	5.8	945	..	910
Kenya	27.8	27	54	20.3	5.2	5.4	550	33	650
Lesotho	2.1	22	58	20.5	..	5.2	455	23	600
Liberia	2.2	48	46	19.4	5.0	6.8	1,150	6	560
Madagascar	15.4	26	56	20.3	4.5	6.1	775	17	660
Malawi	9.8	13	42	17.8	4.3	7.2	865	13	620
Mali	11.1	26	46	16.4	5.0	7.1	945	5	1,250
Mauritania	2.3	52	51	19.4	5.5	5.4	665	4	800
Mauritius	1.1	41	70	21.7	4.8	2.3	230	75	110
Mozambique	17.8	33	46	17.6	4.3	6.5	655	4	1,510
Namibia	1.6	36	56	..	..	5.3	555	29	370
Niger	9.5	22	47	15.8	..	7.4	1,095	4	590
Nigeria	115.0	38	50	18.7	..	6.4	750	6	1,030
Rwanda	5.4	6	42	21.2	4.6	6.5	300	21	1,300
Senegal	8.5	42	49	18.3	..	6.1	775	7	510
Sierra Leone	4.3	35	34		..	6.5	1,060	..	800
Somalia	9.8	28	47	20.1	..	7.0	1,040	..	1,600
South Africa	42.4	50	63	22.8	..	4.1	360	50	400
Sudan	27.3	27	51	18.7	6.3	5.0	295	9	660
Tanzania	30.8	24	50	18.6	..	5.9	670	20	750
Togo	4.2	30	51	18.6	5.1	6.6	630	12	630
Uganda	20.3	12	41	17.7	4.5	7.1	900	5	550
Zaire	46.8	31	52	20.1	5.5	6.7	1,155	8	870
Zambia	8.3	43	44	19.4	5.0	6.0	725	15	230
Zimbabwe	11.4	31	51	20.4	5.2	5.2	645	48	80
Arab States									
Algeria	28.8	55	67	21.0	7.0	4.3	130	51	140
Egypt	63.3	45	64	21.4	5.5	3.8	310	47	170
Iraq	20.6	77	59	20.8	6.3	5.7	245	14	310
Jordan	5.6	71	68	22.6	6.6	5.6	245	35	130
Kuwait	1.7	97	75	22.9	6.5	3.1	205	35	18

Country	Population (millions)	Urban population (as % of total population)	Life expectancy at birth (years)	Average female age at first marriage	Average family size	Total fertility rate	Fertility in young women. Number of births to a thousand women from age 15 to 19	Contraceptive prevalence rate (% of females 15-45)	Maternal mortality rate (per 100,000 live births)
	1996	1994	1995	1980-90	1980-90	1995	1991 to 1996	1990-94	1993
Lebanon	3.1	63	69	..	..	3.1	160	53	300
Libya	5.6	88	63	18.7	..	6.4	550	..	220
Morocco	27.0	48	64	22.3	6.0	3.8	185	42	610
Oman	2.3	13	70	..	..	7.2	610	9	180
Saudi Arabia	18.8	80	70	..	..	6.4	620	..	110
Syria	14.6	55	67	20.7	6.3	4.7	285	40	180
Tunisia	9.2	57	68	24.3	5.6	3.3	85	50	140
U.A.E.	2.3	83	74	18.0	5.2	3.8	395	..	20
Yemen, Rep.	15.7	33	55	17.8	6.8	7.6	510	7	1,470
South Central Asia									
Afghanistan	20.9	22	43	17.8	6.2	6.9	765	2	1,700
Armenia	3.6	69	71	..	..	2.2	260	22	35
Azerbaijan	7.6	56	71	..	..	2.6	110	17	29
Bangladesh	120.1	18	56	16.7	5.7	3.4	690	45	890
Bhutan	1.8	6	51	..	..	5.9	430	..	
Georgia	5.4	58	73	..	..	2.1	255	17	55
India	944.6	27	60	18.7	5.5	3.4	580	41	440
Iran	70.0	58	67	19.7	5.0	5.3	480	65	120
Kazakhstan	16.8	59	68	..	..	2.6	175	30	50
Kyrgyz Rep.	4.5	39	68	..	..	3.6	225	31	43
Nepal	22.0	13	55	17.9	5.8	5.4	460	25	1,500
Pakistan	140.0	34	62	19.8	6.7	5.5	465	12	340
Sri Lanka	18.1	22	72	24.4	5.0	2.2	170	62	30
Tajikistan	5.9	32	67	..	..	4.3	180	21	39
Turkey	61.8	67	67	20.6	5.2	2.7	295	63	180
Turkmenistan	4.2	45	65	..	..	4.0	110	20	55
Uzbekistan	23.2	41	68	..	..	3.8	195	28	43
East Asia									
China	1,232.1	29	69	22.4	4.0	1.9	25	77	120
Hong Kong	6.2	95	78	25.3	3.7	1.3	35	81	7
Japan	125.4	78	79	25.1	3.0	1.5	20	64	18
Korea, Dem.	22.5	..	71	..	..	2.1	25	..	70
Korea, Rep.	45.3	80	71	24.1	4.1	1.6	20	79	30
Mongolia	2.5	60	64	..	..	3.6	155	..	240
Southeast Asia and Oceania									
Australia	18.1	85	78	23.5	3.0	1.9	110	76	9
Cambodia	10.3	24	52	21.3	..	4.9	60	..	900
Indonesia	200.4	34	63	21.1	4.8	2.9	310	55	650
Lao PDR	5.0	21	51	..	..	6.7	255	19	660
Malaysia	20.6	53	71	23.5	5.1	3.6	145	48	34
Myanmar	45.9	26	58	22.4	5.2	3.6	175	17	520
New Zealand	3.6	86	76	22.7	2.9	2.1	170	70	25
P.N.G.	4.4	16	56	..	4.5	5.0	115	5	700
Philippines	69.3	53	66	22.4	5.6	4.0	240	40	210
Singapore	3.4	100	76	26.2	4.7	1.8	40	74	10
Thailand	58.7	20	69	22.7	4.6	1.9	255	66	160
Vietnam	75.2	21	65	..	4.8	3.4	225	65	110

Country	Population (millions)	Urban population (as % of total population)	Life expectancy at birth (years)	Average female age at first marriage	Average family size	Total fertility rate	Fertility in young women. Number of births to a thousand women from age 15 to 19	Contraceptive prevalence rate (% of females 15-45)	Maternal mortality rate (per 100,000 live births)
	1996	1994	1995	1980-90	1980-90	1995	1991 to 1996	1990-94	1993
Latin America and the Caribbean									
Argentina	35.2	88	72	22.9	3.9	2.8	350	74	140
Bolivia	7.6	58	59	22.1	4.4	4.8	410	45	370
Brazil	161.1	77	66	22.6	4.4	2.4	365	66	200
Chile	14.4	86	75	23.6	4.5	2.5	280	43	65
Colombia	36.4	72	70	22.6	5.1	2.9	400	66	110
Costa Rica	3.5	49	76	21.7	4.7	3.1	265	75	60
Cuba	11.0	78	75	19.9	4.1	1.6	335	70	95
Dom. Rep.	8.0	64	70	19.7	4.8	3.1	455	56	110
Ecuador	11.7	58	69	21.1	4.8	3.5	395	57	150
El Salvador	5.8	45	68	19.4	5.0	3.5	525	53	300
Guatemala	10.9	41	65	20.5	5.2	5.4	615	23	460
Haiti	7.3	31	54	23.8	..	4.8	270	18	600
Honduras	5.8	47	68	20.0	5.7	4.9	635	47	220
Jamaica	2.5	55	74	25.2	4.2	2.6	475	62	120
Mexico	92.7	75	71	20.6	5.5	3.1	385	53	110
Nicaragua	4.2	62	66	20.2	..	4.4	745	49	160
Panama	2.7	54	73	21.2	4.6	2.9	455	58	55
Paraguay	5.0	52	69	21.8	5.2	4.5	435	48	180
Peru	23.9	72	67	22.7	5.1	3.4	315	59	280
Trinidad	1.3	66	73	22.3	4.2	2.3	300	53	90
Uruguay	3.2	90	73	22.4	3.3	2.3	310	..	85
Venezuela	22.3	92	72	21.2	5.3	3.3	505	49	200
North America									
Canada	29.7	77	78	26.1	2.8	1.7	130	73	6
U.S.A.	269.4	76	76	23.3	2.6	2.1	315	71	12
Europe									
Albania	3.4	37	71	..	..	2.8	70	..	65
Austria	8.1	55	76	25.7	2.7	1.5	110	71	10
Belarus	10.3	70	70	..	3.8	1.7	140	50	25
Belgium	10.2	97	76	24.9	2.7	1.6	45	79	10
Bosnia	3.6	49	72	23.3	..	1.5	155	..	..
Bulgaria	8.5	70	71	21.9	2.9	1.5	300	76	27
Croatia	4.5	64	71	23.2	..	1.6	160	..	..
Czech Rep.	10.3	65	72	21.5	..	1.7	210	69	15
Denmark	5.2	85	75	28.2	2.4	1.8	45	78	9
Estonia	1.5	73	69	23.0	..	1.6	165	36	41
Finland	5.1	63	76	26.9	2.6	1.8	55	80	11
France	58.3	73	78	26.1	2.7	1.7	45	75	15
Germany	81.9	86	76	26.0	2.4	1.3	65	15	22
Greece	10.5	65	78	24.4	3.1	1.4	90	..	10
Hungary	10.0	64	69	21.6	2.8	1.7	175	73	30
Ireland	3.5	57	76	25.9	3.7	2.0	75	60	10
Israel	5.7	90	77	23.5	3.5	2.9	95	..	7
Italy	57.2	67	77	25.6	3.0	1.2	40	78	12
Latvia	2.5	73	68	22.4	2.4	1.6	175	32	40
Lithuania	3.7	71	70	..	..	1.8	130	20	29

Country	Population (millions)	Urban population (as % of total population)	Life expectancy at birth (years)	Average female age at first marriage	Average family size	Total fertility rate	Fertility in young women. Number of births to a thousand women from age 15 to 19	Contraceptive prevalence rate (% of females 15-45)	Maternal mortality rate (per 100,000 live births)
	1996	1994	1995	1980-90	1980-90	1995	1991 to 1996	1990-94	1993
Macedonia, FYR	2.2	59	71	22.8	..	2.1	220	..	..
Moldova	4.4	51	68	..	..	2.1	195	22	34
Netherlands	15.6	89	77	26.6	2.5	1.6	35	74	12
Norway	4.3	73	77	26.2	2.7	1.9	80	76	6
Poland	38.6	64	71	21.6	3.1	1.9	140	75	19
Portugal	9.8	35	74	24.5	3.3	1.5	110	66	15
Romania	22.7	55	70	22.1	3.1	1.5	235	57	130
Russia	148.1	73	66	..	2.9	1.5	405	67	52
Slovakia	5.3	58	71	21.2	..	1.8	215	74	..
Slovenia	1.9	63	73	24.1	..	1.4	140	92	13
Spain	39.7	76	77	25.3	3.5	1.3	50	59	7
Sweden	8.8	83	78	27.8	2.2	2.0	60	78	7
Switzerland	7.2	61	78	27.3	2.5	1.5	25	71	6
Ukraine	51.6	70	69	17.4	3.7	1.6	215	23	33
U.K.	58.1	89	76	25.7	2.7	1.8	..	72	9
Yugoslavia	10.3	56	72	23.8	..	1.9	205	55	..

Region	Population (millions)	Urban population as % of total population	Life expectancy at birth (years)	Average female age at first marriage	Average family size	Total fertility rate	Fertility in young women. Number of births to a thousand women from age 15 to 19	Contraceptive prevalence rate (% of females 15-45)	Maternal mortality rate (per 100,000 live births)
	1995	1994	1995	1980-90	1980-90	1995	1991 to 1996	1990-94	1993
World	5,750	45	65	21.3	4.5	3.1	325	53	310
Developing	4,570	37	63	20.7	4.9	3.4	360	50	380
Industrial	1,180	74	74	24.1	2.8	1.7	185	63	22
Dev exc India / China	2,390	45	61	20.5	5.2	4.2	445	40	490
Ind exc USA / Russia	760	74	75	24.4	2.9	1.6	90	60	20
Sub-Saharan Africa	600	31	50	19.0	5.2	6.2	750	14	920
Arab States	220	56	65	21.1	6.1	4.7	300	39	320
South Central Asia	1,470	31	61	18.8	5.6	3.7	540	39	450
East Asia	1,430	35	70	22.7	3.9	1.9	25	76	110
Southeast Asia / Oc	520	35	65	21.9	4.9	3.1	245	52	390
Latin Am / Carib	480	74	69	21.9	4.8	3.0	390	59	180
North America	300	76	76	23.6	2.6	2.1	295	71	11
Europe	730	73	73	24.2	2.9	1.6	170	59	28

TABLE 26
MIGRATION AND REFUGEES

| Country | International migrants | | | Remittances from abroad (% of total foreign earnings) | Refugees | |
| | Number (thousands) | Percent female | Percent of total population foreign born | | By country of origin (thousands) | By country of asylum (thousands) |
	1990	1990	1990	1992-94	1995	1995
Sub-Saharan Africa						
Angola	28	49	0.3	..	284	11
Benin	48	49	1.0	17.8	..	70
Botswana	22	44	1.8	2.5	..	1
Burkina Faso	418	52	4.7	28.2	..	50
Burundi	333	50	6.1	..	389	300
Cameroon	269	46	2.4	..	..	44
C.A.R.	57	50	2.0	..	..	48
Chad	11	48	0.3	..	212	(.)
Congo	120	50	5.9	..	..	16
Côte d' Ivoire	3,440	45	29.3	..	..	360
Eritrea	..	..	..	..	422	..
Ethiopia	777	50	12.1	3.7	188	348
Gabon	100	43	8.9	..	..	1
Gambia	101	47	11.2	..	..	2
Ghana	137	46	0.9	1.7	12	119
Guinea	97	50	1.7	..	..	577
Guinea-Bissau	17	50	1.8	2.3	..	24
Kenya	168	50	0.7	1.2	8	252
Lesotho	24	48	1.4	57.0	..	(.)
Liberia	127	45	5.0	..	794	120
Madagascar	35	38	0.3	1.8	..	(.)
Malawi	1,105	50	12.1	..	..	90
Mali	110	50	1.2	22.9	173	16
Mauritania	65	43	3.3	0.5	68	82
Mauritius	9	44	0.8	..	..	..
Mozambique	7	57	0.1	16.0	235	(.)
Namibia	8	48	0.6	..	..	1
Niger	115	52	1.5	4.1	22	15
Nigeria	254	39	0.3	5.3	..	6
Rwanda	69	48	1.0	2.3	2,257	6
Senegal	178	45	2.5	6.5	26	73
Sierra Leone	198	40	5.0	..	275	16
Somalia	622	50	7.2	..	536	..
South Africa	1,118	32	3.1	2.4	..	92
Sudan	803	49	3.3	25.1	399	745
Tanzania	580	50	2.3	..	..	883
Togo	143	52	4.1	5.1	168	12
Uganda	330	43	1.9	..	26	287
Zaire	1,041	48	2.8	..	72	1,724
Zambia	325	49	4.1	..	..	141
Zimbawe	775	45	8.0	0.1	..	2
Arab States						
Algeria	370	49	1.5	1.8	20	219
Egypt	176	47	0.3	31.1	..	7
Iraq	500	33	2.8	..	702	120
Jordan	1,112	50	26.4	26.3	..	1
Kuwait	1,503	43	71.7	..	..	30

| Country | International migrants | | | Remittances from abroad (% of total foreign earnings) | Refugees | |
| | Number (thousands) | Percent female | Percent of total population foreign born | | By country of origin (thousands) | By country of asylum (thousands) |
	1990	1990	1990	1992-94	1995	1995
Lebanon	314	50	11.2	..	..	1
Libya	550	30	12.3	..	..	2
Morocco	42	49	0.2	23.4	167	(.)
Oman	575	28	33.6	0.7	..	..
Saudi Arabia	4,038	33	25.8	..	..	18
Syrian	800	49	6.6	11.3	..	40
Tunisia	38	50	0.5	9.0	..	(.)
U.A.E.	1,478	33	90.2	..	..	(.)
Yemen, Rep.	65	30	0.6	..	..	14
South Central Asia						
Afghanistan	30	33	0.2	..	2,744	19
Armenia	..	..	..	..	202	304
Azerbaijan	..	..	..	..	299	232
Bangladesh	800	46	0.7	25.5	54	116
Bhutan	..	..	..	..	103	..
Georgia	..	..	..	..	..	..
India	8,660	48	1.0	9.3	..	287
Iran	3,588	49	6.2	..	50	2,236
Kazakhstan	..	..	..	..	..	5
Kygyz Rep.	..	..	..	..	..	21
Nepal	401	72	2.1	..	..	123
Pakistan	7,272	47	6.1	14.7	..	1,055
Sri Lanka	21	42	0.1	15.2	77	(.)
Tajikstan	..	..	..	..	42	1
Turkey	1,102	50	2.0	9.6	17	25
Turkmenistan	..	..	..	..	..	15
Uzbekistan	..	..	..	..	29	58
East Asia						
China	346	46	(.)	1.0	109	287
Hong Kong	..	..	40.6	..	..	2
Japan	868	49	0.7	0.1	..	9
Korea, Dem.	39	33	0.2	..	..	..
Korea, Rep.	900	42	2.1	0.5	..	..
Mongolia	10	46	0.5	..	..	..
Southeast Asia and Oceania						
Australia	4,266	49	23.4	2.2	..	32
Cambodia	22	40	0.3	..	1	(.)
Indonesia	96	49	0.1	0.8	9	(.)
Lao PDR	14	46	0.4	2.9	15	..
Malaysia	745	51	4.2	0.2	..	5
Myanmar	100	46	0.2	0.5	204	..
New Zealand	519	50	15.5	7.0	..	10
P.N.G.	27	46	0.7	0.7	..	9
Philippines	38	46	0.1	13.4	..	1
Singapore	418	53	15.5	..	..	(.)
Thailand	314	49	0.6	2.5	..	101
Vietnam	21	49	(.)	..	307	5

Country	International migrants			Remittances from abroad (% of total foreign earnings)	Refugees	
	Number (thousands)	Percent female	Percent of total population foreign born		By country of origin (thousands)	By country of asylum (thousands)
	1990	1990	1990	1992-94	1995	1995
Latin America and the Caribbean						
Argentina	1,661	52	5.1	..	..	12
Bolivia	65	48	1.0	0.4	..	1
Brazil	1,011	47	0.7	0.2	..	2
Chile	106	36	0.8	..	..	(.)
Colombia	101	50	0.3	6.3	..	(.)
Costa Rica	177	61	5.9	..	..	25
Cuba	68	26	0.6	..	1	2
Dominican Rep.	174	36	2.5	13.1	..	1
Ecuador	78	50	0.9	..	..	(.)
El Salvador	50	50	1.0	36.8	17	(.)
Guatemala	44	51	0.5	10.5	45	5
Haiti	18	57	0.3	..	..	..
Honduras	34	50	0.7	10.4	..	(.)
Jamaica	19	56	0.8	9.1	..	(.)
Mexico	339	50	0.4	7.6	..	48
Nicaragua	75	50	2.1	5.5	23	(.)
Panama	61	47	2.6	..	..	1
Paraguay	185	48	4.3	1.7	..	(.)
Peru	67	50	0.3	..	..	1
Trinidad	61	51	5.0	1.2	..	..
Uruguay	93	54	3.0	..	..	(.)
Venezuela	1,027	49	5.3	(.)	..	2
North America						
Canada	4,266	51	15.5	0.7	..	142
United States	19,603	51	7.9	0.1	..	592
Europe						
Albania	13	53	0.4	56.8	..	3
Austria	450	44	5.8	1.5	..	19
Belarus	..	..	..	..	..	2
Belgium	898	46	9.0	..	..	20
Bosnia	..	..	..	..	321	..
Bulgaria	22	53	0.2	..	..	1
Croatia	..	..	..	..	78	184
Czech Rep.	..	..	..	..	..	1
Denmark	211	49	4.1	..	..	27
Estonia	..	..	..	..	..	..
Finland	62	50	1.2	0.1	..	11
France	5,897	49	10.4	1.2	..	152
Germany	5,037	44	6.4	0.4	..	1,005
Greece	322	50	3.2	15.8	..	8
Hungary	30	53	0.3	..	..	3
Ireland	326	50	9.3	..	..	(.)
Israel	1,427	52	30.9	5.6	75	..
Italy	1,549	56	2.7	0.8	..	13
Latvia	..	..	..	..	..	..
Lithuania	..	..	..	..	..	..

Country	International migrants			Remittances from abroad (% of total foreign earnings)	Refugees	
	Number (thousands) 1990	Percent female 1990	Percent of total population foreign born 1990	1992-94	By country of origin (thousands) 1995	By country of asylum (thousands) 1995
Macedonia, FYR	..	..	..	..	..	15
Moldova	..	..	..	..	..	..
Netherlands	1,167	42	7.8	0.5	..	31
Norway	186	50	4.4	0.2	..	10
Poland	1,350	51	3.6	..	..	(.)
Portugal	141	52	1.4	15.1	..	1
Romania	140	57	0.6	0.1	..	1
Russia	..	..	..	..	..	50
Slovakia	..	..	..	..	..	(.)
Slovenia	..	..	..	..	15	30
Spain	719	52	1.8	2.3	..	5
Sweden	761	52	8.9	0.3	..	37
Switzerland	1,092	44	11.0	0.8	..	27
Ukraine	..	..	..	..	..	5
United Kingdom	3,718	52	6.5	..	..	20
Yugoslavia	400	54	1.7	..	39	196

Region	International migrants			Remittances from abroad (% of total foreign earnings)	Refugees	
	Number (millions) 1990	Percent female 1990	Percent of total population foreign born 1990	1992-94	By country of origin (thousands) 1995	By country of asylum (thousands) 1995
	T				T	T
World	111.8	47	2.4	..	..	14.7
Developing	56.3	46	1.6	..	..	12.0
Industrial	55.5	51	6.2	..	..	2.7
Dev exc India / China	47.2	45	2.8	..	..	11.4
Ind exc USA / Russia	35.8	51	5.5	..	..	2.0
Sub-Saharan Africa	14.2	45	3.8	..	6.5	6.5
Arab States	11.6	46	6.3	..	..	0.5
South Central Asia	21.9	48	1.8	..	3.6	4.5
East Asia	2.2	38	0.3	..	..	0.3
Southeast Asia / Oc	6.6	48	1.4	..	..	0.2
Latin Am / Carib	5.5	46	1.3	..	..	0.1
North America	23.9	51	8.7	..	..	0.7
Europe	25.9	51	5.4	..	..	1.9

TABLE 27
ECONOMIC

Country	GNP per capita (US Dollars)	PPP estimates of GNP per capita (Current int'l $)	Ratio of household income share		Labour force participation rates (% age 15-64)	
			Richest 10% to poorest 10%	Richest 20% to poorest 20%	Male	Female
	1995	1995	1980 -94	1980 -94	1995	1995
Sub-Saharan Africa						
Angola	410	1,310	..	..	91	54
Benin	370	1,760	..	..	88	77
Botswana	3,020	5,580	..	16.4	79	39
Burkina Faso	230	780	..	..	94	77
Burundi	160	630	..	..	96	79
Cameroon	650	2,110	..	..	87	41
C.A.R.	340	1,070	..	..	92	70
Chad	180	700	..	..	90	23
Congo	680	2,050	..	..	88	53
Côte d' Ivoire	660	1,580	10.2	6.5	93	51
Eritrea	..	..	..	..	..	..
Ethiopia	100	450	..	4.8	91	53
Gabon	3,490	..	..	..	78	45
Gambia	320	930	..	..	..	..
Ghana	390	1,990	8.0	5.3	78	49
Guinea	550	..	35.2	16.7	96	59
Guinea-Bissau	250	790	84.8	28.0	91	57
Kenya	280	1,380	39.8	18.3	82	51
Lesotho	770	1,780	48.2	21.5	89	60
Liberia	..	..	..	..	85	36
Madagascar	230	640	15.2	8.6	90	55
Malawi	170	750	..	..	94	57
Mali	250	550	..	..	92	16
Mauritania	460	1,540	43.4	12.9	85	26
Mauritius	3,380	13,210	..	..	85	31
Mozambique	80	810	..	..	93	78
Namibia	2,000	4,150	..	..	85	26
Niger	220	750	9.8	5.9	95	80
Nigeria	280	1,220	24.1	12.3	85	43
Rwanda	180	540	5.8	4.0	96	80
Senegal	600	1,780	30.6	16.7	87	52
Sierra Leone	180	580	..	..	89	40
Somalia	..	..	..	..	92	55
South Africa	3,160	5,030	33.8	19.2	75	42
Sudan	..	..	..	..	87	27
Tanzania	120	640	10.4	6.6	86	73
Togo	310	1,130	..	..	88	46
Uganda	240	1,470	11.1	7.1	92	60
Zaire	120	490	..	..	90	47
Zambia	400	930	20.9	12.9	89	36
Zimbabwe	540	2,030	46.9	15.6	82	41
Arab States						
Algeria	1,600	5,300	11.3	6.7	76	8
Egypt	790	3,820	6.8	4.7	84	10
Iraq	..	..	..	..	78	24
Jordan	1,510	4,060	14.5	8.5	72	10
Kuwait	17,390	23,790	..	..	94	25

Country	GNP per capita (US Dollars)	PPP estimates of GNP per capita (Current int'l $)	Ratio of household income share		Labour force participation rates (% age 15-64)	
			Richest 10% to poorest 10%	Richest 20% to poorest 20%	Male	Female
	1995	1995	1980 -94	1980 -94	1995	1995
Lebanon	2,660	..	..	..	77	22
Libya	..	..	..	..	79	10
Morocco	1,110	3,340	10.9	7.0	88	23
Oman	4,820	8,140	..	..	81	10
Saudi Arabia	7,040	9,480	..	..	81	10
Syria	1,120	5,320	..	..	79	17
Tunisia	1,820	5,000	13.3	7.8	83	28
U.A.E.	17,400	16,470	..	..	90	19
Yemen, Rep.	280	..	..	..	90	12
South Central Asia						
Afghanistan	..	..	..	..	85	9
Armenia	730	2,260	..	..	79	69
Azerbaijan	480	1,460	..	..	78	56
Bangladesh	240	1,380	5.8	4.0	84	8
Bhutan	420	1,260	..	..	96	43
Georgia	440	1,470	..	..	80	64
India	340	1,400	7.7	5.0	90	31
Iran	..	5,470	..	..	93	23
Kazakhstan	1,330	3,010	8.0	5.4	82	68
Kyrgyz Rep.	700	1,800	..	22.8	78	65
Nepal	200	1,170	6.3	4.3	91	43
Pakistan	460	2,230	7.4	4.7	90	16
Sri Lanka	700	3,250	6.6	4.4	82	30
Tajikistan	340	920	..	..	78	56
Turkey	2,780	5,580	..	..	87	48
Turkmenistan	920	..	10.0	6.4	81	64
Uzbekistan	970	2,370	..	..	76	64
East Asia						
China	620	2,920	10.3	7.1	96	80
Hong Kong	22,990	22,950	..	8.4	86	50
Japan	39,640	22,110	..	4.3	84	53
Korea, Dem.	..	..	..	..	75	65
Korea, Rep.	9,700	11,450	..	5.7	76	41
Mongolia	310	1,950	..	..	89	15
Southeast Asia and Oceania						
Australia	18,720	18,940	15.2	9.6	86	55
Cambodia	270	..	..	..	95	50
Indonesia	980	3,800	6.6	4.7	85	38
Lao PDR	350	..	6.3	4.2	98	71
Malaysia	3,890	9,020	19.9	11.7	91	52
Myanmar	..	..	..	..	93	51
New Zealand	14,340	16,360	15.0	8.8	89	49
P.N.G.	1,160	2,420	..	..	89	58
Philippines	1,050	2,850	11.5	7.4	85	38
Singapore	26,730	22,770	..	9.6	84	53
Thailand	2,740	7,540	14.8	9.4	86	67
Vietnam	240	..	8.3	5.6	92	77

Country	GNP per capita (US Dollars)	PPP estimates of GNP per capita (Current int'l $)	Ratio of household income share		Labour force participation rates (% age 15-64)	
			Richest 10% to poorest 10%	Richest 20% to poorest 20%	Male	Female
	1995	1995	1980 -94	1980 -94	1995	1995
Latin America and the Caribbean						
Argentina	8,030	8,310	..	..	80	32
Bolivia	800	2,540	13.8	8.6	78	25
Brazil	3,640	5,400	73.3	32.1	82	33
Chile	4,160	9,520	32.9	17.4	82	33
Colombia	1,910	6,130	30.4	15.5	81	23
Costa Rica	2,610	5,850	28.4	12.7	87	26
Cuba	..	..	..	..	84	42
Dom. Rep.	1,460	3,870	24.8	13.3	87	18
Ecuador	1,390	4,220	16.3	9.7	79	20
El Salvador	1,610	2,610	..	..	87	29
Guatemala	1,340	3,340	77.7	30.0	85	19
Haiti	250	910	..	..	79	51
Honduras	600	1,900	27.9	15.1	87	24
Jamaica	1,510	3,540	13.3	8.2	86	75
Mexico	3,320	6,400	24.5	13.5	83	32
Nicaragua	380	2,000	24.9	13.1	88	32
Panama	2,750	5,980	84.4	29.9	83	34
Paraguay	1,690	3,650	..	..	89	24
Peru	2,310	3,770	18.1	10.3	78	26
Trinidad	3,770	8,610	..	..	92	39
Uruguay	5,170	6,630	..	..	83	39
Venezuela	3,020	7,900	30.5	16.2	81	33
North America						
Canada	19,380	21,130	12.1	7.1	87	58
U.S.A.	26,980	26,980	15.9	8.9	86	60
Europe						
Albania	670	..	..	..	86	63
Austria	26,890	21,250	..	..	80	55
Belarus	2,070	4,220	4.0	3.0	82	73
Belgium	24,710	21,680	6.5	4.6	82	47
Bosnia	..	..	..	..	79	47
Bulgaria	1,330	4,480	7.5	4.7	76	68
Croatia	3,250	..	..	..	77	56
Czech Rep.	3,870	9,770	5.1	3.6	82	74
Denmark	29,890	21,230	..	7.1	89	75
Estonia	2,860	4,220	13.0	7.0	78	71
Finland	20,580	17,760	8.3	6.0	80	73
France	24,990	21,030	13.1	7.5	83	57
Germany	27,510	20,070	8.4	5.8	87	57
Greece	8,210	11,710	..	..	79	30
Hungary	4,120	6,410	6.5	3.9	82	67
Ireland	14,710	15,680	10.0	5.9	82	36
Israel	15,920	16,490	..	6.6	84	44
Italy	19,020	19,870	9.7	6.0	79	37
Latvia	2,270	3,370	5.1	3.8	79	71
Lithuania	1,900	4,120	8.2	5.2	79	70

Country	GNP per capita (US Dollars)	PPP estimates of GNP per capita (Current int'l $)	Ratio of household income share		Labour force participation rates (% age 15-64)	
			Richest 10% to poorest 10%	Richest 20% to poorest 20%	Male	Female
	1995	1995	1980 -94	1980 -94	1995	1995
Macedonia, FYR	860	..	..	..	..	..
Moldova	920	..	9.6	6.0	78	53
Netherlands	24,000	19,950	6.6	4.5	83	38
Norway	31,250	21,940	8.5	5.9	90	68
Poland	2,790	5,400	5.5	4.0	84	71
Portugal	9,740	12,670	..	..	84	48
Romania	1,480	4,360	5.3	3.8	78	69
Russia	2,240	4,480	32.3	11.5	82	72
Slovakia	2,950	3,610	3.6	2.6	82	71
Slovenia	8,200	6,230	5.8	4.0	77	65
Spain	13,580	14,520	..	4.4	80	26
Sweden	23,750	18,540	7.4	4.6	89	75
Switzerland	40,630	25,860	16.6	8.6	91	53
Ukraine	1,630	2,400	5.1	3.7	80	70
U.K.	18,700	19,260	18.2	9.6	91	59
Yugoslavia	..	..	..	..	77	55

Region	GNP per capita (US Dollars)	PPP estimates of GNP per capita (Current int'l $)	Ratio of household income share		Labour force participation rates (% age 15-64)	
			Richest 10% to poorest 10%	Richest 20% to poorest 20%	Male	Female
	1995	1995	1980 -94	1980 -94	1995	1995
World	4,970	6,070	14.4	7.9	88	50
Developing	1,120	3,050	14.2	8.2	89	48
Industrial	19,260	17,320	15.0	7.2	84	59
Dev exc India / China	1,760	3,860	21.0	10.6	85	38
Ind exc USA / Russia	19,850	16,360	9.7	5.6	83	55
Sub-Saharan Africa	510	1,400	23.6	11.1	87	50
Arab States	2,040	5,220	..	..	82	14
South Central Asia	480	1,910	7.5	4.9	89	29
East Asia	4,480	4,980	..	6.8	94	76
Southeast Asia / Oc	2,170	5,490	9.7	6.4	88	50
Latin Am / Carib	3,320	5,700	46.0	21.5	82	31
North America	26,230	26,400	15.5	8.7	86	60
Europe	12,840	12,570	14.7	6.9	83	59

TABLE 28
ENVIRONMENT

Country	Total Land area (thousand sq km)	Population density (population per sq km)	Nationally protected areas (% of total area)	Total Forest Area (as %of total land area)	Deforestation	
					(thousand sq km)	(% of total forest area)
	1995	1996	1994	1995	1990 to 95	1990 to 95
Sub-Saharan Africa						
Angola	1,247	9	..	18	12	5.0
Benin	111	49	6.9	42	3	6.0
Botswana	567	3	18.3	25	4	2.5
Burkina Faso	274	39	9.7	16	2	3.5
Burundi	26	224	3.2	12	(.)	2.0
Cameroon	465	29	4.3	42	6	3.0
C.A.R.	623	5	9.8	48	6	2.0
Chad	1,259	5	9.0	9	5	4.0
Congo	342	8	3.4	57	2	1.0
Côte d' Ivoire	318	43	6.2	17	2	3.0
Eritrea	101	28	..	3	(.)	(.)
Ethiopia	1,000	53	5.5	14	3	2.5
Gabon	258	4	3.9	69	5	2.5
Gambia	10	101	7.0	9	(.)	4.5
Ghana	228	75	4.6	40	6	6.5
Guinea	246	31	0.7	26	4	5.5
Guinea-Bissau	28	30	..	82	1	2.0
Kenya	69	48	6.0	2	(.)	1.5
Lesotho	30	68	0.2	(.)	(.)	(.)
Liberia	96	20	..	47	1	3.0
Madagascar	582	26	1.9	26	7	4.0
Malawi	94	83	8.9	36	3	8.0
Mali	1,220	9	3.2	10	6	5.0
Mauritania	1,025	2	1.7	1	(.)	(.)
Mauritius	2	553	2.0	6	(.)	0.2
Mozambique	784	22	(.)	22	6	3.5
Namibia	823	2	12.4	15	2	1.5
Niger	1,267	7	6.6	2	(.)	(.)
Nigeria	911	125	3.2	15	6	4.5
Rwanda	25	205	12.4	10	(.)	1.0
Senegal	193	43	11.1	8	2	3.5
Sierra Leone	72	60	1.1	18	2	15.0
Somalia	627	15	..	1	(.)	1.0
South Africa	1,221	35	5.7	7	1	1.0
Sudan	2,376	11	..	18	18	4.0
Tanzania	884	33	14.7	37	16	5.0
Togo	54	74	11.4	23	1	7.0
Uganda	200	86	8.1	31	3	4.5
Zaire	2,267	20	..	48	37	3.5
Zambia	743	11	8.5	42	13	4.0
Zimbabwe	387	29	7.9	23	3	3.0
Arab States						
Algeria	2,382	12	5.0	1	1	6.0
Egypt	995	63	0.8	(.)	(.)	(.)
Iraq	437	47	..	(.)	(.)	(.)
Jordan	89	57	3.3	1	(.)	12.5
Kuwait	18	95	1.5	(.)	(.)	(.)

Country	Total Land area (thousand sq km) 1995	Population density (population per sq km) 1996	Nationally protected areas (% of total area) 1994	Total Forest Area (as %of total land area) 1995	Deforestation (thousand sq km) 1990 to 95	Deforestation (% of total forest area) 1990 to 95
Lebanon	10	297	..	5	(.)	39.0
Libya	1,760	3	..	(.)	(.)	(.)
Morocco	446	61	0.8	9	1	1.5
Oman	212	11	17.6	(.)	(.)	(.)
Saudi Arabia	2,150	9	2.9	(.)	(.)	4.0
Syria	184	79	..	1	(.)	11.0
Tunisia	155	56	0.3	4	(.)	2.5
U.A.E.	84	27	..	(.)	(.)	(.)
Yemen, Rep.	528	30	..	8	(.)	(.)
South Central Asia						
Afghanistan	652	32	..	2	6	34.0
Armenia	28	122	7.2	12	(.)	13.5
Azerbaijan	87	88	2.2	11	(.)	(.)
Bangladesh	130	834	0.7	8	(.)	4.0
Bhutan	47	39	..	59	(.)	1.5
Georgia	70	78	2.7	43	(.)	(.)
India	2,973	287	4.4	22	(.)	(.)
Iran	1,636	42	5.0	1	1	8.5
Kazakhstan	2,671	6	0.3	4	-10	-9.5
Kyrgyz Rep.	192	23	1.4	4	(.)	(.)
Nepal	137	156	7.9	35	3	5.5
Pakistan	771	176	4.7	2	3	14.5
Sri Lanka	65	276	12.1	28	1	5.5
Tajikistan	141	41	0.6	3	(.)	(.)
Turkey	770	79	1.1	12	(.)	(.)
Turkmenistan	70	9	2.3	8	(.)	(.)
Uzbekistan	414	52	0.5	22	-11	-13.5
East Asia						
China	9,326	128	6.1	14	4	0.5
Hong Kong	1	5,924	..	(.)	(.)	(.)
Japan	377	332	7.3	67	1	0.5
Korea, Dem.	120	186	..	51	(.)	(.)
Korea, Rep.	99	458	7.0	77	1	1.0
Mongolia	1,567	2	3.9	6	(.)	(.)
Southeast Asia and Oceania						
Australia	7,644	2	12.1	5	-1	(.)
Cambodia	77	57	..	56	8	8.0
Indonesia	1,812	105	9.7	61	54	5.0
Lao PDR	231	21	10.3	54	7	6.0
Malaysia	329	62	4.5	47	20	12.0
Myanmar	658	68	0.3	41	19	7.0
New Zealand	270	13	22.7	29	-2	-3.0
P.N.G.	53	..	0.2	82	7	2.0
Philippines	298	231	2.0	23	13	17.5
Singapore	1	5,476	4.8	7	(.)	2.5
Thailand	511	114	13.7	23	16	13.0
Vietnam	325	227	4.0	28	7	7.0

Country	Total Land area (thousand sq km)	Population density (population per sq km)	Nationally protected areas (% of total area)	Total Forest Area (as %of total land area)	Deforestation	
					(thousand sq km)	(% of total forest area)
	1995	1996	1994	1995	1990 to 95	1990 to 95
Latin America and the Caribbean						
Argentina	2,737	13	1.6	12	4	1.5
Bolivia	1,084	7	8.4	45	29	6.0
Brazil	8,457	19	3.8	65	128	2.5
Chile	49	19	18.1	11	1	2.0
Colombia	1,039	32	8.2	51	13	2.5
Costa Rica	51	68	12.5	24	2	15.0
Cuba	110	99	..	17	1	6.0
Dom. Rep.	48	163	21.5	33	1	8.0
Ecuador	277	41	39.2	40	9	8.0
El Salvador	21	278	0.2	5	(.)	16.5
Guatemala	108	100	7.6	35	4	10.0
Haiti	28	262	0.4	1	(.)	17.0
Honduras	112	52	7.7	37	5	11.5
Jamaica	11	227	0.2	16	1	36.0
Mexico	1,909	47	5.0	29	25	4.5
Nicaragua	121	33	6.9	46	8	7.5
Panama	74	35	17.6	38	3	10.5
Paraguay	397	12	3.6	29	16	13.0
Peru	1,280	19	3.2	53	11	1.5
Trinidad	5	253	3.1	31	(.)	7.5
Uruguay	175	18	0.2	5	(.)	(.)
Venezuela	882	24	28.9	50	25	5.5
North America						
Canada	9,221	3	8.3	27	-9	-0.5
U.S.A.	9,159	29	11.1	23	-29	-1.5
Europe						
Albania	27	118	1.2	38	(.)	(.)
Austria	83	97	23.9	47	(.)	(.)
Belarus	207	50	1.2	36	-3	-5.0
Belgium	31	333	2.5	22	(.)	(.)
Bosnia	51	71	..	53	(.)	(.)
Bulgaria	111	76	3.3	29	(.)	(.)
Croatia	56	80	6.8	33	(.)	(.)
Czech Rep.	77	130	13.5	34	(.)	(.)
Denmark	42	122	32.2	10	(.)	(.)
Estonia	42	33	9.8	48	-1	-5.0
Finland	305	15	8.1	66	1	0.5
France	550	106	10.2	27	-8	-5.5
Germany	349	230	25.8	31	(.)	(.)
Greece	129	79	1.7	51	-7	-11.5
Hungary	2	108	6.2	19	(.)	-2.5
Ireland	69	51	0.7	8	-7	-13.5
Israel	21	269	14.6	5	(.)	(.)
Italy	294	190	7.6	22	(.)	-0.5
Latvia	62	39	12.0	46	-1	-4.5
Lithuania	65	57	9.7	31	-1	-3.0

Country	Total Land area (thousand sq km)	Population density (population per sq km)	Nationally protected areas (% of total area)	Total Forest Area (as %of total land area)	Deforestation	
					(thousand sq km)	(% of total forest area)
	1995	1996	1994	1995	1990 to 95	1990 to 95
Macedonia, FYR	25	85	8.4	39	(.)	(.)
Moldova	33	132	0.2	11	(.)	(.)
Netherlands	34	381	10.4	10	(.)	(.)
Norway	307	13	17.1	26	-1	-1.5
Poland	304	119	9.8	29	-1	-0.5
Portugal	92	106	6.3	31	-1	-4.5
Romania	230	95	4.6	27	(.)	(.)
Russia	16,889	9	3.8	45	..	..
Slovakia	46	109	20.7	41	(.)	-0.5
Slovenia	20	95	5.3	54	(.)	(.)
Spain	500	79	8.4	17	(.)	(.)
Sweden	412	20	6.6	59	(.)	(.)
Switzerland	40	175	17.7	29	(.)	(.)
Ukraine	579	85	0.9	16	(.)	-0.5
U.K.	242	238	20.9	10	-1	-2.5
Yugoslavia	102	101	..	17	(.)	(.)

Region	Total Land area (thousand sq km)	Population density (population per sq km)	Nationally protected areas (% of total area)	Total Forest Area (as %of total land area)	Deforestation	
					(thousand sq km)	(% of total forest area)
	1995	1996	1994	1995	1990 to 95	1990 to 95
	T				T	
World	126.8	43	6.5	27	554	1.7
Developing	77.7	56	5.3	24	625	3.4
Industrial	49.1	23	8.1	30	-71	-0.5
Dev exc India / China	65.4	34	5.2	26	621	3.8
Ind exc USA / Russia	23.1	32	10.0	21	-42	-0.9
Sub-Saharan Africa	23.3	25	6.5	23	188	4.0
Arab States	9.3	23	3.6	1	2	1.8
South Central Asia	10.7	118	3.0	11	-7	-0.6
East Asia	11.5	121	5.8	16	6	0.3
Southeast Asia / Oc	12.2	40	10.6	20	148	6.0
Latin Am / Carib	19.0	24	5.6	47	286	3.2
North America	18.4	16	9.7	25	-38	-0.8
Europe	22.4	32	5.2	41	-31	-0.3

TABLE 29
RATIFICATION OF CULTURAL CONVENTIONS AND HERITAGE SITES

Country	Cultural Conventions				Heritage Sites							
	Protection of the world cultural and natural heritage	Protection of cultural property in the event of armed conflict		Means of prohibiting and preventing the illicit import, export and transfer of ownership of cultural property	Properties included in the World Heritage list				Tentative list of world heritage properties	Endangered heritage sites	
		Convention	Protocol		Cultural	Natural	Combined	Total		World heritage committee	World monument fund
Date of convention	1972	1954	1954	1970	1997	1997	1997	1997	1997	1997	1996
Andorra	-	-	-	-	-	-	-	-	-	-	-
Antigua	X	-	-	-	-	-	-	-	-	-	-
Bahamas	-	-	-	-	-	-	-	-	-	-	-
Bahrain	X	-	-	-	-	-	-	-	-	-	-
Barbados	-	-	-	-	-	-	-	-	-	-	1
Belize	X	-	-	X	-	1	-	1	-	-	1
Cape Verde	X	-	-	-	-	-	-	-	-	-	-
Comoros	-	-	-	-	-	-	-	-	-	-	-
Cook Is.	-	-	-	-	-	-	-	-	-	-	-
Cyprus	X	X	X	X	2	-	-	2	-	-	-
Djibouti	-	-	-	-	-	-	-	-	-	-	-
Dominica	X	-	-	-	-	-	-	-	-	-	-
Eq. Guinea	-	-	-	-	-	-	-	-	-	-	-
Fiji	X	-	-	-	-	-	-	-	-	-	-
Grenada	-	-	-	X	-	-	-	-	-	-	-
Guyana	X	-	-	-	-	-	-	-	4	-	1
Iceland	X	-	-	-	-	-	-	-	-	-	-
Kiribati	-	-	-	-	-	-	-	-	-	-	-
Luxembourg	X	X	X	-	1	-	-	1	3	-	-
Maldives	X	-	-	-	-	-	-	-	-	-	-
Malta	X	-	-	-	3	-	-	3	-	-	-
Marshall Is.	-	-	-	-	-	-	-	-	-	-	-
Monaco	X	X	X	-	-	-	-	-	-	-	-
Nauru	-	-	-	-	-	-	-	-	-	-	-
Niue	-	-	-	-	-	-	-	-	-	-	-
Qatar	X	X	-	X	-	-	-	-	-	-	-
St. Kitts	X	-	-	-	-	-	-	-	-	-	-
St. Lucia	X	-	-	-	-	-	-	-	-	-	-
St. Vincent	-	-	-	-	-	-	-	-	-	-	-
Samoa	-	-	-	-	-	-	-	-	-	-	-
San Marino	X	X	X	-	-	-	-	-	-	-	-
Sao Tome	-	-	-	-	-	-	-	-	-	-	-
Seychelles	X	-	-	-	-	2	-	2	-	-	-
Solomon Is.	-	-	-	-	-	-	-	-	-	-	-
Suriname	-	-	-	-	-	-	-	-	-	-	1
Swaziland	-	-	-	-	-	-	-	-	-	-	-
Tonga	-	-	-	-	-	-	-	-	-	-	-
Tuvalu	-	-	-	-	-	-	-	-	-	-	-
Vanuatu	-	-	-	-	-	-	-	-	-	-	-

TABLE 30
REGIONAL AGGREGATES OF CULTURE INDICATORS

INDICATOR	WORLD	DEVEL	INDUST	S.S. AFR	ARAB ST.	S.C. ASIA	E. ASIA	S.E.A. OC.	LAT. AM.	NOR. AM.	EUROPE

Table 1: CULTURAL ACTIVITIES: NEWSPAPERS, BOOKS AND LIBRARIES

INDICATOR	WORLD	DEVEL	INDUST	S.S. AFR	ARAB ST.	S.C. ASIA	E. ASIA	S.E.A. OC.	LAT. AM.	NOR. AM.	EUROPE
Newspapers	97	43	297	10	44	29	89	45	80	213	278
Book copies	..	..	..	..	96	37	..	..	..	..	368
Book titles	18	7	54	..	4	3	13	8	13	26	70
Cultural paper	21	6	83	2	5	2	18	9	10	138	53
Library users	..	..	22	..	..	..	4	..	..	..	24
Library books	..	..	304	..	..	46	35	..	..	..	342

Table 2: CULTURAL ACTIVITIES: RADIO, TELEVISION AND CINEMA

INDICATOR	WORLD	DEVEL	INDUST	S.S. AFR	ARAB ST.	S.C. ASIA	E. ASIA	S.E.A. OC.	LAT. AM.	NOR. AM.	EUROPE
Radios	362	185	1,005	169	251	96	277	201	387	1,990	672
Televisions	204	115	527	33	109	53	249	91	192	796	416
Radios per T.V.'s	1.8	1.6	1.9	5.1	2.3	1.8	1.1	2.2	2.0	2.5	1.6
Cultural Radio	..	..	..	..	..	..	..	..	..	..	..
programmes T.V.	..	..	..	..	..	..	..	..	..	..	..
Cinemas	2.4	2.7	2.0	..	..	3.8	1.4	..	..	3.8	1.3
Long Produced	4,250	2,670	1,570	..	..	1,170	780	..	..	440	830
films Imported	16,350	8,960	7,390	..	1,860	810	880	1,460	..	1,230	5,440
Imports / Total	79	77	82	..	..	41	53	..	..	74	87

Table 3: CULTURAL ACTIVITIES: RECORDED MUSIC

INDICATOR	WORLD	DEVEL	INDUST	S.S. AFR	ARAB ST.	S.C. ASIA	E. ASIA	S.E.A. OC.	LAT. AM.	NOR. AM.	EUROPE
Unit sales	..	..	32.2	..	..	..	5.3	7.6	6.0	45.9	21.3
Domestic pop	..	..	51	..	..	..	93	66	65	..	52
International pop	..	..	44	..	..	..	5	32	33	..	42
Classical	..	..	5	..	..	..	2	2	2	3	6
Piracy	..	..	20	..	..	..	53	12	45	3	29
Tax rates	..	..	18	..	..	..	29	22	24	6	28
CD players	..	..	60	..	..	..	..	..	..	67	55

Table 5: CULTURAL ACTIVITIES: ARCHIVES AND MUSEUMS

INDICATOR	WORLD	DEVEL	INDUST	S.S. AFR	ARAB ST.	S.C. ASIA	E. ASIA	S.E.A. OC.	LAT. AM.	NOR. AM.	EUROPE
Archives	..	..	..	..	..	..	0.4	..	0.3	3.3	..
User per pop'n	..	..	..	..	..	..	9.9	..	..	8.3	..
visits per staff	..	..	..	..	..	..	..	..	..	115	..
Museum per pop'n	..	..	66	..	5	..	..	8	..	..	65
visits per staff	..	..	13	..	9	..	..	..	..	..	9

Table 6: NATIONAL PUBLIC HOLIDAYS

INDICATOR	WORLD	DEVEL	INDUST	S.S. AFR	ARAB ST.	S.C. ASIA	E. ASIA	S.E.A. OC.	LAT. AM.	NOR. AM.	EUROPE
Total	12.2	12.1	12.4	11.0	11.4	12.9	12.5	10.7	14.4	10.5	12.5
January	1.3	1.3	1.3	1.3	1.4	1.4	1.0	1.4	1.2	1.5	1.4
Febrary	1.1	1.1	1.3	0.9	1.0	1.4	1.5	1.3	1.1	0.5	1.4
March	1.6	1.7	1.6	1.5	1.9	1.8	1.3	1.7	1.8	1.0	1.5
April	1.2	1.1	1.3	0.9	0.9	1.4	1.8	0.9	1.3	0.0	1.4
May	1.8	1.9	1.7	2.0	2.1	1.8	1.8	1.7	1.7	1.0	1.6
June	0.4	0.4	0.5	0.3	0.4	0.6	0.3	0.3	0.4	0.0	0.5
July	0.7	0.8	0.4	0.8	1.5	0.8	0.8	0.7	0.7	1.0	0.3
August	0.7	0.8	0.6	0.8	0.5	0.6	0.3	0.4	1.3	0.5	0.7
September	0.4	0.4	0.3	0.3	0.1	0.5	1.0	0.2	0.6	1.0	0.3
October	0.5	0.6	0.3	0.4	0.2	0.9	1.2	0.4	1.0	1.0	0.2
November	0.7	0.8	0.7	0.6	1.1	0.8	0.5	0.4	1.1	1.5	0.7
December	1.6	1.4	2.3	1.5	0.4	1.1	0.8	1.3	2.3	1.5	2.4

INDICATOR	WORLD	DEVEL	INDUST	S.S.AFR	ARABST.	S.C.ASIA	E.ASIA	S.E.A.O.C.	LAT.AM.	NOR.AM.	EUROPE

Table 7: HERITAGE SITES

	WORLD	DEVEL	INDUST	S.S.AFR	ARABST.	S.C.ASIA	E.ASIA	S.E.A.O.C.	LAT.AM.	NOR.AM.	EUROPE
World Cultural	380	176	204	17	42	45	19	18	48	13	178
Heritage Natural	104	61	43	28	2	8	5	6	15	19	21
Sites Combined	19	10	9	1	1	2	3	5	3	..	4
Total	503	247	256	46	45	55	27	29	66	32	203
Tentative list	790	297	493	19	44	37	76	50	85	95	384
Endangered Heritage	23	16	7	8	3	1	..	1	3	2	5
sites Monument	96	43	53	5	5	9	4	7	13	7	46

Table 8: TRADE IN CULTURAL GOODS

	WORLD	DEVEL	INDUST	S.S.AFR	ARABST.	S.C.ASIA	E.ASIA	S.E.A.O.C.	LAT.AM.	NOR.AM.	EUROPE
Cultural Books	..	..	8.2	..	..	..	2.5	3.6	21.1	10.6	9.3
trade Newspapers	..	..	4.2	..	..	..	0.7	1.1	8.3	4.7	5.1
Music	..	..	31.9	..	..	..	44.0	17.4	20.7	36.8	27.5
Visual arts	..	..	6.3	..	..	..	2.5	0.2	1.0	6.4	6.0
Cinema	..	..	14.8	..	..	..	19.0	5.8	20.9	17.2	13.0
Radio / T.V.	..	..	34.6	..	..	..	31.3	72.1	28.0	24.3	39.1

Table 9: INTERNATIONAL TOURISM

	WORLD	DEVEL	INDUST	S.S.AFR	ARABST.	S.C.ASIA	E.ASIA	S.E.A.O.C.	LAT.AM.	NOR.AM.	EUROPE
Foreign visitors	10	3.4	40	2.0	8.4	0.8	3.1	6.3	9.5	21	50
Receipts	829	782	1,007	699	750	1,016	570	1,064	823	1,324	672
National Number	5.6	1.3	22	1.0	2.5	0.4	1.4	3.3	4.6	19	26
departures Expenditures	1,060	919	1,580	1,225	1,066	662	1,271	1,198	715	1,042	1,469

Table 10: COMMUNICATION AND NEW TECHNOLOGY

	WORLD	DEVEL	INDUST	S.S.AFR	ARABST.	S.C.ASIA	E.ASIA	S.E.A.O.C.	LAT.AM.	NOR.AM.	EUROPE
Post offices	13	9	26	3	7	18	7	6	7	23	28
Letter Total	71	12	329	9	10	13	27	23	17	684	180
items Abroad	1.3	0.7	4.2	1.2	3.1	0.3	0.3	1.8	0.8	2.5	5.7
Tele- Lines	137	44	431	11	55	32	80	64	88	623	337
phones Minutes	11	3	43	2	10	1	4	6	5	64	38
Cellular phones	164	27	635	..	24	5	92	124	76	1,242	330
Fax machines	58	5	251	4	14	2	47	17	15	503	107
P.C.'s	..	..	1,555	..	67	..	199	215	174	3,146	860
Internet	31	0.9	135	..	0.2	0.1	5.9	1.7	2.5	366	48

Table 11: CULTURAL TRENDS: BOOKS

	WORLD	DEVEL	INDUST	S.S.AFR	ARABST.	S.C.ASIA	E.ASIA	S.E.A.O.C.	LAT.AM.	NOR.AM.	EUROPE
Book 1981-83	..	..	..	..	..	..	..	..	..	..	..
copies 1991-94	..	..	..	..	..	..	..	..	..	..	..
Rate of change	..	..	..	..	..	..	..	..	..	..	..
Book 1981-83	..	..	49	..	..	..	10	..	..	..	56
titles 1991-94	..	..	54	..	..	..	13	..	..	..	70
Rate of change	..	..	1.0	..	..	..	3.0	..	..	..	2.5
Library 1981-83	..	..	..	..	..	..	..	..	..	..	..
books 1991-94	..	..	..	..	..	..	..	..	..	..	..
Rate of change	..	..	..	..	..	..	..	..	..	..	..

INDICATOR	WORLD	DEVEL	INDUST	S.S. AFR S.T.	ARAB ST.	S.C. ASIA	E. ASIA	S.E. A O.C.	LAT. AM.	NOR. AM.	EUROPE

Table 12: CULTURAL TRENDS: NEWSPAPERS AND CULTURAL PAPER

Indicator		WORLD	DEVEL	INDUST	S.S. AFR S.T.	ARAB ST.	S.C. ASIA	E. ASIA	S.E. A O.C.	LAT. AM.	NOR. AM.	EUROPE
News-	1980	86	36	251	12	27	20	92	39	83	268	242
papers	1994	97	43	297	10	44	29	89	45	80	213	278
Rate of change		0.9	1.3	1.2	-1.4	5.2	3.8	-0.2	1.3	-0.3	-1.7	1.2
Cultural	1980	14	3.0	59	..	3.8	..	7.5	5.0	9.4	107	33
paper	1994	21	6.0	83	..	4.5	..	18	9	10	138	53
Rate of change		4.3	7.4	3.1	..	1.3	..	10.6	6.2	0.5	2.3	4.7

Table 13: CULTURAL TRENDS: RADIO AND TELEVISION

Indicator		WORLD	DEVEL	INDUST	S.S. AFR S.T.	ARAB ST.	S.C. ASIA	E. ASIA	S.E. A O.C.	LAT. AM.	NOR. AM.	EUROPE
Radios	1980	294	97	878	92	164	52	127	143	260	1,869	603
	1994-95	362	185	1,005	169	251	96	277	201	387	1,990	672
Rate of change		1.7	6.5	1.0	6.0	3.8	6.0	8.4	2.9	3.5	0.5	0.8
Tele-	1980	126	26	424	12	55	12	61	38	99	659	350
visions	1994-95	204	115	527	33	109	53	249	91	192	796	416
Rate of change		4.4	24.5	1.7	12.5	7.0	24.4	21.9	10.0	6.7	1.5	1.3
Radios	1980	2.3	3.7	2.1	7.7	3.0	4.3	2.1	3.8	2.6	2.8	1.7
per T.V.'s	1994-95	1.8	1.6	1.9	5.1	2.3	1.8	1.1	2.2	2.0	2.5	1.6

Table 14: CULTURAL TRENDS: CINEMA

Indicator		WORLD	DEVEL	INDUST	S.S. AFR S.T.	ARAB ST.	S.C. ASIA	E. ASIA	S.E. A O.C.	LAT. AM.	NOR. AM.	EUROPE
Cinema	1980-83	..	..	3.1	..	..	..	..	..	..	4.5	3.0
attendances	1990-95	..	..	2.0	..	..	..	..	..	..	3.8	1.3
Rate of change		..	..	-3.0	..	..	..	..	..	..	-1.2	-4.7
Long films	1980-83	..	..	..	..	..	..	..	..	..	..	..
produced	1990-95	..	..	..	..	..	..	..	..	..	..	..
Rate of change		..	..	..	..	..	..	..	..	..	..	..
Long films	1980-83	..	..	..	..	..	..	..	..	..	..	..
imported	1990-95	..	..	..	..	..	..	..	..	..	..	..
Rate of change		..	..	..	..	..	..	..	..	..	..	..

Table 15: CULTURAL TRENDS: COMMUNICATION AND TRAVEL

Indicator		WORLD	DEVEL	INDUST	S.S. AFR S.T.	ARAB ST.	S.C. ASIA	E. ASIA	S.E. A O.C.	LAT. AM.	NOR. AM.	EUROPE
Tele-	1980	74	12	270	..	20	8	36	27	39	414	194
phones	1995	137	44	431	..	55	32	80	64	88	623	337
Rate of change		5.7	17.9	4.0	..	11.3	21.1	8.4	9.2	8.5	3.4	4.9
Foreign visitors	1980	..	..	24	..	..	..	0.6	3.0	6.6	14	38
	1995	..	..	40	..	..	..	3.1	6.3	9.5	21	50
Rate of change		..	..	4.3	..	..	..	23.5	6.9	2.8	3.2	2.0

Table 16: CULTURAL TRENDS: CULTURAL TRADE

Indicator		WORLD	DEVEL	INDUST	S.S. AFR S.T.	ARAB ST.	S.C. ASIA	E. ASIA	S.E. A O.C.	LAT. AM.	NOR. AM.	EUROPE
Cultural US $	1980	67,090	9,240	57,850	..	..	..	16,830	3,780	2,780	13,740	29,480
Trade Mill	1991	196,500	39,230	157,270	..	..	..	46,270	18,940	4,900	45,180	79,260
US$	1980	24	5	84	..	..	..	105	14	9	54	102
per cap	1991	78	38	208	..	..	..	270	185	12	160	246
%	1980	0.6	0.2	0.8	..	..	..	1.2	0.3	0.5	0.4	1.0
of GNP	1991	0.9	0.8	1.0	..	..	..	0.9	2.0	0.6	0.7	1.4
Exports as	1980	50.9	42.9	52.2	..	..	..	86.5	38.6	15.7	38.9	41.7
% of total	1991	47.3	50.7	46.4	..	..	..	70.0	55.6	24.4	33.2	41.8

INDICATOR	W O R L D	D E V E L	I N D U S T	S. S. A F R	A R A B S T.	S. C. A S I A	E. A S I A	S. E. A. O C.	L A T. A M.	N O R. A M.	E U R O P E

Table 17: RATIFICATION OF CULTURAL CONVENTIONS (%)

	W O R L D	D E V E L	I N D U S T	S. S. A F R	A R A B S T.	S. C. A S I A	E. A S I A	S. E. A. O C.	L A T. A M.	N O R. A M.	E U R O P E
Heritage protection	85	82	95	71	84	100	67	92	95	100	94
Armed Convention	54	48	70	34	89	50	17	50	45	0	77
conflict Protocol	47	40	65	29	79	42	0	42	32	0	74
Trade	55	55	55	39	74	75	67	17	73	100	54

Table 18: RATIFICATION OF HUMAN RIGHTS CONVENTIONS (%)

	W O R L D	D E V E L	I N D U S T	S. S. A F R	A R A B S T.	S. C. A S I A	E. A S I A	S. E. A. O C.	L A T. A M.	N O R. A M.	E U R O P E
Econ /Soc/Cultural	81	74	100	83	71	65	67	42	91	100	100
Civil / Political	81	75	98	83	71	65	67	42	95	100	97
Discrim- Racial	86	82	98	88	86	76	67	58	91	100	97
ination Women	87	82	100	85	57	71	67	92	100	100	100
Genocide	73	67	88	44	86	59	67	83	95	100	89
Children	97	95	100	98	79	100	83	100	100	100	100
Torture	64	52	95	46	50	53	33	42	77	100	97
Refugees	69	65	80	90	36	35	50	50	77	50	81

Table 19: TRANSLATIONS AND BOOKS IN FOREIGN LANGUAGES

	W O R L D	D E V E L	I N D U S T	S. S. A F R	A R A B S T.	S. C. A S I A	E. A S I A	S. E. A. O C.	L A T. A M.	N O R. A M.	E U R O P E
Trans- 1980	..	..	..	..	270	..	..	1,080	3,800	1,750	..
lations 1994	..	..	..	..	..	..	..	..	..	..	57,720
Titles	..	..	11.0	..	..	..	..	..	..	..	11.5
Multi-lingual	..	..	3.0	..	..	..	..	..	..	..	2.3

Table 22: EDUCATION

	W O R L D	D E V E L	I N D U S T	S. S. A F R	A R A B S T.	S. C. A S I A	E. A S I A	S. E. A. O C.	L A T. A M.	N O R. A M.	E U R O P E
Primary Boys	90	89	95	60	85	90	97	97	92	99	93
enrolment Girls	82	79	96	49	76	71	95	86	86	100	93
Secondary Boys	61	53	93	27	63	56	65	52	50	98	90
enrolment Girls	54	43	94	22	52	38	57	48	55	97	93
Tertiary	16	9	47	3	14	8	8	13	17	80	39
Expend as % GNP	5.1	3.6	5.4	5.4	5.2	3.6	4.4	4.2	3.3	5.7	5.4

Table 23: THIRD LEVEL EDUCATION ABROAD

	W O R L D	D E V E L	I N D U S T	S. S. A F R	A R A B S T.	S. C. A S I A	E. A S I A	S. E. A. O C.	L A T. A M.	N O R. A M.	E U R O P E
Students abroad	1,250	790	460	90	130	170	280	110	80	50	340
Foreign students	1,380	150	1,230	20	50	30	70	50	20	490	650
Foreign / Abroad	110	19	267	22	38	18	25	..	..	980	191

Table 24: HUMAN CAPITAL

	W O R L D	D E V E L	I N D U S T	S. S. A F R	A R A B S T.	S. C. A S I A	E. A S I A	S. E. A. O C.	L A T. A M.	N O R. A M.	E U R O P E
Adult Total	..	70	..	57	57	54	83	87	87	..	..
literacy Male	..	79	..	67	68	66	90	91	88	..	..
Female	..	62	..	47	44	41	74	83	86	..	..
15-19	..	82	..	66	76	65	..	97	94	..	..
Mean Total	4.9	3.7	10.8	1.6	3.2	2.5	5.7	4.8	5.4	12.4	9.8
years of Male	5.8	4.7	10.9	2.2	4.6	3.5	6.9	5.7	5.5	12.3	10.0
schooling Female	4.1	2.8	10.7	1.0	1.9	1.3	4.5	4.1	5.3	12.5	9.6

INDICATOR	WORLD	DEVEL	INDUST	S.S. AFR	ARAB ST.	S.C. ASIA	E. ASIA	S.E.A. OC.	LAT. AM.	NOR. AM.	EUROPE
Table 25: DEMOGRAPHIC AND HEALTH											
Population	5,750	4,570	1,180	600	220	1,470	1,430	520	480	300	730
Urban	45	37	74	31	56	31	35	35	74	76	73
Life expectancy	65	63	74	50	65	61	70	65	69	76	73
Marriage age	21.3	20.7	24.1	19.0	21.1	18.8	22.7	21.9	21.9	23.6	24.2
Family size	4.5	4.9	2.8	5.2	6.1	5.6	3.9	4.9	4.8	2.6	2.9
Fertility	3.1	3.4	1.7	6.2	4.7	3.7	1.9	3.1	3.0	2.1	1.6
Teenage births	325	360	185	750	300	540	25	245	390	295	170
Contraception	53	50	63	14	39	39	76	52	59	71	59
Maternal mortality	310	380	22	920	320	450	110	390	180	11	28
Table 26: MIGRATION AND REFUGEES											
Migrants Total	111.8	56.3	55.5	14.2	11.6	21.9	2.2	6.6	5.5	23.9	25.9
% female	47	46	51	45	46	48	38	48	46	51	51
% of pop'n	2.4	1.6	6.2	3.8	6.3	1.8	0.3	1.4	1.3	8.7	5.4
Refugees Origin	..	..	..	6.5	..	3.6	..	..	..	..	..
Asylum	14.7	12.0	2.7	6.5	0.5	4.5	0.3	0.2	0.1	0.7	1.9
Table 27: ECONOMIC											
GNP per cap. US$	4,970	1,120	19,260	510	2,040	480	4,480	2,170	3,320	26,230	12,840
GNP per cap. PPP	6,070	3,050	17,320	1,400	5,220	1,910	4,980	5,490	5,700	26,400	12,570
Rich / Poor 10% / 10%	14.4	14.2	15.0	23.6	..	7.5	..	9.7	46.0	15.5	14.7
Income share 20% / 20%	7.9	8.2	7.2	11.1	..	4.9	6.8	6.4	21.5	8.7	6.9
Labour Male	88	89	84	87	82	89	94	88	82	86	83
force Female	50	48	59	50	14	29	76	50	31	60	59
Table 28: ENVIRONMENT											
Land area	126.8	77.7	49.1	23.3	9.3	10.7	11.5	12.2	19.0	18.4	22.4
Pop'n density	43	56	23	25	23	118	122	40	24	16	32
Protected areas	6.5	5.3	8.1	6.5	3.6	3.0	5.8	10.6	5.6	9.7	5.2
Forest areas	27	24	30	23	1	11	16	20	47	25	41
Deforest- Sq Km2	554	625	-71	188	2	-7	6	148	286	-38	-31
ation %	1.7	3.4	-0.5	4.0	1.8	-0.6	0.3	6.0	3.2	-0.8	-0.3

Index and sources of the Culture Indicators

Indicators	Indicator tables[1]	Basic data sources[2]	New *World Culture Report* indicators[3]
Archives, metres	5	UNESCO	×
personnel	5	UNESCO	×
user visits	5	UNESCO	×
Book titles, published	1, 11	UNESCO	×
Books, copies published	1, 11	UNESCO	×
Cinema attendance	2, 14	UNESCO	
Compact-disc players	3	IFPI	
Computers, personal	10	ITU	
Contraceptive prevalence	25	UNFPA	
Cultural conventions			
ratifications, total	17	UNESCO	
ratifications, small countries	29	UNESCO	
Cultural paper, consumption	1, 12	UNESCO	×
Deforestation, total	28	FAO	
as percentage of forest area	28	FAO	×
Education expenditure, public	22	UNESCO	
Enrolment, primary female	22	UNESCO	
primary male	22	UNESCO	
secondary female	22	UNESCO	
secondary male	22	UNESCO	
tertiary total	22	UNESCO	
Exports, cultural	16	UNSTAT, UNESCO	×
Fax machines	10	ITU	
Family size	25	UNPOP	
Fertility, total	25	UNPOP	
young women	25	UNPOP	×
Films, produced	2, 14	UNESCO	
imported	2, 14	UNESCO	
imported as a percentage of total	2	UNESCO	×
Foreign-born population	26	UNPOP	
Foreign language publications	9	UNESCO	×
Foreign remittances	26	IMF	×
Foreign students, total	23	UNESCO	
major countries of origin	23	UNESCO	×
as percentage of students abroad	23	UNESCO	×
Forest area	28	FAO	
GNP per capita, United States dollars	27	WBANK	
International dollars (PPP)	27	WBANK	

Indicators	Indicator tables[1]	Basic data sources[2]	New *World Culture Report* indicators[3]
Heritage sites, total	7, 29	UNESCO	
small countries	29	UNESCO	
cultural	7	UNESCO	
natural	7	UNESCO	
combined	7	UNESCO	
tentative	7	UNESCO	
endangered	7	UNESCO, WMF	
Human rights conventions, ratification	18	UNCHR	
Income share of households			
highest 20% to lowest 20%	27	WBANK	×
highest 10% to lowest 10%	27	WBANK	×
Internet hosts	10	ITU	
Labour-force participation, female	27	ILO	
male	27	ILO	
Land area	28	FAO	
Letters posted	10	UPU	×
Library (public), books	1, 11	UNESCO	×
Library (public), users	1	UNESCO	×
Life expectancy	25	UNPOP	
Literacy (adult), total	24	UNESCO	
female	24	UNESCO	
male	24	UNESCO	
young adult	24	UNESCO	
Marriage (first), female age	25	UNPOP	
Maternal mortality	25	WHO	
Migrants (international), total	26	UNPOP	
female	26	UNPOP	
Museums, attendance	5	UNESCO	×
personnel	5	UNESCO	×
Music (recorded), sales	3	IFPI	×
domestic popular	3	IFPI	
international popular	3	IFPI	
classical	3	IFPI	
piracy	3	IFPI	
tax rates	3	IFPI	×
Newspaper circulation	1, 12	UNESCO	
Performing arts, establishments	4	UNESCO	×
performances	4	UNESCO	×
attendance	4	UNESCO	×
foreign tours	4	UNESCO	×
Population, total	25	UNPOP	
urban	25	UNPOP	
Population density	28	UNPOP	

Indicators	Indicator tables[1]	Basic data sources[2]	New *World Culture Report* indicators[3]
Post offices	10	UPU	
Protected areas	28	FAO	
Public holidays	6	JPM	×
Radios	2, 13	UNESCO	
Radios per televisions	2, 13	UNESCO	×
Radio programmes, cultural	2	UNESCO	×
Refugees, country of origin	26	UNHCR	×
country of asylum	26	UNHCR	
Schooling, mean years total	24	UNESCO, UNDP	×
female	24	UNESCO, UNDP	×
male	24	UNESCO, UNDP	×
Students abroad, total	23	UNESCO	
major countries of study	23	UNESCO	×
Telephones, total	10, 15	ITU	
cellular	10	ITU	
Telephone calls (international), minutes	10	ITU	
major partner	10	ITU	×
Televisions	2, 13	UNESCO	
Television programmes, cultural	2	UNESCO	×
Tourism (foreign), visitors	9, 15	WTO	×
departures of nationals	9	WTO	×
major countries of origin	9	WTO	×
major countries of destination	9	WTO	×
receipts	9	WTO	×
expenditures	9	WTO	×
Translations, total	19	UNESCO	
major languages	19	UNESCO	×
multilingual publications	19	UNESCO	×
original language	20	UNESCO	
major translating language	20	UNESCO	×
authors most translated	21	UNESCO	
Trade (cultural), total	16	UNSTAT, UNESCO	
per capita	16	UNSTAT, UNESCO	×
as percentage of GNP	16	UNSTAT, UNESCO	×
books and pamphlets	8	UNSTAT, UNESCO	×
newspapers and periodicals	8	UNSTAT, UNESCO	×
music-related goods	8	UNSTAT, UNESCO	×
visual arts	8	UNSTAT, UNESCO	×
cinema and photography	8	UNSTAT, UNESCO	×
radio and television	8	UNSTAT, UNESCO	×

1. In addition to being shown in the tables as listed, many indicators are also repeated in aggregated form in Table 30.
2. See list of abbreviations on page 488. The first source listed is the main source for the indicator. Whenever data come originally from more than one source, or when a second organization has published the data in a more convenient form, the leading secondary source follows the main source.
3. New indicator developed by World Statistics Ltd (New York) for the *World Culture Report*.

Key to source abbreviations

FAO	Food and Agriculture Organization of the United Nations
IFPI	International Federation of the Phonographic Industry
ILO	International Labour Organisation
IMF	International Monetary Fund
ITU	International Telecommunication Union
JPM	J. P. Morgan
UNCHR	United Nations Centre for Human Rights
UNDP	United Nations Development Programme
UNESCO	United Nations Educational, Scientific and Cultural Organization
UNFPA	United Nations Fund for Population Activities
UNHCR	United Nations High Commission for Refugees
UNPOP	United Nations Population Division
UNSTAT	United Nations Statistical Division
UPU	Universal Postal Union
WBANK	The World Bank
WMF	World Monuments Fund
WHO	World Health Organization
WTO	World Tourism Organization